REVISED EDITION

The New York Times

COOK BOOK

REVISED EDITION

The New York Times

COOK BOOK

Craig Claiborne

1817

HARPER & ROW, PUBLISHERS, NEW YORK

GRAND RAPIDS, PHILADELPHIA, ST. LOUIS, SAN FRANCISCO
LONDON, SINGAPORE, SYDNEY, TOKYO, TORONTO

My special thanks to Vivian Collyer Bucher
who contributed so much
to the retesting of many recipes
that appear in this book.

Designer: JOEL AVIROM

Library of Congress Cataloging-in-Publication Data
Claiborne, Craig.
     The New York times cook book/by Craig Claiborne.—
Rev. ed.
          p.   cm.

     1. Cookery,   International.   2. Cookery,   American.
I. New York Times.   II. Title.
TX725.A1C5584   1990
641.59—dc20   89–45640

♦

This book is for Joan Whitman,
a devoted friend for many years and a consummate editor.
Without her enthusiasm and scrupulous eye for detail,
this new edition would never have materialized.

♦

Contents

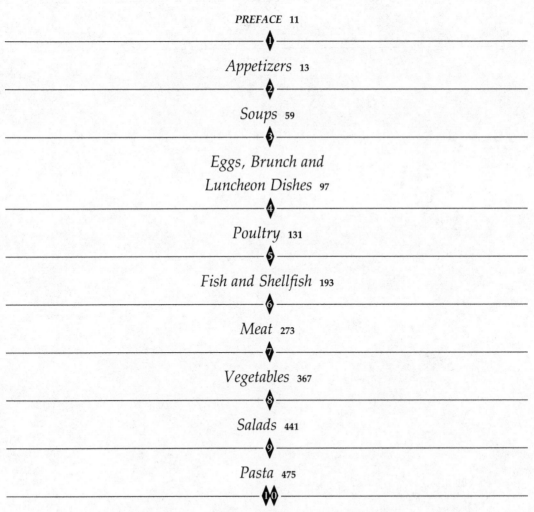

Preface

When I wrote the preface to the original *New York Times Cook Book* in 1960, I quoted M. F. K. Fisher, to my mind the finest writer on food subjects in America. She once noted, I wrote, "that the basis of French cuisine is butter, that of Italy olive oil, of Germany lard, and of Russia sour cream. Water or drippings are attributed to English kitchens, and to those of America, the flavor of innumerable tin cans."

That was written more than two decades ago and, of course, the whole concept of eating and drinking in this country has changed dramatically. We *do* live in a world complete with frozen foods, microwave ovens, fast-foods, and carry-out foods, but America in the last half of the twentieth century has become one of the most sophisticated nations in the world where the kitchen and the table are concerned. We have undergone an absolute revolution in our attitude toward good food and how to prepare it.

It is hard to believe that when the first edition of this book was published, a quiche—lorraine or otherwise—had rarely been heard of on this side of the Atlantic. Pesto sauce was at that time a total novelty, and so were many Japanese foods that today are taken for granted, things like sushi and sashimi, tempura, teriyaki and sukiyaki.

Within the past two decades, such "foreign" foods as paella, ratatouille, moussaka and niçoise salad have become almost as commonplace as apple pie and Boston baked beans. And I hope my food writings over the years have gone a long way toward establishing the popularity of these dishes. I can well recall that a decade or so ago, most Americans would not eat tuna unless it came out of a can.

The shelves of grocery stores, supermarkets and specialty food shops have also undergone a great revolution. When this book was first published, the nation was largely limited to what I have laughingly referred to as ball-park mustard. Today the word *mustard* is almost synonymous with Dijon, with its white-wine base. A short while ago, vinegar was, by and large, something red or white, rarely referred to as "wine" vinegar, and the balsamic version was wholly unknown. A couple of decades ago when the word "lettuce" was used in a recipe, it almost invariably implied the iceberg variety. Even in luxury French restaurants in America, salads were made with the iceberg variety. Today there is an astonishing variety of "new" lettuces to be had in almost every community. They include romaine, Boston, chicory, watercress and endive. Not to mention such elegant varieties as arugula, radicchio, and field salad, or lamb's salad. I remember the early years when fresh ginger was a novelty and you had to search for it, sometimes long distances. When mention was made of shallots, a conscientious food writer felt compelled to list a mail-order source for the product— some small farming operation somewhere in New Jersey or elsewhere. Sun-dried tomatoes were an unknown and unavailable quantity. Fresh coriander, or cilantro, was, until a very short while ago, very much a novelty. And so were jalapeño peppers.

In my early days with *The New York Times*, there was only one major cheese shop in all of Manhattan. Today there are fine cheeses to be had in abundance, East Side, West Side and across the nation, left and right, top to bottom.

Wine has become an accepted part of America's gastronomic culture and it is a universally accepted fact that the nation produces wines on a par with those of France, Germany, Italy, Spain or wherever.

In the new edition of this book, I have attempted to retain the finest recipes of the original while putting it in harmony with modern thinking in the kitchen. Numerous new recipes have been added, and the food processor has been put in its appropriate, prominent place. When this book was first published, the food processor had not been introduced, and that contribution, alone, has altered the whole concept of food preparation from coast to coast.

In my long career as a food writer, I have always thought of myself as a diarist, a historian who has been able to communicate his enthusiasm for good food and food preparation. My major hope is that this book reflects that feeling.

East Hampton, New York

1

Appetizers

Appetizers or hors d'oeuvres are the frivol-ities of a meal, and, like champagne, they are capable of setting a mood. There are several that are almost guaranteed to give a feeling of elegance and richness. These are fresh caviar, genuine foie gras, smoked salmon and thin slices of fine ham such as that of Paris, Parma, Westphalia or Bay-onne. On a lesser but nonetheless appetiz-ing plane are everything from canapés to meat and game pâtés.

♦

SERVING CAVIAR

All caviar, whether fresh or pasteurized, should be served thoroughly chilled. To keep it cold, the serving bowl is usually imbedded in ice.

With fresh caviar, many gourmets de-clare, no embellishments are necessary. They heap it on fresh toast—either but-tered or dry—and relish it as is. Others demand a dash of lemon juice. Caviar is also superb, and obviously more economi-cal, when served with blini, melted butter and sour cream.

Chopped hard-cooked egg yolk, chopped hard-cooked egg white and raw onion rings or chopped raw onion often are offered with both fresh and pasteur-ized caviar. They are particularly recom-mended with the pasteurized product.

For a delicious spread for buttered bread fingers, mix pasteurized pressed caviar with cream cheese and enough sour cream to make it of spreading consistency.

Fresh caviar is highly perishable and must be kept refrigerated. Never put fresh caviar in a home freezer; freezing ruins it.

Two beverages are eminently suited for service with caviar. They are chilled vodka and chilled dry champagne.

SERVING FOIE GRAS

The foie gras should be chilled. Cut it into quarter-inch or half-inch slices and serve with buttered toast. If the foie gras is coated with aspic, serve a little chopped aspic on the side.

SERVING SMOKED SALMON

The best smoked salmon comes from Nova Scotia, Scotland, Norway and Den-mark. Most of that available in the United States is from Nova Scotia. The salmon is generally purchased in wafer-thin slices, and it should be served chilled on chilled plates. Classically, it is served accom-panied by lemon wedges, capers, buttered toast and a pepper mill. It is also served on occasion with a cruet of olive oil, chopped egg and chopped onion.

SERVING HAM

Fine ham, whether it is a domestic ham such as those from Smithfield or an im-ported one from France, Italy or Germany, should be served in thin slices. Ham is complemented by sour gherkins and but-tered toast.

SERVING OYSTERS ON THE HALF SHELL

The flavor of oysters is so delicate they are best savored with a touch of lemon juice and a sprinkling of coarsely ground black pepper or with the delightful mignonette sauce that follows. Mignonette is the name of a white peppercorn traditionally used for this sauce, but any white pepper will do. The oysters should be served on a bed of ice and accompanied by buttered toast or buttered black bread fingers. The classic drink with oysters is a well-chilled chablis or, when it is appropriate to the occasion, stout.

MIGNONETTE SAUCE

6 TABLESPOONS

¼ cup red wine vinegar
2 tablespoons finely chopped shallots
½ teaspoon freshly ground white pepper

Combine all the ingredients and spoon about 1 teaspoon of the sauce over each oyster.

◆

SPICED SPANISH OLIVES

4 TO 6 SERVINGS

1 cup green Spanish olives
¼ cup vinegar
¼ cup olive oil
1 garlic clove, finely chopped
2 tablespoons chopped chives
1 teaspoon paprika
½ teaspoon peppercorns

1 Crush the olives with a hammer or mallet until the pits show.
2 Combine the olives with the remaining ingredients and let stand at room temperature 4 hours. Chill in the refrigerator until ready to serve.

BLACK OLIVES, GRECIAN STYLE

12 TO 18 SERVINGS

2 pounds small, pointed black Greek olives
Vinegar to cover
2 lemons, thinly sliced
2 celery stalks, coarsely chopped
Olive oil

1 Crack the olives with a hammer or mallet until the pits show and cover them with the vinegar. Let stand 2 days.
2 Drain and pack into sterilized jars, arranging the olives alternately with layers of lemon slices and celery. Cover with olive oil and keep in a cool place until ready to serve.

◆

MIXED ITALIAN OLIVES

8 TO 10 SERVINGS

½ pound green olives
½ pound black olives
¼ cup vinegar
¼ cup olive oil
3 celery stalks, chopped
1 green pepper, chopped
1 red pepper, chopped
1 garlic clove, crushed
Freshly ground pepper to taste
Oregano to taste

1 Crack the olives with a hammer or mallet until the pits show.
2 Combine the olives with the remaining ingredients. Let stand at room temperature 2 days. Store in refrigerator in sealed, sterilized jars.

OLIVES WITH DILL

8 TO 10 SERVINGS

2 pounds large green olives
¼ cup vinegar
¼ cup olive oil
3 garlic cloves, crushed
2 red chili peppers
2 dill sprigs
1 bay leaf

1 Drain the olives and crack them with a hammer or mallet until the pits show.

2 Combine the olives with the remaining ingredients and let stand a day or so in a cool place. Place in sterilized jars, seal and store in the refrigerator.

◆

BUTTERED NUTS

ABOUT 2 CUPS

1 pound shelled nuts (pecans, walnuts or almonds)
2 tablespoons melted butter

1 Preheat the oven to 250°F.

2 Place the nuts on a baking sheet and pour the butter over them. Toss the nuts or otherwise shift them around in the butter to coat well.

3 Bake for 10 to 15 minutes, until nuts are crisp and golden brown. Shake the pan occasionally or stir with a spoon to achieve even browning. When the nuts are cool, taste them; if desired, sprinkle with salt.

SARDINE CANAPÉS

ABOUT 12 SMALL CANAPÉS

1 (3¾-ounce) can boneless sardines packed in oil, drained
2 tablespoons lemon juice
1 tablespoon cream
1 tablespoon mayonnaise
½ teaspoon dry mustard
Freshly ground pepper to taste
Few drops of Tabasco sauce
Toast rounds
Hard-cooked egg slices or sliced green olives

Mash the sardines with a fork and mix with the seasonings. Spread on toast rounds and garnish with hard-cooked egg slices or sliced green olives.

◆

SHRIMP CANAPÉS WITH DILL

6 SERVINGS

18 medium shrimp, cooked, shelled and deveined
12 toast rounds
Butter
Mayonnaise
12 dill sprigs
Lemon wedges
Freshly ground pepper

1 Slice each shrimp in half lengthwise.

2 Butter the toast rounds and arrange 3 shrimp halves in a spiral on each round.

3 Garnish the canapés, if desired, with mayonnaise "stars" pressed from a pastry tube. Top with dill sprigs. Serve with lemon wedges and freshly ground pepper.

CURRIED CHEESE CANAPÉS

8 TO 10 CANAPÉS

1 (3-ounce) package cream cheese
8 pitted ripe olives, chopped
¼ teaspoon curry powder
1 teaspoon chopped chives
Toast rounds

Blend the cheese, olives, curry powder and chives and spread on toast rounds. If desired, the mixture may be seasoned with a little lemon juice.

CLAM AND CHEESE CANAPÉS

ABOUT 16 CANAPÉS

1 cup grated cheddar cheese
1 (8-ounce) can minced clams, drained
2 tablespoons chopped parsley
1 tablespoon chopped chives
Pinch of cayenne
Toast rounds

Combine the cheese, clams and seasonings. Spread on toast rounds and broil briefly under a preheated broiler.

BAKED CHEESE CANAPÉS

12 CANAPÉS

1 (3-ounce) package cream cheese
1 teaspoon minced onions
1 egg, beaten
¼ teaspoon Tabasco sauce
12 rounds toasted bread

1 Preheat the oven to 375°F.

2 Combine the cheese, onion, egg and Tabasco and beat with a whisk until light.

3 Spread the mixture on the toast and bake until light brown.

CRABMEAT CANAPÉS

ABOUT 16 CANAPÉS

1 cup fresh lump crabmeat, picked over well to remove any bits of shell or cartilage
¼ cup mayonnaise
1 tablespoon chopped parsley
1 tablespoon chopped chives
1 teaspoon lemon juice
1 teaspoon Worcestershire sauce
Tabasco sauce to taste
Freshly ground pepper to taste
Toast rounds

Combine the crabmeat with the mayonnaise, herbs and seasonings. Spread on rounds of toast and serve immediately.

AVOCADO CANAPÉS

Remove the crusts from very thin slices of white and dark bread. Spread with butter and seasoned mayonnaise. Place wafer-thin slices of cold roast turkey or chicken on white bread and then add a layer of thinly sliced avocado. Top with a slice of dark bread.

Wrap in a damp towel and refrigerate a few hours. Cut into small wedges.

Set upright in tiny pyramids on a tray ringed with parsley. Toothpicks may be used to hold the wedges together.

♦

CUCUMBER SANDWICHES

Slice a cucumber very thin and let soak in vinegar for a few minutes. Drain, season to taste with salt and freshly ground pepper and place between thin slices of well-buttered bread. Trim crusts; cut into strips or triangles.

♦

ROLLED PICNIC SANDWICHES

Using a sharp knife, remove the crusts from a loaf of unsliced white bread. Cut the bread into very thin slices and spread with a little softened butter or softened cream cheese. Cover each slice with chopped watercress leaves or thin slices of scallions and roll like a jelly roll.

Garnish each end, if desired, with a sprig of watercress. Wrap the sandwiches close together in foil or plastic wrap and keep chilled in a dry place until ready to serve.

Roquefort or Danish blue cheese mixed with a little softened butter, or the cheese known as petit Suisse, also make flavorful spreads for these sandwiches.

♦

CURRIED MUSHROOM ROLLS

12 TO 14 ROLLS

12 to 14 thin slices of white bread
Softened butter
½ pound fresh mushrooms, finely chopped
2 tablespoons butter, melted
½ teaspoon curry powder
1 tablespoon lemon juice
½ teaspoon salt
Dash of freshly ground pepper
Dash of cayenne
Additional melted butter

1 Preheat the oven to 425°F.

2 Remove the crusts from the bread slices and roll each slice to ⅛-inch thickness with a rolling pin. Spread the surface of each slice thinly with softened butter and set it aside.

3 Sauté the mushrooms until tender in 2 tablespoons melted butter with the curry powder and lemon juice. Add the salt, pepper and cayenne.

4 Spread about 1 tablespoon of this mixture over each slice of buttered bread. Roll like a jelly roll and fasten the ends with toothpicks. Brush each roll with a little melted butter. Heat in the oven for about 10 minutes, until brown. Serve hot as a first course.

IRMA'S ONION SANDWICHES

The success of this popular appetizer depends on the quality of the brioches or bread used and the thinness of the onion filling, which must be nearly transparent.

18 SMALL SANDWICHES

7 brioches or any fine-textured bread
18 wafer-thin slices of a small onion
¾ cup mayonnaise
Salt to taste
½ cup minced parsley

1 Slice the brioches across in pieces about ¼ inch thick; there should be about 5 slices from each brioche. Cut the slices into rounds with a small biscuit cutter, about 1 inch in diameter.

2 Choose small onions and slice them so that each circle will be a little smaller than the brioche rounds.

3 Spread each piece of brioche with mayonnaise. On half the pieces arrange one onion slice and season with salt. Cover the onion with the remaining pieces of brioche to make sandwiches.

4 Spread the remaining mayonnaise on a wooden board and sprinkle the chopped parsley on another board. Hold each sandwich lightly between thumb and finger so it will turn like a wheel. Roll the edge in mayonnaise, then in parsley. Set the sandwiches, as they are completed, on wax paper and chill thoroughly.

SHRIMP TOAST

24 HOT CANAPÉS

½ pound raw shrimp, shelled and deveined
4 water chestnuts, chopped
1 teaspoon dry sherry
1 teaspoon sugar
1 tablespoon cornstarch
1 egg, lightly beaten
1 tablespoon chopped coriander
6 slices of bread, at least 2 days old
2 cups peanut oil

1 Put the shrimp, water chestnuts, sherry, sugar, cornstarch, and egg in the bowl of a food processor. Purée until a spreadable paste forms. Put in a bowl and stir in the coriander.

2 Trim the crusts off the bread slices and cut each slice into 4 triangles. Spread each triangle with 1 teaspoon of the shrimp mixture.

3 Heat the oil to 375°F. Gently lower bread into the oil with shrimp side down. After 1 minute turn over and fry for a few more seconds, until golden. Fry only a few at a time. Drain.

◆

CHEESE LOG

ABOUT 2 DOZEN SLICES

½ pound sharp American cheese, shredded (2 cups)
⅓ cup crumbled Roquefort cheese
½ garlic clove, minced
¼ cup sour cream, approximately
⅛ teaspoon Tabasco sauce
¼ cup finely chopped ripe olives
½ cup minced parsley

Continued

1 Combine the cheeses, garlic and enough sour cream to bind them together. Add the Tabasco and olives. Chill until firm enough to form into a long roll. Roll in parsley. Wrap in plastic wrap and store in the refrigerator.

2 When ready to serve, cut into ¼-inch slices and serve on toast or crackers.

Stuffed eggs, page 99.

♦

ROQUEFORT AND COGNAC

ABOUT 3 CUPS

1 pound Roquefort or blue cheese
¼ pound butter
Pinch of cayenne
⅓ cup cognac, approximately

1 Put the cheese and the butter in the container of a food processor and blend until creamy.

2 Season the mixture with cayenne and beat in cognac to taste. Add a little more cognac before using to make the mixture spread easily. Serve with toast or toasted crackers.

Note: The mixture will keep several weeks in small jars in the refrigerator.

CARAWAY AND CHEESE SPREAD

ABOUT ½ CUP

1 (3-ounce) package cream cheese
2 tablespoons sour cream
2 tablespoons caraway seeds
1 tablespoon capers
½ garlic clove, crushed, or 1 teaspoon minced onions

Combine all the ingredients in a food processor and blend until well mixed, or use an electric mixer. Serve on miniature rounds of rye bread.

♦

CHEDDAR CHEESE AND SHERRY SPREAD

ABOUT 2 CUPS

¼ pound cheddar cheese, grated
¾ cup sour cream
3 tablespoons dry sherry

Combine the cheese, sour cream and sherry. Beat vigorously with a wooden spoon or in the bowl of an electric beater until light and fluffy. Add more seasonings, such as Tabasco sauce, if desired. Chill and serve with buttered toast or crackers.

TARAMASALATA
A GREEK CARP ROE SPREAD

Most people are familiar with black and red caviar. The Greeks have a word for another kind of caviar and it is *tarama*. It makes an excellent appetizer.

8 GENEROUS SERVINGS

3 slices white bread
3 tablespoons bottled tarama (carp roe)
2 tablespoons lemon juice
½ cup olive oil
¼ cup chopped scallions

1 Trim crusts from the bread and soak the slices in cold water. Squeeze the bread thoroughly.

2 Place the tarama and the lemon juice in the bowl of a food processor and break the bread into the mixture. Pulse on and off until thoroughly blended. Add the oil gradually. The mixture should thicken to the consistency of thick mayonnaise. Stir in the scallions. Serve as a dip in the center of a salad tray ringed with slices of green pepper, tomatoes, cucumbers and olives. Or serve with buttered toast.

♦

BRAZIL NUT–CLAM SPREAD

ABOUT 1 CUP

1 (3-ounce) package cream cheese
Pinch of curry powder
1 cup minced steamed clams
¼ cup finely chopped Brazil nuts

1 Blend the cream cheese with the curry powder.

2 Drain the clams well and add to the cream cheese. Mix thoroughly and stir in the Brazil nuts. Turn into a serving dish and serve with crackers.

♦

SMOKED SALMON DIP

ABOUT ¾ CUP

4 ounces smoked salmon, shredded
⅓ cup cream
½ teaspoon capers (optional)
⅛ teaspoon freshly ground pepper
Tabasco sauce to taste

Put all the ingredients into the container of a food processor and blend until smooth. Grind additional pepper over the top of the dip.

♦

GORGONZOLA DIP

ABOUT ¾ CUP

4 ounces Gorgonzola or other blue cheese
1 (3-ounce) package cream cheese
⅓ cup cognac, or cream

Mash the Gorgonzola, add the cream cheese and mix until smooth. Add the cognac to give a soft consistency. Use for sliced apples, pears or crackers.

SOUR CREAM AND RED CAVIAR

ABOUT 1¼ CUPS

¾ cup sour cream
4 ounces red caviar (salmon roe)

Combine the sour cream with the caviar and chill. Serve as a first course on lettuce leaves, or as a cocktail dip.

♦

SAMBAL DIP

1¾ CUPS

1 (¼-inch-thick) slice of a medium onion
1 garlic clove
2 celery stalks
½ large cucumber, peeled
½ green pepper, seeded
½ teaspoon salt
½ teaspoon turmeric
½ teaspoon ground ginger
⅛ teaspoon chili powder
⅛ teaspoon cumin seed, crushed
1 tablespoon tomato paste
1 cup sour cream

1 Finely chop the onion slice, garlic, celery, cucumber and green pepper in a food processor. Turn into a sieve and press out the juice, then put in a bowl.
2 Sprinkle salt, turmeric, ginger, chili powder and cumin seed over the vegetables and mix thoroughly. Blend in the tomato paste.
3 Add the sour cream and stir until mixed. Chill until ready to serve. Use as a dip for cheese cubes or on crackers.

DEVILED CHICKEN SPREAD

1 CUP

1 cup ground cooked chicken
¼ cup finely chopped scallions
2 tablespoons mayonnaise
2 or 3 drops Tabasco sauce
Salt to taste

Combine all the ingredients until well blended. Chill, if desired, before serving. Use as a spread for canapés.

♦

GUACAMOLE

6 SERVINGS

2 large ripe avocados
Juice of 1 lime
1 teaspoon finely chopped fresh or bottled
    jalapeño chili
1 medium onion, finely chopped
1 garlic clove, minced
1 small tomato, peeled, seeded and finely
    chopped
Salt and freshly ground pepper to taste
¼ cup chopped coriander

1 Peel the avocados and mash the pulp. Combine pulp in a bowl with the lime juice, chili, onion, garlic, tomato, salt, pepper and half the coriander. Blend well.
2 Serve, sprinkled with remaining coriander, as an appetizer or salad.

HUMMUS

2 cups cooked or canned chick-peas, drained
⅔ cup tahini (sesame paste)
¾ cup lemon juice
2 garlic cloves, peeled
Salt and freshly ground pepper to taste
¼ cup finely chopped scallions
Italian parsley leaves

1 Place the chick-peas, tahini, lemon juice, garlic, salt and pepper in a food processor and blend until smooth. Stir in the scallions.

2 Pile into a small bowl and garnish with the parsley leaves. Serve with pita bread.

EGGPLANT AND YOGURT DIP

Eggplant purée plus yogurt is a classic food combination in Greece. The blend makes a marvelous appetizer when served with pita bread or melba toast.

1¼ CUPS

4 (½-inch-thick) slices of eggplant, with skin left on
3 tablespoons olive oil
1 cup yogurt, well drained
1 garlic clove, finely chopped
2 teaspoons lemon juice
1 teaspoon finely chopped mint

1 Preheat the oven to 425°F.

2 Arrange the eggplant slices on a baking sheet and brush the tops on 1 side with 2 tablespoons of the oil. Place in the oven and bake 15 minutes. Using a wide spatula or pancake turner, turn the slices and return the baking sheet to the oven. Bake 5 minutes longer. Remove and let cool.

3 Pull away and discard the outer skin from the eggplant slices. The slices will be quite soft and there should be about 1 cup of pulp. Put the eggplant into the container of a food processor, or blender. Add the yogurt and the remaining 1 tablespoon of oil, garlic, lemon juice and mint. Blend thoroughly. Serve with pita bread or on melba toast.

FONDUE BRUXELLOISE

10 SERVINGS

4 tablespoons butter
6 tablespoons flour
1½ cups milk
2 cups grated Gruyère cheese
1 cup grated Parmesan cheese
½ teaspoon salt
Dash of freshly ground pepper
3 egg yolks, lightly beaten
Flour, egg and fine dry bread crumbs
Oil for deep frying

1 Melt the butter in a saucepan. Stir in the 6 tablespoons flour, using a wire whisk, until blended. Meanwhile, bring the milk to a boil and add all at once to the butter-flour mixture, stirring vigorously with the whisk. Add the cheeses, salt and pepper and cook, stirring, until the cheese has melted. Remove from the heat, correct the seasonings and let cool. Stir in the egg yolks.

2 Pour the mixture into a 9 × 9-inch pan. Chill overnight.

3 Cut into 2-inch fancy shapes. Coat with flour, egg beaten with a little water and finally with the bread crumbs. Let dry at room temperature or in the refrigerator.

4 Heat the fat to 390°F and fry a few at a time until brown. Drain on paper toweling. Serve at once. If desired, accompany with deep-fried parsley.

BEIGNETS AU FROMAGE

ABOUT 3 DOZEN BEIGNETS

¾ cup flour
¼ teaspoon salt
1 tablespoon salad oil
1 egg, beaten
½ cup beer, at room temperature
1 egg white, stiffly beaten
1 pound Gruyère cheese, cut into small cubes
Oil for deep frying

1 Sift ½ cup of the flour with the salt and stir in oil and egg. Add the beer gradually, stirring until the mixture is smooth. Let stand 1 hour. Fold in the egg white.

2 Lightly dredge the cubes of cheese in the remaining flour and coat with the batter. Heat oil to 375°F and fry cheese until brown. Drain on paper toweling and serve piping hot.

◆

HUNGARIAN CHEESE

This is a version of the classic European appetizer known as *Liptauer Käse*.

8 TO 10 SERVINGS

1 cup cottage cheese
½ pound butter
1 tablespoon caraway seeds, crushed or whole
1 tablespoon capers, minced
1 tablespoon minced chives
1 teaspoon dry mustard
1 anchovy, chopped
1 tablespoon paprika

1 Put the cheese through a ricer or fine sieve.

2 Cream the butter with the caraway seeds, capers, chives, mustard and anchovy and gradually stir in the cottage cheese.

3 Form the mixture into a mound, sprinkle with paprika and garnish with salad greens. Serve as a dip for vegetables.

♦

STUFFED FRENCH BREAD

24 TO 36 SLICES

3 (3-ounce) packages cream cheese
1 can anchovy fillets, drained and rubbed
    to a paste
1 tablespoon capers, drained, or chopped
    sour pickle
2 tablespoons chili sauce
1 teaspoon grated onion
1 teaspoon Worcestershire sauce
3 dashes of Tabasco sauce
Salt to taste
¼ pound butter, at room temperature
½ cup minced watercress
1 tablespoon fine, soft bread crumbs
1 loaf French bread

1 Cream the cheese until smooth. Add the anchovy paste, capers, chili sauce, onion, Worcestershire, Tabasco and salt. Thin to a stiff spreading consistency with liquid from the caper or anchovy container.

2 Cream the butter, add the watercress and crumbs and mix.

3 Split the bread lengthwise and remove the center. Spread the entire cavity of the upper half with watercress butter.

Fill the cavity of the lower half with the cheese mixture, piling it up so that when the top half of the loaf is pressed over the lower, the entire cavity will be filled. Wrap in foil and chill well. Using a sharp knife, cut into thin slices before serving.

♦

CHEESE STRAWS

Many southern recipes for cheese straws, a passion since my earliest childhood, call for as much as ½ teaspoon of cayenne. But this can be decreased according to taste.

4 DOZEN STRAWS

¼ pound butter, at room temperature
3 cups fine, soft bread crumbs
2 cups shredded sharp cheddar cheese,
    lightly packed
1½ cups flour
½ cup milk
½ teaspoon salt
¼ teaspoon Tabasco sauce
Dash of paprika
Dash of cayenne
Grated Parmesan cheese

1 Combine all the ingredients except the Parmesan cheese in the container of a food processor. Cover and blend thoroughly.

2 Divide the dough into halves and wrap each half in wax paper. Chill in the refrigerator several hours or overnight.

3 Preheat the oven to 350°F.

4 Between 2 layers of wax paper, roll out half of the dough at a time to ⅛-inch thickness. Using a pastry wheel, cut into strips 6 inches long and ½ inch wide. Sprinkle with Parmesan cheese.

5 Place on greased baking sheets and bake until light brown, 10 to 15 minutes.

GARLIC BREAD

6 TO 8 SERVINGS

2 loaves French bread
1/4 pound butter, softened
1 garlic clove, minced
1 tablespoon Parmesan cheese (optional)
1 tablespoon chopped parsley

1 Preheat the oven to 350°F.

2 Cut the bread diagonally in 1-inch slices without cutting through the bottom crust.

3 To the butter add the garlic, cheese and parsley and brush the cut surfaces of the bread with the garlic butter.

4 Wrap the bread in foil and bake until heated through, about 15 minutes.

♦

HOT HERB BREAD

3 TO 4 SERVINGS

1 loaf French bread
1/4 pound butter, softened
1 large garlic clove, crushed
1 tablespoon chopped basil or other fresh herb
Salt and freshly ground pepper to taste

1 Preheat the oven to 375°F.

2 Slice the bread at 1½-inch intervals, without cutting through the bottom crust.

3 Cream the butter with the remaining ingredients and spread the cut surfaces with the herb butter. Wrap the bread in foil, leaving the top exposed, and heat about 10 minutes. Serve hot.

CREAM CHEESE PASTRY

ENOUGH FOR 4 TO 5 DOZEN TINY PASTRIES

8 ounces cream cheese, at room temperature
1/2 pound butter, at room temperature
2¼ cups flour
1 teaspoon salt

1 Beat the cheese and the butter in an electric mixer, or by hand, until very smooth and creamy. Or do this in a food processor.

2 Gradually mix in the flour and salt with the mixer at low speed, or use a fork to mix in the flour and salt. Knead the dough only until it just clings together.

3 Wrap the dough in wax paper and refrigerate for 3 to 4 hours, or overnight.

4 If the dough has been in the refrigerator overnight, let it stand at room temperature for at least 30 minutes before trying to roll it. Roll out the chilled pastry, one-quarter at a time, on a lightly floured pastry cloth or between 2 sheets of wax paper according to one of the instructions given below.

SLICES Roll out one quarter of the dough into a rectangle (20 × 4 inches). The dough will be about ⅛ inch thick. Place 1 cup of one of the fillings (chicken filling and chicken liver filling take especially well to this method of shaping) down the center of the strip in a sausage shape slightly flattened on top.

Draw one of the edges over the filling and press slightly. Moisten the other edge with egg white and draw up to seal in the filling. Roll the filled pastry onto a cookie sheet with the seam side down. Chill for at least 1 hour. Cut the roll slantwise into 1-inch slices and separate slightly. Brush with lightly beaten egg mixed with 1 tablespoon water and bake in a preheated 325°F oven for 25 to 30 minutes, or until light brown. Or the slices may be frozen and then baked, while still frozen, for 30 minutes, until brown and heated through.

TURNOVERS Roll out one quarter of the pastry until it is about ⅛ inch thick. Cut into 3-inch rounds or squares. Place ½ teaspoon of one of the fillings in the middle of each round or square and fold over to make half-moons or triangles, sealing the edges with egg white or water. Pinch or flute the edges. Place the turnovers on an ungreased baking sheet and chill or freeze before baking. Brush the surface with lightly beaten egg and make a pinpoint hole to allow steam to escape. Bake in a preheated 325°F oven for about 30 minutes, or until light brown.

Each quarter of the dough will make about a dozen pieces. Smaller rounds (2 inches) can be stacked atop each other with the filling in between to give round shapes.

CHICKEN LIVER FILLING
ABOUT 2 CUPS

¼ pound butter
2 onions, finely chopped
1 garlic clove, finely minced
1 pound chicken livers
2 hard-cooked eggs
2 tablespoons cognac
¼ cup finely chopped parsley
Salt and freshly ground pepper to taste

1 Melt the butter in a heavy skillet. Sauté the onions and garlic until tender but not brown.

2 Increase the heat, add the chicken livers, and cook quickly, stirring to brown all sides, for about 3 minutes.

3 Turn the livers onto a chopping board and chop with the eggs until very fine. Mix in the cognac and parsley and add salt and pepper. Cool before using.

CHICKEN FILLING
ABOUT 2 CUPS

1 small onion, finely chopped
4 tablespoons butter
1 egg, lightly beaten
2 cups very finely chopped cooked chicken
½ cup finely chopped parsley
2 tablespoons finely chopped celery
½ teaspoon salt
⅛ teaspoon freshly ground pepper

Sauté the onion in the butter until tender but not brown. Add remaining ingredients and mix well. Cool before using.

SPINACH FILLING
ABOUT 2 CUPS

4 slices of bacon
2 garlic cloves, finely minced
2 small onions, finely chopped
1 pound fresh spinach, washed, or 1 package
    frozen chopped spinach, partially thawed
1 cup pot cheese
Salt and freshly ground pepper to taste
⅛ teaspoon grated nutmeg

1 Dice the bacon and sauté it until crisp. Remove the bacon pieces and reserve.

2 Sauté the garlic and onions until tender but not brown. Add the spinach, cover, and cook until the spinach is tender. If fresh spinach is used, drain excess liquid and chop after cooking.

3 Stir in the pot cheese, seasonings and reserved bacon. Cool before using.

MEAT FILLING
ABOUT 2 CUPS

1 large onion, finely chopped
1/4 pound butter
2 tablespoons chopped chives
2 cups firmly packed cooked ground beef
2 eggs, lightly beaten
1/2 cup chopped parsley
Salt and freshly ground pepper to taste

1 Sauté the onion in the butter until tender but not brown. Add the chives and meat and mix well.

2 Beat in the eggs, stir in the parsley, and season with salt and pepper. The consistency of the filling should be like mashed potatoes; if it is too dry, add another egg. Cool before using.

MUSHROOM FILLING
ABOUT 2 CUPS

3 tablespoons butter
1 large onion, finely chopped
1/2 pound mushrooms, finely chopped
1/4 teaspoon thyme
1/2 teaspoon salt
Freshly ground pepper to taste
2 tablespoons flour
1/4 cup sweet or sour cream

1 In a skillet, heat the butter, add the onion and brown lightly. Add the mushrooms and cook, stirring often, about 3 minutes.

2 Add the thyme, salt and pepper and sprinkle with flour. Stir in the cream and cook gently until thickened. Cool before using.

Pâtés can be as simple as chopped chicken livers with egg or as elegant as a truffled loaf with many meats and seasonings. Even the latter, however, is nothing more than a well-made meat loaf, albeit an expensive one. Incidentally, there is no difference between a pâté and a terrine. Originally, pâtés were baked in earthenware utensils, or terrines.

◆

QUICK CHICKEN-LIVER PÂTÉ

ABOUT 1½ CUPS

1/2 pound chicken livers
Chicken stock to cover
2 hard-cooked eggs
1/2 cup chopped onions
2 tablespoons chicken fat or butter
Salt and freshly ground pepper to taste

1 Simmer the livers in stock until done, 8 to 10 minutes. Drain. Grind them with the eggs, using the medium blade of a food chopper. Or purée in a food processor, using a little of the liquid in which the livers were cooked.

2 Brown the onions lightly in the fat and blend all the ingredients to make a paste. Season with salt and pepper. If desired, season further with a pinch of curry powder or a dash of cognac. Serve on buttered toast fingers or in a lettuce cup.

CHICKEN-LIVER TERRINE

ABOUT 3 CUPS

1 quart boiling salted water
1 celery stalk
2 parsley sprigs
6 whole peppercorns
1 pound chicken livers
1 teaspoon salt
Pinch of cayenne, or ½ teaspoon Tabasco sauce
½ pound soft butter or rendered chicken fat
    (see below)
½ teaspoon grated nutmeg
2 teaspoons dry mustard
¼ teaspoon ground cloves
5 tablespoons minced onions
½ garlic clove, finely chopped
2 tablespoons cognac
2 tablespoons chopped parsley
1 finely chopped truffle (optional)

1 To the boiling water add the celery, parsley and peppercorns. Reduce the heat and simmer 5 minutes. Add the chicken livers and cook, covered, 10 minutes.

2 Drain and grind the livers, using the finest blade of a food grinder. Or purée in a food processor.

3 Add the salt, cayenne, butter, nutmeg, mustard, cloves, onions, garlic and cognac. Blend thoroughly. Add chopped parsley and truffle and mix. Pack the pâté in a 3-cup terrine and chill thoroughly.

4 Garnish the pâté, if desired, with sliced green olives. Serve with buttered toast.

To Render Chicken Fat: Place the fresh fat in the top of a double boiler and heat over boiling water until the fat has been extracted from the tissues. Strain.

TRUFFLED PÂTÉ

24 SERVINGS

1½ pounds fresh pork fat
1 pound lean boneless veal
1 pound boneless pork shoulder
½ pound ham
½ pound tongue
4 chicken breast halves, boned, skinned
    and trimmed
1 pound chicken livers
4 eggs
⅓ cup cognac
½ cup chopped black truffles
½ cup pistachios
2 teaspoons salt
1 teaspoon white pepper
1 teaspoon allspice
½ teaspoon cinnamon
¼ teaspoon ground cloves
⅓ cup flour

1 Preheat the oven to 400°F.

2 Thinly slice ⅔ pound of the pork fat. Grind ⅛ pound each of the veal, pork shoulder, pork fat, ham and tongue. Grind together 3 times or chop in a food processor.

3 Wrap each chicken breast half in a thin strip of sliced pork fat.

4 Line two 1½-quart molds or one 3-quart mold with the remaining thin slices of pork fat, letting long ends hang over outside of the pan.

5 In a food processor, purée half the chicken livers with the eggs and cognac. Gradually add all the ground meats to the processor. Use a little more cognac, an additional egg or a little cream to provide extra liquid if necessary so that the mixture is made as fine as possible.

6 With a sharp knife, cut the remaining pork fat and meats, except the chicken breasts, into cubes less than ⅓ inch in size.

Continued

Combine the finely ground meats with the diced meats. Add the truffles, nuts, seasonings and flour. Mix very well.

7 Fill the molds slightly less than halfway with the pâté mixture. Place wrapped chicken breasts over it. Cover with remaining pâté mixture, filling pans to top.

8 Fold hanging strips of pork fat over the top. Cover each mold tightly with a double thickness of foil. Place in a pan of water and bake 3 hours. Remove the foil and continue baking until the top of the pâté is brown, about 20 minutes longer. Weight the pâté (see below).

How to Weight a Pâté: Firm pâtés should be weighted so they will slice well. Here are instructions for weighting a pâté.

Do not remove molds from underpan after taking from oven. There will be an overflowing of fat after weights are placed on top.

Place a pan that is slightly smaller than the pâté mold right on top of the baked pâté. Fill pan with heavy objects. Do not remove weights until pâté is completely cool. Refrigerate until needed. Pâté will keep several weeks if surrounding fat is not removed.

◆

SHRIMP PÂTÉ

2½ CUPS

3 or 4 tablespoons Pernod
Juice of ½ lemon
1 pound shrimp, cooked, shelled and deveined
1 teaspoon Dijon mustard
½ teaspoon mace
Dash of Tabasco sauce
¼ pound butter, softened
Salt and freshly ground pepper to taste

1 Put the Pernod, lemon juice, shrimp and seasonings into the container of a food processor. Blend until the mixture is coarsely chopped.

2 Stir the blended mixture into the softened butter and add salt and pepper. Place in a mold or bowl and chill.

Note: If desired, dry sherry may be substituted for the Pernod. If sherry is used, add 1 teaspoon chopped tarragon to the seasonings.

◆

FINE LIVER PÂTÉ

24 SERVINGS

1 teaspoon rendered chicken or pork fat
2 pounds chicken or pork livers
3 eggs
⅓ cup cognac
1½ cups cream
⅔ cup diced fresh unrendered chicken fat
  or fresh pork fat
1 onion, coarsely chopped
½ cup flour
2 teaspoons salt
1 teaspoon ground ginger
2 teaspoons white pepper
1 teaspoon allspice

1 Preheat the oven to 325°F.

2 Lightly grease a 3-quart mold with rendered fat.

3 In a food processor, make a fine purée of the livers, eggs, cognac and cream. From time to time add a little diced fat, onion and flour. Add all the seasonings and mix well. Pour into the mold and cover the top with a double thickness of foil.

4 Place in a pan of water and bake 2 to 2½ hours. Cool the pâté, then store it in the refrigerator. It is not necessary to weight it.

◆

COUNTRY PÂTÉ

24 SERVINGS

1½ pounds fresh pork fat
1 pound boneless veal
1 pound boneless pork shoulder
1 pound ham
½ pound chicken or pork livers
8 garlic cloves
¼ cup cream
3 eggs
½ cup cognac
2 teaspoons salt
2 teaspoons white pepper
½ teaspoon allspice
½ teaspoon cinnamon
½ cup flour

1 Preheat the oven to 400°F.
2 Thinly slice ½ pound of the pork fat. Finely grind half of the remaining pork fat with all the veal and pork shoulder. Or chop fine in a food processor.
3 Line a 3-quart mold or two 1½-quart molds with the thin slices of pork fat, letting long ends hang outside of the pan.
4 Grind the ham and remaining pork fat, using the coarse blade of the meat grinder. Or coarsely chop in a food processor.
5 In a food processor, purée the chicken livers with the garlic, cream, eggs and cognac. Gradually add about one third of the finely ground veal-pork mixture.

6 In a mixing bowl combine all the ground and puréed meats and add the remaining seasonings and flour. Mix all the ingredients thoroughly.
7 Fill the prepared mold with the pâté mixture. Fold the overhanging strips of pork fat over the top. Cover tightly with a double thickness of foil. Place the mold in a pan of water and bake 3 hours. Remove the foil and continue baking until the top of the pâté is brown, about 20 minutes longer. Weight the pâté according to the directions given on the opposite page.

Note: If desired, the veal and pork shoulder called for in this recipe may be replaced by any available game, such as venison, hare or pheasant. The amount of garlic used may be varied according to taste.

◆

RABBIT OR HARE PÂTÉ

24 SERVINGS

1 (5-pound) hare or rabbit
1 cup cognac
3 pounds boneless pork
4 shallots
3 leeks, white part only
1 cup sliced celery
2 teaspoons salt
1 teaspoon freshly ground pepper
3 eggs plus 2 egg yolks
½ pound foie gras or liver sausage
¼ teaspoon thyme
¼ teaspoon powdered bay leaf
¾ pound salt pork, sliced
2 egg whites
3 envelopes unflavored gelatin

Continued

1   Reserve the hare liver. Bone the hare and slice the meat, reserving the bones. Add the cognac to the meat and let stand overnight in the refrigerator. Drain, reserving the cognac.

2   Preheat the oven to 325°F.

3   Grind the hare liver, pork and vegetables, using the finest blade of a food grinder. Or finely chop in a food processor. Add the salt, pepper, eggs and yolks and mix. Reserve the egg shells. Line the bottom of a 3-quart casserole with three-quarters of the mixture. Arrange the hare slices and foie gras on top and sprinkle with the seasonings. Cover with the remaining pork mixture and top with the salt pork.

4   Cover the casserole and bake in a pan of hot water 3 hours.

5   Meanwhile, cook the bones of the hare in salted water to cover 2 hours. Drain, reserving the broth.

6   Press any excess liquid from the cooked pâté and add the juice to the broth. Add the cognac marinade. Boil until reduced to 4 cups. Strain and chill. Chill the pâté.

7   Remove the fat from the broth. Beat the egg whites with the reserved crushed egg shells. Add to the broth and boil 5 minutes. Let stand 20 minutes and strain through dampened cheesecloth.

8   Soften the gelatin in ¾ cup of cold water, add to the hot broth and stir until dissolved. Add more cognac to taste.

9   Remove the pâté from the casserole. Wash the dish and oil it. Cover the bottom with a layer of thin gelatin and chill until set. Return the pâté to the dish, pour thin gelatin around the sides and chill.

BEET AND SCALLION APPETIZER

ABOUT 4 SERVINGS

3 medium beets, cooked
¼ cup chopped scallions
½ cup sour cream
½ teaspoon prepared mustard
½ teaspoon lemon juice
Freshly ground pepper or Tabasco sauce to
    taste

1   Cut the beets in thin matchlike strips, or coarsely chop. Add the scallions.

2   Mix the remaining ingredients, add to the beets and blend. Chill. Serve on chilled plates with toast.

♦

CUCUMBER APPETIZER

6 SERVINGS

3 medium cucumbers
Salt
5 scallions, chopped fine
Pinch of freshly ground pepper
¼ teaspoon ground cumin
¼ teaspoon chili powder
¼ teaspoon ground cloves
1 cup yogurt

1   Cut the cucumbers in half lengthwise. Remove seeds and slice cucumbers. Lightly salt the cucumbers and let stand 20 minutes. Press out excess moisture from the cucumbers by spreading on a plate and topping with another plate on which a heavy object, such as an iron, may be rested.

2 Add the scallions, pepper, cumin, chili powder and cloves to the yogurt. Blend well. Chill both the sauce and the cucumbers well. Serve the cucumbers in individual dishes, topped with the yogurt sauce.

◆

ANCHOVIES WITH ONION RINGS

ABOUT 2 CUPS

6 anchovy fillets
1 garlic clove, minced
2 tablespoons chopped parsley
1 teaspoon drained capers
2 tablespoons bread crumbs
1 cup olive oil
¼ cup red wine vinegar
Salt and freshly ground pepper to taste
1 onion, sliced into rings

1 In a mortar, grind the anchovies with 1 tablespoon oil from the can until smooth. Add the garlic, parsley, capers and crumbs and continue grinding until the paste is well blended. Or use a food processor and purée.

2 Add the oil, vinegar, salt and pepper. Blend well and pour the mixture over the onions. Chill. Serve with chilled fish or meats as an hors d'oeuvre.

CELERY WITH RED-CAVIAR STUFFING

Black caviar is the product of the sturgeon. Red caviar comes from salmon and has its virtues, too.

6 SERVINGS

2 bunches celery
8 ounces cream cheese
1 tablespoon grated onion
⅓ cup chopped parsley
⅓ cup red caviar
Salt and freshly ground pepper to taste

1 Use only choice, inner stalks of celery. Wash thoroughly.

2 Mix the softened cream cheese with the onion, parsley, caviar, salt and pepper. Stuff the celery stalks with the mixture and refrigerate until serving time.

◆

CÉLERI RÉMOULADE

8 TO 12 SERVINGS

4 or more celery knobs, enough to make 3 cups
    when shredded
2 egg yolks
1 tablespoon white vinegar
2 tablespoons Dijon or Düsseldorf mustard
¼ teaspoon Tabasco sauce
Salt and freshly ground pepper to taste
1½ cups olive oil (may be part vegetable oil)
Lemon juice to taste
1 teaspoon chopped parsley

Continued

1 Peel the celery knobs and drop them into cold water.

2 Place the egg yolks in a mixing bowl and add the vinegar, mustard, Tabasco, and salt and pepper. Start beating with a wire whisk or an electric beater, gradually adding the oil. Continue beating until all the oil is used and the mayonnaise is thick. Add the lemon juice. If necessary, thin the sauce with a little water, adding it a little at a time.

3 Drain the celery knobs. Cut them into the thinnest possible slices, then cut the slices into the thinnest possible shreds (julienne). Place the shreds in a mixing bowl and add enough mayonnaise to bind thoroughly. Season to taste with salt and pepper. Chill. Serve cold, sprinkled with parsley, as an appetizer or first course.

◆

ROASTED PEPPERS

6 TO 8 SERVINGS

6 large sweet green or red peppers
½ cup finely chopped Italian parsley
⅓ cup olive oil
2 large garlic cloves, coarsely chopped
1 teaspoon finely chopped mint
Salt and freshly ground pepper to taste

1 Put the peppers under the broiler until the skin is black and blistered, turning the peppers as they roast. Put in a paper bag until peppers are cool enough to handle. Peel off the skin and remove the core and seeds. Do not wash the peppers. Cut them into slices.

2 Place the peppers in a mixing bowl and add the remaining ingredients. Refrigerate until ready to serve.

OLD HOUSE CHILES RELLENOS

This is an excellent unusual version of chiles rellenos, a great Mexican specialty. The basic version of the dish is made by filling chilies with cheese or meat, coating with a batter and deep frying. This version, which I sampled in the Old House restaurant in the El Dorado Hotel in Santa Fe, New Mexico, consists of roasting the chilies, filling with three cheeses and baking. They are served piping hot with a cold tomato salsa.

4 SERVINGS

8 medium to large poblano chilies
4 ounces mascarpone cheese
4 ounces goat cheese
4 ounces Asiago, fontina or Gruyère cheese
2 cups fresh tomato-ginger salsa (page 563)
¼ cup diced red pepper
¼ cup diced yellow pepper
¼ cup diced seeded tomatoes

1 Roast the chilies under the broiler or on a charcoal grill, turning often, until the skin is blackened. Place them in a paper bag and close tightly. When chilies are cool enough to handle, pull away and discard the skin. Cut away and discard the stems. Make a small slit down the center of each chili and cut or scrape away the seeds and inside veins.

2 Preheat the oven to 350°F.

3 Put the cheeses into the container of a food processor and blend thoroughly.

4 Spoon equal portions of the cheese mixture into each of the chilies and fold over the sides to seal. Arrange the filled chilies in a baking dish. Place in the oven and bake 10 minutes, or until the filling is piping hot.

5 Arrange 2 chilies on each of 4 hot plates. Spoon the salsa around each serving. Sprinkle the tops of the stuffed chilies with red and yellow peppers and diced tomatoes. Serve immediately.

ANCHOVY AND PIMIENTO SALAD

4 TO 6 SERVINGS

2 hard-cooked eggs
3 pimientos
2 (2-ounce) cans flat anchovy fillets
Romaine lettuce leaves
2 tablespoons lemon juice
1 small onion, minced
⅛ teaspoon freshly ground pepper
⅛ teaspoon oregano
1 tablespoon minced parsley

1 Chop the egg whites fine. Push the yolks through a sieve. Cut the pimientos into strips the same size as the anchovies.

2 Drain off the oil from the anchovies and reserve. Separate the anchovy fillets and place them in a row on the lettuce leaves. Lay the pimiento strips across the fillets to form a lattice pattern.

3 Combine the anchovy oil with the lemon juice, onion and pepper and pour the mixture over the anchovies. Sprinkle with the oregano, chopped egg whites, sieved yolks and parsley.

◆

ANTIPASTO MUSHROOMS

6 SERVINGS

¼ cup finely minced prosciutto
⅓ cup finely chopped parsley
½ cup soft fresh bread crumbs
¼ cup grated Parmesan cheese
Olive oil
18 medium mushroom caps
3 cups basic tomato sauce (page 561)

1 Preheat the oven to 350° F.

2 Mix the prosciutto with the parsley, bread crumbs and cheese. Add enough olive oil to bind the mixture. Spoon a little of the filling into each of the mushroom caps.

3 Spoon three quarters of the tomato sauce over the bottom of a baking dish and arrange the mushrooms over it. Spoon the remaining sauce over the stuffed mushrooms. Bake for 30 minutes. Serve hot or cold.

◆

STUFFED MUSHROOMS

6 TO 8 SERVINGS

24 medium to large mushrooms,
    or 40 tiny ones
¼ cup olive oil
1 (2-ounce) can flat anchovy fillets
1 garlic clove, minced
1 teaspoon lemon juice
¾ cup soft fresh bread crumbs
¼ cup chopped parsley
Freshly ground pepper to taste

1 Preheat the oven to 350°F.

2 Remove the stems from the mushrooms. Chop the stems and sauté them in 3 tablespoons of the oil for 2 or 3 minutes.

3 Chop the anchovies with the garlic. Add the lemon juice, bread crumbs and parsley, then the sautéed mushroom stems; mix. Season with pepper.

4 Fill the caps with the mixture, drizzle remaining oil over them and bake for 15 minutes, or until hot.

MUSHROOMS A LA GRECQUE

The isles of Greece where burning Sappho loved and sung have contributed a splendid hors d'oeuvre.

ABOUT 6 SERVINGS

1½ pounds whole small mushrooms
2 cups water
1 cup olive oil
1 celery stalk
1 frond fennel
1 garlic clove, peeled
Juice of 1 lemon
1 tablespoon white vinegar
¾ teaspoon ground coriander
¾ teaspoon salt
½ teaspoon rosemary
½ teaspoon sage
½ teaspoon thyme
½ bay leaf
8 peppercorns

1 Combine all ingredients and bring to a boil. Simmer, stirring occasionally, 5 minutes.

2 Pour into a bowl and marinate overnight in the refrigerator.

3 Serve the mushrooms on toothpicks or, as a first course, on a bed of lettuce leaves.

Artichokes à la Grecque, page 449.

MARINATED RAW MUSHROOMS

ABOUT 3 CUPS

½ pound very fresh mushrooms
½ cup olive oil
3 tablespoons wine vinegar or lemon juice
½ teaspoon tarragon or oregano, crushed
¼ teaspoon salt
Freshly ground pepper to taste

1 Trim the ends from the stems of the mushrooms. Wash the mushrooms thoroughly, dry and slice.

2 Mix the remaining ingredients together, add to the mushrooms and toss until all the pieces are coated. Let stand at room temperature several hours. Serve with toothpicks as a cocktail accompaniment.

◆

MUSHROOMS STUFFED WITH LIVER

12 APPETIZERS

12 large mushrooms
5 tablespoons olive oil
½ pound chicken livers
1 tablespoon minced onions
1 (3-ounce) package cream cheese, softened
¼ teaspoon tarragon
Salt and freshly ground pepper to taste

1 Remove and chop the mushroom stems. In a skillet heat 3 tablespoons of the oil, add the mushroom caps and sauté 5 minutes, turning frequently. Remove to a platter.

2 Add the remaining oil to the pan and cook the livers, mushroom stems and onions until the livers are light brown. Chop the livers very fine and cool the mixture.

3 Cream the cheese, add the liver mixture and season with the tarragon, salt and pepper. Pile the mixture into the mushroom caps and chill thoroughly.

♦

MUSHROOMS STUFFED WITH SNAILS

6 SERVINGS

¼ pound butter, softened
1 teaspoon minced shallots
1 large garlic clove, crushed
1 tablespoon minced parsley
1 tablespoon minced celery
¼ teaspoon salt
Freshly ground pepper to taste
12 very large mushrooms
12 canned snails, drained

1 Preheat the oven to 375° F.

2 Cream 6 tablespoons of the butter with the shallots, garlic, parsley, celery, salt and pepper.

3 Remove the mushroom stems and reserve for another use. In a skillet, heat the remaining butter, add the mushroom caps and turn to coat on all sides. Arrange in the depressions of a snail pan, in scallop shells or in a shallow baking dish.

4 Place a scant teaspoon of the herb butter in each mushroom cap, add a snail and cover it with a little more butter.

5 Bake about 15 minutes.

Note: Any leftover herb butter may be used for baked or boiled fish.

CREAM CHEESE– STUFFED TOMATOES

ABOUT 2 DOZEN

2 pints cherry tomatoes
3 (3-ounce) packages cream cheese, at room
    temperature
2 ounces Roquefort or Danish blue cheese,
    at room temperature
1 tablespoon lemon juice
Tabasco sauce to taste

1 Cut off a thin slice from the stem end of the tomatoes. Scoop out the seeds and pulp.

2 Combine the remaining ingredients and beat with a fork until the cheeses are well blended. Spoon the mixture into the tomatoes and top with a sprig of parsley.

Note: If desired, ½ cup chopped cucumber or 1 tablespoon chopped chives may be substituted for the Roquefort or blue cheese.

STUFFED SNAILS

Snails can be rinsed and used directly from the can, but I find that the flavor improves enormously if they are simmered briefly with a few seasonings. Either way, they recall one of our first encounters with French-restaurant dining and are simple to prepare in the home.

4 TO 6 SERVINGS

1/4 teaspoon minced garlic
5 tablespoons butter
2 tablespoons chopped parsley
1/2 teaspoon salt
Dash of freshly ground pepper
3/4 cup soft fresh bread crumbs
1 (6 1/2-ounce) can French snails
1 bay leaf
1/2 teaspoon thyme
2 parsley sprigs
2 tablespoons dry white wine
24 snail shells

1 Preheat the oven to 450°F.

2 Sauté the garlic in 3 tablespoons of the butter for about 4 minutes, until limp and transparent. Remove from heat. Add the parsley, half of the salt, the pepper and bread crumbs. Mix lightly.

3 Empty the snails with their liquid into a saucepan and add the bay leaf, thyme, parsley sprigs and wine. Cover and simmer for 10 minutes. Drain and cool slightly.

4 Melt the remaining butter and combine it with the remaining salt. Dip each snail into this mixture and place it in a shell. Fill the rest of the shell with the bread-crumb mixture, using about 1/2 teaspoon for each.

5 Place the snails in snail holders and bake for 5 to 8 minutes.

COOKED PERIWINKLES

ABOUT 1 CUP PERIWINKLE MEATS

1 quart periwinkles
3 tablespoons salt

1 Rinse the periwinkles well and place them in a 1 1/2-quart saucepan. Add water to cover to the depth of 1 inch and the salt.

2 Bring the periwinkles to a boil and simmer until the operculum (a tiny "door" on each periwinkle) falls off. This may require from 10 to 20 minutes.

3 Drain the periwinkles and cool them. Remove the meat from each periwinkle with a pin or nutpick. Serve with toothpicks and cocktail sauce or melted butter on the side.

◆

BAKED STUFFED CLAMS WITH GARLIC BUTTER

4 SERVINGS

2 cups shucked clams
24 empty clam shells
10 tablespoons butter, at room temperature
1 tablespoon minced garlic
1 tablespoon finely chopped shallots
1/4 cup finely chopped parsley
3/4 teaspoon finely chopped thyme, or half the amount dried
1/2 teaspoon hot red pepper flakes
Salt and freshly ground pepper to taste
3 tablespoons fine fresh bread crumbs
3 tablespoons grated Parmesan cheese

1 Cut each clam into 4 or 5 pieces. Fill each clam shell with equal amounts of the clams.

2 Preheat the broiler.

3 Put the butter into a mixing bowl and add the garlic, shallots, parsley, thyme, red pepper flakes, salt and pepper. Spoon equal amounts of the butter onto each filled clam. Smooth over the top.

4 Blend the bread crumbs and cheese and additional pepper to taste. Sprinkle equal amounts of the mixture on top of each stuffed clam.

5 Place the stuffed clams under the broiler 5 or 6 inches from the source of heat. Cook about 3 minutes and turn the oven heat to 450°F. Let cook 2 minutes longer. Serve immediately.

♦

MUSSELS IN BACON

6 SERVINGS

36 mussels
1 cup water
18 slices bacon

1 Scrub the mussels well with a stiff brush or a plastic mesh scrubbing ball. Rinse well and put them into a heavy kettle. Add the water and steam 10 minutes. Discard any mussels that do not open. Use a knife to remove the mussels from the shells.

2 Preheat the oven to 400°F.

3 Cut the bacon slices in half crosswise and cook in a skillet until half done. Drain on paper toweling and cool slightly. Wrap a half slice of bacon around each mussel and secure each with a toothpick.

4 Bake in oven 5 minutes, or until the bacon is crisp. Drain on paper toweling and serve.

MUSSELS RAVIGOTE

6 SERVINGS

2 pounds mussels
2 shallots, coarsely chopped
2 small onions, quartered
2 parsley sprigs
Salt and freshly ground pepper to taste
Pinch of cayenne
1 cup dry white wine
2 tablespoons butter
½ bay leaf
½ teaspoon thyme
Sauce ravigote (see below)

1 Scrub the mussels well to remove all exterior sand and dirt. Place them in a large kettle with the shallots, onions, parsley, salt and pepper, cayenne, wine, butter, bay leaf and thyme. Cover and bring to a boil. Simmer for 5 to 10 minutes, or until the mussels have opened.

2 Lift mussels from the broth and discard any that have not opened. Strain the broth through a sieve lined with cheesecloth and reserve 1 cup for the sauce.

3 Take the mussels out of the shells and spoon into a serving dish. Cover with sauce ravigote.

SAUCE RAVIGOTE
ABOUT 1½ CUPS

3 tablespoons chopped shallots
⅓ cup chopped capers
1 tablespoon chopped tarragon
2 tablespoons chopped parsley
1 cup broth in which mussels cooked
½ cup mayonnaise
3 tablespoons prepared mustard, preferably
*   Dijon or Düsseldorf*
¼ teaspoon Tabasco sauce
Freshly ground pepper to taste

Continued

1 Combine the shallots and capers in a mixing bowl. Add the tarragon and parsley.

2 Reduce the mussel broth by half by boiling over high heat.

3 Add the mayonnaise to the bowl and, using a wire whisk, beat in the hot liquid. Add the mustard, Tabasco and pepper. Cool sauce to room temperature. Pour over shelled mussels and serve.

♦

ANGUILLES QUO VADIS

Eels are available during most of the winter months and may be purchased in many Italian fish markets. One of the finest preparations using them is in this green herb sauce.

8 TO 10 SERVINGS

½ cup olive oil
1½ pounds eel, cleaned, skinned and cut
 into 1½-inch pieces
1 quart boiling chicken stock
1 cup dry white wine
Juice of 1 lemon
Salt and freshly ground pepper to taste
¼ cup chopped parsley
¼ cup chopped mint
¼ cup chopped chives
¼ cup puréed spinach

1 Heat the oil in a skillet, add the eel and cook about 5 minutes. Add the stock and cook 5 minutes longer. Drain.

2 Combine the eel, wine, lemon juice, salt, pepper, herbs and spinach. Bring to a boil. Cool and chill.

CRABMEAT REMICK

6 SERVINGS

2 cups fresh crabmeat in large flakes, picked
 over well to remove any bits of shell
 or cartilage
6 slices bacon, fried until crisp
1 teaspoon dry mustard
½ teaspoon paprika
Few drops of Tabasco sauce
½ cup chili sauce
1 teaspoon tarragon vinegar
1¾ cups mayonnaise

1 Preheat the oven to 350°F.

2 Pile the crab flakes into 6 buttered individual shells or ramekins. Heat in the oven and top with crisp bacon.

3 Blend together the mustard, paprika and Tabasco. Add the chili sauce and vinegar, mix well and add the mayonnaise. Spread the warmed crabmeat with this sauce and brown under a preheated broiler.

The following recipes for oysters and clams call for placing the shells on rock salt. The rock salt, such as that used for freezing ice cream, provides a steady base for the shells and keeps the cooked food warm.

♦

OYSTERS CASINO

6 SERVINGS

3 dozen freshly opened oysters
3 slices bacon
½ cup minced scallions
¼ cup minced green pepper
¼ cup minced celery
1 teaspoon lemon juice
1 teaspoon Worcestershire sauce
2 drops of Tabasco sauce

1 Preheat the oven to 400°F.
2 Place 2 drained oysters on the deep half of 1 shell. Arrange filled oyster shells on a layer of rock salt in 1 large baking pan or 6 individual shallow casseroles.
3 Cook the bacon in a skillet until crisp, remove from the pan, drain and crumble.
4 To the bacon fat add the scallions, green pepper and celery and cook until almost tender. Season with lemon juice, Worcestershire and Tabasco.
5 Spoon the mixture on the oysters in the shells and top with the crumbled bacon. Bake 10 minutes.

OYSTERS ROCKEFELLER I

4 SERVINGS

24 oysters on the half shell
½ pound butter
⅓ cup finely chopped parsley
¼ cup finely chopped celery
¼ cup finely chopped shallots or scallions
½ small garlic clove, minced
2 cups chopped watercress
⅓ cup chopped fennel
⅓ cup fine soft bread crumbs
¼ cup anisette or Pernod
Salt and freshly ground pepper to taste

1 Preheat the oven to 450°F.
2 Fill 4 tin pie plates with rock salt and arrange 6 oysters on the half shell on each.
3 In a skillet heat the butter, add the parsley, celery, shallots and garlic and cook 3 minutes. Add the watercress and fennel and cook until the watercress wilts, about 1 minute.
4 Pour the mixture into the container of a food processor and add the remaining ingredients. Blend until the sauce is thoroughly puréed.
5 Place 1 tablespoon of the sauce on each oyster and spread to the rim of the shell. Bake the oysters just until the sauce bubbles, about 4 minutes.

OYSTERS ROCKEFELLER II

6 SERVINGS

½ pound spinach, washed well and drained
6 or 8 scallions
½ head lettuce
1½ celery stalks
½ bunch of parsley
1 garlic clove
½ pound butter
½ cup fine bread crumbs
1 tablespoon Worcestershire sauce
1 teaspoon anchovy paste
½ teaspoon salt
Few dashes of Tabasco sauce
1 ounce (2 tablespoons) Pernod
36 oysters

1 Put the spinach, scallions, lettuce, celery, parsley and garlic in the container of a food processor and chop fine.

2 Heat the butter and mix in the greens, bread crumbs, Worcestershire sauce, anchovy paste, salt, Tabasco and Pernod. Refrigerate until ready for use.

3 Preheat the oven to 450°F.

4 Spoon the mixture onto 36 oysters on the half shell, set the oyster halves on a bed of rock salt and bake until piping hot. Serve immediately.

CLAMS AUX BLINIS

4 SERVINGS

36 small clams
1 tablespoon finely chopped shallots
½ cup dry white wine
1 teaspoon finely chopped parsley
½ teaspoon finely chopped tarragon
½ teaspoon finely chopped chives
3 egg yolks, beaten
½ cup cream
2 ounces (¼ cup) Pernod
1 tablespoon hollandaise sauce (page 554)
12 blinis (page 658)

1 Have the clams opened and reserve the clams and the clam juice. Discard the shells. Chop the clams and pour the clam juice into a saucepan.

2 Add the shallots and wine and bring to the boil. Cook until wine is reduced by half. Add the parsley, tarragon and chives. Remove the saucepan from the heat.

3 Combine the beaten egg yolks and cream and add to the saucepan. Blend well and return to the lowest possible heat. Stir in half the Pernod and the hollandaise sauce. Stir well and heat thoroughly but do not boil or the sauce may curdle.

4 Add the clams and heat thoroughly. Do not overcook or the clams will toughen. Add the remaining Pernod, blend well and serve immediately on top of warm blinis.

SEA SCALLOPS SEVICHE

Attitudes toward food are frequently droll. Many are those who enjoy raw oysters or clams on the half shell but shudder at the thought of eating fish or other shellfish in an uncooked state. Fresh scallops are delicious when marinated in lime juice and seasonings.

4 SERVINGS

1 cup (about ½ pound) sea scallops
Juice of 4 limes
2 tablespoons chopped onions
1 tablespoon chopped parsley
2 tablespoons chopped green pepper
3 tablespoons olive oil
Salt and freshly ground pepper to taste

1 Cut the raw scallops into quarters and cover with the lime juice. Marinate 1 hour or more in the refrigerator. Drain.

2 Combine the onions, parsley and green pepper with the scallops. Add the olive oil and mix well. Season with salt and pepper. Serve as a first course.

SEVICHE

The essential thing in making this dish is that the fish be as fresh as possible, because the only "cooking" is the action of the lime juice on the raw fish.

6 TO 8 SERVINGS

2 cups of ½-inch cubes of fish fillets (weakfish, bluefish, sea squab, flounder, red snapper, bass, etc.)
2 small hot green peppers, finely chopped
1 large tomato, peeled and chopped
½ cup coarsely chopped onions
¼ cup finely chopped sweet red peppers
1½ garlic cloves, minced
½ cup tomato juice
⅓ cup lime juice
⅓ cup olive oil
1 tablespoon finely chopped parsley
1 tablespoon finely chopped coriander
2 thyme sprigs, finely chopped
Salt and freshly ground pepper to taste

Combine all ingredients and let stand in the refrigerator overnight.

SHRIMP AND MASHED CUCUMBERS

This is an easily made appetizer, a beguiling combination of the flavors of the East and West. It is a creation of Hubert's popular restaurant in Manhattan.

4 SERVINGS

16 medium shrimp
Salt to taste
1 (4-inch) length of cucumber, preferably the
    seedless variety
½ cup soy sauce
½ cup rice vinegar
½ cup Dijon mustard
2 tablespoons honey
2 tablespoons lemon juice

1 Put the shrimp in a saucepan and add salt. Bring to the boil, remove from the heat and let stand until cool. Set aside.

2 Cut the cucumber crosswise into 4 pieces of equal length. Place the cucumber pieces, flat sides down, on a flat surface. Cover with wax paper to prevent splattering. Crush each with a solid blow using a flat mallet or the bottom of a heavy skillet.

3 Arrange equal portions of the cucumber in the center of 4 appetizer plates. Cut each shrimp in half and arrange one fourth of the shrimp halves neatly around the cucumbers.

4 Blend the soy sauce with the rice vinegar, mustard, honey and lemon juice. Shake well. Pour equal portions of this sauce around the shrimp.

SHRIMP RÉMOULADE

4 TO 6 SERVINGS

¾ cup olive oil
¼ cup prepared mustard
¼ cup wine vinegar
1 teaspoon salt
½ teaspoon paprika
1 hard-cooked egg, chopped
½ cup minced celery
1 tablespoon grated onion
2 tablespoons minced parsley
½ tablespoon minced green pepper
2 pounds shrimp, cooked, shelled and deveined

Whip the oil, mustard, vinegar, salt and paprika thoroughly. Fold in the egg, celery, onion, parsley and green pepper. Add the shrimp and chill for several hours until ready to serve.

◆

SHERRIED SHRIMP

4 SERVINGS

24 medium raw shrimp, shelled and deveined
¼ cup soy sauce
¼ cup sherry
¼ cup vegetable oil
1 tablespoon finely chopped fresh ginger
1 garlic clove, finely chopped

1 Marinate the shrimp in the remaining ingredients 1 hour or less.

2 Place the shrimp with a little of the marinade in a skillet and cook 3 or 4 minutes, until the shrimp are done.

SHRIMP WITH HERB SAUCE

6 SERVINGS

36 shrimp, cooked, shelled and deveined
Shredded lettuce
½ cup mayonnaise
1 tablespoon chopped parsley
1 tablespoon chopped chives
1 tablespoon chopped cucumber
1 tablespoon finely chopped fennel
½ teaspoon lemon juice

1 Arrange 6 shrimp for each person on 6 beds of lettuce. Cover with plastic wrap and chill.

2 Combine the remaining ingredients and let stand in the refrigerator 1 hour.

3 Spoon the mayonnaise sauce over the shrimp before serving.

♦

ROQUEFORT-STUFFED SHRIMP

6 SERVINGS

24 jumbo raw shrimp
3 ounces cream cheese
1 ounce Roquefort or Danish blue cheese
½ teaspoon prepared mustard
1 teaspoon finely chopped scallions
1 cup finely chopped parsley

1 Bring 2 quarts salted water to a boil in a saucepan. Add the shrimp and, when the water returns to a boil, cook 3 to 5 minutes.

2 Drain the shrimp, shell and devein. Split the shrimp down the spine about halfway through. Chill.

3 Meanwhile, blend the cheeses, mustard and scallions. Using a knife or small spatula, stuff the cheese mixture into the split backs of the shrimp. Roll the cheese side of the shrimp in parsley and serve chilled.

♦

SHRIMP WITH DILL AND LEMON SAUCE

6 SERVINGS

¼ pound butter
2 pounds raw shrimp, shelled and deveined
1 tablespoon chopped dill
1 teaspoon Worcestershire sauce
Juice of 1 lemon
6 drops of Tabasco sauce
Salt and freshly ground pepper to taste

In a skillet heat the butter, add the shrimp and cook, shaking the skillet occasionally, until the shrimp are red in color and cooked through, about 3 minutes. Sprinkle with the remaining ingredients and serve on toothpicks.

SHRIMP VINAIGRETTE WITH ROSEMARY

4 SERVINGS

24 medium shrimp, cooked
½ cup finely chopped heart of celery
1 bunch watercress, rinsed and drained, with tough stems trimmed away and discarded
2 navel oranges, peeled and sliced, or cut into sections, membranes removed
7 tablespoons shallot vinaigrette (page 577)
½ teaspoon minced rosemary
½ teaspoon paprika

1 Peel and devein the shrimp and chill until ready to use.

2 Put the celery in a small saucepan and add water to cover. Bring to a simmer and cook about 30 seconds, no longer. Drain and set aside to cool.

3 Arrange equal portions of watercress on each of 4 salad plates. Arrange equal amounts of orange pieces and shrimp symmetrically on each bed of watercress. Sprinkle with equal amounts of chopped celery.

4 Blend the vinaigrette sauce with the rosemary and paprika and beat well. Spoon equal portions of the sauce over each serving.

CHILLED SHRIMP WITH DILL SAUCE

6 SERVINGS

1 quart water
1 celery stalk
1 carrot
Juice of ½ lemon
1 tablespoon salt
¼ teaspoon cayenne
1 small garlic clove
24 medium raw shrimp, shelled and deveined
Dill sauce (see following recipe)

1 In a deep saucepan combine all the ingredients except the shrimp and sauce and boil 10 minutes.

2 Drop the shrimp into the boiling liquid, return to a boil and drain. Discard the vegetables and chill the shrimp. Serve with dill sauce.

DILL SAUCE
ABOUT 1 CUP

¾ cup olive oil
3 tablespoon lemon juice
1 tablespoon chopped dill
½ teaspoon dry mustard
Salt to taste
½ garlic clove (optional)

Combine all the ingredients and mix well. Let stand overnight in the refrigerator. Discard the garlic and serve the sauce chilled.

HERRING SALAD

1 salt herring, filleted, or 2 (5-ounce) jars
    Bismarck herring
1½ cups diced boiled potatoes
1½ cups diced cooked beets
½ cup diced peeled apples
¼ cup chopped onions
⅓ cup diced gherkins
¼ cup distilled white vinegar
2 tablespoons water
2 tablespoons sugar
White pepper to taste
½ cup heavy cream, whipped
1 or 2 hard-cooked eggs, sliced
Chopped parsley
Sour cream

1 Soak the herring overnight in cold water. Drain and dice. Mix carefully with the potatoes, drained beets, apples, onions and gherkins.

2 Blend the vinegar, water, sugar and pepper and add to the herring mixture. Add the whipped cream.

3 Pack the mixture into a mold rinsed out in cold water and chill in the refrigerator.

4 Unmold and garnish with hard-cooked eggs and parsley. Serve with sour cream.

Gefilte Fish, page 233.

SCALLOP WALTZ

This is an unusual scallop appetizer, a creation of Len Allison, chef-owner of Hubert's restaurant in Manhattan. Scallops are poached quickly and arranged on a sweet-and-sour fruit sauce made with pineapple, sweet peppers, raisins and a touch of orange rind.

2 SERVINGS

1 cup dry white vermouth
1¼ cups (about 10 ounces) sea scallops
¼ cup diced fresh pineapple
¼ cup diced sweet yellow pepper
¼ cup diced sweet red pepper
2 tablespoons diced green pepper, preferably
    a mildly hot chili poblano
¼ cup finely chopped onions
2 tablespoons golden raisins
½ tablespoon coriander seed, ground in a
    mortar and pestle or in a small pepper mill
¼ cup olive oil
¼ teaspoon finely grated orange rind
2 very thin lemon slices, seeded
2 tablespoons caviar, preferably black,
    although red or golden may be used

1 Combine the vermouth and scallops in a small saucepan and bring the liquid to the boil. Let simmer about 1 minute, no longer, and drain. Let the scallops cool until they are lukewarm. Cut the scallops crosswise into thin rounds.

2 Meanwhile, prepare the sauce. Combine the pineapple; yellow, red and green pepper; onions; raisins; coriander seed; olive oil and orange rind.

3 Spoon half of the sauce into the center of 2 appetizer plates. Arrange half the scallop slices symmetrically in a concentric pattern over the sauce with 1 scallop round in the center.

4 Cover the center round with 1 lemon slice. Spoon 1 tablespoon of caviar on top of each lemon slice.

SCALLOP COCKTAIL

This is a vibrantly colored salad, especially good on a hot summer's day. It makes an excellent first course or a main luncheon course.

4 SERVINGS

½ cup raw scallops
1 cup corn kernels freshly cut from the cob
1½ cups finely chopped red onions
½ cup fresh or bottled clam juice
½ cup cubed sweet red pepper
½ cup cubed sweet yellow pepper
½ cup finely chopped coriander
⅓ cup tomato catsup
⅓ cup lime or lemon juice
¼ cup olive oil
1 tablespoon minced garlic
1 tablespoon minced jalapeño pepper,
    or ¼ teaspoon hot red pepper flakes
Salt and freshly ground pepper to taste

1 If sea scallops are used, cut them into quarters; if bay scallops are used, leave them whole.

2 Put the remaining ingredients in a bowl and blend. Add the scallops and stir to coat.

♦

GRAVLAX

12 OR MORE SERVINGS

1 (3½- to 4-pound) center cut of salmon,
    filleted but with skin left intact
3 tablespoons peppercorns, preferably white
5 tablespoons sugar
3 tablespoons salt, preferably kosher salt
2 to 3 bunches (about ¼ pound) dill sprigs
Marianne Lipsky's mustard sauce (see
    following recipe)

1 Carefully run the fingers over the boned surface of the fillet. Use a pair of pliers or tweezers to pull out and remove any bones that may remain. Discard the bones.

2 Put the peppercorns on a flat surface and crush them coarsely with a mallet or the bottom of a clean skillet. Or crush them in a mortar. Put the pepper in a small bowl and add the sugar and salt.

3 Cut the salmon fillet in half crosswise and place the 2 halves skin side down in one layer. Sprinkle evenly with the salt mixture.

4 Make a generous layer of dill sprigs over the bottom of a flat dish large enough to hold 1 salmon fillet compactly. Place 1 fillet skin side down on the dill. Cover with a generous amount of dill. Place the other salmon piece skin side up over the layer of dill. Cover closely with plastic wrap.

5 Place a smaller flat dish on top of the salmon and add weights, about 10 pounds. Refrigerate overnight.

6 Remove the weights and the top dish from the salmon. Carefully turn over the double-salmon "package," leaving the dill layer at the bottom. Cover with plastic wrap, the top dish and the weights and refrigerate a second time.

7 Repeat this 2 or 3 times during a 12 to 24 hour period.

8 When ready to serve, scrape away all the dill and pat the salmon halves dry. Carve each piece on the diagonal into thin slices, cutting away the skin. Serve with mustard sauce.

MARIANNE LIPSKY'S MUSTARD SAUCE
ABOUT 2¼ CUPS

¼ cup prepared spicy-brown mustard
¼ cup Dijon mustard
6 tablespoons white wine vinegar
6 tablespoons sugar
Salt and freshly ground pepper to taste
1 cup corn, peanut or vegetable oil
1 cup chopped dill
2 tablespoons cognac

1 Put the mustards, vinegar, sugar, salt and pepper into a mixing bowl.

2 Start beating with a wire whisk while adding the oil in a thin, steady stream. When all the oil is added, stir in the dill and cognac.

◆

TUNA CARPACCIO WITH LIME MAYONNAISE

8 SERVINGS

1½ pounds fresh tuna
1½ cups mayonnaise, preferably freshly made
1 tablespoon lime juice
1 tablespoon grated fresh ginger
1 tablespoon finely chopped parsley
1 tablespoon finely chopped tarragon
2 tablespoons cream
8 herb sprigs such as rosemary or tarragon
   for garnish

1 Cut the tuna into very thin slices. Place each slice between 2 sheets of clear plastic wrap or wax paper. Using a flat, heavy mallet, pound the slices until they are almost translucent. Try to avoid making holes in the slices.

2 Arrange an equal number of the slices on each of 8 chilled plates. Arrange the slices slightly overlapping.

3 Put the mayonnaise in a bowl and add the lime juice, ginger, parsley and tarragon. Gradually beat in the cream.

4 Spoon an equal amount of mayonnaise sauce over each serving. Garnish each plate with an herb sprig.

◆

MARINATED TUNA FISH AND VEGETABLES ITALIENNE

There are many ingredients to this recipe but the finished product is worth the effort.

6 SERVINGS

1 teaspoon mixed pickling spice
1 tablespoon tomato paste
3 cups water
1 cup olive oil
½ cup lemon juice
4 garlic cloves, minced
¼ teaspoon whole thyme leaves
1 teaspoon salt
¼ teaspoon freshly ground pepper
1 bay leaf
6 basil leaves
1 large carrot, thinly sliced
1 celery stalk, thinly sliced
12 small white onions
4 mushrooms, quartered
2 green peppers, thinly sliced
2 pimientos, sliced
1 dill pickle, thinly sliced
8 green olives, whole or chopped
8 black olives, whole or chopped
1 (7-ounce) can tuna fish

Continued

1 Tie the pickling spice in a cheesecloth bag. Combine in a heavy saucepan with the tomato paste, water, oil, lemon juice, garlic, thyme, salt, pepper, bay leaf and basil. Bring the mixture to a boil.

2 Add the carrot, celery and onions, reduce the heat and simmer ½ hour.

3 Add the mushrooms and green pepper and cook until pepper is tender, about 10 minutes. Add the pimiento, pickle, olives and tuna fish and cook 5 minutes longer. Discard spice bag. Cool and chill. Drain. Serve as an appetizer on lettuce.

♦

BRANDADE DE MORUE

Salt cod, called *bacalao* in Spain, *baccala* in Italy, and *morue* in France, is the basis of one of the finest of all appetizers, served frequently in my home as part of a New Year's Eve buffet. Pure olive oil and an abundance of garlic are essential to give this mousse its true flavor of Provence.

12 TO 16 SERVINGS

1½ pounds dried salt cod, preferably boneless
1 pound potatoes
2 cups milk
1 bay leaf
1 small onion, peeled and thinly sliced
2 whole cloves
1½ tablespoons minced garlic
Salt and freshly ground pepper to taste
Pinch of grated nutmeg
Pinch of cayenne
1 cup pure virgin olive oil
1½ cups cream

1 Place the salt cod in a pan and add cold water to cover. Let soak, changing the water at 3- or 4-hour intervals for 12 hours or longer.

2 When ready to cook, bake the potatoes at 375°F for 45 minutes or longer, until tender.

3 Meanwhile, drain the fish and put the pieces in a casserole. Add cold water to barely cover. Add the milk, bay leaf, onions and cloves. Bring to the boil and simmer 3 or 4 minutes.

4 Drain the fish and discard the cooking liquid. When the pieces are cool enough to handle, remove the skin and bones. Use only the white flesh of the fish. Flake the flesh and add it to the bowl of a food processor.

5 Scoop out the potato flesh and add it to the fish. Add the garlic, salt, pepper, nutmeg, and cayenne.

6 Heat the oil and cream separately, almost but not quite to the boil.

7 Start blending the fish and gradually add the oil and cream, adding each alternately.

8 Taste the mixture and, if necessary, add a little salt. Serve with toast triangles or thinly sliced French bread.

♦

CARNITAS
MEXICAN PORK CRISPS

This is one of the most easily prepared dishes ever created.

1 Trim fat from fresh pork shoulder or meaty spareribs and cut into 1½-inch cubes.

2 Cook on a baking sheet in a preheated 200°F oven until the cubes are crisp, 1½ to 2 hours. Serve with sauce piquante (page 602) or guacamole (page 22).

MARINATED PORK STRIPS

This hors d'oeuvre is of Korean origin.

32 SLICES

2 pork tenderloins
¾ cup sesame seed
½ cup dark soy sauce
3 tablespoons sugar
2 tablespoons minced onion
1 tablespoon chopped fresh ginger
2 garlic cloves, minced

1 Trim the fat from the tenderloins. If thick, split lengthwise.

2 Combine the remaining ingredients in a bowl. Marinate the pork in the mixture 3 hours in the refrigerator, turning and basting frequently. Drain and reserve the marinade.

3 Preheat the oven to 375°F.

4 Transfer the pork to an oiled roasting pan and roast until tender, about 45 minutes. Simmer the marinade 10 minutes.

5 Cut the pork into thin slices and serve on toothpicks with the marinade.

Swedish meatballs, page 296.

PORK BALLS WITH GINGER

12 TO 16 PORK BALLS

1 pound ground pork
1 cup coarsely chopped water chestnuts
¼ cup finely chopped crystallized ginger
1 egg, lightly beaten
1 teaspoon salt
Cornstarch
Peanut oil for deep frying

1 Mix lightly all the ingredients except the cornstarch and peanut oil.

2 Shape the mixture into small bite-size balls and dust lightly with cornstarch.

3 Heat the peanut oil to 375°F. Deep-fry the pork balls until they are cooked through. Serve hot on toothpicks.

Fricadeller (Danish Pork Balls), page 349.

◆

KEFTEDES
GREEK MEATBALLS

ABOUT 32 MEATBALLS

1½ pounds ground round steak
2 eggs, lightly beaten
2 medium onions, finely chopped
½ cup fine, soft bread crumbs
2 tablespoons chopped parsley
1 tablespoon chopped mint
¼ teaspoon cinnamon
¼ teaspoon allspice
Salt and freshly ground pepper to taste
Oil for pan frying

Continued

Combine all the ingredients except oil and mix thoroughly. Refrigerate for several hours. Shape into small, bite-size balls and fry in hot oil until brown. Serve hot.

Buffalo Chicken Wings, page 147.
Steak Tartare Lausanne, page 276.

♦

BACON AND LIVER APPETIZERS

16 APPETIZERS

¾ cup chicken livers
2 hard-cooked eggs
2 tablespoons butter, at room temperature
1 teaspoon cognac (optional)
½ teaspoon lemon juice
Chopped chives or finely grated onion to taste
Salt and freshly ground pepper to taste
8 slices bacon, cut in half

1 Cook the chicken livers in a small amount of boiling salted water until barely done, 5 to 8 minutes.

2 Rub the livers and hard-cooked eggs through a fine sieve or use a food mill. Blend well and mix with the remaining ingredients except the bacon. Chill.

3 Spread the mixture on the strips of bacon. Roll and fasten with toothpicks. Grill under a preheated broiler until the bacon is crisp. Serve hot.

SPARERIBS AND GINGERED PLUM SAUCE

10 TO 15 APPETIZERS

2 pounds lean spareribs
⅓ cup light soy sauce
5 tablespoons brown sugar
1 tablespoon cornstarch
2 tablespoons vinegar
5 tablespoons candied ginger, chopped fine
1 garlic clove, chopped fine
1 cup pitted, mashed green plums

1 Simmer the spareribs in salted water to cover until tender, about 1 hour, and pull out all the bones. Cut the meat into strips about 1 inch long.

2 Mix the remaining ingredients except the plums and 2 tablespoons of the ginger. Thoroughly coat the meat with the mixture.

3 Arrange in a roasting pan and set the pan 4 to 6 inches from heat. Turn on the broiler to high, leave the door open and watch carefully. When the tops are brown, turn the meat, brush with sauce and brown. Remove from the broiler and drain the meat on paper toweling. Refrigerate for 24 hours.

4 Meanwhile, mix the plums and remaining ginger and let stand 24 hours.

5 When ready to serve the meat, spear each piece with a toothpick. Place the gingered plum sauce in a small bowl and surround with the meat.

Chinese Barbecued Spareribs, page 344.

ROQUEFORT CHEESE STRUDEL

Packaged strudel leaves are available in specialty stores and many supermarkets. If frozen, defrost thoroughly before using.

16 SERVINGS

---

2 packages strudel leaves
¾ cup mashed potatoes
½ cup evaporated milk
¾ cup pot cheese
6 ounces Roquefort cheese, crumbled
2 egg yolks
Salt and freshly ground pepper to taste
½ teaspoon curry powder
2 egg whites
¼ pound butter, melted
Dry bread crumbs

1 Remove the packages of strudel leaves from the refrigerator at least 3 hours before using.

2 In an electric mixer blend the potatoes, milk, cheeses, yolks, salt, pepper and curry powder. Blend in the slightly beaten egg whites.

3 Preheat the oven to 375°F.

4 Spread a large damp towel on a table. Open a sheet of strudel leaves and place on the cloth (keep the remaining dough covered to prevent drying). Brush the leaves with butter and sprinkle with crumbs. Repeat this procedure with 3 more sheets of leaves, placing each on top of the last.

5 Spread the nearest short edge of the leaves with half the cheese mixture, making a strip about 3 inches wide.

6 Roll up the strudel, using the towel as an aid and folding in the sides of the leaves. Roll onto a greased baking sheet and brush the top with butter. Repeat the process with the remaining ingredients for a second strudel.

7 Bake until golden brown, or 25 to 30 minutes. Slide onto a bread board, cut into 2-inch pieces and serve hot as a first course.

◆

SPINACH-FETA STRUDEL

This is a Greek appetizer often served in the home of Mr. and Mrs. Leon Lianides of New York. Mr. Lianides is proprietor of the Coach House, one of the city's best "American" restaurants.

16 SERVINGS

---

2 packages strudel leaves
2 pounds fresh spinach
3 tablespoons olive oil
1½ cups finely chopped onions
4 tablespoons butter
5 eggs, beaten
½ cup chopped scallions, green part included
½ pound feta cheese, chopped
½ cup chopped dill
½ cup finely chopped parsley
Salt and freshly ground pepper to taste
½ pound sweet butter, melted

1 Remove packages of strudel leaves from the refrigerator at least 3 hours before using.

2 Wash the spinach in several changes of water. Dry it and cut into 2-inch lengths. Cook it in oil until wilted. Drain. Brown the onions in the butter.

3 Mix the onions, eggs, scallions, cheese, dill and parsley. Add the spinach and season with salt and pepper.

4 Preheat the oven to 350°F.

Continued

5 Butter two 8 × 8 × 2-inch pans. Cut 2 strudel leaves into 6 squares each by cutting into thirds lengthwise and in half across (keep the remaining strudel leaves covered to prevent drying).

6 Place 1 of the squares in the prepared pan and brush with melted butter. Repeat with the remaining 11 strudel squares, placing each on top of the last. Spread with half the spinach-cheese filling and cover with 12 more strudel squares, brushing each with butter. Repeat the process with the remaining ingredients for a second pan.

7 With a sharp knife, cut through the top to mark it into 2-inch squares. Bake 1 hour, or until brown and very puffy. Cut into squares and serve hot as a first course.

◆

Pirogi and their smaller versions, piroshki, are savory hot Russian turnovers traditionally served at luncheon with a clear borscht or a meat broth. But they also make excellent appetizers. They are either rectangular or shaped like a slice of flattened jelly roll. The turnovers may be made with either raised dough or pastry, which is then filled with a meat or vegetable mixture.

For variation, a combination pirog can be made by filling half of the roll with meat filling, the other half with cabbage-carrot filling. When serving, offer small slices from each end.

PIROG

1 PIROG, ABOUT 12 SERVINGS

1 package (1 tablespoon) yeast
¼ cup lukewarm water
¼ pound butter
1 cup milk, scalded
1 teaspoon salt
2 teaspoons sugar
4½ to 5 cups flour
3 eggs, lightly beaten
Filling (see pages 55–56)
1 egg yolk, lightly beaten

1 Dissolve the yeast in the lukewarm water in a large bowl. Melt the butter in the milk. Add the salt and sugar to the milk and cool to lukewarm. Add the milk mixture to the yeast mixture.

2 Beat in 1 cup of the flour. Beat in the eggs and then gradually beat in enough flour to make a soft dough. Turn the dough out on a lightly floured board and knead until soft and elastic.

3 Place in a lightly greased bowl and turn to grease the top. Cover with a clean cloth and place in a warm place for about 2 hours, until the dough has doubled in bulk.

4 Preheat the oven to 400°F.

5 Roll out the dough on a lightly floured pastry cloth into a rectangle (18 × 14 inches).

6 Place the filling in a meat-loaf shape in the center of the dough, leaving at least 4 inches clear all around.

7 Draw the long edges of the dough together over the filling and pinch to seal. Cut off a triangle from each corner, then fold remaining triangular ends like envelope flaps over the covered filling and seal.

8 Place a lightly greased and floured baking sheet face down on the sealed edges. Holding the pastry cloth firmly, turn the cloth, filled roll, and pan over, all together, so that the smooth dough is uppermost and the seam side is down.

9 Brush pirog with the egg yolk mixed with 2 tablespoons of water. Make 3 or more steam holes in the top. Bake the pirog for 15 minutes, or until brown. Reduce the heat to 350°F and cook for 15 minutes longer, or until bottom dough is cooked.

CABBAGE–CARROT FILLING FOR PIROG
ENOUGH FOR 1 PIROG

5 cups chopped tender white cabbage
2 tablespoons salt
2 onions, chopped
4 tablespoons butter
6 carrots, finely cubed
2 tablespoons chopped parsley
4 hard-cooked eggs, chopped
Salt and freshly ground black pepper to taste

1 Mix the cabbage with the salt; let stand for 15 minutes. Squeeze out water. Blanch the cabbage in a colander over steam for 6 minutes; drain.

2 Sauté the onion in the butter. Add cabbage and carrots and cook slowly for 30 minutes. Add the parsley and eggs and season with salt and pepper. Cool before using.

SALMON FILLING FOR PIROG
ENOUGH FOR 1 PIROG

4 (1-inch-thick) fresh salmon steaks
½ cup finely chopped shallots
1 garlic clove, minced
4 tablespoons butter
¾ pound mushrooms, sliced
2 tablespoons snipped dill
½ cup fish stock
1 teaspoon salt
¼ teaspoon freshly ground pepper
Dash of grated nutmeg
4 cups cold cooked rice
6 hard-cooked eggs, chopped
Salt and freshly ground pepper to taste

1 Poach the salmon and cool it. Remove skin and bones and cut the fish into large pieces.

2 Sauté the shallots and garlic in the butter until tender. Add the mushrooms and dill and cook for 3 to 5 minutes.

3 Add the stock, salt, pepper and nutmeg and bring the mixture to a boil. Consistency should be mushy. If there is excess liquid, evaporate it; if the mixture is dry, add a little more fish stock.

4 Mix the mushroom mixture with the salmon chunks and cool to room temperature.

5 Spread 2 cups of the rice in the middle of the prepared dough. Spread half of the salmon mixture on top of the rice, cover with the chopped eggs, and season with salt and pepper. Pile the remaining salmon and then the remaining rice on top of the eggs, making a meat-loaf shape.

Continued

MEAT FILLING FOR PIROG
ENOUGH FOR 1 PIROG

¼ pound butter
2 large onions, finely chopped
1 garlic clove, finely minced
2 pounds beef chuck, ground
1 pound veal, ground
2 teaspoons salt
½ teaspoon freshly ground pepper
3 tablespoons flour
⅓ cup beef stock
¼ cup finely chopped parsley
4 cups cold cooked rice
4 hard-cooked eggs, chopped
Salt and freshly ground pepper to taste

1 Melt the butter in a large heavy skillet and sauté the onions and garlic in it until tender but not brown.

2 Add the beef and veal and cook, stirring occasionally, until the meat loses all pink color. Drain off the fat.

3 Sprinkle the salt, pepper and flour over the surface and cook, stirring, until the flour disappears. Stir in the stock and parsley and heat until the mixture thickens slightly. Cool to room temperature.

4 Spread 2 cups of the rice in the middle of the prepared dough. Spread half of the meat mixture on top of the rice, cover with the chopped eggs, and season with salt and pepper. Pile the remaining meat and then the remaining rice on top of the eggs, making a meat-loaf shape.

PIROSHKI

36 PIROSHKI

Make the raised dough for pirog (page 54). Prepare any filling for pirog. When the dough is ready, roll it out to ¼-inch thickness. Cut it into 3-inch rounds or rectangles (3 × 2 inches). Place about 1 teaspoon filling in the center of each round or rectangle, moisten the edges, and pinch together to seal. The rectangles will make a pillow shape.

FRIED PIROSHKI

Place the filled piroshki on a flour-sprinkled cloth and cover with another cloth. Let the piroshki rise for about 20 minutes.

Heat deep fat to 375°F. Using a wire basket, gently lower a layer of piroshki into the fat. Fry for about 4 minutes, until golden brown, turning often with a slotted spoon. Drain on paper toweling.

BAKED PIROSHKI

Place the filled piroshki on a greased baking sheet, cover, and let stand for about 20 minutes, until dough is light. Preheat oven to 425°F. Bake the piroshki for 15 minutes. Lower the temperature to 400°F and bake for about 15 minutes longer, until piroshki are golden.

EMPANADAS

Empanadas are a Chilean version of meat turn-overs. The pastry also contains black olives, raisins and hard-cooked eggs.

ABOUT 10 SERVINGS

5 cups flour
¼ pound butter, at room temperature
2 egg yolks
1 tablespoon vinegar
1 teaspoon salt
1 cup water, approximately
Filling (see following recipe)
2 hard-cooked eggs, cut into wedges
1 egg yolk, beaten with a little water

1 Heap the flour on a board. Make a depression in the center and add the butter, yolks and vinegar. Mix well, using the fingers.

2 Dissolve the salt in the water. Begin sprinkling it over the flour mixture and rub the dough between the hands until it is smooth and fairly stiff. Gather the dough into a ball; continue sprinkling with salt water and kneading until the dough is no longer sticky.

3 Using about ¼ cup dough at a time, roll into circles ⅛ inch thick and about 9 inches in diameter.

4 Place about ½ cup filling on each pastry round. Add 2 wedges hard-cooked egg. Dip the fingers in the pan juices from the filling and run them around the pastry near the filling. Fold the dough to make a turnover, press around the filling to seal and cut the edges about 1 inch from the filling, using a pastry wheel to make a half circle. Mold the curved edge of the pastry to make a triangle. Press tightly at the corners and prick the top with a fork. Brush with the egg yolk.

5 Place on an ungreased baking sheet and bake in a preheated 400°F oven until brown, about 15 minutes. Serve hot.

FILLING
ABOUT 4 CUPS

1 tablespoon vegetable oil
1 tablespoon butter
½ cup chopped onions
1 teaspoon finely chopped garlic
½ cup chopped green pepper
½ pound ground top sirloin
¼ teaspoon hot red pepper flakes
1 tomato, peeled, seeded and chopped
8 pitted black olives, quartered
3 tablespoons raisins
¼ teaspoon oregano
Tabasco sauce to taste

1 Heat the oil and butter. Add the onions, garlic and green pepper and brown lightly. Add the sirloin and cook until the meat has lost its raw look. Pour off the fat.

2 Add the red pepper flakes, tomato, olives, raisins, oregano and Tabasco. Cook, stirring, until most of the liquid has evaporated.

COCKTAIL PIZZA

APPROXIMATELY 36 SERVINGS

1 package (1 tablespoon) yeast
⅞ cup lukewarm water
1½ tablespoons vegetable oil
¾ teaspoon salt
2⅔ cups flour
2 pounds (6 or 7 medium) tomatoes
¼ pound Italian sausage
2 tablespoons olive oil
1 teaspoon crushed oregano
1 tablespoon chopped basil
Freshly ground pepper to taste
¾ pound mozzarella cheese, sliced
4 ounces flat anchovies packed in oil, drained

1 Soften the yeast in the lukewarm water.

2 Add the vegetable oil, ¼ teaspoon of the salt and the flour and mix well. The dough should be soft but not sticky. Add a little more flour if necessary.

3 Turn the dough out onto a floured surface and knead until very smooth and elastic.

4 Place in a greased bowl, grease the surface of the dough, cover with a towel and let rise in a warm place (80 to 85°F) until doubled in bulk, about 1½ hours.

5 While the dough is rising, core and peel tomatoes and cut them into wedges. Add the remaining salt and simmer, covered, until very soft, 10 minutes or longer. Drain and set the solid part aside.

6 Cook the sausage in a little water 5 minutes. Drain and continue cooking until light brown. Slice the sausage and set it aside.

7 Preheat the oven to 500°F.

8 Grease a 15 × 10 × 1-inch jelly roll pan.

9 Turn the dough out onto a floured surface and shape into a ball. Roll the dough into a long strip that is about the size of the pan.

10 Place the dough in the pan and press and stretch with the fingers until the dough touches the sides of the pan at all points.

11 Spread the tomatoes over the dough and sprinkle with the olive oil, oregano, basil and pepper.

12 Arrange the sausage over one third of the dough and cheese over the other two thirds. Arrange the anchovies over half of the cheese-covered dough, leaving the other half with cheese only.

13 Bake the pizza on the lower shelf of the oven until it is brown, 15 to 20 minutes. Cut into squares or bars and serve hot.

2

Soups

CONSOMMÉ A LA MADRILÈNE

Tomatoes are frequently related to the cuisine of Madrid. Thus the name *consommé à la madrilène,* or "consommé in the style of Madrid."

ABOUT 2 QUARTS

2½ pounds lean beef, cut into thirds
1½ pounds marrow bone
3¼ quarts cold water
2 onions, each studded with 3 cloves
3 carrots, cut up
2 celery stalks with leaves
3 leeks, sliced lengthwise and washed
2 teaspoons salt
6 peppercorns
2 parsley sprigs
Pinch of thyme
1 garlic clove
1 bay leaf
3 egg whites, beaten
3 crushed eggshells
2 cups tomato purée
2 tablespoons finely chopped onions
½ teaspoon basil

1 In a large kettle combine the beef, bone and water and bring to a boil. Simmer 5 minutes and skim. Cover and simmer 1 hour.

2 Add the onions studded with cloves, carrots, celery, leeks, salt, peppercorns, parsley, thyme, garlic and bay leaf. Cover and cook slowly 4 to 5 hours. Strain through a double thickness of cheesecloth and skim off the fat. Use paper toweling, if necessary, to remove the remaining particles of fat. Discard bone and vegetables and reserve the meat for another purpose.

3 To clarify the consommé, return it to the heat and add the beaten egg whites and eggshells. Bring to a rolling boil and strain once more through 3 thicknesses of cheesecloth.

4 Pour 6 cups of the consommé into a saucepan and reserve the remainder for another use. Add the tomato purée, onions, and basil. Simmer 20 minutes, remove from the heat and strain through cheesecloth. Serve hot.

♦

RED CAVIAR MADRILÈNE

This is an interesting dish. It has unusual eye appeal because it combines the red of salmon roe and madrilène with the white of sour cream and the green of chives. It is served cold, of course.

6 SERVINGS

1 quart consommé à la madrilène (opposite)
2 ounces red caviar
6 tablespoons sour cream
3 teaspoons minced chives

1 Pour the madrilène into 6 bouillon cups. Stir into each cup a heaping teaspoon of caviar. Refrigerate until the madrilène jells.

2 Just before serving, top each cup with 1 tablespoon of sour cream. Sprinkle with minced chives.

MINESTRONE

If Italy can be said to have a national soup, minestrone is it. It is one of the most fortifying of dishes and has few peers for winter meals.

6 GENEROUS SERVINGS

½ pound dried white beans soaked in
  water overnight
1 teaspoon olive oil
⅛ pound salt pork, cut into small dice
  (optional)
1 garlic clove, chopped fine
1 small onion, chopped
1 leek, diced and washed
1 teaspoon chopped parsley
1 teaspoon chopped basil
1 tablespoon tomato paste
3 tomatoes, peeled, seeded and chopped
3 celery stalks, chopped
2 carrots, sliced
2 potatoes, diced
1 small turnip, peeled and diced
¼ small cabbage shredded
2 zucchini, diced
1½ quarts water
Salt to taste
½ teaspoon freshly ground pepper
1 cup elbow macaroni or ditali
6 tablespoons grated Parmesan cheese

1 Drain the beans and boil them in 3 quarts water about 1 hour, or until tender. (Or use quick-soaking method, page 78.) Drain.

2 Place the olive oil in a large kettle and add the salt pork, garlic, onions, leek, parsley, and basil. Brown lightly. Add the tomato paste thinned with a little water and cook 5 minutes. Add the tomatoes, celery, carrots, potatoes, turnip, cabbage, zucchini, water, salt and pepper and cook slowly 45 minutes to 1 hour. Add the beans.

3 Add the macaroni and cook 10 minutes, or until tender. Correct the seasonings and pour into heated bowls. Serve immediately, sprinkled with grated Parmesan cheese.

Note: The number and kinds of vegetables used in making minestrone are optional. They may be varied according to season.

◆

AVOCADO SOUP GERALD

It was a happy day for ripe avocados when the food processor came into being. This is a wonderful cold soup made in seconds.

4 SERVINGS

1 to 2 ripe avocados
Few drops of onion juice
1 cup chicken stock
½ cup sour cream
½ cup half-and-half
Salt and freshly ground pepper

1 Wash and peel enough avocado to make 1 cup.

2 Combine all the ingredients in a food processor, or mash the avocado and beat with the other ingredients until smooth and well blended.

3 Store the mixture in a covered jar in the refrigerator until chilled.

4 Correct the seasonings and top each serving with a sprinkling of paprika.

COLD CURRIED AVOCADO SOUP

4 SERVINGS

1 large or 2 small ripe avocados
2¼ cups chicken stock
1 teaspoon curry powder
¾ teaspoon salt
⅛ teaspoon freshly ground white pepper
½ cup cream
4 thin slices of avocado
2 tablespoons lemon juice

1 Peel and halve the avocado, discarding the pit. Cut avocado into rough pieces. Place the avocado and 1 cup of the stock in the container of a food processor. Add the curry powder, salt and pepper. Purée until smooth.

2 Pour mixture into an enamelware saucepan. Add remaining stock and heat, stirring, to boiling. Cool. Stir in cream and chill.

3 Serve in chilled soup mugs. Garnish each serving with an avocado slice dipped into lemon juice to prevent discoloration.

UKRAINIAN BORSCHT

The only ingredient that is constant in borscht is beets. It can be made with almost any stock except, perhaps, fish stock. Here is a hearty borscht from the Ukraine.

12 SERVINGS

2 pounds soup beef with cracked soup bone
2½ quarts cold water
1 pound lean fresh pork
½ pound smoked pork
1 bay leaf
10 peppercorns
1 garlic clove
Few sprigs of parsley
1 carrot, sliced
1 celery stalk, sliced
1 leek, sliced
8 medium beets
1 cup shredded cabbage
2 large onions, quartered
3 large potatoes, cut into eighths
¼ cup tomato purée
2 tablespoons vinegar
2 teaspoons sugar
½ cup cooked or canned navy beans
5 frankfurters, thickly sliced
Salt to taste

1 In a heavy 6-quart pot, simmer the beef and bone in the water about 1 hour. Add the fresh and smoked pork, bay leaf, peppercorns, garlic, parsley, carrot, celery and leek. Cover tightly and bring to a boil. Reduce the heat and simmer slowly 1½ hours.

2 Meanwhile, boil the beets, unpeeled, until tender. Slip off the skins and cut each into 8 pieces.

3 Remove the bone and meats from the pot and discard the bone. Strain the soup, discarding the vegetables and flavoring materials. Return the meats and liquid to the pot. Add the cooked beets, cabbage, onions, potatoes, tomato purée, vinegar and sugar. Simmer, covered, 40 minutes. Add the beans and frankfurters and simmer, covered, 10 minutes.

4 Skim the excess fat from the soup.

5 Remove the meats, slice and return to the soup. Return to a boil and serve.

◆

RUSSIAN BORSCHT

8 TO 10 SERVINGS

1 pound lean beef, cubed
1½ quarts water
1 tablespoon salt
1½ cup shredded raw beets
¾ cup shredded carrots
¾ cup shredded white turnips or rutabagas
1 medium onion, chopped
2 tablespoons tomato purée
2 tablespoons vinegar
1 teaspoon sugar
2 tablespoons butter
½ small head cabbage, shredded
Freshly ground pepper
2 bay leaves
Sour cream

1 Simmer the beef, covered, in salted water until tender, or about 1½ hours.

2 Meanwhile, in a large saucepan simmer the beets, carrots, turnips, onion, tomato purée, vinegar, sugar and butter, covered, 15 minutes. Stir frequently. Add the cabbage and cook 10 minutes longer.

3 Add the vegetable mixture, pepper and bay leaves to the meat and broth. Adjust seasonings and cook until the vegetables are tender. Add more vinegar, if desired.

4 Before serving, add sour cream to taste.

CHLODNIK
POLISH BORSCHT WITH VEGETABLES AND DILL

This is an exceptional and easily made soup of Polish origin. Pronounced KLOD-nick, it is basically a borscht to which very fresh chopped vegetables including scallions, cucumber and lots of dill are added. Finely cubed cooked shellfish or meat may be added, including shrimp. It is a fine soup for midsummer meals.

4 SERVINGS

1 pound raw beets, trimmed but with 1 or 2 inches of the stems left intact
3 cups chicken stock
3 cups water
Salt to taste
1 cup small shrimp, cooked and peeled (optional)
½ cup sour cream or yogurt
3 tablespoons vinegar, preferably apple cider vinegar
1 tablespoon lemon juice
5 teaspoons sugar
Salt and freshly ground pepper to taste
¾ cup finely diced cucumber
¾ cup finely diced scallions, green part included
½ cup trimmed, thinly sliced radishes (optional)
¼ cup finely chopped dill

1 Rinse the beets well and put them into a saucepan in which they will fit snugly. Add the stock, water and salt. Bring to the simmer. Cook, partly covered, 30 to 40 minutes, or until the beets are tender.

2 Drain but reserve both the beets and their cooking liquid. You will need 1½ to 2 cups of liquid. Using the fingers or a small paring knife, remove and discard the stems and the tender outer skin of each beet. Cut the beets into eighths. There should be about 2 cups.

Continued

3 Put the beet pieces and about ½ cup of the reserved liquid into the container of a food processor. Blend thoroughly. Pour the mixture into a bowl and add the remaining liquid. Let cool then chill thoroughly.

4 Cut the shrimp into small bits and add them to the soup. Add the sour cream, vinegar, lemon juice and sugar and stir to blend. If desired, add more vinegar, lemon juice and sugar, according to taste. Add salt and pepper. Stir in the cucumber, scallions, radishes and dill. Chill.

◆

QUICK COLD BEET SOUP

6 SERVINGS

1 cup sliced cooked beets
½ small onion, sliced
1 teaspoon salt
¼ teaspoon freshly ground pepper
2 tablespoons lemon juice
1 medium boiled potato, or ⅔ cup
   mashed potato
1 cup chicken stock
1 cup sour cream
1 cup cracked ice

1 Put the beets, onions, salt, pepper, lemon juice and potato into the container of a food processor and coarsely chop.

2 With the motor running, pour in the chicken stock and the sour cream.

3 Add the cracked ice and blend briefly.

4 Chill and serve garnished with chopped dill.

Chicken Stock, page 587.

CREAM OF BROCCOLI SOUP

6 SERVINGS

1 medium onion, sliced
1 medium carrot, sliced
1 small celery stalk with leaves, sliced
1 garlic clove
½ cup water
2 cups coarsely chopped cooked broccoli
1 teaspoon salt
Generous pinch of cayenne
½ cup cooked macaroni
1 cup chicken stock
½ cup cream
Sour cream

1 Put the onion, carrot, celery, garlic and water in a covered skillet and simmer for 10 minutes.

2 Transfer to the container of a food processor. Add broccoli, salt, cayenne and macaroni and coarsely chop. With motor running, add the stock and the cream.

3 Chill and serve topped with sour cream.

CREAM OF CARROT SOUP

4 carrots, sliced (1 cup)
1 medium onion, sliced
1 celery stalk with leaves, sliced
1½ cups chicken stock
1 teaspoon salt
Generous pinch of cayenne
½ cup cooked rice
¾ cup cream

1 Place the carrots, onion, celery and ½ cup of the chicken stock in a saucepan. Bring to a boil, cover, reduce the heat and simmer 15 minutes.

2 Transfer to the container of a food processor and add the salt, cayenne and rice. Process briefly and, with the motor running, pour in remaining stock and cream.

3 Chill and serve garnished with diced pimiento.

Note: One cup of almost any fresh vegetable may be substituted for the carrots.

POTAGE CRESSONIÈRE

4 tablespoons butter
1 garlic clove, minced
2 cups chopped onions
4 cups thinly sliced raw potatoes
1 teaspoon salt
¼ teaspoon freshly ground pepper
¾ cup water
1 bunch watercress
1½ cups milk
1½ cups chicken stock
2 egg yolks
½ cup half-and-half

1 Heat the butter in a large saucepan. Add the garlic and onions and sauté until tender, about 5 minutes.

2 Add the potatoes, seasonings and water. Cover and bring to a boil. Reduce the heat and simmer 15 minutes, or until the potatoes are almost tender.

3 Cut the watercress stems into ⅛-inch lengths. Coarsely chop the leaves.

4 To the potato mixture add all the watercress stems, half of the leaves, the milk and stock. Cook 15 minutes. Let cool slightly, then purée in a food processor, in batches if necessary. Return to the saucepan and reheat.

5 Blend together the egg yolks and cream. Gradually stir into the soup and cook, stirring constantly, until slightly thickened. Garnish with the remaining watercress leaves and serve immediately.

CORN AND CRABMEAT CHOWDER

4 SERVINGS

4 ears fresh corn on the cob, or 2 cups thawed
frozen kernels
¾ pound potatoes
3 tablespoons butter
1½ cups finely chopped onions
1½ cups finely chopped heart of celery
2 cups fresh fish stock, or 1 cup bottled clam
juice and 1 cup water
1 cup half-and-half
Salt and freshly ground pepper to taste
½ teaspoon hot red pepper flakes
2 cups (about ¾ pound) fresh lump crabmeat,
picked over well to remove any bits of shell
or cartilage
¼ cup finely chopped coriander

1 Bring enough water to a boil to cover the ears of corn when they are added. Put in the corn and when the water returns to the boil, turn off the heat, cover closely and let stand 5 minutes. Drain and let cool. Scrape the kernels from the cobs; there should be about 2 cups.

2 Peel the potatoes and cut them into ¼-inch cubes. There should be about 1½ cups. Add cold water to cover and set aside.

3 Heat the butter in a saucepan and add the onions and celery. Drain the potatoes and add them. Cook, stirring, until the onions are wilted.

4 Add the fish stock, half-and-half, salt, pepper and red pepper flakes. Add the corn and half of the crabmeat and stir. Let simmer 6 to 8 minutes, or until the potatoes are tender without being mushy. Add the remaining crabmeat and stir gently. When the soup is heated through, ladle it into hot soup bowls and sprinkle each serving with the chopped coriander.

CORN AND WATERCRESS SOUP

6 SERVINGS

1 garlic clove, minced
⅓ cup small onion rings
4 tablespoons butter
1½ cups fresh corn cut off the cobs (3 or 4
ears)
1 teaspoon salt
½ teaspoon sugar
1 cup water
1½ cups milk
1 cup chopped watercress
2 egg yolks, beaten
½ cup cream

1 Sauté the garlic and onion rings in the butter in a saucepan for about 3 minutes, until transparent and limp. Add the corn, salt, sugar and water and bring to a boil. Cover and cook for 15 minutes.

2 Add the milk and watercress. Cover and cook for 5 minutes longer, but do not boil.

3 Remove the mixture from the heat and purée a small amount at a time in a food processor. Blend in the egg yolks and cream. Return the mixture to the stove and heat only until hot. Serve garnished with additional watercress.

COLD CUCUMBER SOUP

4 SERVINGS

2 tablespoons butter
¼ cup chopped onions, or 1 leek sliced
    and cubed
2 cups diced, unpeeled cucumber
2 cups chicken stock
1 cup watercress leaves
½ cup finely diced raw potato
2 parsley sprigs
½ teaspoon salt
¼ teaspoon freshly ground pepper
¼ teaspoon dry mustard
1 cup cream
Chopped chives, cucumber and radishes
    for garnish

1 Melt the butter in a saucepan and cook the onions in it until they are transparent. Add the remaining ingredients except the cream and vegetables for garnish and bring to a boil. Simmer 15 minutes, or until the potatoes are tender.

2 Let cool slightly and purée in a food processor. Correct the seasonings and chill. Before serving, stir in the cream. Garnish with chopped chives, cucumber and radishes.

JULIE WILSON'S WILD RICE AND MUSHROOM SOUP

This is one of the greatest soups ever created. It is a bit time-consuming to prepare but it is incredibly tasty and warming. It might serve as a first course but, even better, as the principal course on a cold winter's day. The ideal accompaniment would be a tossed green salad followed by cheese and a simple dessert.

4 SERVINGS

1 cup (about 1½ ounces) dried mushrooms
    such as shiitake, morels, chanterelles or
    oyster mushrooms, preferably imported
5 cups hot water
2 tablespoons butter
½ cup wild rice
Salt to taste
1½ tablespoons olive oil
½ cup finely chopped onions
2 tablespoons minced garlic
1 cup finely chopped leeks
2½ tablespoons flour
¼ cup dry white wine
¾ cup chicken stock
Freshly ground pepper to taste
¼ teaspoon Tabasco sauce
1 cup half-and-half
3 ounces fresh mushrooms, preferably wild,
    although the cultivated variety may be used
Juice of ½ lemon
1 teaspoon dry sherry
1 teaspoon finely chopped thyme leaves,
    or ½ teaspoon dried
¼ cup finely chopped parsley

1 Put the dried mushrooms in a mixing bowl and add 4 cups of the water. Let soak 20 minutes or longer. Drain but reserve the soaking liquid.

2 Squeeze the drained mushrooms and rinse under cold water to remove any soil or sand. Squeeze dry. Trim off any tough stems. Chop coarsely. Set aside.

Continued

3 Line a mixing bowl with a sieve. Line the sieve with a double thickness of cheesecloth and pour the mushroom soaking liquid through it. Set aside.

4 Meanwhile, bring the remaining 1 cup of water to the boil in a small heavy saucepan and add 1 tablespoon of the butter and the wild rice. Add salt and cover closely. When the water returns to the boil, simmer about 50 minutes, or until the rice "blossoms" and the water is absorbed. Add a little more water if necessary as the rice cooks.

5 Meanwhile, heat the oil in a kettle and add the onions, garlic and leeks. Cook, stirring often, until the onions are softened. Add the chopped mushrooms and sprinkle with flour. Cook over low heat, stirring often, about 4 minutes. Add the white wine, chicken stock, salt, pepper, Tabasco and the liquid in which the mushrooms soaked. Bring to the boil. Simmer uncovered over low heat about 1 hour. There should be 5 to 6 cups of soup.

6 Strain the soup, reserving both the liquid and the solids. Ladle the solids, a little at a time, into the container of a food processor and blend thoroughly. Return the soup to the kettle; add the reserved liquid and half-and-half.

7 Meanwhile, cut the fresh mushrooms into thin slices. There should be about 1½ cups.

8 Heat the remaining tablespoon of butter in a small skillet and add the sliced fresh mushrooms. Sprinkle with lemon juice and cook, stirring, about 1 minute. Sprinkle with sherry.

9 Add the sliced mushrooms and wild rice to the soup and bring to the boil. Add salt and pepper. Sprinkle with thyme and parsley. Serve hot in hot soup bowls.

CREAM OF MUSHROOM SOUP

6 SERVINGS

6 tablespoons butter
1 medium onion, finely chopped
½ pound fresh mushrooms, finely chopped
3 tablespoons flour
3 cups beef stock
1 bay leaf
⅛ teaspoon freshly ground pepper
¾ cup half-and-half

1 Melt the butter in a heavy pan. Add the onions and stir over moderate heat until onions are transparent. Add the mushrooms and cook, stirring, another 4 minutes.

2 Remove the mixture from the heat and blend in the flour. Add the stock slowly, stirring constantly. Add the bay leaf and pepper.

3 Bring the mixture to a boil, reduce heat and simmer 5 minutes. Remove the bay leaf and stir in the cream. If desired, garnish with croutons just before serving.

Beef Stock, page 586.

CREAM OF CURRIED PEA SOUP

1 cup shelled fresh or frozen peas
1 medium onion, sliced
1 small carrot, sliced
1 celery stalk with leaves, sliced
1 medium potato, sliced
1 garlic clove
1 teaspoon salt
1 teaspoon curry powder
2 cups chicken stock
1 cup cream

1 Place the vegetables, seasonings and 1 cup stock in a saucepan and bring to a boil. Cover, reduce the heat and simmer for 15 minutes.

2 Transfer to the container of a food processor and purée. With the motor running, pour in the remaining stock and the cream.

3 Chill and serve topped with whipped cream, if desired.

LA FONDA DEL SOL'S PUMPKIN SOUP

2½ pounds pumpkin, peeled and cut into cubes
5 cups chicken stock
1 cup chopped onions
¾ cup scallions, white part only, chopped
2 cups half-and-half
Salt and freshly ground pepper to taste
Pinch of cayenne
Pinch of grated nutmeg
¾ cup finely chopped scallions, green part only

1 In a large kettle combine the pumpkin, chicken stock, onions, and white part of scallions. Bring to a boil and simmer until the pumpkin is tender. Put the mixture through a fine sieve or purée in a food processor.

2 Stir the half-and-half into the soup and season to taste with salt, pepper, cayenne and nutmeg.

3 Serve the soup at room temperature, garnished with sprinklings of the green part of the scallions.

ONION SOUP WITH CHEESE

The onion is prized today in kitchens around the world, particularly in onion soup. It is the best of soups for cold weather. In France onion soup may be made with stock or with water; it may be enriched with dry white wine or a bit of dry red wine.

10 TO 12 SERVINGS

¼ pound butter
2 pounds sweet onions, thinly sliced
1 tablespoon flour
2 quarts chicken or beef stock
Salt and freshly ground white pepper to taste
1 loaf of French bread, sliced
2 cups dry white wine
4 ounces Swiss cheese, coarsely grated
4 ounces Swiss cheese, sliced

1 Melt half of the butter in a saucepan. Cook the onions in it until they are transparent and golden. Add the flour and stir. Cook for 3 minutes longer. Add the stock and simmer for at least 30 minutes. Add salt and pepper.

2 Toast the bread slices and butter the toast with the remaining butter.

3 Preheat the oven to 375°F.

4 Pour the soup into a large earthenware casserole. Add the wine and half of the grated cheese. Cover the surface with the pieces of buttered toast. Sprinkle all with the remaining grated cheese and add the slices of cheese. The object is to cover the liquid completely with toast and cheese.

5 Place the casserole, uncovered, in the oven for about 15 minutes, until the cheese and bread are brown and crusty.

Variations

Serve the soup without the toast and cheese; just before serving, stir in 2 to 4 tablespoons cognac.

Serve the soup without the toast and cheese; instead beat 2 eggs, blend with a little hot soup, and stir into the boiling soup before serving.

Omit the wine; instead stir in ½ cup dry vermouth along with the stock.

♦

VICHYSSOISE A LA RITZ

Someone should start a campaign to instruct Americans that vichyssoise is not pronounced veeshy-swah! Because this creation of the late Louis Diat has become a national favorite, it seems only just that the final consonant be sounded. It is veeshee-swahze.

8 OR MORE SERVINGS

4 leeks, sliced white part only
1 medium onion, sliced
4 tablespoons butter
5 medium potatoes, thinly sliced
4 cups chicken stock
1 teaspoon salt
3 cups milk
2 cups cream
Chopped chives

1 In a deep kettle, brown the leeks and onions very lightly in the butter. Add the potatoes, stock and salt and boil 35 minutes, or until very tender. Crush and rub through a fine sieve or purée in a food processor.

2 Return the mixture to the kettle, add the milk and 1 cup of the cream and bring to a boil. Cool and rub again through a fine sieve. Chill.

3 Add the remaining cream. Chill thoroughly and serve garnished with chives.

SPINACH SOUP WITH YOGURT

4 SERVINGS

2 large (about ¾ pound) potatoes
1 tablespoon butter
1 tablespoon olive oil
1 cup finely chopped onions
2½ cups chicken stock
Salt to taste
½ cup dry white wine
1 pound spinach in bulk, or 1 (10-ounce)
    package of fresh spinach
⅛ teaspoon grated nutmeg
¼ cup yogurt, well drained

1 Peel the potatoes and cut them into ½-inch-thick slices. Cut slices into strips ½ inch wide. Cut strips into ½-inch cubes. There should be about 2 cups. Cover with cold water to prevent discoloration.

2 Heat the butter and oil in a saucepan and add the onions. Cook, stirring, until the onions are wilted. Drain the potatoes and add them. Add the stock, salt and wine and cook 8 to 10 minutes, or until the potatoes are tender but not mushy.

3 Meanwhile, cut off and discard any tough stems from the spinach. Discard any blemished leaves. There should be about 8 cups. Rinse the spinach thoroughly without patting dry. Put the spinach in a large saucepan with a tight-fitting cover. Cover closely and cook, in only the water that clings to the leaves, stirring the leaves occasionally so that they wilt evenly. Cook only until all the leaves are wilted, 2 to 3 minutes. Drain. Press to extract excess liquid. There should be about 1 cup of spinach, tightly packed.

4 Put the spinach into the container of an electric blender (a food processor may be used, but the soup will not have as fine a texture). Add the potatoes with their liquid, the nutmeg and the yogurt. Blend as fine as possible. Chill before serving.

CREAM OF SPINACH SOUP

6 SERVINGS

4 tablespoons butter
½ cup chopped Bermuda onion
1 pound fresh spinach, or 1 (10-ounce)
    package frozen chopped spinach
3 tablespoons flour
6 cups chicken stock
Salt and freshly ground pepper to taste
2 egg yolks
½ cup cream
Grated nutmeg

1 Melt 3 tablespoons of the butter in a saucepan and cook the onions in it until they are translucent. Do not brown.

2 Pick over the spinach and wash it well; tear off the tough stems and shred the leaves with a knife. Dry on paper toweling. Add the spinach to the saucepan. Cook over low heat, stirring with a 2-pronged fork, just until the leaves are wilted.

3 Sprinkle with the flour. Pour in the stock and, stirring constantly, bring to a boil.

4 Put the soup through a food mill or purée it in a food processor. Return it to the saucepan and add salt and pepper.

5 In a small mixing bowl combine egg yolks and cream. Beat slightly, then add a little of the hot soup. When blended, pour the egg mixture into the saucepan, stirring rapidly.

6 Heat thoroughly, but do not boil or the soup will curdle. Add a little nutmeg and stir in remaining butter. Serve immediately in very hot soup plates.

There are thousands of versions of cold tomato soup. Few of them are more delicious than the two that follow.

♦

COLD TOMATO SOUP I

4 SERVINGS

4 cups drained canned tomatoes
2 celery stalks, sliced
1 onion, sliced
1 bay leaf
2 tablespoons minute tapioca
¼ teaspoon ground ginger
⅛ teaspoon allspice
Salt to taste
Sour cream, hard-cooked eggs, radishes
   and cucumbers for garnish

1 Boil the tomatoes with the celery, onion and bay leaf ½ hour. Strain. Return to a boil.

2 Add the tapioca and cook until clear. Add the seasonings and chill. To serve, garnish each portion with sour cream, slices of hard-cooked egg, radish and cucumber.

COLD TOMATO SOUP II

5 TO 6 SERVINGS

3 cups tomato juice
4 scallions, minced
2 tablespoons tomato paste
2 tablespoons lemon juice
½ teaspoon curry powder
Grated rind of ½ lemon
Pinch of thyme
Salt and freshly ground pepper to taste
Sugar to taste
1 cup sour cream
Chopped parsley

1 Mix all the ingredients except the sour cream and parsley. Chill.

2 Before serving, blend in the sour cream and sprinkle each portion with parsley.

♦

FRESH TOMATO SOUP

One of the most easily made yet delectable of summer soups is a simple creation of cubed red, ripe tomatoes, finely chopped fresh herbs and beef stock, which may be fresh or canned. Served with freshly made toast plus goat cheese, it makes a perfect warm-weather meal.

6 SERVINGS

4 large (about 1¾ pounds) red, ripe tomatoes
2 large (about 1¾ pounds) Bermuda onions
2 tablespoons olive oil
1 tablespoon minced garlic
3½ cups beef stock
Salt and freshly ground pepper to taste
¼ teaspoon hot red pepper flakes
¼ cup finely chopped basil
¼ cup finely chopped parsley

1 Peel and core the tomatoes. Cut them into small cubes. There should be about 4 cups.

2 Peel the onions and cut them into cubes, no larger than ½ inch in diameter. There should be about 5 cups.

3 Heat the oil in a large saucepan and add the onions. Cook, stirring often, with a wooden spoon to prevent sticking or burning. Cook 5 minutes or longer, until the onions have lost their raw smell. Do not brown. Add the garlic for the last minute of cooking.

4 Add the cubed tomatoes and cook, stirring often, about 10 minutes, or until they have become a bit saucelike. Add the stock, salt, pepper, red pepper flakes, basil and parsley. Cook, stirring occasionally, about 20 minutes. Serve hot.

How to Peel Tomatoes: Tomatoes should usually be peeled for soup, and it is easily done. Dip them in boiling water and let them sit for just 10 seconds. If it is longer than that, they start to cook and their texture is spoiled. Remove them from the water and skin them with a paring knife. Then core and seed them as called for in the recipe.

Variations

FRESH TOMATO SOUP WITH OKRA

Prepare the tomato soup. Trim off the stem end of ¼ pound of okra, or more if desired. Cut the pods crosswise into ¼-inch pieces. Bring the soup to the simmer and add the okra, stirring briefly. Let simmer 5 to 6 minutes, or until okra is tender. Do not overcook.

FRESH TOMATO SOUP WITH CORN

Add 2 cups of cooked corn kernels, freshly cut from the cob or frozen, to the cooked soup.

FRESH TOMATO SOUP WITH PESTO

After the soup has cooked, stir in 2 teaspoons or more pesto sauce (page 498), according to taste. If the pesto sauce seems too thick, dilute it with a little beef stock.

◆

CREAM OF TOMATO SOUP

6 SERVINGS

1½ pounds (5 or 6 medium) ripe tomatoes
4 tablespoons butter
1 cup chopped onions
1 cup peeled, seeded and diced cucumber
½ bay leaf
2 cloves
¼ cup flour
3 cups milk (may be part half-and-half)
1 teaspoon salt
Freshly ground pepper to taste

1 Peel, core and chop the tomatoes.

2 Melt the butter in a saucepan and cook the onions in it until wilted. Add the tomatoes, cucumber, bay leaf and cloves. Stir in the flour and mix well. Simmer until the tomatoes are very soft, stirring occasionally.

3 Purée the tomato mixture in a food processor and return to the saucepan. Heat the milk and add to the tomatoes, stirring vigorously until the soup thickens and is smooth. Season with salt and pepper.

GAZPACHO

2 small cucumbers
4 ripe tomatoes
1 red onion
2 teaspoons finely chopped garlic
1½ cups finely diced red and green sweet
    peppers
2 tablespoons red wine vinegar
2 tablespoons lemon juice
¼ cup olive oil
1 egg yolk
Salt to taste
1 teaspoon freshly ground pepper,
    preferably white
¼ teaspoon Tabasco sauce
½ cup tomato juice

GARNISHES

1 cup toasted bread cubes
1 cup finely chopped red and green sweet
    peppers
½ cup chopped, peeled tomatoes
½ cup finely chopped cucumber

1 Peel the cucumbers and cut them into small cubes. There should be about 1½ cups.

2 Peel, core and seed the tomatoes. Cut into small cubes. There should be about 3 cups.

3 Peel and chop the onion. There should be about 1 cup.

4 Put the cucumbers, tomatoes and onion into the container of a food processor. Add the garlic, sweet peppers, vinegar, lemon juice, oil, egg yolk, salt, pepper, Tabasco and tomato juice. Blend as fine as possible. Pour the mixture into a bowl and refrigerate until thoroughly chilled.

5 Serve the soup in chilled bowls with the garnishes on the side.

TOMATO DILL SOUP

3 large tomatoes
1 medium onion, sliced
1 small garlic clove
1 teaspoon salt
¼ teaspoon freshly ground pepper
2 dill sprigs
1 tablespoon tomato paste
¼ cup cold water
½ cup cooked macaroni
1 cup chicken stock
¾ cup cream

1 Peel and slice the tomatoes into a saucepan. Add the onion, garlic, seasonings, dill, tomato paste and water. Cover and simmer 12 to 15 minutes.

2 Transfer to the container of a food processor. Add macaroni and purée. With motor running, add the stock and cream.

3 Chill and serve garnished with chopped dill and chopped tomato.

TURNIP SOUP

Turnip soup? By all means, for it is startlingly good.

6 SERVINGS

2 cups peeled and diced white turnips
4 cups chicken stock
1 cup cream
Salt and freshly ground pepper to taste
2 egg yolks, beaten
1 tablespoon butter

1 Cook the turnips in the stock until tender. Drain, reserving the liquid.

2 Rub the turnips through a sieve or food mill, or purée in a food processor.

3 Add the reserved stock to the puréed turnips and bring to a boil. Remove from the heat, add the cream, and season with salt and pepper. Reheat but do not boil. Remove from the heat and stir in the egg yolks and butter. Serve piping hot.

♦

COLD PEA AND LETTUCE SOUP

6 SERVINGS

1 leek
1 head Boston lettuce
2 tablespoons butter
4 cups hot chicken stock
1½ cups cooked peas
1 small bay leaf
1 whole clove
Salt, freshly ground pepper and grated
    nutmeg to taste
¼ cup heavy cream, whipped
1 tablespoon or more chopped chives

1 Cut the leek in quarters lengthwise and wash thoroughly. Wash the lettuce well.

2 Heat the butter, add the leeks and lettuce and sauté until soft but not brown. Add the stock, peas and seasonings and cook until the peas are very tender. Strain the broth and rub the vegetables through a sieve or food mill, or purée in a food processor. Chill thoroughly.

3 At serving time, fold in the whipped cream and serve garnished with chopped chives.

♦

COLD CREAM OF SORREL SOUP

6 SERVINGS

½ pound sorrel, finely chopped
1 teaspoon butter
5 cups chicken stock
4 egg yolks
2 cups half-and-half

1 Sauté the sorrel in the butter until wilted. Set aside.

2 Heat the stock to a boil. Lightly beat together the egg yolks and half-and-half; remove the stock from the heat and add the egg mixture, stirring with a wire whisk. Cook until slightly thickened, stirring constantly, either over very low heat or over hot water. Do not allow mixture to boil.

3 Remove the mixture from the heat, add the sorrel and set in cracked ice to cool, stirring often. Correct the seasonings. Refrigerate.

Cold fruit soups are not for every palate, but those who admire them are voluble in their praise. The ideal time to drink or dine on such soups is at high noon on the hottest day of the year.

♦

COLD BERRY SOUP

4 OR 5 SERVINGS

2 cups fresh strawberries or raspberries
½ cup sugar, approximately
½ cup sour cream
2 cups ice water
½ cup dry red wine

1 Rub the berries through a fine sieve. Add sugar to taste and the sour cream. Mix.

2 Add the water and wine and correct sweetening. Chill.

♦

CHERRY SOUP

4 TO 6 SERVINGS

1 cup pitted cherries
1 lemon slice
1 stick (2-inch) cinnamon
2 cups water
2 tablespoons sugar, or more
Pinch of salt
1 tablespoon cornstarch
¼ cup cream

1 Boil the cherries, lemon and cinnamon stick in the water for about 10 minutes, until the cherries are very soft. Add the sugar and salt.

2 Mix the cornstarch with a small amount of water, add it to the boiling mixture, and cook, stirring, for 1 minute. Remove the cinnamon stick.

3 Purée the mixture in a food processor, add the cream, mix, and chill. Garnish each serving with additional cherries.

♦

CHILLED FRUIT SOUP

6 SERVINGS

½ cup raisins
6 thin orange slices
6 thin lemon slices
¼ cup lemon juice
1 stick (about 3 inches) cinnamon
2 cups water
2 cups sliced fresh peaches
1½ cups pitted sweet or sour cherries
½ cup sugar, approximately
Dash of salt
1½ tablespoons cornstarch
Whipped cream

1 Simmer the raisins, orange and lemon slices, lemon juice, cinnamon stick and water for 20 minutes. Remove the cinnamon stick.

2 Add the peaches, cherries, sugar and salt to the mixture and bring to a boil.

3 Blend the cornstarch with a little water and add to the fruit. Cook, stirring, until clear, or about 1 minute. Adjust the sweetening, adding more if sour cherries are used. Serve chilled, garnished with whipped cream.

Soups made with dried beans have a particular appeal in cold weather. They are hearty and nutritious. Dried beans have a splendid pantry life; properly stored, they will keep for a year or two. Note, however, that the longer the beans stand, the longer cooking time they require because water penetrates them more slowly. All dried beans can be soaked by the quick method on page 78.

♦

BLACK BEAN SOUP

10 TO 12 SERVINGS

2 cups dried black beans
4 tablespoons butter
2 celery stalks, chopped
2 medium onions, chopped
1 tablespoon flour
¼ cup chopped parsley
Rind and bone from a smoked ham
2 bay leaves
1 teaspoon salt
¼ teaspoon freshly ground pepper
½ cup dry Madeira
2 tablespoons vinegar
Chopped hard-cooked egg whites

1 Pick over and wash the beans. Cover them with water and soak overnight. Drain the beans, add 8 cups of cold water, cover, and simmer for 1½ hours.

2 Melt the butter in a heavy kettle. Add the celery and onions; sauté until tender but not brown. Blend in the flour and cook the mixture, stirring, for 1 minute.

3 Add the parsley, the beans and cooking liquid, the ham rind and bone, bay leaves, salt and pepper. Cover and simmer for 3 hours.

4 Discard the ham bone and rind, but keep any bits of meat. Put the soup through a sieve or purée in a food processor. Add the wine and vinegar. Reheat and serve topped with chopped egg whites.

♦

CALDO GALLEGO

ABOUT 12 SERVINGS

½ pound dried chick-peas
¼ pound lean salt pork, diced
¼ cup diced cooked smoked ham
¼ pound chorizos (Spanish sausages), sliced
2 tomatoes, peeled and chopped
2 garlic cloves, minced
1 ham bone
2 quarts water
1½ teaspoons cumin seed, crushed
Salt and freshly ground pepper to taste
4 small potatoes, peeled and diced
½ pound dandelion greens, spinach or romaine lettuce, washed and cut into large pieces

1 Cover the chick-peas with water, bring to a boil, drain, and discard the water.

2 Sauté the salt pork until light brown. Add the ham and sausages and cook until all the meats are light brown.

3 Put the chick-peas, tomatoes, garlic, ham bone, water, cumin seed, and salt and pepper in a large kettle. Add the browned meats. Cover, bring to a boil, and simmer for about 2½ hours, until chick-peas are tender.

4 Add the potatoes and cook for 25 minutes. Add the greens and cook for 5 minutes longer. Remove the ham bone. Season soup with additional salt and pepper, if desired.

DUTCH SPLIT PEA SOUP

As Canadians are known for yellow pea soup, the Dutch are identified with split pea soup.

6 TO 10 SERVINGS

1 pound dried green split peas
2½ quarts cold water
¼ cup diced salt pork
½ cup chopped leeks
½ cup chopped celery
½ cup celeriac (optional)
½ cup chopped onions
½ bay leaf
1 teaspoon salt
1 pig's knuckle
1 smoked Dutch ring sausage, sliced, or 1 cup
    sliced Polish sausage
Chopped parsley

1   Rinse the peas under cold water and pick over to remove all foreign particles. Place the peas in a large kettle, add the water, cover and let stand overnight. Or use the quick-soaking method (opposite).

2   In a skillet, cook the salt pork 5 minutes. Add the vegetables and cook 10 minutes, until tender but not brown.

3   Add the salt pork mixture, bay leaf, salt and pig's knuckle to the peas. Cover and bring slowly to a boil. Reduce the heat, skim foam from the top and simmer gently 2 hours, or until the meat on the pig's knuckle separates from the bone.

4   Remove the pig's knuckle, shred the meat and reserve. Discard the bone and the bay leaf.

5   Strain the soup and purée the vegetables in a food processor. Return the meat and vegetables to the soup kettle and adjust the seasonings. Add the sliced sausages and simmer 5 minutes longer.

6   Serve the soup piping hot and garnish each portion with chopped parsley.

CANADIAN PEA SOUP

Funny how certain dishes are so closely identified with certain regions. Speak of yellow pea soup—soup aux pois—and the map of Canada immediately comes to mind.

4 SERVINGS

1 pound whole dried yellow peas
3 quarts cold water
½ pound salt pork
½ cup diced carrots and turnips
1 small onion, chopped
Salt and freshly ground pepper to taste

1   Pick over and wash the peas. Soak 12 hours in water with ½ teaspoon baking soda; or use the quick-soaking method (see below).

2   Rinse the peas well and place in a pot with the cold water and salt pork. Bring to a boil, skim and add the vegetables. Let simmer 4 hours; add salt and pepper to taste. A little finely chopped herbs or parsley may be added. Serve unstrained.

Quick-Soaking Method: Start by boiling whole peas or beans with the water for 2 minutes. Remove from the heat, cover and soak 1 hour before cooking as directed.

LENTIL AND MACARONI SOUP

4 TO 6 SERVINGS

1 pound dried lentils
¼ cup olive oil
½ cup diced celery
½ cup chopped onions
1 cup crushed tomatoes
2 cups macaroni or other pasta, broken into
    1-inch pieces
Salt and freshly ground pepper to taste

1 Wash the lentils thoroughly. Place them in a large saucepan with cold water to cover and cook over medium heat for about 1½ hours, until tender.

2 In a separate saucepan, heat the oil. Add the celery and onions and sauté until golden brown. Add the tomatoes and simmer for 10 minutes. Add to the lentils.

3 Bring 2 quarts of salted water to a boil in a kettle. Add the macaroni and cook for 10 minutes. Drain.

4 Add the macaroni to the lentils, season with salt and pepper and simmer slowly until the pasta is tender. Serve accompanied by a tossed green salad and a favorite cheese.

NEW ENGLAND CLAM CHOWDER, SOUTH-OF-BOSTON STYLE

8 TO 10 SERVINGS

4 dozen medium hard-shell clams
6 cups cold water
1 (2-inch) cube salt pork, diced
1 large onion, chopped very fine
4 medium potatoes, diced
Salt and freshly ground pepper to taste
2 cups milk, heated
1 cup cream, heated

1 Wash clams thoroughly. Place them in a deep saucepan with the cold water, bring to a boil and let boil gently 10 minutes, or until the shells open. Discard any clams that do not open. The water should almost cover the clams.

2 Strain the broth through cheesecloth and reserve. Remove the clams from their shells, clean and chop.

3 Fry the salt pork in the deep saucepan. Add the onions and cook slowly until they begin to turn golden brown. Add the clams and reserved broth. Skim well, if necessary.

4 Add the potatoes and season with salt and pepper. Cook until the potatoes are tender.

5 Remove the mixture from the heat and slowly add the warm milk and cream. Serve immediately.

MANHATTAN CLAM CHOWDER

10 TO 12 SERVINGS

2 dozen fresh cherrystone clams or
    chowder clams
4 cups water
¼ pound salt pork, diced
2 onions, finely chopped
1½ cups chopped celery
4 potatoes, peeled and diced
3 cups tomato juice
1 teaspoon salt
¼ teaspoon freshly ground pepper
½ teaspoon thyme

1 Wash the clams well and place in a kettle with the water. Simmer until the shells open. Discard any clams that do not open. Drain and reserve 3 cups of the broth.

2 Sauté the salt pork until it is crisp and light brown. Add the onions and celery and sauté until they are translucent but not brown.

3 Add the potatoes, reserved clam broth, tomato juice, salt and pepper. Bring to a boil, cover, and simmer for about 15 minutes, until potatoes are barely tender.

4 Meanwhile, remove the clams from their shells and chop fine or put through a food grinder using a medium knife.

5 Add the thyme and chopped clams to the potatoes. Cover and cook for 5 minutes longer.

ITALIAN CLAM SOUP

4 SERVINGS

40 littleneck clams
¼ cup olive oil
1 garlic clove
3 anchovy fillets, chopped
1 tablespoon chopped parsley
½ cup dry red wine
1 tablespoon tomato paste
1½ cups warm water
½ teaspoon salt
½ teaspoon freshly ground pepper
¼ teaspoon oregano
8 thin slices Italian bread, fried in olive oil

1 Wash the clams and scrub well with a vegetable brush.

2 Place the oil in a large saucepan, add the garlic and brown. Discard the garlic. Add the anchovies, parsley and wine to the oil and cook 5 minutes.

3 Add the tomato paste, water, salt and pepper and cook 3 to 4 minutes.

4 Add the clams, cover the pan and cook until all the shells are open, or a maximum of 5 minutes. Discard any clams that do not open. Add the oregano and cook 2 minutes longer.

5 To serve, place 2 slices of fried bread in each soup bowl; pour the soup over them.

FISH CHOWDER

4 SERVINGS

4 fish heads, or bones from 4 fish (any kind
    saved when fish were cooked for a meal)
2 cups water
1 small onion, chopped
1 garlic clove, minced
2 tablespoons chopped green pepper
2 tablespoons butter or olive oil
2 cups peeled and chopped ripe tomatoes
2 medium potatoes, finely diced
½ cup minced celery
1 bay leaf
1 teaspoon salt
⅛ teaspoon freshly ground pepper
1 tablespoon minced parsley

1 Wash the heads or bones and simmer
in water 10 minutes. Drain, reserving the
broth. Pick the meat from the bones and
reserve; discard the bones.

2 Sauté the onion, garlic and pepper in
butter until the onions are transparent.
Add the reserved stock, tomatoes, potatoes, celery, bay leaf, salt and pepper to
taste. Cook until the potatoes are tender.

3 Add the reserved fish meat and the
parsley and reheat.

Bouillabaisse, page 234.
Cacciucco, page 235.

FISH SOUP WITH TOMATOES

8 SERVINGS

2 tablespoons olive oil
1 tablespoon minced garlic
2 cups finely chopped onions
2 cups finely chopped leeks
1½ cups finely chopped celery
1 teaspoon turmeric
1 bay leaf
¼ teaspoon hot red pepper flakes
½ teaspoon thyme
¼ teaspoon aniseed
3 cups canned crushed tomatoes
6 cups fish stock
1 cup dry white wine
Salt and freshly ground pepper to taste
½ cup very thin spaghetti, such as
    angel's hair or fidelini
2 pounds skinless, boneless, nonoily fish such
    as monkfish, tilefish, cod or red snapper
16 (about ½ pound) raw shrimp, shelled
2 tablespoons minced parsley

1 Heat the oil in a kettle and add the
garlic and onions. Cook briefly, stirring
until onions are wilted.

2 Add the leeks and celery and continue cooking, stirring, without browning
about 5 minutes. Add the turmeric, bay
leaf, red pepper flakes, thyme, aniseed,
tomatoes, fish stock, wine, salt and pepper. Stir to blend. Bring to the boil and
simmer 20 minutes.

3 Add the spaghetti and cubed fish (if
monkfish is used, cook it 1 minute before
adding any remaining fish). The cooking
time for the fish will depend on its texture.
Cod needs very little cooking; monkfish
demands 3 or 4 minutes cooking time.
Add the shrimp and cook about 3 minutes.
Add the parsley. Stir and ladle into hot
soup plates.

FISH SOUP WITH LEEKS

2 pounds mussels, well cleaned
1 cup dry white wine
1 bay leaf
3 thyme sprigs, or ½ teaspoon dried
4 to 6 (about 1½ pounds) ripe tomatoes, or 3
    cups drained, chopped imported tomatoes
1 pound skinless, boneless monkfish fillets
2 tablespoons olive oil
1 tablespoon minced garlic
1 cup finely chopped onions
4 cups chopped well-cleaned leeks
Salt and freshly ground pepper to taste
½ teaspoon turmeric
¼ teaspoon hot red pepper flakes
¼ teaspoon fennel seed
1 tablespoon flour
5 cups water
¼ cup cream
3 tablespoons finely chopped parsley

1 Put the mussels in a kettle and add the wine, bay leaf and thyme. Cover closely, bring to the boil and cook until the mussels open, 1 minute or slightly longer. Drain and reserve the broth. There should be about 2 cups. Discard any mussels that do not open. Remove the mussels from the shells. Discard the shells.

2 Peel and core the tomatoes. Cut them crosswise in half and squeeze to remove most of the seeds. Cut the tomatoes into ½-inch cubes. There should be about 3 cups.

3 Cut away any bloodspots from the fish. Cut the fish into ½-inch cubes.

4 Heat the oil in a kettle or casserole and add the garlic and onions. Cook, stirring, until onions are wilted. Add the leeks and cook about 2 minutes. Sprinkle with salt, pepper, turmeric, red pepper flakes and fennel seed. Sprinkle with flour and stir to blend. Add the tomatoes and blend.

5 Add the reserved broth and water. Bring to the boil and cook 15 minutes. Add the cubes of fish and cook 4 or 5 minutes.

6 Add the mussels and cream and heat through. Serve sprinkled with parsley.

◆

CREAM OF FISH SOUP WITH VEGETABLES

2 pounds mussels, well cleaned
1 cup dry white wine
4 cups water
2 cups finely chopped leeks
1 cup finely chopped onions
1 cup finely chopped celery
¾ cup finely diced sweet red pepper
¾ cup finely diced sweet green pepper
¾ cup diced carrots
¾ cup diced potatoes
1 tablespoon minced garlic
2 tablespoons olive oil
6 tablespoons flour
½ cup canned crushed tomatoes
Salt and freshly ground pepper to taste
½ teaspoon hot red pepper flakes
2 cups milk
1½ pounds skinless, boneless, white-fleshed,
    nonoily fish, such as cod, cut into
    1-inch cubes
16 (about ½ pound) raw shrimp, shelled
2 tablespoons finely chopped parsley

1 Put the mussels in a kettle and add the wine and water. Bring to the simmer and cook 2 to 3 minutes, or until mussels open. Line a mixing bowl with a sieve and strain the mussels. Discard any that do not open. Set the mussels and liquid aside. There should be about 5 cups of liquid. Remove the mussels from the shells. Discard the shells.

2 Prepare the leeks, onions, celery, red and green peppers, carrots, potatoes, and garlic. Set each aside.

3 Heat the oil in a kettle and add the onions, leeks and garlic. Cook, stirring, until wilted. Add the celery, peppers and carrots and stir. Sprinkle with flour and stir to coat the pieces evenly.

4 Add the reserved mussel liquid, stirring. Add the crushed tomatoes and potatoes. Add salt and pepper and the red pepper flakes. Bring to the boil and cook 10 minutes. Add the milk and continue cooking 10 minutes.

5 Add the cubed fish and the shrimp and shelled mussels. Bring to the boil and let simmer 1 minute or slightly longer. The cooking time of fish depends on its texture. Cod needs very little cooking; monkfish demands 3 or 4 minutes cooking time.

6 Stir in the parsley and serve hot.

CURRIED FISH SOUP WITH CREAM AND TOMATOES

4 TO 6 SERVINGS

5 cups fish stock
2 tablespoons butter
½ cup finely chopped onions
1 teaspoon minced garlic
1 tablespoon curry powder
2 cups chopped fresh ripe or canned tomatoes, preferably imported
½ cup raw long-grain rice
¾ pound white-fleshed, nonoily, skinless, boneless fish fillets, cut into 1-inch cubes
½ cup corn kernels, preferably freshly scraped from the cob
½ cup cream

1 Prepare the fish stock in advance and set aside.

2 Melt the butter in a saucepan and add the onions and garlic. Cook briefly, stirring, until onions are wilted.

3 Add the curry powder and cook briefly, stirring. Add the tomatoes, fish stock and rice and bring to the boil. Let cook 15 minutes, or until rice is thoroughly tender.

4 Pour the mixture into the container of a food processor or blender and blend thoroughly.

5 Add the fish cubes and simmer about 4 minutes. Add the corn and stir. Cook about 1 minute. Add the cream and bring to the boil. Serve piping hot.

Fish Stock, page 589.

MEXICAN SHELLFISH SOUP WITH SALSA

6 SERVINGS

1 (about ½ pound) skinless, boneless fillet of
   fish such as tilefish, flounder or monkfish
5 cups fish stock
1 tablespoon olive oil
¾ cup finely chopped onions
½ teaspoon minced garlic
2 cups canned crushed tomatoes
1 cup cubed carrot
1½ cups cubed hearts of celery
Salt and freshly ground pepper to taste
3 bay leaves
1 cup cubed potato
1 avocado
2 teaspoons lemon juice
18 raw medium shrimp, peeled, deveined and
   cut crosswise into thirds
12 raw oysters
2 cups salsa cruda (page 563)
Lime wedges for garnish
Tabasco sauce or other hot sauce to taste

1 Cut the fish into 1-inch cubes. Refrigerate.

2 Prepare the fish stock and strain. Set aside.

3 Heat the oil in a small kettle or large saucepan and add the onions and garlic. Cook, stirring, until onions are wilted. Add the tomatoes, carrot, celery and fish stock. Add salt and pepper and the bay leaves. Bring to the boil and simmer 20 minutes.

4 Add the potato and cook until tender but not mushy, 10 to 15 minutes.

5 Meanwhile, peel the avocado and discard the seed. Cut the flesh into 1-inch cubes. Toss with lemon juice to prevent discoloration. Set aside.

6 Add the fish cubes and simmer about 3 minutes.

7 At the last minute, add the shrimp and oysters to the soup. Bring just to the simmer (do not overcook or the oysters will toughen) and spoon into very hot soup bowls or, preferably, mugs.

8 Spoon a small amount of salsa on top of each serving. Top each serving with a few avocado cubes. Serve lime wedges and Tabasco on the side.

♦

SPANISH FISH CHOWDER

6 TO 8 SERVINGS

¼ cup olive oil
1 tablespoon paprika
2 large onions, sliced
2 garlic cloves, minced
1 medium green pepper, cut into strips
1 pound tomatoes, sliced
¼ cup chopped parsley
1 cup flaked cooked lobster meat
1 pound shrimp, shelled and deveined
½ cup chopped pimiento-stuffed green olives
2 cups water
2 cups tomato juice
Salt and freshly ground pepper to taste
1 pint shucked oysters

1 Heat the olive oil, add the paprika, and blend. Add the onions and garlic and cook until tender. Add the green pepper, tomatoes and parsley. Cook for 30 minutes, stirring occasionally.

2 Add the lobster, shrimp, olives, water, tomato juice, salt and pepper. Cover and cook over low heat for 30 minutes, stirring occasionally. Add the oysters and mix well. Cook briefly until the edges of the oysters curl.

Seafood Gumbo, page 240.

BILLI BI

This may well be the most elegant and delicious soup ever created. It may be served hot or cold. This is the recipe of Pierre Franey, one of this nation's greatest chefs.

4 SERVINGS

2 pounds mussels
2 shallots, coarsely chopped
2 small onions, quartered
2 parsley sprigs
Salt and freshly ground pepper to taste
Pinch of cayenne
1 cup dry white wine
2 tablespoons butter
½ bay leaf
½ teaspoon thyme
2 cups cream
1 egg yolk, lightly beaten

1 Scrub the mussels well to remove all exterior sand and dirt. Place them in a large kettle with the shallots, onions, parsley, salt, pepper, cayenne, wine, butter, bay leaf and thyme. Cover and bring to a boil. Simmer 5 to 10 minutes, or until the mussels have opened. Discard any mussels that do not open.

2 Strain the liquid through a double thickness of cheesecloth. Reserve the mussels for another use or remove them from the shells and use them as a garnish.

3 Bring the liquid in the saucepan to a boil and add the cream. Return to the boil and remove from the heat. Add the beaten egg yolk and return to the heat long enough for the soup to thicken slightly. Do not boil. Serve hot or cold.

ROGER FESSAGUET'S MUSSEL SOUP

6 SERVINGS

4 pounds mussels
1 pound fish bones
¼ cup olive oil
3 leeks, trimmed, washed well and chopped
3 celery stalks, chopped
1 onion, peeled and quartered
½ garlic clove
3 parsley sprigs
4 tomatoes, peeled, seeded and crushed
½ teaspoon thyme
½ teaspoon aniseed
½ teaspoon saffron
1 bay leaf
2 cups dry white wine
4 cups water
Salt and cayenne to taste
⅓ cup arrowroot

1 Scrub the mussels well and rinse the fish bones under cold running water.

2 Heat the olive oil in a large kettle and add the leeks, celery, onions, garlic and parsley. Cook until the leeks are wilted. Add the tomatoes and seasonings. Add the wine and stir. Add the fish bones and water and cook 45 minutes. Add the mussels and cook for 5 to 10 minutes. Discard any mussels that do not open.

3 Strain the liquid through a sieve lined with a double thickness of cheesecloth and reserve the meat from the mussels. Chop the mussels.

4 Season the soup with salt and cayenne, then thicken it with arrowroot thoroughly blended with a little cold water. Add the mussels and serve piping hot. Garnish, if desired, with toast croutons rubbed with garlic.

MARYLAND CRAB SOUP

Whiskey gives a surprising nuance of flavor to a crab soup.

4 TO 6 SERVINGS

2 tablespoons finely chopped onions
3 tablespoons butter
2 cups crabmeat, picked over well to remove any bits of shell or cartilage
½ teaspoon salt
Freshly ground pepper
3 cups milk
½ cup cream
2 tablespoons Scotch whiskey
Chopped parsley

1 Cook the onions in the butter until they are transparent. Stir in the crabmeat, salt and pepper and cook over low heat 10 minutes, stirring occasionally.

2 Add the milk and cook over boiling water 15 minutes. Add the cream and, when the mixture is piping hot, stir in the whiskey. Serve immediately sprinkled with chopped parsley.

CRÈME ST. JACQUES

In the world of cuisine *St. Jacques* is synonymous with scallops. The following is a cream of scallop soup.

8 SERVINGS

1½ quarts water
1 pound (3 or 4 medium) potatoes, peeled and quartered
2 medium onions, coarsely chopped
½ bay leaf
¼ teaspoon thyme
Salt and freshly ground pepper to taste
1 cup sea scallops, coarsely chopped
1 teaspoon chopped garlic
2 egg yolks
½ cup cream

1 Bring the water to a boil and add the potatoes, onions, bay leaf, thyme, salt and pepper. Simmer 50 minutes. Add the scallops and cook 5 minutes longer. Add the garlic.

2 Remove the bay leaf and purée the soup in a food processor until smooth. Return the soup to the heat and bring to a boil. Turn the heat off and stir in the egg yolks blended with the cream. Serve hot but do not allow the soup to boil.

SHRIMP SOUP

4 SERVINGS

1 small onion, chopped
1 small carrot, sliced
¼ teaspoon thyme
1 bay leaf
1 tablespoon chopped parsley
2 tablespoons chopped celery leaves
3 tablespoons butter
1¼ pounds shrimp
4½ cups chicken stock
½ cup dry white wine
¼ cup raw rice, or 4 slices white bread
    without crusts
Salt and freshly ground pepper to taste

1 Sauté the onions, carrot, thyme, bay leaf, parsley and celery leaves in 2 tablespoons of the butter until light brown.

2 Shell and devein the shrimp. Cook, covered, in 1 cup of the stock and the wine 5 minutes. Strain. Reserve 8 shrimp for garnish.

3 Combine the remaining stock with the sautéed vegetables and bring to a boil. Add rice or bread. Cook until rice is tender or bread has blended well with the broth. Purée in a food processor along with the cooked shrimp. Reheat and season with salt and pepper. Add the remaining butter and the shrimp garnish.

LOBSTER BISQUE

ABOUT 5 SERVINGS

1 (1½-pound) live lobster
5 tablespoons butter
¼ cup diced carrot
1 small onion, chopped
½ bay leaf
Pinch of thyme
2 parsley sprigs
3 tablespoons cognac
⅓ cup dry white wine
½ cup fish or chicken stock
1 tablespoon sherry or Madeira wine
¼ cup flour
3 cups milk
3 tablespoons cream, approximately
1 tablespoon tomato paste

1 Have the lobster split and cleaned at the market. Crack the claws and cut the body and tail into 4 or 5 pieces.

2 Melt 2 tablespoons of the butter and sauté the carrot and onions in it until the onions are transparent. Add the bay leaf, thyme, parsley and lobster. Sauté until the lobster turns red, or about 5 minutes, shaking the pan occasionally.

3 Add 2 tablespoons of cognac and ignite. Add the wine and stock and simmer 20 minutes.

4 Remove the lobster, cool and remove the meat from the shell. Dice the meat fine, add the sherry and set aside. Reserve the shell and broth.

5 Melt the remaining 3 tablespoons of butter in a saucepan, add the flour and blend with a wire whisk. Meanwhile, bring the milk to a boil and add all at once to the butter-flour mixture, stirring vigorously with the whisk.

6 Grind or crush the lobster shell and add to the sauce. Add the reserved broth with the vegetables and simmer, covered, about 1 hour. Strain through a fine sieve.

Continued

7 Bring the sauce to a boil, and add enough cream to give the desired consistency. Stir in the tomato paste.

8 Add the reserved lobster meat, correct the seasonings and add the remaining 1 tablespoon of cognac.

◆

QUICK SEAFOOD BISQUE

8 SERVINGS

1½ quarts water
4 medium potatoes, peeled and quartered
2 medium onions, coarsely chopped
½ bay leaf
½ teaspoon thyme
¼ teaspoon minced garlic
1 teaspoon salt
⅛ teaspoon freshly ground pepper
1 cup chopped sea scallops, shrimp, lobster or crabmeat
2 egg yolks
½ cup cream
Paprika

1 Bring 2 cups of the water to a boil. Add the potatoes, onions, bay leaf, thyme, garlic, salt and pepper and simmer until the vegetables are barely tender, about 15 minutes, adding the selected seafood during the last 5 minutes of cooking.

2 Remove the bay leaf and purée the mixture in a food processor.

3 Return the puréed mixture to the saucepan and add the remaining water. Bring to a boil and correct the seasonings.

4 Turn off the heat and stir in the egg yolks blended with the cream. Serve hot or chill. Garnish with paprika.

OYSTER CHOWDER

4 TO 6 SERVINGS

2 medium potatoes, diced
1 carrot, finely chopped
2 celery stalks, chopped
1 quart milk
1 tablespoon chopped onions
Salt and freshly ground pepper to taste
2 tablespoons flour
6 tablespoons butter
1 pint shucked oysters with liquor
2 tablespoons chopped parsley

1 In a large saucepan, boil the potatoes, carrot and celery in a small amount of boiling salted water until tender. Drain. Add the milk, onions, salt and pepper and bring to a boil.

2 Cream the flour with 2 tablespoons of the butter and gradually add to the boiling mixture. Cook, stirring, until thickened.

3 Cook the oysters with their liquid in the remaining butter until the edges curl. Add to the soup and serve immediately sprinkled with parsley.

HANK KETCHAM'S OYSTER SOUP

Hank Ketcham, the creator of "Dennis the Menace," is, of course, one of America's best-known cartoonists. He was, some years ago, a participant in a March of Dimes cooking contest, held in Monterey, California. His contribution was a first-rate oyster soup said to be of Virginia origin. This prizewinner is easy to make.

8 SERVINGS

1¼ pints shucked oysters with their liquid
1 pound spinach in bulk, or 2 (10-ounce) packages fresh spinach
1 teaspoon butter
2 scallions, ends trimmed and chopped
½ cup finely chopped hearts of celery, leaves included
¼ teaspoon aniseed, crushed as fine as possible
2 tablespoons finely chopped parsley
1¾ cups chicken stock
2 drops Tabasco sauce
2 cups half-and-half
Salt and freshly ground pepper to taste
1 to 2 tablespoons Pernod, Ricard or Herbsaint

1 As a refinement, you may cut away the muscle of each oyster. To some minds the muscles tend to toughen when cooked. Or leave the oysters whole. Put the oysters into the container of a food processor or blender. Blend as thoroughly as possible. Scrape the oysters into a bowl and chill until ready to use.

2 Pick over the spinach to remove any tough stems and blemished leaves. Drop the spinach into a quantity of boiling water. Stir until wilted and drain thoroughly in a sieve, pressing to extract as much liquid as possible.

3 Heat the butter in a small skillet and add the scallions, celery and aniseed. Cook, stirring briefly, until wilted.

4 Put the spinach, scallion mixture, parsley and stock into the container of a food processor and blend as thoroughly as possible.

5 Pour the mixture into a saucepan. Add the Tabasco, half-and-half, salt and pepper. Cook, stirring, about 5 minutes. Add the oysters. Bring just to the simmer and add the Pernod.

◆

OYSTER STEW

Nothing is easier to make and few things are more warming and delicious than a rich oyster stew. Care should be taken not to overcook the oysters.

4 SERVINGS

4 tablespoons butter
1 pint shucked oysters with liquor
1½ cups milk
½ cup half-and-half
½ teaspoon salt
⅛ teaspoon freshly ground pepper or paprika
2 tablespoons chopped parsley (optional)

In the top of a double boiler over boiling water, place the butter, oysters with their liquor, milk, half-and-half, salt and pepper. When the oysters float, the butter has melted and the milk and cream are hot, add the parsley, if desired. Serve hot.

Note: A richer stew may be made by increasing the half-and-half to 1 cup and decreasing the milk by ½ cup.

CHICKEN CORN SOUP

This soup is a gift from the Pennsylvania Dutch.

10 TO 12 SERVINGS

1 (3½-pound) chicken, cut into pieces
3 quarts water
1 teaspoon salt
¼ teaspoon saffron
4 ounces noodles
2 cups fresh corn cut from the cob
Freshly ground pepper
Chopped parsley
2 hard-cooked eggs, chopped

1 Cover the chicken with water, add the salt and saffron and bring to a boil. Lower the heat and simmer, covered, until tender, about 2 hours.

2 Remove the chicken from stock and take the meat from the skin and bones. Chop the meat and return to the stock.

3 Bring to a boil, add the noodles and corn and cook until the noodles are tender. Add pepper and salt to taste, a little chopped parsley and the eggs.

♦

CHICKEN SOUP WITH MUSHROOMS

12 SERVINGS

3 pounds chicken wings
3 quarts water
3 scallions, trimmed
1 celery stalk, leaves included
3 parsley sprigs
1 teaspoon salt
1 piece of fresh ginger, crushed
2 mushrooms, thinly sliced

1 Simmer chicken, water, scallions, celery, parsley, salt and ginger in a large kettle for 1 to 1½ hours. Strain the broth and discard wings and vegetables.

2 Boil broth to concentrate flavor.

3 Serve hot in hot cups or soup bowls. Float mushroom slices on each serving.

Note: Leftover broth can be frozen for later use.

Chicken-Okra Gumbo, page 154.

♦

CREAMED CHICKEN SOUP

6 SERVINGS

2 pounds chicken backs and wings
6 cups water
1 celery stalk
1 small bay leaf
1 small onion, sliced
1 teaspoon salt
6 peppercorns
1 cup half-and-half
1 cup milk
3 tablespoons butter
3 tablespoons flour

1 Cook the chicken, covered, in the water with the celery, bay leaf, onions, salt and peppercorns, about 2 hours. Strain, reserving meat and broth. Remove skin and bones from the chicken and discard.

2 Add the half-and-half and milk to the broth and heat to a boil. Cream the butter and flour together, add to the soup and cook, stirring, until the mixture boils. Add the chicken meat and reheat.

3 Garnish with chopped parsley, watercress, shredded ham, sliced celery, toasted slivered almonds or cubed avocado.

AVGOLEMONO SOUP
GREEK EGG AND LEMON SOUP

6 TO 8 SERVINGS

2 quarts strong, strained chicken stock
½ cup rice
4 eggs
Juice of 2 lemons

1 Bring the stock to a boil and add the rice. Cook until the rice is tender, about 20 minutes.

2 Remove the stock from the heat. Just before serving, beat the eggs with a rotary beater until they are light and frothy. Slowly beat in the lemon juice and dilute the mixture with 2 cups of the hot soup, beating constantly until well mixed.

3 Add the diluted egg-lemon mixture to rest of soup, beating constantly. Bring almost to the boiling point, but do not boil or soup will curdle. Serve immediately.

♦

CHICKEN AND CUCUMBER SOUP

4 SERVINGS

1 large cucumber
1 chicken breast, skinless and boneless
4 cups chicken stock
2 to 4 tablespoons sherry

1 Peel the cucumber, cut it lengthwise into halves, and remove the seeds. Slice it into thin rings.

2 Cut the chicken into thin, bite-size slices.

3 Heat the stock to boiling. Add the cucumber and chicken and boil for 2 minutes. Add the sherry.

ESCAROLE CHICKEN SOUP

8 SERVINGS

1 (4- to 5-pound) chicken, cut into pieces
2½ quarts water
4 celery stalks, sliced
2 carrots, sliced
2 onions, sliced
1 cup canned tomatoes
1 teaspoon salt
1 bay leaf
½ teaspoon peppercorns
2 cups small pasta bows or shells
4 cups coarsely shredded escarole

1 Simmer the chicken, covered, in water with the celery, carrots, onions, tomatoes, salt, bay leaf and peppercorns until tender, about 4 hours.

2 Remove the chicken pieces and save for another use. Strain the broth and skim off the excess fat. Heat to boiling and adjust the seasonings.

3 Add the pasta and the escarole and boil until both the pasta and the escarole are tender, about 10 minutes.

SENEGALESE SOUP

Curried soup, anyone? Here is a refreshing one to be served well chilled on a hot summer day. A tossed green salad and crusty bread are all that is needed.

10 SERVINGS

4 tablespoons butter
2 medium onions, coarsely chopped
3 celery stalks, chopped
1 tablespoon curry powder
1 cup chopped leeks
1 garlic clove, finely chopped
1 cup diced bananas
1½ cups peeled, cubed potatoes
2 apples, peeled and chopped
Tabasco sauce to taste
8 cups chicken stock
1 cup diced cooked chicken
1 cup cream, chilled

1 Melt the butter in a skillet, add the onions and celery and cook until the vegetables are limp. Add the curry powder and stir to coat.

2 Add the leeks, garlic, bananas, potatoes, apples, Tabasco and stock. Stir well and simmer for 20 minutes.

3 Cool slightly and purée the mixture in a food processor. Pour into a bowl and chill.

4 When ready to serve, stir in the chicken and cream.

COCK-A-LEEKIE

6 SERVINGS

1 (3½-pound) frying chicken, cut up
3 quarts water
3 onions, sliced
4 parsley sprigs, tied together
1 bay leaf
1 teaspoon salt
1 teaspoon peppercorns, crushed
8 to 12 leeks
6 medium potatoes, peeled and cubed, or
    ½ cup rice

1 Simmer the chicken, covered, in the water with the onions, parsley, bay leaf, salt and peppercorns for about 1 hour, until tender. Remove the chicken and cool.

2 Split the leeks lengthwise and wash thoroughly. Cut into 1-inch lengths, using both the white and green portions. Add to the chicken stock. Add the potatoes and rice and boil for about 20 minutes, until tender. Remove the parsley and bay leaf.

3 Meanwhile, remove the skin and bones of the chicken and cut the meat into large bite-size pieces. Add to the soup, adjust seasonings, and reheat.

HOT AND SOUR SOUP

The "hot" of this seductive Chinese soup comes from the white pepper, not oil, and the "sour" comes from vinegar.

6 TO 8 SERVINGS

2 tablespoons (4 or 5) dried Chinese fungi (tree ears)
3 or 4 medium-size dried Chinese mushrooms
8 dried tiger lily buds
4 cups chicken stock
1/3 cup shredded bamboo shoots
1/3 cup lean boneless pork shreds
1 teaspoon dark soy sauce
1/2 teaspoon sugar
1 teaspoon salt
1/2 teaspoon freshly ground white pepper
2 tablespoons red wine vinegar
2 tablespoons cornstarch
3 tablespoons water
1 (1/2-pound) pad soft bean curd, cut into thin strips
1 egg, lightly beaten
1 teaspoon sesame oil
2 tablespoons chopped scallions

1 Soak the fungi, mushrooms and tiger lily buds in warm water for 20 minutes. After trimming off any tough stems, cut the fungi and mushrooms into slices. With the fingers, shred the tiger lily stems.

2 Place the fungi, mushrooms, tiger lily buds, stock, bamboo shoots and pork shreds in a saucepan. Bring to a boil and simmer for 10 minutes.

3 Add the soy sauce, sugar, salt, pepper and vinegar. Combine the cornstarch with the water.

4 Add a little of the hot soup to the cornstarch, return all to the pan, and heat to boiling, stirring. Add the bean curd and cook for 1 to 2 minutes.

5 Just before serving, turn off the heat, add the egg, and stir a few times in a circular motion. Add the oil. Sprinkle each serving with scallions.

◆

CHINESE WATERCRESS AND PORK BALL SOUP

6 SERVINGS

2 ounces cellophane noodles (bean thread)
1/2 pound ground lean pork
1 teaspoon grated fresh ginger
1/2 teaspoon sugar
1 teaspoon cornstarch
Salt to taste
1 teaspoon freshly ground pepper, preferably white
1 tablespoon dry sherry or shao hsing wine
2 tablespoons beaten egg (beat 1 egg and measure the proper amount)
6 cups chicken stock
2 bunches of watercress

1 Put the noodles in a mixing bowl and add warm water to cover. Let stand at least 20 minutes.

2 Meanwhile, put the pork in another bowl and add the ginger, sugar, cornstarch, salt, pepper, sherry and beaten egg. Blend well with the fingers.

3 Lightly oil a plate that will fit in the top rack of a steamer. Shape the pork mixture into 18 to 20 round balls. Arrange them on the oiled plate and place in the top rack of the steamer.

4 Partially fill the bottom of the steamer with water and bring to the boil. Arrange the filled rack over the water and cover closely. Let steam for 20 minutes.

Continued

5 Meanwhile, bring the chicken stock to the simmer.

6 In a separate saucepan, bring enough water to the boil to cover the watercress when added. Trim off and discard the tough stems of the watercress. Add the tender leaves to the saucepan. Turn off the heat and let stand 2 minutes. Drain and chill immediately under cold running water. Drain well and set aside.

7 Drain the noodles and cut them approximately in half with scissors. Put them in a saucepan and add cold water. Bring to the boil and let simmer 10 minutes. Place the noodles and watercress in the bottom of a heated soup tureen. Pour the meatballs and stock into the tureen. Sprinkle with a little more pepper, preferably white, and serve.

◆

LIVER DUMPLINGS IN SOUP

There is something very middle-European and old-fashioned about liver dumplings in soup. It is also delicious.

8 SERVINGS, OR 3 TO 4 DOZEN DUMPLINGS

¼ pound liver (beef, calf, lamb, pork or chicken)
½ small onion
1 egg yolk
¼ teaspoon salt
Pinch of freshly ground pepper
Pinch of thyme
Pinch of grated nutmeg
1½ tablespoons minced parsley
1½ slices bread without crusts
Milk or water
½ cup sifted flour, approximately
2 quarts soup stock

1 Trim the liver and grind with the onion, using the finest knife of food grinder. Add the egg yolk, salt, pepper, thyme, nutmeg and parsley.

2 Soak the bread in milk or water to moisten and squeeze out excess liquid. Add to the liver. Add enough flour to make a soft dough.

3 Bring the soup stock to a boil. Dip a teaspoon in the soup, then fill it with liver batter and drop the batter into the soup. Redip spoon in broth before shaping each dumpling. Cover the pot and simmer 10 to 15 minutes, depending on the size of the dumplings.

◆

ALBÓNDIGAS
A MEXICAN MEATBALL AND TOMATO SOUP

4 SERVINGS

½ pound ground sirloin (or use a mixture of ground beef and pork)
1 very small (less than ¼ pound) zucchini
2 tablespoons vegetable oil
1¼ cups finely chopped onions
2 teaspoons minced garlic
¼ cup finely chopped coriander leaves
¼ teaspoon oregano
½ teaspoon cumin
1 egg, lightly beaten
Salt and freshly ground pepper to taste
1½ cups chopped, peeled and seeded ripe tomatoes, or canned imported crushed tomatoes
1 chile chipotle, finely chopped (available in cans in Spanish and Mexican markets)
4 cups chicken stock
1 cup tomato juice

1 Put the meat in a mixing bowl.

2 Trim off the ends of the zucchini. Cut the vegetable lengthwise into slices about ⅛ inch thick. Stack the slices and cut them into strips about ⅛ inch wide. Stack the strips and cut them into ⅛-inch cubes. Add this to the meat.

3 Heat 1 tablespoon of the oil in a small skillet and add ¼ cup of the onions and 1 teaspoon of the garlic. Cook, stirring, until the onions wilt. Let cool briefly and add this to the meat. Add the coriander, oregano, cumin, egg, salt and pepper. Blend well.

4 Shape the mixture into 24 meatballs of equal size.

5 Heat the remaining oil in a saucepan and add the remaining onions and garlic. Cook, stirring, until wilted.

6 Add the tomatoes and the chile chipotle and let simmer about 10 minutes, stirring often. Pour the mixture into the container of a food processor and blend thoroughly. Return the tomato mixture to a saucepan.

7 Add the stock and tomato juice and bring to the boil. Add the meatballs and let simmer about 20 minutes. Carefully skim the surface as the soup cooks. Serve in hot soup bowls garnished with additional chopped coriander.

PHILADELPHIA PEPPER POT

12 SERVINGS

1 pound fresh honeycomb tripe
½ cup diced salt pork
½ cup chopped onions
1 green pepper, cored, seeded, and chopped
½ cup chopped celery
½ cup chopped carrots
2 garlic cloves, minced
1 small hot green pepper, trimmed and chopped
12 cups water
5 pounds veal knuckles
Salt and freshly ground pepper to taste
1 bay leaf
1 sprig thyme, or ½ teaspoon dried
1 cup diced potatoes
1 teaspoon paprika
2 tablespoons butter
2 tablespoons flour
½ cup cream

1 Rinse the tripe under cold running water and drain it.

2 Place the tripe on a flat surface and cut it into thin shreds. Chop the shreds into 1-inch lengths. Set aside.

3 Heat the salt pork in a kettle and, when it is rendered of fat, add the onions. Cook, stirring, until onions are wilted. Add the tripe shreds, green pepper, celery, carrots and garlic and cook briefly. Stir in the hot pepper and water and add the veal knuckles, salt, pepper, bay leaf and thyme. Bring to a boil and simmer partially covered 3 hours.

4 Add the potatoes and continue to cook about 1 hour, or until the tripe is thoroughly tender. It should not be chewy. Sprinkle with paprika.

Continued

5 Blend the butter with the flour and stir it, bit by bit, into the soup. When the mixture is thickened slightly and boiling, stir in the cream.

♦

SCOTCH BROTH WITH MUSHROOMS

6 TO 8 SERVINGS

2 pounds meaty lamb bones
10 cups cold water
½ cup finely chopped onions
¾ cup diced carrots
½ cup diced celery
¾ cup diced white turnips
Salt and freshly ground pepper to taste
1 bay leaf
1 garlic clove, minced
½ cup medium pearled barley
1½ tablespoons butter
¼ pound mushrooms, cut into ¼-inch cubes

1 Place the bones in a kettle and add cold water to cover. Bring to the boil. Drain. Chill thoroughly and return to a clean kettle.

2 Add the 10 cups of water, onions, carrots, celery, turnips, salt, pepper, bay leaf and garlic. Bring to the boil and simmer 1 hour.

3 Add the barley; cook 45 minutes.

4 Meanwhile, heat the butter in a skillet and add the mushrooms. Cook to wilt and add this to the soup. Continue cooking the soup 15 minutes.

MATZO BALLS

4 SERVINGS, OR 16 DUMPLINGS

4 large eggs
1 teaspoon salt
½ teaspoon freshly ground white pepper
½ teaspoon ground ginger
⅓ cup vegetable oil
½ cup water
1¼ cups matzo meal
¼ teaspoon baking powder
1 quart chicken stock

1 Combine the eggs, salt, pepper and ginger in a china, glass, or enamelware mixing bowl. Beat well with a wire whisk or use a blender. Beat in the oil, water, matzo meal and baking powder.

2 Chill the mixture for 30 minutes or longer, or chill overnight.

3 Bring a large quantity of salted water to a boil. Shape the mixture into 16 balls and drop them into the water. Simmer for 30 minutes. Serve in hot chicken stock.

3

Eggs, Brunch and Luncheon Dishes

There are people in the world who literally do not know how to boil water. There are also those who cannot scramble an egg. Not properly, that is. Eggs, for the most part, should be cooked slowly, which is the treatment they deserve. The one exception is in making French omelets, when the eggs must be cooked over high heat.

♦

BAKED OR SHIRRED EGGS

Butter
Eggs at room temperature

1 Preheat the oven to 350°F.
2 Melt 1 teaspoon butter in an individual ramekin or any small heatproof dish. Break 1 or 2 eggs into each dish and bake 10 to 12 minutes, until the white is milky and still creamy.

Note: There are many variations of this dish. To make shirred eggs Florentine, for example, buttered ramekins are lined with cooked, well-drained buttered spinach over which the eggs are broken.

Other ingredients that may be combined with the eggs to be shirred are tongue slices, cooked sausages, chicken livers or shrimp and other seafood.

Hot chicken gravy or veal gravy flavored with tarragon may be poured over the eggs after they are cooked.

FRIED EGGS

Butter or bacon fat
Eggs at room temperature

1 Melt enough butter or bacon fat in a heavy skillet to cover the bottom. Break the eggs, 1 at a time, into a saucer and slip them carefully into the pan.
2 Cook over low heat, basting the eggs with the hot fat until the whites are set. If the eggs are to be cooked on both sides, turn with a spatula.

♦

OEUFS AU BEURRE NOIR

The most famous fried-egg dish, other than plain fried eggs, is the French specialty, fried eggs *au beurre noir*, or "in black butter." Eggs are fried in butter and transferred to a warm serving dish. A little additional butter is added to the pan and cooked quickly until dark brown. A few drops of vinegar are added for each egg and the mixture is poured over the eggs. Each egg is garnished with ½ teaspoon capers.

HARD- OR SOFT-COOKED EGGS

Water
Eggs at room temperature

1 In a saucepan bring enough water to a rapid boil to cover the eggs to be cooked.

2 Place each egg on a spoon and lower it into the water. Reduce the heat until the water barely simmers and cook the eggs to the desired degree of doneness. For soft-cooked eggs, leave in the water 3 to 4½ minutes. For hard-cooked eggs, leave in the water 10 minutes, drain immediately and plunge the eggs into cold water; this causes a jacket of steam to form between the egg and shell to facilitate peeling.

Variation

EGGS MOLLET

Eggs soft-cooked in the above fashion for exactly 6 minutes are called eggs mollet. The white is set and firm and the yolks remain liquid. They are shelled and used in much the same way as poached eggs. Plunge the eggs immediately into cold water after removing from the pan to arrest the cooking process.

STUFFED EGGS

12 STUFFED EGG HALVES

6 hard-cooked eggs
Small cubes of ham, olive or pimiento
3 tablespoons butter, at room temperature
2 tablespoons mayonnaise
1 teaspoon Worcestershire sauce
Salt and freshly ground pepper to taste

1 Peel and cut the eggs in half lengthwise and remove the yolks. Arrange the egg halves on a cake rack and add a cube of ham, olive or pimiento to each cavity.

2 Force the egg yolks through a food mill or fine sieve. Add the remaining ingredients and beat well with a wire whisk. Beat until the mixture is perfectly smooth.

3 Fit a pastry bag with a large star tube and spoon the egg yolk mixture into it. Hold the pastry bag close to and almost parallel with the cavity. Force the mixture through the tube, moving in a zigzag fashion to form a "Turk's head."

Note: The eggs may also be cut in half widthwise and stuffed. If they are to be stuffed in this fashion, use a sharp paring knife to trim off a bit of the round bottom portion of each half and discard. This will permit the egg halves to stand upright. To fill the halves, arrange them on a cake rack and hold the pastry tube directly over the cavity. Fill the halves to produce a spiral effect. At the height of the spiral, raise the tube quickly to form a small peak.

Continued

Variations

OLIVE-STUFFED EGGS

Combine the egg yolks with ½ teaspoon dry mustard, 3 tablespoons butter at room temperature, 2 tablespoons finely chopped olives, salt and freshly ground pepper to taste and 2 tablespoons mayonnaise. Fill the egg white halves with the mixture and top each with an olive half.

MUSHROOM-STUFFED EGGS

Mince 6 medium mushrooms and sprinkle with lemon juice. Cook in 1 tablespoon butter until they give up their liquid, then until all liquid evaporates. Cool and combine with egg yolks, 3 tablespoons butter at room temperature, 1 tablespoon finely chopped dill and salt and freshly ground pepper to taste. Fill the egg white halves with the mixture.

SALMON-STUFFED EGGS

Combine the egg yolks with ¼ cup flaked salmon, 1 teaspoon minced onion, 1 chopped pimiento, ¼ cup mayonnaise, 1 tablespoon lemon juice and ¼ teaspoon cayenne. Fill the egg white halves with the mixture.

TUNA-STUFFED EGGS

Combine the egg yolks with ¼ cup flaked tunafish, 1 teaspoon Dijon mustard, 2 tablespoons butter at room temperature, 1 tablespoon minced parsley, ½ garlic clove, minced, and 1 tablespoon mayonnaise. Season with lemon juice and Tabasco sauce. Fill the egg white halves with the mixture and top each with a caper.

POACHED EGGS

Water
3 tablespoons white vinegar
1 teaspoon salt
Eggs at room temperature

1 Put water to a depth of 1 inch in a skillet, add the vinegar and salt and bring to a boil.

2 Reduce the heat immediately. Break the eggs one at a time into a saucer, then slip them gently into the water. Let the eggs set until the whites are firm.

3 Using a slotted spoon or pancake turner, remove the eggs and drain on paper toweling. Trim with a knife or cookie cutter. Serve topped with butter.

Note: Eggs may be poached in advance and reheated briefly in boiling salted water, about 30 seconds, just before serving. This is advantageous if a quantity of eggs are to be poached for a special occasion.

◆

EGGS BENEDICT

3 OR 6 SERVINGS

6 slices cooked ham
3 English muffins, halved and toasted
6 poached eggs
Hollandaise sauce (page 554)

Sauté ham briefly in butter. Place each slice on a toasted English muffin half and top each with a poached egg. Cover with hollandaise sauce. If desired, garnish with a truffle slice.

SCRAMBLED EGGS

6 eggs, at room temperature
2 tablespoons butter
2 tablespoons cream
Salt to taste

1 Break the eggs into a small bowl and beat with a fork, whisk or egg beater until well mixed but not frothy.

2 Melt the butter in the top of a double boiler or skillet and add the eggs. Place the skillet over low heat, or the double boiler over boiling water. Cook, stirring constantly, until the eggs begin to set. Add the cream and continue stirring until the desired degree of firmness is reached. Season with salt and serve immediately.

Note: Tarragon, chives, parsley or chervil cooked with scrambled eggs complements their flavor. Garnishes include sautéed mushroom caps, anchovy fillets and chicken livers.

♦

It is best to make an omelet for one person at a time. The preparation requires less than a minute, and with a bit of practice you may turn out omelets for six or more in less than five minutes. Have your plates ready and the fillings next to the stove. Use individual bowls for beating the eggs for each omelet. To serve six or more, get out six or more bowls and have them ready.

BASIC TECHNIQUE FOR MAKING AN OMELET FOR ONE

2 eggs
Salt and freshly ground pepper to taste
2 teaspoons butter
2 to 4 tablespoons of omelet filling
  (see pages 102–103)

1 Break the eggs into a small mixing bowl. (If you are making 2 or more omelets, break 2 eggs into each of 2 or more bowls. Have a fork or forks ready for beating each batch as well as butter and omelet filling.) Before you start cooking, beat the eggs, adding salt and pepper.

2 Select a small, well-cured omelet pan or use a nonstick pan.

3 Heat the pan and the butter. Swirl the pan around, to coat bottom and sides. Do this as rapidly as possible so the butter does not burn. Immediately add the batch of beaten egg and cook quickly over moderately high heat, stirring rapidly with a fork holding the tines parallel to the bottom of the pan. The moment the egg starts to set on the bottom, tilt the pan to a slight angle and tap the bottom of the pan firmly against the stove burner. This makes the omelet slide about an inch away from the hand and handle. This should "curve" the omelet.

4 Rapidly spoon the filling along the curved portion, holding the pan at an angle and, using the fork, folding the top of the omelet over to give the omelet a neat, oval shape. Turn the omelet, seam side down, onto a warmed plate. Serve immediately. You may garnish the top of the omelet with a spoonful or so of the filling.

Continued

OMELET FILLINGS

CHICKEN LIVERS WITH SAGE
FILLING FOR 4 OMELETS

½ pound very fresh chicken livers
2 tablespoons vegetable oil
Salt and freshly ground pepper to taste
3 tablespoons butter
2 tablespoons finely chopped onions
½ teaspoon sage
1 tablespoon Madeira wine or brandy

1 Pick over the livers to remove any tough connecting veins. Cut each liver in half.

2 Heat the oil in a heavy skillet and when it is quite hot add the livers. Sprinkle with salt and pepper and cook over high heat 2 to 3 minutes, shaking the skillet and tossing the livers so that they cook on all sides. Drain in a colander.

3 Heat 2 tablespoons of the butter in a skillet and add the onions. Cook, stirring often, about 10 minutes without browning. The onions should be quite soft.

4 Heat the remaining tablespoon of butter in a clean skillet and when it is very hot add the livers and onions. Sprinkle with sage and cook, stirring, about 2 minutes longer. Sprinkle with Madeira.

5 Use 2 to 4 tablespoons of the livers to fill each omelet.

Note: The chicken livers also can be served as an appetizer. Spread on buttered toast triangles and sprinkle lightly with grated Parmesan cheese.

OMELET CHASSEUR
FILLING FOR 6 OMELETS

6 tablespoons butter
2 teaspoons chopped shallots or scallions
3 chicken livers, cut into 3 or 4 pieces
3 mushrooms, sliced
Salt and freshly ground pepper to taste
1½ teaspoons flour
3 tablespoons dry white wine or chicken stock
18 small mushroom caps
Chopped parsley

1 In a skillet melt 3 tablespoons of the butter and add the shallots. Cook, stirring, 1 minute. Add the chicken livers and mushroom slices and sprinkle with salt and pepper. Cook gently, stirring, 1 minute, or until the livers are brown.

2 Sprinkle the mixture with flour and stir in the wine. Use 2 to 4 tablespoons to fill each omelet.

3 Melt the remaining 3 tablespoons butter in a skillet and in it sauté the mushroom caps. Garnish each omelet with 3 caps and sprinkle with parsley.

Salsa Cruda, page 563.
Pico de Gallo, page 564.

SPINACH AND SOUR CREAM FILLING
FILLING FOR 6 OMELETS

2 pounds fresh spinach
Salt to taste
1½ tablespoons butter
¼ teaspoon grated nutmeg
Freshly ground pepper to taste
1 cup sour cream
Paprika

1 Trim off the tough stems from the spinach and discard. Wash the spinach leaves thoroughly in several changes of cold water until free from sand. Drain. Place the moist spinach in a saucepan, sprinkle with salt and cover tightly. Cook over moderate heat, stirring once or twice, 6 minutes or until tender. Drain and coarsely chop.

2 Add the butter, nutmeg, additional salt and pepper to taste and half the sour cream. Reheat gently over low heat without boiling.

3 Reserve 6 tablespoons of the mixture. Use 2 to 4 tablespoons to fill each omelet. Spoon the reserved mixture along the top of the folded omelets and top with the remaining sour cream. Sprinkle with paprika.

SPANISH OMELET
FILLING FOR 6 OMELETS

6 fresh tomatoes
3 tablespoons vegetable oil
1 onion, chopped
1 green pepper, chopped
1 celery stalk, chopped
1 leek, chopped
½ fennel bulb, chopped, or
   ½ teaspoon crushed fennel seed
1 garlic clove, minced
3 parsley sprigs, chopped
1 clove
½ teaspoon thyme
½ teaspoon oregano
½ bay leaf
Pinch of saffron
Salt and freshly ground pepper to taste

1 Peel the tomatoes, cut in half and gently press out the seeds and liquid. Chop the tomatoes.

2 Heat the oil in a pan and add the onions, green pepper, celery, leek, fennel, garlic and parsley. Sauté 5 minutes. Add the tomatoes and season with the clove, thyme, oregano, bay leaf, saffron and salt and pepper.

3 Simmer the mixture gently until the vegetables are tender, about 10 minutes. Discard the clove and bay leaf. Use 2 to 4 tablespoons to fill each omelet.

FRITTATA

One of the great, delicate yet substantial dishes for a crisp autumn or cold winter day is the Italian dish known as *frittata*. It is often referred to as an Italian omelet. Unlike the French omelet, it is not folded but it is left flat out of the skillet. There is no limit to the ingredients that may be used in preparing it. The most common —and many think the best—are potatoes and onions. Some people use leftover spaghetti, cubed ham and numerous vegetables such as sweet peppers. Here is a basic potato and onion version.

4 TO 6 SERVINGS

¾ pound potatoes
½ pound onions
Salt to taste
¼ cup vegetable oil
Freshly ground pepper to taste
1 cup diced sweet red pepper
6 eggs
2 tablespoons butter
1 tablespoon red wine vinegar

1 Peel the potatoes and cut them into ¼-inch cubes. There should be about 2 cups. Drop the potatoes into cold water to prevent discoloration.

2 Peel the onions and cut into the thinnest possible slices. This is best done by using the thinnest slicing blade of a food processor. You will need 1 cup somewhat firmly packed.

3 Drain the potatoes and put into a saucepan with cold water to cover. Add salt. Bring to the boil and cook until tender but not mushy, 6 to 8 minutes. Do not overcook. Drain immediately.

4 Heat the oil in a well-cured omelet pan and add the potatoes and salt and pepper. Cook, stirring often but gently, until the potatoes are golden brown.

Continued

Using a slotted spoon transfer the potato cubes to paper toweling to drain. Leave the oil in the pan, adding a little more, if necessary, to cook the onions.

5 Add the onions and sweet pepper to the pan and cook stirring, until the onions are golden brown. Using a slotted spoon transfer the mixture to a plate lined with paper toweling.

6 Pour off the oil from the pan and wipe the pan clean with paper toweling.

7 Break the eggs into a mixing bowl and add salt and pepper.

8 Heat the butter in the omelet pan and when it melts return the potatoes and the onion mixture to the pan. Increase the heat to high and pour in the eggs, stirring with a fork as you would an ordinary omelet. Cover closely and cook over moderate heat about 2 minutes. The omelet will remain slightly unfirm on top. Sprinkle the top with vinegar.

9 Invert a plate slightly larger than the rim of the pan over the pan. Holding the plate tightly over the omelet, quickly and carefully let the omelet fall onto the plate. Serve warm or at room temperature.

CHEESE AND MUSHROOM OMELET

1 OR 2 SERVINGS

1 small potato
2 tablespoons vegetable oil
Salt and freshly ground pepper to taste
1 tablespoon plus 2 teaspoons butter
½ cup thinly sliced mushrooms
2 eggs
1 tablespoon finely diced Gruyère or
  Swiss cheese
2 teaspoons finely chopped chives

1 Peel the potato and cut it into ¼-inch dice. There should be about ½ cup. Put the cubes into a small amount of cold water to prevent discoloration.

2 Drain the potato and pat dry with paper toweling.

3 Heat the oil in a small skillet and add the potato. Sprinkle with salt and pepper. Cook, shaking the skillet and stirring, until the potatoes are cooked on all sides, about 10 minutes. Drain well.

4 Heat 1 tablespoon of butter in a clean skillet and add the mushrooms. Cook until they give up their liquid. Cook until the liquid evaporates.

5 Beat the eggs in a mixing bowl and add the potato, mushrooms, cheese, chives, salt and pepper. Blend well.

6 Heat 2 teaspoons of butter in a small omelet pan and add the egg mixture. Cook over relatively high heat, shaking the skillet and stirring, until the omelet is set on the bottom. Invert the omelet onto a hot round serving dish and serve.

SALMON SOUFFLÉ

3 SERVINGS

3 tablespoons butter
3 tablespoons flour
1 cup milk
4 eggs, separated
2 egg whites
Salt, dry mustard and Worcestershire sauce
    to taste
1 cup cooked salmon
Hollandaise sauce (page 554)

1 Preheat the oven to 375°F.
2 Melt the butter in a saucepan, stir in
flour and blend with a wire whisk. Meanwhile, bring the milk to a boil and add all
at once to the butter-flour mixture, stirring
with the whisk until thickened and
smooth. Cool the mixture.
3 Beat in, 1 at a time, the 4 egg yolks,
and cook briefly, stirring constantly with a
whisk. Season with salt, mustard and
Worcestershire.
4 Flake the salmon and blend well into
the white sauce and egg mixture.
5 Using a rotary beater or an electric
mixer, beat the 6 egg whites until they
stand in peaks. Do not overbeat. Fold the
whites gently into the salmon mixture
with a rubber spatula or wooden spoon,
being careful not to overblend.
6 Pour into a buttered 2-quart soufflé
dish, place in oven and bake 30 to 40 minutes. Serve with hollandaise sauce, if desired.

CHEESE SOUFFLÉ

4 TO 6 SERVINGS

4 tablespoons butter
¼ cup flour
1½ cups milk
Salt, Worcestershire sauce and cayenne
    to taste
½ pound cheddar cheese, finely grated
4 eggs, separated
2 egg whites

1 Preheat the oven to 375°F.
2 In a saucepan melt the butter over
low heat and add the flour; stir with a wire
whisk until blended. Meanwhile, bring
the milk to a boil and add all at once to the
butter-flour mixture, stirring vigorously
with the whisk. Season to taste with salt,
Worcestershire and cayenne.
3 Turn off the heat and let the mixture
cool 2 to 3 minutes. Add the cheese and
stir until melted. Beat in the egg yolks 1 at
a time and cool.
4 Beat the 6 egg whites until they stand
in peaks, but do not overbeat. Cut and
fold the egg whites into the mixture. Turn
into a buttered 2-quart soufflé dish and
bake 30 to 45 minutes.

Note: You may add ¾ cup ground cooked
ham to the white sauce along with the
cheese.

HERBED EGG TIMBALES

4 SERVINGS

1½ cups half-and-half or milk, scalded
5 eggs, slightly beaten
¾ teaspoon salt
Freshly ground pepper to taste
1 teaspoon grated onion
1 tablespoon minced parsley
1 tablespoon minced tarragon or dill
1 cup tomato sauce, heated

1 Preheat the oven to 325°F.
2 Add the scalded half-and-half to the eggs, stirring. Mix in the remaining ingredients except the tomato sauce.
3 Pour the mixture into greased custard cups, filling the cups slightly more than three-quarters full.
4 Place the filled cups on a rack in a deep pan and pour simmering water around them. Bake until a knife inserted in the center comes out clean, 20 minutes or longer.
5 To serve, turn the timbales out on a serving dish and pour tomato sauce over them. Garnish with parsley or chopped chives.

EGGS FLORENTINE

This is a foremost luncheon dish. It may be prepared in advance and reheated quickly in a hot oven. The dish is poached eggs on a bed of spinach covered with a cream sauce.

6 SERVINGS

4 tablespoons butter
¼ cup flour
1 cup milk
1 cup cream
Salt and freshly ground pepper to taste
1½ pounds spinach, cooked and puréed
¼ teaspoon grated nutmeg
12 poached eggs
Grated Parmesan cheese

1 In a saucepan melt the butter, add the flour and stir with a wire whisk until blended. Meanwhile, bring the milk and cream to a boil and add all at once to the butter-flour mixture, stirring vigorously with the whisk until thickened. Season with salt and pepper.
2 Combine the hot drained spinach with ½ cup of the sauce and season with nutmeg. Pour the spinach mixture into a shallow casserole and arrange the eggs on top. Spoon the remaining sauce over the eggs, sprinkle with Parmesan cheese and brown lightly under a broiler; or bake in a preheated 400°F oven until brown.

CRABMEAT QUICHE

6 TO 10 SERVINGS

Pastry for a 1-crust 9-inch pie
1 tablespoon butter
1 tablespoon chopped celery
1 tablespoon chopped onions
1½ cups crabmeat, picked over well to remove
    any bits of shell or cartilage
2 tablespoons finely chopped parsley
2 tablespoons sherry
4 eggs, lightly beaten
1 cup milk
1 cup cream
¼ teaspoon grated nutmeg
½ teaspoon salt
¼ teaspoon white pepper

1 Preheat the oven to 375°F.
2 Line a 9-inch pie plate with pastry and line the pastry with foil. Add dried beans to weight the bottom down and bake 30 minutes. Remove the foil and beans.
3 Melt the butter in a skillet and sauté the celery and onions until wilted. Add the crabmeat and cook over high heat until any liquid has evaporated. Stir in the parsley and sherry.
4 Sprinkle the inside of the baked pastry shell with the crabmeat mixture.
5 Combine the eggs, milk, cream, nutmeg, salt and pepper and strain over the mixture in the pie shell.
6 Bake 45 minutes, or until knife inserted 1 inch from the pastry edge comes out clean. Cut into wedges and serve immediately.

Variation

BAY SCALLOPS QUICHE

Substitute ¾ pound bay scallops for the crabmeat.

QUICHE LORRAINE

This very special French pie, rich custard with cheese and bacon, may be served either as an appetizer or as a main luncheon dish. Swiss cheese, which the Swiss know as *Emmenthal*, may be used in making this dish, but Gruyère has more flavor. Gruyère is available wherever fine cheeses are sold.

6 TO 10 SERVINGS

Pastry for a 1-crust 9-inch pie
4 strips of bacon
1 onion, thinly sliced
1 cup cubed Gruyère or Swiss cheese
¼ cup grated Parmesan cheese
4 eggs, lightly beaten
1 cup cream
1 cup milk
¼ teaspoon grated nutmeg
½ teaspoon salt
¼ teaspoon white pepper

1 Preheat the oven to 375°F.
2 Line a 9-inch pie plate with pastry and line the pastry with foil. Add dried beans to weight the bottom down and bake 30 minutes. Remove the foil and beans.
3 Cook the bacon until crisp and remove it from the skillet. Pour off all but 1 tablespoon of the fat remaining in the skillet. Cook the onions in the remaining fat until they are transparent.
4 Crumble the bacon. Sprinkle the bacon, onions and cheeses over the inside of the baked shell.
5 Combine the eggs, cream, milk, nutmeg, salt and pepper and strain over the onion-cheese mixture.
6 Bake the pie 45 minutes, or until a knife inserted 1 inch from the pastry edge comes out clean. Cut into wedges and serve immediately.

EGG AND SPINACH PIE

6 TO 8 SERVINGS

Pastry for a 1-crust 8-inch pie
1 pound spinach, cooked
4 eggs
1 cup sour cream
¾ cup soft bread crumbs
1 tablespoon butter, melted
2 tablespoons grated Parmesan cheese

1 Preheat the oven to 375°F.

2 Line a pie plate with the pastry and line the pastry with foil. Add dried beans to weight the bottom down and bake for 30 minutes. Remove the foil and beans.

3 Coarsely chop the spinach and drain well. Spread over the baked pie shell. Break the eggs over the spinach and cover with sour cream.

4 Toss the crumbs in the butter and cheese and sprinkle over the top. Bake until the eggs are set, about 15 minutes.

LEEK AND SAUSAGE PIE

6 SERVINGS

9 leeks
2 cups chicken stock
6 tablespoons butter
6 tablespoons flour
½ teaspoon salt
⅛ teaspoon freshly ground pepper
½ cup cream
Freshly grated horseradish to taste
1 9-inch baked pie shell
½ pound pork sausages, fully cooked
*   and drained*
1 8-inch round of pastry, baked

1 Trim the roots and green leaves from the leeks. Split lengthwise, wash carefully and cut into julienne strips.

2 Cook the leeks in the chicken stock until just tender but not mushy, about 15 minutes. Drain and reserve the liquid.

3 Melt the butter, blend in the flour, salt and pepper. Add 2 cups of the reserved liquid slowly, while stirring. Bring to a boil, cover, and then cook over hot water, stirring occasionally, for 30 minutes.

4 Preheat the oven to 375°F.

5 Add the cream and leeks to the sauce and reheat. Season with horseradish and place in the baked pie shell.

6 Arrange the sausages like spokes of a wheel over the sauce mixture and place the pastry round on top.

7 Reheat the pie in the oven for 10 minutes. Serve immediately.

FONDUTA

6 SERVINGS

12 ounces fontina cheese, diced
3 cups milk, approximately
2 tablespoons butter
6 egg yolks
¼ teaspoon white pepper
1 white truffle, sliced paper thin (optional)

1 Place the cheese in a dish and cover with the milk. Let stand at least 6 hours in the refrigerator.

2 Place 1 tablespoon of the butter and the egg yolks in the upper part of a double boiler, add the cheese and milk and place over boiling water. Beat with a rotary beater while the cheese melts and until it begins to harden. When the cheese begins to thicken, remove from the boiling water, add the pepper, truffle and remaining butter and mix well. Serve on toast or with rice or polenta.

◆

MOZZARELLA IN CARROZZA

4 SERVINGS

8 large slices Italian bread
4 (¼-inch-thick) slices mozzarella cheese
Light olive oil
2 eggs, lightly beaten
Flour
Anchovy sauce (page 570)
4 lemon slices

1 Remove the crusts from the bread. Place each slice of cheese between 2 slices of bread.

2 Pour enough olive oil in a skillet to make a depth of 1 inch. Heat until hot but not smoking.

3 Dip the sandwiches in the eggs then in flour and fry in the hot oil, turning once, until the bread turns pale gold and the cheese starts to ooze out. Pour hot anchovy sauce over the sandwiches and garnish each with a lemon slice.

◆

WELSH RABBIT

I subscribe to the story that a Welshman went hunting and returned home empty-handed. His wife concocted a dish with melted cheese and dubbed it "rabbit." Thus, Welsh rabbit, not rarebit.

4 TO 6 SERVINGS

2 teaspoons Worcestershire sauce
½ teaspoon dry mustard
Dash of cayenne
Dash of paprika
½ cup ale or beer
1 pound sharp natural cheddar cheese, shredded

Mix the seasonings in a skillet. Add the ale and let stand over very low heat until the ale is hot. Add the cheese and stir until it has melted. Serve on hot toast.

SHRIMP FONDUE

4 SERVINGS

1 pound shrimp, shelled and deveined
2 tablespoons butter
½ teaspoon dry mustard
4 slices bread, crusts removed
1½ cups grated Gruyère cheese
2 eggs, beaten
1 cup milk
½ teaspoon salt
Freshly ground pepper to taste

1 Preheat the oven to 350°F. Cook shrimp, covered, in ½ cup water 5 minutes. Drain, reserving the broth.

2 Cream the butter with the mustard and spread on the bread. Cut into cubes. Arrange the bread cubes, cheese and shrimp in layers in a greased 1-quart casserole.

3 Mix the eggs, milk, reserved shrimp broth, salt and pepper and pour over the shrimp mixture. Set in a pan of hot water and bake until a knife inserted in the center comes out clean, 1 hour or longer. Serve immediately.

SWISS FONDUE

The traditional wine for this dish is a Fendant or Neuchâtel.

8 SERVINGS

1 garlic clove
1½ cups dry white wine
1 pound natural Gruyère cheese, grated
    (do not used processed Gruyère)
2 teaspoons cornstarch
3 tablespoons kirsch
Freshly ground pepper to taste

1 Rub the bottom and sides of an earthenware casserole or chafing dish with the garlic. Add the wine and heat to the boiling point, but do not boil.

2 Add the cheese, stirring constantly with a wooden spoon. When the cheese is creamy and barely simmering, add the cornstarch blended with the kirsch. Stir until the mixture bubbles. Season with pepper.

3 Place the casserole over an alcohol burner with a slow flame. Keep the fondue hot but not simmering. If it becomes too thick, add a little more wine.

4 To serve, accompany with cubes of crusty bread and long forks for dipping into the melted cheese.

BAKED KIPPERED HERRING

Baked kippered herring is a wonderful idea for Sunday brunch. Serve the herring with scrambled eggs to which a little whipped cream has been added, broiled tomato halves, and toast. Pickled walnuts provide a flavorful garnish. Serve tea with lemon or cups of piping hot coffee.

6 SERVINGS

6 plain smoked kippered herring, canned
   or packaged
Butter
Juice of ½ lemon
Few drops of Tabasco sauce
Worcestershire sauce (optional)
Chopped parsley

1 Preheat the oven to 400°F.

2 Line a heavy skillet with foil and arrange the herring on it. Dot with butter and bake until the butter melts and the fish is heated through, 5 to 10 minutes.

3 In a small saucepan or butter warmer, combine 3 tablespoons butter, the lemon juice, Tabasco and Worcestershire. Pour over the hot herring and serve sprinkled with chopped parsley.

♦

KEDGEREE

One of the finest dishes I know for brunch is the British creation called kedgeree. Actually, it is of Anglo-Indian origin and is made with smoked fish fillets, rice and hard-cooked eggs with a curry flavor. The best recipe for the dish is Jane Garmey's. This is a variation of kedgeree found in her book *Great British Cooking: A Well Kept Secret.*

4 SERVINGS

¾ pound smoked haddock fillet
1 tablespoon vegetable oil
1 cup finely chopped onions
¾ cup long-grain or basmati rice
4 teaspoons curry powder
4 teaspoons butter
½ cup finely chopped hard-cooked egg
⅓ cup finely chopped parsley
4 thin lemon slices, seeded

1 Put the haddock in a saucepan or skillet, large enough to hold it without crowding. Pour enough boiling water over the fish to cover. Bring to the boil and let simmer 12 minutes or longer until the fish flakes easily with a fork. Do not overcook the fish or it will lose flavor and texture.

2 Drain the fish but reserve 1⅓ cups of the cooking liquid.

3 Heat the oil in a saucepan and add the onions, stirring. Cook briefly until onions are wilted. Bring to the simmer and add the rice and curry powder and stir over low heat about 1 minute.

4 Add the cooking liquid and bring to the boil. Cover and let simmer 17 minutes. Cook only until the liquid is absorbed.

5 Flake the fish, discarding any bones or pieces of skin.

6 Add the fish, butter, egg and parsley to the rice. Stir. Serve on 4 plates, garnishing each portion with a lemon slice.

Note: Cooked salmon may be substituted for the smoked haddock. Nutmeg may be substituted for the curry powder.

ARTICHOKES MOCK BENEDICT

4 SERVINGS

4 rounds of buttered toast or toasted
    English muffins
4 small slices of ham, preferably Smithfield
4 artichoke bottoms, freshly cooked and hot
4 eggs, poached
2 cups cheddar cheese sauce (page 550)
Paprika
Watercress for garnish

Place a toast round on each of 4 hot plates
and top each with a slice of ham. Place a
cooked artichoke bottom on the ham and
fill the center with a poached egg. Spoon
cheese sauce over each serving and sprinkle with paprika. Garnish with watercress
and serve immediately.

♦

SEAFOOD SALAD WITH TARRAGON

6 SERVINGS

1 cup cooked lobster meat
1 cup crabmeat, picked over well to remove
    any bits of shell or cartilage
1 cup bite-size pieces of cooked shrimp
¼ cup finely chopped scallions
2 tablespoons finely chopped chives
1 tablespoon vinegar, preferably tarragon
    vinegar
1 tablespoon minced tarragon, or more
Mayonnaise
Lobster claws for garnish

1 Combine all ingredients except lobster claws. Use just enough mayonnaise to
bind the mixture.
2 Serve on a bed of lettuce and garnish
with lobster claws.

♦

LOBSTER-STUFFED TOMATOES

6 SERVINGS

2 cups diced cooked lobster meat
½ cup diced celery
1½ tablespoons minced green pepper
1 tablespoon minced onions
2 tablespoons chopped green olives
3 tablespoons mayonnaise
3 tablespoons finely chopped tomato
2 teaspoons lime juice
1½ teaspoons salt
1 tablespoon snipped dill
⅛ teaspoon freshly ground pepper
⅛ teaspoon cayenne
6 firm ripe tomatoes
Bibb lettuce

1 Combine lobster, celery, green pepper, onions and olives. Mix well. Blend
together the mayonnaise, chopped tomato, lime juice, salt, dill, pepper and cayenne. Stir dressing into the lobster
mixture.
2 Cut a 1-inch-thick slice from the bud
end of each tomato and reserve the slices.
Cut tomatoes into wedges, leaving the
wedges attached at the base. Spread the
wedges apart to look like flower petals. Fill
with some of the lobster mixture, mounding it in the center.
3 Serve on Bibb lettuce, topping each
mound of lobster with the reserved slice
of tomato.

LOBSTER AND AVOCADO SALAD

4 TO 6 SERVINGS

2 (2½-pound) lobsters
Salt to taste
1 head romaine lettuce
1 cup finely chopped scallions
2 (¾-pound) firm unblemished avocados
1 tablespoon lemon juice
2 tablespoons finely chopped basil
1 tablespoon Dijon mustard
¼ cup wine vinegar
2 tablespoons finely chopped shallots
Salt and freshly ground pepper to taste
1 hard-cooked egg, finely chopped
½ cup vegetable oil
½ cup olive oil

1 Bring enough water to the boil to cover the lobsters when they are added. Add salt to taste. Add the lobsters and cover closely. When the water returns to the boil, let the lobsters cook 20 minutes. Let stand 5 to 10 minutes and drain well.

2 Meanwhile, cut away and discard the core of the lettuce. Cut the lettuce lengthwise into quarters. Cut the leaves into very thin shreds. There should be 6 to 7 cups.

3 Remove the meat from the lobster shells. Cut the meat into bite-size pieces. There should be about 4 cups.

4 Put the lettuce in a salad bowl. Arrange the lobster pieces on top and sprinkle with scallions. Toss lightly.

5 Cut the avocados in half lengthwise. Discard the pits. Peel the halves. Cut each half lengthwise into thin strips. Sprinkle with lemon juice.

6 Arrange the avocado slices neatly over the salad. Sprinkle with basil.

7 To make the salad dressing, put the mustard, vinegar, shallots, salt and pep-per in a mixing bowl. Add the egg. Blend the oils and add gradually, while beating.

8 Serve the salad and salad dressing separately, if desired. Or toss the salad with the dressing.

◆

CURRIED LOBSTER SALAD

6 SERVINGS

3 (1½- to 2-pound) lobsters
1 (9-ounce) package frozen artichoke hearts
1 cup diced celery
1 cup mayonnaise
¼ cup lime juice
1 teaspoon curry powder, or more
¼ teaspoon dry mustard
Salt and freshly ground pepper to taste
Salad greens
Radish roses

1 Plunge the lobsters into a large kettle of boiling water. Boil for 15 minutes, or until tender. Remove and cool.

2 Cook the artichoke hearts according to package directions. Cool. Cut each heart into 6 pieces.

3 Split lobsters into halves. Remove and reserve the meat, liver and coral from each. Remove and discard the sac and large vein from each, but retain the shells.

4 Dice the lobster meat and coral, and toss with the liver, artichoke hearts and celery. Mix mayonnaise with lime juice, curry powder and mustard. Add to lobster mixture and mix well. Season with salt and pepper.

5 Place the salad greens in a large serving bowl. Pile the lobster mixture into the shells. Arrange shells on the greens, pyramid fashion. Garnish with radish roses.

HOT CRAB SALAD

6 SERVINGS

2 (7½-ounce) cans Alaska king crab
½ cup diced celery
½ cup mayonnaise
¼ cup finely chopped green pepper
2 tablespoons chopped shallots or scallions
2 tablespoons chopped parsley
2 tablespoons lemon juice
¼ teaspoon salt
Dash of Tabasco sauce
½ cup buttered soft fresh bread crumbs

1 Preheat the oven to 400°F.
2 Drain the crab, slice the leg sections, and pick over for cartilage. Combine the crab with the remaining ingredients except the buttered crumbs.
3 Spoon the mixture into shells or individual ramekins. Top with the buttered crumbs and bake for 10 minutes, or until heated through and light brown.

CRAB-STUFFED AVOCADOS

6 SERVINGS

4 large ripe avocados
⅓ cup lime juice
1 cup mayonnaise
3 tablespoons chopped chives
½ teaspoon salt
¼ teaspoon freshly ground pepper
1 pound lump crabmeat
Boston lettuce leaves
3 tablespoons capers
Stuffed green olives

1 Peel and halve the avocados, discarding pits. Dip all surfaces of the avocados into lime juice to prevent discoloration. Cut 2 avocado halves into small cubes.
2 Combine the lime juice with mayonnaise, chives, salt and pepper. Pick over crabmeat to remove pieces of shell and cartilage, taking care not to break up the crabmeat too much. Add crabmeat and avocado cubes to mayonnaise. Mix gently.
3 Place lettuce leaves on a serving platter. Arrange the remaining avocado halves on lettuce. Pile crabmeat mixture into the halves. Garnish with capers and olives.

CHEESE ROULADE WITH CRABMEAT

This is an uncommonly appealing crabmeat roulade that may be served as a first course or a main luncheon course. The roulade, flavored with two kinds of cheese, is actually a "fallen soufflé," filled with lump crabmeat, rolled and sliced. The recipe was given to me by an excellent caterer, Sanda Cooper of Jackson, Mississippi.

4 TO 6 SERVINGS

¾ cup fine fresh bread crumbs
3 tablespoons butter
¼ cup flour
1¼ cups milk
Salt and freshly ground pepper to taste
¼ teaspoon grated nutmeg
5 eggs, separated
⅛ teaspoon cream of tartar
¼ cup grated Parmesan cheese
1½ cups grated Gruyère cheese
1 pound crabmeat, preferably lump meat
3 cups tomato sauce with herbs (page 562)

1 Preheat the oven to 425° F.
2 Line a jelly roll pan measuring about 11 × 17 inches with 2 overlapping sheets of wax paper. Rub the top sheet with a generous amount of butter and sprinkle lightly with flour, shaking to remove excess. Set aside.
3 Scatter the crumbs over a pie plate or sheet of foil and place in the oven. Bake 7 to 10 minutes, checking frequently, until crumbs are golden brown. Set aside.
4 Meanwhile, melt the butter in a saucepan and add the flour, stirring rapidly with a wire whisk. When the mixture is smooth, add the milk, stirring briskly with the whisk. Stir in the salt, pepper and nutmeg. Set aside to cool briefly.
5 Add all the egg yolks at once, beating vigorously with the whisk. Scrape the mixture into a mixing bowl.

6 Beat the egg whites with the cream of tartar until stiff. Add about half of the whites to the sauce and beat briskly with the whisk. Add the remaining whites and fold them in carefully. Fold in the cheeses.
7 Pour and scrape the mixture into the prepared pan and smooth over the surface. Place the pan on the middle rack of the oven. Bake 12 to 15 minutes, or until the soufflé has puffed and the top is light brown and slightly cracked. When ready, the edges of the soufflé should have pulled away slightly from the sides of the pan.
8 Sprinkle the reserved crumbs evenly over the top of the soufflé. Place a lightly buttered sheet of foil over the top of the soufflé. Quickly but carefully invert the pan, letting the soufflé fall onto the foil. Let stand 5 minutes. Carefully remove and discard the wax paper. Cover with plastic wrap until ready to fill and roll.
9 Pick over the crabmeat to remove any bits of cartilage or shell. Leave the lumps as large as possible.
10 Heat 1 cup of the tomato sauce and add the crab. Heat gently.
11 Spoon the crab and tomato sauce over the soufflé. Carefully pull up the foil and roll the soufflé as though you were making a jelly roll.
12 Serve sliced with additional hot tomato sauce on the side.

CRAB LOUIS

4 SERVINGS

1 cup mayonnaise
⅓ cup basic vinaigrette (page 576)
¼ cup chili sauce
2 tablespoons minced chives
2 tablespoons minced green olives
1 teaspoon horseradish
1 teaspoon Worcestershire sauce
Salt and freshly ground pepper
Chilled lettuce, torn into bite-size pieces
3 cups cooked crabmeat, flaked and picked over
    well to remove any bits of shell or cartilage
4 hard-cooked eggs, quartered
Quartered tomatoes
Capers

1 Combine the mayonnaise, French dressing, chili sauce, chives, olives and seasonings. Chill.

2 Arrange the lettuce in a shallow, chilled salad bowl and mound the crabmeat on top. Spoon the dressing on top and garnish with hard-cooked egg, tomato quarters and capers.

CHICKEN SALAD A LA CHINOISE

6 SERVINGS

3 cups diced cooked chicken
1 cup fresh or canned bean sprouts, drained
2 celery stalks, diced
½ teaspoon salt
Freshly ground pepper to taste
Basic vinaigrette (page 576)
¾ cup mayonnaise
Dash of soy sauce
Lettuce
Olives

1 Combine the chicken with the bean sprouts, celery, salt and pepper. Moisten with French dressing. Chill in the refrigerator.

2 Flavor the mayonnaise with the soy sauce. Mix with the chicken mixture.

3 Pile into crisp lettuce cups. Garnish with olives.

Scallop Cocktail, page 48.

CHICKEN SALAD WITH ALMONDS

5 SERVINGS

4 cups lightly packed ¾-inch cubes of cooked
   chicken meat
2 cups thinly sliced celery
1 to 2 tablespoons minced onions
1 tablespoon lemon juice
¾ cup mayonnaise
¼ cup cream
Salt and freshly ground white pepper to taste
¼ to ½ cup toasted almonds

   1 Toss the chicken and celery together.
   2 Mix the onions, lemon juice, mayonnaise and cream. Add to the chicken and toss until the pieces of chicken and celery are coated with the dressing.
   3 Season with salt and pepper and stir in the almonds, or reserve them to use as a garnish. Chill.
   4 Serve on a bed of lettuce or other salad green.

♦

CHICKEN OR SHRIMP SALAD FOR ONE

1 SERVING

1 cup cooked chicken or shrimp
¼ cup mayonnaise, approximately
1 teaspoon capers
3 tablespoons chopped celery
Lemon juice to taste
Freshly ground pepper to taste

Cut the chicken or shrimp into bite-size pieces. Place in a bowl. Add mayonnaise, capers and celery. Sprinkle lemon juice and pepper over the salad. Stir just to coat chicken or shrimp and blend ingredients. Serve on lettuce leaves.

♦

CHICKEN MOUSSE

8 TO 10 SERVINGS

6 tablespoons butter
¾ cup soft bread crumbs
½ teaspoon salt
¼ teaspoon grated nutmeg
2 cups half-and-half
3 cups chopped cooked chicken
6 eggs, well beaten
½ cup dry sherry
3 large avocados, peeled and cubed
1½ cups mayonnaise

   1 Preheat the oven to 350°F.
   2 Melt the butter in a double boiler and add the crumbs, salt and nutmeg. Add the half-and-half and cook over hot water 10 minutes, stirring often. Mix the chicken, eggs and sherry and add to the sauce.
   3 Pour the mixture into a buttered 2-quart mold, cover and bake until firm, or about 50 minutes. Cool and chill.
   4 Toss the avocados with the mayonnaise. Unmold the mousse and surround with the avocado mixture.

COLD CRABMEAT MOUSE

8 SERVINGS

4 tablespoons butter
¼ cup flour
1 cup hot chicken stock
1 cup hot milk
2 envelopes (2 tablespoons) unflavored gelatin
¼ cup cold water
1 pound crabmeat, picked over well to remove any bits of shell or cartilage
1 tablespoon lemon juice
1 tablespoon chopped parsley
½ teaspoon paprika
½ teaspoon dry mustard
Salt and freshly ground pepper to taste
2 cups heavy cream, whipped

1 In a saucepan melt the butter, add the flour and stir with a wire whisk until blended. Meanwhile, bring the stock and milk to a boil and add all at once to the butter-flour mixture, stirring vigorously with the whisk.

2 Soften the gelatin in the cold water and add to the sauce. Cook, stirring, until the gelatin has dissolved.

3 Add all the remaining ingredients except the cream and refrigerate until the mixture starts to set.

4 Meanwhile, tie a band of wax paper or foil around the top of a straight-sided 6-cup bowl. Let the band rise 2 inches above the bowl.

5 Fold the cream into the partly set mixture. Turn into the prepared dish (the mixture may come to the level of the paper) and refrigerate until set.

6 To serve, remove the paper to expose the top of the mousse. Garnish the top as desired with lobster claws, green pepper rings, etc.

CHICKEN LOAF NIVERNAISE

6 TO 8 SERVINGS

CHICKEN MOUSSE

1 envelope (1 tablespoon) unflavored gelatin
⅓ cup boiling chicken stock
½ very small onion
½ garlic clove
1 cup (6½ ounces) cubed cooked chicken
1 cup cream
½ teaspoon salt
¼ teaspoon grated nutmeg
¼ teaspoon freshly ground pepper
¼ teaspoon tarragon

1 Put the gelatin, stock, onion, and garlic in the container of a food processor and blend.

2 Add the remaining ingredients and blend for a few seconds until well combined.

3 Pour the mixture into a 9 × 5 × 3-inch loaf pan and chill until set.

CARROT MOUSSE

1 envelope (1 tablespoon) unflavored gelatin
⅓ cup boiling water
2 cups sliced cooked carrots
3 tablespoons mayonnaise
⅛ teaspoon freshly ground pepper

1 Put the gelatin and boiling water into the container of a food processor and blend for a few seconds.

2 Add the carrots, mayonnaise and pepper and blend until carrots are puréed.

3 Pour the mixture into the loaf pan over the chicken mousse and chill until set.

4 When ready to serve, unmold on a cold serving platter and garnish with salad greens and small cutouts of sliced cooked carrot. Serve with mayonnaise.

Veal Rollatine, page 311.

♦

SALMON MOUSSE WITH SOUR CREAM–DILL SAUCE

8 SERVINGS

1 envelope (1 tablespoon) unflavored gelatin
¼ cup cold water
½ cup boiling water
½ cup mayonnaise
1 tablespoon lemon juice
1 tablespoon grated onion
½ teaspoon Tabasco sauce
¼ teaspoon paprika
Salt to taste
2 cups finely chopped cooked salmon
1 tablespoon chopped capers
½ cup heavy cream
Sour cream–dill sauce (page 560)

1 Soften the gelatin in the cold water, add the boiling water and stir until the gelatin has dissolved. Cool.

2 Add the mayonnaise, lemon juice, onion, Tabasco, paprika and salt and mix well. Chill to the consistency of unbeaten egg white.

3 Add the salmon and capers and beat well. Whip the cream, fold into the salmon mixture and turn into a 2-quart oiled fish mold. Chill until set.

4 Unmold on a serving platter and garnish with watercress, lemon slices and salmon roe. Serve with sour cream–dill sauce.

AVOCADO-WATERCRESS RING

An avocado-watercress ring filled with shrimp and mushrooms is an ideal luncheon dish for summer.

6 SERVINGS

6 ounces cream cheese
3 cups mashed avocado (about 3 avocados)
⅓ cup lime juice
¾ teaspoon salt
1 cup milk
1 envelope (1 tablespoon) unflavored gelatin
¼ cup cold water
1 bunch of watercress
1 pound shrimp, cooked, peeled and deveined
1 cup sliced raw mushrooms
Basic vinaigrette (page 576) to taste
½ teaspoon crushed tarragon

1 Let the cream cheese soften at room temperature in a mixing bowl.

2 Combine the mashed avocado, lime juice and salt.

3 Mash the cheese with the back of a wooden spoon. Gradually blend in the avocado mixture and milk.

4 Soften the gelatin in the water 5 minutes, then dissolve it over boiling water.

5 Meanwhile, chop the watercress stems into ⅛-inch lengths. Add to the avocado mixture. Save the leaves for garnish.

6 Add the dissolved gelatin to the avocado mixture. Mix well. Turn into an oiled 6-cup ring mold. Chill.

7 Combine the shrimp and mushrooms with the French dressing and tarragon. Mix well and chill.

8 To serve, unmold the avocado ring on a serving plate. Fill the center with marinated shrimp and mushrooms and garnish with watercress.

HAM MOUSSE

6 SERVINGS

2 envelopes (2 tablespoons) unflavored gelatin
2 tablespoons dry vermouth
1 teaspoon lemon juice
½ cup hot chicken stock
2 eggs, separated
½ cup mayonnaise
5 dashes of Tabasco sauce
1 cup diced cooked ham
½ cup cream

1 Put the gelatin, vermouth, lemon juice and hot stock in the container of a food processor. Blend for a few seconds.

2 Add the egg yolks, mayonnaise, Tabasco and ham. Blend for a few seconds longer.

3 With the motor running, gradually pour in the cream.

4 In a mixing bowl beat the egg whites until stiff. Pour the blended mixture over the egg whites and fold gently until mixed.

5 Pour into a 4-cup mold and chill for about 1 hour, until set.

TOMATOES ANTIBOISE

6 SERVINGS

6 ripe medium tomatoes
Salt
1 (7-ounce) can tuna fish
2 hard-cooked eggs, chopped
2 tablespoons capers
1 tablespoon finely chopped parsley
1 tablespoon finely chopped chives, or scallions
2 tablespoons mayonnaise
1 teaspoon anchovy paste, or chopped anchovy

1 Cut out the core of each tomato and use a small sharp knife or scoop to cut out most of the seeds. Sprinkle the interiors of the tomatoes with salt and invert them on a rack to drain.

2 Mash the tuna fish and blend it well with the eggs, capers, parsley, chives, mayonnaise and anchovy paste.

3 Use the tuna mixture to stuff the tomatoes, piling it high in a dome shape. Serve with heated pita bread.

SALADE NIÇOISE

6 TO 10 SERVINGS

2 teaspoons mustard, preferably Dijon
  or Düsseldorf
2 tablespoons wine vinegar
1½ teaspoons salt
1 or 2 garlic cloves, minced
6 tablespoons peanut or vegetable oil
6 tablespoons olive oil
Freshly ground pepper to taste
1 teaspoon chopped thyme,
  or ½ teaspoon dried
2 pounds green beans
2 green peppers
4 celery stalks, approximately
1 pint cherry tomatoes
5 medium red-skinned potatoes, cooked,
  peeled, and sliced
3 (7-ounce) cans tuna fish
1 (2-ounce) can flat anchovies
10 stuffed olives
10 black olives, preferably imported
  Greek or Italian
2 small or 1 large red onion
2 tablespoons chopped basil,
  or 1 teaspoon dried
⅓ cup finely chopped parsley
¼ cup finely chopped scallions
6 hard-cooked eggs, quartered

1 In a mixing bowl, combine the mustard, vinegar, salt, garlic, peanut oil, olive oil, pepper and thyme. Beat with a fork until well blended and set aside.

2 Pick over the beans and break them into 1½-inch lengths. Place in a saucepan and cook in salted water to cover until tender but crisp. Drain and run under cold water, then drain in a colander and set aside.

3 Remove the cores, seeds and white membranes from the green peppers. Cut the peppers into thin rounds and set aside.

4 Trim the celery stalks and cut crosswise into thin slices. There should be about 2 cups of sliced celery. Set aside.

5 Bring a quart of water to a boil. Drop in the cherry tomatoes and let stand for exactly 15 seconds, no longer, or they will become mushy. Drain immediately. Using a paring knife, pull off the tomato skins. Set the tomatoes aside.

6 In a large salad bowl, make a more or less symmetrical pattern of the green beans, peppers, celery, tomatoes and potatoes. Flake the tuna and add to the bowl. Arrange the anchovies on top and scatter the olives over all.

7 Peel the onions and cut into thin, almost transparent slices. Scatter the onion rings over all. Sprinkle with basil, parsley and scallions. Garnish with hard-cooked eggs.

8 Toss the salad with the dressing after the garnished bowl has been presented to the guests for their enjoyment. Serve with a crusty loaf of French or Italian bread.

Crêpes are, without question, one of the finest creations of Western cuisine, admirable on many counts. Primary among these is the contrast between their texture and flavor and whatever they are allied with. There are many ways to fold crêpes. They may be folded in quarters to make a fan shape. They may be rolled into a cigar shape with the filling in the center. And they may be folded into a lily shape, with the top open slightly and the bottom pointed.

♦

BASIC CRÊPES

8 OR 9 CRÊPES

1 egg
½ cup flour
Salt to taste
½ cup plus 2 tablespoons milk
2 tablespoons butter

1 Put the egg, flour and salt into a mixing bowl and start beating and blending with a wire whisk. Add the milk, stirring.

2 Melt 1 tablespoon of the butter in a 7- or 8-inch nonstick pan. When it is melted, pour the butter into the crêpe batter.

3 Line a mixing bowl with a sieve and pour the batter into the sieve. Strain the batter, pushing any solids through with a rubber spatula.

4 Melt the remaining tablespoon of butter and use this to brush the pan each time, or as necessary, before making a crêpe.

5 Brush the pan lightly and place it on the stove. When the butter is hot but not burning, add 2 tablespoons of the batter

(preferably with a small ladle with a 2-tablespoon capacity) and swirl it around neatly to completely cover the bottom of the pan. Cook over moderately high heat for 30 to 40 seconds, or until light brown on the bottom. Turn the crêpe and cook the other side for about 15 seconds. Turn the crêpe out onto a sheet of wax paper.

6 Continue making crêpes, brushing the pan lightly as necessary to prevent sticking, until all the batter is used. As the crêpes are made, turn them out, edges slightly overlapping, onto the wax paper.

Variation

CRÊPES WITH FINES HERBES

Add 1 teaspoon each chopped tarragon, parsley and chives to the crêpe batter.

♦

SEAFOOD CRÊPES

4 SERVINGS

Butter
1 tablespoon finely chopped shallots
¼ cup dry white wine
1 teaspoon each finely chopped chives, parsley and tarragon
1 cup finely diced cooked lobster or crabmeat
1 cup finely diced cooked shrimp
Salt and freshly ground pepper to taste
8 basic crêpes (page 122)
1 cup curry sauce (page 571)

1 Heat 1 tablespoon of the butter and add the shallots. Cook briefly, stirring, then add the wine. Cook to reduce by half.

2 Add the herbs and seafood and stir to blend. Sprinkle with salt and pepper and cook, stirring, just until heated through.

3 Preheat the oven to 200°F.

4 Spoon equal portions of the mixture into the center of each crêpe and roll. Arrange the crêpes on a platter and brush with melted butter. Butter a sheet of wax paper and place it, buttered side down, over the crêpes. Cover and bake briefly, just until heated through.

5 Serve on hot plates, spooning a little of the curry sauce on each crêpe.

◆

CHICKEN AND SPINACH CRÊPES

8 SERVINGS

1 (¾-pound) chicken breast
2½ cups chicken stock
10 ounces fresh spinach
½ pound mushrooms
7 tablespoons butter
2 shallots, finely chopped
5 tablespoons flour
2 cups milk
1 cup cream
Salt and freshly ground pepper to taste
⅛ teaspoon cayenne
¼ teaspoon grated nutmeg
1½ cups finely grated Gruyère or fontina
    cheese
16 basic crêpes (opposite page)
½ cup grated Parmesan cheese

1 Place the chicken breast in a saucepan and add the stock to cover. Bring to a boil and simmer, partly covered, about 20 minutes. Let the chicken cool in the liquid.

2 When the chicken has cooled, remove and discard the skin and bones. Chop the chicken meat, then cover and set aside.

3 Meanwhile, pick over the spinach and wash it under cold running water. Cook the spinach, covered, in the water that clings to the leaves, only until wilted, stirring once or twice. Drain well. When cool enough, press the spinach between the hands to extract most of the liquid. Chop and set aside.

4 Wipe the mushrooms, then chop fine.

5 Heat 2 tablespoons of the butter in a skillet. Add the shallots and cook briefly. Add the mushrooms and cook until they give up their liquid. Continue to cook, stirring frequently, until all the liquid evaporates.

6 Heat the remaining butter and stir in the flour, using a wire whisk. Add the milk, stirring rapidly with the whisk. When the mixture is thickened and smooth, stir in the cream, salt, pepper, cayenne and nutmeg.

7 Combine the chicken, spinach and mushrooms. Add ½ cup of the sauce, or enough to make the mixture hold together.

8 Heat the oven to 350°F.

9 Add the Gruyère cheese to the remaining sauce. Spoon a thin layer of sauce over the bottom of an ovenproof baking dish.

10 Spoon a little of the chicken and mushroom mixture onto each of the crêpes, then roll the crêpes. Arrange the rolled crêpes close together in the baking dish. Spoon the remaining sauce on top. Sprinkle with the Parmesan cheese and bake 30 to 40 minutes.

Although the United States could be called a sandwich festival from one end of the year to the other, it is the summer season, naturally, when the fête reaches its zenith. The consensus seems to be that midday, in particular, is the time for a cool brow and a cold stove, and a sandwich with a tall drink just fills the bill.

5 Using a sharp slicing knife, cut each sandwich diagonally. Secure each half with toothpicks and serve with chilled bread-and-butter pickles.

Note: Tomato peelings can make an interesting garnish for sandwiches. Roll them around loosely to resemble roses.

♦

CLUB SANDWICH

4 SANDWICHES

12 large slices of firm white bread, toasted
½ cup mayonnaise
1 teaspoon prepared mustard
16 slices of crisp bacon
2 tomatoes, sliced
4 lettuce leaves
4 slices of ham
8 slices of chicken breast
1 cucumber, peeled and thinly sliced
Salt and freshly ground pepper to taste
Bread-and-butter pickles

1 Trim the toast and arrange the slices on wax paper.
2 Combine the mayonnaise and mustard and spread the toast on one side.
3 Arrange 4 slices of bacon on each of 4 slices of toast. Place tomato slices on the bacon and top with 1 lettuce leaf. Top this with another slice of toast, mayonnaise side up.
4 Arrange 1 ham slice on each sandwich and top each with 2 chicken slices. Add the cucumber and sprinkle with salt and pepper. Finish with the last slices of toast, mayonnaise side down.

♦

LOBSTER ROLL

4 SANDWICHES

3 tablespoons olive oil
1 tablespoon vinegar
Salt and freshly ground pepper
½ cup mayonnaise
2 tablespoons chili sauce
2 teaspoons chopped dill
2 tablespoons finely chopped scallions
⅔ cup finely chopped celery
Tabasco sauce to taste
2 cups bite-size pieces of lobster meat
8 Kaiser rolls, toasted
Lettuce leaves

1 Combine the oil and vinegar in a mixing bowl and add a sprinkling of salt and pepper. Mix well with a fork.
2 Stir in the mayonnaise, chili sauce, dill, scallions and celery. Add Tabasco and the lobster meat. Blend well.
3 Use as a filling for toasted Kaiser rolls. Garnish each sandwich with lettuce leaves.

SHRIMP SALAD SANDWICH

4 SANDWICHES

2 cups shelled cooked shrimp
¼ cup chopped chives
5 tablespoons Dijon or Düsseldorf mustard
2 tablespoons chopped capers
3 tablespoons mayonnaise
2 (5-ounce) cans water chestnuts, drained
 and chopped
Salt and freshly ground pepper to taste
1 teaspoon lemon juice
Tabasco sauce to taste
4 white or whole wheat pita breads
Slices of hard-cooked egg, watercress and
 stuffed olives for garnish

1 Chop the shrimp coarsely and combine with the chives, mustard, capers, mayonnaise, water chestnuts, salt, pepper and lemon juice. Add more mayonnaise if necessary to make a spreadable mixture. Add Tabasco and blend well.

2 Spread the filling over the insides of the pitas. Garnish the sandwiches with egg slices, watercress sprigs and olives.

OPEN-FACE TOMATO SANDWICH

6 SANDWICHES

6 slices of firm bread
Butter, softened
12 thin slices mozzarella
2 large firm ripe tomatoes
½ teaspoon oregano
⅛ teaspoon freshly ground pepper
1 tablespoon butter, melted
Salt to taste
¼ cup grated Parmesan cheese
18 flat anchovy fillets

1 Spread one side of each bread slice with softened butter. Cover each with slices of mozzarella cheese.

2 Cut the tomatoes into 6 slices ½ inch thick. Place 1 slice on each of the sandwiches.

3 Combine the oregano, pepper and melted butter and brush over tomato slices. Sprinkle with salt and Parmesan cheese. Top each sandwich with 3 anchovy fillets.

4 Place the sandwiches under the broiler until cheese is melted and bubbly. Serve hot, garnished with parsley.

Some of the best sources for sandwich fillings are Italian grocery stores, which offer such delicacies as thin-sliced prosciutto, hot pickled peppers, assorted salami, tuna fish in olive oil and a multitude of cheeses. These flavorful ingredients make superior hero sandwiches.

♦

TUNA AND PEPERONCINI HERO

4 TO 6 SERVINGS

1 crusty loaf of French or Italian bread
2 (7-ounce) cans tuna fish packed in olive oil
8 to 12 Tuscan peppers (peperoncini)
Juice of 1 lemon

1 Slice the bread from one end to the other but do not cut all the way through. Leave one edge of the bread as a "hinge."

2 Empty the undrained tuna fish down the middle of the loaf and arrange the pickled peppers on top. Squeeze the lemon juice over the tuna fish. Close the sandwich, slice into individual portions, and serve.

HERO WITH EVERYTHING

4 TO 6 SERVINGS

1 crusty loaf of Italian or French bread
¼ cup olive oil
1 garlic clove, crushed
2 tablespoons grated Parmesan cheese
¼ pound or less thinly sliced salami
¼ pound or less thinly sliced prosciutto
¼ pound or less thinly sliced mortadella
¼ pound or less thinly sliced capicola
4 ounces or less thinly sliced provolone
   or fontina cheese
6 to 8 Tuscan peppers (peperoncini)
3 roasted sweet peppers, preferably red
5 or 6 crisp lettuce leaves
1 ripe tomato, cored and sliced (optional)
Salt and freshly ground pepper to taste
2 teaspoons red wine vinegar (optional)

1 Preheat the broiler.

2 Slice the bread lengthwise. Combine the olive oil and garlic. Stir briefly. Brush the split halves of the bread with the oil and garlic. Sprinkle each half with Parmesan cheese. Run the bread under the broiler, split side up, until cheese is golden.

3 Arrange layers of salami, prosciutto, mortadella, capicola, provolone, Tuscan peppers, sweet peppers, lettuce and tomatoes on one of the bread halves. Sprinkle with salt and pepper. Sprinkle, if desired, with more oil and vinegar. Cover with the remaining bread half and slice into serving portions.

EGG AND TOMATO HERO

4 TO 6 SERFVINGS

1 crusty loaf of French or Italian bread
2 ripe red tomatoes, cored and sliced
Salt and freshly ground pepper to taste
3 hard-cooked eggs, sliced
6 flat anchovy fillets
1 onion, thinly sliced
Wine vinegar
Olive oil

1 Slice the bread from one end to the other but do not cut all the way through. Leave one edge of the bread as a "hinge."

2 Arrange the tomato slices down the middle of the bread and sprinkle with salt and pepper. Arrange the sliced eggs over the tomatoes. Cover with the anchovy fillets and onion slices. Sprinkle the filling lightly with vinegar and generously with olive oil. Close the sandwich, slice into individual portions, and serve.

BAGEL WITH CREAM CHEESE AND SALMON

This is a wonderful New Year's Day sandwich, using smoked fish and caviar from the night before. But it is, of course, good any time of the year.

1 SERVING

1 bagel
1 tablespoon cream cheese
1 slice red onion, about ¼ inch thick or
   slightly less
1 generous but thin slice smoked salmon
   or Nova Scotia salmon
1 tablespoon or more fresh caviar (optional)
1 generous but thin slice smoked sturgeon
2 teaspoons drained capers

1 Cut the bagel horizontally through the center, sandwich fashion.

2 Toast each bagel half on the cut side and, if desired, on both sides.

3 Spread each half with an equal amount of the cream cheese.

4 Top one cheese-smeared half with the onion slice. Leave the salmon slice whole but cover the onion slice with half of it. Cover the salmon-and-onion half with caviar. Fold over the other half of the salmon.

5 Leave the smoked sturgeon slice whole but cover the smoked salmon with half of it, and spoon the capers over it in the center. Fold over the other half of the sturgeon.

6 Top with the remaining cheese-smeared bagel half.

REUBEN SANDWICH

4 SERVINGS

8 slices fresh rye bread or pumpernickel
8 teaspoons butter, melted
½ cup Russian dressing (page 578)
½ pound very lean corned beef, cut into the
    thinnest possible slices
¼ pound drained sauerkraut
⅓ pound Gruyère or Swiss cheese,
    thinly sliced

1 Preheat the oven to 400°F.
2 Place the bread slices on a flat surface and brush one side of each with the melted butter.
3 Turn the slices over and spread the other side with Russian dressing. Arrange equal amounts of corned beef on 4 of the slices smeared with Russian dressing. Add equal amounts of sauerkraut over the corned beef. Arrange an equal number of slices of cheese over the sauerkraut. Cover the layered slices with the remaining 4 slices of bread, Russian dressing side touching the filling.
4 Place the sandwiches on a hot griddle or in a large skillet in the oven and bake briefly, just until the cheese is melted.

SMØRREBRØD

Lunch in Denmark is a selection of delicious sandwiches called smørrebrød, literally "butter and bread." These sandwiches do not have tops, for they are too fat, and usually have garnishes as well. The important thing is that they must be made of the finest ingredients, including the freshest butter, and the sandwiches must not only taste good, but look good. The breads must be firm; rye bread is especially favored. Any of these sandwiches could be made in miniature to serve as canapés, but in the usual size they are as filling as a standard American sandwich for all the daintiness of their appearance.

SHRIMP SANDWICH
1 SERVING

Butter a thin slice of dark or light rye bread and cover copiously with tiny bay shrimp (may be purchased in jars). Garnish with a small lettuce leaf and a slice of lemon.

SMOKED EEL SANDWICH
1 SERVING

Butter a thin slice of dark or light rye bread and cover with thin slices of smoked eel. Top with a small spoonful of cold scrambled egg. Garnish with a radish rose and a small lettuce leaf.

MATJES HERRING SANDWICH
1 SERVING

Butter a thin slice of dark or light rye bread and cover with slices of matjes herring. Garnish with grated orange rind, quartered orange slices and a thin lettuce leaf.

DANISH CHEESE SANDWICH
1 SERVING

Butter a thin slice of dark or light rye bread and cover with thin slices of Danish cheese such as Danish blue, Samsø, havarti or King Christian IX.

LUMPFISH CAVIAR SANDWICH
1 SERVING

Butter a thin slice of dark or light rye bread and cover with a spoonful of imported lumpfish caviar (may be purchased in jars). Garnish with a small lettuce leaf and twist of lemon.

ROAST CHICKEN SANDWICH
1 SERVING

Butter a thin slice of dark or light rye bread and cover with thin slices of roast chicken. Decorate with a liver paste pushed through a pastry tube. Garnish with tiny triangle of pineapple.

SMOKED SALMON SANDWICH
1 SERVING

Butter a thin slice of dark or light rye bread and cover with thin slices of smoked salmon. Garnish with lemon wedges.

LIVER PÂTÉ SANDWICH
1 SERVING

Butter a thin slice of dark or light rye bread and cover with thin slices of liver pâté, either purchased or homemade. Top with a thin slice of a clear firm aspic and shreds of cooked beets. Garnish with cucumber slices and lettuce.

HAM AND EGG SANDWICH
1 SERVING

Butter a thin slice of dark or light rye bread and cover it with overlapping thin slices of Danish ham. Top with a spoonful of cold scrambled egg. Garnish with white asparagus tips and slivers of tomato.

FRESH PORK SANDWICH
1 SERVING

Butter a thin slice of dark or light rye bread and cover with thin slices of roast fresh pork. Top with a spoonful of cold orange-flavored red cabbage and a cooked prune. Garnish with quartered thin orange slices.

ROAST DUCK SANDWICH
1 SERVING

Butter a thin slice of dark or light rye bread and cover with slices of roast duck with crisp skin. Top with a spoonful of cold orange-flavored red cabbage and garnish with quartered thin orange slices.

BISMARCK HERRING SANDWICH
1 SERVING

Butter a thin slice of dark or light rye bread and cover with bits of Bismarck herring and thin onion rings. Garnish with a thin lettuce leaf, finely chopped parsley and bits of pimiento.

Continued

TONGUE SANDWICH
1 SERVING

Butter a thin slice of dark or light rye bread
and cover with overlapping thin slices of
tongue. Cover this with a spoonful of cold
vegetable salad mixed with mayonnaise.
Garnish with white asparagus tips, a small
lettuce leaf and slivers of tomato.

SARDINE SANDWICH
1 SERVING

Butter a thin slice of dark or light rye bread
and cover with small imported sardines in
tomato sauce. Garnish with a small lettuce
leaf, a twist of lemon and parsley sprigs.

STEAK TARTARE SANDWICH
1 SERVING

Butter a thin slice of dark or light rye bread
and cover with a large spoonful of freshly
ground raw beef such as sirloin or tenderloin. Garnish with a raw egg yolk in half
of an eggshell, grated fresh horseradish,
chopped onion, capers, anchovy fillets
and a small lettuce leaf.

EGG AND TOMATO SANDWICH
1 SERVING

Butter a thin slice of dark or light rye
bread, cover with thin slices of hard-
cooked egg, and top with thin slices of
tomato. Garnish with freshly grated horseradish and a small lettuce leaf.

4

Poultry

Chicken

ROAST CHICKEN

4 SERVINGS

1 (4-pound) roasting chicken, at room
    temperature
½ lemon
Salt and freshly ground pepper to taste
1 small onion, peeled
Herbs, such as ½ teaspoon of thyme or
    rosemary, 1 bay leaf, 1 sprig of tarragon
    or parsley
2 to 4 tablespoons butter, softened

1 Preheat the oven to 350°F.

2 Rub the inside of the chicken with
the lemon half and sprinkle with salt and
pepper. Add onion to the cavity and the
herbs, or stuff with desired stuffing. Truss
the chicken and place it in a roasting pan.
Rub the softened butter over the skin of
the chicken.

3 Bake 18 to 20 minutes per pound, or
about 1¼ hours for a 4-pound bird, 1½
hours if stuffed. Baste the chicken as it
roasts with the pan juices. Test for doneness by moving the leg of the chicken up
and down. If it moves easily the chicken is
done.

ROAST CHICKEN WITH WILD RICE

Wild rice is, conceivably, the most luxurious of
all native American products. It has a nuttiness
and texture that are incomparable. It makes an
exceptional stuffing for roast chicken.

4 SERVINGS

1 (4-pound) roasting chicken
Salt and freshly ground pepper to taste
½ cup wild rice
1½ cups water
⅓ cup cashew nuts
½ pound mushrooms
3 chicken livers (about ¼ pound)
4 tablespoons butter
½ cup finely chopped onions
¼ cup dry white wine
2 tablespoons vegetable oil
1 small whole onion, peeled

1 Sprinkle the chicken inside and out
with salt and pepper.

2 Put the wild rice in a saucepan and
add 1 cup of the water and some salt.
Bring to the boil, cover and simmer 40 to
45 minutes, or until rice "blooms" and is
tender. Drain thoroughly.

3 Meanwhile, preheat the oven to
450°F. Put the cashews in a skillet and
place in the oven. Bake, stirring often,
until golden brown, 5 minutes or longer.

4 Cut the mushrooms into ½-inch
cubes. There should be about 3 cups. Cut
the livers into ¼-inch cubes. There should
be about ½ cup.

5 Heat 2 tablespoons of the butter in a
saucepan and add the chopped onions.
Cook, stirring, until wilted. Add the
mushrooms, salt and pepper and cook,
stirring often, about 5 minutes. Add the
wine and cook, stirring often, until the liquid is almost totally evaporated.

6 Add the chicken livers and cook, stirring, until livers lose their raw look.

7 Add the cooked wild rice, cashews and 1 tablespoon of butter to the mushroom mixture. Stir to blend. Let cool.

8 Stuff the chicken in the body and in the crop with the wild rice mixture. Truss the chicken and rub on all sides with the oil. Place the chicken on one side in a roasting pan. Scatter the whole onion, neck and gizzard around the chicken.

9 Place the chicken in the oven and bake 25 minutes. Turn the chicken onto the other side and bake 25 minutes. Turn the chicken breast side up and continue roasting, basting often, about 10 minutes. Reduce the oven heat to 400°F.

10 Pour off the fat from the pan. Add 1 tablespoon of butter and then ½ cup of water, stirring to dissolve the brown particles that cling to the bottom of the pan.

11 Return the chicken to the oven and bake 15 minutes longer. The total roasting time is 1¼ hours.

◆

CHICKEN ROASTED IN A BAG

5 OR 6 SERVINGS

1 (5-pound) roasting chicken
1 teaspoon salt
¼ teaspoon freshly ground pepper
1 teaspoon fresh rosemary, or ½ teaspoon dried
½ teaspoon ground cumin
¼ cup olive oil
½ teaspoon paprika
1 garlic clove, minced

1 Truss the chicken.

2 Combine the salt, pepper, rosemary, cumin, oil, paprika and garlic. Set this mixture aside for about 30 minutes.

3 Preheat the oven to 325°F.

4 Rub the entire surface of the chicken with the seasoned oil mixture. Put chicken into a heavy brown paper bag, close the bag, and put it in a roasting pan. Bake for 2½ to 3 hours, or until done.

Note: If a well-browned chicken is desired, the paper bag may be removed for the last 30 minutes of roasting.

◆

POACHED CHICKEN

3 TO 4 SERVINGS, OR 2 TO 3 CUPS DICED CHICKEN

1 (2- to 3½-pound) chicken, trussed
1 small onion, studded with 2 cloves
1 celery stalk, trimmed and quartered
1 carrot, scraped and quartered
1 parsley sprig
½ bay leaf
Pinch of thyme
Salt to taste
10 peppercorns
Sauce poulette (page 566)

1 Place the chicken in a small kettle or a large saucepan and add cold water to cover.

2 Add the remaining ingredients and bring to a boil. Reduce heat, cover partly and simmer until the chicken is tender, 30 minutes or longer depending on size. Serve the poached chicken with sauce poulette, or cut up and use for other dishes calling for cooked chicken.

Chicken Salad à la Chinoise, page 116.
Chicken Salad with Almonds, page 117.

BROILED CHICKEN FOR ONE

1 SERVING

¼ cup lemon or lime juice, or equal parts
    lemon juice and dry white wine
¼ cup vegetable oil
1 teaspoon tarragon
¼ teaspoon Tabasco sauce
½ (1 to 1½ pounds) broiling chicken

1 Combine the lemon juice, oil, tarragon and Tabasco and marinate the chicken for at least 1 hour.

2 Preheat the broiler.

3 Place the chicken, skin side up, on a broiler rack. Place the rack 4 to 6 inches from the source of heat. Cook, basting at frequent intervals with the marinade, until chicken is brown.

4 Turn the chicken with tongs and continue to broil and baste for 40 minutes to 1 hour, depending on the size of the chicken. It may be necessary to reduce the heat as the chicken cooks.

LIME BROILED CHICKEN

6 SERVINGS

3 (2½-pound) broiler-fryer chickens, quartered
Lime barbecue sauce (see following recipe)

1 Put the chicken in a bowl and pour the sauce over. Marinate for several hours.

2 Preheat the broiler.

3 Place chicken skin side up on rack 6 inches from broiler heat. Cook slowly until tender, turning and basting frequently, about 45 minutes.

LIME BARBECUE SAUCE

½ cup corn oil
½ cup lime juice
2 tablespoons chopped onions
1 tablespoon chopped tarragon, or 2
    teaspoons dried
1 teaspoon salt
½ teaspoon Tabasco sauce

Combine all ingredients in a blender or food processor until smooth.

ROSEMARY BROILED CHICKEN

4 SERVINGS

2 (2½-pound) broiling chickens,
    split for broiling
Salt and freshly ground pepper to taste
¼ pound butter
½ cup lemon juice
1 teaspoon chopped rosemary
¼ teaspoon Tabasco sauce
1 teaspoon Worcestershire sauce

1 Preheat the broiler.

2 Sprinkle the chickens on all sides with salt and pepper.

3 Melt the butter and add the lemon juice, rosemary and Tabasco to make a basting sauce.

4 Place the chickens, bony side down, on the broiler rack. Brush chickens with the sauce and place them under the broiler. Cook the chickens for 35 minutes to 1 hour, until they are done, basting and turning them often. Do not let the chickens burn. Adjust the broiler heat as necessary while they cook. When cooked, the chickens should be a nice brown on all sides.

5 Transfer the chickens to a hot serving platter. Add the Worcestershire sauce to the liquid in the broiler pan. Stir lightly. Pour the sauce over the chickens and serve.

BARBECUED CHICKEN

4 SERVINGS

2 (2-pound) broiling chickens,
    halved for broiling
Vegetable oil
1 (14-ounce) bottle tomato catsup
½ teaspoon chili powder, or more
¼ cup vegetable oil
½ teaspoon ground cumin
Juice of 1 lemon
3 lemon slices, unpeeled
1 tablespoon Worcestershire sauce, or more
Tabasco sauce to taste
1 garlic clove, flattened
1 cup chicken stock
Salt and coarsely cracked pepper to taste

1 Rub all surfaces of the chickens with oil.

2 Combine the remaining ingredients and simmer briefly.

3 Place chickens, bony side down, on a grill over a charcoal fire. Using a pastry brush, baste chickens with the sauce during broiling, turning several times. To achieve a slight crust, place grill closer to coals toward end of cooking time.

4 When chickens are thoroughly cooked, remove them to a heatproof platter and spoon any remaining sauce over them.

Note: The cooked chicken may be kept hot in a 200°F oven for 1 hour.

FRIED CHICKEN

6 SERVINGS

½ cup flour
1½ teaspoons salt
1 teaspoon freshly ground pepper
2 (2-pound) frying chickens, cut into pieces
Oil for deep frying

1 In a paper bag combine the flour, salt and pepper. Add a few chicken parts at a time and shake to coat well with the seasoned flour.
2 Pour oil to a depth of 1 inch in a heavy skillet and heat to 375°F. Drop the chicken pieces into the fat and cook until golden brown on one side. Turn and cook the other side until brown. Drain on paper toweling.

Variations

HERB FRIED CHICKEN

Add ½ teaspoon crushed rosemary to the seasoned flour.

CHILI FRIED CHICKEN

Place the chicken pieces in a mixing bowl and add milk barely to cover. Sprinkle with 2 tablespoons chili powder, stir briefly, and let stand overnight. When ready to cook, lift the pieces from the milk, drain briefly, and coat with seasoned flour. Fry as above.

SOUTHERN FRIED CHICKEN

4 SERVINGS

1 (2½- to 3-pound) chicken, cut into
    serving pieces
Milk
¼ teaspoon Tabasco sauce
1 cup flour
1½ to 2 teaspoons salt
2 teaspoons freshly ground pepper
1 pound lard, or 2 cups corn oil
¼ pound butter

1 Put the chicken pieces in a bowl and add milk to cover. Add the Tabasco sauce and stir. Refrigerate 1 hour or longer.
2 Combine the flour, salt and pepper (the flavor of pepper in this recipe is important) in a flat baking dish. Blend well.
3 Remove the chicken pieces, 2 or 3 at a time, and dip them into the flour mixture, turning them in the flour to coat well.
4 Heat the lard and butter in a skillet, preferably a black iron skillet large enough to hold the chicken pieces in one layer without touching, over high heat. Add the chicken pieces, skin side down, and cook until golden brown on one side. Turn the pieces and reduce the heat to medium-low. Continue cooking until pieces are golden brown and cooked through. The total cooking time should be 20 to 30 minutes. As the pieces are cooked, transfer them to paper toweling to drain.

INDONESIAN FRIED CHICKEN

4 SERVINGS

1 (2½- to 3-pound) chicken, cut into
   serving pieces
1 teaspoon salt
2 teaspoons light soy sauce
1 teaspoon sugar
1 teaspoon lemon juice
1 tablespoon ground cumin
½ tablespoon turmeric
Oil for deep frying

1 Place the chicken in a mixing bowl and add the salt, soy sauce, sugar, lemon juice, cumin and turmeric. Massage well so that the pieces are thoroughly coated. Cover with plastic wrap and refrigerate for 2 hours.

2 Heat the oil for deep frying to 370°F. Add the chicken pieces one at a time and cook until golden brown. Drain on paper toweling.

HERBED BAKED CHICKEN

4 TO 6 SERVINGS

2 plump broiling chickens, quartered
Flour for dredging
Salt and freshly ground pepper to taste
4 teaspoons chopped tarragon,
   or 1 teaspoon dried
4 teaspoons chopped parsley
4 teaspoons chopped chives
Juice of ½ lemon
¼ pound butter
¼ cup lemon juice
½ cup dry sherry

1 Preheat the oven to 250°F. Remove the necks and backbones from the chicken parts and reserve for another use.

2 In a paper bag combine the flour, salt, pepper and 2 teaspoons each of the tarragon, parsley and chives. Add a few chicken parts at a time and shake to coat well with the seasoned flour. Place the chicken, skin side down, in a shallow buttered baking dish. Sprinkle with the juice from ½ lemon and cover with foil.

3 In a saucepan combine the butter, ¼ cup lemon juice, sherry and the remaining herbs. Heat until the butter melts.

4 Bake the chicken 1 to 1½ hours, lifting the foil and basting every 20 minutes with the butter sauce. Toward the end of the cooking time, increase the oven temperature to 400°F, remove the foil and turn the chicken to let it brown lightly. If necessary add a little more wine or water to the pan so that there will be ample sauce.

5 Sprinkle the chicken with additional freshly chopped herbs and serve with the pan juices.

BAKED CHICKEN, SUMMER STYLE

4 SERVINGS

1 (3-pound) frying chicken, cut into
    serving pieces
2 tablespoons olive oil
2 tablespoons butter
3 slices of bacon, cut into halves
6 slices of fresh ripe tomatoes
2 teaspoons chopped basil
2 teaspoons chopped parsley
1 garlic clove, minced
Salt and freshly ground pepper to taste
½ cup dry white wine

1 Preheat the oven to 350° F.
2 Brown the chicken on all sides in the oil and butter. Transfer the chicken to a baking dish and cover each piece with ½ slice of bacon and 1 slice of tomato. Sprinkle with a mixture of the basil, parsley, garlic, salt and pepper. Add the wine to the pan and place the chicken in the oven.
3 Bake the chicken for 30 minutes, basting occasionally with the fat in which the chicken was browned. The chicken is done when it is tender when pricked with a fork.

TO BONE CHICKEN BREASTS

Boneless chicken breasts are the basis for many of the world's most elegant dishes. Boning them is easily done in the home; here is how to go about it.

Buy 1 whole chicken breast split in two for each 2 people to be served. Place the halved chicken breasts on a flat surface and, using the fingers, pull off the skin of the chicken. It has a tenuous attachment to the flesh and comes off with a minimum of effort.

Using a paring knife, make a small incision between the meat and the breast-bones at a point away from the main wing portion. Using the fingers and the knife, carefully pull and scrape the meat away from the bones, taking care not to tear the meat.

If the breasts are to be boned "French-style," the butcher must be instructed to leave the main wing bones attached to the breasts.

♦

CHICKEN BREASTS ALL' ALBA

This is one of the most incredible of dishes when made with white Italian truffles and topped with fontina cheese. These ingredients are available wherever fine Italian delicacies are sold.

4 SERVINGS

2 whole chicken breasts, boned and halved
Flour for dredging
2 tablespoons butter
Salt and freshly ground pepper to taste
Slices of white or black truffles, or 4 sliced
    mushrooms sautéed in a little butter
4 slices of fontina cheese

1 Remove and discard skin from chicken breasts. Place the chicken breasts between pieces of wax paper and pound until thin.
2 Dredge the chicken in flour. In a skillet heat the butter, add the chicken and cook until tender, 5 to 6 minutes on each side. Remove to a shallow pan and sprinkle with salt and pepper. Arrange on each breast half a dozen small slices of truffles or mushrooms and cover with a slice of cheese.
3 Place the chicken breasts under a hot broiler just long enough to melt the cheese. Serve at once.

BREADED CHICKEN BREASTS

6 SERVINGS

3 whole chicken breasts, boned and halved
Salt and freshly ground pepper to taste
Flour
2 eggs
1 teaspoon water
2 cups soft fresh bread crumbs
¼ pound butter
Lemon wedges and parsley

1 Place each breast half between pieces of wax paper and pound thin with the flat side of a heavy knife.

2 Sprinkle the chicken with salt and pepper and dredge in flour. Combine the eggs with the water and beat lightly with a fork. Dip the chicken into the egg mixture and then into the bread crumbs. Pound lightly with the flat side of a knife to make the crumbs adhere. Place the breaded chicken on a rack and dry briefly in the refrigerator so crumbs will adhere.

3 Melt the butter in a large skillet and cook the chicken over moderate heat until it is golden brown on all sides. If the chicken breasts are thin, further cooking will not be necessary. If they are relatively thick, place them in a preheated 350°F oven for 5 to 10 minutes. Serve hot, garnished with lemon wedges and parsley.

Variations

VIENNESE CHICKEN BREASTS

Top each cooked breaded chicken breast with a slice of lemon, 1 anchovy fillet stuffed with capers and chopped parsley.

CHICKEN PARMESAN

Put cooked breaded chicken breasts in a shallow roasting pan. Top each with a slice of mozzarella cheese. Pour ¾ cup tomato sauce over all. Sprinkle with 1½ teaspoons oregano and 3 tablespoons Parmesan cheese. Bake at 350°F for 20 minutes.

♦

BREAST OF CHICKEN FLORENTINE

As will be noted many times throughout this book, Florentine means spinach. This is breast of chicken on a bed of spinach. The dish is also called Gismonda.

8 SERVINGS

Flour for dredging
Salt and freshly ground pepper to taste
4 whole chicken breasts, boned and halved
1 egg
1 tablespoon water
¼ cup grated Parmesan cheese
½ cup dry bread crumbs
¼ pound plus 4 tablespoons butter
2 pounds spinach, cooked and drained
1 tablespoon lemon juice
1 pound mushrooms, sliced
Chopped parsley

1 Mix the flour, salt and pepper and dredge the chicken breasts with the seasoned flour. Dip them in the egg lightly beaten with the water and then coat with a mixture of the cheese and crumbs. Refrigerate 1 hour or more.

2 In a large skillet heat ¼ pound of the butter, add the chicken and brown on both sides. Lower heat, cover and cook until tender, about 25 minutes.

Continued

3 Meanwhile, chop the spinach coarsely and season with the lemon juice. Pile the spinach on a platter, arrange the chicken breasts on top and keep hot.

4 To the skillet add 2 tablespoons of the remaining butter and the mushrooms and sauté until the mushrooms are tender. Spoon over the chicken.

5 Brown the remaining butter in the same pan and pour through a fine sieve over the dish. Sprinkle with chopped parsley.

◆

BREAST OF CHICKEN EN PAPILLOTE

En papillote means roughly "baked in a bag." This is breast of chicken baked in foil.

6 SERVINGS

3 chicken breasts, halved
Chicken stock or lightly salted water
4 tablespoons butter
2 tablespoons flour
½ cup milk
½ cup dry white wine
1 egg yolk
Salt and freshly ground pepper to taste
Pinch of cayenne
Pinch of mace or grated nutmeg
Pinch of ground cloves
¼ cup finely chopped mushrooms
1 teaspoon chopped chives

1 Place the chicken breasts in a small kettle and add chicken stock barely to cover. Bring to a boil, reduce the heat, cover and simmer gently until the meat is tender, 25 to 40 minutes, depending on the size of the breasts. Remove the chicken from the broth and cool. Carefully remove skin and the meat from the bones. Reserve ½ cup of the broth.

2 Preheat the oven to 400°F.

3 Cut 6 pieces of foil large enough to make an envelope for each breast half and spread the foil with half the butter.

4 In a saucepan melt the remaining 2 tablespoons butter, add the flour and stir with a wire whisk until blended. Meanwhile, bring the milk, wine and reserved chicken broth to a boil and add all at once to the butter-flour mixture, stirring vigorously with the whisk until the sauce is thickened and smooth. Add the egg yolk lightly beaten with a little of the hot sauce, stirring gently until thickened. Do not let boil. Add the seasonings and stir in the mushrooms and chives.

5 Place half a chicken breast in the center of each square of foil and spoon some sauce over the top. Fold the edges of the foil and seal tightly by crimping the edges. Arrange on a baking sheet and bake 10 minutes. Serve wrapped in the foil.

CHICKEN BREASTS WITH TARRAGON

White wine, cream and the delicate herb known as tarragon are three of the foundations for classic French cuisine.

6 SERVINGS

3 whole chicken breasts, boned and halved
Salt and freshly ground pepper to taste
1/4 cup flour
2 tablespoons butter
1 tablespoon chopped shallots
1/4 cup dry white wine
1 teaspoon freshly chopped tarragon,
    or 1/2 teaspoon dried
1/4 cup chicken stock
1/4 cup cream

1 Sprinkle the chicken breasts with salt and pepper and dredge in the flour. Reserve the remaining flour.

2 In a large skillet heat the butter, add the chicken and brown on both sides. Transfer to a heated platter. Add the shallots to the skillet and sauté briefly. Add the wine.

3 Cook the liquid over high heat until it is nearly evaporated, while scraping loose all the brown particles.

4 Add the reserved flour and stir to make a thick paste. Sprinkle with the tarragon and stir in the chicken stock.

5 Return the chicken to the skillet, cover and cook until tender, about 25 minutes. Transfer the chicken to a heated platter and keep hot. Add the cream to the skillet; heat, stirring, and pour the sauce over the chicken.

CHICKEN BREASTS VÉRONIQUE

6 SERVINGS

3 whole chicken breasts, skinned and halved
Flour for dredging
1/2 teaspoon salt
1/4 teaspoon freshly ground pepper
1/4 teaspoon tarragon
4 tablespoons butter
2 tablespoons vegetable oil
1/4 cup finely chopped onions
1/2 cup chicken stock
1/2 cup dry white wine
1/2 pound mushrooms, sliced
2 cups seedless green grapes

1 Preheat the oven to 375°F.

2 Coat the chicken pieces with the flour mixed with the salt, pepper and tarragon. Brown the chicken on all sides in 2 tablespoons of the butter and the oil in a skillet. Place the pieces in a single layer in a shallow baking pan.

3 Add the onions to the butter left in the skillet and cook until tender. Pour in the stock and wine and bring to a boil. Pour around the chicken. Bake, uncovered, for 30 minutes.

4 Sauté the mushrooms in the remaining 2 tablespoons butter and add along with the grapes to the chicken. Bake for 8 to 10 minutes longer.

Chicken and Cucumber Soup, page 91.
Creamed Chicken Soup, page 90.

KASHMIR CHICKEN BREASTS

Cooked potatoes puréed in a liquid can replace cream in a recipe; they give an oddly pleasant, smooth and creamy texture to this curry sauce.

4 SERVINGS

2 whole chicken breasts, split
Freshly ground pepper to taste
3 tablespoons olive oil
2 tablespoons finely chopped shallots
2 tablespoons dry vermouth or dry white wine
½ cup thinly sliced onions
2 teaspoons minced garlic
½ cup finely chopped leeks
1 tablespoon curry powder
1 bay leaf
1 medium-size (about ¼ pound) potato, sliced
    as thin as possible
1½ cups chicken stock
½ cup dry white wine

1 Sprinkle the breast pieces with pepper.

2 Heat 2 tablespoons of the oil in a heavy skillet and add the pieces, skin side down. Cook 5 minutes, or until nicely browned on one side. Turn the pieces and cover closely with a lid. Continue cooking about 10 minutes, turning the pieces occasionally.

3 Pour off the fat from the skillet and scatter the shallots around the chicken pieces. Add the vermouth and cook until the liquid has almost evaporated. Remove from the heat.

4 Meanwhile, heat the remaining 1 tablespoon oil in a saucepan and add the onions, garlic and leeks. Cook, stirring, until the onions are wilted. Sprinkle with curry powder and stir to blend. Add the bay leaf and potato slices and stir. Add the stock and the wine. Bring to a boil and simmer 10 minutes. Remove and discard the bay leaf.

5 Pour the mixture into the container of a food processor and blend until smooth. Pour the sauce over the chicken breasts. Bring to the boil and simmer about 1 minute.

♦

STIR-FRY CHICKEN WITH SNOW PEAS

4 SERVINGS

1 pound snow peas
2 whole chicken breasts, boned but with
    skin left on
2 tablespoons cornstarch
3 tablespoons dry sherry
8 to 10 large dried black mushrooms
1 tablespoon light soy sauce
1 tablespoon dark soy sauce
2 teaspoons sugar
Salt to taste
1 cup peanut or vegetable oil
2 teaspoons water

1 Pinch off the stem ends of the snow peas and, if necessary, string them.

2 Cut the chicken breasts into bite-size pieces and put them in a bowl. Add 1 tablespoon of the cornstarch and 1 tablespoon of the sherry and stir to coat the pieces.

3 Place the mushrooms in a bowl and add boiling water to cover. Let stand 20 minutes, then drain and squeeze to remove excess liquid. Cut off and discard the stems.

4 Combine the soy sauces, sugar, salt and remaining 2 tablespoons sherry and stir to blend. Stir in the remaining 1 tablespoon of cornstarch.

5 Heat the oil in a wok or skillet until it is hot and almost smoking. Add the chicken and cook over high heat, stirring, 3 to 4 minutes. Remove the chicken pieces with a slotted spoon but leave the oil in the pan.

6 Add the mushrooms and the snow peas to the hot oil and cook, stirring, about 30 seconds. Remove the vegetables with a slotted spoon.

7 Pour off all but 2 tablespoons of oil from the wok. Return to the heat and stir in the soy sauce mixture. Stir about 5 seconds and add the chicken and water and turn the heat to high.

8 Add the snow peas and mushrooms and cook, stirring, about 30 seconds. Serve immediately.

INDIAN CHICKEN

10 OR MORE SERVINGS

2 tablespoons butter
2 tablespoons vegetable oil
8 small chicken breasts, skinned, boned and quartered
1 cup chopped onions
1 garlic clove, chopped
1 teaspoon salt
1 tablespoon ground ginger
¼ teaspoon chili powder
½ cup drained canned tomatoes
1 cup clear chicken stock, or yogurt
½ cup ground cashews
½ cup flaked coconut
2 tablespoons cornstarch
1 cup cream

1 In a 3½-quart Dutch oven or deep skillet heat the butter and oil. Brown the chicken, about 8 pieces at a time, and drain on paper toweling.

2 To the pan add the onions and garlic and cook 5 minutes. Return the chicken to the pan.

3 Add the salt, ginger, chili powder, tomatoes and stock. Mix lightly, cover and cook 15 minutes.

4 Add the nuts and coconut, cover and cook over low heat until the chicken is tender, about 10 minutes longer.

5 To the cornstarch slowly add the cream, then stir into the cooking liquid. Stir constantly until the sauce returns to a boil. Simmer over low heat another 5 minutes. If desired, cool and refrigerate. Near serving time, bring up to room temperature. Reheat over very low heat. Serve with basmati rice.

KUNG PAO CHICKEN

This spiced dish, redolent with garlic and chili paste, was named for a high-ranking Chinese official who fled Sichuan as a political refugee a few hundred years ago. It became popular in many provinces where the inhabitants dote on hot foods.

4 SERVINGS

1 large whole chicken breast, boned but with
  skin left on
½ egg white (beat the egg white lightly,
  then divide in half)
2 teaspoons cornstarch
Salt to taste
2 tablespoons bean sauce
1 tablespoon hoisin sauce
1 tablespoon chili paste with garlic
1½ teaspoons sugar
1 tablespoon dry sherry
1 tablespoon red wine vinegar
4 garlic cloves, peeled and flattened
1 cup peanut or vegetable oil
1 cup shelled unsalted peanuts
12 dried hot red peppers, cut in half

1 Cut the chicken into bite-size cubes. Combine with the egg white, cornstarch and salt. Refrigerate for 30 minutes.

2 Combine the bean sauce, hoisin, chili paste, sugar, sherry, vinegar and garlic in a small bowl.

3 Heat the oil in a wok or skillet until it is hot but not smoking. Turn off the heat and add the peanuts. The peanuts will turn light golden brown. Remove with a slotted spoon and drain on paper toweling.

4 Heat the oil again and add the chicken mixture. Cook about 45 seconds, stirring, until the chicken becomes translucent. Do not brown. Remove the chicken and drain well.

5 Pour off all but 2 tablespoons of the oil from the wok. Add the peppers to the wok and cook until dark, about 15 seconds. Add the sauce and the chicken and cook about 1 minute. Serve sprinkled with the peanuts.

◆

NASI GORENG

6 SERVINGS

3 onions, cut into thin slices
2 garlic cloves, finely minced
Peanut oil
2 cups cubed raw chicken
¼ cup bumbu nasi goreng (mixed spices)
8 cups (about 1 pound raw) steamed rice
1 pound shrimp, cooked, peeled, deveined and
  cut into bite-size pieces
4 eggs, lightly beaten
¼ cup water
Salt and freshly ground pepper to taste
1 sweet red pepper, cut into strips
1 sweet Italian-style green pepper,
  cut into strips
½ cup shredded cooked ham

1 Sauté two of the onions and the garlic in 3 tablespoons peanut oil until soft and tender.

2 Add the chicken cubes and cook over high heat, stirring frequently, for 5 minutes.

3 Barely cover the bumbu nasi goreng with hot water and simmer for 15 minutes. Add to the chicken mixture.

4 Add the rice and shrimp and heat gently, stirring.

5 Pour 2 teaspoons oil into a small skillet. Combine the eggs, water, salt and pepper and pour one quarter of the mixture into the skillet. Tilt the pan so that the

egg covers the bottom. Cook until set. Remove and cut into strips. Repeat 3 times with the remaining egg mixture and add more oil if necessary. Add three quarters of the egg strips to the chicken mixture. Season with salt and pepper.

6 Fry the red and green pepper strips in 1 tablespoon oil. Separate the remaining onion slices into rings and fry the onion rings in 1 tablespoon oil until brown.

7 Pile the rice mixture in the center of a dish. Ring with remaining egg strips. Top with the ham, fried red and green pepper strips, and fried onion slices.

Cannelloni alla Nerone, page 483.

♦

CHICKEN LEGS STUFFED WITH WILD RICE

4 SERVINGS

*4 chicken legs with thighs attached
   (about 2 pounds)*
2 tablespoons butter
½ cup finely chopped onions
1 cup diced mushrooms
2 tablespoons toasted pine nuts
¾ cup cooked wild rice
Freshly ground pepper to taste
Asparagus sauce (page 572)

1 Bone the chicken legs with thighs, or have them boned by the butcher. To bone them, place skin side down on a flat surface. Using a small paring or boning knife, cut down to the bone from the top of each thigh down to the knoblike bone at the bottom of each leg. Do not cut through the skin. Cut and scrape the flesh from the meat, leaving the bones as bare as possible. Using a sharp heavy knife or a meat cleaver, hack off the bottom of the end of each leg bone, leaving the knoblike bone intact.

2 Heat the butter in a small skillet and add the onions. Cook, stirring, until wilted. Add the mushrooms and cook, stirring, about 1 minute. Add the pine nuts, wild rice and pepper. Stir to blend. Let cool.

3 Lay out the legs with thighs attached opened up and skin side down. Spoon equal portions of the filling into the center of each. Fold over the outer skin neatly and compactly to enclose the filling.

4 Lay out four 8-inch squares of plastic wrap and place one stuffed leg in the center of each. Fold over the plastic wrap to enclose compactly. Prick the plastic wrap in several places to allow the liquid that will accumulate to drain.

5 Place the 4 packages in the top of a steamer. Bring water to the boil in the bottom of the steamer. Place the top rack over the water and cover with a tight-fitting lid. Let steam 20 to 25 minutes, or until done. Carefully unwrap each package onto a dinner plate, letting any accumulated liquid flow out. Discard the liquid.

6 Spoon equal portions of the asparagus sauce over each serving. Garnish, if desired, with a fresh herb such as basil leaves or finely chopped parsley or the cooked tips of asparagus spears.

EGYPTIAN KEBABS

4 SERVINGS

2 whole chicken breasts, skinned and boned
1 tablespoon yogurt
¼ teaspoon salt
¼ teaspoon turmeric
⅛ teaspoon dry mustard
½ teaspoon curry powder
⅛ teaspoon ground cardamom
1 teaspoon lemon juice
1 teaspoon vinegar
8 thin onion slices
4 small tomatoes, halved

1 Cut each chicken breast into 16 squares. Combine with the yogurt, salt, turmeric, mustard, curry powder, cardamom, lemon juice and vinegar and let stand ½ hour.

2 Thread on skewers 2 chicken pieces, 1 slice of onion, 2 chicken pieces, ½ tomato. Repeat until all the ingredients are used.

3 Cook slowly, turning occasionally and brushing with the marinade, over hot coals or under the broiler until the chicken is tender, about 10 minutes.

4 Transfer to a hot platter, sprinkle with lemon juice and garnish with fresh tomatoes, green pepper rings and fresh mint or parsley.

DEEP-FRIED CHICKEN WINGS SATAY

4 TO 6 SERVINGS

12 to 18 large, meaty chicken wings
1 tablespoon soy sauce
1 teaspoon sugar
2 teaspoons lemon or lime juice
2 tablespoons curry powder
Satay sauce (see following recipe)
Oil for deep frying

1 Cut each chicken wing into 3 pieces, main wing bone, second joint and wing tip. Discard the tips.

2 Put the wings in a mixing bowl and add the soy sauce, sugar, lemon juice and curry powder. Cover closely and let stand for ½ hour or longer.

3 Meanwhile, prepare the satay sauce and set aside.

4 Heat the oil in a kettle or deep fryer to 360°F. It may be best to cook only half the chicken pieces at a time. Drop them into the deep fat and cook until golden brown and crisp. Remove and drain on paper toweling. Repeat as necessary.

5 Serve hot or cold with satay sauce.

SATAY SAUCE
1¾ CUPS

1 large (about ½ pound) sweet red pepper
1 tablespoon vegetable oil
3 tablespoons thinly sliced shallots
2 tablespoons curry powder or curry paste
1 cup coconut cream (opposite page)
½ cup chunky peanut butter
1 teaspoon sugar

1 Preheat the broiler to high or heat a charcoal grill. Cook the pepper, turning at intervals, so that it chars evenly on all sides. Place the pepper in a brown paper bag and let stand until cool enough to handle. Remove and discard the skin, core and seeds of the pepper. Cut into small cubes.

2 Heat the oil in a small skillet and add the shallots. Cook briefly, stirring, and add the curry powder. Cook briefly, stirring, and add the cubed pepper. Remove from the heat.

3 Bring the coconut cream to the simmer. Pour and scrape the pepper cubes into the cream. Add the peanut butter and sugar and stir. Let simmer about 5 minutes.

4 Pour the mixture into the container of a food processor or blender. Blend thoroughly. Return the mixture to a saucepan and bring to the simmer. The sauce may be thinned if desired with a little water or chicken stock.

HOW TO PREPARE COCONUT MILK AND COCONUT CREAM

Using a hammer or mallet crack a coconut, discarding the liquid. Crack the shell further to produce 4 or 5 large pieces. Place these pieces, shell side down, over a gas, charcoal or electric burner about 1 minute, or until the flesh is easily loosened from the shell. Using a knife or other sharp instrument pry the flesh from the shell. Discard the shell pieces.

Using a swivel-bladed vegetable scraper or paring knife, scrape away the dark outer coating of the flesh, leaving only the white meat. Cut the meat into small pieces. There should be about 3 cups.

Put the coconut meat into the container of a food processor or blender and add 2 cups of hot water. Blend until the meat is finely pulverized.

Line a bowl with a sieve and line the sieve with cheesecloth. Pour in the coconut mixture. Press to extract as much liquid as possible. There should be about 2 cups. The white creamlike substance that rises to the top of the liquid on standing is coconut cream. The bottom layer is coconut milk. Both will last as long as ordinary milk when covered and refrigerated.

♦

BUFFALO CHICKEN WINGS

This curiously compelling dish was first served in a bar in Buffalo and almost overnight gained nationwide popularity. The chicken is served with celery sticks, which are dipped in blue cheese dressing, to counteract the spiciness of the hot sauce.

6 SERVINGS

4 pounds chicken wings
Salt and freshly ground pepper to taste
Oil for deep frying
4 tablespoons butter
3 to 5 tablespoons bottled red hot sauce
1 tablespoon white wine vinegar
2½ cups blue cheese dressing (see following recipe)
Celery sticks

1 Discard the wing tips and cut the chicken wings into 2 pieces at the joint. Sprinkle with salt and pepper.

2 Heat the oil in a wok or deep fryer to 375°F. Add half of the wings and cook, stirring occasionally, about 10 minutes, until crisp and golden. Remove with a slotted spoon and drain well. Repeat with the remaining wings.

3 Melt the butter and add hot sauce to taste and the vinegar. Pour over the chicken wings and serve with blue cheese dressing and celery sticks.

Continued

BLUE CHEESE DRESSING
2½ CUPS

1 cup mayonnaise, preferably homemade
½ cup sour cream
¼ cup crumbled blue cheese
4 tablespoons finely chopped parsley
2 tablespoons chopped onions
1 tablespoon lemon juice
1 tablespoon white wine vinegar
1 teaspoon finely chopped garlic
Salt and freshly ground pepper to taste
Cayenne to taste

Combine all the ingredients and chill until ready to serve.

◆

MADRAS CHICKEN CURRY

4 TO 6 SERVINGS

1 (3- to 3½-pound) chicken
¼ cup flour
Salt and freshly ground pepper to taste
5 tablespoons butter, at room temperature
1½ cups finely chopped onions
1 teaspoon minced garlic
2 tablespoons curry powder
1½ cups chicken stock
2 tablespoons finely chopped chutney
2 tablespoons raisins or dried currants
*8 peppercorns, coarsely but thoroughly
   crushed*
¼ cup blanched almonds
½ cup cream
2 teaspoons sugar
1 tablespoon lime or lemon juice

1 Remove and discard the skin of the chicken. Using a sharp knife, cut the flesh away from the bones. Cut into fairly large bite-size pieces, but use the smaller pieces as well.

2 Dredge the pieces in flour seasoned with salt and pepper and shake off excess.

3 Heat 3 tablespoons of the butter in a skillet and add the chicken pieces. Cook, shaking the pan and stirring, so that the pieces brown evenly. Using a slotted spoon, transfer the pieces to a warm platter.

4 To the butter in which the chicken pieces cooked, add the onions and garlic. Cook, stirring, until wilted. Set aside.

5 Heat 1 tablespoon of butter in a separate skillet and add the curry powder. Cook briefly, stirring, until the curry powder has lost its raw taste, less than a minute. Add the chicken stock, chutney, raisins, peppercorns and salt to taste. Add the chicken pieces and cover. Cook over gentle heat about 20 minutes.

6 Meanwhile, heat 1 tablespoon of butter in a small saucepan or skillet and add the almonds. Cook, stirring, until the almonds are light brown. Put the almonds and cream into the container of a food processor or blender and blend as thoroughly as possible. Pour and scrape this mixture into a small saucepan and cook over gentle heat about 5 minutes. Add this to the chicken. Stir in the sugar. Add and stir in the onion and garlic mixture.

7 Uncover and cook until the sauce has become medium thick. Sprinkle with lime juice.

POULET AU VINAIGRE

One of the recently fashionable dishes in French restaurants is this chicken sauté with vinegar. The chicken is sautéed briefly and a touch of vinegar is added. It is simmered slowly and at the end a bit of tomato, tarragon, parsley and vinegar complete the dish.

4 SERVINGS

1 (3-pound) chicken, cut into serving pieces
Salt and freshly ground pepper to taste
2 tablespoons vegetable oil
½ cup red wine vinegar
¼ cup water
1 teaspoon finely chopped garlic
2 teaspoons tomato paste
1 tablespoon chopped parsley
1 teaspoon chopped tarragon,
    or ½ teaspoon dried

1 Sprinkle the chicken with salt and pepper. Heat the oil in a skillet and add the chicken, skin side down. Brown on one side and turn to brown on the other, about 10 minutes in all.

2 Pour in half the vinegar and the water. Cover and cook over medium heat about 20 minutes. Transfer the chicken to a warm platter.

3 Add the garlic to the skillet and cook about 1 minute. Add the remaining ¼ cup vinegar and boil quickly to reduce, about 1 minute. Add the tomato paste and salt and pepper. Cook just to heat through.

4 Pour the sauce over the chicken and sprinkle with parsley and tarragon. Serve hot.

LEMON CHICKEN SAUTÉ

3 OR 4 SERVINGS

1 (3-pound) frying chicken, cut into
    serving pieces
Salt and freshly ground pepper to taste
2 tablespoons vegetable oil
⅓ cup chopped shallots or onions
¼ cup chopped parsley
½ teaspoon marjoram
⅓ cup lemon juice
Grated rind of 1 lemon

1 Sprinkle the chicken with salt and pepper and brown it on all sides in the hot oil.

2 Sprinkle the pieces with chopped shallots, parsley and marjoram. Pour the lemon juice over, cover the skillet, and simmer for about 15 minutes, until the chicken is tender. Sprinkle grated lemon rind over the chicken and serve hot or cold.

VIVIAN BUCHER'S BSTEEYA

One of the world's finest and most interesting dishes is a great specialty of Morocco, Tunisia and Algeria. The name of the dish is *bsteeya* (sometimes spelled pastilla and bstilla). It is a pigeon pie made with crisp flaky dough and sprinkled, oddly enough, with confectioners' sugar and cinnamon. In North African kitchens the dough is made at home, but the Greek pastry sheets known as phyllo pastry create the same result. Chicken also makes an admirable substitute for pigeon.

6 TO 8 SERVINGS

1 (2½-pound) chicken, cut into serving pieces
Salt and freshly ground pepper to taste
2 tablespoons vegetable oil
3 cups coarsely chopped onions
2 cups water
1 cup finely chopped parsley
1 teaspoon or less thread saffron
3 eggs (about ¾ cup liquid)
12 phyllo pastry sheets
¼ pound butter, melted
½ cup coarsely chopped walnuts
2 tablespoons confectioners' sugar
½ teaspoon cinnamon

1 It is essential that the filling for this pie be prepared 1 day in advance or overnight.

2 Sprinkle the chicken pieces with salt and pepper. Heat the oil in a kettle and brown the pieces on all sides. Transfer the pieces to a bowl.

3 To the oil remaining in the kettle, add the onions and cook, stirring, until they become translucent. Add water, parsley and saffron and stir to dissolve the brown particles that cling to the bottom and sides of the kettle. Cover closely and let simmer 1 hour. Let cool.

4 Beat the eggs thoroughly and pour them into the cooled liquid, blending well. Cook over low heat, stirring constantly over the bottom with a wooden spoon. When ready, the mixture will have the consistency of a fairly thick custard. The cooking time will be from 15 to 20 minutes.

5 Remove the flesh and skin from the chicken bones and shred it. Add this to the sauce. Pour the mixture into a bowl and refrigerate overnight. The sauce will be easier to handle once it is chilled and slightly congealed.

6 Preheat the oven to 400°F.

7 Brush a 12-inch round pizza pan or other dish with a small amount of butter. Line the dish with 2 sheets of phyllo pastry and cover with another layer of 2 sheets; the pastry sheets should overlap the rim of the dish. Brush the surface of each sheet with melted butter. Repeat with 2 more sheets of pastry, brushing them with butter. Spoon the filling into the dish and smooth it over. Cover with 2 more sheets of phyllo brushed with butter. Sprinkle the walnuts over the phyllo and cover with 2 sheets of pastry, brushed with butter. Blend the sugar with cinnamon and sprinkle it as evenly as possible over the phyllo. Cover with 2 final sheets of pastry, brushed with butter. Bring up and fold over the pastry sheets to enclose the filling completely. Brush with butter.

8 Place the dish in the oven and bake 45 minutes. Cut into wedges and serve hot.

MOROCCAN-STYLE CHICKEN

4 SERVINGS

1 lemon
1 (3-pound) frying chicken, cut into
  serving pieces
Salt and freshly ground pepper to taste
2 tablespoons butter
2 tablespoons olive oil
2 shallots or scallions, finely chopped
½ teaspoon minced garlic
¾ cup chicken stock
¼ cup chopped parsley
1 teaspoon oregano

1 With a swivel-bladed vegetable scraper pare away half the lemon rind and cut it into very thin strips. Reserve. Squeeze the lemon and reserve the juice.

2 Sprinkle the chicken parts with salt and pepper. Heat the butter and the oil in a skillet. Brown the chicken pieces in it on all sides and transfer them to a warm plate.

3 Add the shallots and garlic to the skillet in which the chicken was browned. Cook, stirring, until golden. Add the stock and stir to dissolve all brown particles clinging to the bottom and sides of the skillet. Cook until the liquid is reduced by half.

4 Return the chicken to the skillet and sprinkle with the parsley, oregano, lemon rind and lemon juice. Cover and cook slowly for about 30 minutes, until the chicken is tender.

CHICKEN CACCIATORE

4 SERVINGS

1 (2½- to 3½-pound) chicken, cut into
  serving pieces
Salt and freshly ground pepper to taste
5 tablespoons butter
3 tablespoons olive oil
¼ pound sliced prosciutto, cut into bite-size
  pieces
1 tablespoon fresh or dried leaf sage (preferably
  with stems)
¾ cup dry white wine

1 Sprinkle the chicken pieces with salt and pepper.

2 Heat 3 tablespoons of the butter and the oil in a large skillet and cook the chicken pieces until golden brown all over. Pour off most of the fat from the skillet and add the prosciutto, sage and wine. Cover and cook until tender, about 20 minutes. Remove the chicken to a hot platter.

3 Bring the pan juices to a boil, then remove the skillet from the heat. Swirl in the remaining butter by rotating the pan gently and serve the sauce separately.

STEWED CHICKEN WITH PARSLEY DUMPLINGS

6 SERVINGS

1 (4-pound) stewing fowl, cut into pieces
Salt
10 peppercorns, bruised
1 celery stalk, with leaves
1 medium onion, peeled
1 carrot, scraped
1/2 bay leaf
Parsley dumplings (see following recipe)
3 tablespoons flour, approximately

1 Rinse the chicken pieces under cold running water. Place in a heavy kettle or Dutch oven and barely cover with water. Sprinkle with a little salt and the peppercorns.

2 Add the celery, onion, carrot and bay leaf and cover. Bring to a boil, reduce the heat and simmer gently until the chicken meat begins to loosen from the bones, 2 to 3 hours.

3 Drop the dumpling dough from a wet tablespoon onto the boiling stew, letting the dumplings rest on the meat. Cover tightly, reduce the heat and cook, without raising the cover, 15 minutes.

4 Transfer the dumplings to a hot platter and thicken the stew with flour mixed with water. Serve immediately, using the dumplings as a border around the chicken.

PARSLEY DUMPLINGS
12 DUMPLINGS

1 1/2 cups flour
2 teaspoons baking powder
3/4 teaspoon salt
2 tablespoons chopped parsley
1/2 teaspoon crushed rosemary
3 tablespoons vegetable shortening
3/4 cup milk, approximately

1 Sift together the flour, baking powder and salt. Add the parsley and rosemary and mix.

2 Chop in the shortening until the mixture resembles coarse cornmeal. Add enough milk to make a thick batter that can be mounded up in a spoon and dropped.

♦

CHICKEN PAPRIKASH

Chicken paprikash is best when made with genuine Hungarian rose paprika.

4 SERVINGS

2 tablespoons butter
1/2 cup chopped onions
1 garlic clove, minced
1 1/2 tablespoons paprika
1 teaspoon salt
1 tomato, peeled and chopped
1 green pepper, seeded and chopped
3/4 cup chicken stock
1 (3-pound) broiler-fryer chicken,
    cut into pieces
1/4 cup flour
1/4 cup half-and-half
1/2 cup sour cream

1 In a heavy kettle heat the butter, add the onions and garlic and sauté until light brown. Add the paprika, salt, tomato, green pepper and stock. Cover and cook 10 minutes.

2 Add the chicken, cover and cook until tender, about 40 minutes. Remove the skin from the chicken breast and thighs and return the meat to the kettle. Add water or additional chicken stock, if necessary, to make 1¼ cups broth.

3 Add the flour blended with the half-and-half and a little of the hot sauce and cook, stirring, until thickened.

4 Add the sour cream and cook until heated through. Do not let boil. Serve over noodles or rice.

♦

POULE AU POT

French cookery is celebrated for its elaborate creations, but equally famous is the bourgeois dish, the *poule au pot*, or "chicken in a pot." In the French provinces it is a traditional Sunday dinner dish that is as nourishing as it is delicious.

6 TO 8 SERVINGS

4 pounds of beef (brisket, rump, shin, plate, chuck or round)
2 onions, each stuck with 1 whole clove
2 celery stalks
14 leeks, well washed
12 carrots, scraped and cut into thirds
4 parsley sprigs
1 bay leaf
¼ teaspoon thyme
2 garlic cloves
12 peppercorns
Salt
1 (5-pound) roasting chicken, stuffed and trussed
6 to 8 potatoes, peeled and halved
12 small white turnips, peeled
Sauce gribiche (page 558)

1 Place the beef in a heavy kettle and add water to cover by 3 inches. Add the onions, celery, 2 of the leeks and 2 of the carrots. Tie the parsley, bay leaf, thyme, garlic and peppercorns in a piece of cheesecloth and add it to the kettle. Add about 1 tablespoon of salt. Bring the mixture to a boil, skimming frequently. Reduce the heat and simmer, covered, for 3 to 4 hours, depending on the cut of beef.

2 Wash the chicken and dry thoroughly. Sprinkle inside with salt and pepper. Stuff the bird with sausage stuffing for chicken (page 190) or with any flavorful stuffing. Sew the openings tight and truss the bird.

3 About 1½ hours before the beef is done, remove it from the kettle. Strain the broth and discard the cooked vegetables and the spice bag. Return broth and meat to the kettle. Add the chicken, cover, bring to a boil and simmer for 1 hour.

4 Tie the remaining carrots and leeks in bundles to help retain their shape. Add them to the kettle with the potatoes and turnips. Adjust the seasoning if necessary. Continue to cook for 30 minutes longer, until the chicken and beef are cooked and the vegetables tender but not mushy.

5 Slice the beef and carve the chicken. Arrange the meats on a large platter and surround them with the vegetables in neat piles. Serve with sauce gribiche.

Note: If desired, the broth may be served as soup at the same meal. If not, save it for other uses as it will be a rich and flavorful stock.

CHICKEN-OKRA GUMBO

8 TO 10 SERVINGS

2 tablespoons butter
1 (3- to 3½-pound) chicken, cut into pieces
1½ to 2 pounds ham slices, cut into
    1-inch cubes
1 onion, chopped
1 hot red pepper, seeded
1 thyme or parsley sprig, chopped
6 large tomatoes, peeled and chopped
1 pound okra, sliced
3 quarts boiling water
1 bay leaf
Salt and cayenne to taste

1 Heat the butter in a heavy kettle or Dutch oven, add the chicken and ham and cook, covered, about 5 minutes.

2 Add the onion, red pepper, thyme and solid part of the tomatoes, reserving the juice. Simmer a few minutes, stirring often.

3 Add the okra and simmer, stirring, until brown.

4 Add the reserved tomato juice, the boiling water and bay leaf. Season with salt and cayenne and simmer, covered, about 1 hour. Serve with rice.

Escarole Chicken Soup, page 91.
Cock-a-Leekie, page 92.

BRUNSWICK STEW

This dish, which comes from Brunswick County, Virginia, was originally made with squirrel, but chicken makes a practical and delicious substitute.

4 TO 6 SERVINGS

1 (4-pound) chicken, cut into serving pieces
2 teaspoons salt
Paprika to taste
2 tablespoons vegetable oil
2 medium onions, sliced
1 medium green pepper, diced
3 cups water
2 cups canned tomatoes, undrained
2 tablespoons chopped parsley
½ teaspoon Tabasco sauce
1 tablespoon Worcestershire sauce
2 cups whole-kernel corn
2 cups lima beans
1 pound potatoes, peeled and quartered

1 Sprinkle the chicken with 1 teaspoon of the salt and paprika.

2 Heat the oil in a deep kettle and brown the chicken on all sides. Add the onions and green pepper and cook until the onions are transparent.

3 Add the water, the tomatoes with their liquid, the parsley, remaining salt, the Tabasco and Worcestershire and bring to a boil. Cover, reduce the heat and simmer for 30 minutes.

4 Add the corn and lima beans and cook 20 minutes longer.

5 Meanwhile, cook the potatoes until tender and put through a food mill or ricer. Add the mashed potatoes to the kettle and stir. Cook 10 minutes longer.

6 Serve in flat soup plates, with hot rice if desired.

CHICKEN SAUTÉ CHASSEUR

4 SERVINGS

1 (2½- to 3-pound) frying chicken,
    cut into pieces
Flour for dredging
Salt and freshly ground pepper to taste
Thyme to taste
2 tablespoons vegetable oil
¼ cup chopped shallots or onions
¼ pound mushrooms, chopped
½ cup white wine
¾ cup canned tomatoes
2 tablespoons chopped parsley
1 teaspoon chopped tarragon,
    or ¼ teaspoon dried

1 Dredge the chicken in the flour seasoned with the salt, pepper and thyme. In a large skillet heat the oil, add the chicken and brown on all sides.

2 Add the shallots and mushrooms and cook briefly. Add the wine, tomatoes and herbs. Cover and cook slowly until the chicken is tender, 30 to 45 minutes.

POULET MARENGO

Poulet Marengo, like chicken chasseur, contains tomatoes and mushrooms. This dish, according to *Larousse Gastronomique*, was created by Napoleon's chef after the battle of Marengo. The original creation was garnished with crawfish and fried eggs.

6 SERVINGS

½ cup flour
1 teaspoon salt
½ teaspoon freshly ground pepper
1 teaspoon tarragon
1 (3-pound) roasting chicken, cut into pieces
¼ cup olive oil
4 tablespoons butter
1 cup dry white wine
2 cups canned tomatoes
1 garlic clove, finely chopped
8 mushrooms, sliced
Chopped parsley

1 Preheat the oven to 350°F.

2 Mix the flour, salt, pepper and tarragon and dredge the chicken in the seasoned flour. Reserve the remaining flour.

3 In a large skillet heat the olive oil and butter, add the chicken and brown on all sides.

4 Remove the chicken to a heavy casserole. Add the reserved flour to the fat remaining in the skillet and, using a wire whisk, gradually stir in the wine. When the sauce is thickened and smooth, pour over the chicken and add the tomatoes, garlic and mushrooms. Cover the casserole with a heavy lid and bake until the chicken is tender, about 45 minutes. Before serving, sprinkle with chopped parsley.

CHICKEN VALLE D'AUGE

4 SERVINGS

2 tablespoons butter
2 tablespoons vegetable oil
2 small broiling chickens, quartered
¼ cup warmed Calvados (or other
    apple brandy)
2 small white onions, minced
1 tablespoon minced parsley
Pinch of thyme
Salt and freshly ground pepper to taste
6 tablespoons cider
6 tablespoons cream

1 In a large skillet heat the butter and oil, add the chicken and brown on all sides. Continue cooking, uncovered, 20 minutes. Add the Calvados and ignite. When the flame has subsided, add the onions, parsley, thyme, salt, pepper and cider. Cover tightly and cook over low heat until the chicken is tender, about 20 minutes.

2 Remove the chicken to a warm platter and keep hot. Slowly stir the cream into the pan and heat thoroughly, but do not boil. Correct the seasonings. Pour some of the sauce over the chicken and serve the remainder separately.

CHICKEN IN SAFFRON CREAM SAUCE

4 SERVINGS

1 (3½-pound) frying chicken
Salt and freshly ground pepper to taste
3 tablespoons butter
¼ teaspoon thyme
½ bay leaf
½ teaspoon thread saffron
1 cup cream
2 teaspoons tomato paste

1 Season the chicken with salt and pepper and brown it on all sides in butter. Sprinkle with thyme and add the bay leaf, saffron and cream. Stir in the tomato paste until smooth.

2 Cover the skillet and simmer for 25 to 30 minutes, or until chicken is tender. Taste the sauce for seasoning and add more salt and pepper if necessary.

CHICKEN WITH ALMONDS

4 SERVINGS

2 tablespoons butter
2 tablespoons vegetable oil
1 (2½- to 3-pound) frying chicken, cut into
  serving pieces
1 garlic clove, chopped
2 tablespoons chopped onions
1 tablespoon tomato paste
2 tablespoons flour
1½ cups chicken stock
2 tablespoons sherry
2 tablespoons slivered almonds
Salt and freshly ground pepper to taste
1 teaspoon tarragon
¾ cup sour cream
1 tablespoon grated Parmesan cheese

1 In a skillet heat the butter and oil, add the chicken and brown on all sides. Remove the chicken and keep hot. To the pan add the garlic and onions and cook over low heat 3 minutes. Add the tomato paste and flour and stir with a wire whisk until the mixture is smooth.

2 Stir in the stock and sherry. When the mixture returns to a boil return the chicken to the pan and add the almonds, salt, pepper and tarragon. Cover and simmer slowly 45 to 50 minutes.

3 Transfer the chicken to a shallow casserole. Stir the sour cream into the sauce remaining in the pan and heat thoroughly. Do not boil. Pour the sauce over the chicken and sprinkle with the cheese. Brown lightly under a preheated broiler.

COUNTRY CAPTAIN

Country Captain sounds as though it originated in the southern United States. It is, according to authoritative sources, a dish from India, and the word *captain* is a corruption of *capon*.

4 SERVINGS

1 (2½-pound) frying chicken, cut into
  serving pieces
¼ cup flour
1 teaspoon salt
¼ teaspoon freshly ground pepper
2 tablespoons vegetable oil
⅓ cup finely diced onions
⅓ cup finely diced green peppers
1 garlic clove, crushed
1½ teaspoons curry powder
½ teaspoon thyme
2 cups canned stewed tomatoes
3 tablespoons dried currants, washed
  and drained
Blanched toasted almonds
Chutney

1 Dredge the chicken pieces in the flour seasoned with the salt and pepper.

2 Heat the oil in a large skillet and brown the chicken parts on all sides. Remove the chicken from the skillet and add the onions, green peppers, garlic, curry powder and thyme. Cook briefly, stirring, until the onions wilt. Add the tomatoes with the liquid from the can. Return the chicken to the skillet, skin side up. Cover and cook until tender, 20 to 30 minutes. Stir the currants into the sauce.

3 Serve with blanched toasted almonds and chutney.

CHICKEN IN PARMESAN CREAM SAUCE

One of the simplest and most flavorful of cheeses is that from the region around Parma. Known as *Parmesan*, it should be freshly grated —either by hand or in a food processor.

4 TO 6 SERVINGS

1 (3-pound) frying chicken, cut into
    serving pieces
Salt and freshly ground pepper to taste
2 tablespoons vegetable oil
2 tablespoons butter
2 tablespoons flour
¾ cup half-and-half
½ cup grated Parmesan cheese
3 egg yolks, beaten
½ cup fresh bread crumbs

1 Season the chicken with salt and pepper. In a skillet heat the oil, add the chicken pieces, skin side down, and cook until brown. Turn the pieces, partly cover the skillet and cook until the chicken is tender, about 30 minutes.

2 Preheat the oven to 350°F.

3 In a saucepan, melt the butter, add the flour and stir with a wire whisk until blended. Bring the half-and-half to a boil and add all at once to the butter-flour mixture, stirring vigorously with the whisk until the sauce is thickened and smooth. Stir in 1 tablespoon of the cheese. When it has melted, stir in the egg yolks lightly beaten with a little of the hot sauce.

4 Sprinkle the bottom of a flat casserole with ¼ cup of the cheese, arrange the chicken on the cheese and spoon the sauce over the top. Place the casserole in the oven and bake 5 minutes, or until thoroughly heated.

5 Combine the remaining cheese with the crumbs, sprinkle over the chicken and broil until golden brown.

Chicken Corn Soup, page 90.
Chicken Loaf Nivernaise, page 118.
Pastel de Choclo, page 294.

◆

COQ AU VIN

4 SERVINGS

1 (3½-pound) frying chicken or 2 (2-pound)
    broilers
Salt and freshly ground pepper to taste
½ cup diced salt pork
2 tablespoons butter
½ pound small onions
½ pound mushrooms
2 to 3 chopped shallots, or ½ cup
    chopped scallions
1 garlic clove, minced
2 tablespoons flour
2 cups dry red wine
3 parsley sprigs
½ bay leaf
⅛ teaspoon thyme
2 tablespoons chopped parsley

1 Cut the fryers into quarters, or the broilers into halves, and season with salt and pepper.

2 Parboil the salt pork 5 minutes, drain and sauté in the butter until brown. Remove pork and reserve. Sauté the chicken in the fat left in the pan until brown on all sides.

3 Add the onions and mushrooms. Cover pan and cook slowly until the onions are partly tender and beginning to brown. Remove the chicken to a hot platter. Pour off all but 2 or 3 tablespoons of the fat. Add the shallots and garlic and cook 1 minute. Blend in the flour. Add the wine and cook, stirring, until boiling.

4 Return the chicken to the pan. If the wine does not cover the meat, add water. Tie parsley sprigs, bay leaf and thyme in cheesecloth and add to the chicken. Add reserved diced pork.

5 Simmer on top of the stove or cook, covered, in a 400°F oven until the chicken is tender, 30 minutes or longer. Remove the herb bag and skim the fat from the surface. Arrange the chicken, onions and mushrooms on a platter, cover with sauce and sprinkle with chopped parsley.

PORTUGUESE CHICKEN

4 SERVINGS

3 tablespoons vegetable oil
1 (2-pound) frying chicken, cut into pieces
1 tablespoon chopped onions
1 tablespoon flour
1 garlic clove, finely chopped
¼ cup dry white wine or water
½ cup chicken stock
½ cup canned tomatoes, drained
Salt and freshly ground pepper to taste
2 fresh tomatoes, peeled and chopped
Chopped parsley

1 In a large skillet heat the oil, add the chicken and brown on all sides. Remove chicken and keep hot.

2 Add the onions to the skillet and cook slowly, stirring occasionally, 3 to 4 minutes. Add the flour and garlic and, stirring with a wire whisk, add the wine and stock and cook until the mixture is thickened and smooth.

3 Add the canned tomatoes, salt and pepper. Return the chicken to the skillet, cover and simmer until tender, about 30 minutes.

4 Remove the chicken from the skillet to a warm serving platter and keep hot. Add the fresh tomatoes to the skillet and simmer 15 minutes. Pour the sauce over the chicken and serve sprinkled with chopped parsley.

ARROZ CON POLLO

Arroz con pollo is "chicken with rice."

6 TO 8 SERVINGS

1 (4-pound) frying chicken, cut into
   serving pieces
1¼ teaspoons salt
½ teaspoon pepper
⅛ teaspoon paprika
¼ cup olive oil
1 garlic clove, minced
1 medium onion, chopped
2 cups chicken stock
3½ cups canned whole tomatoes
½ teaspoon oregano
½ teaspoon thread saffron
1 bay leaf
2 cups rice
1 package frozen peas or artichoke hearts,
   defrosted
3 pimientos, cut into pieces

  1 Preheat the oven to 350°F.

  2 Season the chicken with 1 teaspoon of the salt, the pepper and paprika. In a skillet heat the oil, add the chicken and brown on all sides. Remove to a baking dish.

  3 To the skillet add the garlic and onions and sauté until the onions are tender. Add the stock and heat while scraping loose any brown particles that are stuck to the bottom and sides of the skillet. Add the tomatoes and their liquid, seasonings and remaining salt. Bring to a boil and pour over the chicken. Add the rice and stir. Cover tightly.

  4 Bake 25 minutes. Uncover and toss the rice. Stir in the peas, arrange the pimientos on top, cover and cook 10 minutes longer.

Senegalese Soup, page 92.

MIZUTAKI

Undoubtedly the most popular of all Japanese dishes in America is sukiyaki. Equally delicious in its own way is a simmered chicken dish known as mizutaki. To prepare it, uncooked chicken is cut into bite-size pieces and simmered in chicken stock. Vegetables are added and everything is served piping hot with chopsticks and a soy and lemon sauce. A word of warning: The dish must be eaten with chopsticks or it loses character.

2 TO 4 SERVINGS

1 (3-pound) broiler-fryer chicken
Chicken stock or water to cover
Salt to taste
6 scallions, cut into 1-inch lengths
1 medium onion, peeled and sliced thin
1 bunch watercress, trimmed
¼ cup lemon juice
¼ cup light soy sauce
¼ cup Japanese wine (sake)

  1 Have the butcher divide the chicken in half and cut or chop both halves into 1½-inch cubes with the bones.

  2 Place the pieces in a heavy saucepan and cover with chicken stock or water. Add a little salt and simmer gently, uncovered, 45 minutes after the boiling point is reached.

  3 Bring to the table in the cooking utensil and place over a charcoal or alcohol burner so that the liquid barely boils.

  4 When the guests are seated, commence adding the vegetables to the simmering broth, a few at a time. To serve, spoon a few portions of the meat and barely cooked vegetables into small serving bowls. Using chopsticks, guests dip bite-size pieces of chicken into a sauce made by combining the lemon juice, soy sauce and sake.

CHICKEN AND KIDNEY BEAN CASSEROLE

10 SERVINGS

1 pound dried red kidney beans
6 cups cold water
1 teaspoon salt
2 (3½-pound) frying chickens, cut into
    serving pieces
¼ teaspoon freshly ground pepper
¼ cup vegetable oil
1 onion, sliced
2 garlic cloves, minced
3 canned green chilies, chopped
1 cup tomato sauce
1 bay leaf
¼ teaspoon thyme
Chicken stock

1 Pick over the beans, wash thoroughly, and cover with the water. Allow to soak overnight; or see quick-soaking method (page 78).

2 Add ½ teaspoon of the salt, bring to a boil, cover, and simmer for about 1½ hours, or until the beans are tender. Drain and reserve the liquid.

3 While the beans are cooking, season the chicken pieces with the remaining salt and the pepper and brown on all sides in the oil in a heavy skillet. Transfer to a large heavy casserole or Dutch oven.

4 Sauté the onion and garlic in the oil remaining in the skillet until soft but not brown. Add the chilies, tomato sauce, bay leaf and thyme. Stir to loosen the brown pieces adhering to the pan. Pour over the chicken and add the drained beans. Measure the reserved bean liquid and add enough chicken stock to measure 2 cups.

Add to the casserole. Cover, bring to a boil, and simmer gently for about 45 minutes, or until chicken is tender. Any excess liquid may be removed by boiling rapidly with the cover off or may be absorbed by mashing some of the beans.

♦

MEXICAN CHICKEN

6 OR MORE SERVINGS

4 tablespoons butter
4 medium onions, chopped
4 green peppers, seeded and chopped
¼ cup flour
2 cups chicken stock
4 cups stewed tomatoes, undrained
2 cups pitted ripe olives
2 cups whole-kernel corn, frozen, canned or
    cut from the cob
3 cups diced poached chicken (page 133)
6 slices bacon

1 In a skillet heat the butter, add the onions and green peppers and cook until the vegetables are wilted. With a wire whisk stir in the flour, add the chicken stock, tomatoes and olives and cook, stirring, until thickened and smooth.

2 Preheat the oven to 400°F.

3 Place a layer of corn in a buttered baking dish, add a layer of chicken and a layer of the tomato mixture. Repeat the process until all the ingredients are used, ending with a layer of corn.

4 Place bacon on the top and bake until the bacon is crisp, about 20 minutes.

CHICKEN TAMALE PIE

4 TO 6 SERVINGS

2 cups chicken stock
½ cup yellow cornmeal
2 tablespoons butter
¼ cup chopped onions
1 garlic clove, finely chopped
2 ripe tomatoes, peeled and chopped
¼ teaspoon oregano
¼ teaspoon thyme
¼ teaspoon tarragon
Chili powder to taste
1½ cups whole-kernel corn, fresh,
    frozen or canned
Salt to taste
3 cups diced poached chicken (page 133)
½ cup grated Monterey Jack or cheddar cheese

1 In a saucepan bring 1½ cups of the stock to a boil. Combine the cornmeal with the remaining broth, stir into the boiling stock, cover and cook until the mixture thickens, 10 to 15 minutes.

2 Preheat the oven to 350°F. Cool the mush slightly and use to line the bottom and sides of a 2½-quart casserole.

3 Meanwhile, melt the butter and cook the onions and garlic in it until the onions are transparent. Add the tomatoes and seasonings and simmer 15 minutes. Add the corn and salt.

4 Spread the chicken over the center of the mush-lined casserole and cover with the tomato and corn mixture. Sprinkle with cheese and bake 30 minutes.

POLLO EN SALSA TONNATO
CHICKEN IN TUNA SAUCE

6 SERVINGS

4 large chicken breasts, halved and skinned
1¼ cups dry white wine
1 onion, finely chopped
1 garlic clove, finely minced
1 (7-ounce) can tuna fish
6 anchovy fillets, chopped
½ teaspoon salt
¼ teaspoon freshly ground black pepper
1 teaspoon grated lemon rind
¼ cup olive oil
3 tablespoons lemon juice
4 cups cooked white rice, at room temperature
3 tablespoons chopped parsley
Capers

1 Combine the chicken with the wine, onion, garlic, tuna, anchovies, salt, pepper and lemon rind in a heavy saucepan. Cover, bring to a boil, and simmer gently for 25 minutes, or until chicken is tender.

2 Transfer the chicken to a bowl. Put the sauce in which the chicken was cooked into the container of a food processor and purée it. Add the oil and lemon juice, and pour over chicken. Cover and let stand until ready to serve.

3 Spread the rice on a serving platter. Slice the chicken into large oval pieces, discarding the bones. Place chicken atop rice. Add parsley to the sauce, pour over chicken and rice, and sprinkle with capers.

CHICKEN DIVAN

This rich dish is said to have originated many years ago in a New York restaurant, the Divan Parisien. It is poached chicken on broccoli with a hollandaise sauce. Turkey may be substituted for the chicken.

6 SERVINGS

1 (5-pound) stewing chicken
2 teaspoons salt
4 tablespoons butter
3 tablespoons flour
2 cups milk
½ teaspoon grated nutmeg
1 large bunch broccoli
1 cup grated Parmesan cheese, approximately
½ cup hollandaise sauce (page 554)
½ cup heavy cream, whipped
3 tablespoons sherry
1 teaspoon Worcestershire sauce

1 Place the chicken on a rack in a large kettle. Add about 5 cups boiling water and the salt. Bring to a boil, lower the heat, cover and simmer until tender, about 3 hours. Cool the chicken in the broth.

2 Meanwhile, make a white sauce: In a saucepan melt the butter, add the flour and stir with a wire whisk until blended. Bring the milk to a boil and add all at once to the butter-flour mixture, stirring vigorously with the whisk until the sauce is thickened and smooth. Stir in the nutmeg. Keep hot.

3 When the chicken has cooled, remove the skin and slice the breast and leg meat. Reserve the remainder of the chicken for another purpose.

4 Cook the broccoli in salted water until tender, drain and arrange on a deep heatproof serving platter. Sprinkle lightly with some of the cheese. Arrange the chicken meat on the broccoli.

5 Combine the hollandaise sauce with the white sauce. Add the whipped cream, sherry and Worcestershire sauce. Pour the sauce over the chicken and broccoli and sprinkle with the remaining cheese.

6 Place about 5 inches below high heat in a preheated broiler and broil until brown and bubbly.

◆

CHICKEN NEWBURG

How often has the story been told about Mr. Wenburg who was much admired by a chef? A lobster dish was named after Mr. Wenburg but he had a falling-out with the chef and the dish became forevermore *newburg*. Here is a similar dish made with chicken.

4 SERVINGS

2 tablespoons butter
¼ cup sliced mushrooms
2 cups cubed, cooked chicken (pieces should be fairly large)
¼ cup dry sherry
¼ teaspoon salt
Dash of white pepper
1 cup half-and-half
3 egg yolks
Hot cooked fluffy rice or noodles
Paprika

1 In a skillet heat the butter, add the mushrooms and cook until almost tender. Add the chicken, half the sherry, the salt and pepper and cook slowly until the mushrooms are tender.

2 Transfer the mixture to the top of a double boiler, add the half-and-half and heat thoroughly over boiling water.

3 Add the remaining sherry and the egg yolks lightly beaten with a little of the hot sauce. Cook, stirring, until thickened. Correct the seasonings. Serve on rice or noodles and sprinkle with paprika.

SCALLOPED CHICKEN

4 SERVINGS

2¼ cups chicken stock
6 tablespoons butter
1 tablespoon chopped onions
⅓ cup rice
¼ pound mushrooms, sliced
3 tablespoons flour
½ cup cream
¼ teaspoon salt
⅛ teaspoon freshly ground pepper
¼ teaspoon thyme
2 cups diced cooked chicken, or turkey
¼ cup chopped pimiento
¼ cup sliced pitted ripe olives
⅓ cup buttered soft fresh bread crumbs

1 Preheat the oven to 350°F.
2 Place ¾ cup of the stock, 1 tablespoon of the butter, the onions, and the rice in a small pan. Cover and bring to a boil. Reduce the heat and simmer gently for about 15 minutes, or until the liquid has been absorbed and the rice is tender. Add ½ cup additional stock. Set rice aside, covered.
3 Sauté the sliced mushrooms in 2 tablespoons of the butter and add to rice.
4 Melt the remaining 3 tablespoons butter and blend in the flour. Stir in remaining stock and the cream. Bring to a boil, stirring, and cook for 2 minutes. Add the salt, pepper, thyme, chicken, pimiento and olives. Mix well.
5 Alternate layers of the chicken mixture with the rice mixture in a buttered 1½-quart casserole, ending with the chicken mixture. Top with buttered crumbs and bake for about 30 minutes, or until hot, bubbly and light brown.

CHICKEN TETRAZZINI

Luisa Tetrazzini, the coloratura soprano, was distinctly Italian. This dish, named for her, is quite good but distinctly American.

6 SERVINGS

1 (5-pound) stewing chicken, cut into
    serving pieces
1 onion studded with 2 cloves
2 celery stalks with leaves
Salt
½ bay leaf
1 carrot
3 cups water
7½ tablespoons butter
¼ cup flour
Tabasco sauce to taste
½ pound mushrooms, sliced
1 egg yolk, lightly beaten
1 tablespoon dry sherry
3 tablespoons half-and-half
½ pound spaghetti
2 tablespoons grated Parmesan cheese
Toasted almonds (optional)

1 In a heavy kettle place the chicken, onion, celery, 1 tablespoon salt, the bay leaf, carrot and water. Bring to a boil, reduce the heat and simmer, covered, until the chicken is tender, 3 to 4 hours. Remove the chicken from the broth and let cool. Remove the meat from the bones, discarding skin and bones.
2 Skim the fat from the top of the broth and discard. Place 4 tablespoons of the butter in a saucepan. Add the flour and salt to taste, stirring with a wire whisk until blended. Meanwhile, bring 2 cups of the strained chicken broth to a boil and add all at once to the butter-flour mixture, stirring vigorously with the whisk until the sauce is thickened and smooth. Season with Tabasco.

3 In a skillet heat 3 tablespoons of the remaining butter, add the mushrooms and cook until brown.

4 To the sauce add the egg yolk lightly beaten with a little of the hot sauce and stir in the sherry, half-and-half, chicken and mushrooms. Cook, stirring, until heated through. Do not let boil.

5 Cook the spaghetti according to package directions. Place alternate layers of spaghetti and sauce in a buttered casserole, sprinkle with grated Parmesan cheese and dot with approximately 1 teaspoon butter. Brown quickly in a preheated broiler and serve with toasted almonds, if desired.

Chicken Mousse, page 117.
Chicken and Spinach Crêpes, page 123.

CHICKEN CROQUETTES

9 OR 10 CROQUETTES

3 tablespoons butter
⅓ cup flour
1 cup milk
1½ cups minced cooked chicken
1 tablespoon minced onion
2 tablespoons chopped parsley
2 eggs
2 tablespoons sherry
Salt and freshly ground pepper to taste
1 tablespoon water
Sifted fine dry bread crumbs
Oil for deep frying
Onion-pimiento sauce (page 567), or sauce poulette (page 566)

1 Melt the butter, blend in the flour, and add the milk. Cook, stirring with a wire whisk, until the mixture boils and thickens.

2 Add the chicken, onion, parsley, 1 egg, the sherry, salt and pepper. Cook, stirring, until thickened. Chill.

3 Use ¼ cup of the mixture to shape a croquette—cone, cylinder or as desired. Continue until all the mixture is used. Beat remaining egg lightly with the water. Coat the croquettes with crumbs, then with beaten egg, and again with crumbs. Dry on a rack for 30 minutes.

4 Fry in oil heated to 380°F. Drain on paper toweling. Serve with onion-pimiento sauce or sauce poulette.

CHICKEN BURGERS

4 SERVINGS

1½ pounds skinless, boneless chicken breasts
⅛ teaspoon grated nutmeg
⅓ cup finely chopped parsley
Salt and freshly ground pepper to taste
¾ cup fine, fresh bread crumbs
3 tablespoons chicken stock
3 tablespoons vegetable oil

1 Using a small sharp knife, cut away and discard any pieces of fat, nerve fibers and cartilage from the chicken pieces. Cut the chicken into 1-inch cubes.

2 Put the cubes into the container of a food processor and blend. The meat should be coarse-fine without becoming a paste.

3 Scrape the chicken into a mixing bowl and add the nutmeg, parsley, salt, pepper, crumbs and stock. Blend thoroughly with the fingers. Chill the mixture.

4 Divide mixture into 8 portions of equal weight. Using moistened hands, flatten each portion into a round patty.

5 Heat the oil in a nonstick skillet and cook the patties about 4 minutes on one side. Turn the patties and cook 4 to 5 minutes on the other side.

CHICKEN HASH

6 SERVINGS

1 (3½-pound) chicken
Salt to taste
12 peppercorns
¾ cup coarsely chopped onions
½ cup coarsely chopped celery
½ cup coarsely chopped carrots
1 bay leaf
½ teaspoon thyme
6 parsley sprigs
6 ounces mushrooms
5 tablespoons butter
5 tablespoons flour
3 cups chicken stock
¼ cup finely chopped shallots
¼ cup dry sherry
½ cup cream
⅛ teaspoon cayenne
¼ teaspoon grated nutmeg
1 egg yolk
3 tablespoons grated Gruyère cheese

1 Put the chicken in a kettle and add water to cover and salt.

2 Add the peppercorns, onions, celery, carrots, bay leaf, thyme and parsley. Bring to the boil and let simmer uncovered about 45 minutes, or until tender.

3 Remove the chicken and let cool. Strain the stock and set aside.

4 Rinse the mushrooms and pat dry. Cut them into ½-inch cubes. There should be about 2 cups.

5 Heat 4 tablespoons of the butter in a saucepan and add the flour, stirring with a wire whisk. Add the stock, stirring rapidly with the whisk.

6 Heat the remaining 1 tablespoon of butter in a saucepan and add the shallots. Cook briefly, stirring, and add the mushrooms. Cook, stirring often, about 5 minutes. Add the sherry and cook, stirring, until the liquid has almost evaporated.

Add the white sauce and stir to blend. Add the cream and stir, cooking briefly. Add the cayenne, nutmeg and the egg yolk, stirring rapidly to prevent curdling.

7 Meanwhile, remove and discard the skin and fat of the chicken. Cut the flesh into 1-inch cubes or slightly smaller. There should be 3 to 3½ cups. Add this to the sauce and stir to blend.

8 Preheat the broiler.

9 Spoon and scrape the mixture into a baking dish and smooth over the top. Sprinkle evenly with cheese and place under the broiler. Broil about 5 minutes, or until nicely glazed on top.

♦

CHICKEN LIVERS MARSALA

4 SERVINGS

1 pound chicken livers
2 tablespoons butter
½ teaspoon sage
½ teaspoon salt
¼ teaspoon freshly ground pepper
2 slices of prosciutto, diced
8 bread triangles, sautéed
¼ cup Marsala wine

1 Cut the livers in half and simmer in butter, together with the seasonings and prosciutto, 5 minutes.

2 Remove the livers from the pan and place them on the bread triangles. Add the wine to the pan gravy, cook 3 minutes and pour over the livers.

BROILED CHICKEN LIVERS

6 SERVINGS

18 chicken livers
Salt and freshly ground pepper to taste
10 slices of bacon
¾ cup fine dry bread crumbs
4 tablespoons butter
1 tablespoon lemon juice
2 tablespoons finely chopped parsley

1 Cut the livers into quarters or thirds depending on size. Sprinkle with salt and pepper.

2 Cook the bacon in a skillet for about 1 minute, turning once. Reserve bacon drippings. Cool the bacon and cut each slice into sixths.

3 Alternate pieces of liver and bacon on skewers. Brush with bacon fat and sprinkle with crumbs.

4 Melt the butter and add the lemon juice and parsley.

5 Broil liver and bacon under the broiler or over hot coals, turning occasionally, until done. Brush with butter sauce and serve.

CHICKEN LIVERS MADEIRA

6 SERVINGS

1 pound chicken livers
1 tablespoon butter
Salt and freshly ground pepper to taste
2 tablespoons flour
3 shallots, diced
1 cup chicken stock
2 tablespoons chopped parsley
¼ cup Madeira wine

1 Trim, wash and dry the chicken livers. Cut them into halves. Sauté the livers in the butter and season with salt and pepper. Cook over high heat, shaking the pan frequently so the livers do not stick. Do not overcook; the livers should be tender, but not dry.

2 Sprinkle the livers with the flour, add the shallots, shake the pan, and let cook for ½ minute.

3 Add the stock and bring to a boil, stirring gently. Add the parsley, wine and additional salt and pepper to taste, stirring just to heat through. Serve on a bed of rice.

Tomatoes Stuffed with Chicken Livers, page 430.
Pasta with Chicken Livers and Mushrooms, page 501.

CHICKEN LIVERS EN BROCHETTE

6 SERVINGS

1 pound chicken livers
12 medium-size mushrooms
6 slices of bacon
6 cherry tomatoes
6 white onions, cooked
¼ cup flour
⅓ cup olive oil
½ teaspoon salt
¼ teaspoon freshly ground pepper
1 teaspoon Dijon mustard

1 Preheat the broiler.

2 On each of 6 small skewers alternate chicken livers with mushrooms, folded half strips of bacon, tomatoes and onions.

3 Roll the skewers in the flour. Brush livers and vegetables lightly with the olive oil mixed with the salt, pepper and mustard.

4 Broil the filled skewers 3 inches from the source of heat until brown on all sides, turning frequently and basting with remaining olive oil if necessary. Serve the skewers atop a bed of rice with a homemade tomato sauce.

SAMBAL GORENG
SPICED CHICKEN LIVERS WITH
VEGETABLES

Sambal Goreng is an Indonesian dish that is
made with chicken livers, vegetables, spices
and a great deal of garlic.

6 SERVINGS

1 pound chicken livers, cut in half
3 tablespoons peanut oil
10 garlic cloves, minced
1 teaspoon minced fresh ginger
3 shallots, or 1 small onion, minced
1 pound string beans, cut into ½-inch pieces
1 cup chicken stock
¼ cup ground Indonesian almonds (optional)
2 tablespoons tamarind pulp, or juice
    of 2 lemons
1 tablespoon dark soy sauce
1 tablespoon salt
2 teaspoons dark molasses
2 teaspoons turmeric
2 teaspoons seren leaves (optional)
1½ teaspoons kentjur (optional)
1 teaspoon cayenne
½ teaspoon laus (optional)

1 In a large skillet sauté the chicken livers in peanut oil over high heat until light
brown, stirring constantly. Remove the
livers from the skillet.

2 Reduce the heat and add the garlic,
ginger and shallots. Cook until the vegetables are soft, stirring occasionally. Add
the string beans and cook 3 minutes.

3 Add the remaining ingredients,
cover the pan and cook over low heat until
the string beans are just tender, about 10
minutes.

4 Return the livers to the pan and cook
5 minutes longer.

CHICKEN GIBLETS
WITH MUSHROOMS

4 SERVINGS

2 tablespoons butter
1 pound mushrooms, sliced
1 medium onion, sliced thin
½ pound chicken livers
½ pound chicken gizzards and hearts,
    cooked and trimmed
Salt and freshly ground pepper to taste
½ cup dry white wine
4 slices toasted bread

1 Heat the butter, add the mushrooms
and onion and cook until brown, stirring
occasionally.

2 Add the chicken livers and cook 3
minutes. Add the gizzards and hearts and
cook about 3 minutes longer. Season with
salt and pepper, add the wine and cook 2
minutes. Serve hot on toast squares.

Turkey

Season a stuffed turkey with salt and place it on its side in a roasting pan fitted with a rack. Place slices of fat salt pork over the breast and spread the bird generously with butter. Cook in a preheated (425°F) oven 15 minutes, then turn on the other side and cook 15 minutes longer.

Reduce the oven heat to 375°F and continue roasting, turning the bird from side to side and basting often with fat from the pan. If the fat tends to burn, add a few tablespoons of water.

Allow 15 minutes a pound for roasting.

Place the turkey on its back for the last 15 minutes of cooking. Pierce the thigh for doneness; if the juice that runs out is clear with no tinge of pink, the bird is done.

Note: For stuffing directions and recipes, see pages 187–192.

LOW-TEMPERATURE
ROASTING OF TURKEY
ALLOW ¾ TO 1 POUND PER SERVING

Place stuffed turkey, breast side up, on a rack in an open roasting pan. Grease the surface well with shortening and place a butter-moistened cheesecloth—large enough to drape down over the sides of the bird—on top.

Roast in a constant 325°F oven. Do not add water; baste only once or twice with drippings in the pan. Remove the cloth for the last half hour to brown.

Allow 2 to 2½ hours for a 4- to 8-pound turkey, 2½ to 3 hours for an 8- to 12-pound turkey and 3 to 4 hours for a 12- to 16-pound turkey.

To test for doneness, move the leg joint up and down. It should give readily or break. Or, using a cloth or paper, press the fleshy part of the drumstick. It should feel soft.

Note: For stuffing directions and recipes, see pages 187–192.

◆

GIBLET GRAVY

ABOUT 3 CUPS

Giblets from 1 turkey or chicken
4 tablespoons pan drippings from roast turkey
   or chicken
¼ cup flour
½ cup cream (optional)
1 hard-cooked egg, chopped (optional)
Salt and freshly ground pepper to taste

1 Clean the giblets well and simmer, covered, in salted water until tender, about 1 hour. Drain, reserving the broth. Cool the giblets and chop.

2 After bird has been removed to a serving platter, pour 4 tablespoons of the pan drippings into a saucepan. If necessary, add enough butter to make the 4 tablespoons. Add 2 cups of the giblet broth to the drippings in the roasting pan and scrape loose all the brown particles. If necessary, add enough water to make 2 cups.

3 Add flour to the drippings in the saucepan and cook, stirring, until brown. Gradually add the giblet broth from the roasting pan and cook, stirring, until thickened.

4 Add the cream, chopped giblets and hard-cooked egg, season with salt and pepper and reheat.

TURKEY FLORENTINE

6 SERVINGS

3 tablespoons butter
3 tablespoons flour
1 cup milk
½ cup cream
Salt and freshly ground pepper to taste
3 tablespoons chopped onions
1 tablespoon olive oil
2 pounds spinach, cooked and chopped
¼ teaspoon grated nutmeg
Sliced cooked turkey, enough for 6 servings
2 tablespoons grated Parmesan cheese

1 Melt the butter in a saucepan, add the flour and stir with a wire whisk until blended. Meanwhile bring the milk and cream to a boil and add all at once to the butter-flour mixture, stirring vigorously with the whisk until the sauce is thickened and smooth. Season with salt and pepper.

2 In a skillet sauté the onions in the oil until wilted. Add the spinach and sauté briefly until the moisture has evaporated. Add the nutmeg and ½ cup of the sauce. Heat thoroughly but do not let boil.

3 Spoon the spinach onto a warm heat-proof platter and arrange the sliced turkey on top.

4 Stir a little Parmesan cheese into the remaining sauce and spoon over the turkey slices. Sprinkle with additional Parmesan cheese, dot with additional butter and brown lightly under the broiler.

TURKEY-FILBERT CASSEROLE

6 SERVINGS

¼ pound butter
½ pound mushrooms, sliced
3½ tablespoons flour
1 cup milk
1 cup half-and-half
Salt and freshly ground pepper to taste
¼ teaspoon celery seed
2 cups noodles, cooked and drained
2 cups coarsely diced cooked turkey
5 thin slices of Bermuda onion, separated
    into rings
½ lemon, sliced very thin
⅓ cup sliced or chopped filberts, toasted
½ teaspoon paprika

1 Preheat the oven to 350°F.

2 Melt 2 tablespoons of the butter and sauté the mushrooms in it until tender.

3 Melt 4 tablespoons of the butter and blend in the flour. Gradually stir in the milk and the half-and-half. Bring to a boil, stirring. Add the mushrooms and season with salt and pepper to taste.

4 Add the celery seed to the noodles and place half of them in a greased shallow casserole. Top with the turkey and half of the mushroom sauce. Add remaining noodles and arrange the onion rings and lemon slices over the top.

5 Pour the remaining sauce over all. Dot with the remaining butter and sprinkle with the filberts and paprika. Bake for 30 minutes, or until hot and bubbly.

TURKEY PIE WITH SAGE CORNMEAL PASTRY

6 SERVINGS

5 tablespoons butter
½ cup chopped onions
1 garlic clove, minced
⅓ cup flour
1½ cups turkey stock
1 cup half-and-half
2 cups diced cooked turkey
1 teaspoon salt
¼ teaspoon ground sage
⅛ teaspoon freshly ground pepper
⅛ teaspoon mace
1 teaspoon lemon juice
Sage cornmeal pastry (see following recipe)

1 Preheat the oven to 425°F.
2 Melt the butter in a saucepan and cook the onions and garlic in it until golden. Blend in the flour. Remove from the heat and stir in the turkey stock and half-and-half. Cook, stirring, until the mixture is medium thick. Add the turkey, seasonings and lemon juice. Turn into a 1-quart casserole.
3 Top the casserole with sage cornmeal pastry. Trim, turn under, and flute the edges of the pastry. Cut 2 or 3 gashes in the top to allow for escape of steam. Bake for about 20 minutes, until brown.

SAGE CORNMEAL PASTRY

½ cup flour
½ cup cornmeal
1 tablespoon sage
½ teaspoon salt
⅓ cup vegetable shortening
3 tablespoons water

In a mixing bowl mix together the flour, cornmeal, sage and salt. Add shortening and cut it in until the mixture resembles coarse crumbs. Add the water. Mix lightly to form a ball. Turn out onto a lightly floured board. Roll to ⅛-inch thickness and 1 inch larger than the circumference of the casserole.

♦

TURKEY TURNOVERS

6 SERVINGS

3 tablespoons butter
2 teaspoons minced onions
3 tablespoons flour
¼ teaspoon celery salt
¼ teaspoon salt
⅛ teaspoon freshly ground pepper
⅛ teaspoon ground ginger
1 cup milk
2 cups chopped cooked turkey
Basic pie pastry (page 663)
Mushroom sauce (page 565)

1 Preheat the oven to 450°F.
2 Melt butter; add onions and flour and stir until smooth. Add the seasonings. Slowly add the milk, stirring constantly, and cook until thickened. Add the turkey; adjust the seasonings. Let mixture cool.

3 Meanwhile, roll out the pastry to ⅛-inch thickness. Cut dough into 3-inch circles or squares, place a rounded tablespoon of the turkey mixture over one half and fold the other half over the filling, pressing the edges together. Or put the turkey mixture in the center of a square or circle, place another square or circle over the top and press the edges together to seal. Slash the top crust to allow the steam to escape.

4 Place on a cookie sheet and bake until attractively brown, or 20 to 30 minutes. Serve with mushroom sauce or with a creamed vegetable.

◆

FRICASSEE OF TURKEY WITH HERBS

Turkey parts are increasingly available in supermarkets and can be used in place of chicken in almost any recipe. A boneless and skinless turkey breast will yield about twelve slices (cut on the bias) that can be used in place of veal scaloppine. This turkey fricassee is delicious and relatively inexpensive.

---

8 SERVINGS

---

3 cups chicken stock
1 onion studded with 4 cloves
1 large carrot, sliced
3 peppercorns
1 tablespoon chopped chives
2 tablespoons chopped parsley
1 teaspoon salt
1 bay leaf
4 pounds turkey (legs, thigh, wings),
    cut into pieces
6 tablespoons flour
2 tablespoons vegetable oil
6 tablespoons butter
12 small white onions, peeled and left whole
1 tablespoon chopped dill

1 tablespoon chopped parsley
3 tablespoons cream
1 teaspoon lemon juice

1 In a heavy kettle combine the stock, onion studded with cloves, carrot, peppercorns, chives, parsley, salt and bay leaf. Bring to a boil.

2 Dredge the turkey pieces in 3 tablespoons of the flour. In a skillet, heat the oil and 3 tablespoons of the butter, add the turkey and brown on all sides. Add to the simmering stock and cook, covered, over low heat until the turkey is tender, about 1¼ hours.

3 Remove the turkey pieces to a warm platter and keep hot. Strain the stock, return it to the heat and add the small onions. Cover and cook 20 minutes. Remove the onions to the platter and keep hot.

4 In a heavy saucepan melt the remaining 3 tablespoons butter, add the remaining 3 tablespoons flour and stir with a wire whisk until blended. Measure 2 cups of the simmering chicken stock and add all at once to the butter-flour mixture, stirring vigorously with the whisk until the sauce is thickened and smooth.

5 Add the herbs, cream and lemon juice to the sauce, stirring until heated through. Pour over the turkey and serve.

TURKEY HASH

4 SERVINGS

3 cups ground cooked turkey
3 cups finely chopped cooked potatoes
½ cup finely chopped onions
3 tablespoons chopped green pepper
1 teaspoon salt
Freshly ground pepper to taste
¾ cup turkey or chicken stock
4 poached eggs
Tabasco sauce

   1 Preheat the oven to 350°F.
   2 Mix together the turkey, vegetables, seasonings and stock. Place in 1 large greased casserole or 4 individual greased casseroles. Cover.
   3 Bake 1 hour for large casserole, or about 40 minutes for individual casseroles. Halfway through the baking, remove cover to permit browning.
   4 Arrange poached eggs on top of the hash and serve with Tabasco sauce.

Duck

People will turn to duck as main fare in the winter months more than in other seasons. It is a versatile meat that can be roasted with a wide variety of seasonings or turned into a fine ragout.

◆

ROAST DUCK

4 OR 5 SERVINGS

1 (5-pound) duck
Salt and freshly ground pepper to taste
¼ teaspoon thyme
5 small onions, peeled
1 carrot, scraped and cut into ¼-inch rounds

   1 Preheat the oven to 450°F.
   2 Sprinkle the duck inside and out with salt and pepper. Sprinkle the cavity with the thyme and add one of the onions. Truss the duck and place it, breast side up, in a roasting pan.
   3 Arrange the carrot rounds and remaining onions around duck. Roast for 15 minutes. It is not necessary to baste the duck as its cooks.
   4 Reduce the oven heat to 350°F.
   5 Turn the duck on its side and roast for 30 minutes longer. Remove most of the fat from pan as it accumulates.
   6 Turn the duck on its other side. Roast for 15 minutes and turn it breast side up again. Roast for 15 minutes longer. Lift the duck so that the juices in the cavity run into the pan. When the thigh is pricked and the juices run pale yellow, the duck is done.

ROAST DUCK WITH GRAPE STUFFING

4 SERVINGS

1/3 cup chopped onions
4 tablespoons butter
4 cups toasted bread cubes (croutons)
2 tablespoons chopped parsley
1 cup chopped celery
Salt and freshly ground pepper
1 teaspoon thyme
1/3 cup duck or chicken stock
1 cup seedless grapes
1 (4- to 5-pound) duck
1/2 lemon
Giblet gravy (see following recipe)

1 Preheat the oven to 325°F.

2 Sauté the onions in the butter. Mix bread cubes with onions, parsley, celery, 1 teaspoon salt, 1/2 teaspoon pepper, the thyme, stock and grapes.

3 Sprinkle the inside of the duck with salt and pepper. Fill crop and body cavities with grape stuffing. Close openings with skewers. Lace tightly with a strong string. Rub the outside of the skin with the lemon.

4 Place the duck on a rack in a shallow pan, such as a jelly roll pan. Bake for 2 to 2½ hours. Serve with giblet gravy.

DUCK STOCK
2 CUPS

Put duck neck and giblets in 2 cups water with 1/2 teaspoon salt, 3 peppercorns and 1 parsley sprig. Cook, covered, until tender. Lift out the cooked giblets and strain the stock.

GIBLET GRAVY
2½ CUPS

Blend 1 tablespoon flour with 2 cups of the stock made from giblets. Stir and cook until slightly thickened. Chop giblets and add. Season with salt and freshly ground pepper to taste.

◆

DUCK A L'ORANGE

4 SERVINGS

1 (4- to 5-pound) duck
Salt and freshly ground pepper
2 tablespoons sugar
2 tablespoons white vinegar
1 orange
1 lemon
1/2 cup brown sauce (page 551)
1 tablespoon red currant jelly
1 tablespoon orange liqueur (Cointreau, Grand Marnier or Triple Sec) (optional)

1 Preheat the oven to 375°F.

2 Sprinkle the inside of the duck with salt and pepper. Place the bird on a rack in a roasting pan, place in the oven, and roast for 15 to 20 minutes per pound, depending on the doneness desired. Baste frequently with pan drippings and pour the fat from the pan as it accumulates.

Continued

3 Meanwhile, combine the sugar and vinegar in a saucepan. Cook over moderate heat until the sugar caramelizes and becomes amber in color; do not overcook.

4 Peel the orange and lemon with a swivel-bladed vegetable scraper. Using a sharp knife, cut the orange rind and half of the lemon rind into the thinnest possible strips. Discard the remaining lemon rind but save the fruit.

5 Combine the slivers of orange and lemon rinds in a saucepan and cover with water. Bring to a boil, remove from the heat, and let stand for 3 minutes. Drain and reserve the rinds.

6 Squeeze the juice from the orange and combine it with 1 tablespoon lemon juice; reserve.

7 Pour off any fat remaining in the roasting pan. Remove the duck and keep it warm on a hot serving platter. Add a little water to the roasting pan and swirl it around to dissolve any brown particles clinging to the bottom and sides of the pan. Pour this mixture over the caramelized sugar and bring to a boil. Cook over high heat for 3 minutes; strain.

8 Add the orange and lemon juices and the brown sauce to the strained mixture. Cook over high heat for 10 minutes. Add the orange and lemon rinds and the currant jelly. Cook until the jelly dissolves. Add the orange liqueur.

9 If desired, the duck may be cut into quarters before serving. Spoon part of the orange sauce over the bird and serve the rest in a sauceboat. Garnish the platter with peeled orange slices and watercress sprigs.

CHINESE ROAST DUCK

4 SERVINGS

1 (4- to 5-pound) duck
Salt
2 tablespoons chopped onions
2 tablespoons finely chopped celery
1½ teaspoons sugar
¼ teaspoon cinnamon
⅛ teaspoon aniseed
⅓ cup plus 1½ teaspoons light soy sauce
2 cups plus 2 teaspoons water
2 tablespoons honey
2 tablespoons cider vinegar
1 teaspoon cornstarch

1 Preheat the oven to 325°F.

2 Wash the duck and remove excess fat from the body and neck cavities. Rub the inside lightly with salt.

3 Combine the onion, celery, sugar, cinnamon, aniseed, ⅓ cup of the soy sauce and 1 cup of the water. Bring to the boiling point.

4 Tie the duck's neck tightly with a string so the sauce will not seep out while cooking. Pour the hot sauce inside the duck. Sew up the vent tightly. Rub the outside of the duck with a little salt. Place breast side up on a rack in a roasting pan. Roast for 20 minutes.

5 Heat 1 cup water with the honey, vinegar, remaining soy sauce and 1 tablespoon salt. Brush this mixture over the skin of the bird. Continue to cook until the duck is done, about 1½ hours, basting at 20-minute intervals with this sauce.

6 Remove the duck from the oven. Drain the sauce into a saucepan and thicken it with cornstarch mixed with 2 teaspoons water. Cook until slightly thickened. Serve separately as gravy.

ROTISSERIE CHINESE DUCK

This is a splendid recipe developed for an electric rotisserie. When done the duck should be crisp on the outside and almost jet black.

4 SERVINGS

1 (5- to 6-pound) duck
Salt to taste
Few sprigs of parsley
½ lemon
¼ cup dark molasses (preferably Chinese bead molasses available in most Oriental grocery stores)
½ cup light soy sauce
½ cup sherry
1 small garlic clove, minced

1 Wash the duck and dry well with paper toweling inside and out. Sprinkle the cavity with salt and insert the parsley and lemon. Truss the bird securely. Fold the wings under and tie close to the body. Tie the legs together, then bring the cord under the tail and over the breast and tie securely. Make certain the thighs are tied close to the body so they will not break away during cooking.

2 In a saucepan combine the molasses, soy sauce, sherry and garlic and cook over low heat 5 minutes.

3 Insert the spit rod through the center of the duck cavity, balancing it carefully. Be sure one set of skewers is inserted firmly into the legs before tightening the screws.

4 Roast until tender, about 2 hours, basting every 15 minutes with the sauce. The duck skin will darken considerably while cooking. When done, the drumstick meat is soft when pressed with the fingers and the thigh joint moves easily.

LONG ISLAND DUCK IN PORT

4 SERVINGS

1 (5- to 6-pound) duck
3 tablespoons vegetable oil
1 cup port or dry red wine
½ cup orange juice
2 teaspoons lemon juice
1 tablespoon cognac
1 tablespoon cornstarch
½ teaspoon salt
Dash of freshly ground pepper
⅛ teaspoon Tabasco sauce
Pinch of allspice
2 tablespoons pâté de foie gras or the duck liver, cooked and puréed (optional)

1 With a sharp pointed knife, cut through the duck skin along the center of the breasts from neck to vent. Loosen the skin by pulling away from the flesh and at the same time running the knife underneath. Cut the skin where necessary but keep the flesh intact. Quarter the skinned duck.

2 In a skillet heat the oil, add the duck and brown on all sides. Add half of the port, cover and cook until the duck is tender, about 45 minutes. Remove the duck to a warm platter and keep hot.

3 Blend together and stir into the pan the remaining ingredients. Cook, stirring constantly, until the sauce thickens. Return the duck to the sauce and simmer over low heat 5 minutes. Serve with a garnish of orange slices and watercress.

CONFIT DE CANARD
PRESERVED DUCK

Americans, at times, are late to accept many coveted and delectable foods from other cultures, even French. That is the case with what is known as *confit de canard*, or "preserved duck," and *confit d'oie*, or "preserved goose." They have within the past decade become very much in vogue in this country. Homemade confit is a bit tedious to prepare but it is worth it. Here is a recipe for preserved duck, which makes an excellent ingredient for salad as well as an ingredient for the traditional cassoulet.

4 SERVINGS

1 (4-pound) duck
2 tablespoons salt
2 teaspoons freshly ground pepper
½ teaspoon thyme
2 bay leaves
4 peeled garlic cloves, cut in half lengthwise
1 pound lard

1 Cut the duck as follows: 2 legs with thighs attached, 2 pieces of back, each of about the same size, 2 wings, each breast split lengthwise in half, 1 gizzard, 1 heart, 1 kidney, 1 neck, cut crosswise in half.

2 Combine the salt and pepper in a small bowl. It is best if you can pulverize the thyme and bay leaves in a bowl. Take care, however, that the bay leaves are totally pulverized and have no sharp edges or they could be injurious. Otherwise leave the bay leaves whole. Add the spices to the salt and pepper.

3 Arrange half the pieces of duck in large bowl and sprinkle with a portion of the salt mixture. Arrange another layer of duck and the remaining salt mixture. Rub the pieces of duck so that they are evenly coated.

4 Stick the garlic cloves between the pieces of duck. Cover closely with plastic wrap and refrigerate for a minimum of 24 hours.

5 Heat the lard in a large heavy kettle and add the duck pieces skin side down. When the pieces start to brown, cover closely and cook 1¼ hours.

6 Transfer the pieces skin side down to a casserole or other container. Pour the fat overall to cover the solids completely. Add a weight to the solids to make certain they are thoroughly immersed in the fat. Let cool to room temperature.

7 Cover the casserole and refrigerate until ready to use. The ducks will keep for weeks under proper refrigeration. You may use as much of the duck as you wish for one preparation. Keep the remainder completely covered with fat and under refrigeration.

Note: Melted leftover fat in which the ducks cooked should be strained. It will keep well under refrigeration. It can be used to prepare more ducks.

HOW TO COOK PRESERVED DUCK PIECES

It is preferable to use a heavy skillet for cooking the duck pieces. Heat about 4 tablespoons of the fat in which the duck was cooked. Add pieces of duck—the amount will depend on how many you wish to serve—skin side down. Cook until the skin is crisp and a nice brown. Turn the pieces and cook until brown on the other side. The total cooking time will be from 5 to 10 minutes, depending on the size of the pieces.

Mixed Green Salad with Preserved Duck, page 446.

CASSOULET

4 cups (2 pounds) small dried pea beans
2 quarts water
1 tablespoon salt
2 garlic cloves, minced
2 carrots, quartered
2 onions, each studded with 3 whole cloves
1 bouquet garni (parsley, celery, bay leaf and
    thyme tied in cheesecloth)
½ cup diced salt pork
3 tablespoons duck drippings or vegetable oil
1½ pounds lean pork, cubed
1 pound boneless lamb, cubed
2 Bermuda onions, chopped
1 cup chopped shallots
1 cup thinly sliced celery
1 (8-ounce) can tomato sauce
1 cup dry white wine
1 garlic or Polish sausage
1 confit de canard (preserved duck), removed
    from the bone and cut into bite-size pieces
    (opposite page), or canned preserved goose

1 Combine the beans, water and salt in a large kettle, and let stand overnight. Or use the quick-soaking method (page 78).

2 Add the garlic, carrots, onions studded with cloves, bouquet garni and salt pork. Bring to a boil. Reduce the heat and cook gently 1 hour. Skim the foam from the surface.

3 Heat the duck drippings in a skillet. Add the pork and lamb and sauté until brown. Transfer to the bean mixture.

4 Sauté the Bermuda onions, shallots and celery in the remaining drippings until tender. Add the tomato sauce and wine and simmer 5 minutes. Add to the beans. Add the garlic sausage, cover and simmer until the meats and beans are tender, about 1 hour, adding water if necessary to cover the beans. Skim off the excess fat. Discard the bouquet garni.

5 Transfer the mixture to a large earthenware casserole. Add the pieces of preserved duck. Bake, uncovered, in a preheated 350°F oven 35 minutes.

♦

DUCK WITH BEANS

1 pound dried pea or marrow beans
2 teaspoons salt
4 parsley sprigs
2 celery tops with leaves
1 bay leaf
2 garlic cloves
1 (5-pound) duck, cut into serving pieces
6 strips of bacon
1 onion, chopped
½ teaspoon thyme
Tabasco sauce or cayenne to taste

1 Soak the beans overnight in water to cover. Or use the quick-soaking method (page 78).

2 Add the salt and additional water to cover if necessary. Add the parsley, celery, bay leaf and 1 sliced clove of garlic all tied in a piece of cheesecloth. Cook, covered, until tender, for 2 hours or longer. Drain, reserving the broth and beans.

Continued

3 Sprinkle the duck lightly with additional salt. Broil in a preheated broiler, skin side up, until brown. Turn, brush the other side with the drippings in the pan and broil until brown. (If desired, the duck may be pan fried.)

4 Reduce the oven heat to 300°F.

5 Rub the inside of an earthenware casserole with the remaining clove of garlic and place 3 strips of bacon on the bottom of the casserole. Add the onion, thyme and Tabasco to the beans and place half the mixture in the casserole. Add the broiled duck and cover with the remaining beans.

6 Pour off the fat from the broiler pan, add 1 cup bean broth to the pan and scrape loose all the brown particles. Pour over the beans. Place the remaining bacon on top.

7 Cover and bake until the duck is tender, or about 1½ hours. The cover may be removed during the last 15 minutes to crisp the bacon.

Goose

HIGH-TEMPERATURE ROASTING OF GOOSE

Stuff the goose (see page 192) and truss as directed on page 187. Rub the outside with a little salt, place in a shallow roasting pan on its side and brush with 2 tablespoons goose fat. Pour 1 cup hot water into the pan and roast in a 425°F oven, allowing 15 to 16 minutes for each pound ready-to-cook weight. Baste often. If the water evaporates and juice that comes out of the bird gets too brown, add a little hot water to the pan. Skim off the fat from time to time. After the first hour turn the bird on the other side, then turn every ½ hour, roasting the goose the last 15 minutes on its back so that the breast will brown. To test for doneness, move the legs up and down—they should move freely.

LOW-TEMPERATURE ROASTING OF GOOSE

After stuffing and trussing the goose, place the bird, breast up, on a rack in a shallow open pan and roast in a 325°F oven until the leg joints move readily or twist out. Toward the end of cooking time, test by moving the drumstick up and down. During the roasting, spoon or siphon off the fat as it gathers in the pan. Save the fat for use in other cooking.

An 8-pound goose (ready-to-cook weight) will take 4 hours to roast; a 10-pound goose will take 4¼ hours; a 12-pound goose will take 5 hours and a 14-pound goose, 6 hours.

DANISH ROAST GOOSE

8-POUND GOOSE SERVES 6 TO 8

Greenings or other tart apples
Prunes
Ready-to-cook goose
Salt to taste

1 The amount of stuffing depends on the size of the goose. Allow 1 cup for each pound of the bird, ready-to-cook weight. Apples and prunes may be used in equal measure.

2 Soak the prunes 2 hours or longer, drain and remove the pits. Peel, core and slice the apples. Mix the fruits and sweeten to taste.

3 Preheat the oven to 325°F.

4 Sprinkle the goose inside with salt and fill its cavities with the fruits. Truss as directed on page 187, tying the legs loosely to the tail.

5 Place the goose, breast side up, on a rack in an open roasting pan and roast until the leg joints move easily and the flesh is soft. Remove the fat from the pan as it is extracted. See high- or low-temperature roasting of goose (opposite page) for roasting time.

6 Make a gravy from the drippings in the pan. Danish cooks sometimes finish off the gravy for roast goose by stirring in a little tart currant jelly.

Game Birds

A squab is a cultivated pigeon too young to fly and is one of the finest of esculents. The flavor is more gamelike than any other bird raised in captivity. Rock Cornish game hens may be substituted for squabs, which are expensive.

◆

ROAST STUFFED SQUABS

3 SERVINGS

3 (1-pound) squabs
½ lemon
Salt and freshly ground pepper to taste
3 tablespoons butter
9 chicken livers, halved
½ cup chopped mushrooms
¼ cup ham cut in thin strips
¼ cup shelled pistachios
12 bacon strips

1 Preheat the oven to 350°F. Rub the squabs with the lemon half and sprinkle inside and out with salt and pepper.

2 In a skillet heat 2 tablespoons of the butter, add the chicken liver halves and cook until barely done. Remove from the pan and chop fine.

3 Heat the remaining butter in the same skillet, add the mushrooms and cook briefly. Combine the livers, mushrooms, ham and nuts and stuff the squabs lightly with the mixture. Close the opening with skewers and string and tie the legs with string.

Continued

4 Place the birds, breast side up, on a rack in an open roasting pan and cover the breasts with the bacon slices. Roast, basting occasionally with the pan drippings, until tender, 45 minutes to 1 hour. Serve hot or cold.

♦

PAKISTANI PIGEONS AND PILAU

6 SERVINGS

4 tablespoons butter
6 (1-pound) squabs
5 cups water
2 pieces fresh ginger
2 garlic cloves
2 teaspoons coriander seed
2 teaspoons fennel seed
1 small onion, quartered
½ cup chopped onions
6 cloves
¼ teaspoon ground cardamom
2 tablespoons chopped candied or preserved ginger
¾ teaspoon cumin seed
¼ teaspoon saffron
1½ cups long-grain rice
2 tablespoons pistachios, chopped
1 cup sultana raisins

1 In a heavy kettle heat 2 tablespoons of the butter, add the squabs and brown on all sides.

2 Remove the kettle from the heat and pour the water over the birds. Add the fresh ginger, garlic, coriander seed, fennel seed and the quartered onion. Return the kettle to the heat and bring the liquid to a boil. Cover the kettle tightly, reduce the heat and simmer until the birds are tender, about 30 minutes.

3 Remove the birds from the kettle, place on a warm platter and keep hot.

4 Strain the liquid from the kettle into a saucepan and wash the kettle. Return the kettle to the heat, melt the remaining 2 tablespoons of butter, add the chopped onions and cook until golden.

5 Add the cloves, cardamom, candied ginger, cumin seeds, saffron and rice and stir until all the ingredients are thoroughly mixed. Add 3 cups of the strained liquid in which the birds were cooked and bring to a boil. Cover the kettle, reduce the heat to the lowest point and cook until the rice is tender, 15 to 20 minutes. Stir in the nuts and the raisins.

6 Cut each squab in half and arrange on top of the rice mixture. Cover and keep hot until ready to serve.

♦

ROAST SQUABS WITH MADEIRA SAUCE

6 SERVINGS

6 (1-pound) squabs, with livers
2 tablespoons butter
¼ cup Madeira or port wine
¼ cup brown sauce (page 551)
2 tablespoons cold butter
6 pieces of toast

1 Preheat the oven to 400°F.

2 If the birds are not trussed by the butcher, truss them. Fold the wing tips back under the bird. Then take a length of twine and tie the legs tightly together at the ends. Make a loop around the tail. Cross the strings over the back and bring string across the wings to hold them firmly to the body. Make another loop to tie the neck skin.

3 Select a large skillet that can be placed in the oven. Heat the 2 tablespoons butter in the skillet and cook the squabs in it until they are golden brown on all sides.

4 Place each squab on its side and place the skillet in the oven. Roast for 10 minutes, basting once or twice, then turn each squab on the other side. Roast for 10 minutes longer, basting once or twice, then turn each squab on its back. Add squab livers.

5 Turn off the oven heat. Using a 2-pronged fork, drain the liquid from the cavity of each squab into the skillet. Remove the trussing strings and transfer birds to a heatproof serving platter. Return them to the oven but leave oven door ajar.

6 Place the skillet on the stove. Chop the livers, add them to the skillet, and add the wine and brown sauce. Stir to blend. Turn off the heat under the skillet and add the cold butter to the sauce. Swirl the butter around until it melts and is well incorporated in the sauce. Place the squabs on toast and serve immediately with the sauce.

POTTED SQUABS

6 SERVINGS

6 (1-pound) squabs
Flour
Salt and freshly ground pepper
4 tablespoons butter
1 small onion, chopped
1 carrot, scraped and diced
1 celery stalk, chopped
¼ teaspoon thyme
1 bay leaf
1 cup chicken stock

1 Preheat the oven to 350°F.

2 Mix a little flour with salt and pepper and dredge the squabs in it. Brown the birds on all sides in the butter and place them in a casserole or Dutch oven.

3 Add onion, carrot, celery, thyme and bay leaf to the skillet in which squabs were browned. Cook, stirring, for about 3 minutes. Add the stock. Bring the mixture to a boil and pour it over the squabs.

4 Cover the casserole closely and bake the birds for 45 minutes to 1 hour. Strain the sauce and serve it with the squabs. Serve with steamed white rice or wild rice.

PHEASANT SMITANE

¼ teaspoon thyme
1 garlic clove
1 (3-pound) pheasant
Salt and freshly ground pepper to taste
3 thick slices of bacon
¼ cup finely chopped shallots
⅓ cup dry white wine
⅓ cup cream
⅔ cup sour cream
1 tablespoon butter

1 Preheat the oven to 450°F.

2 Put the thyme and garlic in the cavity of the pheasant and truss. Sprinkle the bird with salt and pepper and place it on a rack in a baking dish. Cover with the bacon. Roast for 10 minutes, basting occasionally.

3 Reduce the heat to 350°F and continue to roast for about 35 minutes. Baste the pheasant and turn it occasionally as it cooks. Do not let the bacon burn. If the bacon starts to get too brown, remove it from the oven and reserve.

4 When pheasant is cooked and golden brown all over, remove it from the oven. Cut it into serving pieces and keep warm.

5 Pour off most of the fat from the pan and add the shallots. Cook, stirring with a wooden spoon, until they are translucent. Add the wine and continue to cook and stir until liquid is reduced almost by half.

6 Add the cream and sour cream and stir, shaking pan, until sauce boils once. Do not overcook or sauce may curdle. Quickly add the butter and shake the pan in a swirling motion until it is incorporated into the sauce. Strain the sauce over the pheasant, garnish with bacon and serve immediately.

ROAST PHEASANT

1 (2- to 3-pound) pheasant
Salt and freshly ground pepper to taste
1 bay leaf
1 garlic clove
A few celery leaves
1 lemon slice
4 bacon slices
Melted butter
1 cup chicken stock
2 tablespoons flour
2 tablespoons butter
2 to 3 tablespoons Madeira wine

1 Preheat the oven to 350°F.

2 Sprinkle the pheasant inside and out with salt and pepper. Place the bay leaf, garlic, celery leaves and lemon in the cavity. Tie the legs together with string and turn the wings under.

3 Cover the breast with bacon and a piece of cheesecloth soaked in melted butter. Place the pheasant, breast up, on a rack in a baking pan and roast until tender, about 30 minutes per pound, basting frequently with melted butter.

4 Remove the pheasant to a warm serving platter and add chicken stock to the roasting pan. Stir over moderate heat, scraping loose the brown particles. Blend the flour with the butter and stir into the gravy bit by bit. When the gravy is thickened and smooth, add the wine and the pheasant liver.

5 Remove the cheesecloth and string from the pheasant. Carve and serve with sauce.

Quail rate high on any gourmet's list of the finest winged delicacy. They were once a rarity (to be found mostly in hunting season) but they are now available in many fine grocery stores, supermarkets and gourmet shops.

◆

PAN-ROASTED QUAIL WITH PROSCIUTTO AND ROSEMARY

4 SERVINGS

8 semiboneless quails, ¼ pound each
8 neat rectangles of prosciutto
8 rosemary sprigs, or 4 teaspoons dried
Salt and freshly ground pepper to taste
2 tablespoons butter
2 tablespoons vegetable oil
6 tablespoons dry white wine
2 tablespoons cognac or other brandy

1 Rinse the quails inside and out with water. Pat dry with paper toweling.

2 Stuff each quail with 1 piece of prosciutto and 1 rosemary sprig, or ½ teaspoon dried. Sprinkle each bird with salt and pepper.

3 Heat the butter and oil in a skillet large enough to hold the quails in 1 layer. Place each quail on one side in the hot fat and brown. Turn the birds and continue cooking until they are brown all over, about 5 minutes. Add the wine to the skillet. Let simmer about 1 minute, or until most of the liquid evaporates.

4 Pour the cognac over all and cover closely with a tight-fitting lid. Cook about 5 minutes and serve.

GRILLED QUAIL

2 TO 4 SERVINGS

4 fresh quails, ¼ pound each, boned but with
    the leg and thigh bones left intact
2 tablespoons Dijon mustard
2 tablespoons vegetable oil
1 teaspoon minced garlic
1 teaspoon finely chopped thyme,
    or ½ teaspoon dried
4 teaspoons coarsely ground pepper
Salt to taste

1 Place the quails skin side up on a flat surface and press to make the birds lie flat.

2 In a small bowl combine the mustard, oil, garlic, thyme, pepper and salt. Rub the birds on all sides with the mixture.

3 Preheat a charcoal grill or the oven broiler to high. If a grill is to be used, scrape it firmly on top to remove any residue from previous use. Brush the top of the grill lightly with oil.

4 Arrange the quails skin side down and flat on a grill. Or if a broiler is to be used, place a rack on a baking dish or tray and arrange the quails skin side up. If a grill is used, cook about 5 minutes on one side and turn. Cook 3 to 5 minutes longer. If a broiler is used, place the quails about 4 inches from the source of heat. Broil about 4 minutes and turn. Broil 3 to 5 minutes longer.

Salad with Hot Grilled Quail, page 447.

ROAST WILD GOOSE

1 (6- to 8-pound) young wild goose
Juice of 1 lemon
Salt and freshly ground pepper to taste
4 tablespoons butter
¼ cup chopped onions
1 cup chopped tart apples
1 cup chopped dried apricots
3 cups fine, soft bread crumbs
4 to 6 bacon slices
Melted butter

1 Preheat the oven to 325°F.

2 Sprinkle the goose inside and out with lemon juice, salt and pepper.

3 In a large saucepan, heat the butter, add the onions and cook until tender. Stir in the apples, apricots, crumbs, ½ teaspoon salt and ⅛ teaspoon pepper.

4 Spoon the stuffing lightly into the goose cavity. Close the opening and truss with skewers and string. Cover the breast with bacon slices and cheesecloth soaked in melted butter. Place the goose, breast up, on a rack in an open roasting pan.

5 Roast until tender, 2 to 3 hours, basting frequently with the drippings in the pan. If the age of the goose is uncertain, pour 1 cup water into the pan and cover for the last hour of cooking. Remove the cheesecloth, skewers and string before carving.

WILD DUCKS WITH MADEIRA

4 wild ducks, 1 to 2 pounds each
Olive oil or melted butter
Salt and freshly ground pepper
4 apples, peeled, cored and cut into eighths
4 onions, peeled and cut into eighths
1 cup chopped celery
4 slices of bacon, each halved
2 tablespoons A.1. Sauce
4 orange slices
4 lemon slices
2 celery stalks with leaves, quartered
½ cup Madeira wine
2 tablespoons flour

1 Preheat the oven to 275°F.

2 Clean the ducks well and rub them with oil or butter. Sprinkle inside and outside with salt and pepper. Stuff the cavities with equal quantities of apples, onions and chopped celery. Truss the ducks and place them side by side, breast up, in a roasting pan just large enough to hold them.

3 Arrange 2 pieces of bacon on each breast and add ½ inch of water to the pan. Stir in the A.1. and arrange the orange and lemon slices and the quartered celery around the ducks. Bake for about 3 hours, basting occasionally, or until birds are tender.

4 Thirty minutes before ducks are done, remove the bacon strips and add the wine. Baste frequently.

5 When done, remove ducks to a serving platter and strain the juices. Blend the flour with about 2 tablespoons of the juice to make a paste. Stir this into the sauce, using a wire whisk, until sauce boils up and is thickened. Season with salt and pepper to taste and serve with the ducks.

Stuffings

POULTRY STUFFINGS

Stuffing for poultry can be moist or dry and can be made as family tradition indicates, with a basis of white bread, corn bread, rice or even sauerkraut. Preparing a stuffing consumes precious time Thanksgiving or Christmas morning and many cooks like to make it the day before. Stuffings are highly perishable, however, and have been suspected in food-poisoning outbreaks. The American Institute of Baking suggests the following safe-for-health procedures:

MOIST STUFFINGS Prepare the liquid ingredients and refrigerate. Prepare the dry ingredients and store at room temperature. Combine the two just before stuffing and roasting the bird.

DRY STUFFINGS Combine the ingredients except raw egg, oysters and other such moist foods and refrigerate. Stuff the bird just before roasting.

BREAD CRUMBS

Freshly made bread crumbs are superior to packaged crumbs. Some stuffing recipes call for very small bread cubes, but crumbs are even smaller.

SOFT FRESH BREAD CRUMBS Trim the crusts from slices of fresh bread and tear the bread into small pieces. Drop the pieces into the container of a food processor and blend to the desired size. If no food processor is available, bread from a firm loaf may be crumbled in an old-fashioned grater. Trim off the crusts and rub the bread through the coarse side of the grater. If the loaf is soft, allow it to dry for a day or two before grating.

Note: Do not use a food grinder to make fresh bread crumbs. The moisture in the fresh bread will make it come out of the grinder more like a paste than crumbs.

FINE DRY BREAD CRUMBS Trim the crusts from slices of fresh bread and arrange the slices in a single layer on a baking sheet. Bake the bread in a 250 to 275°F oven until the bread is very dry, but do not let it brown at all. When the bread is dry, crumble it in a food processor. Or put the dried bread through a food grinder.

TO TRUSS POULTRY

Allow ¾ to 1 cup of stuffing for each pound of ready-to-cook bird. Stuff wishbone cavity lightly and skewer or sew the skin to the back. Shape the wings akimbo, bringing tips onto back of wings. Sprinkle the body cavity with salt and fill lightly with stuffing. Do not pack it, as it expands on cooking. To close the cavity, place skewers across it and lace it closed with cord. Tie the drumsticks securely to the tail. (Many frozen birds do not require trussing nowadays because the legs are held in place through a slit made in the skin.)

BASIC BREAD CRUMB STUFFING

5 CUPS

1 small onion, chopped
1 celery stalk with leaves, chopped
4 tablespoons butter
2 tablespoons chopped parsley
1 to 2 teaspoons sage
½ teaspoon salt
Freshly ground pepper
5 cups stale bread cubes or crumbs
Water, milk or giblet stock (optional)

1 Sauté the onions and celery in the butter until tender but not brown.
2 Combine the seasonings and the crumbs, toss together with the onion mixture and, if a moist dressing is desired, add just enough liquid to moisten crumbs.

Variations

MUSHROOM STUFFING

Cook ½ pound sliced mushrooms with the onions and celery and proceed as directed.

BRAZIL NUT–MUSHROOM STUFFING

Add ½ cup chopped Brazil nuts to the sliced mushrooms and cook with the onions and celery.

NEW ENGLAND DRESSING

Cook ½ cup diced peeled tart apples with the onions and celery.

GIBLET STUFFING

Simmer giblets in water until tender. Chop and measure. Substitute for an equal amount of the crumbs.

OLD-FASHIONED BREAD AND EGG DRESSING

8 SERVINGS

¼ cup chopped onions
¼ cup chopped celery
4 tablespoons butter or drippings
5 cups stale bread cubes or crumbs
1 hard-cooked egg, chopped
1 teaspoon mixed herbs (sage, thyme and marjoram)
¾ teaspoon salt
⅛ teaspoon pepper
1 egg, beaten
¾ cup giblet stock

1 Sauté the onions and celery in the butter until the onions are transparent. Mix with the bread, hard-cooked egg and seasonings.
2 Blend the beaten egg with the stock and stir into the bread mixture.
3 Turn into a greased pan and place in the oven with the turkey about 1 hour before the turkey is done. Bake, uncovered, until the dressing is a deep golden brown. Cut into pieces to serve.

CHESTNUT STUFFING

12 CUPS

8 cups chestnuts
6 cups beef stock
2 onions, chopped
2 tablespoons butter
2 pounds sausage meat
1 tablespoon chopped parsley
1 tablespoon chopped chives
1 teaspoon thyme
½ teaspoon marjoram
½ teaspoon sage
Salt and freshly ground pepper to taste
1½ cups soft bread crumbs
½ cup cognac

1 Cut gashes in the flat side of each chestnut. Cover the chestnuts with water and bring to a boil. Simmer for about 5 minutes. Drain and let cool. Remove the shells and inner skins.

2 Cook the chestnuts in the stock 20 minutes, or until tender. Drain, reserving the stock for soup. Chop half the chestnuts coarsely and mash the rest. Set aside.

3 Cook the onions in the butter until golden brown. Add the sausage and seasonings and cook, stirring constantly, 4 to 5 minutes. Add to the chestnuts.

4 Soften the crumbs in milk or water. Press out the excess liquid and add to the chestnuts. Add the cognac and mix well.

CORN BREAD STUFFING

8 CUPS

4 cups finely crumbled corn bread
4 tablespoons butter
2 cups finely chopped onions
1 tablespoon minced garlic
1 turkey gizzard
1 turkey liver
1 turkey heart
1 cup finely chopped sweet green peppers
1 cup finely chopped celery
1 cup finely chopped parsley
1 cup canned cream-style corn
2 hard-cooked eggs, coarsely chopped
¼ pound (about ⅔ cup) finely cubed
    Gruyère or cheddar cheese
2 eggs, well beaten
Salt and freshly ground pepper to taste
½ cup rich turkey or chicken stock

1 Crumble the corn bread and set aside.

2 Heat the butter in a deep skillet and add onions and garlic. Cook, stirring, until onions are wilted.

3 Trim the tough membranes from the gizzard, liver and heart. Finely chop soft parts. There should be ⅓ to ½ cup. Add to the onion mixture and cook, stirring often, about 2 minutes.

4 Add the green peppers and celery and cook, stirring often, about 3 minutes. Remove from heat and let stand briefly. Add parsley, corn bread, corn, hard-cooked eggs, cheese and beaten eggs. Blend well. Add salt and a generous grinding of pepper. Add broth and blend well.

OYSTER STUFFING

6 CUPS

2 tablespoons bacon fat or vegetable oil
1 tablespoon chopped parsley
2 teaspoons chopped chives
4 cups stale bread cubes or crumbs
1 teaspoon marjoram or thyme
1 teaspoon salt
Freshly ground pepper to taste
25 oysters, drained, liquor reserved

1 Melt the bacon fat, add the parsley and chives and cook until wilted. Add the mixture to the bread and season with marjoram, salt and pepper.

2 Lightly mix in the oysters. If the stuffing seems too dry, moisten with a little of the liquor that had been drained from the oysters.

SAUSAGE STUFFING

10 CUPS

8 cups cubes of day-old bread with crusts
    removed
1/2 pound sausage meat
1 cup finely chopped onions
3/4 cup finely chopped celery, including leaves
1/4 pound butter
1 teaspoon sage
3/4 teaspoon thyme
Salt and freshly ground pepper to taste

1 Preheat the oven to 350°F.

2 Spread the bread cubes on a baking sheet and bake until dry. Do not brown.

3 In a skillet cook the sausage meat, stirring, until it loses color. Pour off most of the fat.

4 Sauté the onions and celery in the butter and reserved fat until the onions are transparent. Add the sausage, bread cubes, herbs and seasonings. Mix well and let cool.

◆

WILD RICE STUFFING

6 CUPS

1/2 green pepper, cut into strips
3 celery stalks, chopped
2 medium onions, quartered
1/4 pound mushrooms, sliced
2 cups chicken stock
1/2 cup vegetable oil
1 1/2 cups uncooked wild rice
1 teaspoon salt
1/2 teaspoon freshly ground pepper

1 Place the vegetables in the container of a food processor. Add stock and blend until vegetables are chopped. Drain; reserve stock.

2 Heat the oil in a skillet. Add the rice and sauté for 10 minutes. Stir in the reserved stock and the salt and pepper. Cover, bring to a boil, and cook for 45 minutes. Add the chopped vegetables.

♦

POTATO STUFFING

ABOUT 7 CUPS

¼ *pound butter, melted*
1 *teaspoon salt*
½ *teaspoon freshly ground pepper*
½ *teaspoon sage*
2 *medium onions, quartered*
¼ *cup parsley clusters*
6 *cups diced cooked potatoes (see note)*

1 Place the butter, salt, pepper, sage, onions and parsley in the container of a food processor. Blend until smooth.

2 Pour the sauce over the potatoes and mix lightly.

Note: Select potatoes that are of the same size so that the cooking time will be the same for all. Wash them well, cover with water, and add 2 teaspoons salt for each quart of water. Cook until tender. Peel and dice.

CALIFORNIA WALNUT STUFFING

10 CUPS

¼ *pound butter*
1 *cup chopped onions*
1 *cup chopped celery*
8 *cups of ½-inch cubes of soft bread*
½ *cup diced cooked turkey liver*
1 *cup chopped walnuts*
2 *teaspoons sage*
1½ *teaspoons salt*
¼ *teaspoon freshly ground pepper*
½ *cup water (optional)*
½ *cup brandy (optional)*

1 Melt the butter in a large skillet. Add the onions and celery and sauté for 15 minutes.

2 Combine bread cubes, liver, walnuts and seasonings. Add to onion-celery mixture. This gives a dry stuffing. For a moist stuffing, add the water and brandy.

NOODLE STUFFING

5 CUPS

4 ounces very fine egg noodles
2 tablespoons butter
½ cup fine white bread crumbs
¼ cup chopped parsley
¼ cup pine nuts
¼ cup chopped fennel or celery
½ teaspoon oregano
½ teaspoon salt
¼ teaspoon freshly ground pepper

1 Cook the noodles in boiling salted water for about 8 minutes. Do not overcook. Drain and rinse thoroughly with cold water.

2 Toss the noodles lightly with the butter. Add remaining ingredients and mix lightly. Cool before using.

STUFFING A GOOSE

When stuffing a goose, Germans sometimes use mashed potatoes, sometimes sauerkraut and sometimes quartered apples, cored and peeled or not, as preferred.

The French like chestnuts and at least two chefs I know use them in combination with pork sausage and cognac. Sausage is an unusual ingredient, because goose is so fatty that a tart or at least dry stuffing is better than one containing fat.

TANGERINE STUFFING FOR GOOSE

8 CUPS

4 tablespoons butter
½ cup diced celery with leaves
3 tangerines
4 cups prepared bread stuffing
½ pound chestnuts, cooked and chopped
  (there should be 1 cup)
½ teaspoon sage
3 cups cooked rice
½ cup stock or water

1 Melt the butter in a skillet, add the celery and cook over medium heat about 10 minutes.

2 Meanwhile, peel the tangerines, removing the white membranes. Cut the sections into halves and remove the seeds.

3 Combine the tangerines, bread stuffing, chestnuts (to prepare see page 188), sage, rice and stock. Add the cooked celery and butter and mix together lightly with a fork.

5

Fish and Shellfish

FISH

BAKED FISH FILLETS

4 TO 6 SERVINGS

2 tablespoons plus 4 teaspoons butter
Salt and freshly ground pepper to taste
2 tablespoons finely chopped shallots
2 pounds fish fillets (fluke, flounder or sole)
½ cup dry white wine
2 teaspoons Dijon mustard
6 tablespoons fine fresh bread crumbs
¼ cup finely chopped parsley
Lemon wedges

1 Preheat oven to 400°F.

2 Butter a baking dish large enough to hold the fish in 1 layer with the 2 tablespoons of butter. Sprinkle with salt, pepper and shallots.

3 Arrange the fish pieces over the shallots and sprinkle with half of the wine. Blend the remaining wine with the mustard and brush the tops of the fish with the mixture. Sprinkle with crumbs and dot with the 4 teaspoons butter. Bake for 5 minutes.

4 Turn the broiler to high and run the baking dish under it. Broil until the fish flakes easily when tested with a fork. Sprinkle with chopped parsley. Serve each portion with a lemon wedge.

BREADED FISH FILLETS

4 TO 6 SERVINGS

2 pounds fish fillets (tilefish, striped bass)
¼ cup flour
Salt and freshly ground pepper to taste
1 egg, lightly beaten
3 tablespoons plus 1 teaspoon vegetable oil
2 tablespoons water
¾ cup fresh bread crumbs
1 tablespoon butter
Lemon wedges

1 Cut the fish into serving pieces. Combine the flour, salt and pepper.

2 Beat the egg with the 1 teaspoon of the oil, the water and salt and pepper.

3 Coat the fish pieces in the seasoned flour. Dip them into the egg, then coat them all over with the crumbs.

4 Heat the remaining 3 tablespoons of oil and the butter in a heavy skillet. Cook the fish pieces until golden brown on both sides, basting with the oil and butter in the skillet, from 5 to 10 minutes depending on the thickness of the fish.

5 Serve the fish with lemon wedges.

POACHED FISH FILLETS

4 TO 6 SERVINGS

2 pounds fish fillets (cod, whitefish or tilefish)
2 cups water
½ cup milk
2 cloves
1 bay leaf
Salt to taste
Melted butter

1 Place the fillets in a heatproof dish and add the water, milk, cloves, bay leaf and salt. Cover and bring to the simmer, spooning the liquid over the fish. Cook for about 1 minute.

2 Drain and serve with melted butter.

◆

STEAMED FISH FILLETS

4 TO 6 SERVINGS

2 pounds fish fillets (blackfish, red snapper, weakfish)
Salt and freshly ground pepper
1 tablespoon finely chopped basil or tarragon
Melted butter

1 Place the fillets skin side down in the top of a steamer. Sprinkle with salt, pepper and basil.

2 Pour water in the bottom of the steamer and bring to a boil.

3 Place the steamer top securely over the boiling water and cover tightly. Steam for 3 to 5 minutes, depending on the thickness of the fish.

4 Serve with melted butter.

BAKED WHOLE FISH

4 SERVINGS

1 (2-pound) whole fish (bluefish, porgy, mackerel or flounder)
3 tablespoons olive oil
½ teaspoon salt
¼ teaspoon freshly ground pepper
3 tablespoons chopped parsley
2 tablespoons finely chopped onions
2 tablespoons butter
1 tablespoon lemon juice

1 Preheat the oven to 350°F.

2 Wash and dry the fish. Coat with the oil and season with salt and pepper. Place fish on greased foil (see below) and bake for 10 minutes, or until the fish flakes easily when tested with a fork.

3 Combine the parsley, onions, butter and lemon juice and spread over the cooked fish. Place the fish under the broiler and cook until light brown.

Preparing Whole Baked Fish: The following procedure will prevent the cooked fish from breaking when it is transferred from the pan to the serving platter: Line a greased baking dish with heavy duty foil, allowing foil to overlap at both ends. Grease the foil, place the fish on it and bake as directed. When fish is done, use the foil as handles to transfer the fish to a heated serving platter.

POACHED WHOLE FISH

6 SERVINGS

1 (4-pound) whole fish (striped bass,
    grouper or weakfish)
4 quarts cold water
1 carrot, scraped and cut into ½-inch lengths
1 celery stalk, cut into 1-inch lengths
4 teaspoons salt, or more
12 peppercorns
1 bay leaf
Pinch of thyme

1 Leave the fish whole and keep it cold until ready to cook. It must be thoroughly cleaned and scaled. Rinse in cold water and pat dry with a towel. Wrap the fish loosely in foil. Do not seal the foil because the water must penetrate the flesh. Or wrap it in cheesecloth.

2 Place the foil-wrapped fish in the water and add remaining ingredients. Bring to a boil and reduce the heat. Cook the fish for exactly 12 minutes. Let stand in the cooking liquid until ready to serve.

STRIPED BASS STUFFED WITH TOMATOES AND MUSHROOMS

6 SERVINGS

6 tablespoons butter
¼ cup chopped onions
1 cup chopped mushrooms
1 tomato, peeled, seeded and chopped
1 teaspoon chopped chives
1 tablespoon chopped parsley
¾ cup fresh bread crumbs
Salt and freshly ground pepper to taste
1 (3-pound) striped bass
1 tablespoon lemon juice
½ cup dry white wine or water

1 Preheat the oven to 400°F.

2 In a skillet heat half the butter, add the onions and cook until they are transparent. Add the mushrooms and cook until wilted. Add the tomato and simmer 5 minutes. Add the chives, parsley, crumbs, salt and pepper and mix. Stuff the fish loosely with the mixture and close the opening with skewers and string.

3 Place the fish in a baking pan lined with foil (page 195) and sprinkle with the lemon juice, wine and additional salt and pepper. Dot with the remaining butter and bake, uncovered, basting occasionally, until the fish flakes easily when tested with a fork, 20 to 30 minutes. Sprinkle with additional butter and lemon juice.

STUFFED STRIPED BASS WITH SHRIMP-WINE SAUCE

6 SERVINGS

1 (4- to 5-pound) striped bass,
    dressed for baking
Salt and freshly ground pepper to taste
Shrimp stuffing (see following recipe)
1 carrot, sliced
1 cup sliced celery
1 small onion, minced
1½ cups dry white wine
1 bay leaf
2 tablespoons butter, melted
Shrimp-wine sauce (see following recipe)

1 Preheat the oven to 400°F.
2 Sprinkle the inside of the fish with salt and pepper and stuff loosely with shrimp stuffing. Close with skewers and lace with string.
3 Line an open roasting pan with foil (page 195). On it make a bed of the carrot, celery and onion. Add the wine and bay leaf and place the fish on the vegetables. Brush the fish with butter. Bake, uncovered, until the fish flakes easily when tested with a fork, 20 to 30 minutes. Baste frequently during baking with any remaining butter and with the liquid in the pan.
4 Place the fish on a hot platter and serve with shrimp-wine sauce.

SHRIMP STUFFING
3 CUPS

1¼ pounds raw shrimp, shelled and deveined
4 tablespoons butter
1 small onion, minced
½ cup minced celery
½ cup chopped parsley
2 tablespoons dry white wine
1½ cups soft bread crumbs or cubes
Salt and fresh ground pepper to taste

1 Coarsely chop enough of the shrimp to yield ½ cup and reserve for the sauce. Chop the remaining shrimp in small pieces.
2 In a skillet heat the butter, add the onions and celery and cook until the onions are transparent. Add the shrimp pieces and cook until they are pink. Add the parsley and cook until wilted.
3 Remove the pan from the heat, add the wine, mix, and add the crumbs. Season to taste with salt and pepper.

SHRIMP-WINE SAUCE
3 CUPS

Dry white wine
2 teaspoons flour
½ cup chopped raw shrimp (reserved from
    the stuffing)
2 egg yolks, lightly beaten
1 cup cream
Salt and freshly ground pepper to taste

1 Strain the pan drippings from the fish and rub the vegetable residue through a fine sieve.
2 Add enough wine to the strained portion to make 1¼ cups. Blend the flour with a little wine and add, stirring, to the mixture. Add the shrimp and bring to a boil.
3 Mix the egg yolks and the cream. Add to the shrimp mixture and cook over the lowest heat, stirring constantly, until the mixture thickens. Do not let boil. Season with salt and pepper.

SEA BASS STUFFED WITH CRABMEAT

6 SERVINGS

1 (3- to 4-pound) sea bass
Salt to taste
1 pound crabmeat, picked over well to remove
    any bits of shell or cartilage
½ cup fresh bread crumbs
¼ cup cream
¼ cup chopped chives or scallions
¼ cup chopped parsley
4 tablespoons butter, melted
3 tablespoons chopped celery
Freshly ground pepper to taste
Olive or vegetable oil
Rémoulade sauce I (page 560)

1 Preheat the oven to 400°F.
2 Sprinkle the fish inside and out with salt. Combine the remaining ingredients, except the oil and sauce. Stuff the fish with the mixture and close with skewers and string. Sprinkle the fish with oil and place in a foil-lined baking pan (page 195).
3 Bake, uncovered, until the fish flakes easily when tested with a fork, 30 to 40 minutes. Serve with rémoulade sauce to which has been added ½ cup crabmeat.

BAKED SEA BASS FILLETS IN WHITE WINE SAUCE

6 SERVINGS

2 pounds sea bass fillets
Salt and freshly ground pepper
3 shallots, chopped
1 small onion, chopped
3 tablespoons finely chopped parsley
1 garlic clove, minced
3 large mushrooms, thinly sliced
4 tablespoons butter
2 cups dry white wine

1 Preheat the oven to 350°F.
2 Butter an oven dish. Season the fish with salt and pepper and place it in the buttered dish. Spread with the shallots, onions, parsley, garlic and mushrooms. Dot the fish well with 3 tablespoons of the butter and pour the wine over it.
3 Bake for 20 to 30 minutes, basting frequently. Remove the fish to a heated platter.
4 Add the remaining 1 tablespoon of cold butter to the sauce in the baking dish to bind it. Do not heat. Pour the sauce over the fish without straining. Decorate, if desired, with lemon slices and additional chopped parsley.

BLACKFISH FILLETS WITH GINGER

6 SERVINGS

3 tablespoons olive oil
3 tablespoons butter
6 blackfish fillets
1 garlic clove, chopped
12 wafer-thin slices fresh ginger
1½ tablespoons sugar
1 tablespoon cider vinegar
2½ tablespoons soy sauce
1 tablespoon cornstarch
6 tablespoons water
2 scallions, cut in thin diagonal slices

1 In a skillet, heat the olive oil and butter. Add the fish fillets and cook until the fish flakes easily when tested with a fork, 3 to 4 minutes on each side. Transfer the fish to a warm serving platter.

2 To the fat remaining in the skillet, add the garlic and ginger. Add the sugar mixed with vinegar and soy sauce.

3 Combine the cornstarch and water and gradually stir into the liquid in the skillet. Cook, stirring with a wire whisk, until the sauce is smooth and thickened. Pour the sauce over the fish, sprinkle with the scallions and serve immediately.

BLUEFISH AU VIN BLANC

This dish actually improves after several hours of refrigeration, or overnight, making it ideal for a buffet.

6 SERVINGS

2 cups thinly sliced onions
1 tablespoon peanut oil
3 garlic cloves
2 thyme sprigs, or 1 teaspoon dried
2 parsley sprigs
2 bay leaves
Tabasco sauce to taste
⅓ cup white vinegar
3 cups dry white wine
Salt and freshly ground pepper to taste
6 bluefish or mackerel fillets
2 lemons, thinly sliced
1 carrot, scraped and thinly sliced

1 Preheat the oven to 350°F.

2 Cook the onions in the oil in a skillet until barely wilted. Do not brown. Add the garlic, thyme, parsley, bay leaves, Tabasco, vinegar and white wine. Season with salt and pepper. Simmer for 15 minutes.

3 Oil a shallow baking dish large enough to accommodate the fish fillets without overlapping. Arrange the fillets on the dish and spoon the hot sauce over. Sprinkle with additional salt and pepper. Arrange the lemon slices and carrots neatly over the fish. Bring to a boil.

4 Cover the dish with foil and place it in the oven. Bake for 20 to 25 minutes, depending on the size of the fish. Remove from the oven and let stand in the marinade until cool. Serve at room temperature or chilled.

FILLETS WITH MUSHROOMS AND TOMATOES

6 SERVINGS

2 tablespoons butter
1 teaspoon chopped shallots or onions
6 large mushrooms, thinly sliced
1 tablespoon chopped parsley
6 medium tomatoes, peeled, seeded
    and chopped
6 fillets of bluefish, weakfish, or other fish
Salt and freshly ground pepper
1/4 cup dry white wine
1 or 2 egg yolks
1/2 cup cream
1 teaspoon chopped chives

1 In a large skillet melt the butter and add the shallots, mushrooms, parsley and tomatoes.

2 Season the fillets with salt and pepper and arrange side by side on the tomatoes. Pour the wine over the top.

3 Cover with a circle of buttered wax paper. Bring to a boil, cover the pan, reduce the heat and simmer until the fish flakes easily when tested with a fork, 10 to 12 minutes. Remove the fillets to a serving dish.

4 Cook the sauce in the pan until it is reduced about one-half. Add the egg yolk lightly beaten with a little of the hot liquid and the cream. Combine by swirling it in, moving the pan in a circular motion.

5 Reheat the sauce but do not let boil. Pour over the fish and garnish with chopped chives.

CARP IN RED WINE

4 TO 6 SERVINGS

1 (5-pound) carp, dressed
1 cup water
1 cup red wine
1 slice each lemon and orange
1 tablespoon chopped parsley
Pinch of marjoram
Pinch of thyme
2 medium onions, chopped
2 anchovy fillets, chopped
2 tablespoons flour
2 tablespoons butter
1 egg yolk, lightly beaten

1 Combine the carp head, water, wine, fruit, parsley and herbs and simmer, uncovered, 20 minutes; strain.

2 Preheat the oven to 350°F.

3 Place the onions in a foil-lined baking dish (page 195) and place the fish on top. Add the seasoned wine and anchovies and bake, uncovered, until the fish flakes easily, 20 to 30 minutes. Baste often with the pan liquid.

4 Transfer the fish to a hot platter. Strain the liquid and reheat. Stir in the flour creamed with the butter and boil 1 minute. Add a little of the hot mixture to the egg yolk, then return this to the sauce. Heat but do not boil. Adjust the seasonings and pour over the fish.

DEEP-FRIED CATFISH

4 SERVINGS

Oil for deep frying
¾ cup white cornmeal
Salt and freshly ground pepper to taste
1½ pounds catfish fillets
Lemon halves

1 Heat the oil to 370°–375° for deep frying.

2 Combine cornmeal, salt and pepper.

3 Cut each fillet in half and dredge in the cornmeal. Pat to make the coating adhere.

4 Cook the fillets in the hot oil for 5 to 10 minutes, until crisp and brown. Serve with lemon halves.

◆

POACHED SALT COD

ABOUT 4 SERVINGS

Soak 1½ pounds salt cod for several hours, changing the water 3 times. Drain and cut into 3-inch squares. Place in a skillet and cover with fresh water. Bring to a boil and simmer gently for not longer than 8 minutes. Remove the skin and bones. Flake the fish or leave it whole, as desired. Serve warm with buttered potatoes and aïoli sauce (page 557). The cod also may be served with lemon juice, chopped parsley and brown butter, or it may be creamed. It also may be served hot in a curry or creole sauce.

Brandade de Morue, page 50.

COD PROVENÇALE

8 SERVINGS

¼ cup olive oil
1 large onion, sliced thin
2 garlic cloves, chopped
1 green pepper, shredded
1 (2-ounce) can anchovies with oil, chopped
½ cup black olives, pitted
¼ teaspoon fennel seed
8 thin cod steaks
4 tomato slices
Salt and freshly ground pepper to taste
½ cup tomato purée
1 cup red wine
Chopped parsley

1 Preheat the oven to 400°F.

2 In a skillet, heat half the oil, add the onions, garlic and green pepper and cook until the onions are transparent. Add the anchovies, olives and fennel seed.

3 Place 4 cod steaks in a greased baking dish, spread with the anchovy mixture and top each with a slice of the remaining cod and then with a slice of tomato. Brush with the remaining oil and season with salt and pepper.

4 Mix the tomato purée with the wine and pour over the fish. Bake about 20 minutes, basting often. Sprinkle with parsley.

BAKED COD WITH POTATOES

4 TO 6 SERVINGS

10 to 14 tablespoons butter
Salt and freshly ground pepper to taste
4 (2-inch-thick) cod steaks with skin on
1½ pounds baking potatoes
1 small onion, thinly sliced (about ½ cup)
1 small garlic clove, finely chopped
3 tablespoons finely chopped parsley
3 tablespoons fresh bread crumbs

1 Preheat the oven to 400°F.
2 Butter a metal baking dish large enough to hold the fish and potatoes when added with 2 or 3 tablespoons of butter. Sprinkle with salt and pepper. Arrange the cod steaks in 1 layer on the bottom.
3 Peel and thinly slice the potatoes, plunging the slices immediately into cold water to prevent them from discoloring. Drain the potatoes in a colander.
4 Neatly scatter the potato slices around and between the pieces of fish, not on top. Scatter the onion slices over the potatoes. Season the fish and vegetables with salt and pepper. Dot everything with the remaining butter. Do not add liquid; the fish provides its own.
5 Place the baking dish on top of the stove and bring to the boil. When it starts to boil, put the dish in the oven and bake uncovered 10 minutes. Baste the fish and potatoes and continue baking 10 minutes longer, basting occasionally.
6 Meanwhile, combine the garlic, parsley and crumbs and sprinkle the mixture over the fish and vegetables. Bake 10 minutes longer, or until crumbs are brown.

CODFISH LOAF

6 SERVINGS

2½ cups cooked cod, flaked
¼ cup chopped onions
3 tablespoons chopped celery
3 tablespoons chopped green pepper
⅓ cup chopped walnuts
¼ cup chopped parsley
2 toast slices, crumbled
Salt and freshly ground pepper to taste
Few drops of Tabasco sauce
1 teaspoon Worcestershire sauce
1 teaspoon tarragon
2 eggs, separated
½ cup half-and-half
¼ pound butter, melted

1 Preheat the oven to 375°F.
2 Combine the fish, onions, celery, green pepper, walnuts, parsley, toast crumbs, salt, pepper, Tabasco, Worcestershire and tarragon.
3 Beat the egg yolks until light and lemon colored and add them to the mixture. Add the half-and-half and melted butter. Fold in the egg whites, stiffly beaten, and pour the mixture into a buttered ring mold or bread pan.
4 Set in a pan of hot water and bake until the loaf is set, about 40 minutes. Unmold on a hot plate and serve with egg sauce.

Salt cod is a staple food all around the Mediterranean. Some salt cod dishes have become classics, especially **brandade de morue,** *a purée of cod made with milk and olive oil. But there are many other ways to serve this salty dried fish; when properly prepared, it is delicious.*

◆

SALT COD, PORTUGUESE STYLE

6 SERVINGS

3 tablespoons butter
1 cup chopped onions
2 garlic cloves, minced
1 green pepper, cored, seeded and chopped
¼ teaspoon thyme
1 bay leaf
2 cups canned Italian plum tomatoes
Salt and freshly ground pepper to taste
1 large eggplant
¼ cup olive oil
1½ pounds salt cod, poached (page 201)
1 cup rice, cooked
½ teaspoon cumin seed, crushed,
　　or ¼ teaspoon ground cumin
3 tablespoons capers

1 Melt 2 tablespoons of the butter and cook the onions, garlic, green pepper, thyme and bay leaf until the vegetables are tender. Add the tomatoes and simmer for 30 minutes, or until mixture has thickened somewhat. Season with salt and pepper.
2 Preheat the oven to 400°F.
3 Peel the eggplant and cut it into ½-inch slices. Place the slices on a greased baking sheet and brush with oil. Bake for about 12 minutes, until the eggplant is tender, turning once. Brush with more oil as necessary.

4 When the eggplant is tender, line the bottom of a baking dish with the slices. Cover with the poached salt cod.
5 Combine the cooked rice with the cumin seed and capers. Spoon it over the fish. Add the tomato sauce and dot with remaining butter. Cover and bake for 10 minutes. Uncover and continue to bake for 10 to 15 minutes longer. Serve from the baking dish.

Note: Fresh cod fillets may be substituted for the salt cod. Simmer in water for 5 minutes, then proceed with the recipe.

◆

CURRIED COD

6 SERVINGS

¾ cup flour
¼ cup curry powder
2 pounds cod fillets, cut into 2-inch strips
¼ pound butter
Chopped parsley

1 Mix the flour and curry powder and dip the fish strips into the mixture.
2 Heat the butter in a skillet over moderate heat and brown fish on both sides. Serve sprinkled with chopped parsley.

Cream of Fish Soup with Vegetables, page 82.

CODFISH CAKES

4 SERVINGS

½ pound salt cod, soaked overnight
1 cup mashed potatoes
1 or 2 eggs
Freshly ground pepper to taste
Butter
Flour or crumbs, if desired

1 Cut the cod into small pieces, cover with water and bring to a boil. Taste for saltiness; if excessively salty, discard the water and repeat until the water is almost fresh.

2 Mix the fish with the potatoes, eggs and pepper. Form into 8 cakes and sauté in plenty of hot butter. Or roll in flour or crumbs and fry in deep fat heated to 370°F.

Note: A little ground ginger does wonders for codfish cakes.

EELS IN TOMATO SAUCE

6 SERVINGS

3 pounds fresh eels, cleaned and skinned
½ cup olive oil
1 onion, minced
2 garlic cloves, crushed or minced
1 tablespoon minced parsley
½ cup boiling rich meat or fish stock
2 tablespoons tomato paste, or ¾ cup
*   tomato purée*
Salt and freshly ground pepper to taste

1 Cut the eels into small sections. Wash and dry thoroughly.

2 Heat the oil in a skillet, add the onions, garlic and parsley and cook until the onions are transparent. Add the eels and cook very slowly, turning the sections so they absorb the flavor of the sauce.

3 When the sauce has almost cooked away, slowly add the stock and blend in the tomato paste. Add salt and pepper, bring to a boil and cook 5 to 10 minutes over low heat. Serve very hot.

Anguilles Quo Vadis, page 40.

EELS A L'ORLY

3 pounds fresh eels, cleaned and skinned
2 tablespoons lemon juice
2 tablespoons cognac
Salt and freshly ground pepper to taste
1 cup flour
½ teaspoon baking powder
1 egg, beaten
½ cup milk
Oil for deep frying

1 Cut the eels into 3-inch lengths. Wash and drain. Add the lemon juice, cognac, salt and pepper. Let stand 1 hour or longer.

2 Sift together the flour, baking powder and ¼ teaspoon salt. Mix the egg and milk and combine with the dry ingredients. Stir until smooth.

3 Dip the eels in batter and fry in deep fat heated to 360°F until brown.

◆

FINNAN HADDIE IN CREAM SAUCE

6 SERVINGS

2½ to 3 pounds finnan haddie
5 tablespoons butter
4 tablespoons flour
3½ cups milk
Salt and freshly ground pepper
1 (½-inch-thick) onion slice
1 bay leaf
½ cup cream
¼ teaspoon grated nutmeg, or more to taste
⅛ teaspoon cayenne or Tabasco sauce to taste

1 Cut the finnan haddie into 6 pieces more or less the same size.

2 Prepare the sauce before cooking the haddie. Melt 3 tablespoons of the butter in a saucepan and stir in the flour, using a wire whisk. When blended, add 2½ cups of the milk, stirring constantly with the whisk. When the sauce is blended and smooth, add salt and pepper. Cook, stirring frequently, for 20 to 30 minutes.

3 When the sauce is almost done, place the fish pieces in a large dish for poaching and add water to cover (the fish will swell slightly as it cooks). Do not add salt. Add the remaining milk, onion slice and bay leaf. Bring to a boil and cook briefly, just until the fish is piping hot throughout. Do not cook for an extended period, because the fish will toughen.

4 Just before serving, finish the sauce. Add to the sauce 1 cup of liquid in which the fish cooked and the cream. Add nutmeg and cayenne and stir to blend. When the sauce returns to the boil, remove from the heat and swirl in the remaining 2 tablespoons of butter.

5 Drain the fish, 1 piece at a time, using a slotted spoon. Transfer 1 piece at a time to a hot dinner plate and spoon the sauce over. Serve with grilled tomatoes and buttered new potatoes, if desired.

FLOUNDER FILLETS IN WHITE WINE SAUCE

6 SERVINGS

6 flounder fillets
1 cup boiling water or court bouillon
Salt and freshly ground pepper to taste
6 tablespoons butter
2 shallots, chopped, or 1 tablespoon
    chopped onion
½ cup dry white wine
1 tablespoon flour
½ cup cream

1 Halve the fillets lengthwise and roll each half. Fasten with toothpicks and place in a skillet. Add the water, salt, pepper, half the butter, the shallots and wine. Bring to a boil, reduce the heat and simmer until the fish is white in the center, about 5 minutes. Remove to a hot platter and keep warm.

2 Boil the liquid in the pan until reduced to one-third. Add the flour blended with the cream, then the remaining butter. Heat, stirring, until smooth. Strain and pour over the fish.

Kedgeree, page 111.

GULF COAST STUFFED FLOUNDER

6 SERVINGS

4 tablespoons butter
2 tablespoons chopped green pepper
¼ cup finely chopped onions
1 cup crabmeat, picked over well to remove
    any bits of shell or cartilage
1 teaspoon chopped parsley
Salt and freshly ground pepper to taste
1 tablespoon lemon juice
Tabasco sauce to taste
6 (1-pound) flounders, backbones removed

1 In a saucepan heat the butter, add the green pepper and onions and cook until the onions are transparent. Add the crabmeat, parsley, salt, pepper, lemon juice and Tabasco and mix well.

2 Stuff the flounders loosely with the mixture and close with skewers and string. Arrange the fish on a buttered baking pan and sprinkle with salt and pepper.

3 Broil slowly on both sides in a preheated broiler, basting frequently with lemon juice and additional butter, until golden brown.

HADDOCK WITH HERBED CRUMBS

4 TO 6 SERVINGS

2 pounds haddock fillets
Salt to taste
¼ pound butter, melted
3 cups soft fresh bread crumbs
½ teaspoon crumbled oregano
½ teaspoon crumbled marjoram
¼ teaspoon freshly ground pepper

1 Preheat the oven to 350°F.
2 Cut the fish into 4 or 6 serving pieces. Arrange the pieces in a buttered baking pan. Sprinkle with salt and pour half of the melted butter over the fish.
3 Blend all the remaining ingredients and sprinkle the mixture over the fish. Bake for 20 minutes, or until fish flakes easily when tested with a fork.

CURRIED HADDOCK

6 SERVINGS

2 pounds haddock fillets
1 cup water
1 cup dry white wine
½ bay leaf
3 tablespoons butter
¼ cup finely chopped shallots or onions
¼ cup finely chopped green pepper
1 celery stalk, finely chopped
1 tablespoon curry powder
3 tablespoons flour
½ cup dry white wine
Tabasco sauce to taste
Salt and freshly ground pepper to taste
Chopped parsley

1 Wipe the fillets with a damp cloth and place in a skillet. Cover with the water and wine and add the bay leaf. Cover closely with foil and simmer over low heat until the fish flakes easily with a fork, about 10 minutes. Drain and reserve the stock. Transfer fish to a heated serving dish and keep warm.
2 In a saucepan, heat the butter and add the vegetables. Cook over low heat 10 minutes. Stir in the curry powder and flour. Bring the reserved stock and wine to a boil and, using a wire whisk, add the stock all at once to the vegetable mixture, stirring vigorously until the sauce is thickened and smooth.
3 Simmer gently 5 minutes and season with Tabasco, salt and pepper. Strain or not, as desired, and pour the sauce, piping hot, over the fish. Garnish with chopped parsley.

BROILED HADDOCK WITH LEMON SAUCE

6 SERVINGS

2 pounds haddock fillets
3 tablespoons lemon juice
Salt and freshly ground pepper to taste
2 tablespoons butter
½ cup olive oil
½ teaspoon dry mustard
1½ teaspoons water

1 Preheat broiler.
2 Cut the fish into serving pieces and place on an oiled broiler pan. Brush with 1 tablespoon of the lemon juice and season with salt and pepper. Dot with the butter.
3 Broil for about 7 minutes, or until the fish flakes easily when tested with a fork.
4 Combine the oil, mustard, water, additional salt to taste and the remaining lemon juice. Heat, stirring well to blend, and pour over the fish.

NORTHWEST-STYLE HALIBUT

6 SERVINGS

2 pounds halibut steaks
¼ cup flour
1 teaspoon salt
¼ teaspoon freshly ground pepper
⅛ teaspoon grated nutmeg
4 tablespoons butter, melted
1½ cups milk
⅓ cup grated Parmesan cheese
½ teaspoon Worcestershire sauce
1 (10-ounce) package frozen chopped spinach,
    cooked and drained
Paprika

1 Preheat the oven to 350°F.
2 Remove the skin and bones from the fish and cut the fish into serving pieces.
3 Blend the flour, salt, pepper, nutmeg and butter together in a small pan. Gradually stir in the milk and bring to a boil, stirring. Add the cheese and Worcestershire.
4 Combine the spinach with half of the sauce and spread in the bottom of a well-greased shallow baking dish.
5 Arrange the fish over the top of the spinach. Pour remaining sauce over the fish. Sprinkle with paprika and bake for 15 to 20 minutes, or until the fish flakes easily when tested with a fork.

HALIBUT STEAKS WITH MUSHROOMS

4 SERVINGS

5 tablespoons butter
4 (1-inch-thick) halibut steaks
Salt and freshly ground pepper
1 tablespoon minced shallots
½ pound mushrooms, chopped
3 tablespoons dry white wine
1 tablespoon lemon juice
1 tablespoon chopped parsley

1 Preheat the oven to 400°F.

2 Lightly grease the center of 4 pieces of heavy-duty foil with 1 tablespoon of the butter. Place a steak on each piece of foil. Season with salt and pepper.

3 Sauté the shallots in the remaining butter until translucent. Add the mushrooms. Cook for 5 minutes.

4 Add the wine, lemon juice and parsley and continue to cook until most of the liquid has evaporated. Spoon the mixture over the fish. Season with salt and pepper to taste.

5 Draw the edges of the foil together and seal the packages. Bake for 15 minutes, or until fish flakes easily when tested with a fork. Serve in the foil.

Baked Kippered Herring, page 111.
Herring Salad, page 47.

HALIBUT STEAK AU BEURRE BLANC

6 SERVINGS

Salt to taste
1 tablespoon crab boil (available on grocery spice shelf)
1 (1½-inch-thick) halibut steak (about 3 pounds)
Beurre blanc (page 555)

1 Pour water into a fish cooker to a depth of 2 inches. There should be enough water to cover the halibut steak when it is added later. Add salt to taste and the crab boil. If crab boil is not available, add 1 teaspoon thyme and 1 bay leaf to the poaching liquid. Cover and bring to a boil. Simmer for 15 minutes.

2 Add the halibut steak to the poaching liquid. Return to the boil, partially cover the kettle, and simmer the fish for 10 to 15 minutes, until it flakes easily when tested with a fork. Do not overcook. Drain the fish well and serve immediately with beurre blanc.

MACKEREL WITH OLIVES

4 SERVINGS

4 small mackerel
Small pitted green olives
Freshly ground pepper to taste
Black Italian or Greek olives
Lemon slices

1 Preheat the oven to 350°F. Lightly grease the bottom of a shallow glass or earthenware baking dish with vegetable oil.
2 Stuff each mackerel with 5 or 6 green olives. Arrange the fish in the baking dish, sprinkle with a little more oil and with pepper. Scatter the black olives around the fish.
3 Bake, uncovered, until the fish flakes easily when tested with a fork, 15 to 20 minutes. Garnish the mackerel with lemon slices and serve from the baking dish.

BROILED MACKEREL

3 TO 4 SERVINGS

1 (3-pound) mackerel
Flour
Butter
Salt and freshly ground pepper
Paprika to taste
Lemon wedges
Chopped parsley

1 Preheat the broiler.
2 Split the mackerel, dust with flour, place skin side down in a greased baking pan and dot heavily with butter. Sprinkle with salt, pepper and paprika.
3 Broil the fish 2 to 3 inches from the source of the heat, basting occasionally. Cook until the fish flakes easily when tested with a fork, 6 to 10 minutes.
4 Serve immediately with lemon wedges and, if desired, sprinkle with chopped parsley.

BAKED STUFFED MACKEREL

1 (3-pound) mackerel
4 tablespoons butter
½ onion, chopped
¼ cup chopped celery
2 cups crumbs of day-old bread, lightly toasted
3 tablespoons finely chopped parsley
½ teaspoon crumbled thyme
¼ cup toasted sesame seed
1 teaspoon salt
½ teaspoon freshly ground pepper
2 bacon slices, cut into halves
Lemon slices and parsley sprigs for garnish

1 Have fish cleaned but leave tail and head intact. Wash the fish well and pat it dry with paper toweling.

2 Preheat the oven to 350°F.

3 Heat the butter and in it cook the onions until they are wilted. Combine with the celery, crumbs, parsley, thyme, sesame seed, half of the salt and half of the pepper.

4 Sprinkle the inside of the fish with the remaining salt and pepper. Spoon the filling into the cavity of the fish and skewer the opening. Place the fish in a baking dish and cover with the bacon slices.

5 Bake for about 30 minutes, or until the fish flakes easily when tested with a fork. Garnish the fish with lemon slices and parsley, and serve.

MARINER'S STEW

2 cups canned Italian plum tomatoes
1 tablespoon flour
1½ cups of onion rings
1 teaspoon salt
½ teaspoon freshly ground pepper
2 tablespoons chopped parsley
⅓ teaspoon oregano
¼ teaspoon dry mustard
¼ teaspoon allspice berries
1 small piece of fresh ginger
2 pounds monkfish or cod steak, diced
2 tablespoons butter
2 eggs, lightly beaten
2 tablespoons lime or lemon juice

1 In a large skillet break up the tomatoes with a fork. Add the flour and stir until all the lumps disappear. Add the onion rings, salt, pepper, parsley, oregano and mustard. Tie the allspice and ginger in a cheesecloth bag and add to the skillet. Cook, covered, for 15 minutes.

2 Add the fish and cook for 5 to 10 minutes, until flaky. Remove from the heat and discard spice bag. Stir in the beaten eggs and lime juice. Return to heat and cook for 2 or 3 minutes, until slightly thickened. Serve hot.

Fish Soup with Tomatoes, page 81.
Fish Soup with Leeks, page 82.
Fish Chowder, page 81.

SAUTÉED WALLEYED PIKE

ABOUT 6 SERVINGS

1 small (5- to 6-pound) walleyed pike
½ cup milk
Flour or cornmeal
Salt and freshly ground pepper to taste
2 tablespoons vegetable oil
4 tablespoons butter
1 tablespoon lemon juice
1 teaspoon chopped parsley

1 Cut fillets from the pike and cut the fillets into serving pieces. The thicker portions should be split if more than 1 inch thick.

2 Dip the pieces of fish in the milk and then in flour or cornmeal seasoned with salt and pepper.

3 In a skillet heat the oil and sauté the fish in it until brown on both sides. Cook until the fish flakes easily when tested with a fork.

4 Cream the butter with the lemon juice and dot over the hot, cooked fish. Sprinkle with the chopped parsley. Serve with broiled tomatoes and marinated cucumbers.

POMPANO A LA SIEPI

4 SERVINGS

4 Florida pompano, cleaned
Salt and fresh ground pepper to taste
Olive oil
4 tomatoes
8 anchovy fillets
4 tablespoons butter
2 teaspoons dry mustard
2 teaspoons chopped chives
2 tablespoons lemon juice

1 Season the pompano lightly with salt and pepper and brush with olive oil.

2 Broil the fish about 3 inches from the source of heat in a preheated broiler 5 minutes on each side. Brush the second side with oil after turning the fish.

3 Cut a slice from the top of each tomato and discard. Season the tomatoes lightly with salt and pepper and brush with olive oil. Place on the broiler rack after turning the fish and broil until hot but not soft. Place 2 anchovy fillets on each tomato.

4 In a small saucepan, melt the butter and add the mustard and chives. Add the lemon juice just before serving.

5 To serve, place the fish on a hot platter, garnish with the tomatoes and pour the sauce over the fish, or serve separately.

PORGY SAUTÉ MEUNIÈRE

6 SERVINGS

6 porgies, cleaned
Milk
Flour
Salt and freshly ground pepper to taste
Vegetable oil
Lemon juice
Chopped parsley
6 slices peeled lemon
4 tablespoons butter

1 Dip the fish in milk, then in flour seasoned with salt and pepper.

2 In a skillet add oil to a depth of ¼ inch and heat until very hot. Add the fish and cook until golden brown, about 3 minutes on a side.

3 Remove the fish to a warm serving platter and sprinkle with lemon juice and chopped parsley. Place a slice of lemon on top. Heat the butter until it is light brown and pour over the fish.

SALMON FLORENTINE

4 SERVINGS

2 cups cooked or canned salmon
4 tablespoons butter
¼ cup flour
1½ cups milk (if canned salmon is used, the liquid from the can may be substituted for part of the milk)
½ teaspoon dry mustard
¼ teaspoon salt
¼ teaspoon Tabasco sauce
1½ cups grated Gruyère cheese
2 cups cooked spinach, drained

1 Preheat the oven to 425°F.

2 Flake the salmon.

3 In a saucepan melt the butter, add the flour and stir with a wire whisk until blended. Meanwhile, bring the milk to a boil and add all at once to the butter-flour mixture, stirring vigorously with the whisk until the sauce is thickened and smooth. Season with the mustard, salt and Tabasco and mix in 1 cup of the cheese.

4 Place the spinach in 4 individual greased casseroles, top with the salmon and sauce and sprinkle with the remaining cheese. Bake, uncovered, 15 minutes.

POACHED SALMON STEAK

6 SERVINGS

2 tablespoons butter
⅓ cup chopped onions
⅓ cup chopped carrots
⅓ cup chopped celery
4 cups water
½ cup dry white wine, or ¼ cup vinegar
Salt to taste
Peppercorns to taste
1 (3-pound) salmon steak
Hollandaise sauce (page 554), or green
    mayonnaise (page 556)

1 In a large skillet heat the butter, add the vegetables and cook 5 minutes. Add the water, wine and seasonings and simmer 5 minutes.

2 Wrap the salmon in cheesecloth and place in the boiling liquid. Lower the heat, cover and simmer gently about 15 minutes, or 5 minutes per pound.

3 Remove the salmon carefully, unwrap and serve hot with hollandaise sauce or cold with green mayonnaise.

BROILED SALMON STEAKS

8 SERVINGS

8 (¾-inch-thick) salmon steaks
¾ cup dry vermouth
¾ cup olive or vegetable oil
1½ tablespoons lemon juice
1 tablespoon minced parsley
¾ teaspoon salt
¼ teaspoon thyme
¼ teaspoon marjoram
⅛ teaspoon sage
Dash of freshly ground pepper

1 Place the salmon steaks in a large pan. Mix the remaining ingredients and pour over the top. Allow to stand 3 to 4 hours, turning once.

2 Preheat the broiler. Remove the steaks from the marinade, reserving the marinade. Place the fish on a greased broiler rack and broil until brown. Turn carefully and brown on the other side. Cook until fork tender, or about 5 minutes a side, brushing frequently with the reserved marinade.

Note: The salmon steaks may be grilled over charcoal.

WHOLE SALMON BAKED IN FOIL

Here is a dish for a New England Fourth of July feast. Salmon and peas are traditional in that region on Independence Day.

ABOUT 12 SERVINGS

1 (7- to 10-pound) salmon, cleaned
¾ cup dry white wine, or equal parts lemon juice and water
3 minced shallots, or 1 small onion, minced
Celery leaves from a small stalk
8 basil leaves
3 tarragon sprigs
2 rosemary sprigs
2 lemon slices with peel
¼ teaspoon thyme
Salt
White wine sauce (see following recipe)

1 Leave the salmon whole or remove the head. Rinse under cold running water and place on paper toweling to dry.

2 Place the wine in a saucepan and add the remaining ingredients, except the salt and wine sauce. Let the mixture simmer, uncovered, ½ hour without boiling.

3 Preheat the oven to 375°F.

4 Place the fish lengthwise on a long sheet of foil, bring up the edges and pour the wine mixture over the fish. Sprinkle with salt.

5 Completely enclose the fish, crimping the foil to seal the edges tightly. Place the foil-wrapped fish in a large baking pan and transfer to the oven. Bake until the fish flakes easily when tested with a fork, about 1 hour.

6 Serve hot with white wine sauce.

Note: A small 3- or 4-pound center cut of salmon may be baked in exactly the same manner as the whole salmon. For a center cut of that size, use half the wine-herb mixture and prepare half the amount of sauce. Cook 10 minutes a pound in a 375°F oven.

WHITE WINE SAUCE
6 CUPS

¼ pound butter
2 shallots, minced
6 tablespoons flour
Liquid in which salmon was baked
Equal parts dry white wine and boiling water
½ cup cream
Salt and freshly ground pepper to taste
2 egg yolks

1 While the salmon is baking, melt the butter in a saucepan and add the shallots. Cook until transparent but not brown. Using a wire whisk, stir in the flour until it is well blended. Cook over low heat 3 minutes. Let stand until the fish is done.

2 When the fish is removed from the oven, use a large spoon to dip out the juices and add to the butter mixture in the saucepan, stirring constantly over moderate heat. Continue stirring vigorously and add enough wine and boiling water to make 5 cups of liquid.

3 Cook the liquid, stirring, until thickened and smooth. Add the cream and season with salt and pepper. Strain through a fine sieve. Just before serving, reheat and add the egg yolks lightly beaten with a little of the hot sauce. Cook 2 minutes over low heat but do not let boil.

BROILED SALMON WITH ASPARAGUS SAUCE

4 SERVINGS

1½ pounds skinless, boneless 1-inch-thick
    fillet of salmon, or use a white-fleshed
    nonoily fish
3 tablespoons olive oil
2 tablespoons lemon juice
Salt and freshly ground pepper to taste
Asparagus sauce (page 572)

1 Cut the salmon into 4 pieces of equal
size. Put the pieces in a flat dish, add the
olive oil, lemon juice, salt and pepper.
Turn the fish in the oil and set aside until
ready to cook.
2 Place a wire rack in a flat, heatproof
baking dish. Arrange the salmon pieces on
the rack. Place the fish pieces about 4
inches from the source of heat. Leave the
broiler door partly open. Broil about 1½
minutes on one side and turn the pieces.
Broil on the other side 2 to 5 minutes, depending on the thickness of the fillets.
3 Heat the asparagus sauce. Spoon
equal amounts on each of 4 warmed plates
and arrange 1 piece of salmon fillet on
each serving. Garnish each serving with a
sprig of fresh herb such as basil or rosemary or with finely chopped parsley.

SALMON VERTE

6 SERVINGS

⅓ cup dry white wine
1 tablespoon lemon juice
¼ cup water
¼ teaspoon peppercorns
½ bay leaf
1 teaspoon salt
3 (8-ounce) salmon steaks (about 1 inch thick)
1 cup mayonnaise
2 tablespoons finely chopped chives
2 tablespoons finely chopped parsley
2 tablespoons finely chopped cooked spinach
Cucumber and tomato slices (optional)

1 In a large skillet bring to a boil the
wine, lemon juice, water, peppercorns,
bay leaf and salt. Add the salmon steaks,
cover, and poach for 5 to 8 minutes, or
until the salmon flakes easily when tested
with a fork. Cool. Drain the salmon and
arrange it on a serving dish.
2 Combine the mayonnaise, chives,
parsley and spinach and spoon over the
salmon. Chill. Garnish with cucumber and
tomato slices, if desired.

Gravlax, page 48.
Salmon Soufflé, page 105.
Salmon Mousse with Sour Cream-Dill Sauce, page 119.
Salmon Ravioli, page 507.

SALMON ARCHIDUC

Salmon archiduc is salmon in a sherry and cream sauce.

4 TO 6 SERVINGS

¼ cup minced onions
4 tablespoons butter
4½ tablespoons flour
1½ cups milk (if canned salmon is used, the
    liquid from the can may be substituted for
    part of the milk)
½ teaspoon salt
¼ teaspoon freshly ground pepper
Dash of cayenne
½ cup cream
¼ cup sherry
2 tablespoons cognac
2 cups cooked salmon
1 tablespoon finely chopped parsley

1 In a saucepan sauté the onions in butter until they are transparent. Using a wire whisk, stir in the flour. Meanwhile, bring the milk to a boil and add all at once to the butter-onion mixture, stirring vigorously with the whisk until the sauce is thickened and smooth.

2 Stir in the salt, pepper, cayenne, cream, sherry and cognac. Stir in the flaked salmon and parsley and heat until very hot. Serve over rice.

SARDINES ORIENTALE

4 SERVINGS

2 tablespoons olive oil
2 leeks (white part only), cut into thin strips
1 onion, cut into thin rings
2 garlic cloves, crushed
2 tomatoes, peeled and chopped
1 cup white wine
Pinch of saffron
Salt and freshly ground pepper to taste
4 (3¾-ounce) cans sardines, packed in oil

1 Preheat the oven to 350°F.

2 In a skillet heat the oil, add the leeks and onions and cook 10 minutes. Add the garlic, tomatoes, wine and saffron. Simmer, uncovered, about 25 minutes. Season with salt and pepper.

3 Place all but 15 of the drained sardines in an earthenware dish. Pour the sauce over the top and arrange the reserved sardines over the sauce. Bake 5 minutes. Serve hot in the baking dish.

BREADED SEA SQUABS

6 SERVINGS

18 sea squabs (blowfish), cleaned
2 eggs, lightly beaten
1 tablespoon water
2 cups soft fresh bread crumbs
1/4 pound butter

   1 Dip the sea squabs into a mixture of eggs and water, then roll them in the crumbs.
   2 Heat the butter and cook the fish on all sides until golden brown.

SEA SQUAB PROVENÇALE

6 SERVINGS

18 sea squabs (blowfish), cleaned
Milk
Seasoned flour
Vegetable oil
3 tablespoons butter
1 garlic clove, minced
Lemon juice
Finely chopped parsley

   1 Dip the sea squabs into milk, then dredge them in seasoned flour.
   2 Pour oil into a skillet to a depth of 1/4 inch; heat. When hot, cook the sea squabs on all sides for 6 to 8 minutes, until they are just cooked through.
   3 Transfer the sea squabs to a hot platter. Pour off and discard the oil from the skillet. Add the butter to the skillet and cook to a golden brown. Quickly add the garlic, then pour the butter over the fish. Sprinkle with lemon juice and chopped parsley and serve immediately.

Shad and shad roe are among the noblest gifts of spring. Despite the delicate texture and flavor of shad, however, it is loaded with bones, so be sure to deal with an experienced fish boner, who will charge accordingly.

◆

BAKED SHAD WITH SHAD ROE DRESSING

6 TO 8 SERVINGS

1 (4-pound) shad, boned
1 pair shad roe
¾ teaspoon salt
1 tablespoon vinegar
1 tablespoon butter
1 small onion, minced
1 tablespoon chopped parsley
1 tablespoon lemon juice or dry white wine
Freshly ground pepper

1 Prepare boned shad for stuffing.
2 Preheat the oven to 400°F.
3 Simmer shad roe in water to cover with ½ teaspoon of the salt and the vinegar for 10 minutes. Drain, skin and chop.
4 In a skillet heat the butter, add the onions and cook until they are transparent.
5 Mix roe, onions and the remaining ingredients until well blended.
6 Sprinkle the fish with additional salt, stuff with roe mixture, sew cut surfaces together loosely and place in a foil-lined baking dish (page 195). Bake until the fish flakes easily when tested with a fork, about 30 minutes.

SHAD ROE POACHED IN BUTTER

3 TO 6 SERVINGS

3 pairs of shad roe
Salt and freshly ground pepper to taste
6 tablespoons butter
1 teaspoon lemon juice
¼ cup chopped parsley
Lemon wedges

1 Wipe the shad roe with a damp cloth and sprinkle them with salt and pepper. Prick them all over with a needle or pin.
2 Melt the butter in a heavy skillet and add the shad roe. Cook over low heat for 10 to 15 minutes, until a delicate brown, turning once. Remove the roe to a warm platter.
3 Add the lemon juice to the pan drippings and pour over the roe. Sprinkle with chopped parsley and serve with lemon wedges.

Variation

SHAD ROE AUX FINES HERBES

Poach the shad roe in butter and remove to a warm platter. Add 2 teaspoons lemon juice, 1 tablespoon chopped parsley, 2 teaspoons chopped chives, 1 teaspoon chopped tarragon and 1 teaspoon chopped chervil to the pan drippings. Heat, stirring, and pour over the roe.

BROILED MARINATED SHAD

4 TO 6 SERVINGS

2 tablespoons lemon juice
1 bay leaf, crushed
⅛ teaspoon thyme
¼ cup vegetable oil
¼ teaspoon salt
Freshly ground pepper to taste
2 pounds boneless shad fillets
3 tablespoons melted butter
1 lemon, thinly sliced

1 Combine the lemon juice, bay leaf, thyme, oil, salt and pepper in a shallow pan. Add the fish and marinate for 30 minutes, turning once. Drain.
2 Preheat the broiler.
3 Place the fish on the broiler rack and broil for 5 to 10 minutes, or until fish flakes easily when tested with a fork. Transfer fish to a hot platter. Sprinkle with melted butter and garnish with lemon slices.

◆

FRIED SHAD ROE WITH BACON

Allow 2 slices bacon per serving. Fry bacon and set aside. Blend 1 beaten egg with 1 tablespoon milk or water. Dip poached roe into the egg mixture, then in flour, cornmeal or sifted crumbs. Fry in the bacon fat until brown on both sides, turning the roe carefully. Garnish with the bacon.

SHAD BAKED IN CREAM

6 SERVINGS

1 (3-pound) boned shad
Butter
Salt and freshly ground pepper to taste
1 cup cream
Chopped parsley

1 Preheat the oven to 400°F.
2 Butter a baking dish and place the shad on it. Dot with butter and sprinkle with salt and pepper. Bake, uncovered, 10 minutes.
3 Add the cream and bake 10 minutes longer, basting occasionally with the cream. Sprinkle with chopped parsley.

TO POACH SHAD ROE

Handle the roe carefully in pairs with the membrane intact. Cover with boiling water and for each quart of water add 1 tablespoon vinegar or lemon juice, ½ teaspoon salt and, if desired, ½ teaspoon pickling spice. Lower the heat and simmer until white and firm, from 5 to 20 minutes depending on size. Drain, cover with cold water, cool and drain again. Remove the membrane or not, as desired.

◆

BROILED SHAD ROE

Dry poached roe. Dredge with flour and baste generously with melted butter. Broil about 2 inches from the source of heat in a very hot preheated broiler about 3 minutes on one side and 5 minutes on the other.

SKATE PROVENÇALE

4 SERVINGS

4 skinless, boneless skate wings (about
    2½ pounds)
½ cup milk
Salt and freshly ground pepper to taste
¾ cup flour
¼ cup olive oil
2 tablespoons butter
1 tablespoon minced garlic
1 tablespoon finely chopped shallots
2 cups of ½-inch cubes of peeled,
    seeded tomatoes
1 teaspoon finely chopped rosemary,
    or ½ teaspoon dried
½ teaspoon finely chopped thyme,
    or ¼ teaspoon dried
1 bay leaf
2 tablespoons white vinegar
1 tablespoon finely chopped basil
1 tablespoon finely chopped parsley

1 Put the skate wings in a shallow pan and add the milk. Sprinkle with salt and pepper.

2 Put the flour in a shallow dish and dredge the milk-coated skate wings in it to coat all over. Shake off excess flour.

3 Unless you have a skillet large enough to hold the skate wings, use 2 skillets. To a large skillet add the oil and butter. If smaller skillets are used, heat half of the oil and half of the butter in each. Add the skate wings and cook over moderately high heat about 3 minutes, or until golden brown on one side. Turn the pieces and continue cooking 3 to 5 minutes. The length of cooking time will depend on the thickness of the fish pieces. When ready, transfer the skate wings to a platter.

4 If 2 skillets have been used, pour the oil from one skillet to the other. Add the garlic and shallots and cook briefly, stirring. Add the tomatoes, salt, pepper,

rosemary, thyme, bay leaf and vinegar. Cook over moderately high heat, stirring, about 2 minutes. Spoon the sauce over the fish and sprinkle with basil and parsley.

♦

GILBERT LE COZE'S SKATE WITH BLACK BUTTER SAUCE

2 OR MORE SERVINGS

2 skate wings with skin and inner cartilage
    intact (about 1½ pounds)
1 large bay leaf
3 thyme sprigs, or ¾ teaspoon dried
Salt to taste
1 teaspoon whole peppercorns
⅓ cup fish stock or bottled clam juice
6 tablespoons butter
2 tablespoons drained capers
⅓ cup white vinegar

1 Put the skate in a skillet in which it will fit without crowding. Add water to barely cover the fish and add the bay leaf, thyme, salt and peppercorns. Bring to the boil and reduce the heat. Let simmer about 15 minutes. Lay out a sheet of paper toweling. Lift the fish out of the water and reserve the cooking liquid. Place the fish dark skin side up on the toweling.

2 In a small skillet heat the fish stock and the reserved cooking liquid. Bring to the simmer.

3 Place the butter in a small heavy skillet and cook over high heat about 2 minutes or slightly longer. Watch carefully. When the butter has turned the color of dark caramel, verging on black, add the capers, vinegar and the hot stock. The color of the sauce will lighten somewhat. Pour the sauce over the fish.

PAN-FRIED SMELTS

6 SERVINGS

3 pounds smelts
1 tablespoon salt
¼ teaspoon freshly ground pepper
¾ cup flour
2 eggs
2 tablespoons water
1½ cups fine fresh bread crumbs
½ cup vegetable oil

1 Wipe the smelts with a damp cloth. Mix salt and pepper with the flour and sprinkle the mixture over the fish. Dip floured fish into the eggs lightly beaten with the water and then roll in the crumbs.

2 In a shallow skillet, heat the oil, add the smelts and cook until brown on both sides, about 5 minutes. Turn the fish carefully with a spatula.

POACHED RED SNAPPER

6 TO 8 SERVINGS

1 (4-pound) red snapper
2 celery stalks
4 parsley sprigs
2 teaspoons salt
1 bay leaf
1 teaspoon thyme
10 peppercorns
Green mayonnaise (page 556)

1 Have the red snapper thoroughly cleaned and scaled but leave the head and tail intact. Wrap the fish in cheesecloth to facilitate removing it from the pan when cooked.

2 Place the fish in a large oval baking pan or fish cooker. Add enough water to cover and the remaining ingredients.

3 Bring to a boil and simmer for about 15 minutes, until the fish flakes easily when tested with a fork. Very carefully remove the fish from the cooking liquid, using the cheesecloth as handles. Place the fish on a long oval platter and remove the cheesecloth carefully.

4 Chill the fish and serve with green mayonnaise.

BAKED RED SNAPPER

6 SERVINGS

1 (4-pound) red snapper
Salt and freshly ground pepper
6 tablespoons butter
1 small onion, chopped
4 cups fine stale bread crumbs
1 cup chopped cucumber
2 teaspoons capers or chopped sour pickle
¾ teaspoon sage
½ cup white wine

1 Preheat the oven to 400°F.
2 Sprinkle the fish inside with salt and pepper.
3 In a skillet heat 4 tablespoons of the butter, add the onions and brown lightly. Add the crumbs, cucumber, capers, sage and half the wine and mix. Stuff the fish with the mixture and close with skewers and string.
4 Place the fish in a well-greased shallow pan lined with foil (page 195).
5 Bake, uncovered, until the fish flakes easily when tested with a fork, about 30 minutes. Baste frequently with additional butter and wine. Serve with the pan drippings seasoned to taste.

BAKED RED SNAPPER WITH SHRIMP STUFFING

6 TO 8 SERVINGS

1 (4- to 6-pound) red snapper, cleaned
Salt and freshly ground pepper
¼ pound butter
3 tablespoons minced onions
1 tablespoon flour
½ teaspoon crumbled basil
1 tablespoon minced parsley
½ cup milk
½ pound shrimp, chopped
1 cup cooked rice
3 tablespoons lemon juice
Lemon slices and watercress for garnish

1 Wipe the fish with damp paper toweling. Sprinkle inside generously with salt and pepper.
2 Melt half of the butter in a skillet. Add the onions and cook until transparent. Stir in the flour, basil and parsley. Season with salt and pepper. Gradually add milk, stirring to form a thick sauce. Add shrimp, rice and lemon juice. Stir until blended. Remove stuffing from heat.
3 Preheat the oven to 400°F.
4 Place the fish in a foil-lined pan. Place skewers through both edges of body cavity and fill cavity with stuffing. Lace closed with string. Cover tail with foil to prevent burning.
5 Melt remaining butter and pour over fish. Bake for about 30 minutes, or until fish flakes easily when tested with a fork. Baste occasionally with pan drippings, or with more butter if needed. Serve garnished with lemon slices and watercress.

RED SNAPPER WITH LEMON BUTTER

4 TO 6 SERVINGS

3 pounds red snapper fillets
Flour
Salt and freshly ground pepper
¼ cup vegetable oil
4 tablespoons butter
2 tablespoons lemon juice
4 slices of lemon
2 tablespoons chopped parsley

1 Dredge the fish lightly on both sides in flour, salt and pepper.

2 Heat the oil in a skillet and cook the fish until golden brown on both sides, 3 to 5 minutes on a side. Do not overcook. The fish is done when the flesh flakes easily when tested with a fork.

3 Meanwhile, melt the butter and add lemon juice. Simmer briefly. Transfer the fish to a hot platter, pour the butter over it, and garnish with lemon and parsley.

SOLE TURBANS WITH CRAB STUFFING

6 SERVINGS

6 sole or flounder fillets
Salt and freshly ground pepper
½ pound crabmeat, picked over well to remove any bits of shell or cartilage
1 tablespoon minced onions
1 tablespoon chopped parsley
1 tablespoon chopped celery
6 tablespoons butter, melted
½ cup cracker crumbs
1 egg

1 Preheat the oven to 375°F.

2 Sprinkle fish with salt and pepper. Coil each fillet inside a buttered muffin tin or 6-ounce custard cup. If necessary, trim top of each fillet to make it even. Flake the crabmeat.

3 Sauté onions, parsley and celery in 2 tablespoons of the butter until tender. Remove from heat. Add crumbs, crabmeat and egg. Mix well and season with salt and pepper.

4 Spoon crabmeat mixture into center of fillets. Brush with remaining butter. Bake for 5 to 8 minutes, or until fish flakes easily when tested with a fork. Remove fillets carefully with 2 spoons.

SOLE MEUNIÈRE

6 SERVINGS

6 fillets of sole or flounder
Milk
Seasoned flour
Peanut oil
3 tablespoons butter
Lemon juice
Finely chopped parsley
Lemon slices

1 Divide the sole down the center line and discard the tiny bone structure from the center line. Add milk barely to cover and let stand about 15 minutes.

2 Pat the fillets dry and dredge in seasoned flour. Add peanut oil to a large skillet to a depth of ¼ inch. When it is hot, cook the fillets on both sides until golden brown. Use a spatula to transfer the fillets to a hot dish and pour off and discard the oil in the skillet.

3 Add the butter to the skillet and when it starts to brown, pour it over the sole fillets. Sprinkle with lemon juice and chopped parsley and garnish with lemon slices dipped in parsley.

Variation

SOLE AMANDINE

Add toasted slivered almonds to the skillet with the butter and when hot and foamy, pour over the fish.

PAUPIETTES OF SOLE WITH MUSHROOM SAUCE

6 SERVINGS

1 (7¾-ounce) can salmon, drained, boned and flaked
2 tablespoons minced parsley
2 tablespoons chopped chives
½ teaspoon tarragon
½ teaspoon paprika
1 tablespoon lemon juice
6 sole or flounder fillets
1 tablespoon butter, melted
Mushroom Sauce (page 565)

1 Preheat the oven to 350°F.

2 Mix the salmon, parsley, chives, tarragon, paprika and lemon juice.

3 Spread some of the salmon filling on each piece of sole to within ¼ inch of the edge. Roll up the sole in jelly roll fashion, starting with the tail end. Secure with toothpicks.

4 Place the sole in a buttered shallow baking dish. Brush the sole with melted butter and bake for about 10 minutes, or until the fish flakes easily when tested with a fork. Drain sole and remove toothpicks. Arrange on a serving dish and top with mushroom sauce.

SOLE DUGLÉRÉ

In French cuisine the name *Dugléré* indicates the presence of tomatoes.

4 SERVINGS

4 fillets of sole or flounder
2 tablespoons butter
¼ cup finely chopped onions
¼ cup fish stock or bottled clam juice
½ cup dry white wine
½ cup peeled and coarsely chopped tomatoes
Tabasco sauce to taste
2 tablespoons minced parsley or coriander
⅛ teaspoon freshly ground pepper

1 Roll the fillets and secure with toothpicks. In a skillet heat the butter, add the onions and cook until they are transparent.

2 Arrange the fillets in the pan and pour the fish stock and wine over them. Add the tomatoes, Tabasco and parsley and bring to a boil. Reduce the heat and cook gently until the fish flakes easily when tested with a fork, 5 to 8 minutes. Turn carefully once while cooking.

3 Remove the fillets to a serving dish, remove toothpicks and keep warm. Stir the sauce over high heat 2 or 3 minutes, until slightly reduced. Add the pepper and pour the sauce over the fillets.

SWORDFISH STEAK WITH ROSEMARY

4 SERVINGS

1 (2-inch-thick) swordfish steak
Flour
1 teaspoon rosemary
Olive oil
6 tablespoons butter
Salt to taste
¼ cup white wine

1 Dredge the steak in the flour. Press the rosemary into the fish and brush with oil.

2 Heat 5 tablespoons of the butter in a skillet, add the fish and cook, turning once, until the fish flakes easily when tested with a fork, about 15 minutes. Sprinkle with salt and remove the fish to a hot platter.

3 Add the wine and remaining butter to the pan and heat. Pour over and around the fish.

SWORDFISH BAKED IN FOIL

4 SERVINGS

1 cup sliced mushrooms
1 medium onion, sliced
2 tablespoons chopped green pepper
2 tablespoons olive oil
2 tablespoons lemon juice or wine vinegar
Salt and freshly ground pepper to taste
1 teaspoon chopped dill
1½ pounds swordfish steak, cut into
    4 servings
4 small pieces of bay leaf
4 thick tomato slices

1 Preheat the oven to 425°F.
2 Cook the mushrooms, onion and green pepper in the oil until wilted. Add the lemon juice, salt, pepper and dill.
3 Line a baking pan with foil, spread half the seasoning mixture over the bottom and add the swordfish steaks.
4 Sprinkle the fish with salt and pepper, place a piece of bay leaf and a slice of tomato on each steak and cover with remaining seasoning mixture.
5 Cover the pan with foil and bake until the fish flakes easily when tested with a fork, about 30 minutes.
6 To serve, remove cover and set pan of fish on a tray or platter. Serve juices and vegetables in the pan as a sauce for the fish.

SWORDFISH WITH CAPERS

4 SERVINGS

1½ pounds swordfish (about 1½ inches thick)
Salt and freshly ground pepper to taste
¼ cup olive oil
2 tablespoons finely chopped shallots
1 garlic clove, minced
3 cups peeled, seeded and chopped ripe or
    canned tomatoes
⅓ cup dry white wine
1 teaspoon lemon juice
2 tablespoons chopped celery
1 tablespoon chopped parsley
1 tablespoon capers

1 Preheat the oven to 400°F.
2 Season the fish with salt and pepper and brown quickly on all sides in the oil. Place in a buttered shallow baking dish.
3 Top with the shallots, garlic, tomatoes, wine, lemon juice, celery and parsley. Bake for 10 to 15 minutes, or until the fish flakes easily when tested with a fork. Transfer the fish to a warm platter.
4 Pour the sauce over the fish and top with the capers.

BROILED SWORDFISH WITH SALMORIGLIO SAUCE

One of the simplest and best sauces for fish is Sicilian in origin and is called *salmoriglio*. It is a combination of olive oil, lemon juice and oregano, best suited to swordfish although another white-fleshed nonoily fish may be used.

4 SERVINGS

1¼ pounds (1-inch-thick) swordfish steak
5 tablespoons olive oil
Salt and freshly ground pepper to taste
1½ tablespoons lemon juice
¾ teaspoon oregano

1 Preheat the broiler.
2 Brush the swordfish on both sides with 2 tablespoons of the olive oil and sprinkle with salt and pepper.
3 Place a wire rack inside a heatproof baking dish. Arrange the swordfish on top and place under the broiler 4 or 5 inches from the source of heat. Leave the broiler door partly open and cook 4 to 5 minutes.
4 Turn the fish and broil 4 to 5 minutes longer.
5 Meanwhile, combine the remaining oil with the lemon juice, oregano, salt and pepper in a saucepan. Heat gently without simmering. Pour the sauce over the fish and serve.

NIKA HAZELTON'S SPANISH TROUT

4 SERVINGS

4 whole trout, cleaned
½ lemon
Salt and freshly ground pepper to taste
2 tablespoons olive oil
½ cup soft fresh bread crumbs
1 garlic clove, minced
2 tablespoons finely chopped parsley
⅓ cup dry sherry

1 Preheat the oven to 350°F.
2 Rub the trout with the lemon, then squeeze the lemon and reserve the juice. Season the fish with salt and pepper.
3 Heat the oil. Remove it from the heat and stir in the crumbs, garlic and parsley. Sprinkle half of this mixture over the bottom of a greased shallow baking dish. Place the trout on top. Sprinkle the fish with the remaining crumb mixture. Sprinkle with the reserved lemon juice.
4 Bake the fish for 5 minutes, then add sherry. Continue to bake for 5 to 8 minutes, basting occasionally with the sherry. When the fish is done, it should flake easily when tested with a fork.

BROOK TROUT MEUNIÈRE

6 SERVINGS

6 brook trout
Milk
⅓ cup flour
½ teaspoon salt
Freshly ground pepper to taste
Peanut oil
4 tablespoons butter
Lemon slices
Chopped parsley

1 Clean the trout, remove the fins but leave the heads and tails on. Dip in milk and drain well but do not dry.

2 Mix flour, salt and pepper. Roll fish in mixture.

3 Heat enough peanut oil in a skillet to cover the bottom to a depth of about ¼ inch. When hot, add trout and brown well on both sides. When cooked, remove to a hot serving platter.

4 Pour off the fat from the skillet and wipe well with paper toweling. Add the butter and cook until it is hazelnut brown. Pour the butter over the trout. Garnish with lemon and parsley.

BROILED TILEFISH WITH LEMON-MUSTARD SAUCE

4 SERVINGS

1 teaspoon grated lemon rind
¼ cup lemon juice
¼ cup vegetable oil
¼ teaspoon salt
⅛ teaspoon freshly ground pepper
1 tablespoon chopped parsley
2 teaspoons prepared mustard, preferably Dijon
1½ pounds tilefish fillets
Lemon quarters and parsley sprigs for garnish

1 Combine the rind, juice, oil, salt, pepper, parsley and mustard.

2 Brush the tilefish well with the sauce; place skin side down on a greased shallow broiling pan. Broil, 4 to 5 inches from the heat, for about 8 minutes, brushing frequently with the sauce, until the fish flakes easily when tested with a fork. It is not necessary to turn the fish.

3 Serve garnished with the lemon quarters and parsley sprigs.

TRUITES AU BLEU LUCHOW

This dish can be made only if you are fortunate enough to have freshly caught trout.

2 SERVINGS

1 pound fish bones and heads
¼ onion, chopped
¼ carrot, chopped
¼ celery heart, chopped
2 cups water
¼ cup white vinegar
2 tablespoons wine vinegar
½ teaspoon salt
Juice of ½ lemon
½ bay leaf
1 clove
2 peppercorns
2 fresh brook trout

1 Combine all the ingredients except the trout and bring to a boil. Lower the heat and simmer 20 minutes. Strain the mixture through cheesecloth.

2 While the liquid is boiling, clean the fish. Do not wash, and handle as little as possible.

3 Bring the strained liquid to a boil, reduce the heat, add the trout and simmer, uncovered, until the trout turns blue and the fish flakes easily when tested with a fork, 7 or 8 minutes. Remove from the liquid and serve with boiled potatoes.

TILEFISH FILLETS BONNE FEMME

Bonne femme means that "the good wife" cooked with mushrooms.

6 SERVINGS

2 shallots, chopped, or 1 small onion
¾ cup sliced mushrooms
Salt and freshly ground pepper to taste
2 pounds tilefish fillets
1 cup dry white wine
¼ cup cream
1 tablespoon butter
1 tablespoon chopped chives
1 tablespoon chopped parsley

1 Preheat the oven to 350°F.

2 Butter a heatproof baking dish. Arrange the shallots and mushrooms on the bottom of the dish and sprinkle with salt and pepper. Place the fish on top, add the wine and cover with buttered wax paper or foil.

3 Bake until the fish flakes easily when tested with a fork, about 10 minutes.

4 Drain the juices from the baking dish into a saucepan. Cook over moderately high heat until reduced about one-half. Add the cream and cook until the sauce has thickened a little. Add the butter in little curls, rotating the pan all the time; this incorporates the butter without rapidly melting it.

5 Pour the sauce over the fish and sprinkle with the chives and parsley.

GRILLED TUNA WITH GINGER SAUCE

There was a time, not many years ago, when most Americans considered tuna solely as something that came out of a can. Today it is one of the most popular American fish, purchased and eaten raw (sushi and sashimi) or cooked (grilled, broiled and sautéed). Grilled tuna is excellent when served in a ginger-flavored sauce. This is the invention of Len Allison, the chef-owner of Hubert's restaurant in Manhattan.

4 SERVINGS

8 scallions, ends trimmed
3 cups dry red wine
½ cup red wine vinegar
1 cup soy sauce
½ cup sesame oil
3 tablespoons paprika
20 slices fresh ginger
16 garlic cloves
2 pounds raw tuna in 1 piece
¼ cup peeled and shredded fresh ginger
½ cup dry white wine
½ cup rice vinegar
½ cup finely chopped shallots
½ cup cream
¾ pound butter
Salt and freshly ground pepper to taste

1 To prepare the tuna, place the scallions over a low flame, an electric burner or charcoal. Cook until they are slightly charred all over, turning as necessary. Remove from the heat and place them in a large bowl.

2 Add the red wine, red wine vinegar, soy sauce, sesame oil, paprika, sliced ginger and garlic.

3 Cut the tuna lengthwise into 4 portions of equal size and weight. Add the slices to the marinade and let stand for 2 hours.

4 To prepare the sauce, combine the shredded ginger, white wine, rice vinegar and shallots and cook 10 to 15 minutes, until the liquid is reduced to about 3 tablespoons. Add the cream and cook down about 5 minutes. Gradually add the butter, beating vigorously and constantly with a wire whisk. Add salt and pepper.

5 When ready to cook the tuna, preheat a charcoal, gas or electric grill. When it is very hot, brush lightly with oil. Add the tuna strips and cook 1½ to 2 minutes on one side. Turn and cook 1½ to 2 minutes on the other side, or to the desired degree of doneness.

6 Slice the tuna on the diagonal into ¼-inch-thick slices. Arrange the slices, slightly overlapping and in a fan shape on a plate. Spoon the sauce over the base of the "fan."

Tuna Carpaccio with Lime Mayonnaise, page 49.
Spaghetti with Fresh Tuna Sauce, page 491.

◆

GRILLED TUNA WITH HERBS

4 SERVINGS

4 (1-inch-thick) tuna steaks
Salt and freshly ground pepper to taste
¼ cup olive oil
1 tablespoon minced garlic
1 teaspoon chopped thyme,
    or ½ teaspoon dried
1 teaspoon finely grated lemon rind
¼ teaspoon hot red pepper flakes
2 tablespoons butter
2 tablespoons lemon juice

1 Preheat an outdoor grill or preheat the oven broiler to high.

2 Sprinkle the tuna pieces on all sides with salt and pepper.

Continued

3 Combine the oil, garlic, thyme, lemon rind and red pepper flakes. Blend well and brush the fish all over with the mixture.

4 Scrape the remaining oil mixture into a small saucepan and add the butter and lemon juice.

5 If the fish is to be cooked on an outdoor grill, place the pieces directly on the grill. Cook, turning often, 5 to 6 minutes. If it is to be cooked under the broiler, place it in a dish about 2 inches from the source of heat. Leave the broiler door partly open. Let cook 3 minutes and turn. Cook the other side 2 to 3 minutes.

6 Put the steaks on individual plates or on a platter. Heat the oil and butter mixture and pour it over the fish.

♦

PAN-FRIED WHITING

4 SERVINGS

4 (¾- to 1-pound) whole whiting
½ teaspoon salt
Freshly ground pepper to taste
½ cup milk
½ cup white cornmeal
½ cup shortening (may be half butter)
⅛ teaspoon rosemary or thyme
Lemon wedges

1 Sprinkle inside of the fish with salt and pepper. Dip in the milk, and then roll in the cornmeal.

2 Heat the shortening in a skillet and fry the fish in it until brown on one side. Sprinkle with the rosemary, turn carefully and cook until the fish flakes easily when tested with a fork. Serve with lemon wedges.

BAKED WEAKFISH, SOUTHERN STYLE

6 TO 8 SERVINGS

1 weakfish
Butter
Salt and freshly ground pepper to taste
Pinch of thyme
1 bay leaf
¾ cup chopped celery
1 cup chopped green peppers
½ cup chopped parsley
¼ pound butter
1 onion, thinly sliced
2 garlic cloves, minced
¼ cup flour
4 cups canned tomatoes, preferably Italian style with basil

1 Preheat the oven to 325°F.

2 Have the weakfish thoroughly cleaned and scaled but leave the head and tail intact.

3 Rub the fish with butter and sprinkle both inside and outside with salt and pepper. Place the fish in a pan lined with heavy-duty foil.

4 Sprinkle the fish with thyme, bay leaf, celery, green peppers and parsley.

5 Heat the butter and sauté the onions and garlic in it until golden but not brown. Stir in the flour; when it is blended, stir in the tomatoes. When the mixture comes to a boil and is slightly thickened, season with salt and pepper.

6 Pour the sauce over the fish and place pan in the oven. Bake, basting frequently, for about 30 minutes, until the fish flakes easily when tested with a fork. Serve with steamed potatoes or rice.

Seviche, page 43.

FISH CURRY

1 cup yogurt
¼ cup chopped onions
1 garlic clove, minced
2 teaspoons lemon juice
1 teaspoon ground coriander
1 teaspoon cayenne
1 teaspoon ground ginger
1 teaspoon oregano
½ teaspoon turmeric
¼ teaspoon curry powder
4 weakfish fillets
½ cup olive or vegetable oil
⅛ teaspoon cumin seed

1 Preheat the oven to 350°F.

2 Put all ingredients except the fish fillets, oil and cumin seed in a food processor and blend until thoroughly mixed.

3 Cut the fish into halves and arrange in a shallow baking dish.

4 Combine the oil and cumin seed in a skillet and heat until dark brown. Add the blended ingredients, stirring constantly. Pour the mixture over the fish and bake for 10 to 15 minutes.

GEFILTE FISH

There are nearly as many recipes for gefilte fish as there are for bouillabaisse.

5 pounds fish fillets (equal amounts
of whitefish and pike plus a small amount
of carp)
Heads, bones and trimmings from fish
5 onions, sliced
1 celery stalk, sliced
2 large carrots, sliced
Salt and freshly ground pepper to taste
3 or 4 eggs, depending on size
2 tablespoons matzo meal
Horseradish

1 Have butcher grind the fish or put it through the finest blade of a food grinder.

2 In a large kettle, combine heads, bones and trimmings of fish with 4 of the onions, the celery and carrots. Cover with water and season with salt and pepper. Bring to a boil.

3 Meanwhile, place the remaining sliced onion and the eggs in a food processor or blender and blend well. Add the onion-egg mixture to the ground fish and blend well. Add matzo meal and salt and pepper. Add ¼ cup of water and blend well.

4 Shape the fish mixture into balls and drop into simmering fish broth. Lower the heat so that the broth barely simmers and cook, covered, 2 hours. When cool, remove the balls to a platter. Garnish with the cooked carrots and strain the fish broth. Chill. Serve the gefilte fish with the jellied fish broth and horseradish.

FISH PUDDING

6 SERVINGS

1 pound fish fillets, cut into small pieces
1½ cups milk
2 tablespoons potato starch or cornstarch
2 eggs
1 cup cream
¼ teaspoon grated nutmeg
Sour cream–dill sauce (page 560)

1 Preheat the oven to 325°F.

2 Put the fish fillets, 1 cup of the milk, the starch and eggs into the container of a food processor and blend well. With the motor on, gradually add the remaining milk. Pour in the cream, add the nutmeg, and pulse just to combine.

3 Pour the mixture into a buttered 1-quart mold. Set the mold in a pan containing warm water about 1 inch deep and bake for 1 hour. Turn out and serve with sour cream–dill sauce.

Shellfish

BOUILLABAISSE

In some circles it is impossible to mention bouillabaisse without someone telling you that you cannot make this fish stew unless you are from Marseille or the region from Nice to Menton. They add that the reason it cannot be made elsewhere is that the ugliest fish in the world swims in the waters of that area. It is called *rascasse*, and it is essential in a genuine bouillabaisse. Nevertheless, here is an adapted recipe for the dish, about which William Makepeace Thackeray could not make up his mind as to whether it is "a soup or broth, or brew, or hotchpotch."

6 SERVINGS

¼ cup olive oil
1 celery stalk, chopped
1 medium onion, chopped
1 garlic clove, finely chopped
1 leek, diced
½ teaspoon thyme
½ bay leaf
2 cups crushed tomatoes
1 cup bottled clam juice
1 cup dry white wine
¼ cup chopped fennel, or ½ teaspoon crushed
    fennel seed
Pinch of saffron
Salt and freshly ground pepper to taste
2 tablespoons chopped parsley
12 mussels, well scrubbed and debearded
12 raw shrimp, shelled and deveined
12 scallops
1 small lobster, cut into pieces (see page 248)
1 pound red snapper or cod, cut into serving
    pieces

1 In a large kettle heat the oil, add the celery, onion, garlic, leek, thyme and bay leaf and cook 5 minutes.

2 Add the tomatoes, clam juice, wine, fennel, saffron, salt, pepper and parsley and simmer 15 minutes.

3 Add the seafood and cook 15 minutes longer. Serve in large soup bowls.

Curried Fish Soup with Cream and Tomatoes, page 83.

◆

CACCIUCCO
ITALIAN SEAFOOD STEW

Lobster is sometimes used in cacciucco, but squid are always customary. Although Americans hold them in somewhat nervous regard, they are delicious. One old Boston fisherman holds they are "twice as sweet as lobster and only half the trouble to fix." Squid, sometimes known as *cuttlefish*, or *calamari* in Italian, are plentiful and inexpensive.

Those who never have cleaned squid would do well to enlist assistance from a fish dealer. The general procedure is to remove the spiny portion, which looks like a translucent rod. Then the head and legs are pulled from the envelopelike covering. The ink sac at the base of the head may be retained or removed. Europeans think the ink adds to the flavor.

4 SERVINGS

½ cup olive oil
1 garlic clove, minced
1 hot red pepper
½ pound raw shrimp, shelled and deveined
½ pound squid, skinned and cleaned
½ cup dry white wine
2 tablespoons tomato paste
3 cups water
½ teaspoon salt
1 pound cod fillet, cut into pieces
½ pound scallops, cut into pieces
½ pound halibut, cut into pieces
4 slices of Italian bread
1 garlic clove, cut

1 In a deep kettle heat the oil, add the minced garlic and red pepper and brown the garlic lightly.

2 Cut the shrimp and squid into small pieces and add. Cover the pan and cook over low heat until the squid is tender, about 30 minutes. Add the wine and continue cooking, uncovered, until the wine evaporates. Add the tomato paste, water and salt and cook 5 minutes longer.

3 Add the remaining fish. Cover and simmer until tender, about 10 minutes. Add more water if necessary; the stew must be thick.

4 While the stew is cooking, toast the bread and rub with the cut garlic. Place a slice of bread in each soup bowl.

5 Remove the hot red pepper from the stew and correct the seasonings. Ladle a generous serving of stew over the bread.

CHUPE

Chupe is a Chilean seafood casserole that is thickened with bread soaked in milk. It is a splendid buffet dish. The chupe below was served on occasion in the home of Leonard Bernstein, the conductor of the New York Philharmonic. His late wife, the former Felicia Montealegre, was born in Montevideo.

10 SERVINGS

3 small loaves French bread (about 5 cups cubed)
5 cups milk
4 cups water
1 tablespoon salt
1 bay leaf
2 pounds scallops, washed
1 pound raw shrimp, shelled and deveined
2 tablespoons paprika
1 teaspoon Tabasco sauce
4 tablespoons butter, melted
½ teaspoon oregano
¼ teaspoon freshly ground pepper
1 onion, sliced
2 large lobster tails
½ pound crabmeat, picked over well to remove any bits of shell or cartilage
½ pound mozzarella cheese, diced
Butter
4 hard-cooked eggs, cut into wedges
Grated Parmesan cheese

1 Cut the bread into cubes and soak in the milk.

2 Bring the water with the salt and bay leaf to a boil. Add the scallops and cook about 3 minutes. Remove the scallops, add the shrimp and cook until pink. Remove the shrimp.

3 Add about 1½ cups of the broth to the bread mixture. Add the paprika, Tabasco and 4 tablespoons of melted butter. Mix well and press through a sieve, or purée in a food processor.

4 Add enough water to the remaining broth to make about 3 quarts. Add the oregano, pepper and onion and bring to a boil. Add the lobster tails and boil about 8 minutes. Cool the lobster, remove from shell and cut the meat into 1-inch slices.

5 Discard the broth, wash the pot and place in it all the seafood, bread purée, mozzarella and 3 tablespoons of butter. Mix.

6 Spread half the mixture in two shallow buttered 3-quart casseroles. Add the eggs and the remaining seafood mixture. Sprinkle with Parmesan and dot with bits of butter.

7 Bake in a preheated 400°F oven until golden brown, about 20 minutes. If prepared ahead and chilled, let warm to room temperature before baking.

◆

TEMPURA

Almost every nation has some version of the "mixed fry" in which many foods are dipped in a batter and deep fried. In Japan it is known as *tempura*; in Italy *fritto misto*. Both include bits of fish, seafood and vegetables.

ABOUT 6 SERVINGS

18 medium shrimp
2 flounder fillets
1 medium squid (optional)
6 sea scallops
1 carrot
12 long string beans
1 sweet potato
4 cups vegetable oil or, preferably, 3 cups vegetable oil and 1 cup sesame seed oil
Tempura batter (see following recipe)
Tempura sauce (see following recipe)

1 Insert the small blade of a pair of scissors under the shell of each raw shrimp. Starting at the head portion, cut down to, but not through, the last tail segment.

2 Peel the shrimp, leaving the tail segment intact. Cut off the lower half of the tails. Split the peeled shrimp down the backs and rinse under cold running water to remove sand and intestinal tract.

3 Using a sharp knife, make shallow cuts across the underside of each shrimp in 3 equidistant places. This permits "straightening" the shrimp lengthwise.

4 Cut the flounder into small sections measuring about 2 x 3 inches. Remove the tentacles from the squid and peel off the outer and inner skins. Cut into square bite-size pieces. Cut the scallops into quarters.

5 Cut the carrot into ⅛-inch-thick slices. Cut string beans into 3-inch lengths. Peel the sweet potato and cut into ⅛-inch-thick slices and cut each slice into quarters.

6 Dry all the seafood and vegetables well between clean cloths or paper towels.

7 Using a deep fryer or electric skillet, heat the oil to 375°F. This temperature must be maintained for the entire frying process. Hold shrimp by the tail, dip into the batter and gently drop, one at a time, into the hot fat. Deep fry a few shrimp at a time until the batter is golden brown, or 30 seconds to 1 minute. Dip the flounder in the batter and cook the same length of time. Continue with remaining seafood and vegetables.

8 Remove the deep-fried foods, as they are cooked, to paper napkins or other toweling to drain briefly. To eat tempura, dip the fried food in tempura sauce.

TEMPURA BATTER

3 egg yolks
2 cups cold water
2½ cups flour

Combine the egg yolks with the water and mix well. Gradually stir in the flour, stirring from the bottom of the bowl, preferably with thick chopsticks. Do not overstir; this is the secret of a light batter. Flour should still float on top of the batter.

TEMPURA SAUCE
ABOUT 2 CUPS

1 cup water
2 tablespoons dried bonito flakes
⅓ cup soy sauce
⅓ cup mirin, or ⅓ cup sake mixed with 1
  teaspoon sugar
Freshly grated Japanese white radish
Grated fresh ginger

1 In a saucepan, bring the water to a boil and add the bonito flakes. Cook 3 minutes and strain. This stock is known as dashi.

2 Combine the dashi with the soy sauce and mirin. Pour a little of the sauce into individual serving bowls and let guests add radish and ginger to taste.

PEIXADA

A *peixada*, pronounced *pay-SHAH-dah*, is a Brazilian specialty that includes a fish not available in North American waters, but red snapper will do.

8 SERVINGS

1 (4-pound) red snapper
6 medium tomatoes, peeled and chopped
2 scallions, sliced, green part included
¼ cup chopped parsley
2 bay leaves
1 teaspoon ground coriander
¼ teaspoon freshly ground pepper
2 teaspoons salt
2 pounds small raw shrimp, shelled and
    deveined
Tabasco sauce to taste

1 Clean the red snapper and remove the head. Cut the body into slices about 1 inch thick. Place the slices and the head, if desired, in a large saucepan and add the tomatoes, scallions, parsley, bay leaves, coriander, pepper and salt. Let stand several hours in the refrigerator.

2 Add water just to cover the fish and bring to a boil. Reduce the heat and simmer, covered, until the fish flakes easily when tested with a fork, about 10 minutes. Carefully remove the fish steaks to a hot platter. Discard the bay leaves and the fish head, if used.

3 Add the shrimp to the mixture in which the fish was poached and add Tabasco and additional salt and pepper to taste. Simmer until the shrimp are pink, about 3 minutes. Serve the sauce over the fish.

FRITTO MISTO

6 TO 8 SERVINGS

2 cups sifted flour
1½ teaspoons salt
¼ teaspoon freshly ground pepper
4 eggs, separated
1 (12-ounce) can of beer
4 tablespoons butter, melted
Pieces of vegetables, fish, seafood, cheese
Oil for deep frying

1 Sift together the flour, salt and pepper.

2 Beat the egg yolks until light. Add the beer and mix into the dry ingredients, stirring only until well blended.

3 Stir in the butter. Let stand at room temperature 1½ hours. Beat the egg whites until stiff, then fold into the batter.

4 Heat the fat to 375°F. Dip pieces of vegetables, fish, seafood and cheese into the batter and fry until golden brown, 2 or 3 minutes.

Variations

Almost any vegetable, fish or seafood is suitable in one form or another for a mixed fry. The following are especially recommended.

ONIONS Cut into ¼-inch rings and coat with flour before dipping into the batter.

EGGPLANT Slice without peeling into half-moons or rectangular fingers about ½ inch thick. Coat with flour before dipping into the batter.

CAULIFLOWER Break into flowerets.

BROCCOLI Peel stems and cut vegetables into bite-size flowerets.

TOMATOES Do not peel. Cut into ½-inch slices. Discard the seeds and coat with flour before dipping into the batter.

SHRIMP Shell and devein raw shrimp, leaving the last segment of the tail intact, if desired. To "butterfly" shrimp, slit deeply down the back with a sharp knife, without cutting through. Wash and dry with paper toweling. Dust with flour before dipping into batter.

CRABMEAT Select large pieces of lump crabmeat. Dust with flour before dipping into batter.

OYSTERS Use whole. Dust with flour before dipping into batter.

LOBSTER OR ROCK LOBSTER TAIL Cut meat into ½-inch medallions and dust with flour before dipping into the batter.

FISH FILLETS Cut into strips about 1 inch wide. Dust with flour before dipping into the batter.

CHEESE Use Gruyère, Swiss or fontina cheese cut into 1-inch squares ½-inch thick.

Seafood Salad with Tarragon, page 112.

SEAFOOD IN RAMEKINS

4 SERVINGS

5 tablespoons butter
½ cup raw shrimp, cut into bite-size pieces
½ cup crabmeat, flaked and picked over well to remove any bits of shell or cartilage
½ cup bay or sea scallops, cut into bite-size pieces
1 tablespoon finely chopped onions
2 tablespoons sherry
½ teaspoon salt
¼ teaspoon freshly ground pepper
3 tablespoons flour
1½ cups milk
½ cup bread crumbs
¼ cup grated Parmesan cheese

1 Preheat the oven to 400°F.
2 In a large skillet heat 2 tablespoons of the butter, add the seafood and onions and cook 4 minutes, stirring occasionally. Sprinkle with the sherry, salt and pepper.
3 In a saucepan melt the remaining 3 tablespoons butter, add the flour and stir with a wire whisk until blended. Meanwhile, bring the milk to a boil and add all at once to the butter-flour mixture, stirring vigorously with the whisk until the sauce is thickened and smooth. Combine the sauce with the seafood mixture.
4 Spoon the mixture into individual buttered ramekins or shells and sprinkle with the crumbs mixed with the cheese.
5 Bake 10 to 12 minutes, or brown under a broiler. Garnish with lemon wedges.

SEAFOOD GUMBO

6 TO 8 SERVINGS

4 tablespoons butter
1 pound okra, sliced
2 onions, finely chopped
1½ tablespoons flour
1 cup tomatoes
12 oysters in liquor
2 teaspoons salt
1 garlic clove, crushed
Pinch of cayenne, or ¼ pod red pepper
1 pound raw shrimp in shells
Tabasco sauce to taste
Worcestershire sauce to taste
½ pound crabmeat, picked over well to remove
    any bits of shell or cartilage
Boiled rice

1 Heat 2 tablespoons of the butter in a soup kettle, add the okra and cook, stirring frequently, until tender.

2 Stir in onions and cook for several minutes, then stir in flour until the mixture is smooth. Add tomatoes and cook the mixture for several minutes longer.

3 Add enough water to the oyster liquor to make 8 cups of liquid. Stir this into the okra mixture and add salt, garlic and cayenne. Simmer for 1 hour.

4 Meanwhile, shell the shrimp and sauté in the remaining 2 tablespoons of butter just until they turn pink.

5 Ten minutes before serving add the shrimp and oysters and cook over low heat until edges begin to curl. Add Tabasco, Worcestershire and the crabmeat and heat through. Serve gumbo in soup bowls over boiled rice.

WASHBOILER CLAMBAKE

8 SERVINGS

Wet seaweed, well washed
4 cups water
4 Idaho potatoes, wrapped in foil
2 chickens cut up, each part wrapped in
    cheesecloth
2 (1½-pound) lobsters
4 ears of corn, husked and wrapped in foil
24 steamer clams

1 Fill the bottom of a washboiler or large enamel pot with a layer of washed seaweed. Add the water and place over high heat. When water boils, add potatoes and more washed seaweed. Cover.

2 About 15 minutes later, add the chicken and a layer of seaweed. Cover.

3 Fifteen minutes later, add the lobster and more seaweed. Cover.

4 About 8 minutes later add the corn.

5 Ten minutes later add the clams. Cover and steam until clams open. Serve with butter and kettle liquid as a dip.

STUFFED QUAHOGS

2 dozen quahogs (chowder clams)
1/4 cup water
1/4 cup minced onions
1/4 cup finely chopped celery
1/4 cup chopped green pepper
2 cups soft fresh bread crumbs
12 slices of bacon, each cut into halves
Parsley for garnish

1 Preheat the oven to 450°F.

2 Wash the clams well and place them in a kettle with the water. Steam over moderate heat just until the clams open wide. Remove the meat and reserve half the shells for stuffing. Reserve the clam broth.

3 Grind the clams or process briefly in a food processor. Combine with the onions, celery, green pepper and crumbs. Dampen the mixture with clam broth, just enough to bind. Stuff the 24 reserved clamshells.

4 Lay half a slice of bacon across the top of each stuffed clam and arrange the clams on a baking dish. Bake until bacon is crisp. Garnish each stuffed clam with a parsley sprig and serve hot, with lemon wedges if desired.

CLAM FRITTERS

1½ cups flour
½ teaspoon salt
3 tablespoons butter
3 eggs, lightly beaten
¾ cup beer
2 dozen fresh cherrystone clams, or 2 cups
    drained minced canned clams
3 egg whites, stiffly beaten
½ cup vegetable oil
Lemon wedges and parsley sprigs for garnish

1 Place the flour and salt in a mixing bowl. Melt the butter and add with the eggs to the bowl. Mix well. Gradually stir in the beer. Allow the batter to stand in a warm place, such as atop the stove, for 1 hour.

2 Open the clams, remove the meat, and chop fine. Reserve the clam liquor for use in chowder. Fold the minced clams and the egg whites into the batter.

3 Heat the oil in a heavy skillet. When it is hot but not smoking, drop in the batter by spoonfuls. When the undersides of the fritters are light brown, turn and brown the other sides. Drain on paper toweling.

4 Place fritters on a warm platter and keep warm until all are cooked. To serve, garnish with lemon wedges and parsley sprigs.

CLAMS MEXICAINE

4 scallions, trimmed and chopped
1 large green pepper, cored, seeded
*   and chopped*
¼ cup olive oil
1 cup rice
1 cup Italian plum tomatoes, drained
1 cup tomato juice
2 cups chopped clams with their juice
Salt to taste
1 teaspoon chili powder, or more

1 Cook the scallions and pepper in the oil for 3 minutes. Add the rice and cook, stirring, for 3 minutes longer.

2 Add the tomatoes, tomato juice and 1 cup clam juice. If necessary, add enough water to make the cup of liquid. Season the mixture with salt and chili powder; cover. Simmer for 20 minutes, or until rice is tender. Stir in the clams and heat through. Serve immediately.

Baked Stuffed Clams with Garlic Butter, page 38.
Clams aux Blinis, page 42.
New England Clam Chowder, page 79.
Manhattan Clam Chowder, page 80.
Italian Clam Soup, page 80.
Linguine with Clams and Basil, page 494.
Pasta with Anchovy and Clam Sauce, page 496.
Pasta with Red Clam Sauce, page 495.

STEAMED CLAMS

4 quarts soft-shell clams
½ cup water
¼ pound butter
2 tablespoons lemon juice
Salt and freshly ground pepper to taste
Dry white wine (optional)

1 Wash clams under cold running water until free of sand. Scrub with an abrasive sponge or cloth to remove remaining grime.

2 Bring the water to a boil in a large pot and add clams. Cover the pot and lower the heat to minimum. Steam until clams barely open. Stir occasionally so that clams cook evenly.

3 Remove clams from the pot, discarding clams that have not opened, and reserve broth. Strain the broth through cheesecloth. Place ½ cup broth in a small bowl for each serving.

4 Melt the butter and add lemon juice, salt and pepper and a little white wine if desired. Divide among small bowls and serve with a slice of lemon or a sprig of watercress.

5 Heap clams into soup bowls and serve with dry white wine. Provide finger bowls and a large bowl for shells.

BURGUNDIAN CLAMS

20 large clams
4 tablespoons butter, at room temperature
¼ cup fine dry bread crumbs
1 tablespoon finely chopped parsley
2 garlic cloves, minced
2 teaspoons finely chopped shallots
Freshly ground pepper to taste
3 tablespoons finely chopped Swiss cheese

1 Have clams opened and leave them on the half shell.
2 Preheat the oven to 425°F.
3 Combine the butter, crumbs, parsley, garlic, shallots, pepper and Swiss cheese and work the mixture to a paste.
4 Using a small spatula, spread the mixture over the opened clams. Arrange the clams on pie plates and bake for 8 to 10 minutes, until the clams are thoroughly heated and bubbling. Serve piping hot.

◆

SOFT-SHELL CRABS SAUTÉ

2 CRABS PER SERVING

Kill the crabs by piercing between the eyes with a knife. Lift the pointed ends of the shells and scrape out the spongy portions between the shells and the body. Put the crabs on their backs and cut off the tails.

Wash thoroughly and dry. Sprinkle with salt and pepper and dip in flour. Fry quickly in hot shallow butter until golden brown.

Sprinkle crabs with chopped parsley.

SOFT-SHELL CRABS AMANDINE

4 TO 6 SERVINGS

8 to 12 soft-shell crabs, dressed for cooking (preceding recipe)
Flour
6 to 8 tablespoons butter
1 teaspoon Worcestershire sauce
Salt and freshly ground pepper to taste
½ cup blanched, sliced almonds
Lemon wedges

1 Dip the crabs in flour. In a skillet heat the butter, add the crabs and Worcestershire and cook until the crabs are a delicate brown and crisp on the edges, 3 to 4 minutes on each side. Remove the crabs to a hot serving dish and sprinkle with salt and pepper.
2 Add the almonds to the butter in the pan in which the crabs were cooked. Sauté until golden, then pour them, with the butter, over the crabs. Serve with lemon wedges.

◆

DEEP-FRIED SOFT-SHELL CRABS

2 CRABS PER SERVING

Prepare the crabs as for sauté (opposite) and season with salt and pepper. Dip in flour, then in slightly beaten egg that has been mixed with a little water, and then in sifted cracker or bread crumbs.

Fry the crabs in deep fat heated to 370°F until golden brown. Drain on paper toweling.

BROILED SOFT-SHELL CRABS

12 soft-shelled crabs, dressed for cooking
   (page 243)
Flour for dredging
¼ pound butter, at room temperature
½ cup chopped parsley
1 tablespoon finely chopped chives
2 teaspoons paprika
1 teaspoon salt
Melted butter
Lemon juice and lemon wedges

1 Dredge the crabs lightly in flour. Arrange them in a flat broiling dish or on a broiling rack.

2 Cream the butter with the parsley, chives, paprika and salt and dot the crabs with the mixture.

3 Broil the crabs about 3 inches from the source of heat in a preheated broiler 5 to 8 minutes. Baste often and turn once during cooking. Serve with melted butter and lemon juice. Garnish with lemon wedges.

HARD-SHELL CRABS

2 TO 3 CRABS PER SERVING

Wash live crabs in several changes of cold water, handling them with tongs. Plunge them head first into boiling salted water to cover and boil 15 to 20 minutes, or until shells turn red. Drain, plunge into cold water, drain again and cool. To clean crabs, break off claws and legs close to the body; crack the claws with a nutcracker and remove the meat. Break off the pointed apron, or tail. Take the crab in both hands and pull the upper and lower shells apart, beginning at tail. Wash away loose matter under running water and remove membranous covering round side. Remove meat between sections, picking out any cartilage. Six crabs yield about 1 cup of meat.

HERBED CRABMEAT

6 SERVINGS

4 tablespoons butter
1½ pounds crabmeat, picked over well to
   remove any bits of shell or cartilage
Salt and coarsely ground pepper to taste
Juice of ½ lemon
1 tablespoon chopped chives
1 tablespoon chopped parsley
1 teaspoon chopped tarragon

1 Heat the butter until it bubbles and cook the crabmeat in it just until heated through.

2 Season the crab with salt, pepper, lemon juice and the herbs. Serve on noodles or angel's hair pasta.

CRABMEAT SAUTÉED WITH ALMONDS

4 SERVINGS

7 tablespoons butter
1 pound crabmeat, picked over well to remove
    any bits of shell or cartilage
2/3 cup almonds, blanched and split in half
Salt and freshly ground pepper to taste
1/2 cup cream
3 tablespoons chopped parsley

1 In a medium-size skillet heat 4 table-spoons of the butter, add the crabmeat and toss lightly until a delicate brown.

2 Meanwhile, in a separate skillet heat the remaining butter, add the almonds and cook over brisk heat until light brown. Add the salt and pepper, then add the crabmeat.

3 Add the cream and parsley and bring the mixture to a boil. Reduce the heat and simmer 2 minutes. Serve on rice.

Corn and Crabmeat Chowder, page 66.
Crab-Stuffed Avocados, page 114.
Hot Crab Salad, page 114.
Crab Louis, page 116.
Cold Crabmeat Mousse, page 118.
Maryland Crab Soup, page 86.
Spaghetti with Crabmeat, page 493.
Crabmeat Remick, page 40.

DEVILED CRAB

6 SERVINGS

2 tablespoons butter
2 tablespoons flour
1/2 cup milk
1/2 cup cream
1/4 teaspoon grated nutmeg
1/4 teaspoon dry mustard
2 egg yolks
1/4 cup sherry
Salt and freshly ground pepper to taste
3 cups crabmeat, picked over well to remove
    any bits of shell or cartilage
Buttered bread crumbs
Lemon wedges

1 Preheat the oven to 400°F.

2 In a saucepan melt the butter, add the flour and stir with a wire whisk until blended. Meanwhile, bring the milk and cream to a boil and add all at once to the butter-flour mixture, stirring vigorously with the whisk until the sauce is smooth.

3 Remove the sauce from the heat and stir in the nutmeg and mustard. Add the egg yolks lightly beaten with a little of the hot sauce and heat, stirring, until thickened. Add the sherry, salt, pepper and crabmeat.

4 Spoon the mixture into individual crab shells, flameproof ramekins or a baking dish. Sprinkle with buttered crumbs and bake until the crab is thoroughly hot and the crumbs are brown, 5 to 10 minutes. Serve with lemon wedges.

Cheese Roulade with Crabmeat, page 115.

CRABMEAT STEW

6 SERVINGS

2 cups crabmeat, picked over well to remove
    any bits of shell or cartilage
½ cup dry sherry
2 tablespoons butter
1 garlic clove, crushed
1½ tablespoons flour
½ teaspoon rosemary
¼ cup finely chopped onions or chives
3 tablespoons finely chopped green pepper
¾ cup peeled, chopped tomato
Salt and freshly ground pepper to taste
1 cup cream

1 Marinate the crabmeat in the sherry 1 hour in the refrigerator. In a skillet heat the butter, add the garlic and sauté. Add the flour, rosemary, onions, green pepper, tomato, salt and pepper and simmer 5 minutes.

2 Stir in the crabmeat with the sherry and add the cream.

3 Cook 5 to 10 minutes longer, adding more cream if necessary. Correct the seasonings and serve with rice.

PEPPERY STUFFED CRAB, GUADELOUPE STYLE

6 SERVINGS

1 cup fine fresh bread crumbs
1 cup milk
1½ tablespoons finely chopped bacon
1 teaspoon minced garlic
1 small hot fresh green pepper, seeded and
    finely chopped
1 tablespoon finely chopped shallots
1 pound fresh lump crabmeat, picked over to
    remove any bits of shell or cartilage
4 tablespoons butter, melted
4 dashes of Tabasco sauce
2 tablespoons lime juice
2 tablespoons olive oil
½ cup fine dry bread crumbs

1 Preheat the oven to 375°F.

2 Put the fresh crumbs in a bowl and add the milk. Blend and let stand.

3 Heat the bacon in a skillet and add the garlic, hot pepper and shallots. Cook briefly, stirring.

4 Add the crabmeat to the bread mixture. Add the garlic mixture, half the butter, Tabasco and lime juice. Blend thoroughly, striving not to break up the lumps of crabmeat any more than necessary.

5 Brush the insides of 6 crab shells or individual ramekins with olive oil. Fill the shells with equal portions of the crab mixture. Sprinkle equally with the dry crumbs and remaining 2 tablespoons of melted butter.

6 Place the shells on a baking sheet and bake about 20 minutes.

CRABMEAT CHASSEUR

6 SERVINGS

3 tablespoons butter
4 large mushrooms, sliced
2 teaspoons finely chopped shallots
2 tablespoons tomato paste
1¼ cups cream, approximately
1 pound lump crabmeat, picked over to remove
    any bits of shell or cartilage
Salt and freshly ground pepper to taste
2 egg yolks
1 teaspoon chopped parsley
1 teaspoon chopped chives
1 teaspoon chopped tarragon
Cognac (optional)

1 Melt the butter in a skillet or chafing dish. Add the mushrooms and cook, stirring, for 5 minutes.

2 Add the shallots. Stir until most of liquid given up by mushrooms evaporates. Add the tomato paste and cook for 5 minutes longer.

3 Pour in approximately 1 cup of the cream and cook, stirring, until ingredients are thoroughly heated.

4 Add the crabmeat to the mixture and season with salt and pepper. Stir gently and heat well, but do not break up pieces of crabmeat.

5 Mix egg yolks with ¼ cup of the cream. Add this mixture and the chopped herbs to the crabmeat. Heat to thicken slightly but do not allow to come to a boil. To heighten the flavor of the dish, a generous dash of cognac may be added.

6 Keep hot over water bath or chafing dish. Serve with rice and a tossed green salad.

VIRGINIA CRAB CAKES

6 SERVINGS

1 pound crabmeat, picked over well to remove
    any bits of shell or cartilage
3 eggs
½ cup mayonnaise
¼ cup minced scallions, green part included
2 tablespoons minced celery with leaves
1 teaspoon Worcestershire sauce
1 tablespoon lemon juice
½ cup coarse, fresh bread crumbs
¾ cup flour
Fine fresh bread crumbs
Oil
Butter

1 Mix the crabmeat, 1 egg, mayonnaise, scallions, celery, Worcestershire, lemon juice and the coarse crumbs. Place in a sieve and drain.

2 Place the flour on one sheet of wax paper, fine crumbs on another. Beat the remaining 2 eggs lightly. Heat equal parts of oil and butter to a depth of ¼ inch in a large heavy skillet.

3 Shape the crab mixture into rounded teaspoonfuls and drop into the flour. Coat with flour, then with egg and finally with crumbs.

4 Brown on both sides in hot oil.

CRABMEAT CASSEROLE

6 SERVINGS

1 green pepper, seeded
¾ pound mushrooms
3 small white onions
2 tablespoons chopped parsley
1½ pounds fresh crabmeat, picked over well to
    remove any bits of shell or cartilage
6 tablespoons butter
5 tablespoons flour
1½ cups milk
½ cup half-and-half
½ teaspoon salt
Freshly ground pepper to taste
Few grains of cayenne
½ cup dry sherry
½ cup dry bread crumbs

1 Chop fine the pepper, mushrooms, and onions and mix with the parsley and crabmeat, which has been broken into small pieces.

2 Preheat the oven to 350°F.

3 In a saucepan melt the butter, add the flour and stir with a wire whisk until blended. Meanwhile, bring the milk and half-and-half to a boil and add all at once to the butter-flour mixture, stirring vigorously with the whisk until the sauce is thickened and smooth.

4 Combine the sauce with the crabmeat mixture and season with salt, pepper and cayenne. Remove from the heat and add the sherry. Pour into a buttered casserole, sprinkle with crumbs, dot with additional butter and bake 30 minutes.

Crabmeat Quiche, page 107.

BOILED LIVE LOBSTER

1 LOBSTER PER SERVING

Plunge the lobster, head first, into a large pot of rapidly boiling salted water. Cover the pot, return to a boil and boil 12 to 15 minutes for a 1½- to 2-pound lobster. When done, remove from water with tongs and place the lobster on its back. Slit the undershell lengthwise with a sharp knife or scissors. Remove and discard the dark vein, the sac near the head and spongy tissue, but save the green liver and coral, if any. Serve hot, cut side up, with melted butter. Garnish with parsley and lemon wedges.

To Cut Up Live Lobster: Wash the lobster and cut its spinal cord by inserting a knife where the tail and body meet. Turn lobster on its back and split lengthwise. Clean as above. Cut each tail crosswise into three pieces. Cut off the claws and crack them.

HOMARD A L'ABSINTHE

2 TO 3 SERVINGS

2 (1½-pound) live lobsters
2 teaspoons chopped tarragon
2 teaspoons chopped chervil
Chopped parsley
4 egg yolks
¼ pound butter, at room temperature
¼ cup cream
1 teaspoon salt
Dash of white pepper
1 cup dry white wine
3 tablespoons Pernod or Ricard
2 cups half-and-half
Dash of Tabasco sauce

1 Kill the lobsters (opposite page) and cut the lobster tails into pieces about 1 inch thick. Remove the large front claws and cut each in half. Split the body lengthwise, scrape out the liver, near the head, and reserve. Remove the waste near the head. Remove the small claws for another use.

2 Mix the lobster liver with the herbs, ½ teaspoon parsley, the egg yolks, 3 tablespoons of the softened butter and the cream. Blend together and set aside.

3 Heat a skillet over high heat. Add the remaining butter and cook the cut-up lobster in it over high heat only until the shell turns red, shaking the pan almost constantly. Season with salt and a dash of white pepper.

4 Meanwhile, turn the creamed butter mixture into a saucepan, add the wine and cook, uncovered, over medium heat about 15 minutes. (The wine will evaporate.) Heat 2 tablespoons of the Pernod. Add to the lobster and ignite.

5 While the lobster is cooking, heat a 2½-quart casserole. Heat the half-and-half over low heat.

6 Turn the cooked lobster into the heated casserole and keep warm.

7 Add the heated half-and-half and the Tabasco to the saucepan in which the lobster was cooked. Remove from the heat and add the liver mixture, stirring vigorously with a wire whisk. Cook over low heat, stirring constantly, until the sauce has just thickened.

8 Stir in the remaining Pernod and pour the sauce over the lobster. Sprinkle with chopped parsley. Serve with oyster forks.

Lobster-Stuffed Tomatoes, page 112.
Curried Lobster Salad, page 113.
Lobster and Avocado Salad, page 113.
Spanish Fish Chowder, page 84.
Seafood Crêpes, page 122.
Lobster Ravioli, page 506.
Linguine with Lobster, page 493.
Fettuccine with Oriental Lobster Sauce, page 492.

LOBSTER
A L'AMÉRICAINE

Arguments have raged for decades over the origin of this lobster and tomato dish. American chefs say it was created by an American and French chefs say no such thing unless it was a Frenchman lured to this country by the Yankee dollar.

4 TO 6 SERVINGS

2 (1½-pound) live lobsters
¼ cup olive oil
3 tablespoons butter
¼ cup finely chopped onions
1 garlic clove, finely chopped
6 firm tomatoes, peeled, seeded and chopped
3 tablespoons chopped parsley
1 tablespoon chopped tarragon
Thyme to taste
½ bay leaf
¾ cup dry white wine, or water
3 tablespoons tomato paste
Cayenne to taste
Salt to taste
¼ cup warmed cognac

1 Kill the lobsters by plunging a knife into the thorax (see page 248). Cut through the markings on the tail to make round medallions. Cut the body in half, clean it and save the coral and liver for the sauce. (If the lobster is to be cooked shortly after it is purchased, these preparations may be made by the fish dealer; in this case the lobster must be kept cold to prevent spoilage.)

2 In a large heavy skillet, heat the olive oil and add the lobster pieces. Toss and stir the pieces until the shells turn red and the meat is seared. Transfer the meat and shells to a hot platter.

3 Heat the butter in the skillet and cook the onions and garlic until the onions are wilted. Add the tomatoes, herbs and wine and simmer ½ hour. Add the tomato paste, cayenne and salt.

4 Pour the cognac over the lobster pieces and ignite. Transfer the lobster to the sauce, cover and simmer 15 to 20 minutes. Just before serving, stir in the liver and lobster coral.

Note: If desired, the lobster meat may be removed from the shell before it is transferred to the sauce. The shells, however, give the sauce additional flavor.

♦

LOBSTER THERMIDOR

Created and first served to the public on the evening of January 24, 1894, by the owner of Chez Maire, a once-famous Paris restaurant, now defunct, lobster thermidor was named for the drama *Thermidor,* by Victorien Sardou. Sardou's play, a highly controversial work, opened and closed the same evening; lobster thermidor is a still-running hit.

4 SERVINGS

4 (1½-pound) live lobsters
¼ pound butter
1 cup chopped mushrooms
Salt and freshly ground pepper to taste
½ cup soft bread crumbs
1 tablespoon Worcestershire sauce
Tabasco sauce to taste
4 teaspoons chopped parsley
4 teaspoons chopped pimiento
¾ cup sherry
¼ cup cognac
2 cups cream
4 egg yolks
½ cup grated Parmesan cheese
Paprika

1 Cook and clean the lobsters as for boiled live lobster (page 248). Twist off the claws, reserving the small claws for garnish. Remove meat from the bodies and cut into small pieces. Crack the large claws, remove meat and cube. Reserve the shells.

2 Preheat the oven to 350°F.

3 Heat 6 tablespoons of the butter, add the mushrooms and cook 3 minutes. Season with salt and pepper.

4 Add the lobster meat, crumbs, Worchestershire, Tabasco, parsley, pimiento, sherry, cognac, cream and egg yolks. Mix well.

5 Fill the lobster shells with the mixture, sprinkle with cheese, dot with the remaining 2 tablespoons butter and sprinkle with paprika.

6 Place in a shallow pan and bake 15 minutes. Serve immediately.

Lobster Bisque, page 87.

MOULES MARINIÈRE

8 TO 12 SERVINGS

¼ *pound butter*
1½ *cups finely chopped shallots*
½ *cup finely chopped onions*
½ *cup finely chopped parsley*
8 *quarts mussels, scrubbed and debearded*
3 *cups dry white wine*
1 *teaspoon salt*
2 *teaspoons freshly ground pepper*

1 In a large heavy kettle, melt the butter and add the shallots, onions and parsley. Cook, stirring, without browning, until the onions are wilted and cooked.

2 Add the mussels, wine, salt and pepper. Cover closely and cook, shaking the kettle and stirring occasionally, about 15 minutes.

3 Serve the mussels hot, sprinkled with parsley, with the broth on the side.

Mussels Ravigote, page 39.
Billi Bi, page 85.
Roger Fessaguet's Mussel Soup, page 85.
Mussels with Linguine, page 497.

DEEP-FRIED MUSSELS WITH DILL SAUCE

4 SERVINGS

40 (about 4 cups or 1½ pounds) mussels
3 cloves
1 bay leaf
1 teaspoon peppercorns
¼ cup plus 2 tablespoons water
1 egg
2 cups plus 1 tablespoon vegetable oil
½ cup flour
1½ cups fine fresh spread crumbs
Oil for deep frying
¾ cup dill sauce (see page 573)
Lemon wedges for garnish

1 Pull off the stringy "beard" from each mussel. Rinse and scrub the mussels thoroughly. Drain well.

2 Put the cloves, bay leaf, peppercorns and ¼ cup of the water in a kettle and add the mussels. Cover closely and bring to the boil. Cook 4 minutes or longer until all the mussels are open. Drain. If desired, reserve the cooking liquid for another use such as for fish soup. Remove the mussels from their shells and set aside.

3 Break the egg into a small mixing bowl and beat well while adding 1 tablespoon of oil and the remaining 2 tablespoons of water. Pour this into a flat dish and set aside.

4 Pour the flour into another flat dish and the crumbs into a third dish.

5 Dip the mussels in flour and shake off excess. Dip the flour-coated mussels in the egg mixture. Dip the egg-coated mussels in the crumbs and shake off excess.

6 Heat 2 cups of oil in a skillet to 360°F. Add the mussels, a few at a time, without crowding. Cook until the mussels are golden brown. Using a slotted spoon, remove the cooked mussels to paper toweling to drain well. Continue until all the mussels are cooked. Serve hot with dill sauce on the side. Garnish the mussels with lemon wedges.

Mussels in Bacon, page 39.

♦

FRENCH-FRIED OYSTERS

4 TO 6 SERVINGS

Oil for deep frying
2 eggs
2 tablespoons cream
1 teaspoon salt
Freshly ground pepper
1 quart shucked oysters
Flour
Cracker crumbs, or cornmeal

1 Heat the oil to 380°F.

2 Beat the eggs lightly and add the cream, salt and pepper.

3 Dredge the oysters individually in flour, dip in the egg mixture and roll in crumbs.

4 Fry the oysters until golden brown, about 2 minutes. Drain on paper toweling and sprinkle with additional salt and pepper.

OYSTERS EN BROCHETTE

6 SERVINGS

24 shucked oysters
Lemon juice
Salt and freshly ground pepper to taste
12 strips of bacon, cut in half
12 mushroom caps
Melted butter
Minced parsley

1 Sprinkle the oysters with lemon juice, salt and pepper. Wrap half a strip of bacon around each oyster.

2 Using 6 long brochettes, arrange on each a mushroom cap, 4 bacon-wrapped oysters and another mushroom. Brush with butter and broil over charcoal or under a broiler until the bacon is crisp. Serve sprinkled with parsley.

Oysters Casino, page 41.
Oysters Rockefeller, page 41.

BROILED BREADED OYSTERS

4 TO 6 SERVINGS

1 cup soft fresh bread crumbs
2 tablespoons finely chopped parsley
1 teaspoon tarragon
¼ teaspoon cayenne
Salt to taste
3 dozen raw oysters, shucked
¼ pound butter, melted
Lemon wedges

1 Preheat the broiler for 15 minutes.

2 Combine the crumbs, parsley, tarragon, cayenne and salt. Drain the oysters and roll them in the seasoned crumbs. Place them in a single layer in a buttered baking dish.

3 Pour half of the butter over the oysters and broil them briefly, just until they are golden on top. Turn each oyster carefully and pour the remaining butter over them. Broil briefly until brown. Serve with lemon wedges.

Oysters on the Half Shell, page 14.
Oyster Stew, page 89.
Hank Ketcham's Oyster Soup, page 89.

OLD-FASHIONED SCALLOPED OYSTERS

4 SERVINGS

⅔ cup soft bread crumbs
1 cup fine cracker crumbs
¼ pound butter, melted
1½ pints small shucked oysters, or
    18 large oysters
Salt and freshly ground pepper to taste
2 tablespoons chopped parsley
½ teaspoon Worcestershire sauce
3 tablespoons milk or cream

   1 Preheat the oven to 350°F.
   2 Mix the bread crumbs, cracker crumbs and butter.
   3 Place half of the crumb mixture on the bottom of a greased 1-quart casserole. Add half of the oysters, reserving the liquor, and sprinkle with salt, pepper and half of the parsley. Add the remaining oysters and sprinkle with salt, pepper and remaining parsley.
   4 Mix ⅓ cup oyster liquor with the Worcestershire and milk and pour over the oysters. Top with the remaining crumb mixture.
   5 Bake, uncovered, until puffy and brown, about 30 minutes.

CORNMEAL-FRIED OYSTERS WITH MUSTARD SAUCE

4 SERVINGS

20 large oysters, with liquor reserved
5 tablespoons finely chopped shallots
1 tablespoon minced garlic
¼ cup white vinegar
¼ cup dry white wine
¾ cup cream
⅓ cup Dijon mustard
1 teaspoon Worcestershire sauce
6 tablespoons cold butter, cut into small cubes
1 cup white cornmeal, preferably stone-ground
Salt and freshly ground pepper to taste
2 teaspoons paprika
1½ cups vegetable oil, approximately
Watercress sprigs for garnish

   1 Drain the oysters and measure the liquor. If there is less than 1 cup add enough clam juice to make 1 cup.
   2 Put the shallots, garlic, vinegar, wine, cream and oyster liquor in a saucepan and bring to a boil. Let simmer 30 to 40 minutes, or until reduced to about 1 cup.
   3 Stir in the mustard and Worcestershire and bring to the simmer. Add the butter, a few pieces at a time, stirring with a wire whisk. Line a small bowl with a fine sieve and pour in the sauce, pressing with the back of a spoon to extract as much flavor as possible from the solids. Discard the solids. There should be about 1 cup of sauce. Place the saucepan in a basin of simmering water to keep it hot.
   4 Blend the cornmeal with salt, pepper and paprika in a small bowl or dish. Dredge the oysters in the cornmeal to coat thoroughly. Shake off excess.

5 Heat 1 cup of the oil in a skillet and add the oysters a few at a time without crowding. Cook until golden brown on the bottom and turn. Cook briefly and transfer the oysters to paper toweling to drain. Repeat with the remaining oysters, adding a little more oil as necessary.

6 Spoon equal portions of the sauce on 4 small plates and place 5 oysters on top of the sauce. Garnish with sprigs of watercress.

◆

PAN ROAST
GRAND CENTRAL

This is only a variation of the genuine pan roast served at the Oyster Bar in Grand Central Terminal. To make the real McCoy, one would have to own one of the round-bottom aluminum cooking utensils used by the chefs there.

1 SERVING

8 freshly opened oysters
2 tablespoons butter, at room temperature
1 tablespoon chili sauce
1 teaspoon Worcestershire sauce
Few drops of lemon juice
Paprika to taste
½ cup cream
1 piece of dry toast

1 Boil the oysters with their liquor, 1 tablespoon butter, chili sauce, Worcestershire, lemon juice and paprika 1 minute, stirring constantly.

2 Add the cream, return to a boil and pour the oysters over the toast. Top with remaining butter and sprinkle with additional paprika.

Oyster Chowder, page 88.

BROILED MARINATED
SCALLOPS

Scallops in vermouth is an unusual and good idea.

4 SERVINGS

1½ pounds scallops
½ cup dry vermouth
½ cup olive oil
½ teaspoon finely chopped garlic
½ teaspoon salt
2 tablespoons minced parsley

1 Marinate the scallops in the vermouth mixed with the remaining ingredients several hours in the refrigerator.

2 When ready to serve, place the scallops and the marinade in a shallow pan. Place under a preheated broiler, 2 inches from the source of heat, and broil 5 to 6 minutes, turning once.

Sea Scallops Seviche, page 43.
Bay Scallops Quiche, page 107.

PAN-FRIED SCALLOPS

4 SERVINGS

1½ pounds sea scallops
¾ cup fine dry bread crumbs
6 tablespoons butter
Salt and freshly ground pepper to taste
Paprika to taste
2 tablespoons lemon juice
3 tablespoons chopped parsley

   1 Roll the scallops in the crumbs.
   2 Melt 4 tablespoons of the butter in a heavy skillet and add the scallops. Cook, turning the scallops gently, until golden brown on all sides. Remove the scallops to paper toweling and sprinkle with salt, pepper and paprika.
   3 Add the remaining butter to the skillet. When it melts, add lemon juice and parsley. Do not brown. Arrange the scallops on a hot platter. Pour the sauce over them and serve immediately.

COQUILLES SAINT-JACQUES

6 SERVINGS

1½ pounds bay or sea scallops
2 thyme sprigs
1 bay leaf
1 parsley sprig
8 peppercorns
Salt to taste
½ cup water
½ cup dry white wine
7 tablespoons butter
3 tablespoons flour
2 egg yolks
1 teaspoon lemon juice
Cayenne
Grated Parmesan cheese

   1 Preheat the oven to 400°F.
   2 Combine the scallops, thyme, bay leaf, parsley, peppercorns, salt, water and wine in a small saucepan and bring to a boil. Cover and simmer exactly 2 minutes. Remove the parsley, bay leaf and thyme and drain, but reserve the cooking liquid. Let the scallops cool. If bay scallops are used, cut them in half and set aside. If sea scallops are used, cut them into thin slices and set aside.
   3 Melt 2 tablespoons of the butter and stir in the flour with a wire whisk. When blended, add the scallop liquid (about 1½ cups), stirring vigorously.
   4 Remove the sauce from the heat and beat vigorously with an electric beater. Add the remaining butter, a little at a time, very gradually. Beat in the egg yolks, lemon juice and cayenne; continue beating until cool.

5 Spoon a little of the mixture into 6 to 8 large scallop shells or ramekins. Top with equal parts of scallops. Cover with the remaining sauce and sprinkle with cheese.

6 Bake 5 to 10 minutes, or until bubbling and golden brown. If necessary, glaze under the broiler.

◆

SCALLOPS EN BROCHETTE

4 SERVINGS

1 pound sea or bay scallops
8 strips of bacon
3 tablespoons butter, melted
½ teaspoon salt
⅛ teaspoon freshly ground black pepper
Lemon wedges

1 Wash the scallops and dry thoroughly. Preheat the broiler.

2 On each of 4 skewers, intertwine a strip of bacon with about 3 sea scallops or 4 to 6 bay scallops. Brush the scallops with the melted butter and sprinkle with salt and pepper.

3 Broil 3 to 5 inches from the source of heat 5 to 10 minutes, turning once. Serve with lemon wedges.

SCALLOPS WITH TOMATO AND SHALLOTS

4 TO 6 SERVINGS

2 pounds sea scallops
Salt and freshly ground pepper to taste
½ cup flour
3 tablespoons olive oil
2 tablespoons butter
1¼ cups zucchini cut into ½-inch cubes
⅓ cup finely chopped shallots
¾ cup peeled, seeded tomato cut into
    ½-inch cubes
1 tablespoon lemon juice

1 Place the scallops in a flat dish large enough to hold them without crowding. Sprinkle the scallops with salt and pepper. Dredge the scallops in flour and shake off excess.

2 Heat the oil and butter in a heavy skillet. The skillet must be large enough to hold the scallops without crowding; the pieces when added should not touch. Or cook the scallops in two batches.

3 When the oil is hot, add the scallops and cook, shaking the skillet and stirring, until they start to take on color, 4 minutes or less. Add the zucchini pieces and shallots and cook, stirring, 1 minute longer. Add the tomatoes and stir. Add salt and pepper and lemon juice. Cook, stirring, about 15 seconds and serve.

Scallop Waltz, page 47.
Scallop Cocktail, page 48.
Crème St. Jacques, page 86.

SCALLOPS
SAUCE VERTE

This is a cold scallop dish in which they are served with a green mayonnaise sauce.

6 TO 8 SERVINGS

½ cup dry vermouth
½ onion, chopped
1 parsley sprig
1 bay leaf
Salt and freshly ground pepper to taste
1 pound sea scallops, halved
1 cup mayonnaise, approximately
¼ cup finely chopped parsley
½ cup finely chopped spinach
¼ cup chopped chives or scallions
1 tablespoon chopped dill
Lettuce leaves

1 In a saucepan heat the vermouth with the onions, parsley, bay leaf, salt and pepper. Add the scallops and simmer gently until tender, shaking the pan occasionally, about 7 minutes. Drain and cool.

2 Meanwhile, blend the mayonnaise, chopped parsley, spinach, chives and dill. Add more mayonnaise, if desired.

3 Place the scallops in a bowl lined with lettuce leaves, cover with the green sauce and top with a sprinkling of additional finely chopped parsley. Chill.

BAY SCALLOPS
WITH WHITE WINE

4 SERVINGS

2 tablespoons butter
1 pound bay scallops
Salt and freshly ground pepper to taste
2 tablespoons finely chopped shallots
1 small garlic clove, minced
4 mushrooms, thinly sliced
¼ cup dry white wine
½ cup cream
1 tablespoon finely chopped parsley

1 Heat the butter in a skillet and add the scallops. Cook quickly, shaking the pan; sprinkle with salt and pepper. Continue cooking and stirring with a wooden spoon and add the shallots, garlic and mushrooms. Cook, stirring, for about 1 minute, then transfer scallops to a warm dish.

2 Add the wine to the skillet and cook over high heat, stirring, for about 1 minute. Add the cream and cook over high heat, for 2 minutes. Return the scallops to the skillet and sprinkle with parsley. Serve over freshly made noodles or rice.

SCALLOP SAUTÉ

This is a delectable scallop creation that is quickly prepared.

4 SERVINGS

1 pound sea or bay scallops
4 tablespoons butter
½ teaspoon salt
⅛ teaspoon freshly ground pepper
¼ teaspoon paprika
1 garlic clove, minced
1 tablespoon minced parsley
3 tablespoons lemon juice

1 Wash the scallops and dry thoroughly. If sea scallops are used, cut them into thirds or quarters.

2 In a large skillet heat 2 tablespoons of the butter and add the salt, pepper, paprika and garlic.

3 Add enough scallops to cover the bottom of the skillet without crowding. Cook quickly over high heat, stirring occasionally, until golden brown, about 5 minutes. Transfer the scallops to a heated platter. Repeat the process until all the scallops are cooked.

4 In the same skillet place the parsley, lemon juice and remaining butter. Heat until the butter melts and pour over the scallops.

SCALLOPS SAUTÉED IN GARLIC BUTTER

4 SERVINGS

4 tablespoons butter
1 small garlic clove, split
1 pound scallops
Salt and freshly ground pepper to taste
Tartar sauce
Lemon wedges

In a saucepan heat the butter and garlic slowly. Discard garlic. Add the scallops and cook 5 minutes. Season with salt and pepper and serve immediately with tartar sauce and lemon wedges.

◆

BROILED SHRIMP MARINATED IN BEER

6 SERVINGS

2 pounds shrimp, shelled and deveined
1 (12-ounce) bottle or can of beer
1 tablespoon chopped chives
1 tablespoon chopped parsley
2 teaspoons basil
2 teaspoons dry mustard
1 teaspoon finely chopped garlic
½ teaspoon freshly ground pepper
½ teaspoon celery salt

1 Marinate the shrimp in the remaining ingredients at least 8 hours in the refrigerator, stirring frequently. Drain.

2 Place the shrimp in a preheated broiler pan 3 inches from the source of heat and broil about 5 minutes, turning once.

SHRIMP BOILED IN BEER

Beer makes a marvelous cooking liquid for shrimp.

4 SERVINGS

2 pounds shrimp
2 (12-ounce) bottles or cans of beer
1 garlic clove, peeled
2 bay leaves
1 tablespoon chopped parsley
2 teaspoons salt
1 teaspoon celery seed
½ teaspoon thyme
⅛ teaspoon cayenne
Juice of ½ lemon

1 Wash the shrimp, if desired, but do not remove the shells.

2 Combine the remaining ingredients and bring to a boil. Add the shrimp. Return to a boil, reduce the heat and simmer, uncovered, for 2 to 5 minutes, depending on the size of the shrimp.

3 Drain and serve hot with plenty of melted butter seasoned with lemon juice and Tabasco sauce; or cold with a mayonnaise and cognac sauce for shrimp. The shrimp may, of course, be shelled and deveined before serving.

BOILED SHRIMP

4 SERVINGS

4 cups water
1 carrot, sliced
1 small white onion, sliced
½ celery stalk, sliced
Juice of ½ lemon
1 teaspoon salt
½ teaspoon freshly ground pepper
1 pound shrimp, shelled and deveined

1 In a large saucepan bring the water to a boil, add the remaining ingredients except the shrimp and boil 15 minutes.

2 Add the shrimp to the boiling liquid. Turn off the heat and let cool in the liquid.

Cold Rice with Shrimp, page 471.

CHIVE SHRIMP IN SHELLS

5 OR 6 SERVINGS

1½ cups dry white wine
½ teaspoon salt
¼ teaspoon white pepper
1½ pounds shrimp
2 tablespoons butter
2 tablespoons flour
1 cup milk
¼ cup chopped mushrooms
2 tablespoons grated Parmesan cheese
1 tablespoon chopped chives
½ cup buttered soft fresh bread crumbs

1 Place wine, salt and pepper in a saucepan and bring to a boil. Add the shrimp and simmer just until they turn pink. Drain, reserving the cooking liquid.

2 Shell and devein the shrimp and cut into bite-size pieces. Melt the butter, blend in the flour, and then gradually stir in the reserved liquid and the milk.

3 Bring to a boil, stirring, and cook until thickened. Add the shrimp, mushrooms, cheese and chives and cook for 2 minutes longer.

4 Fill buttered shells or ramekins with the mixture; sprinkle with the buttered crumbs. Broil until the surface is light brown.

SHRIMP WITH TARRAGON

4 SERVINGS

1 garlic clove
½ teaspoon salt
¼ pound butter, at room temperature
2 teaspoons finely chopped parsley
1 teaspoon minced tarragon,
    or ½ teaspoon dried
¾ cup soft fresh bread crumbs
2 tablespoons white rum or dry sherry
1 pound shrimp, shelled and deveined

1 Preheat the oven to 400°F.

2 Chop the garlic and salt together until they are almost a purée. Cream the purée with the butter, parsley, tarragon, crumbs and rum. Spread half the mixture in the bottom of 4 ovenproof ramekins.

3 Arrange equal portions of shrimp in the ramekins. Spread the remaining butter mixture over the shrimp. Bake about 8 minutes, until shrimp are heated through and crumbs are brown.

BROILED SHRIMP WITH HERBS

2 pounds jumbo shrimp, shelled and deveined
3 garlic cloves, finely chopped
½ cup olive oil or vegetable oil
¼ cup chopped parsley
Juice of 1 lemon
1 teaspoon basil
1 teaspoon dry mustard
1 teaspoon salt

1 Place the shrimp in a bowl with the remaining ingredients and let marinate at room temperature several hours.

2 Broil the shrimp over charcoal or in a preheated broiler 4 or 5 minutes, or until the shrimp are just cooked through. Turn once.

ORIENTAL SHRIMP

2 tablespoons vegetable oil
2 pounds shrimp, shelled and deveined
1 scallion or small onion, chopped
½ cup hot chicken stock
½ cup thinly sliced water chestnuts
1 package frozen peas
3 thin slices fresh ginger
2 tablespoons light soy sauce
2 tablespoons sherry
2 teaspoons cornstarch
1 tablespoon water

1 In a skillet heat the oil, add the shrimp and onions and cook, stirring, until the shrimp turn pink and the onions are tender but not brown, about 1 minute.

2 Add the stock, water chestnuts, peas and ginger. Cover and cook until the peas and shrimp are tender, about 3 minutes.

3 Remove the cover and stir in the soy sauce, sherry and cornstarch dissolved in the water. Cook until the sauce is clear and slightly thickened.

SHRIMP MARENGO

ABOUT 8 SERVINGS

½ pound sliced lean bacon, diced
2 garlic cloves, minced
1 cup chopped onions
1 cup chopped celery
1 pound mushrooms, sliced
1 (35-ounce) can (4½ cups) Italian-style
   plum tomatoes
1 (6-ounce) can tomato paste
1½ teaspoons crumbled rosemary
1¼ teaspoons crumbled basil
1 bay leaf
1 teaspoon salt
¼ teaspoon freshly ground pepper
1 tablespoon sugar
3 or 4 drops of Tabasco sauce
3½ pounds shrimp, shelled and deveined
2 green peppers, seeded and cut into large
   cubes

1 Sauté the bacon in a large skillet or Dutch oven until crisp. Remove and reserve.

2 Add the garlic and onions to bacon drippings and sauté until tender and golden but not brown. Add celery and mushrooms and cook for 5 minutes.

3 Return the bacon to the skillet. Add tomatoes, tomato paste, rosemary, basil, bay leaf, salt, pepper, sugar and Tabasco. Bring to a boil and simmer, uncovered, for 20 to 30 minutes.

4 Add the shrimp and green peppers. When the mixture comes to a boil, simmer for 2 to 3 minutes, or until shrimp are tender.

Note: This dish may be prepared ahead by making the sauce as directed through step 3. Reserve the sauce. Ten minutes before serving time, continue with recipe.

SHRIMP WITH DILL-FLAVORED CREAM SAUCE

4 SERVINGS

5 tablespoons butter
1 tablespoon chopped shallots or onions
1 pound shrimp, shelled and deveined
¾ cup white wine
3 tablespoons flour
1½ cups milk
1½ teaspoons chopped dill

1 In a saucepan heat 2 tablespoons of the butter, add the shallots, shrimp and wine and cook about 2 minutes.

2 In a separate saucepan melt the remaining butter, add the flour and stir with a wire whisk until blended. Meanwhile, bring the milk to a boil and add all at once to the butter-flour mixture, stirring vigorously with the whisk until the sauce is thickened and smooth.

3 Add the sauce and the dill to the shrimp mixture and cook slowly 5 minutes longer. Serve immediately over green pasta.

FRIED SHRIMP

1 pound shrimp, shelled and deveined
1 tablespoon cognac, rum or lemon juice
½ teaspoon Worcestershire sauce
Frying batter (see following recipe)
Oil for deep frying

1 Marinate the shrimp in the cognac and Worcestershire about 15 minutes.

2 Dip a few shrimp at a time in the batter and fry in deep fat heated to 375°F until golden brown. Drain on paper toweling. Serve with mayonnaise seasoned with horseradish or capers.

FRYING BATTER (WITH BEER)

½ cup flour
Pinch of salt
1 tablespoon butter, melted
1 egg, beaten
½ cup beer
1 egg white, stiffly beaten

1 Sift the flour and salt into a mixing bowl. Stir in the butter and egg. Add the beer gradually, stirring only until the mixture is smooth.

2 Let the batter stand in a warm place 1 hour, then fold in the beaten egg white.

Shrimp and Mashed Cucumbers, page 44.
Shrimp Rémoulade, page 44.
Sherried Shrimp, page 44.
Shrimp with Herb Sauce, page 45.
Roquefort-stuffed Shrimp, page 45.
Shrimp with Dill and Lemon Sauce, page 45.
Shrimp Vinaigrette with Rosemary, page 46.
Shrimp Soup, page 87.
Shrimp Fondue, page 110.
Mexican Shellfish Soup with Salsa, page 84.
Shrimp-stuffed Artichokes, page 370.
Pasta with Shrimp, page 494.
Fried Rice with Shrimp, page 535.

SCAMPI

6 tablespoons butter
¼ cup olive oil
2 tablespoons chopped parsley
2 garlic cloves, minced
½ teaspoon salt
2 tablespoons lemon juice
1 pound large shrimp

1 Preheat the oven to 450°F.

2 Melt the butter and add the olive oil, parsley, garlic, salt and lemon juice. Mix well.

3 Shell and devein the shrimp, leaving the tails attached. Split down the inside lengthwise, being careful not to cut through the shrimp. Spread open to simulate butterflies.

4 Place in a shallow baking pan, tail end up. Pour sauce over all. Bake for 5 minutes. Place under broiler for 5 minutes longer to brown.

SHRIMP BAKED WITH FETA CHEESE

4 SERVINGS

3 cups imported canned Italian plum tomatoes
¼ cup olive oil
1 teaspoon finely chopped garlic
¼ cup fresh fish broth, or bottled clam juice
1 teaspoon crushed oregano
1 teaspoon hot red pepper flakes
2 tablespoons capers, drained
Salt and freshly ground pepper to taste
3 tablespoons butter
1 pound (about 24) shrimp, shelled and
    deveined
¼ pound feta cheese
¼ cup ouzo (a Greek anise-flavored liqueur
    widely available in wine and spirits shops)
    (optional)

1 Preheat the oven to 350°F.
2 Put the tomatoes in a saucepan and cook until reduced to about 2 cups. Stir often to prevent burning and sticking.
3 Heat the olive oil in another saucepan or deep skillet and add the garlic, stirring. Add the tomatoes, using a rubber spatula to scrape them out.
4 Add the fish broth, oregano, red pepper flakes, capers and salt and pepper.
5 Heat the butter in a heavy saucepan or skillet and add the shrimp. Cook briefly, less than 1 minute, stirring and turning the shrimp until they turn pink.
6 Spoon equal portions of half of the sauce in 4 individual baking dishes and arrange 6 shrimp plus equal amounts of the butter in which they cooked in each dish. Spoon remaining sauce over the shrimp.
7 Crumble the cheese and scatter it over all. Place the dishes in the oven and bake for 10 to 15 minutes, or until bubbling hot.

8 Remove the dishes from the oven and sprinkle each dish with 1 tablespoon ouzo, if desired, and ignite it. Serve immediately.

♦

SHRIMP WITH SAFFRON

4 SERVINGS

1 pound shrimp, shelled and deveined
1 cup dry white wine
1 tablespoon olive oil
1 cup tomato juice
Juice of 1 lemon
2 parsley sprigs
1 fennel branch or celery stalk
1 thyme sprig
½ bay leaf
2 garlic cloves, crushed
6 peppercorns
1 teaspoon powdered saffron
Salt to taste

1 Combine all the ingredients and cook, covered, over high heat 8 to 10 minutes. Correct the seasonings, which should be sharp.
2 Chill the shrimp. Serve cold with the sauce strained over the top.

PAUPIETTES OF SHRIMP WITH LEEKS

Leeks can make an elegant wrapping to be cooked with a shrimp mousse. This recipe for paupiettes of shrimp with leeks is the creation of Josef "Seppi" Renggli, the distinguished chef of The Four Seasons Restaurant in Manhattan.

6 SERVINGS

3 large leeks (about 2¼ pounds)
Salt to taste
1 pound medium-size shrimp, shelled
1 tablespoon coarsely chopped tarragon, or 1
    teaspoon dried
2 tablespoons finely chopped shallots
1 large egg
⅛ teaspoon cayenne
⅛ teaspoon grated nutmeg
Freshly ground pepper to taste
1 cup cream
Beurre blanc (pages 555–556) with 2
    teaspoons chopped tarragon

1 Trim off the ends of the leeks. Cut the leeks crosswise in half and discard the top green half or use it for another purpose such as soups.

2 Carefully peel off 12 of the largest outer leaves of the leeks, which will be used for wrapping the ground shrimp mixture. Save the inner portions of the leeks for another use. Carefully rinse the outer leaves and pat them dry.

3 Bring 3 quarts of water to the boil and add salt. Drop in the leek leaves and cover. Let simmer 5 minutes and drain. Run under cold water and drain once more. Handle carefully and pat dry. Arrange the leaves in one layer on a flat surface with the bottom facing you. They are to be rolled bottom to top so that you can cut easily through the soft fiber when they are rolled.

4 Put the shrimp into the container of a food processor with the tarragon, shallots, egg, cayenne, nutmeg, salt and pepper. Blend thoroughly about 1 minute, stirring down and clearing the sides with a rubber spatula.

5 Gradually add the cream while processing.

6 Sprinkle the opened up leek leaves with salt and pepper.

7 Spoon about ¼ cup of the shrimp mixture onto each leek leaf, placing it about 1 inch from the bottom of each leaf. Roll over the bottom of the leek and continue rolling until the leaf is a neat sausage-shaped package. As the packages are rolled, arrange them seam side down on the rack of a steamer. Refrigerate until ready to cook.

8 Bring water to the boil in the bottom of the steamer. Add the rack containing the leek rolls and cover closely. Cook 4 minutes. Turn off the heat and let the shrimp rolls rest, covered, about 5 minutes. Serve hot with the beurre blanc spooned over.

KUNG PAO SHRIMP WITH CASHEW NUTS

One of the best of all Sichuan dishes is called Kung Pao Chicken (page 144), a stir-fried dish made with bean sauce, chili paste with garlic, hot peppers and fried peanuts. Here is a version of that dish made with shrimp.

4 TO 6 SERVINGS

3 cups vegetable oil
1 cup raw, unsalted cashews
14 to 16 large shrimp
1 tablespoon cornstarch
¼ cup red wine vinegar
Salt to taste
2 tablespoons light soy sauce
5 teaspoons sugar
2 tablespoons minced garlic
2 tablespoons minced scallions,
   white part only
1½ tablespoons finely chopped ginger

1 Heat the oil in a wok or skillet and when it is almost boiling hot, but not smoking, turn off the heat and add the nuts. The nuts should turn light golden brown from retained heat, but if they don't, turn on the heat and cook briefly, watching carefully, until golden brown. They will cook very quickly. Drain immediately and reserve the oil.

2 Shell, devein and rinse the shrimp. Pat them dry with paper toweling. Place them in a small mixing bowl and add the cornstarch. Work with the fingers until all the shrimp are lightly coated.

3 In another small bowl combine the vinegar, salt, soy sauce and sugar.

4 Combine the garlic, scallions and ginger.

5 Heat the reserved oil in a wok or skillet and add the shrimp. Cook, stirring, about 1½ minutes. Drain in a sieve-lined bowl to catch the drippings. Discard all but 1½ tablespoons of the oil.

6 Put this oil in the wok or skillet and when it is hot, add the garlic mixture, stirring. Add the vinegar sauce and when it boils, add the shrimp and nuts. Stir until the shrimp and nuts are coated with sauce. Serve hot with rice.

◆

SHRIMP WITH RICE

4 TO 6 SERVINGS

¼ pound butter
1 large onion, finely chopped
1 cup sliced mushrooms
1 green pepper, finely chopped
1¼ cups rice
¼ teaspoon grated nutmeg
1 teaspoon salt
½ teaspoon freshly ground pepper
1 cup dry white wine
3 cups hot chicken stock or water
2 tablespoons chopped parsley
¼ teaspoon thyme
½ bay leaf
2 pounds shrimp, shelled and deveined

1 In a large skillet heat the butter, add the onions, mushrooms, green pepper, rice, nutmeg, salt and pepper and cook, stirring, until the rice is golden brown.

2 Add the wine and simmer 5 minutes. Add the stock, parsley, thyme and bay leaf, cover and cook 10 minutes, stirring occasionally.

3 Add the shrimp and simmer 5 to 10 minutes, depending on the size of the shrimp.

4 Remove the bay leaf and serve immediately.

SINGAPORE-STYLE SHRIMP WITH NOODLES

This is an excellent dish, encountered often in East Asian kitchens. It is a fine blend of noodles, shrimp, pork and bean sprouts with easily made omelet rings sprinkled over.

4 TO 6 SERVINGS

6 tablespoons vegetable oil, approximately
3 tablespoons coarsely chopped garlic
4 eggs
1½ pounds lean boneless pork, cut into
   5 portions of equal size
Salt to taste
1 cup or more chicken stock
½ pound medium egg noodles
1 cup finely chopped heart of celery
1 pound (about 2 cups) small shrimp, peeled
   and deveined
¼ cup cored, seeded hot red or green chilies,
   cut into the thinnest possible slivers
¾ pound plucked-over bean sprouts (see note)
1 cup finely chopped scallions
½ cup finely chopped coriander

1 Heat about 2 tablespoons of the oil in a small skillet and add the garlic. Cook over low heat, stirring, until the garlic starts to take on color, about 5 minutes. Drain in a small sieve and set aside.

2 Put the eggs in a mixing bowl and beat well. Rub the bottom of an omelet pan, preferably nonstick, with a small amount of oil. Pour in the eggs and let them cook until set on the bottom. Turn the eggs carefully and cook briefly until set on the other side. Slide the "omelet" onto a flat surface and let cool. Roll the omelet like a jelly roll. Cut it crosswise into thin slices. Set aside.

3 Put the pieces of pork in a kettle and add cold water to cover and salt. Bring to the simmer and let cook about 10 minutes. Drain, reserving both the meat and the broth. Pour the broth into a measuring cup. Add enough chicken stock to make 2 cups.

4 Bring a quart or more water to the boil in a kettle and add salt. Drop in the noodles and stir. Cook until the noodles are tender, 4 to 5 minutes. Drain. Return the noodles to the kettle and pour in about 1 tablespoon oil, stirring to blend.

5 Cut the pork into very thin slices. Stack the slices and cut into very thin strips. There should be about 2½ cups.

6 Heat about 4 tablespoons oil in a wok or large skillet and add the slivers of pork and the celery. Cook, stirring rapidly, about 1 minute.

7 Add the shrimp, chili slivers and bean sprouts and cook, stirring, until the shrimp lose their raw look. Add the pork and chicken broth mixture and bring to the boil. Cook about 30 seconds.

8 Ladle equal amounts of the mixture into 4 to 6 hot soup bowls and sprinkle the top of each serving with the fried garlic, omelet rings, scallions and coriander.

Note: Fresh bean sprouts are sold by the pound and should be plump and very white. The entire sprout is edible, but in fine Chinese cooking it is customary to pluck off and discard both the small yellow nubbin at the top and the threadlike root at the bottom. This is a tedious task, however, and is optional. At the least, the sprouts should be rinsed and picked over, discarding any bruised ones.

GRILLED SHRIMP WITH OLIVE OIL AND HERB SAUCE

4 SERVINGS

2 tablespoons finely chopped shallots
1 tablespoon minced garlic
2 teaspoons Dijon mustard
⅓ cup dry white wine
⅓ cup lemon juice
¾ cup olive oil
1 teaspoon finely chopped rosemary leaves
1 tablespoon finely chopped parsley
¼ cup finely chopped basil
Salt and freshly ground pepper to taste
2 pounds (about 28) shrimp, shelled and
    deveined
Buerre blanc (pages 555–556)

1 In a large bowl comine the shallots, garlic, mustard, wine, lemon juice, oil, rosemary, parsley, basil, salt and pepper.

2 Add the shrimp and stir to blend. Refrigerate and let stand a minimum of 2 hours.

3 When ready to cook, preheat a cleaned, well-scrubbed outdoor grill to high. Brush the grill lightly with oil.

4 Arrange an equal number of the shrimp—perhaps 7 or 8—on 4 skewers. Arrange them so that they will lie flat and touching when placed on the grill.

5 Place the skewered shrimp on the grill and cook 1½ to 2 minutes, or until the shrimp can be lifted from the grill without sticking. Turn the shrimp and cook them 1½ to 2 minutes, or until done. Remove the shrimp from the skewers and arrange them, edges slightly overlapping, on each of 4 plates. Serve as is with lemon wedges or, if you wish, with a beurre blanc, or white butter sauce, spooned over.

SHRIMP CURRY

6 OR MORE SERVINGS

2 tablespoons butter
4 large onions, chopped
3 garlic cloves, chopped
3 cups water
3 large tomatoes, peeled and chopped
2 large apples, peeled and chopped
1 cup chopped celery
1 tablespoon shredded coconut
1 tablespoon chopped ginger
1 tablespoon sugar
1½ tablespoons curry powder, or more
1½ tablespoons flour
1 teaspoon salt
¼ teaspoon freshly ground pepper
3½ pounds raw shrimp, shelled and deveined

1 In a large skillet heat the butter, add the onions and garlic and cook until light brown. Add the water and bring to a boil.

2 Add the tomatoes, apples, celery, coconut and ginger.

3 Blend the sugar, curry powder, flour, salt and pepper. Add enough cold water to make a paste and add gradually, stirring, to the boiling mixture. Simmer, partially covered, stirring occasionally, until the vegetables are very tender, about 40 minutes.

4 Add the shrimp and cook 5 minutes longer. Serve over rice.

STIR-FRIED SQUID, CHINESE STYLE

4 TO 6 SERVINGS

2 pounds small fresh squid
2 tablespoons peanut or vegetable oil
2 scallions, trimmed and cut into 1-inch
    lengths
2 slices of fresh ginger
2 tablespoons light soy sauce
2 tablespoons dry sherry
1 tablespoon cornstarch
2 tablespoons water

1 Have the squid thoroughly cleaned. Rinse well under cold running water and dry. Cut off and reserve the tentacles and cut the squid into 1-inch pieces.

2 Heat the oil; when it is hot, add all the squid. Add the scallions and ginger and cook, stirring, for 1 minute. Add soy sauce and sherry and cook, stirring, for 2 minutes longer.

3 Mix cornstarch and water, stir it into the squid, and cook until the sauce is boiling and translucent. Serve immediately.

STUFFED SQUID

4 TO 6 SERVINGS

1 (1-pound) tender fresh squid
2 or 3 onions, chopped
2 or 3 garlic cloves, minced
½ cup olive oil
Salt and freshly ground pepper to taste
1 cup tomato sauce
1 bay leaf, crumbled
½ cup rice
Dried currants (optional)
Chopped parsley or dill to taste
1½ cups boiling water

1 Have the squid thoroughly cleaned; chop the tentacles and set aside. Wash squid and soak in water until ready to use.

2 Brown the onions and garlic in the oil. Add salt, pepper, tomato sauce and bay leaf. Mix well. Add rice, currants, parsley and the chopped tentacles.

3 Stuff the squid with this mixture. Place in an oiled casserole and pour any remaining stuffing on top. Add the boiling water. Simmer, covered, for 25 minutes.

ITALIAN-STYLE SQUID WITH TOMATOES

4 TO 6 SERVINGS

2 pounds small fresh squid
1 garlic clove, minced
¼ cup olive oil
½ cup dry sherry
1 cup canned Italian plum tomatoes
1 tablespoon finely chopped parsley
¼ teaspoon hot red pepper flakes, or more
Pinch of thyme
Salt and freshly ground pepper to taste

1 Have the squid thoroughly cleaned. Rinse well under cold running water and dry. Cut off and reserve the tentacles and cut the squid into 1-inch pieces.

2 Cook the squid and garlic in the olive oil, stirring, for about 5 minutes. Add the sherry, cover, and cook over low heat for 10 minutes. Add the remaining ingredients, cover, and cook for 15 minutes, or until squid are tender. Serve with rice.

A frog is neither a fish nor a shellfish, but an amphibian; however, one finds recipes for this delicacy along with those for other aquatic creatures. The flavor and texture of frogs' legs most closely resembles that of tender young chicken.

♦

FROGS' LEGS PROVENÇALE

6 SERVINGS

18 jumbo frogs' legs, trimmed
Milk
Seasoned flour for dredging
Peanut oil
3 tablespoons butter
1 garlic clove, finely chopped
Lemon juice to taste
Finely chopped parsley

1 Soak the frogs' legs in water to cover for 2 hours. Drain and dry well. Dip the frogs' legs in milk, then dredge in seasoned flour.

2 Add peanut oil to a skillet to the depth of ¼ inch. When it is hot, cook the frogs' legs on all sides, 6 to 8 minutes.

3 Transfer the frogs' legs to a hot platter and pour off and discard the oil from the skillet. Add the butter to the skillet and cook to a golden brown. Add the garlic, then pour the butter over the frogs' legs. Sprinkle with lemon juice and chopped parsley and serve immediately.

SOUFFLÉED FROGS' LEGS

3 OR 4 SERVINGS

1 pound frogs' legs
Milk
Seasoned flour
Batter (see following recipe)
Oil for deep frying

1 Soak the frogs' legs in milk to cover for 30 minutes.

2 Dry the frogs' legs and dredge them in seasoned flour. Dip them into the batter and fry them in deep oil heated to 370°F for about 3 minutes, until puffed and golden brown. Drain on paper toweling.

BATTER

½ cup flour
½ teaspoon baking powder
¼ cup oil
½ cup milk
1 egg, separated

Sift the flour and baking powder into a bowl. Add the oil and combine thoroughly. Pour in milk and lightly beaten egg yolk. Beat with a rotary beater until smooth. Beat the egg white until stiff but not dry. Fold it gently into the mixture.

6

Meat

Beef

HIGH-TEMPERATURE ROASTING OF BEEF

Preheat the oven to 450°F.

Wipe the roast with a damp cloth and rub it with salt and freshly ground pepper. Insert a meat thermometer, if one is available, in the thickest part of the roast. Place the meat on a rack in a roasting pan. It is not necessary to baste the roast. Cook the meat 25 minutes and reduce the heat to 300°F. Cook the meat until the thermometer registers 125°F for rare beef. For medium-rare beef, cook to 130°–135°F, for well done, to 145°F. If a meat thermometer is not used, cook it according to the following table.

Roasting Timetable for a Standing Rib Roast Cooked According to the High-Temperature Method

Rare	12 to 14 minutes per pound
Medium rare	14 to 16 minutes per pound
Well done	20 to 25 minutes per pound

LOW-TEMPERATURE ROASTING OF BEEF

Preheat the oven to 300°F.

Wipe the roast with a damp cloth and rub it with salt and freshly ground pepper. Insert a meat thermometer, if one is available, in the thickest part of the roast. Place the meat on a rack in a roasting pan. It is not necessary to baste the roast. Cook the meat until the thermometer registers 125°F for rare beef. For medium-rare beef, cook to 130°–135°, and for well done, to 145°. If a meat thermometer is not used, cook it according to the following table.

Roasting Timetable for a Standing Rib Roast Cooked According to the Low-Temperature Method

Rare	18 to 20 minutes per pound
Medium rare	20 to 22 minutes per pound
Well done	27 to 30 minutes per pound

♦

YORKSHIRE PUDDING

4 SERVINGS

2 eggs
1 cup milk
1 cup sifted flour
½ teaspoon salt
Beef drippings

1 Preheat the oven to 450°F.

2 Beat the eggs with the milk. Sift together the flour and salt and stir this into the egg mixture. Beat the batter until well blended.

3 Discard most of the fat from the pan in which the beef was roasted. Heat an 11 × 7-inch baking pan or ring mold and pour into it ¼ cup of the beef drippings. Pour in the pudding mixture and bake 10 minutes. Reduce the oven temperature to 350°F and bake 15 to 20 minutes longer, or until puffy and a delicate brown. Cut into squares and serve immediately with roast beef.

BROILED STEAK

The best method for broiling a steak in the home is in a skillet. Heat the skillet until it is piping hot and sprinkle it with salt. If the skillet is hot enough it should not be necessary to add fat. Sear the meat quickly on one side, then reduce the heat. Turn the steak and sear on the other side. Cook to desired degree of doneness. The cooking time will depend on the thickness of the steak and the temperature of the skillet. Serve the steak with melted butter seasoned to taste with lemon juice, salt and pepper, Worcestershire sauce, Tabasco sauce and freshly chopped parsley.

♦

MINUTE STEAKS IN PARSLEY BUTTER

4 SERVINGS

4 tablespoons butter, softened
1/4 cup finely chopped parsley
4 to 8 minute or cubed steaks

1 With a fork, blend the butter and parsley thoroughly.

2 Heat a heavy skillet and sprinkle with salt. Brown the steaks on one side about 2 minutes over high heat, turn and brown on the other side about 1 minute. Top immediately with small balls of the butter-parsley mixture.

STIR-FRY BEEF WITH LEEKS

Although leeks are not common in Chinese cooking, they make a delicious addition to stir-fried beef. This is a creation of the late Virginia Lee.

4 SERVINGS

3/4 pound flank steak
1 tablespoon cornstarch
1 egg white
1 tablespoon sesame oil
1/2 pound leeks
1/4 cup vegetable oil
2 tablespoons shao hsing or dry sherry
1/2 teaspoon ground pepper, preferably white

1 Cut the beef on the bias into very thin strips. It will facilitate the slicing if the beef is partly frozen.

2 Put the beef in a bowl and add the cornstarch, egg white and sesame oil. Blend well with the fingers.

3 Trim off the ends of the leeks. Cut off most of the green part and use for soup. Cut the leeks crosswise into 1½-inch pieces. Cut each piece lengthwise into quarters. Separate the leaves and drop into cold water. Rinse well and drain. There should be almost 4 cups.

4 Heat the oil in a wok and add the beef, stirring quickly to separate the pieces. Using a slotted spoon, scoop the beef into a bowl, leaving as much oil as possible in the wok.

5 Add the leeks to the oil in the wok and cook, stirring, for about 2 minutes. Add 1 tablespoon of wine and cook, stirring, for about 30 seconds.

6 Add the beef and cook, stirring, for 30 seconds. Add the pepper and continue cooking and stirring for 30 seconds. Add the remaining wine and cook for 10 seconds. Spoon the mixture into a serving dish.

BEEF SUKIYAKI

4 SERVINGS

4 large dried mushrooms
¼ cup oil
3 medium onions, thinly sliced
3 celery stalks, thinly sliced
3 cups spinach leaves
1 bunch scallions, cut into 2-inch lengths
½ cup canned bamboo shoots, sliced
1 pound tender beef, sliced thin
¾ cup beef stock
½ cup light soy sauce
1 tablespoon sugar
1 (½-pound) pad soft bean curd, cut into
    1-inch cubes
⅓ cup cellophane noodles

1 Soak the mushrooms in boiling water for about 20 minutes. Drain, trim off any tough stems, and slice.

2 Heat the oil in a heavy cast-iron pan, 9 or 10 inches in diameter. Add the onions, celery, spinach, scallions, mushrooms and bamboo shoots.

3 Arrange the meat over the vegetables and add the stock, soy sauce, sugar, bean curd and noodles. Let simmer uncovered over low to medium heat until the meat is tender and the vegetables are cooked but still crisp. Stir gently 2 or 3 times during the cooking. Serve with boiled rice.

STEAK TARTARE LAUSANNE

This is a very special version of steak tartare. The fresher the beef, the redder it will remain. After the meat is ground, serve it as expeditiously as possible. It is best, therefore, to grind it at home, using a meat grinder or a food processor. Take care not to let the meat become mushy if a food processor is used.

4 SERVINGS

2 pounds raw, ground top-quality beef fillet,
    sirloin or round steak
4 egg yolks
8 anchovy fillets
Capers
½ cup finely chopped onions
4 teaspoons chopped parsley
Salt and freshly ground pepper to taste
Rose paprika
Cayenne
Tomato catsup
Worcestershire sauce
1 lemon, quartered
Prepared mustard
Cognac or port to taste
Buttered toast

1 Divide the raw beef into 4 portions and shape into patties. Place the patties on chilled plates. Make a small indentation in the center of each and place 1 egg yolk in each.

2 Garnish each serving with 2 anchovies and sprinkle with capers, onion and parsley.

3 Serve immediately accompanied by the remaining seasonings and buttered toast. Each guest stirs the seasonings into his steak tartare according to his taste. Or one or more of the seasonings may be stirred into the ground steak before it is served to guests.

BEEF FILLETS WITH SHRIMP

One of the winning recipes at a March of Dimes gathering in Monterey, California, was that of Artie Early, one of the town's civic leaders. It is an excellent and novel version of "surf and turf." It is made with beef and shrimp and the sauce in which they are bathed includes tomatoes and dill plus shredded lemon peel for garnish.

4 SERVINGS

4 (3-ounce) slices of fillet of beef, trimmed of
   all fat
Flour for dredging
Salt and freshly ground pepper to taste
4 large prawns or shrimp, shelled and
   deveined
4 tablespoons butter
1 tablespoon finely chopped shallots
2 teaspoons finely chopped chives
1 teaspoon finely chopped dill
¼ cup dry sherry
½ cup beef stock
4 cherry tomatoes, quartered
1 teaspoon lemon juice
1 tablespoon finely chopped parsley
4 lemon peel shreds

1 Dredge the beef in flour seasoned with salt and pepper. Shake off excess.

2 Partially split each prawn in half to "butterfly" it.

3 Heat half of the butter in a heavy skillet and when it is quite hot but not brown, add the beef slices. Cook 2 to 2½ minutes on each side, or until brown. Transfer the slices to a warm platter.

4 Add the shallots, chives and dill to the skillet, stirring without browning. Add the sherry and stir until almost all the liquid evaporates. Add the beef stock and reduce by half. Swirl in the remaining butter and add the tomatoes, lemon juice and prawns. Cook briefly, just until the prawns turn red and are heated through.

5 Arrange 1 prawn on each piece of beef and spoon the sauce overall. Garnish with parsley and the lemon shreds.

♦

BEEF STROGANOFF

ABOUT 4 SERVINGS

1½ pounds beef fillet, sirloin or porterhouse
   steak
Salt and freshly ground pepper to taste
3 tablespoons butter
1 tablespoon flour
1 cup beef stock
1 teaspoon prepared mustard
2 tablespoons oil
1 onion, sliced
3 tablespoons sour cream, at room temperature

1 Remove all the fat and gristle from the meat. Cut into narrow strips about 2 inches long and ½ inch thick. Season the strips with salt and pepper and refrigerate 2 hours.

2 In a saucepan melt 1½ tablespoons of butter, add the flour and stir with a wire whisk until blended. Meanwhile, bring the stock to a boil and add all at once to the butter-flour mixture, stirring vigorously with the whisk until the sauce is thickened and smooth. Stir in mustard.

3 In a separate pan heat the oil and brown the meat quickly on both sides. Remove the meat to a hot platter. Add the remaining butter to the pan and sauté the onions until soft. Spoon the onion slices over the meat.

4 Add the sour cream to the mustard sauce and heat over a brisk flame for 3 minutes. Pour sauce over meat and serve.

STEAK AU POIVRE

Coarsely ground black pepper in generous quantity is the secret of the success of this enormously appealing dish. The method listed below is for pan frying. Or try it over charcoal and serve the steaks with plenty of melted butter that has been seasoned with lemon juice, parsley and chives.

6 SERVINGS

6 club steaks
2 tablespoons coarsely ground pepper
Salt
6 teaspoons butter
Tabasco sauce to taste
Worcestershire sauce to taste
Lemon juice to taste
2 tablespoons cognac (optional)
Chopped parsley
Chopped chives

1 Sprinkle the sides of each steak with pepper and, with the heel of the hand, press the pepper into the meat. Let stand 30 minutes.

2 Heat a heavy skillet and sprinkle a light layer of salt over the bottom. When the salt begins to brown, add the steaks. Cook until well browned on one side. To produce a very rare steak, cook 30 seconds at high heat. Turn the steaks, lower the heat to moderate and cook 1 more minute. Adjust the heat and time to cook the steaks to a greater degree of doneness.

3 Place a teaspoon of butter on each steak and add Tabasco, Worcestershire and lemon juice.

4 Turn the heat to low, blaze with cognac and transfer steaks to a platter. Swirl the sauce in the skillet and pour over the meat. Sprinkle the steaks with parsley and chives.

LONDON BROIL

4 TO 6 SERVINGS

1 (2-pound) flank steak
1 garlic clove
Vegetable oil
Salt and freshly ground pepper to taste

1 Rub the steak on both sides with the cut garlic. Brush with oil and place on a preheated greased broiler rack, 1½ to 2 inches from the source of heat. Broil 5 minutes. Season with salt and pepper.

2 Turn the steak and broil 5 minutes on the other side. Cut in very thin slices diagonally across the grain.

FLANK STEAK WITH HERB STUFFING

4 TO 6 SERVINGS

1 (2-pound) flank steak
2 tablespoons butter
½ large onion, chopped
1 garlic clove, minced
½ cup chopped mushrooms
¼ cup pistachios, coarsely chopped (optional)
¼ cup chopped parsley
1½ cups soft bread cubes
¼ teaspoon basil
¼ teaspoon oregano
½ teaspoon salt
Freshly ground pepper to taste
1 egg, slightly beaten
½ cup water, dry white wine or beef stock

1 Preheat the oven to 350°F. Pound the steak or score it lightly on both sides.

2 In a skillet heat the butter, add the onion and garlic and cook until light brown. Add the mushrooms and cook 3 minutes. Add the nuts, parsley, bread cubes, basil, oregano, salt, pepper and egg and mix.

3 Spread the mixture on the steak. Roll lengthwise, like a jelly roll, and tie with string at 2-inch intervals.

4 Brown the meat on both sides in a little fat in a skillet or heavy Dutch oven. Add the liquid, cover and bake 2 hours. To serve, cut into 1-inch slices and serve with the pan drippings.

TERIYAKI

Teriyaki is Hawaiian for steak marinated in soy sauce, garlic and ginger and broiled, preferably over charcoal.

6 SERVINGS

2 pounds (¼-inch-thick) sirloin steak
1 tablespoon finely chopped fresh ginger
2 garlic cloves, finely chopped
1 medium onion, finely chopped
2 tablespoons sugar
1 cup light soy sauce
½ cup sherry

1 Cut the steak into thin slices or strips.

2 Combine the ginger, garlic, onion, sugar, soy sauce and sherry and pour the mixture over the meat. Let stand 1 to 2 hours.

3 Thread the meat on skewers and broil quickly on both sides over charcoal or in a preheated broiler. Serve hot.

ÉMINCÉ OF BEEF BOURGEOIS

Slivers of beef quickly cooked and served with a chicken liver sauce.

4 TO 6 SERVINGS

4 tablespoons butter
½ pound chicken livers
1 bay leaf
¼ teaspoon thyme
1 truffle, finely chopped (optional)
2 pounds beef tenderloin tips
Salt and freshly ground pepper to taste
¼ cup cognac, heated

1 In a skillet heat half the butter, add the chicken livers, bay leaf and thyme and sauté quickly, shaking the pan occasionally, until the livers are barely cooked.

2 Remove the bay leaf. Place the chicken livers and chopped truffle in the container of a food processor.

3 Cut the beef into very thin strips across the grain. Sprinkle with the salt and pepper and sear quickly in the remaining butter to seal in the juices, 1 minute or less.

4 Pour the warm cognac over the meat and ignite it. Remove the meat to a warm serving platter. Add the beef juices to the container of the food processor and blend until smooth. If necessary, add canned beef broth to make a smooth sauce.

5 Reheat the sauce and pour over the beef. Serve immediately.

STUFFED BEEF BIRDS

4 SERVINGS

2 pounds (⅜-inch-thick) round steak
¼ cup flour
1½ teaspoons salt
¼ teaspoon freshly ground pepper
2 tablespoons butter
2 tablespoons chopped onions
1 tablespoon chopped green pepper
½ cup soft fresh bread crumbs
1 (10½-ounce) can whole kernel corn, drained
¼ teaspoon basil
2 tablespoons oil
½ cup beef stock
1 bay leaf
Chopped parsley

1 Pound the steak with the edge of a plate or a mallet until very thin. Cut it into 8 pieces, each approximately 2 × 4 inches.

2 Dredge the meat in the flour, mixed with 1 teaspoon of the salt and ⅛ teaspoon of the pepper.

3 Melt the butter and sauté the onions for 5 minutes. Add the green pepper, crumbs, corn, basil and remaining salt and pepper.

4 Divide the mixture among the pieces of meat and roll up each one to enclose the stuffing. Secure the rolls with fine string or toothpicks.

5 Heat the oil and brown the rolls on all sides. Add the stock and bay leaf. Cover and simmer for 1 hour, until the rolls are tender. Garnish with chopped parsley.

RUMP ROAST WITH CARAWAY SEEDS

6 TO 8 SERVINGS

1½ cups chopped onions
1 teaspoon salt
2 tablespoons caraway seeds
4 pounds rolled rump roast
5 strips bacon
2 to 3 pounds beef bones, sawed into pieces
⅓ cup wine vinegar
1 tablespoon flour

1 Preheat the oven to 325°F.

2 Combine ½ cup of the onions with the salt and 1 tablespoon of the caraway seeds. Using a spoon and spatula, work the mixture into the folds of the roast.

3 In a large roasting pan cook the bacon until crisp. Add the remaining onions and cook, stirring, until the onions are transparent. Place the beef bones around the edge of the pan and add the meat. Sprinkle with the remaining caraway seeds and the vinegar and add enough water to cover the bottom of the pan to a depth of ½ inch. Bake until tender, about 2 hours, basting frequently. Remove the meat to a warm platter and keep hot.

4 Mix the flour with a little water and stir into the boiling liquid. Cook until the gravy thickens. Strain and serve with the roast.

Note: Bones give additional body and flavor to gravy.

POT ROAST WITH WINE

6 GENEROUS SERVINGS

Flour for dredging
Salt and freshly ground pepper to taste
3 pounds boneless chuck or beef rump roast
¼ cup oil
½ cup chopped onions
½ cup chopped celery
½ cup chopped carrots
1 garlic clove, finely chopped
¼ teaspoon thyme
¼ teaspoon marjoram
1 bay leaf
¼ cup chopped parsley
2 cups canned tomatoes, undrained
½ cup dry red wine

1 Mix flour, salt and pepper. Dredge the meat in seasoned flour. In a Dutch oven heat the oil, add the meat and brown well on all sides. Pour off the fat.

2 Add the onions, celery, carrots and garlic. Stir until onions begin to brown and then add the remaining ingredients. Cover tightly and simmer until tender, about 2½ hours. Remove the meat to a heated platter. Reduce the liquid to the desired consistency. Thicken the gravy, if desired, with a little flour mixed with water.

RIB ROAST BRAISED IN WINE

ABOUT 12 SERVINGS

1 (5-pound) boned and rolled rib roast
Flour for dredging
¼ cup vegetable oil
½ cup chopped onions
½ cup chopped leeks
½ cup chopped carrots
1 garlic clove, crushed
2 cups dry red wine, approximately
Salt to taste
8 crushed peppercorns
1 bay leaf
½ teaspoon thyme
¼ teaspoon marjoram
2 tablespoons cognac, warmed

1 Preheat the oven to 325°F.

2 Dredge the roast in flour. In a Dutch oven, heat the oil, add the meat and brown on all sides.

3 Add the onions, leeks, carrots and garlic and sauté until brown.

4 Add the wine and seasonings. Ignite the cognac and add. Cover and bake until the meat is tender, about 4 hours. If necessary, add more wine.

5 Transfer the meat to a warm platter and keep hot. Strain the sauce, correct the seasoning and pour over the beef.

Note: Five pounds boneless chuck or rump roast may be substituted for rib roast.

POTTED BEEF, ITALIAN STYLE

4 GENEROUS SERVINGS

¼ cup olive oil
3 pounds chuck or rump roast of beef
1 carrot, chopped
1 celery stalk, chopped
1 onion, chopped
2 garlic cloves, chopped
2 bay leaves
Salt and freshly ground pepper to taste
1 ounce dried mushrooms
1 cup red wine
1 (6-ounce) can tomato paste
2 cups warm beef stock

1 In a heavy saucepan, heat the oil and brown the beef quickly on all sides. Add the carrot, celery and onions and sauté until the onions are golden brown. Add the garlic, bay leaves, salt and pepper. Continue cooking over low heat.

2 Soak the mushrooms in warm water several minutes. Drain off the water, trim off any tough stems, chop the mushrooms and add to the meat and vegetables. Cook, uncovered, over low heat 4 minutes. Add the wine and the tomato paste diluted with the warm stock, cover and bring to a boil. Continue cooking, covered, until the meat is tender, about 2½ hours. Stir occasionally, basting the meat from time to time. If the gravy becomes too thick, add more warm stock.

3 When the meat is done, remove from the pan and serve separately. Serve the gravy, unstrained, over any kind of pasta, polenta or gnocchi.

SAUERBRATEN

6 SERVINGS

4 pounds boneless chuck or rump roast
Salt and freshly ground pepper to taste
2 cups wine vinegar
2 cups water
1 garlic clove
¾ cup sliced onions
1 bay leaf
10 peppercorns
¼ cup sugar
3 whole cloves
Flour
2 tablespoons vegetable oil
1½ cups sour cream

1 Season the meat with the salt and pepper and place in a large bowl.

2 Bring the vinegar and water to a boil and add the garlic, onions, bay leaf, peppercorns, sugar and cloves. Pour the marinade over the beef, cover and refrigerate 2 hours or overnight.

3 Remove the meat and dry thoroughly with paper toweling. Reserve the marinade. Dredge the meat in flour.

4 In a heavy kettle heat the oil, add the meat and brown on all sides. Add 2 cups of the marinade, cover tightly and simmer gently until the meat is tender, 2½ to 3 hours. Remove the meat to a warm platter and keep hot. Thicken the gravy with a little flour mixed with water. Stir in the sour cream and serve over the sliced meat.

GLAZED CORNED BEEF

8 TO 10 SERVINGS

5 to 6 pounds corned beef brisket
3 onions, sliced
2 or 3 garlic cloves, finely minced
6 whole cloves
3 bay leaves
1 tablespoon Düsseldorf mustard
⅓ cup light brown sugar

1 Place the corned beef in a Dutch oven. Barely cover corned beef with boiling water.

2 Add the onions, garlic, cloves and bay leaves. Bring the mixture to a boil. Cover the Dutch oven tightly with foil and the lid. Simmer gently, but do not allow to boil, for 50 minutes per pound of meat, or until meat is tender when pricked with a fork.

3 Preheat the oven to 350°F.

4 Remove the meat from the liquid and drain. Place the meat in a shallow pan, fat side up. Score the fat. Spread the top with the mustard and then with the sugar. Bake for 15 to 20 minutes, or until well glazed. Serve corned beef hot or cold.

Variation

CORNED BEEF AND CABBAGE

Core a 3½-pound cabbage and cut the cabbage into 8 or 10 wedges. Peel 2½ pounds small new potatoes. Fifteen minutes before the corned beef is cooked, add the cabbage and potatoes to the simmering liquid. Serve the corned beef sliced with the cabbage and potatoes. Do not glaze the beef.

HOME-CURED CORNED BEEF

TO CURE

7 quarts water
3 cups kosher salt, approximately
1 raw egg in the shell for testing brine
1 (6- to 9-pound) beef brisket
3 garlic cloves, peeled
20 cloves
20 peppercorns
1 bay leaf
6 thyme sprigs, or 1 teaspoon dried
½ tablespoon saltpeter, available in
  drug stores

TO COOK

1 bay leaf
1 onion, sliced
6 thyme sprigs, or 1 teaspoon dried
16 peppercorns
1 garlic clove, sliced
1 carrot, scraped and cut into 3-inch lengths
2 celery stalks, trimmed and cut into
  3-inch lengths

1 To cure the brisket, you will need a large earthenware, enamel or stainless-steel crock. Pour the water into the crock and add the salt, stirring to dissolve it. Add the egg. The egg is used to test the salt content of the brine. If the egg floats in the solution, it is ready. If it does not float, continue adding salt a little at a time, stirring to dissolve, until the egg floats. Remove the egg.

2 Add the brisket to the brine. Add 3 cloves of garlic, cloves, 20 peppercorns, 1 bay leaf, 6 thyme sprigs and saltpeter. Stir well. Place a clean, heavy weight on the meat to make certain it is covered. Place a lid on the crock and refrigerate for 8 to 12 days. Turn the brisket occasionally, but keep it weighted down.

3 When ready to cook the corned beef, remove it from the brine and rinse it well.

4 Put the corned beef in a kettle and add water to come 1 inch above the beef. Add 1 bay leaf, the onion, 6 thyme sprigs, 16 peppercorns, 1 garlic clove, the carrots and celery. Do not add salt. Bring to a boil and simmer 2 to 3 hours, or until tender.

5 Remove the corned beef and cut it into the thinnest possible slices. Serve with rye bread and mustard and butter. Serve with garlic pickles on the side.

♦

CORNED BEEF HASH

2¾ pounds corned beef
3 potatoes (about 1½ pounds)
Salt to taste
1 tablespoon butter
1 cup finely chopped onions
½ cup finely chopped green pepper (optional)
1 egg
1 egg yolk
1 teaspoon Worcestershire sauce
Freshly ground pepper to taste
8 teaspoons butter or vegetable oil

1 Put the corned beef in a kettle and add water to cover to a depth of about 2 inches. Bring to a boil and let simmer uncovered 1 hour. Cover closely and continue cooking 3 hours.

2 Meanwhile, put the potatoes in a saucepan and add cold water to cover and salt. Cook until almost tender but relatively firm, 20 to 30 minutes. The potatoes must not be overcooked or they will not cube properly. Drain and let cool. Peel the potatoes and cut them into very small dice. There should be about 3½ cups.

3 When the corned beef is cooked, remove and let cool.

4 Heat the butter in a skillet and add the onions and green pepper. Cook, stirring, until wilted.

5 Trim away and discard the fat from the corned beef. Cut the corned beef into very thin slices and cut the slices into very small cubes. There should be about 5 cups. Put the cubed meat into a mixing bowl and add the potatoes and onion mixture. Add the egg and egg yolk, Worcestershire, salt and pepper and blend thoroughly with the fingers. Press down with the fingers to make the mass compact. Cover with clear plastic wrap and refrigerate overnight.

6 Shape the mixture into 8 portions of more or less equal size. (Or, if you prefer, heat butter or oil in a nonstick skillet and cover the bottom with hash.) Flatten each portion into patties. Heat 1 teaspoon of butter or oil for each patty to be cooked. Cook 2 or 3 minutes on one side, or until brown. Turn the patty and cook 2 or 3 minutes on the other side, or until brown. Serve, if desired, with a poached egg atop each patty.

Variation

RED FLANNEL HASH

When the corned beef has been prepared, add 2 cups of finely diced cooked beets to the mixture and blend well. Shape into 10 patties. Cook the red flannel hash exactly as you would corned beef hash.

BOILED BEEF

There is many a man with a sophisticated palate who, when asked to name the dish for his desert island, would nominate boiled beef. It has a classic simplicity, and almost every nation has a version of it.

6 SERVINGS

3 pounds lean first-cut beef brisket
2 leeks, trimmed and washed well
1 carrot, scraped and left whole
1 medium onion, peeled
1 small celery stalk with leaves
12 peppercorns, slightly bruised
1 bay leaf
½ teaspoon thyme
Salt to taste
Sauce verte (page 559), or horseradish sauce
    (page 568)

1 Place the brisket in a Dutch oven or heavy skillet in which it will fit compactly. Pour over it boiling water barely to cover.

2 Return to a boil and reduce the heat. Spoon off all the grease and scum.

3 Add the leeks, carrot, onion, celery, peppercorns, bay leaf, thyme and salt and cover lightly. Simmer 3 to 4 hours, until the meat is tender. Serve sliced with sauce verte or horseradish sauce.

Note: Use remaining broth for soups, or freeze for future use.

BOLLITO MISTO

A *bollito misto* is Italian for "mixed boil." It is everything in a pot from chicken to beef to vegetables.

12 SERVINGS

1 (3-pound) stewing chicken
1 pound boned beef rump or boneless veal
2 pounds zampone or cotechino sausage
3 bunches medium carrots, scraped
2 pounds (12 medium) onions, quartered
8 small yellow turnips, peeled and quartered
25 small leeks
Salt and freshly ground pepper to taste
1 bay leaf
Pinch of thyme
Pinch of marjoram
1 (1-pound) veal tongue
4 pounds (12 medium) potatoes, peeled
Sauce verte (page 559), or horseradish sauce
    (page 568)

1 Place the chicken, beef and sausage in a large pot with 1 sliced carrot, 1 quartered onion, 1 quartered yellow turnip and 1 chopped leek and cover with cold water. Bring to a boil, skim and season with salt, pepper, bay leaf, thyme and marjoram. Reduce the heat, cover and simmer 1 hour. Add the veal tongue and continue simmering 1 hour longer.

2 Thirty minutes before the meats have finished cooking, put the remaining carrots, onions and turnips and the potatoes in a separate pot of boiling salted water. After cooking 10 minutes, add the remaining leeks and cook all the vegetables 20 minutes longer. Drain the vegetables and keep warm.

3 Remove the cooked chicken and meats from the pot. Disjoint the chicken, slice the tongue and sausage and cut the beef into bite-size pieces. Correct the seasonings and moisten the meats with a little more of the strained broth in which they were cooked. Keep hot.

4 When ready to serve, arrange the meats in a large, deep platter with the vegetables and some of the hot broth poured over all. Serve with sauce verte or horseradish sauce on the side.

◆

VIENNESE BOILED BEEF

8 SERVINGS

6 celery stalks, sliced
3 carrots, sliced
2 onions, chopped
1 leek, trimmed and washed well
1 teaspoon salt
4 parsley sprigs
1 bay leaf
6 whole peppercorns
4 allspice berries
1 veal knuckle
3 pounds chicken parts (feet, necks,
    backs, wings)
1 large unpeeled onion
4 pounds beef brisket

1 Place the vegetables, seasonings, veal knuckle and chicken parts in a large covered saucepan, cover with water and simmer 2 hours.

2 Meanwhile, bake the unpeeled onion in a preheated 350°F oven for 30 minutes.

3 Place the brisket in a Dutch oven or heavy kettle and strain the stock over it. Add more water if necessary to cover the meat. Add the baked onion, cover and simmer about 3 hours.

POT AU FEU

The French version of boiled beef is *pot au feu*.

6 SERVINGS

4 pounds beef with bone (brisket, rump, shin, plate, chuck or round)
3 quarts beef stock or water
1 teaspoon salt
1 bouquet garni (1 bay leaf, ¼ teaspoon thyme, ½ teaspoon peppercorns, 3 cloves, 4 parsley sprigs and a few celery leaves tied in a cheesecloth bag)
2 cups mixed chopped vegetables (onions, carrots, celery, white turnips, parsnips)
6 leeks, well washed, white part only
6 cabbage wedges
6 potatoes, whole or quartered
3 carrots, quartered

1 Place the meat in a large soup kettle. Add the stock, salt, bouquet garni and chopped vegetables. Bring to a boil, skimming frequently. Reduce the heat and simmer, covered, until the meat is almost tender, 4 hours or longer.

2 Remove the meat and strain the broth. Return meat and broth to the kettle and add the remaining vegetables. Simmer until tender, about 45 minutes longer. Correct the seasonings.

3 To serve, remove the meat to a warm serving platter and surround with the large pieces of vegetables. Serve with coarse salt.

Note: If a fatty cut of meat is used, the dish is best made a day in advance, refrigerated and the fat removed before reheating the pot au feu and serving.

RAGOÛT OF BEEF

6 SERVINGS

1½ tablespoons butter
1 medium onion, chopped
1 garlic clove
2 pounds beef shank or bottom round, cut into 1-inch cubes
1 teaspoon paprika
Salt and freshly ground pepper to taste
2 large tomatoes, chopped
1 cup celery, diced
½ ounce dried black mushrooms
1¼ cups water
2 tablespoons flour

1 In a large skillet heat the butter, add the onion and garlic and sauté until the onion is transparent. Discard the garlic. Add the meat, paprika, salt and pepper. Cook over medium heat, stirring, until the meat is brown. Add tomatoes. Cover and simmer very gently 1 hour. Add the celery.

2 Meanwhile, wash mushrooms and soak in 1 cup of the water for 20 minutes. Boil for 3 minutes in their soaking liquid. Fifteen minutes after the celery is added, add the mushrooms and their liquid and continue to simmer gently until tender. The total time is 1½ to 2 hours.

3 When the meat is tender, blend the flour with ¼ cup of the water and add, stirring, to the ragoût. Cook, stirring, until thickened. Serve with steamed rice, buttered noodles or polenta.

BEEF EN CASSEROLE

4 large white mushrooms
3 tablespoons butter
1½ pounds top sirloin or round beef, cut into
    1-inch cubes
¼ cup cognac
12 small white onions, peeled and left whole
6 small carrots, scraped
6 small white turnips, peeled
1 celery heart, quartered
½ teaspoon tomato paste
3 teaspoons potato flour, or 3 tablespoons flour
1½ cups beef stock
¼ cup red wine
Salt and freshly ground pepper to taste
1 bay leaf

1 Quarter the mushrooms through the stem without disconnecting stem and cap. Do not peel the mushrooms.

2 In a heavy saucepan heat 1 tablespoon of the butter, add the meat and brown on all sides. Heat the cognac, ignite it and add to the meat. Remove the meat from the pan.

3 Heat the remaining butter in the pan, add the onions, carrots, turnips and celery and sauté until brown. Add the mushrooms and cook 1 to 2 minutes longer.

4 Remove the pan from the heat and blend in the tomato paste and flour. Add the stock and wine, return to low heat and stir until the mixture boils. Season with salt and pepper.

5 Return the meat with the juices to the pan and add the bay leaf. Cover and simmer until the meat is tender, 1 to 1½ hours. Discard bay leaf.

BOEUF BOURGUIGNONNE

5 pounds chuck beef, cut into large cubes
Flour
¼ cup olive oil
Salt and freshly ground pepper to taste
¼ cup cognac, warmed
½ pound bacon, diced
3 garlic cloves, coarsely chopped
2 carrots, coarsely chopped
2 leeks, coarsely chopped
3 cups coarsely chopped onions
2 tablespoons chopped parsley
1 bay leaf
1 teaspoon thyme
1 bottle Burgundy wine
5 tablespoons butter
36 whole small onions
Dash of sugar
36 mushroom caps
Juice of ½ lemon

1 Roll the beef cubes in flour and brown them on all sides in a skillet over high heat in the olive oil.

2 Sprinkle the meat with salt and pepper, pour the cognac over it and ignite. When the flame dies, transfer meat to a 3-quart casserole. Add a little water to the skillet and deglaze over high heat, scraping up the brown particles clinging to the pan. Pour over the meat.

3 Preheat the oven to 350°F.

4 To the skillet add the bacon, garlic, carrots, leeks, chopped onions and 2 tablespoons chopped parsley. Cook, stirring, until the bacon is crisp and the vegetables are light brown. Transfer to the casserole with the meat and add the bay leaf, thyme, Burgundy and enough water to barely cover the meat. Cover and bake 1½ hours.

5 Prepare a beurre manié by blending 1 tablespoon each butter and flour and stir into the casserole bit by bit. Return the casserole to the oven and continue cooking 2 to 3 hours longer.

6 Brown the small onions in 2 tablespoons butter with a dash of sugar. Add a little water, cover and cook until the onions are almost tender.

7 Sauté the mushrooms in 2 tablespoons of the butter until light brown on one side. Sprinkle with lemon juice and turn to brown the other side.

8 To serve, add the onions to the casserole and garnish with the mushrooms and additional chopped parsley.

◆

BOEUF EN DAUBE

This classic French stew was traditionally cooked in a *daubière*, or earthenware pot. But any heavy casserole will do.

6 SERVINGS

3 pounds chuck or stewing beef, cut into
   2-inch cubes
1½ cups red wine
¼ cup cognac
2 tablespoons peanut oil
Salt and freshly ground pepper to taste
½ teaspoon thyme
1 bay leaf
1 large onion, coarsely chopped
2 garlic cloves, crushed
2 cups thinly sliced scraped carrots
½ cup coarsely chopped celery
½ pound sliced lean bacon, each slice cut
   into halves
Flour

2½ cups canned Italian plum tomatoes,
   or fresh ripe tomatoes, cored, peeled
   and chopped
2 cups thinly sliced mushrooms
2 cups beef stock

1 Place the beef in a large mixing bowl and add the wine, cognac, oil, salt, pepper, thyme, bay leaf, onion, garlic, carrots and celery. Cover and refrigerate for 3 hours or longer.

2 Preheat the oven to 350°F.

3 Place the bacon in a saucepan and add water barely to cover. Simmer for 5 minutes and drain.

4 Line a heatproof casserole with 3 or 4 pieces of bacon. Drain the beef and reserve the marinade.

5 Dredge each cube of beef in flour; shake to remove excess flour. Arrange a layer of beef in the casserole, add a layer of the marinated vegetables, one third of the tomatoes and one third of the mushrooms. Continue making layers until all the ingredients are used; end with vegetables and bacon. Sprinkle all with salt and pepper. Add the stock and enough of the marinade to cover.

6 Cover the casserole and bring the liquid to a boil on top of the stove. Place in the oven and bake for 15 minutes. Reduce oven heat to 300°F and continue to cook for 3 to 4 hours. Reduce heat as necessary so that the casserole barely simmers. Cook until meat is fork tender. Skim the fat from the surface and serve with rice or noodles.

BEEF STEW WITH WINE AND HERBS

4 TO 5 SERVINGS

2 pounds stewing beef, cut into 2-inch cubes
1 cup red wine
1 large bay leaf
1 garlic clove, sliced
1 teaspoon salt
½ teaspoon freshly ground pepper
2 tablespoons bacon drippings or other fat
1½ cups beef stock
1 celery stalk with leaves, diced
1 onion, sliced
Few sprigs of parsley
¼ teaspoon thyme
8 cloves
1 piece fresh ginger
Cornstarch

1 Place the meat in a large bowl and add the wine, bay leaf, garlic, salt and pepper. Marinate in the refrigerator several hours, turning frequently.

2 Remove the meat and dry thoroughly with paper toweling. Reserve the marinade. In a Dutch oven heat the drippings, add the meat and brown on all sides.

3 Simmer together for 10 minutes the reserved marinade, stock and the celery, onions, herbs and spices tied in a cheesecloth. Combine with the meat, cover and simmer until tender, 2½ to 3 hours. Add water if necessary. If desired, when meat is just tender, vegetables such as peas, carrots and onions may be added. Cook until vegetables are tender.

4 Discard the herb bag and remove the meat to a hot platter.

5 Thicken the gravy with cornstarch mixed with a little cold water, using ½ tablespoon cornstarch for each cup of broth. Boil, stirring, 2 minutes. Serve the sauce over the meat with the vegetables, if used, arranged attractively around it.

♦

CARBONNADES FLAMANDE
BEEF COOKED IN BEER

6 SERVINGS

3 pounds boneless chuck in one piece
¼ pound lean bacon
3 large (about 1½ pounds) onions
3 tablespoons butter
3 garlic cloves, finely chopped
Salt and freshly ground pepper to taste
2 thyme sprigs, or ½ teaspoon dried
2 bay leaves
1 tablespoon brown sugar
2 cups light beer
1 cup beef stock
3 slices of French bread, crusts removed
3 tablespoons Dijon mustard
2 tablespoons red wine vinegar

1 Preheat the oven to 325°F.

2 Place the meat on a flat surface. Cut it into slices about ¾ inch thick. Cut the slices into strips about 2 inches wide. Cut the strips into 2-inch lengths. Set aside.

3 Cut the bacon into small pieces. Cook the pieces in a large skillet until light brown and crisp. Using a perforated spoon, transfer the pieces to a large heavy casserole, leaving the fat in the skillet.

4 Peel and quarter the onions. Cut each quarter into thin slices. There should be about 7 cups. Set aside.

5 Add the butter to the fat in the skillet. Add one quarter of the cubed meat and cook over high heat, turning the pieces so that they cook evenly. As the meat browns, transfer the pieces to the casserole. Add more meat and continue cooking until all the meat has been browned and added to the casserole.

6 Add the onions to the skillet and cook, stirring occasionally, until light brown. Add the onions to the meat.

7 Add the garlic, salt, pepper, thyme, bay leaves, brown sugar, beer and stock.

8 Spread the bread on both sides with the mustard. Place the slices on top of the stew. Cover closely. Bring to the boil. Place in the oven and bake for 1½ to 2 hours. Cooking time will depend on the tenderness of the meat.

9 Stir the vinegar into the sauce and place on top of the stove. Simmer for about 2 minutes. Pour the stew into a sieve and strain the sauce into a saucepan. Skim off the fat and bring back to the boil. Arrange the meat on a warm serving platter and spoon the sauce over the meat.

◆

PICADILLO WITH RICE AND BEANS

Picadillo is a Mexican meat hash. It is used in Mexico as a filling for pies, tamales, enchiladas and tacos.

6 TO 8 SERVINGS

1 onion, chopped
½ green pepper, chopped
1 tablespoon oil
1½ pounds chopped beef
2 cups canned plum tomatoes, undrained
1 tablespoon raisins
1 teaspoon capers

Salt and freshly ground pepper to taste
1 hard-cooked egg white, chopped
6 cups cooked rice
4 bananas, sautéed in butter
Black beans (see following recipe)

1 Sauté the onions and green pepper in the oil until brown. Add the beef, tomatoes, raisins, capers, salt and pepper. Cook, stirring, until the mixture is almost dry.

2 Add the egg white and arrange the mixture on a warm platter with the rice. Garnish with the bananas. Serve with black beans.

BLACK BEANS
2½ CUPS

1 cup dried black beans
3 cups water
1 (½-pound) ham hock
½ teaspoon salt
1 small onion, chopped
1 tablespoon chopped green pepper
1 large garlic clove, chopped
1 tablespoon oil

1 Boil the beans in 3 cups of water 2 minutes, or use quick-soaking method on page 78. Cover and let stand overnight.

2 Add the ham hock and salt and simmer, covered, until the beans are tender, about 2 hours. Add more water if necessary.

3 Brown the onion, green pepper and garlic in the oil. Add to the beans and serve with picadillo and rice.

SOUTHWEST BEEF AND BEANS

6 SERVINGS

1 pound dried pea beans
6 cups water
Salt and freshly ground pepper to taste
1 pound smoked pork sausage links
2 cups chopped onions
3 garlic cloves, minced
2 pounds boneless stew beef, cut into cubes
½ teaspoon rosemary
1 bay leaf
Pinch of thyme
¾ cup chopped tomatoes
Chopped parsley

1 Soak the beans in a large quantity of water overnight, or use the quick-soaking method on page 78. Drain them and add the 6 cups water and salt and pepper. Bring to a boil and simmer for 1½ hours, until beans are tender without being mushy. Drain the beans and measure the cooking liquid. Reserve 1½ cups of the liquid.

2 Preheat the oven to 300°F.

3 Cut the sausages into quarters and fry them in a skillet until they are light brown. Remove them from the skillet and reserve until ready to use.

4 Pour off all but 2 tablespoons of fat from the skillet and add the onions and garlic. Cook, stirring, until onions are wilted. Remove onions, add a little more fat to the skillet and brown the beef cubes.

5 Place the beef, rosemary, bay leaf and thyme in a 3-quart casserole. Add the onions, garlic and tomatoes and cover closely. Bake for 2 hours.

6 Add the beans, sausage and reserved cooking liquid from the beans. Cover. Bake for 1 hour longer, or until beans and meat are thoroughly tender. Stir occasionally while casserole bakes. Serve sprinkled with chopped parsley.

Russian Borscht, page 63.
Albóndigas, page 94.

♦

BEEF WITH OLIVES

6 TO 8 SERVINGS

3 pounds chuck beef, cut into 1½-inch cubes
Flour
Salt and freshly ground pepper to taste
3 tablespoons olive oil
12 small white onions, peeled and left whole
1 garlic clove, finely chopped
½ teaspoon thyme
1½ cups beef stock
1 cup pitted green olives
¼ cup chopped parsley
2 tablespoons butter
2 tablespoons flour

1 Preheat the oven to 300°F.

2 Dredge the meat in flour seasoned with salt and pepper. In a Dutch oven heat the oil, add the meat and brown on all sides. Add the onions and garlic and brown lightly. Sprinkle with the thyme and add the stock.

3 Cover and bake 1½ hours. Add the olives and parsley, cover and cook until the meat is tender, 30 to 45 minutes longer.

4 Blend the butter with the flour and add it, bit by bit, to the simmering liquid in the casserole, stirring constantly until thickened. Correct the seasonings.

PRAGUE THREE-MEAT GOULASH

4 TO 6 SERVINGS

1½ pounds onions, coarsely chopped
    (about 4 cups)
¼ cup shortening
1½ pounds chuck beef, cubed
1 teaspoon salt
1 (6-ounce) can tomato paste
½ pound veal shoulder, cubed
½ pound fresh pork shoulder, cubed
1 cup dry white wine
1 cup sour cream

1 In a heavy 3-quart saucepan or Dutch oven, sauté the onions in the fat until the onions are golden. Add the beef and cook over medium heat until it loses its bright redness.

2 Add the salt and tomato paste, reduce the heat, cover and simmer slowly 30 minutes. Add the veal and pork and continue to simmer slowly, covered, 1 hour. Add the wine.

3 Simmer, covered, 30 minutes longer, or until the meats are tender. Stir in the sour cream and heat for a few minutes; do not boil.

BUDAPEST BEEF GOULASH

4 SERVINGS

2 tablespoons oil
2 large onions, chopped
1 small tomato, chopped
1 small green pepper, seeded and chopped
1 tablespoon sweet paprika
2 pounds chuck beef, cubed
1 teaspoon tomato paste
1 teaspoon salt
1 cup boiling water
2 large raw potatoes, diced

1 In a heavy 2½-quart saucepan, heat the oil, add the onions and cook until golden brown. Add the tomato, green pepper, paprika, beef, tomato paste and salt. Cook, stirring, over medium heat until the beef loses its bright redness.

2 Reduce the heat, add the water, cover and simmer 1½ hours. Remove the meat, strain the gravy and return to the pan with the meat. Add the potatoes and simmer until tender, about 1 hour.

BEEF WITH SOUR CREAM

6 SERVINGS

⅓ cup flour
1 teaspoon salt
1 teaspoon freshly ground pepper
2 pounds boneless chuck, cut into 1-inch cubes
¼ cup vegetable oil
1 cup tomato juice
3 tablespoons grated onions
½ teaspoon thyme
½ bay leaf
1 (10-ounce) package frozen peas
1 cup sour cream
1 tablespoon horseradish

1 Mix the flour, salt and pepper. Dredge the meat in the seasoned flour. In a Dutch oven heat the oil, add the meat and brown quickly on all sides. Add the tomato juice, onions, thyme and bay leaf. Cover tightly and simmer gently about 2¼ hours, or until meat is tender.

2 Add the peas and simmer about 10 minutes, or until done. Stir in the sour cream and horseradish and heat but do not let boil.

PASTEL DE CHOCLO

This is a hearty and unusual Chilean casserole that contains an amplitude of beef, chicken and corn.

10 TO 12 GENEROUS SERVINGS

3 cups chopped onions
4 tablespoons vegetable oil
6 tablespoons butter
1½ pounds lean round steak, cut into ¼-inch cubes
2 teaspoons salt
1 teaspoon paprika
1½ teaspoons oregano
½ to ¾ teaspoon Tabasco sauce
6 black olives, pitted
2 hard-cooked eggs, quartered
2 pounds chicken, cut into serving pieces
1 small onion, sliced
3 ears corn, grated (there should be 2½ cups)
2 teaspoons sugar, approximately
1 egg yolk

1 In a 3-quart heavy kettle, sauté the chopped onions in 1 tablespoon of the oil and 2 tablespoons of the butter until golden.

2 In a heavy skillet, heat 2 tablespoons of the oil and brown the beef. Season with 1 teaspoon salt, the paprika, ½ teaspoon oregano and the Tabasco. Cover and cook, stirring often, until the meat is tender. Transfer the beef to the kettle with the chopped onions.

3 Arrange the olives and the quartered eggs over the beef.

4 Heat 1 tablespoon of the oil and 2 tablespoons of the butter in the skillet and brown the chicken on all sides. Add the sliced onion, ½ teaspoon salt and 1 teaspoon oregano and sauté until onion is golden brown. Transfer the chicken to the kettle, arranging it on top of the eggs.

5 In the same skillet, combine the grated corn with 1 teaspoon of the sugar and the remaining ½ teaspoon salt and 2 tablespoons butter. Cook, stirring constantly, until the mixture boils and thickens. Transfer to the kettle and spoon over the chicken. Paint the corn with the egg yolk diluted with 1 teaspoon of water and sprinkle very lightly with sugar.

6 Bake in a preheated 400°F oven until top is golden brown, about 25 minutes.

♦

WESTERN BEEF AND RICE CASSEROLE

4 TO 6 SERVINGS

1 cup pitted ripe olives
1 pound ground lean beef
2 tablespoons oil
½ cup chopped onions
1 cup sliced celery
¼ cup chopped green pepper
1 cup rice
2½ cups canned tomatoes
1 cup water
2 teaspoons salt
2 or 3 teaspoons chili powder
½ teaspoon Worcestershire sauce
¼ teaspoon freshly ground pepper

1 Preheat the oven to 325°F.

2 Cut the olives into large pieces.

3 Brown the beef in the oil. Remove the meat from the pan and add the onions, celery, green pepper and rice. Cook, stirring, until light brown.

4 Add the tomatoes, water, seasonings, meat and olives and bring to a boil. Pour into a 2-quart casserole and cover. Bake 45 minutes to 1 hour.

GROUND BEEF WITH EGGPLANT

4 TO 6 SERVINGS

12 (½-inch-thick) eggplant slices
2 pounds ground beef
3 tablespoons olive oil
¼ cup chopped onions
¼ cup chopped green pepper
2 tablespoons flour
2 teaspoons salt
¼ teaspoon freshly ground pepper
½ teaspoon oregano
2 cups canned tomato sauce
1½ cups grated cheddar cheese

1 Preheat the oven to 300°F.

2 Cook the peeled eggplant slices in boiling salted water until tender, about 5 minutes.

3 Brown the meat in 2 tablespoons of the oil, stirring occasionally. Cook the onions and green pepper in the remaining oil until the vegetables are wilted. Combine the meat and vegetables in the skillet and stir in the flour, salt, pepper and oregano. Add the tomato sauce and cook until thickened.

4 Arrange half the eggplant slices in a shallow, 2-quart buttered baking dish. Spoon over them half the meat mixture and half the cheese. Repeat the layers and bake, uncovered, for 30 minutes.

SWEDISH MEATBALLS

4 SERVINGS

2 tablespoons butter
3 tablespoons minced onions
1 cup fresh bread crumbs
¾ cup milk, or half-and-half
¾ pound ground round steak
¼ pound ground veal
¼ pound ground pork
1 egg
Salt and freshly ground pepper to taste
¼ cup flour
¾ cup cream or evaporated milk

1 In a large skillet melt the butter and sauté the onions until they are golden brown.

2 Soak the crumbs in the milk, add the meats, egg, onions, salt and pepper and mix thoroughly. Shape the mixture into balls about 1½ inches in diameter and roll in the flour. Reserve 1 tablespoon of the flour.

3 Melt enough additional butter in the skillet to cover the bottom and brown the meatballs over medium heat. Shake the pan occasionally so the meatballs will retain their round shape. Remove to a serving dish and keep warm.

4 Combine the reserved flour with the cream and, using a wire whisk, stir gradually into the pan juices. Simmer 3 to 4 minutes, stirring occasionally. Pour the gravy over the meatballs and serve hot.

Stuffed Eggplant, page 401.
Meat-Stuffed Green Peppers, page 419.
Beef and Macaroni Casserole, page 504.
Beef-Stuffed Artichokes, page 369.
Keftedes (Greek Meatballs), page 51.

GRILLED HAMBURGER FOR ONE

1 SERVING

¼ pound round steak, ground
½ teaspoon butter (optional)
Worcestershire sauce
Tabasco sauce
1 teaspoon lemon juice
1 teaspoon chopped parsley
Salt and freshly ground pepper to taste

1 Shape the beef into a large patty.

2 Grill the meat over charcoal. Or cook in a very hot skillet lightly sprinkled with salt and without the further addition of fat.

3 When cooked, brush lightly with the butter and sprinkle with Worcestershire, Tabasco, lemon juice, parsley and salt and pepper.

Variations

HAMBURGER WITH DILL

Combine the meat lightly with 1 teaspoon chopped fresh dill. Omit the parsley garnish.

ROQUEFORT HAMBURGER

Blend 2 tablespoons Roquefort cheese with 1 teaspoon finely chopped chives or scallions and shape into a flattened round. Divide the meat and shape into 2 patties. Place Roquefort round in the center of 1 patty and top with the second. Seal the edges.

HAMBURGER AU POIVRE

Sprinkle each side of the beef patty with ½ teaspoon coarsely ground pepper. With the heel of the hand, press the pepper into the meat and let stand 30 minutes before cooking.

HAMBURGER POTATO ROLL

One of the most frequently requested recipes ever printed in the *New York Times* is this novelty: a hamburger roll filled with mashed potatoes.

4 SERVINGS

1 tablespoon vegetable oil
1 medium onion, chopped
1 small garlic clove, crushed
1 pound ground chuck beef
1 egg, lightly beaten
2 slices bread, crusts removed
1 teaspoon salt
¼ teaspoon oregano, rosemary or basil
Freshly ground pepper to taste
2 tablespoons dry bread crumbs
1½ cups seasoned mashed potato
1 tablespoon minced parsley
3 strips bacon

1 Preheat the oven to 350°F.
2 Heat the oil, add the onions and garlic and sauté until the onions are transparent. Remove to a mixing bowl and add the ground beef and the egg.
3 Soften the bread in water, press out the excess, and add bread to the meat. Add the salt, oregano and pepper. Mix thoroughly.
4 Sprinkle a piece of wax paper with crumbs. Press the meat out on the crumbs to make a rectangle about ½ inch thick.
5 Beat the mashed potatoes with the parsley and spread on top of the meat. (If leftover potato is used, reheat it in a double boiler before spreading.)
6 Using the wax paper as an aid, roll the meat and potatoes, jelly roll fashion, and place in a loaf pan or on a shallow baking pan. Grease the pan if the meat is very lean. Place the bacon on top.

7 Bake about 1 hour, basting at least once during baking. Serve with a brown sauce made from the pan drippings, or with mushroom, tomato or other sauce.

Stuffed Cabbage, page 385.

♦

BEEF KEBABS

4 SERVINGS

1½ pounds lean beef, cut into 1½-inch cubes
½ cup finely chopped onions
1 small garlic clove, minced
¼ cup lemon juice
1 teaspoon dry mustard
1 teaspoon chili powder
1 teaspoon turmeric
1 teaspoon honey
½ teaspoon ground ginger
Salt and freshly ground pepper to taste

1 Place the meat in a mixing bowl. Combine the remaining ingredients and pour over the meat; mix thoroughly. Let stand for 30 minutes or longer.
2 Thread the meat on skewers. Broil, turning occasionally, until cooked to the desired degree of doneness. Or grill over charcoal.

Note: Cubed pork or lamb may be substituted for the beef. If pork is used, it should be cooked until well done.

HERBED MEAT LOAF

6 SERVINGS

1 pound ground beef
½ pound ground veal
½ pound ground lean pork
2 eggs
¼ cup coarsely chopped green pepper
½ cup fine bread crumbs
¾ cup chopped parsley
¼ cup finely chopped chives
2 tablespoons finely chopped basil
1 teaspoon salt
½ teaspoon freshly ground pepper
Bacon slices to cover top
Mushroom sauce (page 565), or basic tomato
  sauce (page 561)

1 Preheat the oven to 350°F.
2 In a mixing bowl combine all the ingredients except the bacon slices and sauce. Using the hands, blend well; do not overwork the meat or it will produce a meat loaf that is too tightly packed.
3 Line a 9-inch pie plate with aluminum foil. Shape the meat mixture into an oval loaf, place on the foil and cover with bacon slices.
4 Bake 1½ hours. Serve with mushroom sauce or fresh tomato sauce.

ARMENIAN BEEF LOAF

6 SERVINGS

2 pounds fresh spinach, or 2 (10-ounce)
  packages frozen chopped spinach
1 pound round steak, ground
¾ cup finely chopped onions
Salt and freshly ground pepper to taste
½ teaspoon grated nutmeg
¼ teaspoon cinnamon
1 cup cooked rice
2 eggs, lightly beaten
3 bacon slices

1 Preheat the oven to 350°F.
2 If fresh spinach is used, rinse it well in several changes of cold water. Drain, place in a kettle, and cook in only the water that clings to the leaves. Chop well. If frozen spinach is used, just defrost it and squeeze out excess moisture.
3 Combine the spinach, beef, onions, salt, pepper, nutmeg, cinnamon, rice and eggs. Pack the mixture into a buttered 9 × 5-inch loaf pan. Arrange the bacon on top. Bake for 1 hour, or until firm. Serve with a tomato sauce.

CHILI CON CARNE I

12 SERVINGS

5 pounds lean chuck
½ cup olive oil
½ cup flour
½ cup chili powder
2 teaspoons ground coriander
2 teaspoons ground cumin
2 teaspoons dried oregano
6 to 8 garlic cloves, minced
4 cups beef stock
Salt and freshly ground pepper to taste

1 Trim the meat of all fat and cut the meat into ½-inch cubes.

2 Heat the oil in a deep kettle and add the cubed meat. Cook, stirring, just until the meat loses its red color.

3 Sift together the flour and chili powder and sprinkle it over the meat, stirring constantly so that the pieces are evenly coated.

4 Place the coriander, cumin and oregano in the palm of one hand. Rub the spices between your palms, sprinkling them over the meat. Add the garlic and stir. Add the broth, stirring the meat constantly. Add salt and pepper and bring to the boil. Partly cover and simmer 3 to 4 hours, or until the meat almost falls apart. If necessary, add more stock as the meat cooks. The chili should not be soupy, however.

CHILI CON CARNE II

4 SERVINGS

3 tablespoons butter or olive oil
1 large onion, minced
2 garlic cloves, minced
1 pound chopped beef
1⅓ cups canned tomatoes, with juice
1 green pepper, minced
1 cup water
2 tablespoons chili powder
1 teaspoon cumin seed, crushed
1 teaspoon salt
½ teaspoon celery seed
⅛ teaspoon cayenne
⅛ teaspoon basil
1 small bay leaf

1 Heat the butter in a large skillet, add the onions and garlic and sauté until golden brown. Add the meat and brown.

2 Add the remaining ingredients, bring to a boil, reduce the heat and simmer, uncovered, until the sauce is as thick as desired, or about 3 hours. If desired, add 1 can of kidney beans and just heat through.

HALLACAS

Hallacas are the Venezuelan version of tamales. They are normally wrapped in banana leaves, but foil is a reasonable substitute.

12 TO 16 HALLACAS

4 cups beef stock
2 tablespoons paprika
¼ pound butter
3 cups white cornmeal
Filling (see following recipe)
Garnishes:
    2 hard-cooked eggs, sliced and each slice
        cut in half
    Pitted ripe olives, sliced
    Stuffed green olives, sliced
    Raisins

1 Combine the stock and paprika and bring to a boil.
2 Add the butter and, when it has melted, gradually stir in the cornmeal. Cook, stirring, until the mixture is smooth and thick, 10 to 15 minutes. Remove from the heat and set aside.
3 Prepare the filling.
4 Tear off a strip of heavy-duty foil about 8 inches wide. Place it on a flat surface. Pinch off a small amount of the hallaca paste and flatten it on the foil to make a strip 5 inches long, 2½ inches wide, and ¼ inch thick. Top the dough with about 2 tablespoons of the filling and flatten it out. Add a little of each garnish.
5 Pinch off enough of the paste to top the hallaca, flatten it and pinch the top and bottom edges of the paste together to seal in the filling.
6 Pull up the ends of the foil and fold the lengthwise edges over themselves several times. Twist the ends firmly and pull the twisted ends under the hallaca. The idea is to make a watertight seal. Continue with the remaining paste and filling.

7 Drop the foil-wrapped hallacas into boiling water to cover and cook 1 hour. Unwrap and serve.

FILLING
ENOUGH FOR 12 TO 16 HALLACAS

3 tablespoons olive oil
2 garlic cloves, finely chopped
1 onion, chopped
1 pound ground round steak
1 (3-pound) chicken, simmered until tender,
    or 3 cups cooked chicken
6 scallions, sliced
2 tablespoons capers
2 teaspoons sugar
1 teaspoon salt
1 chili pepper, chopped, or ¼ teaspoon hot
    red pepper flakes
¼ cup wine vinegar
4 ripe tomatoes, peeled and chopped
½ cup dry sherry
⅓ cup soft bread crumbs
¼ cup minced parsley

1 Heat the oil in a large skillet. Add the garlic, onions and round steak and brown.
2 Add the chicken, which has been removed from the bones and cut up coarsely, the scallions, capers, sugar, salt, chili pepper and vinegar.
3 Simmer 10 minutes. Stir in the remaining ingredients and cook 5 minutes longer. Remove from the heat.

Empanadas (Chilean Meat Turnovers), page 57.
Pirog (Russian Meat Turnover), page 54.

BRAISED SHORT RIBS OF BEEF

4 SERVINGS

3 tablespoons flour
2 teaspoons salt
Freshly ground pepper to taste
¼ teaspoon rosemary
3 pounds short ribs of beef, cut into
    serving pieces
2 tablespoons vegetable oil
½ cup chopped onions
½ cup chopped celery
1½ cups boiling beef stock

1 Preheat the oven to 300°F.
2 Combine the flour, salt, pepper and rosemary. Dredge the ribs in the seasoned flour.
3 In a skillet, heat 1 tablespoon of oil, add the onions and celery and sauté 5 minutes. Transfer the vegetables to a heavy kettle with a lid.
4 Add the remaining tablespoon of oil to the skillet and brown the ribs well on all sides. Transfer them to the kettle. Add the boiling stock and cover tightly.
5 Bake 2½ hours. If desired, skim off excess fat and thicken the juices by stirring in a little of the seasoned flour mixed with cold water. Simmer 5 minutes and serve with the meat.

Note: The ribs may also be simmered slowly on top of the stove over low heat.

DEVILED SHORT RIBS

4 SERVINGS

3 pounds short ribs, cut into serving pieces
¼ cup oil
1 small onion, chopped
1 garlic clove, crushed
2 tablespoons prepared mustard
2 tablespoons lemon juice
2 teaspoons salt
½ teaspoon chili powder
½ teaspoon sugar
Freshly ground pepper to taste
⅔ cup stock or water
Flour (optional)

1 Place the short ribs in a deep bowl. Mix the remaining ingredients, except the stock and flour, and pour over the ribs. Cover and refrigerate several hours, turning the meat once or twice. Drain, reserving the marinade.
2 Preheat the oven to 425°F. Arrange the ribs on a rack in a roasting pan and bake until brown, about 30 minutes. Reduce the oven temperature to 350°F. Add the reserved marinade to the ribs, cover and bake until tender, about 1½ hours. Pour off the fat from pan. Add stock to the pan. Boil for 2 minutes. If desired, thicken the broth with flour mixed with a little water and serve with the ribs.

LENTIL AND SHORT RIB STEW

3 GENEROUS SERVINGS

3 pounds short ribs, cut into 3-inch pieces
3 cups water
1 teaspoon salt
1 bay leaf
1 garlic clove, minced
1 onion, chopped
1 small celery stalk, chopped
1 cup dried lentils, washed and picked over
1/4 teaspoon thyme or oregano
1 cup elbow macaroni, cooked (optional)

1 Place short ribs in a heavy saucepan and add water, salt, bay leaf, garlic, onion and celery. Simmer, covered, until the meat is tender, about 2 hours.

2 Add the lentils and thyme and continue cooking, stirring often, until the lentils are tender, about 30 minutes longer. Correct the seasonings and add macaroni. Reheat.

3 If the bones have separated from the short ribs, remove them before serving.

ROAST BEEF HASH

6 SERVINGS

1 1/2 pounds (about 3 cups chopped) cold roast beef
1 pound (about 2 cups) cooked diced potatoes
1 large onion, grated
1/4 green pepper, chopped
1 cup beef stock or gravy
1/3 cup tomato paste
Salt and freshly ground pepper to taste

1 Chop or grind the roast beef, add the remaining ingredients and mix well.

2 Turn the mixture into a greased preheated frying pan and cook, stirring occasionally, until the hash is thoroughly hot. Let cook until brown and crusted underneath.

3 Fold the hash over as you would an omelet and turn out on a hot platter.

CREAMED CHIPPED BEEF WITH NUTMEG

6 SERVINGS

2 (4-ounce) jars chipped beef
4 tablespoons butter
¼ cup flour
1½ cups milk, scalded
½ cup cream
½ teaspoon grated nutmeg
¼ teaspoon cayenne
Freshly ground pepper to taste
Worcestershire sauce to taste

1 Place the chipped beef in a colander and pour boiling water over it. Pull beef apart with the fingers and let stand until ready to use.

2 Melt the butter and stir in the flour with a wire whisk. Add the milk, stirring rapidly with the whisk. When the mixture is thickened and smooth, cook, stirring, for 3 or 4 minutes. Add the cream and seasonings. Add the chipped beef and stir just enough to mix the meat with the sauce. Heat thoroughly and serve on toast points.

Veal

Veal of the best quality is milk-fed veal. This is the flesh of a calf that is eight to ten weeks old when slaughtered. In its prime condition for cooking, it is fine grained and velvety in texture and has a delicate pink-white color, the whiter the better. Europeans in general have a special fondness for veal. Some of the most elegant preparations in Italian, Austrian and French cooking are based on veal.

◆

ROAST LEG OF VEAL

6 SERVINGS

1 (4-pound) boneless leg of veal
Salt and freshly ground pepper
½ pound salt pork
2 garlic cloves
1 carrot, coarsely chopped
1 onion, quartered
Pinch of thyme
1 bay leaf
¼ pound butter, melted
1 cup dry white wine

1 Preheat the oven to 300°F.

2 Rub the roast with salt and pepper and cover it with thin strips of salt pork if there is no fat on the veal.

3 Place the veal in a roasting pan and insert a meat thermometer in the thickest part of the roast. Surround the meat with the garlic, carrot, onion, thyme and bay leaf. Roast the meat, basting frequently with melted butter and wine, until the meat thermometer registers 170°F, about 2 hours. Skim fat from surface of sauce.

BRAISED LEG OF VEAL

ABOUT 8 SERVINGS

¼ pound plus 2 tablespoons butter
1 garlic clove, minced
1 teaspoon salt
¼ teaspoon rosemary
Pinch of thyme
Freshly ground pepper to taste
1 small (about 5 pounds) leg of veal, boned
    and tied
2 cups thinly sliced onions
2 celery stalks, trimmed and cut into 2-inch
    lengths
1 carrot, scraped and cut into 1-inch lengths
1 bay leaf
Veal or chicken stock
1 tablespoon cornstarch
¼ cup dry sherry

1 Preheat the oven to 375°F.
2 Cream 2 tablespoons of the butter with the garlic, salt, rosemary, thyme and pepper. Rub this over the meat.
3 Place the remaining butter, the onions, celery, carrot and bay leaf in a heavy casserole or Dutch oven. Put the meat on the bed of vegetables and cover. Bake for about 2 hours, until meat is very tender. Turn the meat several times as it cooks. If necessary, add a little stock to keep it from becoming dry.
4 Remove the meat and strain the broth. Measure it and add enough stock to make 2 cups. Boil the liquid rapidly. Blend the cornstarch with the wine and stir it into the boiling sauce. Cook, stirring, until smooth. Serve the meat with the sauce.

VEAL RUMP WITH SOUR CREAM

6 TO 8 SERVINGS

1 (4-pound) boned rump of veal
2 garlic cloves, crushed
1½ tablespoons anchovy paste
¼ teaspoon basil
5 tablespoons butter
2 cups dry white wine
2 tablespoons cornstarch
½ cup sour cream
2 tablespoons capers
Salt and freshly ground pepper to taste
Watercress

1 Place the roast flat with the boned surface up. Cream together the garlic, anchovy paste, basil and 2 tablespoons of butter. Spread over the meat, roll and tie securely.
2 Place the veal in a bowl, add the wine and marinate 4 hours or longer, turning occasionally.
3 Remove and dry the meat with paper toweling, reserving the marinade. Heat the remaining 3 tablespoons butter in a Dutch oven, add the meat and brown on all sides. Place a rack under the meat, add the marinade, cover and let simmer until the meat is tender, about 2 hours.
4 Slice the veal and arrange the slices on a hot serving platter. Blend the cornstarch with a little water and add, stirring, to the broth. Boil 1 minute.
5 Stir in the sour cream, capers, salt and pepper and heat but do not let boil. Pour over the veal or serve separately. Garnish the platter with watercress.

SAVORY POT ROAST OF VEAL

3½ tablespoons vegetable oil
1 (5-pound) rolled veal rump
Flour
3 dried mushrooms
1 medium onion, chopped
1 garlic clove, crushed
¼ cup chopped celery
1 tablespoon minced parsley
1 teaspoon tomato paste
1 cup concentrated beef stock
1 cup water

1 Preheat the oven to 450°F. Place 2 tablespoons of the oil in a baking pan and heat in the oven.

2 Dredge the veal in flour. Brown in the baking pan in the oven, turning veal over once so both sides brown. Remove from the oven, drain off the fat and lower the oven temperature to 300°F.

3 Meanwhile, soak the mushrooms in boiling water for 15 minutes. Discard any tough stems. Drain and chop.

4 Heat the remaining oil in a skillet, add the onions, garlic, celery and parsley and cook slowly until the onions are transparent. With a slotted spoon, remove the vegetables and add to the veal. Add the tomato paste, mushrooms, stock and water. Cover.

5 Bake about 4 hours, adding more stock if necessary to keep the bottom of the pan covered with liquid. Turn the meat over when the cooking is half finished. When the veal is tender, transfer it to a hot platter and keep warm.

6 Strain the liquid in the pan, skim off the fat, thicken with a little flour mixed with water and serve with the veal.

VEAL ROAST WITH ROSEMARY

1 (3-pound) veal rump roast, boned,
    rolled and tied
Salt and freshly ground pepper to taste
Flour
2 tablespoons vegetable oil
½ cup water
½ cup white wine
1 garlic clove, chopped
1 teaspoon rosemary
3 medium onions, halved
3 carrots, halved

1 Sprinkle the roast with salt and pepper and dredge in flour.

2 Melt the oil in a heavy kettle or roasting pan, add the meat and brown on all sides. Place a rack under the meat, add the water, wine, garlic and rosemary.

3 Cover the kettle or pan and cook slowly over surface heat or in a 350°F oven for 2 hours. Thirty minutes before the meat is done, add the onions and carrots.

4 Remove the roast and vegetables to a hot platter. Slice meat and serve with unthickened sauce remaining in pan.

BREADED VEAL CHOPS

4 SERVINGS

1 cup fine, dry bread crumbs
1 tablespoon chopped parsley
1 teaspoon oregano
½ cup grated Parmesan cheese
4 loin veal chops
Salt and freshly ground pepper to taste
1 egg, well beaten and diluted with 2
    tablespoons water
¼ cup vegetable oil

1 Combine the crumbs, parsley, oregano and cheese.
2 Sprinkle the chops with the salt and pepper, dip them into the beaten egg and roll in the crumb mixture.
3 Heat the oil in a skillet, add the chops and cook over moderate heat until tender, about 10 minutes on a side.

VEAL CHOPS SAUTÉ

4 SERVINGS

4 (½-inch-thick) veal rib chops
Flour for dredging
Salt and freshly ground pepper to taste
3 tablespoons vegetable oil
6 tablespoons dry white wine
1 teaspoon lemon juice
4 tablespoons firm butter
Minced parsley

1 Dredge the chops in flour seasoned with salt and pepper. Heat the oil in a heavy skillet, add the meat and brown on both sides.
2 Reduce the heat to low, cover the pan and cook about 20 minutes. Turn the chops 2 or 3 times. Transfer to a hot platter and keep warm.
3 To the juices in the pan add the wine. Reduce by cooking uncovered over fairly high heat 2 or 3 minutes. Add the lemon juice.
4 Add the firm butter to the sauce in little curls, swirling the pan to incorporate the butter without its melting rapidly.
5 When the butter has barely melted, pour the sauce over the chops and sprinkle with minced parsley.

VEAL CHOPS WITH MUSHROOM STUFFING

6 SERVINGS

½ pound spinach
2 tablespoons butter
¼ cup finely chopped prosciutto
3 tablespoons finely chopped onions
2 tablespoons finely chopped shallots
    or scallions
½ cup chopped mushrooms
1 small garlic clove, minced
3 tablespoons soft fresh bread crumbs
⅓ cup grated Parmesan cheese
Salt and freshly ground pepper to taste
1 egg yolk
¼ teaspoon grated nutmeg
6 double-rib veal chops
⅓ cup vegetable oil
½ cup chicken stock

1 Trim the spinach and wash thoroughly. Place the drained spinach in a saucepan with a tight-fitting lid. Do not add additional water. Simmer, covered, for 3 to 5 minutes, until spinach is wilted.

2 Drain the spinach and let cool. When cool enough to handle, press it between the hands, then chop.

3 Preheat the oven to 375°F.

4 Melt the butter and add the prosciutto, onions, shallots, mushrooms and garlic. Cook, uncovered, until almost all the liquid has evaporated. The mixture should be lightly browned.

5 Add the spinach and stir well. Add the crumbs, cheese, salt and pepper. Remove the saucepan from the heat and let cool slightly. Add the egg yolk and nutmeg and mix rapidly. Use the mixture to stuff the veal chops.

6 Season the chops with salt and pepper and brown quickly in the oil in a heavy casserole.

7 Add enough stock to the casserole to keep chops from sticking to the pan. Transfer the casserole to the oven. Bake, uncovered, for about 1 hour. Add more stock if the pan becomes too dry.

8 Transfer the chops to a warm serving platter. Add the remaining stock to the casserole. Scrape the bottom and sides and cook over high heat for 2 minutes. Pour the pan juices over the chops.

◆

BARBECUED VEAL CHOPS

6 SERVINGS

6 veal chops
1 small onion, minced
1 garlic clove, sliced
½ cup cider vinegar
¼ cup vegetable oil
¼ cup catsup
1½ teaspoons salt
½ teaspoon thyme
½ teaspoon ground cumin
½ teaspoon chili powder
¼ teaspoon hot red pepper flakes

1 Have the butcher cut the veal chops 1½ inches thick.

2 Combine the remaining ingredients in a mixing bowl. Add the meat to the marinade and let stand 2 to 3 hours.

3 Broil the chops slowly over a charcoal fire or under a medium broiler flame until brown on both sides, basting with the sauce left in the bowl as often as the meat looks dry.

VEAL BREAST WITH SPINACH STUFFING

6 SERVINGS

3 tablespoons butter
1 medium onion, chopped
½ pound mushrooms, chopped
1 pound spinach, cooked
½ teaspoon rosemary or basil
½ teaspoon salt
Freshly ground pepper to taste
1 cup cooked rice
1 egg, lightly beaten
1 (3-pound) boned veal breast cut
    with a pocket
4 slices salt pork
1 cup water or stock

1 Heat the butter, add the onions and cook until they are transparent. Add the mushrooms and cook, stirring often, about 3 minutes.

2 Chop the spinach and drain thoroughly.

3 Preheat the oven to 350°F.

4 Mix the vegetables with the seasonings, rice and egg. Use the mixture to fill the pocket in the veal breast and close with metal skewers.

5 Place the meat on a low rack in a roasting pan. Arrange the salt pork over the veal and add the water to the pan. Cover with aluminum foil and bake 2 hours. Uncover and bake 30 minutes longer.

VEAL SHOULDER WITH CHICKEN LIVER STUFFING

6 TO 8 SERVINGS

¼ pound ground pork
¼ pound chicken livers, chopped
¼ cup chopped onions
¼ cup fine, soft bread crumbs
½ pound mushrooms, chopped and cooked
    in a little butter
Pinch of thyme or marjoram
1 egg, lightly beaten
Salt and freshly ground pepper to taste
1 (3-pound) boneless veal shoulder
2 tablespoons vegetable oil
2 cups chicken stock

1 Combine the pork, chicken livers, onions, crumbs, mushrooms, thyme, egg, salt and pepper and mix well. If mixture seems dry, add a little water or dry white wine, tossing it lightly.

2 Spread the meat out on a board, skin side down. If desired, sprinkle with salt and pepper. Cover with the stuffing and roll. Tie into a neat shape.

3 Heat the oil in a Dutch oven, add the meat and brown on all sides. Add the chicken stock, cover closely and simmer gently over low heat until the veal is fork tender, 2 to 3 hours. Turn the meat occasionally as it cooks.

4 Transfer the meat to a hot platter and keep warm. Cook the sauce, uncovered, over moderate heat until it is reduced to 1 cup. Strain and serve with the meat.

BREAST OF VEAL WITH HERB STUFFING

5 TO 6 SERVINGS

1 (3- to 4-pound) boned veal breast,
   cut with a pocket
Salt and freshly ground black pepper to taste
1 medium onion, chopped
1 garlic clove, crushed
4 tablespoons butter
3 cups soft bread crumbs
2 tablespoons minced parsley
½ teaspoon summer savory, rosemary
   or marjoram
¼ teaspoon basil or thyme
Flour
¼ cup vegetable oil
¼ cup water
¼ cup sour cream

   1 Sprinkle the inside of the veal pocket with salt and pepper.
   2 Sauté the onions and garlic lightly in the butter. Mix the crumbs with the parsley, herbs and salt and pepper to taste. Add the onions with the butter in the pan and mix. Stuff the veal breast with the mixture and skewer to close.
   3 Dredge the meat in flour and brown well in the oil in a Dutch oven. Add the water, cover and simmer until tender, about 2 hours.
   4 Remove the veal to a warm serving platter. Add the sour cream to the pan drippings and serve with the sliced veal.

There are few dishes in anyone's repertoire more easily prepared than the thin slices of veal called **scaloppine** *by the Italians,* **escalopes de veau** *by the French,* **Wienerschnitzel** *by the Austrians, and* **veal scallops** *by us. In each country there are many versions of the basic dish. Because these thin slices may be quickly sautéed, they are ideal for summer menus.*

ESCALOPES DE VEAU PANÉES
BREADED VEAL SCALLOPS

4 SERVINGS

4 (6-ounce) veal cutlets
Salt and freshly ground pepper to taste
Flour for dredging
1 egg
1 teaspoon water
1 cup fresh bread crumbs
4 tablespoons butter
1 tablespoon capers
Lemon wedges

   1 Pound the cutlets until thin and sprinkle lightly on both sides with salt and pepper. Dredge them lightly but thoroughly in flour.
   2 Beat the egg lightly with the water and dip the floured cutlets in the mixture; coat with the crumbs. Using the side of a kitchen knife, tap the cutlets lightly so crumbs will adhere well to the meat. Transfer them to a wire rack. Refrigerate 1 or 2 hours. This will help the breading to adhere to the cutlets when they are being cooked.

Continued

3 Heat the butter in a large skillet and, when it is hot but not brown or smoking, sauté the cutlets in it until golden brown on both sides.

4 Arrange the cutlets on a heated serving platter and garnish with capers and lemon wedges. Serve immediately.

Variations

ESCALOPES DE VEAU A LA VIENNOISE

Cook the cutlets as above. Garnish each cutlet with a lemon slice and top each slice with a rolled fillet of anchovy stuffed with a caper. Sprinkle with chopped parsley. If desired, garnish one end of the platter with sieved egg white and the other end with sieved egg yolk.

ESCALOPES DE VEAU A LA HOLSTEIN

Cook veal cutlets as above. Top each slice with an egg fried in butter. Top the egg, if desired, with crossed flat fillets of anchovy.

ESCALOPES DE VEAU A LA MILANAISE

Cook cutlets as above. Arrange them on a bed of cooked spaghetti covered with basic tomato sauce (page 561).

VEAL SCALOPPINE ALLA MARSALA

3 SERVINGS

1 pound veal, cut into thin, even slices
Flour for dredging
Salt and freshly ground pepper to taste
3 tablespoons butter
¼ cup Marsala wine
2 tablespoons chicken stock

1 Pound the veal lightly until very thin. Dredge in flour seasoned with salt and pepper.

2 Heat the butter in a skillet, add the veal and brown on both sides. Add the Marsala and cook 1 minute longer over moderately high heat. Transfer the meat to a warm platter.

3 Add the stock to the pan drippings. Scrape loose all the brown particles and bring to a boil. Pour over the veal.

Variations

VEAL SCALOPPINE WITH PROSCIUTTO

Cook the veal as above. Transfer to a warm serving platter. Add ⅛ pound slivered prosciutto to the drippings in the skillet. Sauté briskly 1 or 2 minutes, adding more butter if needed. Arrange the prosciutto on the veal. Add to the drippings 2 tablespoons stock, 1 teaspoon chopped parsley and 1 teaspoon lemon juice. Bring to a boil and pour over the meat.

VEAL SCALOPPINE WITH MUSHROOMS

Sauté ½ pound sliced mushrooms in 2 tablespoons butter. Arrange mushrooms on a warm platter. Add 3 tablespoons butter to the pan and in it cook the scaloppine as above. Serve the veal and sauce on the same platter with the mushrooms.

Saltimbocca is a whimsically named dish —the exact translation is "jump in the mouth." No one can offer a satisfactory explanation of how it got its name, but it is one of the best-known and best-tasting veal dishes in Italian cookery.

◆

SALTIMBOCCA

4 SERVINGS

8 (4-ounce) slices of boneless veal
Salt and freshly ground pepper to taste
8 sage leaves, or dried to taste
12 thin slices of prosciutto
4 tablespoons butter
¼ cup Marsala wine or sweet vermouth

1 Place the veal slices between pieces of wax paper and pound slices thin with a mallet or rolling pin. Sprinkle the slices on both sides with salt and pepper. Top each slice with a leaf of fresh sage or sprinkle with dried sage. Cover with a slice of prosciutto. Skewer with toothpicks.

2 Melt the butter in a skillet and brown the meat quickly in it on both sides. Add the wine to the skillet, cook rapidly to reduce slightly, and serve the meat hot with pan gravy over all.

Variation

SALTIMBOCCA ALLA ROMANA

Cook 1½ pounds well-trimmed spinach in boiling water for a few seconds. Drain and squeeze out excess liquid. Heat 2 tablespoons oil and 2 peeled garlic cloves. When the garlic begins to take on color, add the spinach and a little freshly ground pepper. Cook, stirring, just to heat through. Discard the garlic. Spoon the spinach down the center of a serving dish. Arrange the veal, cooked as above, around it and pour the pan gravy over all.

◆

VEAL ROLLATINE

Years ago, the late Paula Peck was celebrated for, among a few thousand other good things, her veal rollatine. It is an excellent buffet dish when served cold. In fact, she preferred it that way. If served hot, it may be served with tomato sauce.

6 OR MORE SERVINGS

¾ pound veal, cut into 4 thin slices of
    approximately the same size
½ pound Italian sausage in a casing
¼ pound thinly sliced prosciutto
¼ pound thinly sliced Genoa-style salami
1½ cups fine fresh bread crumbs
½ cup finely chopped parsley
½ cup grated Parmesan cheese
Freshly ground pepper to taste
6 tablespoons olive oil
6 large eggs
Salt to taste
7 slices lean bacon

1 Preheat the oven to 375°F.

2 Arrange 2 large sheets of plastic wrap with edges overlapping on a flat surface. Arrange the slices of veal, edges overlapping, so that you have a large rectangle of meat. Cover with more plastic wrap and pound the meat with a flat mallet until quite thin, without breaking the meat. Remove the top sheet of plastic wrap.

3 Broil the sausage or fry it in a skillet, turning as necessary until done. Drain well.

Continued

4 Arrange the slices of prosciutto over the veal, leaving a small margin all around. Overlap the slices. Similarly, make a layer of salami over the prosciutto.

5 In a mixing bowl, combine the crumbs, parsley, cheese and pepper. Add 4 tablespoons of oil and blend with the fingers. Spoon and smooth this all over the layer of salami.

6 Heat the remaining 2 tablespoons of oil in a skillet. Beat the eggs well and add them to the skillet. Add salt to taste. Cook, stirring well, until the soft-scrambled stage. Spoon the hot scrambled eggs over the bottom third of the crumbs over the shorter width of the rectangle.

7 Arrange the cooked sausage across the center of the eggs.

8 Start rolling the rectangle, beginning with the egg end. Lift up the plastic wrap as you work to facilitate rolling. When completely rolled, discard the plastic wrap. Cover the meat roll lengthwise with bacon. Tie the meat securely in 3 or 4 places with string.

9 Arrange the roll on a rack fitted inside a shallow baking pan. Place in the oven and bake 45 minutes. Reduce oven heat to 350°F and continue cooking 15 to 30 minutes longer.

10 Serve hot, sliced, with a tomato sauce. Or let cool, refrigerate, and serve cold.

BLANQUETTE DE VEAU
VEAL IN A WINE AND CREAM SAUCE

8 OR MORE SERVINGS

4 pounds boneless shoulder of veal
Salt and freshly ground pepper to taste
4 tablespoons butter
1 cup finely chopped onions
1 garlic clove, minced
⅓ cup flour
¼ pound mushrooms, rinsed, drained and quartered
4 large carrots, trimmed, scraped and cut into ½-inch lengths
1 cup dry white wine
1¾ cups chicken broth
2 thyme sprigs, or ½ teaspoon dried
1 bay leaf
12 to 24 peeled small white onions
1 cup freshly shelled peas
1 cup cream
2 egg yolks
¼ teaspoon grated nutmeg
Juice of ½ lemon

1 Preheat the oven to 350°F.

2 Cut the veal into 1½-inch cubes and sprinkle with salt and pepper.

3 In a deep heavy kettle or Dutch oven, heat 2 tablespoons of the butter and add the veal. Cook, stirring frequently, about 5 minutes. Sprinkle with the chopped onions and garlic and continue cooking about 5 minutes. Sprinkle with flour and cook, stirring to distribute the flour evenly, about 5 minutes.

4 Add the mushrooms and carrots. Add the wine and broth, stirring constantly. Add the thyme, bay leaf, salt and pepper. Cook 10 minutes on top of the stove and cover. Put the dish in the oven and bake about 1½ hours, stirring occasionally.

5 In a small saucepan, heat the remaining 2 tablespoons butter and add the white onions and peas. Cover and cook over low heat about 15 minutes. Add to the veal.

6 Blend the cream with the egg yolks, nutmeg and lemon juice and stir this into the veal. Cook on top of the stove, stirring, just until the sauce starts to boil.

♦

BRACIOLETTE RIPIENE
STUFFED VEAL ROLLS

4 TO 6 SERVINGS

12 small slices of veal cut from the leg
12 small thin slices of lean ham
3 tablespoons pine nuts
1 cup chopped parsley
2 tablespoons raisins
2 tablespoons grated Parmesan cheese
Salt and freshly ground pepper to taste
2 tablespoons olive oil
2 tablespoons butter
½ cup dry white wine

1 Pound the veal slices until flattened. Place a slice of ham on each slice of veal. Combine the pine nuts, parsley, raisins, cheese, salt and pepper. Place a spoonful of the mixture in the center of the ham. Roll the veal, ham and filling in jelly-roll fashion. Skewer or tie with strings.

2 Brown the stuffed rolls on all sides in the oil and butter in a skillet. Add the wine, cover and simmer for 15 to 20 minutes. Remove the skewers or string from the rolls before serving.

ITALIAN VEAL BIRDS

6 SERVINGS

1½ pounds veal, cut into thin, even slices
¾ cup finely chopped ham
1 garlic clove, finely chopped
2 tablespoons chopped parsley
Salt and freshly ground pepper to taste
Flour for dredging
3 tablespoons butter
3 tablespoons olive oil
¼ cup dry white wine
2 cups chicken stock
½ cup finely chopped onions
½ cup finely chopped carrot
½ cup finely chopped celery
½ teaspoon rosemary

1 Pound the veal slices lightly until very thin.

2 Combine the ham, garlic, parsley, salt and pepper. Spoon a little of the mixture onto the veal slices, roll and fasten securely with toothpicks.

3 Dredge the meat in flour and brown on all sides in the butter and oil. Add the wine and cook until it is almost completely reduced. Add the chicken stock and simmer gently 20 minutes. Add the vegetables and rosemary and cook 20 minutes longer. Remove the toothpicks before serving the veal birds with some of the sauce spooned over.

VEAL GOULASH

3 pounds shoulder or rump of veal, cut into
   1½-inch cubes
Flour for dredging
¼ cup vegetable oil
1 bay leaf
1 tablespoon caraway seed
1 tablespoon dill seed
1 tablespoon salt
½ tablespoon peppercorns
2 cups veal or beef stock
3 cups onion rings
3 tablespoons butter
2 tablespoons Hungarian paprika, or more
1 cup sour cream

1 Dredge the veal in flour and brown the meat in the oil in a deep saucepan or Dutch oven.

2 Add the bay leaf, caraway seed, dill seed and salt. Tie the peppercorns in a cheesecloth bag and add along with the stock. Cover and cook slowly for 1 to 1½ hours, until meat is tender.

3 Meanwhile cook the onion rings in the butter until they are wilted. Add them to the meat 20 minutes before the end of cooking time.

4 Discard the bag of peppercorns and remove the veal from the heat. Stir in the paprika and sour cream and heat thoroughly but do not boil.

VEAL STEW A LA PROVENÇALE

4 SERVINGS

2 pounds veal, cut into 1½-inch cubes
Flour for dredging
¼ cup olive oil
1 cup chopped onions
2 garlic cloves, minced
½ cup dry white wine
4 medium tomatoes, peeled and chopped
Salt and freshly ground pepper to taste
Chopped parsley

1 Dredge the veal in flour. Heat the oil in a skillet, add the veal and brown on all sides. Remove the veal to a warm platter.

2 Add the onions and garlic to the skillet and cook until onions are wilted. Add the wine and deglaze the pan, scraping up the brown particles. Return the veal to the skillet.

3 Add the tomatoes to the veal and season with salt and pepper. Cover and simmer about 1 hour.

4 Serve the stew sprinkled with chopped parsley.

VEAL STEW MILANESE

One of the finest blend of herbs is known in the Italian kitchen as *gremolata*. This is typically made with finely chopped parsley, minced garlic and finely diced lemon peel. It is most often added to the Italian dish called *ossobuco*, made with veal shanks, but it could be served in or on almost any white-meat stew. In this recipe, the herb blend includes finely chopped rosemary (a small amount of the dried herb could be substituted). This easily made stew could also be made with lean, cubed lamb.

4 SERVINGS

2 pounds lean veal, cut into 1½-inch cubes
Freshly ground pepper to taste
⅓ cup flour
4 tablespoons olive oil, approximately
1 tablespoon butter
1½ cups finely chopped onions
1½ tablespoons minced garlic
1 cup diced carrot
1 cup diced celery
½ cup dry white wine
1½ cups chicken stock
1½ cups canned, crushed tomatoes
2 tablespoons tomato paste
¼ teaspoon hot red pepper flakes
10 teaspoons gremolata (see following recipe)

1 Sprinkle the veal all over with a generous grinding of pepper.

2 Dredge the pieces in flour and shake off excess.

3 Heat 3 tablespoons of the oil and the butter in 1 or 2 nonstick skillets large enough to hold the pieces of meat without crowding. If the meat is crowded it will not brown properly. As the meat cooks, it may be necessary to add a little more oil. As the pieces brown, transfer them to a 2-quart saucepan.

4 When all the pieces are brown, pour off any fat that may remain in the skillet. Add the remaining 1 tablespoon olive oil to 1 skillet and add the onions and garlic.

Cook briefly, stirring, about 1 minute. Add the carrot and celery and cook, stirring, about 1 minute. Pour in the wine and cook until the wine has been almost totally evaporated. Add the stock, tomatoes, tomato paste and red pepper flakes and stir to blend. Pour and scrape the mixture over the meat. Stir to blend.

5 Bring to the boil and cover closely. Cook about 45 minutes, or until the meat is thoroughly tender. Stir in 4 teaspoons of the gremolata and heat 1 minute longer. Serve the remaining gremolata on the side to be sprinkled over in small amounts as desired.

GREMOLATA
AN HERB MIXTURE
3½ TABLESPOONS

5 teaspoons grated or finely chopped
    lemon rind
2 teaspoons finely chopped rosemary,
    or 1 teaspoon dried
2 teaspoons finely chopped parsley
1 teaspoon finely chopped garlic

1 To prepare the lemon rind, it is best to use a swivel-bladed vegetable scraper and pare off several strips of the outer rind without cutting into the white pulp. Stack the strips and cut into the finest possible strips. Cut the strips into the finest possible pieces. Chop to make the pieces even smaller. Put the lemon rind in a small bowl.

2 Add the rosemary, parsley and garlic and stir to blend. This mixture, tightly covered with plastic wrap, will keep for several days in the refrigerator.

VEAL WITH PEPPERS, ITALIAN STYLE

4 SERVINGS

5 tablespoons olive oil
4 large green peppers, seeded and cut into
    thin slices
1 medium onion, chopped
1 garlic clove, minced
6 green olives, chopped
1 tablespoon capers
1 or 2 anchovies, chopped (optional)
Salt and freshly ground pepper to taste
2 pounds veal, cut into 1½-inch cubes
Flour
1 cup chicken stock

   1 In a skillet heat 3 tablespoons of the oil, add the peppers, onions and garlic and sauté until tender, stirring often. Transfer to a bowl, add the olives, capers, anchovies, salt and pepper. Keep warm.

   2 Dredge the veal lightly in flour. Heat the remaining 2 tablespoons oil in the same skillet, add the veal and brown on all sides. Add the stock and deglaze the pan, scraping up any brown particles. Cover and simmer over low heat for 40 minutes.

   3 Add the pepper mixture to the veal and cook for about 20 minutes, until well blended and tender.

VITELLO TONNATO
COLD VEAL WITH TUNA MAYONNAISE

8 TO 12 SERVINGS

3 pounds veal rump in 1 large piece
10 anchovies
6 cups veal or chicken broth
1½ cups dry white wine
6 peppercorns
2 cups coarsely chopped onions
1 cup coarsely chopped celery
1 cup chopped leeks (optional)
½ cup coarsely chopped carrot
2 garlic cloves
1 bay leaf
¼ teaspoon thyme
6 parsley sprigs
1 (7-ounce) can tuna fish packed in oil,
    drained
1½ cups very thick homemade mayonnaise
2 tablespoons capers
4 or more cornichons or other pickles, sliced
Quartered hard-cooked eggs, cut into wedges
    (optional)
Sprigs of rosemary or parsley

   1 If necessary, tie the veal in several places with string to keep it whole. Put in a kettle with cold water to cover and bring to the boil. Drain well.

   2 Make numerous gashes with the pointed thin blade of a small knife over the surface of the meat. Cut 2 or 3 of the anchovies into 4 pieces. Insert the pieces into the gashes.

   3 Return the meat to a clean kettle and add the broth, wine, peppercorns, onions, celery, leeks, carrot, garlic, bay leaf, thyme, parsley and remaining anchovies. Do not add salt at this time. Simmer 45 minutes and turn the meat in the broth. Let the meat cool in the broth.

4 Remove the meat and chill it. If the sauce has jellied, scrape it off the meat and return it to the kettle.

5 Heat the cooking liquid. Strain it into a clean kettle or saucepan, pressing with the back of a heavy spoon to extract the juices. Reduce the cooking liquid to 2 cups. Let cool. It must be quite cool but not jellied.

6 Put the tuna in the container of a food processor or blender and process to a fine purée. Scrape it into a bowl.

7 Gradually add 1 cup of the cooking liquid, stirring constantly. Add the mayonnaise, gradually, beating. Gradually beat in the remaining liquid. Stop adding if the sauce becomes too thin. It should be of a consistency to coat the meat when sliced. Taste for seasoning.

8 Cut the meat into very thin slices. Arrange them neatly and symmetrically over a cold serving dish. Spoon the sauce over, reserving about 1½ cups. Garnish with capers, cornichons, hard-cooked egg wedges and the herb sprigs.

OSSOBUCO

6 SERVINGS

3 whole shanks of veal, cut by a butcher into
*   3-inch pieces*
Flour for dredging
½ cup olive oil, approximately
1 onion, sliced thin
1 bay leaf
2 small carrots, sliced thin
1 celery stalk, diced
½ cup dry white wine
2½ cups canned tomatoes, undrained
1 teaspoon tomato paste
1½ tablespoons chopped parsley
1 garlic clove, crushed
1 tablespoon grated lemon peel
Salt and freshly ground pepper to taste

1 Dredge the shanks in flour. Heat the oil in a skillet, add the shanks and brown on all sides. Remove to a warm platter.

2 If necessary, add more oil to the skillet. Add the onions, bay leaf, carrots and celery and cook over medium heat 5 minutes. Add the wine and simmer until all the wine has evaporated.

3 Add the shanks, tomatoes and tomato paste, cover and simmer until tender, about 1½ hours. If necessary, add a small amount of wine or water during cooking.

4 Remove the shanks from the skillet and strain the sauce. Place the meat and the sauce back in the pan and stir in the parsley, garlic, lemon peel, salt and pepper. Simmer 5 minutes longer. Serve with risotto.

VEAL CROQUETTES

Like many good things in the world of cuisine, croquettes began in a French kitchen. The name derives from *croquer,* which means "to crunch"; and of course a successful croquette has a crunchy exterior hiding the tender and flavorful contents. Croquettes are an ideal way to use leftover cooked foods.

4 TO 6 SERVINGS

1½ cups diced cooked veal
1½ cups veal or chicken stock
6 tablespoons butter
1 medium onion, finely chopped
1 teaspoon salt
½ teaspoon finely ground pepper
1 garlic clove, minced
¾ cup flour
1 egg, beaten with a little milk or water
1 cup fine fresh bread crumbs
Oil for deep frying
Basic tomato sauce (page 561), or mustard hollandaise sauce (page 554)

1 Put the veal and stock in the container of a food processor and blend to a purée.

2 Over low heat melt the butter and add the onions. Cook gently for 4 or 5 minutes. Add the salt, pepper and garlic. Stir in ½ cup of the flour and cook, stirring, until the mixture is a smooth paste.

3 Add the blended meat to the pan. Mix and stir over low heat until all is quite thick. Pour the mixture into a shallow dish and chill.

4 Form the chilled mixture into round cakes or cylinders. Roll them in the remaining flour, dip them into the beaten egg, and roll in the crumbs. Chill the cakes again until they are firm.

5 Fry the croquettes in deep fat heated to 360°F. When they are nicely browned, drain on paper toweling. Serve with tomato sauce or mustard hollandaise sauce.

Note: This recipe may be used to make croquettes of fish, chicken or beef, as well as vegetable croquettes. The seasoning may be varied accordingly and any appropriate flavorful sauce may be served with the croquettes.

♦

VEAL AND MUSHROOM LOAF

8 OR MORE SERVINGS

3 pounds ground veal
2 tablespoons butter
1 cup finely chopped onions
1 garlic clove, minced
1 cup finely diced celery
1 pound mushrooms, sliced thin
1 cup fine fresh bread crumbs
¼ teaspoon grated nutmeg
1 cup finely chopped parsley
2 eggs
Salt and freshly ground pepper to taste

1 Preheat the oven to 375°F.

2 Place the meat in a mixing bowl and set it aside.

3 Melt the butter in a skillet and add the onions, garlic and celery. Cook briefly until onions wilt. Add the mushrooms and cook until they give up their liquid. Continue cooking until this liquid evaporates. Let cool. Add this mixture to the veal.

4 Add the remaining ingredients and blend well. Put the mixture into a standard 9¼ × 5¼ × 2¾-inch loaf pan. Smooth it over. Place the pan in a baking dish and pour boiling water around the pan, about 1½ inches deep. Bake from 1 to 1¼ hours. Serve hot or cold.

Spaghetti with Veal-and-Dill Meatballs, page 489.
Pattypans Stuffed with Veal, page 425.

Lamb

Lamb is eaten less than other meats in the United States. Historically, it has been considered a spring delicacy, a notion that probably developed from its growth patterns in other days when lamb was a tender meat that appeared at the time of the first jonquil. After the season passed, it was allowed to grow into mutton. Today the quality of lamb in the United States is fairly standard from one season to the other and tender legs of lamb are generally available whenever they are desired. The term **spring lamb** refers to those animals that are three to five months old when slaughtered.

Lamb is a wonderfully versatile meat, from riblet to chop to roast, and it deserves greater popularity. It is the basis for countless stews of many nationalities.

♦

ROAST LEG OF LAMB

6 TO 8 SERVINGS

1 (5-pound) leg of lamb, trimmed
1 garlic clove, sliced
1 teaspoon rosemary
Lemon juice
Salt and freshly ground pepper to taste

1 Preheat the oven to 300°F.
2 Cut small slits in the lamb and insert the garlic. Rub the meat with rosemary and lemon juice and sprinkle with salt and pepper.
3 Place the meat on a rack in a roasting pan and roast, uncovered, 18 minutes per pound for medium (170°F on meat thermometer), 12 for rare (140°F).

4 Transfer the lamb to a warm serving tray and let stand for 20 minutes before carving. Serve with pan gravy, a white bean casserole and tossed green salad.

Variation

ROAST LAMB WITH HERBS

Combine crushed garlic clove, 1 teaspoon salt, 1 teaspoon pepper, ½ teaspoon ground ginger, 1 bay leaf, and ½ teaspoon each thyme, sage and marjoram with 1 tablespoon soy sauce and 1 tablespoon vegetable oil. Make slits in the lamb and rub the sauce thoroughly over and into the meat. Proceed as above.

♦

LEG OF LAMB A LA MOLLY ELLSWORTH

6 TO 8 SERVINGS

1 (5-pound) leg of lamb
2 tablespoons butter
¼ pound mushrooms, chopped
1 garlic clove, chopped
¼ pound ham, chopped
1 teaspoon chopped parsley
1 tablespoon chopped onions
Grated rind of 1 lemon
Pinch of grated nutmeg
Salt and freshly ground pepper to taste
¼ cup soft fresh bread crumbs
4 egg yolks, beaten
3 cups chicken or meat stock
¼ cup olive oil
2 garlic cloves, chopped
2 bay leaves
Pinch of thyme
Pinch of marjoram

Continued

1 Have the butcher bone the lamb. Trim and save any lean scraps.

2 Preheat the oven to 325°F.

3 Melt the butter in a skillet, add the mushrooms, garlic, ham, parsley, onions, lemon rind, nutmeg, salt and pepper and cook until the mushrooms wilt.

4 Chop the scraps of lamb. Combine with the crumbs and egg yolks and add to the mushroom mixture. Spread the mixture over the boned side of the lamb. Roll the meat and tie in several places.

5 Heat the oil in a casserole and brown the meat on all sides. Add the remaining ingredients and cover tightly. Cook 3 hours, turning the lamb occasionally.

6 When the meat is tender, remove to a hot platter and keep warm. Remove the strings. Strain the gravy and boil until reduced to one-half the original quantity.

7 Brown the lamb under a broiler, basting occasionally with the gravy, until it acquires a brown glaze. Serve sliced with remaining gravy.

SWEDISH LAMB

6 TO 8 SERVINGS

1 teaspoon salt
1 tablespoon freshly ground pepper to taste
1 (5-pound) leg of lamb
3 onions, sliced
3 carrots, sliced
1 cup hot beef stock
1½ cups hot strong coffee
½ cup cream
1 tablespoon sugar

1 Preheat the oven to 425°F.

2 Rub the salt and pepper into the lamb and place the meat on a rack in a roasting pan surrounded with the onions and carrots. Roast 30 minutes, then skim off the fat.

3 Reduce the oven temperature to 350°F and add the stock, coffee, cream and sugar. Continue roasting, basting frequently, 40 minutes to 1 hour, depending on desired degree of doneness.

4 Transfer the lamb to a warm platter and force the gravy through a sieve, or purée in a food processor.

CROWN ROAST OF LAMB

8 SERVINGS

1 crown roast of lamb, at room temperature
Salt and freshly ground pepper to taste
Center stuffing (see note)

1 Have the butcher prepare a crown roast with rib sections of 2 loins of lamb by tying the sections together in a crown shape.

2 Preheat the oven to 325°F.

3 Cover the tips of the roast's bones with foil to prevent them from charring as the roast cooks. Place the meat on a rack in an open roasting pan.

4 Season the roast with salt and pepper and cook it about 1 to 1¼ hours. It should be rare when served.

5 Remove the foil and replace with paper frills, if desired. Fill the center with the desired stuffing and serve immediately.

Note: Recommended stuffings include buttered or creamed whole onions, mushrooms cooked lightly in butter and puréed peas.

BUTTERFLIED LAMB WITH ROSEMARY

8 SERVINGS

1 (5½- to 6-pound) boned leg of lamb in
*   1 piece*
¼ cup olive oil
1 tablespoon lemon juice
1 tablespoon crumbled rosemary
2 teaspoons coarsely ground pepper
1 bay leaf

1 Trim off most of the surface fat and tough outer coating of the lamb. Place the lamb in a shallow pan that will hold it snugly.

2 Combine the oil, lemon juice, rosemary, pepper and bay leaf. Blend well and rub the mixture all over the lamb. Cover and let stand for 2 hours or longer, unrefrigerated but in a cool place. Turn the meat occasionally as it stands.

3 Prepare a charcoal fire or preheat the broiler. Place the lamb on the fire or under the broiler, as far from the broiler heat as the rack allows. Grill or broil the meat to the desired degree of doneness. Turn the meat several times as it cooks. Cooking time will depend on whether the grill is covered. It should vary from about 20 minutes for rare meat to 40 minutes for medium well done. Let stand for 20 minutes covered with foil. Serve sliced with a little melted butter and lemon juice spooned over the lamb.

ARNI PSITO
ROAST LEG OF LAMB, GREEK STYLE

Lamb is most loved by the Greek people. *Arni tou galatos psito*, or "roast baby lamb," is traditional at Easter and is a dish of great delicacy.

6 SERVINGS

1 (5-pound) leg of lamb
Salt and freshly ground pepper to taste
1 tablespoon oregano
1 garlic clove, halved
4 tablespoons butter
Juice of 1 large lemon
2 small onions, chopped
3 or 4 parsley sprigs
2 or 3 dried mushrooms, washed and chopped
1 cup water

1 Preheat the oven to 500°F.

2 Place lamb, skin side up, on a rack in an open roasting pan. Rub the meat with salt, pepper, oregano and garlic.

3 Melt the butter, add the lemon juice and pour over the meat. Add onions, parsley, mushrooms and ½ cup of the water to the pan. Place in the oven and roast 20 minutes.

4 Add the remaining ½ cup water, lower the oven temperature to 350°F and roast to desired degree of doneness (140°F on a meat thermometer for rare, 170°F for medium). Baste occasionally.

CUSHION SHOULDER OF LAMB WITH CHICKEN LIVER STUFFING

6 TO 8 SERVINGS

1 (3- to 4-pound) cushion lamb shoulder
Salt and freshly ground pepper to taste
½ pound chicken livers, coarsely chopped
2 tablespoons butter
2 cups soft bread cubes or crumbs
¾ cup finely chopped celery
⅓ cup cream or stock
2 tablespoons chopped chives
2 tablespoons sherry
1 tablespoon grated onion
1 egg, slightly beaten

1 Have the butcher remove the bones from a square-cut lamb shoulder to form a cushion roast. Close 3 sides of the roast with metal skewers. Season the pocket lightly with salt and pepper.

2 Brown the chicken livers lightly in the butter.

3 Add the remaining ingredients, mix well and season with additional salt and pepper. Fill the pocket with the mixture, without packing. Fasten the edges together with skewers.

4 Place the roast, fat side up, in an open roasting pan and roast about 2½ hours (170°F for medium on a meat thermometer). Serve with the pan drippings, from which the excess fat has been removed.

STUFFED SHOULDER OF LAMB

6 SERVINGS

3 tablespoons butter
1 cup diced mushrooms
½ pound ham, finely chopped
1 garlic clove, minced
¼ cup finely chopped onion
¼ cup soft fresh bread crumbs
2 eggs, lightly beaten
1 tablespoon finely chopped parsley
Grated rind of 1 lemon
Salt and freshly ground pepper to taste
1 boned shoulder of lamb prepared
    for stuffing

1 Preheat the oven to 300°F.

2 In a large skillet, melt the butter, add the mushrooms and sauté until brown. Add the remaining ingredients, except the lamb, and mix. Stuff the shoulder with the mixture and tie securely with string.

3 Place the shoulder on a rack in a roasting pan and roast approximately 40 minutes per pound.

LEG OF LAMB, MIDDLE EASTERN STYLE

6 SERVINGS

1 (5-pound) leg of lamb, trimmed
Salt and freshly ground pepper to taste
1 bunch scallions, chopped
8 stalks mint, chopped
1 cup chicken stock

1 Preheat the oven to 450°F. Rub the meat with salt and pepper.

2 Place the roast on a rack in an open pan and bake until brown, about 15 minutes. Reduce the temperature to 325°F and continue roasting until the meat is rare (140°F on a meat thermometer).

3 Cover the lamb with the scallions and mint. Add the stock to the pan and return the meat to the oven. Roast until done (170°F on a meat thermometer), basting frequently with the broth in the pan.

4 Serve the meat with the cooked scallions around and on top of it. Make a gravy, if desired, from drippings in the pan.

LEG OF LAMB WITH TURNIPS

8 SERVINGS

1 (6- to 8-pound) leg of lamb, trimmed
Salt to taste
2 tablespoons olive oil
3 onions, sliced
3 carrots, sliced
2 celery stalks, sliced
3 parsley sprigs
1 bay leaf
½ teaspoon thyme
1 tablespoon flour
1 to 2 cups water or stock
1 cup canned tomatoes, undrained
12 white turnips, quartered and parboiled
12 small white onions, peeled and parboiled

1 Preheat the oven to 400°F. Season the meat with salt.

2 In a heavy kettle or Dutch oven place the oil, sliced onions, carrots, celery, parsley, bay leaf and thyme. Sprinkle with flour and place the lamb on top.

3 Roast uncovered, turning frequently, until the lamb is brown on all sides. Add the water and tomatoes, cover closely and reduce the oven temperature to 325°F. Braise the lamb 3 to 3½ hours, basting the meat occasionally. Fifteen minutes before the lamb is done, add the parboiled turnips and onions and cook until done.

4 Remove the lamb to a hot platter and keep warm. Strain the gravy and skim the fat from the surface. Thicken the gravy with a little flour mixed with water.

5 Slice the lamb and serve with the vegetables and gravy.

BROILED LAMB CHOPS

6 SERVINGS

6 double lamb chops
5 tablespoons olive oil
1 garlic clove, sliced
Salt and freshly ground pepper to taste
Chopped dill or parsley
Lemon juice

1 Marinate the lamb chops in the olive oil with the garlic for at least 1 hour.

2 Broil on a rack about 2 inches from the source of heat in a very hot preheated broiler. Brown both sides, cooking a total of 10 minutes for rare, 15 for medium, or 20 for well done. Transfer to a warm platter, season with salt and pepper and sprinkle with dill or parsley and lemon juice.

Variations

HERB-STUFFED LAMB CHOPS

Before cooking, slit the chops in the thickest part. Cream a little butter with parsley, tarragon or rosemary and stuff the chops with the mixture. Seal the opening with toothpicks. Broil and serve as indicated above.

MARINATED LAMB CHOPS

Marinate chops for several hours in a mixture of ¾ cup red wine, ¼ cup olive oil, 2 crushed garlic cloves, 1 teaspoon salt, 6 peppercorns, and 1 teaspoon of oregano. Broil as above.

HERBED LAMB CHOPS

Rub chops with a cut clove of garlic on each side, then rub with olive oil. Combine 1 tablespoon basil and 1 tablespoon marjoram and sprinkle the chops with the mixture. Refrigerate, covered, about 2 hours before cooking. Broil as above.

♦

BARBECUED LAMB RIBS

6 SERVINGS

6 pounds breast of lamb, left whole or cut into small pieces
2 quarts water
1 cup cider vinegar
1 onion, sliced
2 bay leaves
1 garlic clove, minced
1 teaspoon salt
1 cup barbecue sauce (page 584)

1 Place the ribs in a heavy pan and add the water, vinegar, onions, bay leaves, garlic and salt. Bring to a boil, cover, and simmer for 45 minutes to 1 hour, or until lamb is tender.

2 Drain the ribs and arrange on a broiler pan. Brush with barbecue sauce and broil slowly until crisp and brown.

SHASHLIK

Skewered meat dishes are called *shish kebab* in Armenian and *shashlik* in Russian.

6 SERVINGS

1 small leg of lamb
1 cup red wine
¼ cup olive oil
2 garlic cloves, crushed
1 teaspoon salt
Freshly ground pepper to taste
1 teaspoon oregano
Mushroom caps
Tomato wedges
Green pepper squares
Onion squares
Eggplant cubes

1 Trim the leg of lamb and remove the bone, gristle and remnants of fat. Cut the meat into 2-inch cubes and marinate overnight in a mixture of the wine, oil, garlic, salt, pepper and oregano.

2 Preheat the broiler. String the meat on skewers, alternating with mushrooms, tomato, green pepper, onion and eggplant.

3 Brush with the marinade and broil beneath high heat 5 minutes on each side.

SATAY KAMBING MADURA

Satay kambing madura is an Indonesian dish that is, in effect, skewered lamb in a peanut and red pepper sauce. It is a very special version of shish kebab.

6 SERVINGS

¾ cup hot water
1 cup Indonesian soy sauce, or ½ cup regular soy sauce mixed with 1 teaspoon dark molasses
½ cup roasted peanuts, ground
⅓ cup peanut butter
1 garlic clove, minced
1 teaspoon hot red pepper flakes
Juice of 1 lemon
3 pounds well-trimmed leg of lamb, boned and cut into 1-inch cubes
Hot sauce (see following recipe)

1 Combine all ingredients, except lamb and hot sauce, in a saucepan. Bring to a boil and stir until smooth. Cool to room temperature.

2 Pour half the mixture over the lamb cubes. Mix well and let stand 1 hour. Reserve remaining marinade for the hot sauce.

3 Preheat broiler. Arrange the lamb on small skewers, broil quickly on all sides and serve with hot sauce.

HOT SAUCE

Reserved marinade
½ cup tomato sauce
¼ cup water or stock
1 teaspoon Tabasco sauce
Juice of 1 lemon

Combine all ingredients and bring to a boil. Use as a dip for skewered lamb.

JULIE SAHNI'S INDIAN KEEMA WITH GINGER

The word *keema* refers to almost any ground meat casserole in Indian cuisine. It takes many flavors but this version is one of the best. The recipe was given to me by Julie Sahni, the well-known Indian chef and cookbook author. A principal flavor is grated fresh ginger.

4 TO 6 SERVINGS

2 tablespoons vegetable oil
⅔ cup finely chopped onions
4 teaspoons minced garlic
1½ tablespoons finely chopped ginger
2 hot green chilies, seeded and chopped
1 pound lean ground lamb, or beef
¼ teaspoon turmeric
Salt to taste
½ cup boiling water
2 teaspoons garam masala (see note)
2 teaspoons lemon juice
2 tablespoons chopped coriander

1 Heat the oil in a skillet and add the onions. Cook, stirring, about 10 minutes, or until they are caramel colored.

2 Add the garlic, ginger and chilies and cook 2 minutes longer. Add the ground meat and cook, stirring and chopping with the side of a heavy metal spoon to break up any lumps. Cook until the meat loses its raw look and starts to brown.

3 Sprinkle with turmeric and salt and stir. Add the water, cover and cook over low heat about 25 minutes, stirring often to prevent browning and sticking. When ready, all the liquid should be absorbed. If it is not, uncover and cook until all the liquid has evaporated.

4 Stir in the garam masala, lemon juice and coriander.

Note: Garam masala is available where specialty spices are sold or in shops specializing in Indian foods. If it is not available, substitute curry powder or curry paste and add it along with the turmeric and salt.

Julie Sahni's Stuffed Cabbage with Ginger Sauce, page 387.

♦

LAMB CURRY

4 SERVINGS

¼ cup vegetable oil
4 onions, chopped
1 garlic clove, minced
2 pounds boneless lamb shoulder, cut into
    2-inch cubes
½ cup white wine
1 cup yogurt
2 teaspoons ground coriander
1 teaspoon ground ginger
½ teaspoon ground cardamom
¼ teaspoon cinnamon
¼ teaspoon ground cloves

1 Heat the oil in a heavy kettle. Add the onions and garlic and sauté until the onions are tender and transparent. Remove onions and garlic.

2 Add the meat to the kettle and brown on all sides. Add the wine and deglaze the pan, scraping up all the brown particles clinging to the pan. Return the onions to the pot and add the yogurt and remaining ingredients. Simmer until tender, about 1 hour. If desired, thin the sauce with water before serving.

RICHARD KENT'S BENGAL LAMB CURRY

4 TO 5 SERVINGS

2½ pounds lean lamb shoulder
1 tablespoon butter
⅔ cup finely chopped onions
2 tablespoons vegetable oil
3 tablespoons chopped preserved or
    crystallized ginger
½ teaspoon sugar
⅛ teaspoon freshly ground pepper
2 teaspoons salt
2 to 3 tablespoons curry powder
¼ teaspoon crushed mint
2 cups milk
½ cup fresh coconut milk (page 147)
½ cup freshly grated coconut
½ cup lime juice
½ cup cream

1 Cut the lamb into 1-inch cubes, removing the bones and fat.

2 Melt the butter in a large heavy pan. Add the onions and cook until tender, about 5 minutes. Remove with a slotted spoon and set aside.

3 Add the oil to the pan and brown the lamb cubes in it. Return the onions and add the ginger, sugar, pepper, salt, curry powder, mint and milk. Mix well. Cover and simmer over low heat 1 hour.

4 Add the coconut milk and coconut. Cover and cook 5 minutes. Gradually stir in the lime juice and cream, adding them alternately. Cook without boiling 10 to 15 minutes, or until the lamb is tender.

NAVARIN D'AGNEAU

The most famous of all lamb stews is the *navarin d'agneau* of French cuisine. A *navarin* is a savory ragoût with vegetables.

6 SERVINGS

3 pounds lean lamb shoulder, cut into
    serving pieces
3 tablespoons olive oil
1 tablespoon sugar
Salt and freshly ground pepper to taste
3 tablespoons flour
2 to 3 cups chicken stock
2 tomatoes, peeled, seeded and chopped
2 garlic cloves, minced
¼ teaspoon thyme
1 bay leaf
12 small potatoes, peeled
6 carrots, scraped and cut into
    1½-inch lengths
6 small white turnips, peeled and halved
12 small white onions
1 cup shelled fresh peas, or 1 (10-ounce)
    package frozen peas
1 cup green beans cut into ½-inch lengths

1 Preheat the oven to 375°F.

2 Brown the meat on all sides, a few pieces at a time, in the oil. Transfer to a heavy heatproof casserole.

3 Sprinkle the meat with the sugar and place the casserole over moderately high heat for 4 to 5 minutes. Season the meat with salt and pepper and sprinkle with the flour. Cook for 3 to 5 minutes longer, stirring constantly.

4 Add enough stock to cover the meat. Add the tomatoes, garlic, thyme and bay leaf and bring to a boil. Cover and bake in the oven 1 to 1½ hours, or until meat is almost tender.

5 Remove the meat to a clean casserole. Strain the sauce, skim off excess fat, and pour the sauce over meat.

6 Add the potatoes, carrots, turnips and onions. Cover and bake for 25 minutes, or until vegetables are almost tender.

7 Add the peas and beans and bake for 10 minutes longer. If frozen peas are used, add them only for the last 5 minutes of the baking time.

♦

TUNISIAN COUSCOUS

Couscous is a fine-grained pasta, made with ground semolina and water. The flour and water are blended and rolled by hand or machine until tiny pellets are formed. The word *couscous* also refers to the main course stew that it is served with. To make an authentic couscous, it is best to steam it with the stew to get the full flavor, rather than using the commercially available precooked, or quick cooking product.

8 TO 10 SERVINGS

1 cup dried chick-peas
3 to 4 pounds cubed leg of lamb
1 cup olive oil
1 teaspoon salt
½ teaspoon freshly ground pepper
1 (6-ounce) can tomato paste
2 garlic cloves, minced
3 quarts lamb stock
1 tablespoon caraway seed, crushed in a
    mortar
3 or 4 hot red peppers, crushed
½ teaspoon ground cumin, or more
2 cups couscous (not quick cooking)
½ cup water
6 turnips, cut into pieces
6 small white onions
12 carrots, cut into pieces
2 small zucchini, sliced
½ small head of cabbage, cut into wedges
1 large green pepper, seeded and cut into
    strips
Sauce piquante (page 602)

1 Soak the chick-peas in water overnight, or use the quick-soaking method (page 78). Drain.

2 Place the lamb cubes, olive oil, salt, black pepper and tomato paste in a large deep kettle or in the bottom part of a large steamer. Cook for 10 to 15 minutes over medium heat, stirring occasionally.

3 Add the garlic, stock, caraway seed, hot peppers, cumin and drained chick-peas. Bring the mixture to a boil, cover, and cook for 1 to 2 hours.

4 Meanwhile, spread the couscous on a large tray or platter and sprinkle with the water. Mix lightly with the fingers until all the grains are moistened. Line the top of the steamer or a colander that will fit over the kettle with muslin. Drop the moistened grain into the prepared container. Do not pack down.

5 About 1 hour before the meat and chick-peas are done, lower the grains into the top of the steamer or kettle. Cover tightly. The grains will cook in the steam from the lamb and will absorb the flavors. Stir once or twice during the cooking to break up any lumps.

6 Add the turnips, onions and carrots to the lamb. Cook for 15 minutes longer. Add the zucchini, cabbage and green pepper. Cook for 10 minutes, or until vegetables are tender. Taste the sauce; if necessary, adjust the seasoning.

7 Spread the cooked couscous on a large deep serving platter. Gradually add the liquid from the lamb stew, stirring the couscous until it will not absorb any more. Cover and let stand for 5 to 7 minutes. Add more liquid from the stew to the couscous, again stirring until it will not absorb any more.

8 Push the grain into a rounded mound in the center of the tray. Arrange the lamb and vegetables in an attractive pattern around the mound. Serve with sauce piquante.

Note: If canned chick-peas are used, add them (2 cups, or a 1-pound can, drained) when adding the zucchini and cabbage.

◆

GORMEH SABZEE
LAMB AND PARSLEY STEW

This is a Persian stew made with meat and parsley, mostly parsley.

6 TO 8 SERVINGS

4 tablespoons butter
12 cups chopped parsley
16 scallions, chopped
¼ cup vegetable oil
3 pounds lean lamb, cut into 1-inch cubes
Salt and freshly ground pepper to taste
3 lemons
5 cups canned kidney beans, undrained

1 In a heavy 4-quart pot or Dutch oven, heat the butter, add the parsley and scallions and cook until the parsley is dark green.

2 In a large skillet, heat the oil, add the meat and brown lightly. Season with salt and pepper. Combine with the vegetable mixture in the pot and add water to cover, the juice of 2 of the lemons and quarters of the third. Cover and simmer until the meat is almost tender, 1 to 1½ hours.

3 Add the kidney beans and correct the seasonings. Continue cooking until the lamb is tender, about 30 minutes longer.

Note: Beef may be substituted for the lamb.

LAMB STEW

2 pounds shoulder of lamb, cut into
    1½-inch cubes
3 tablespoons vegetable oil
3 tablespoons flour
6 cups water
Salt and freshly ground pepper to taste
2 tomatoes, peeled and diced
2 tablespoons butter
18 small whole white onions, peeled
6 small whole carrots, scraped, or 3 large
    carrots, scraped and cut into quarters
1 medium turnip, peeled and cut into
    1-inch cubes
18 small potatoes, peeled, or 6 medium
    potatoes, cut up
1 pound freshly shelled peas
2 teaspoons chopped parsley

1 Brown the meat on all sides in the oil
in a hot skillet. Transfer to a Dutch oven
or heavy kettle.

2 Sprinkle the lamb with flour and add
the water, salt, pepper and tomatoes.
Bring slowly to a boil, cover, reduce the
heat and simmer 1½ hours.

3 Heat the butter in the skillet, add the
onions, carrots and turnip and sauté until
the onions are light brown.

4 Add the browned vegetables and the
potatoes to the stew. Cook, uncovered,
until the potatoes are tender, 30 to 40 minutes. Twenty minutes before the potatoes
are done, add the peas. Serve sprinkled
with chopped parsley.

LAMB STEW WITH OKRA

¼ cup olive oil
2 pounds lamb shoulder, cut into 2-inch cubes
½ cup finely chopped onions
1 pound trimmed fresh okra, or 1 package
    frozen okra, thawed
4 large tomatoes, peeled and chopped, or 3
    cups canned tomatoes, drained and chopped
1 cup water
1 lemon, sliced and seeded
1 tablespoon chopped parsley
½ teaspoon thyme
Salt and freshly ground pepper to taste

1 Heat the oil in a heavy kettle, add the
meat and brown on all sides. Add the onions and cook until light brown.

2 Add the remaining ingredients,
cover and simmer gently until tender,
about 1¼ hours. Serve with fluffy rice.

RAGOÛT OF LAMB

4 SERVINGS

2 pounds lean lamb, cut from the leg, in
    1½-inch cubes
¼ cup flour
½ teaspoon salt
Freshly ground pepper to taste
¼ cup olive oil
1½ cups beef stock, approximately
⅓ cup Spanish sherry
1 garlic clove, crushed
2 tablespoons lemon juice
2 tablespoons chopped parsley

1 Preheat the oven to 350°F.
2 Dredge the lamb in the flour seasoned with the salt and a generous grinding of pepper. Heat the oil in a Dutch oven
and sauté the lamb in it until lamb is
brown on all sides. Stir in the oil, stock,
sherry and garlic.
3 Cover the casserole and bake until
the lamb is tender, 1 to 1½ hours. Stir in
lemon juice and garnish with the parsley.

BRAISED LAMB SHANKS

6 SERVINGS

6 lamb shanks
Flour for dredging
Salt and freshly ground pepper to taste
½ teaspoon oregano
⅓ cup vegetable oil
¾ cup chopped onions
¾ cup chopped celery
¾ cup chopped carrots
1 garlic clove, finely chopped
Pinch of thyme
¾ cup dry red wine
¾ cup beef stock

1 Preheat the oven to 350°F.
2 Wipe the lamb shanks well with a
damp cloth and remove any fat. Combine
flour, salt, pepper and oregano and
dredge the lamb shanks in the seasoned
flour. Brown in the oil and transfer to a
large earthenware casserole or Dutch
oven. Add the vegetables, garlic and
thyme to the skillet and cook, stirring, 5
minutes.
3 Pour the vegetables over the lamb
and add the liquids. Cover and bake 1½
hours, or until the meat is tender.
4 Remove the shanks to a warm platter. Cook the pan sauce over high heat
until reduced slightly, then pour over the
shanks.

LAMB PILAU

8 TO 10 SERVINGS

2 pounds lean lamb shanks
½ cup yogurt
2 cups cold water
1½ teaspoons salt
2 tablespoons butter
4 whole cardamom pods
6 whole cloves
1 (2-inch-long) cinnamon stick
¼ teaspoon caraway seeds
1 bay leaf
¼ pound mushrooms, sliced
2 cups rice

1 Trim off all excess fat from the lamb shanks. Marinate the meat in the yogurt for 30 minutes.

2 Put the lamb and yogurt in a large saucepan. Add the water and 1 teaspoon of the salt. Cover and simmer for 3 hours.

3 Cool the meat and stock. Trim all lean meat from the bones. Discard the bones and reserve the meat.

4 When stock is cold, lift off all the hardened fat and discard it. Add enough water to the stock to make 4 cups. Reserve the stock.

5 Melt the butter in a 4-quart saucepan. Tie the spices in a cheesecloth bag and add to the butter. Add the mushrooms and sauté for 2 minutes.

6 Put the rice in the saucepan and cook, stirring, for 3 to 4 minutes. Add the reserved stock, the remaining salt, the reserved meat and the mushrooms.

7 Cover the saucepan. Bring the liquid to a boil and boil for 15 minutes, until the rice is tender and the grains stand apart. Do not stir. Lift out the spice bag and discard. Serve the pilau hot.

SHEPHERD'S PIE

One of the world's greatest dishes to be made with leftovers is that British creation known as shepherd's pie. It is traditionally made with leftover roast lamb although any other cooked solid meats may be used, including beef, veal or pork. It is actually a casserole dish made of cubed or ground cooked meat in a light sauce topped with mashed potatoes and baked with grated cheese on top.

4 TO 6 SERVINGS

1 pound cooked very lean meat, preferably
    roast lamb
2 tablespoons butter
1 cup finely chopped onions
½ cup finely chopped carrots
½ cup finely chopped celery
2 tablespoons finely chopped parsley
3 tablespoons flour
2 tablespoons tomato paste
½ cup dry white wine
1½ cups chicken stock
1 teaspoon Worcestershire sauce
Freshly ground pepper to taste
1 cup cooked fresh or frozen corn kernels
2 or more cups mashed potatoes
½ cup grated sharp cheddar cheese

1 Cut the meat into ¼-inch cubes. There should be about 3 cups. Set aside.

2 Heat the butter in a saucepan and add the onions, carrots, celery and parsley. Cook, stirring, until the onions are wilted.

3 Sprinkle with flour and stir with a wire whisk. Add the tomato paste, wine, stock, Worcestershire and pepper, stirring rapidly with the whisk. Let simmer 10 minutes and stir in the cubed meat and the corn. Cook 5 minutes longer.

4 Preheat the oven to 350°F.

5 Put the meat and sauce in a 7-cup baking dish or casserole. Outfit a pastry bag with a round pastry tube—No. 7 or 8—and spoon mashed potatoes into the bag. Pipe the potatoes neatly and evenly on top of the meat mixture, covering it completely. Sprinkle evenly with cheese and place the dish in the oven. Bake 30 to 45 minutes, or until the dish is piping hot throughout and the cheese is melted. If necessary run the dish briefly under the broiler to glaze the top.

◆

MOUSSAKA A LA TURQUE

Moussaka, pronounced *moos-ah-KAH*, is a meat and eggplant dish found in many Middle Eastern countries. Here is a Turkish version.

8 SERVINGS

4 medium eggplants
¾ cup vegetable oil
1 tablespoon lemon juice
6 tablespoons hot water
Coarse salt
½ cup flour
1 tablespoon butter
1 garlic clove, minced
3 tablespoons minced onions
½ cup chopped mushrooms
2 tablespoons minced parsley
1½ cups (2 medium) diced fresh tomatoes
1 cup ground or diced cooked lamb
2 teaspoons salt
½ teaspoon freshly ground pepper
2 eggs, slightly beaten
Basic tomato sauce (page 561)

1 Cut 3 of the eggplants into halves lengthwise. Run a sharp pointed stainless steel knife around the inside of the skins, separating them from the pulp. Score the pulp deeply, cutting almost through but being careful not to pierce the skin.

2 In a large skillet heat 2 tablespoons of the oil, add 2 eggplant halves, cut side down, and cook 1 minute. Combine 1 teaspoon of the lemon juice with 2 tablespoons of the hot water and add. Cover and cook over medium heat 10 minutes. Remove from the pan and scoop out the pulp, leaving the skins intact. Place the pulp in a bowl and reserve. Repeat the process, using the remaining eggplant halves.

3 Peel the fourth eggplant and cut into slices ½ inch thick. Put the slices in a colander, sprinkle with coarse salt and let drain for 30 minutes. Pat dry with paper toweling. Coat the slices lightly with flour and brown on both sides in the remaining oil, adding 2 tablespoons at a time.

4 Preheat the oven to 375°F.

5 In a skillet heat the butter, add the garlic, onions and mushrooms and sauté until the onions are transparent. Combine the mixture with the cooked eggplant pulp. Stir in the parsley, tomatoes, lamb, salt, pepper and eggs.

6 Line an oiled 2-quart charlotte mold or casserole with the eggplant skins, having the purple exterior next to the sides of the mold and extending over the edge. Place a 1-inch layer of the eggplant-and-lamb mixture in the bottom of the mold. Over this place a layer of fried eggplant slices. Repeat until the mold is filled, ending with a layer of the mixture.

7 Bring the skins, which extend over the side of the mold, toward the center. If the skins are not long enough to cover the top, place a piece of foil over the uncovered portion.

8 Place the mold in a pan of hot water and bake 1½ hours. Remove from the oven and let stand 10 minutes. Unmold onto a serving plate and serve hot with tomato sauce.

MOUSSAKA A LA GRECQUE

This moussaka, an eggplant and meat casserole of Greek origin, is a splendid item for buffets because it should be prepared in advance. It may be served lukewarm or at room temperature.

8 TO 10 SERVINGS

3 medium-size eggplants
½ cup vegetable oil
3 large onions, finely chopped
2 pounds ground lamb or beef
3 tablespoons tomato paste
½ cup red wine
½ cup chopped parsley
¼ teaspoon ground cinnamon
Salt and freshly ground pepper to taste
¼ pound butter
6 tablespoons flour
1 quart milk
4 eggs, beaten until frothy
Grated nutmeg
2 cups ricotta or cottage cheese
1 cup fine bread crumbs
1 cup grated Parmesan cheese

1 Peel the eggplants and cut them into slices about ½ inch thick. Brown the slices quickly in ¼ cup of the oil. Set aside.

2 Heat the remaining oil in the same skillet and cook the onions until they are brown. Add the ground meat and cook 10 minutes. Pour off excess fat. Combine the tomato paste with the wine, parsley, cinnamon, salt and pepper. Stir this mixture into the meat and simmer over low heat, stirring frequently, until all the liquid has been absorbed. Remove the mixture from the fire.

3 Preheat the oven to 375°F.

4 Make a white sauce by melting the butter and blending in the flour, stirring with a wire whisk. Meanwhile, bring the milk to a boil and add it gradually to the butter-flour mixture, stirring constantly. When the mixture is thickened and smooth, remove it from the heat. Cool slightly and stir in the beaten eggs, nutmeg and ricotta.

5 Grease an 11×16-inch pan and sprinkle the bottom lightly with crumbs. Arrange alternate layers of the eggplant and the meat sauce in the pan, sprinkling each layer with Parmesan and crumbs. Pour the ricotta sauce over the top and bake 1 hour, or until top is golden. Remove from the oven and cool 20 to 30 minutes before serving. Cut into squares and serve.

Note: The flavor of this dish improves on standing 1 day. Reheat before serving.

LAMB HASH

4 SERVINGS

1 tablespoon butter
1 large onion, minced
3 parsley sprigs, chopped
1 garlic clove, minced
2 slices bacon, minced
3 cups chopped cooked lamb
1 cup meat gravy or stock
½ cup canned tomato sauce
Salt and freshly ground pepper to taste
1 cup cream, approximately
2 tablespoons grated Parmesan cheese

1 Preheat the oven to 325°F.
2 Melt the buttter in a heavy skillet, add the onion and sauté until golden. Add the parsley, garlic and bacon and cook briefly.
3 Mix in the remaining ingredients except the cream and cheese and bake, covered, 1 hour, stirring from time to time.
4 Place the hash in 4 greased individual deep casseroles, cover with cream and sprinkle with cheese. Brown under a preheated broiler.

EGGPLANT-LAMB CASSEROLE

6 SERVINGS

2 medium eggplants, pared and diced
1 pound mushrooms
2 tablespoons vegetable oil
½ cup chopped onions
1 garlic clove, crushed
3 tablespoons butter
2 tablespoons flour
½ cup chopped green pepper
2 cups diced cooked lamb, or ½ pound cooked ground lamb
1 teaspoon oregano
½ cup soft bread crumbs

1 Cook the eggplant in boiling salted water 15 minutes. Drain well and mash.
2 Peel and stem the mushrooms. Simmer the stems and peelings in 2½ cups water 15 minutes.
3 Preheat the oven to 400°F.
4 Coarsely chop the mushroom caps and sauté in the oil.
5 Sauté the onions and garlic in 2 tablespoons of the butter until the onions are golden. Add the flour and blend. Add stock drained from the mushroom stems and stir until smooth and thick.
6 Add the eggplant, sautéed mushrooms, green pepper, lamb and oregano. Pile the mixture in a buttered 2-quart casserole.
7 Cover the mixture with the crumbs and dot with the remaining butter. Bake, uncovered, 30 minutes.

MERGUEZ
GROUND LAMB PATTIES WITH CUMIN FLAVOR

One of the tastiest of all sausages is a specialty of Morocco and it is called *merguez*. It is a trifle spicy and one of its typical flavors is that of cumin. Traditionally, the meat is stuffed in casings and broiled or grilled. But it is delicious as patties, either grilled or cooked in a skillet.

---

4 SERVINGS

---

1 pound ground lean lamb
¾ teaspoon ground cumin
½ teaspoon thyme
⅛ teaspoon grated nutmeg
½ teaspoon hot red pepper flakes
1 teaspoon minced garlic
Freshly ground pepper to taste
1 tablespoon vegetable oil
1 tablespoon butter, melted

1 In a mixing bowl, combine the lamb, cumin, thyme, nutmeg, red pepper flakes, garlic and pepper. Blend well with the fingers.

2 Shape the mixture into 4 patties of equal size.

3 If a grill is to be used, preheat it to high and brush the grill surface with oil. If a skillet is to be used, it is best to use the nonstick variety. Add the oil to the skillet. Cook the patties 3 to 4 minutes on one side. Turn and cook the other side 3 to 4 minutes, or to the desired degree of doneness.

4 Transfer 1 patty to each of 4 plates. Brush the top of each lightly with melted butter and serve.

Pork

ROAST PORK

---

6 SERVINGS

---

1 (4-pound) pork loin
Salt and freshly ground pepper to taste
1 cup chicken stock
Flour (optional)

1 Preheat the oven to 350°F.

2 Rub the meat with salt and pepper and place, fat side up, on a rack in an uncovered roasting pan. Roast about 2 hours, or 30 minutes per pound (170°F on a meat thermometer).

3 When the meat is done, remove roast to a hot platter and pour off the fat in the roasting pan. Add stock to the pan and bring to a boil. Thicken, if desired, with a little flour mixed with water. Serve with the meat.

Variation

ROAST PORK WITH THYME

Combine 3 tablespoons olive oil, 2 tablespoons lemon juice, 1 tablespoon fresh thyme (or 1 teaspoon dried) and 1 garlic clove, finely chopped, with salt and freshly ground pepper to taste. Rub the mixture into the pork loin and roast as above.

PORK LOIN WITH CUMIN FLAVOR

Although few people seem to realize it, cumin is the principal flavor of commercially produced chili powder. It is, otherwise, a little used spice in American kitchens, but it adds a fine flavor for many meats, including a boneless pork loin.

6 SERVINGS

1 (1¾- to 2-pound) boneless pork loin,
    trimmed of surface fat
Freshly ground pepper to taste
1 tablespoon vegetable oil
1 teaspoon ground cumin
1 teaspoon paprika
¼ teaspoon cayenne
⅛ teaspoon grated nutmeg
1 tablespoon Dijon mustard
1 teaspoon minced garlic
½ cup chicken stock
2 tablespoons sour cream

1 Preheat the oven to 375°F.

2 Sprinkle the meat with pepper.

3 Blend the oil with the cumin, paprika and cayenne. Brush the loin on all sides with the mixture.

4 Place the pork in a shallow heatproof skillet or baking dish in which it will fit comfortably. Sprinkle the top with nutmeg and place it in the oven.

5 Meanwhile, blend the mustard with the garlic and set aside.

6 Bake 15 minutes and turn the meat. Bake 15 minutes longer and remove the meat temporarily. Pour off all fat from the baking dish.

7 Place the baking dish on the stove and add the stock stirring with a whisk to dissolve the brown particles that cling to the bottom of the pan.

8 Return the pork to the baking dish and brush the top with the mustard mixture. Return the meat to the oven and continue baking 15 minutes, or until the internal temperature reaches 160°F on a meat thermometer.

9 Remove the meat to a warm platter and heat the sauce. Stir the sour cream into the sauce.

10 Cut the meat on the diagonal into thin slices and serve with very small amounts of sauce spooned over.

♦

LOIN OF PORK WITH PRUNES

The Swedes enjoy braised pork stuffed with prunes. It is not only delicious to dine on but it has a most interesting design.

6 TO 8 SERVINGS

1 (4- to 5-pound) loin of pork
20 prunes, pitted
2 teaspoons salt
½ teaspoon white pepper
¼ teaspoon ground ginger

1 Have the meat boned and a pocket cut to the center along the length of the roast.

2 Cover prunes with hot water and soak 30 minutes. Drain, reserving the liquid.

3 Insert the prunes in the pocket. Season the meat with the salt, pepper and ginger and tie it into a good shape with a string.

4 In a Dutch oven brown the meat on all sides. Cover and cook over low heat until tender, about 1½ hours, basting occasionally with the prune juice. Serve the meat sliced with the strained pan juices in a gravy boat.

PORK CHOPS CHARCUTIÈRE

6 SERVINGS

6 lean pork chops
Salt and freshly ground pepper to taste
2 tablespoons vegetable oil
¼ cup each finely chopped shallots and onions
   (or all onions if shallots are not available)
¾ cup dry white wine
1½ cups brown sauce (page 551) or canned
   beef gravy
2 tablespoons cold butter
1 tablespoon Dijon or Düsseldorf mustard
3 sour gherkins, cut into julienne strips

1 Trim the pork chops, leaving a ¼-inch layer of fat. Sprinkle with salt and pepper.

2 Heat the oil in a skillet and brown the chops on both sides. Cook 20 minutes, or until cooked through. Transfer to a warm platter. Pour off all but 2 tablespoons of fat from the pan and add the shallots and onions to the skillet. Cook, stirring, 2 minutes.

3 Add the wine to the skillet and stir to dissolve brown particles in the bottom of the pan. Cook until the wine is almost totally reduced. Add the brown sauce and cook about 12 minutes.

4 Turn off the heat and stir in the cold butter. Add the mustard and stir. Do not reheat. Add the gherkins. Spoon a little sauce over each chop and serve the remainder in a sauceboat.

PORK CHOPS WITH RYE BREAD STUFFING

6 SERVINGS

6 (1-inch-thick) loin pork chops
2 tablespoons butter
1 medium onion, chopped
1 large garlic clove, minced
1½ cups soft rye bread crumbs
¾ teaspoon salt
½ teaspoon caraway seed
¼ cup chopped parsley
1 egg, lightly beaten
3 tablespoons water
Freshly ground pepper to taste
1 cup stock or water
2 tablespoons flour

1 Have the butcher cut pockets in the pork chops. Preheat the oven to 350°F.

2 In a skillet, heat the butter and sauté the onions and garlic about 5 minutes. Remove from heat. Combine with the crumbs, salt, caraway seed, parsley, egg and water and mix well. Stuff the chops with the mixture, closing the openings with toothpicks.

3 Place the chops in a baking pan and season to taste with additional salt and pepper. Cover closely and bake 30 minutes. Uncover and continue baking until brown and tender, about 30 minutes longer. Remove chops to a heated platter.

4 Pour off fat from the pan. Add stock to the pan and bring to a boil. Thicken with flour mixed with a little water.

PORK CHOPS PIQUANTE

4 thick loin pork chops
2 tablespoons butter
½ cup finely chopped onions
1½ cups tomato purée
1 cup dry white wine
Pinch of thyme
½ bay leaf
Salt and freshly ground pepper to taste
½ cup finely chopped parsley
2 garlic cloves, minced
2 teaspoons grated lemon rind

1 Brown the pork chops on both sides in the butter in a skillet. Transfer chops to a platter and keep warm. Pour off most of the fat.

2 To the fat remaining in the skillet add the onions and cook briefly, stirring until onions are wilted. Add the tomato purée, wine, thyme, bay leaf, salt and pepper.

3 Return the chops to the skillet and turn them in the sauce. Cover and cook for 1 hour, basting occasionally, until chops are fork tender.

4 Mix the parsley, garlic and lemon rind together and sprinkle over the chops.

PORK CHOPS WITH CAPER SAUCE

4 SERVINGS

4 (1-inch-thick) rib or loin pork chops
3 tablespoons flour
2 tablespoons butter
Salt and freshly ground pepper to taste
½ cup beef stock
2 teaspoons prepared mustard
3 tablespoons capers
¼ cup water
½ cup sour cream

1 Sprinkle the chops with 2 tablespoons of the flour. Brown chops in the butter. Pour off the drippings. Season the chops with the salt and pepper.

2 Add the stock to the pan along with the mustard and capers. Cover tightly and simmer for 45 minutes to 1 hour. Remove the chops to a warm platter.

3 Stir the sour cream into the drippings and cook just until heated through. Serve the sauce over the chops.

PORK LOAF

6 SERVINGS

2 pounds lean pork, ground
½ cup soft fresh bread crumbs
½ cup pistachios
2 eggs, lightly beaten
1 tablespoon sage rubbed through the fingers
1 teaspoon salt
¼ teaspoon freshly ground pepper
Basic tomato sauce (page 561), or mushroom
    sauce (page 565)

1 Preheat the oven to 325°F.
2 Mix all the ingredients except sauce together lightly. Pack in a 9 × 5 × 3-inch loaf pan or form into a loaf shape and place in a baking pan. Bake for 1½ to 2 hours. Serve with tomato sauce or mushroom sauce.

Chinese Watercress and Pork Ball Soup, page 93.
Ukrainian Borscht, page 62.
Pork Ravioli, page 508.
Pork Fried Rice with Ginger, page 535.

The creation of music in honor of food and drink is not new. Bach wrote a cantata in praise of coffee and Schubert a trout quintet. One of the most unusual tributes to food was a musical essay written by one of South America's most illustrious composers, the late Heitor Villa-Lobos.

Once when he was a guest in the home of Doña Dora Vasconcellos, the Brazilian consul general in New York, Maestro Villa-Lobos was served a special feijoada, Brazil's national dish. It was prepared by Noemia Faris, a shy, good-humored woman, the head of Doña Dora's kitchen staff.

The meal was an outstanding success and the composer was inspired to pen a brief composition in Miss Faris's autograph book titled "A Fugue without End." The composer wrote beneath the piece that it was a "feijoada set to music for Noemia to remember Villa-Lobos." The composition was in four parts as any good feijoada should be. They were "Farina," "Meat," "Rice," and "Black Beans."

A feijoada pronounced fay-ZHWAH-dah, is a most interesting meal, not too difficult to prepare and an excellent idea for autumn and winter entertaining.

Noemia Faris's feijoada consists of black beans; several meats including sun-dried beef, sausage and salt pork; fluffy rice; sweet orange slices; chopped collards; and onions marinated in a powerfully hot French dressing. Roast pork usually accompanies the beans. Each of the foods is served from separate dishes to dinner plates and all is sprinkled liberally with an uncooked farina the Brazilans call farinha de mandioca.

The linguiça defumada (sausage), carne sêca (dried meat) and black beans can be obtained from many Spanish markets.

FEIJOADA

6 SERVINGS

3 cups dried black beans
1 pound carne sêca (sun-dried salted beef)
2 pounds raw smoked tongue
½ pound linguiça defumada (Portuguese
    sausage)
½ pound chuck beef
½ pound salt pork
Salt and freshly ground pepper to taste
2 large garlic cloves, chopped
2 teaspoons vegetable oil
Braised pork loin (opposite)
Collards (opposite)
Onions in sauce (page 342)
Long-grain rice
Shortening
Vinegar

1 Wash the beans well and soak them overnight in water to cover. Soak the dried beef separately in water to cover. Drain the beans. Add 6 cups water and cook, covered, adding water as needed, until the beans are tender, or about 2½ hours. As soon as the beans are cooking, begin adding the other ingredients.

2 Cut the carne sêca into 1½-inch squares and add to the beans.

3 Peel the tongue and cut it into large cubes. Cover with water and bring to a boil. Simmer 2 minutes, drain and add to beans.

4 Prick the sausages with a fork, cover with water, boil a few minutes, drain and add to the beans.

5 Cut the chuck in half and add to the beans.

6 Cut the salt pork into ½-inch slices and add to the beans. Season the stew with salt and pepper.

7 When the beans are tender, brown the garlic lightly in the oil. Add about 1 cup of the beans, mash and return to the large pot of beans. Adjust the seasonings.

8 Remove the pieces of meat to a hot platter and turn the beans into a chafing dish or bowl. Serve with braised pork loin, collards, onions in sauce, sweeteend orange slices and hot rice. Cook the rice according to package directions, adding 1½ tablespoons shortening and ½ teaspoon vinegar for each 2 cups uncooked, long-grain rice.

BRAISED PORK LOIN FOR A FEIJOADA
6 SERVINGS

1 (4-pound) pork loin (10-inch cut)
1 lemon
1 garlic clove
Tabasco sauce to taste
Salt to taste
¼ cup vegetable oil
1 bay leaf

1 Have the butcher bone the loin and reserve the bone rack. Rub the meat with lemon juice, garlic, Tabasco and salt.

2 Brown the loin in the oil, turning to brown on all sides. Replace meat in bone rack and stand in a Dutch oven.

3 Add the bay leaf and a little water to the pot, cover and braise until tender, or about 1¼ hours.

COLLARDS FOR A FEIJOADA
6 SERVINGS

1 tablespoon chopped onions
2 tablespoons vegetable oil
1½ pounds collards, finely shredded
Salt to taste

1 Sauté the onions in the oil until they begin to brown.

2 Add the collards and salt and cook over low heat, stirring frequently, until the collards are tender, or about 15 minutes.

Continued

ONIONS IN SAUCE FOR A FEIJOADA
6 SERVINGS

1 large onion, sliced thin
3 tablespoons Tabasco sauce
3 tablespoons olive oil
2 tablespoons vinegar
¼ teaspoon salt

1 Cover the onions with boiling water, drain and rinse in cold water. Drain well.

2 Add the remaining ingredients and let stand at room temperature 30 minutes or longer.

PORK SATAY

This Indonesian masterpiece may be cooked over charcoal or under a broiler flame. The marinade is made with ground Brazil nuts.

4 SERVINGS

8 shelled Brazil nuts
1 garlic clove, finely chopped
¼ cup light soy sauce
3 tablespoons lemon juice
2 tablespoons ground coriander
2 tablespoons finely chopped onions
1 tablespoon brown sugar
1 teaspoon salt
¼ teaspoon freshly ground pepper
⅛ teaspoon cayenne
1½ pounds lean pork
Olive oil or melted butter

1 Grind the Brazil nuts very fine, using a food mill, mortar and pestle or blender. Mix with the remaining ingredients except the pork and olive oil.

2 Cut the pork into 1½-inch cubes and add to the marinade. Mix well and let stand 2 or 3 hours.

3 String the meat on skewers and broil slowly over a charcoal fire or under a broiler flame, turning to brown on all sides. Cook 20 to 25 minutes, or until meat is well done. While cooking, baste often with olive oil or butter. Serve hot.

MALAYAN PORK

1 pound boneless pork loin
Salt and freshly ground pepper to taste
1 cup coconut milk (page 147)
2 teaspoons brown sugar
Satay sauce (see following recipe)

1 Cut the pork into bite-size cubes. Sprinkle with salt and pepper. Thread on skewers and marinate in coconut milk at least 1 hour.

2 Drain, sprinkle with sugar and barbecue or broil 15 to 20 minutes, turning frequently and basting often with coconut milk. Serve with satay sauce.

SATAY SAUCE
2½ CUPS

1 garlic clove
1 small onion, chopped
1 cup water, approximately
1 cup shelled peanuts
3 dried hot chili peppers, or ½ teaspoon
   hot red pepper flakes
2 pieces preserved or candied ginger
1 tablespoon light soy sauce
1 teaspoon turmeric
½ teaspoon salt
Juice of ½ lemon

1 Put all the ingredients in a food processor and blend 30 seconds.

2 Pour the sauce into the top part of a double boiler, place over direct heat and bring to a boil, stirring. Place over boiling water and cook 30 minutes, stirring occasionally. Thin to desired consistency with more water or with coconut milk.

Marinated Pork Strips, page 51.

PORK WITH WATERCRESS

4 large bunches watercress
¼ cup peanut oil
1 small garlic clove, chopped
1 pound pork shoulder, cut into thin slices
3 tablespoons light soy sauce

1 Wash the watercress well and drain. Cut off the bottoms of the stems. Soak in cold salted water to cover 30 minutes. Drain, rinse in fresh water and dry gently.

2 In a skillet heat the oil, add the garlic and pork and brown the meat quickly on all sides.

3 Add the soy sauce and watercress. Cook, stirring, until the mixture reaches a boil. Cover and cook 2 minutes longer. Serve immediately.

SPICY PORK
AND BEAN CURD

8 SERVINGS

6 (½-pound) pads soft bean curd
2 tablespoons Sichuan peppercorns
1 pound ground pork
2 tablespoons chili paste with garlic
2 tablespoons dark soy sauce
2 teaspoons sugar
½ cup vegetable oil
¼ cup finely diced fresh ginger
¼ cup minced garlic
1 cup chicken stock
⅔ cup minced scallions, green part only
2 tablespoons cornstarch
¼ cup water
2 tablespoons sesame oil
Fresh coriander for garnish

1   Soak the bean curd pads in boiling water for 3 minutes, then drain and cut into ½-inch pieces.

2   Place the peppercorns in a small skillet and cook over moderate heat, stirring and shaking the skillet until they are roasted, then put them into the container of a spice grinder or blender and blend until fine. Measure out 2 teaspoons and set aside. (The remainder may be kept indefinitely in a covered container.)

3   Blend together the pork, chili paste, soy sauce and sugar.

4   Heat the oil in a wok or skillet and add the pork mixture. Cook, stirring to separate the grains of the meat, about 30 seconds. Add the ginger and garlic and cook briefly. Add the chicken stock and cook about 1 minute.

5   Add the bean curd pieces and stir gently, because they break easily. Cook just to heat through, about 2 minutes. Add the peppercorn powder and scallions.

Blend the cornstarch and water and add it, stirring gently. (No matter how gently you stir, the bean curd will inevitably break up to some degree.) When the dish is thickened, transfer it to a serving dish and sprinkle with the sesame oil. Garnish with fresh coriander.

♦

CHINESE BARBECUED
SPARERIBS

6 SERVINGS

2 racks of spareribs
2 garlic cloves, crushed
2 tablespoons catsup
2 tablespoons soy sauce
2 tablespoons hoisin sauce
2 tablespoons dry sherry
1 tablespoon grated fresh ginger
1 tablespoon honey

1   Preheat the oven to 300°F.

2   Cut the spareribs into individual ribs and arrange them on a rack in a baking pan. Bake for 45 minutes.

3   Combine the remaining ingredients and brush the spareribs lightly with the mixture. Bake for 30 minutes longer and turn the spareribs. Brush with more sauce and bake for 30 minutes longer, or until ribs are nicely browned.

BARBECUED SPARERIBS WITH BEER AND HONEY

8 SERVINGS

8 pounds spareribs, cut into serving pieces
3 cups beer
1 cup honey
2 tablespoons lemon juice
2 teaspoons chili powder
2 teaspoons sage
1½ teaspoons dry mustard
1 teaspoon salt

1 Place the ribs in a large shallow pan. Mix the remaining ingredients and pour over the ribs. Let stand in the refrigerator 24 hours, turning at least once.

2 Remove the ribs from the marinade. Reserve the liquid. Weave the spareribs on a spit or long skewers or place flat on the rack of a hot charcoal grill or broiler, about 4 inches from the heat. Cook, turning frequently and brushing with the marinade, until brown, about 1¼ hours. Or bake in a preheated 350°F oven about 1½ hours, or until ribs are brown and glazed, basting frequently.

Spareribs and Gingered Plum Sauce, page 52.

SPARERIBS AND KRAUT

3 OR 4 SERVINGS

3 pounds spareribs
3 to 4 cups sauerkraut
1 tart apple, peeled, cored and sliced
1 teaspoon caraway seed

1 Cut the spareribs into individual portions and brown in a heavy pan. Add the juice from the sauerkraut and enough water barely to cover. Simmer, covered, about 45 minutes.

2 Add the sauerkraut, pushing it down into the liquid in the pan.

3 Add the apple and caraway seed and cook 30 minutes to 1 hour longer. The liquid should evaporate during cooking.

Note: If desired, this dish may be baked in a 350°F oven.

PIERRE FRANEY'S CHOUCROUTE GARNIE

When winter is without and the appetite rages within, there are few things more gratifying to the taste buds than the aromatic flavor of sauerkraut. The most famous sauerkraut dish is *choucroute garnie*, or "garnished sauerkraut." Almost any smoky meat product can be used in this dish. A characteristic seasoning is juniper berries, and a dry white Alsatian wine is often used as the cooking liquid. It is customary to accompany the dish with various kinds of mustards, including the mustards of Düsseldorf or Dijon, tarragon-flavored mustards, hot mustards made with a paste of dry mustard and water or beer, and mild mustards.

ABOUT 8 SERVINGS

---

3 to 3½ pounds sauerkraut
12 thin slices of fat back (available at pork
    stores and many meat markets)
1 bottle dry white wine
½ teaspoon ground cumin
2 cups chicken stock
2 small onions, each stuck with 4 cloves
2 large carrots, trimmed and scraped
1 bay leaf
12 juniper berries
12 peppercorns
Pinch of thyme
1 garlic clove
2 pounds smoked pork shoulder butt
1 pound lean bacon, in 1 piece, with rind
    removed
1 garlic sausage
8 frankfurters

1 Preheat the oven to 325°F.

2 Drain the sauerkraut and empty it into a basin of cold water. Rinse well and squeeze dry. Pull the sauerkraut apart to loosen any lumps.

3 Line a large kettle with fat back and add the sauerkraut. Add the wine, cumin, stock, onions and carrots. Tie the bay leaf, juniper berries, peppercorns, thyme and garlic in a small cheesecloth bag. Add it to the kettle. Bring the sauerkraut to a boil, cover, and place the kettle in the oven. Simmer for about 3 hours.

4 Meanwhile, put the pork butt and bacon in a large saucepan. Add cold water to cover, bring to a boil and cover. Simmer for 30 minutes. Add the pork butt and bacon to the sauerkraut for the last 2 hours of cooking.

5 Add the sausage to the sauerkraut for the last hour of cooking and then the frankfurters for the last 30 minutes.

6 Remove the onions and cheesecloth bag from the sauerkraut and discard them. Spoon the sauerkraut onto a hot serving platter and garnish with sliced pork butt, sliced bacon, sliced garlic sausage and frankfurters. Slice the carrots and use as a garnish.

Variations

Many combinations of meats may be used in the preparation of this dish.

PIG'S KNUCKLES

Cook on the sauerkraut 3 hours.

KNOCKWURST

Add for the last 45 minutes of cooking.

COOKED HAM SLICES

Heat through in a little white wine.

PIG'S KNUCKLES WITH SAUERKRAUT

6 pig's knuckles
2 quarts sauerkraut
1 tablespoon caraway seed
Dry white wine or water
1 onion studded with 2 cloves
12 medium potatoes, peeled
6 to 12 frankfurters (optional)

1 Scrub the pig's knuckles thoroughly and drain. Place, with alternate layers of sauerkraut, in a large heavy kettle. Sprinkle throughout with the caraway seed.

2 Add enough white wine to cover. Insert the onion, cover and simmer gently until the kunckles are tender, 3 to 4 hours.

3 One-half hour before the knuckles are done, add the potatoes. Replace the cover and continue cooking until done. If desired, add frankfurters to the kettle 5 minutes before the knuckles are done.

GRILLED PIG'S FEET

4 pig's feet
1½ quarts water
1 carrot, sliced
1 onion, sliced
1 garlic clove
1 thyme sprig, or a pinch of dried
2 parsley sprigs
1 bay leaf
3 or 4 cloves
1 teaspoon salt
6 peppercorns
2 tablespoons butter, melted
Fine dry bread crumbs

1 Have the butcher prepare the pig's feet for cooking. Wash them well.

2 Prepare a stock with the water, the carrot, onion, garlic, thyme, parsley, bay leaf, cloves, salt and peppercorns. Bring to a boil and simmer ½ hour.

3 To keep the skin on the pig's feet from breaking, tie each foot tightly in cheesecloth before cooking. Add the pig's feet to the stock and let simmer until very tender, 4 to 5 hours. Cool in the liquid and, when cooled, drain. (Reserve and freeze broth for soups.) Remove the cheesecloth.

4 Brush the pig's feet with melted butter and roll in crumbs. Broil slowly until golden brown on all sides or roast in a 450°F oven until brown. Serve with strong mustard.

ROAST SUCKLING PIG

8 TO 12 SERVINGS

1 (10- to 15-pound) pig
1 tablespoon salt
1 teaspoon freshly ground pepper
¾ teaspoon thyme
Fruit-almond stuffing (see following recipe)
1 potato
2 teaspoons dry mustard
3 tablespoons water

1 Preheat the oven to 350°F.

2 Wash the pig thoroughly under cold running water and dry inside and out with paper toweling. Mix the salt, pepper and thyme and rub the mixture over the inside of the pig. Fill the cavity with the stuffing and run skewers through both sides of opening, lacing it with string to close. Place a raw potato or a tightly packed ball of foil the size of an apple in the pig's mouth. Cover the ears with small pieces of brown paper.

3 Place a piece of heavy-duty foil about 12 inches longer than the pig on a rack placed diagonally in an open roasting pan. Place the pig on the foil with the back legs forward. Turn the foil up loosely around the pig.

4 Place in the oven and roast 3½ to 4 hours, or about 18 minutes per pound. About 15 minutes before the pig is done, mix the mustard with the water and brush over the skin.

5 Transfer the pig to a hot platter and remove the skewers, lacings and covering on the ears. Replace the foil in the mouth with a small apple. Place cranberries or cherries in the eyes and parsley in or around the ears.

6 Pour the drippings in the foil into a saucepan and skim off the fat. Reheat and serve as a sauce.

7 For carving purposes, place the platter before the host with the head to his left.

Note: The pig's bones should separate easily at the joints. There is more meat on the shoulders than on the hind legs. Cut along the backbone to remove the chops.

FRUIT-ALMOND STUFFING FOR SUCKLING PIG

1 pound almonds
1½ pounds prunes
10 large apples
4 tablespoons butter
Salt and freshly ground pepper to taste

1 Drop the almonds in boiling water and let stand until the skins slip off easily. Drain, remove the skins and shred the almonds lengthwise.

2 Cook the prunes in water to cover until just tender. Drain and pit.

3 Peel, core and slice the apples. Cook in the butter over moderately high heat until half tender. Mix the apples, almonds, prunes, salt and pepper.

TOURTIÈRE
PORK PIE

The French-Canadian pork and spice pie is known as *tourtière*.

6 SERVINGS

1 pound ground lean pork (shoulder or leg)
1 teaspoon salt
¼ teaspoon freshly ground pepper
¼ teaspoon grated nutmeg
⅛ teaspoon mace
1½ teaspoons cornstarch
1 cup water
1 small onion, minced
1 garlic clove, minced
1 tablespoon vegetable oil
Pastry for a 2-crust (8-inch) pie

1 In a saucepan combine pork, seasonings, cornstarch and water. Cover and simmer 30 minutes. Uncover and cook 10 minutes more.

2 Sauté the onion and garlic in the oil until soft. Combine with the pork mixture.

3 Preheat the oven to 425°F.

4 Line an 8-inch pie plate with pastry; pour in the mixture and cover with remaining pastry. Press edges together and prick top to allow steam to escape.

5 Bake the pie 10 minutes, reduce heat to 350°F and bake 30 minutes longer. Serve hot.

FRICADELLER

These Danish pork balls appear on many Scandinavian buffets.

24 TO 36 PORK BALLS

2 pounds lean pork, ground
½ cup flour
1 egg
1 small onion, grated
Salt and freshly ground pepper to taste
¾ cup club soda, or plain water
2 tablespoons butter

1 In a mixing bowl combine the ground pork with the flour, egg, onion, salt and pepper. Work with a fork until the ingredients are well blended.

2 Stir in the club soda, a little at a time, and shape the meat mixture into small balls or patties.

3 Melt butter in a skillet. Brown the balls on all sides in the butter, turning gently with a fork or a spatula. Continue to cook over low heat, uncovered, until the pork is cooked through.

Pork Balls with Ginger, page 51.
Carnitas (Mexican Pork Crisps), page 50.

PHILADELPHIA SCRAPPLE

Scrapple, a Pennsylvania Dutch specialty, is traditionally made with pork trimmings of whatever nature. It can be a genuine culinary tour de force.

12 SERVINGS

4 large pig's knuckles, or 3½ pounds meaty spareribs
½ pound lean pork
3 quarts water
Salt to taste
1 dried hot red pepper
½ pound fresh chicken livers, picked over and cut into quarters
½ teaspoon freshly ground pepper
1 teaspoon sage, rubbed fine
2¾ cups cornmeal, preferably stone ground, available in health food stores

1 Combine the pig's knuckles, lean pork, water, salt and red pepper in a kettle and bring to the boil. Cook, covered, about 2½ hours. Add the chicken livers and continue cooking about 20 minutes, or until meat of the knuckles is almost falling off the bone. Drain and reserve knuckles, lean pork, liver and broth.

2 Remove the meat from the bone. Combine the meat and chicken liver pieces and discard the bones and any bits of gristle. Grind the meat and livers or put them into the container of a food processor and add 1 cup of reserved broth. Blend thoroughly.

3 Put 7 cups of the reserved broth in a kettle and add the meat, pepper and sage. Bring to the boil.

4 Put the cornmeal in a mixing bowl and add 3 cups of cold broth, stirring rapidly with a wire whisk. Blend thoroughly and add this to the boiling broth and meat mixture. Cook over low heat, preferably using a metal ring such as a Flame Tamer, 30 minutes, stirring often from the bottom to prevent sticking.

5 Pour and scrape the mixture into 2 standard-size (9 × 5 × 3-inch) loaf pans. Let stand until cool. Refrigerate until ready to serve.

6 Unmold and cut into thin crosswise slices. Cook the slices in a small amount of oil or, if using a nonstick skillet, use no fat at all.

◆

KNOCKWURST IN BEER

8 SERVINGS

8 knockwurst
1 pint beer
2 tablespoons vinegar
1 to 2 teaspoons sugar

1 Simmer the knockwurst in the beer very slowly 15 minutes. Remove to a heated shallow baking dish.

2 Reduce the beer to ⅓ cup, by rapid boiling, and stir in the vinegar and sugar. Pour over the knockwurst and broil briefly, turning to brown on all sides.

Sausage casings, available in specialty pork stores, are normally preserved in salt. When ready to use, put them in a basin of cold water and let stand. Drain and return to the basin of cold water. Lift up one end of a casing and blow into it. It will expand, balloonlike. This is how you determine if the casings have holes in them.

•

BASIC SAUSAGE RECIPE

There are several good commercial pork sausages on the market. None, however, can compare with homemade versions.

ABOUT 9 POUNDS

9 pounds fresh lean pork
3 tablespoons salt
1½ tablespoons freshly ground pepper
1½ tablespoons sage
¾ teaspoon cayenne
6 yards sausage casing

1 Cut the meat into cubes and grind, using the fine knife of the meat grinder. Sprinkle the seasonings over the ground meat and mix well.

2 Remove the cutting blade from the grinder and attach the sausage stuffer. Using a yard of casing at a time, work all but a few inches of casing onto the sausage stuffer. Tie a knot at the end of the casing.

3 Refeed the meat through the grinder and into the casing. Twist into links.

Note: This sausage should be kept refrigerated because it is perishable.

Leek and Sausage Pie, page 108.

CREOLE PORK SAUSAGE

ABOUT 7 POUNDS

7 pounds fresh pork
2 large onions, chopped
1 garlic clove, crushed
2 tablespoons salt
2 teaspoons freshly ground pepper
1 teaspoon crushed chili pepper
½ teaspoon paprika
½ teaspoon cayenne
½ teaspoon allspice
¼ teaspoon powdered bay leaf
3 parsley sprigs, chopped
5 yards sausage casing

1 Grind the pork, using the coarse knife of a meat grinder. Add the onions and garlic and regrind. Add the seasonings and mix thoroughly.

2 Remove the cutting blades from the grinder and attach the sausage stuffer. Attach casing as in basic sausage recipe (opposite). Refeed the mixture into the grinder and through the sausage stuffer.

CHORIZO
SPANISH HOT SAUSAGE

ABOUT 2 POUNDS

---

2 pounds lean pork
3 garlic cloves, crushed
2 small hot red peppers, minced, or
   ½ teaspoon hot red pepper flakes
¼ cup vinegar
2 tablespoons chili powder
2 teaspoons salt
1 teaspoon oregano
1 teaspoon freshly ground pepper
¼ teaspoon ground cumin
1 yard sausage casing

  1 Grind the pork, using the coarse blade of the meat grinder. Add the remaining ingredients and mix thoroughly. Attach casing as in basic sausage recipe (page 351).
  2 Force the mixture through the sausage stuffer into casings and twist into links. If desired, hang the links in a cool place to dry. The dried sausage may be kept for several weeks. Cook as you would fresh sausage.

ITALIAN PEPPER SAUSAGE

ABOUT 6 POUNDS

4½ pounds lean pork
1½ pounds fat pork (fresh pork siding)
1 medium onion, chopped
1 large garlic clove, minced
3 tablespoons salt
2 tablespoons hot red pepper flakes
1½ tablespoons freshly ground pepper
2 teaspoons fennel seed
1½ teaspoons paprika
½ teaspoon crushed bay leaf
¼ teaspoon thyme
Pinch of coriander
⅔ cup red wine or water
2½ yards sausage casing

  1 Grind the lean and fat pork, onion and garlic. Add the seasonings and mix thoroughly. Add the wine and mix well.
  2 Force through a sausage stuffer into casing as in basic sausage recipe (page 351).

Ham

BAKED GLAZED HAM

ALLOW ½ POUND PER SERVING

1 uncooked tenderized ham
Whole cloves
1 cup brown sugar, packed
2 teaspoons dry mustard

1 Preheat the oven to 300°F.
2 Place the ham under cold running water and scrub the rind well with a stiff brush.
3 Dry the ham and place it in a roasting pan with the skin and fat side up. Insert meat thermometer through fat side into the thickest part of the ham.
4 Bake the ham, uncovered, 18 to 20 minutes a pound, or until it registers 160°F on a meat thermometer. Hams weighing 15 pounds or more need only be baked about 15 minutes a pound.
5 When the ham is done, remove it from the oven and, using ordinary kitchen shears or a sharp knife, cut off the rind. Score the fat diagonally about ⅛ inch deep to make a diamond pattern. Stud the corners of the diamond pattern with cloves. Combine brown sugar with dry mustard and a little of the ham fat from the roasting pan. Spread this mixture over the top of the ham.
6 Increase the oven heat to 425°F and return the ham to the oven. Bake until the sugar forms a glaze, about 15 minutes.

BAKED HAM IN BEER

25 SERVINGS

1 (13-pound) canned ham
¾ cup raisins
Whole cloves
2 teaspoons dry mustard
½ cup molasses
1 pint beer
2½ tablespoons cornstarch
2 tablespoons wine vinegar

1 Preheat the oven to 350°F.
2 Remove the top of the ham can and heat the ham in the oven until the gelatin softens. Invert the ham on a rack in a pan, punch holes in the bottom of the can and lift it off. Pour off the can liquid.
3 Cover the raisins with warm water.
4 Score the ham in diamonds and stud with cloves. Mix the mustard and molasses and spread on the ham. Bake 1 hour, basting with the beer.
5 Transfer the ham to a platter and boil the drippings until reduced to 1½ cups. Drain the water from the raisins into a measuring cup and add more water to make 1 cup. Add to the drippings and bring to a boil.
6 Mix the cornstarch with ⅓ cup water, add to the boiling broth and boil, stirring, 1 minute. Add the vinegar and raisins and serve the sauce with the ham.

BAKED COUNTRY HAM

ALLOW ½ POUND PER SERVING

Scrape mold and pepper from the surface of a country-cured Smithfield or Virginia ham. Wash well with baking soda, soap and hot water and rinse thoroughly. Soak the ham overnight in water to cover and then drain.

Place ham in a deep kettle. Add water to cover, bring to a boil and simmer until tender, about 20 minutes per pound. Cool in the water.

Remove the skin and excess fat. Score the remaining fat, stud with cloves and glaze with brown sugar or honey (see instructions for baked glazed ham, page 353). Bake in a preheated 425°F oven, basting with the pan drippings, until well glazed, about 15 minutes.

COUNTRY-FRIED HAM

Cut ham slices about ¼ inch thick and place in a heavy cold skillet. Cook over moderate heat, turning often, until the ham is brown and the fat is crisp.

If the ham is very salty, first simmer briefly in water to cover, turning frequently. Pour off the water and fry as directed.

Serve with red-eye gravy (see below), grits and hot biscuits.

RED-EYE GRAVY

Drain off the excess fat in the pan after the ham is removed. To the drippings left in the pan add a little water and 1 tablespoon of strong coffee. Bring to a boil and serve hot.

BOILED HAM

Place a whole, scrubbed ham in a kettle or other container large enough to hold it and add water to cover. Bring to a boil and lower the heat until the water barely simmers. Cook 15 to 20 minutes to the pound. The broth in which the meat has cooked may be used in dried bean soups or casseroles.

SLICED HAM WITH ASPARAGUS SPEARS AND EGG SAUCE

6 SERVINGS

6 tablespoons butter
6 tablespoons flour
2 cups milk, or half-and-half
Salt and freshly ground pepper to taste
¼ cup grated Parmesan cheese
3 hard-cooked eggs, sliced
6 slices baked ham
12 toast triangles
30 asparagus spears, trimmed and cooked

1 Melt the butter in a saucepan, add the flour and stir with a wire whisk until blended. Meanwhile, bring the milk to a boil and add all at once to the butter-flour mixture, stirring vigorously with the whisk. When thickened, reduce the heat and simmer 1 minute. Season to taste with salt and pepper, turn off the heat and add the cheese, stirring until smooth. Gently stir in the egg slices to complete the sauce.

2 Sauté the ham slices in a little butter until heated through. Place on toast triangles and top each slice with 5 freshly cooked and drained asparagus spears.

3 Spoon the egg sauce over the asparagus spears and serve immediately.

Ham Mousse, page 120.
Zucchini Stuffed with Ham, page 438.
Rice and Ham Vinaigrette, page 472.

Specialty Cuts

BRAINS IN BLACK BUTTER

6 SERVINGS

3 veal brains
1 cup beef stock
1 carrot, sliced
¼ cup sliced celery
1 onion, halved
1 bay leaf
¼ teaspoon thyme
¼ pound butter
1 teaspoon cider vinegar
1 tablespoon capers

1 Soak the brains in water to cover with 2 teaspoons salt for 15 minutes. Remove the covering membrane and veins.

2 Drop the brains into boiling stock and add the carrot, celery, onion, bay leaf and thyme. Reduce heat and simmer, covered, for 30 minutes.

3 Remove the brains, slice and place on a hot serving dish. Brown the butter, add the vinegar and capers and pour over the brains.

STEAK AND KIDNEY PIE

6 SERVINGS

1¾ teaspoons salt
4¼ cups flour, approximately
3 medium eggs, lightly beaten
½ cup milk
½ pound butter
2 pounds round steak, cut ½ inch thick
½ pound beef kidney
½ teaspoon freshly ground pepper

1 Mix ¼ teaspoon of the salt with 4 cups of the flour. Mix the eggs with the milk and reserve about 4 tablespoons for a glaze. Add the milk mixture to the flour and stir together to form a stiff dough. Knead until smooth.

2 Roll into a thin sheet and dot with 4 tablespoons of butter. Sift a light dusting of flour over the butter. Fold the corners of the dough to the center, fold in half, pound to flatten and roll into a sheet. Repeat process until all the butter has been folded in. Chill between each rolling if the butter softens. When all the butter has been used, chill the dough.

3 Preheat the oven to 425°F.

4 While the pastry is chilling, cut the steak into 3-inch squares and pound lightly. Place a piece of kidney on each slice of beef and roll jelly-roll fashion. Mix 1 tablespoon flour, 1½ teaspoons salt and the pepper and sprinkle over the rolls. Stand the rolls on end in a shallow 6- to 8-cup casserole.

5 Roll the chilled pastry to about ¼-inch thickness and cut out a shape that is 1 inch larger than the top of the casserole. Cut a 1-inch hole in the center of the pastry. Cut 6 small "leaves" from scraps of pastry and use the balance of the pastry scraps to line the rim of the casserole.

Place top on pie loosely, moisten the rim and seal the edge. Brush bottoms of leaves with the diluted reserved egg and arrange the leaves as a trim on top of pie. Brush whole of top with the egg.

6 Bake at 425°F 12 minutes, then lower the heat to 325°F; bake 2 hours longer.

◆

BEEF KIDNEY STEW

2 TO 4 SERVINGS

1 beef kidney
3 tablespoons wine vinegar
Salt and freshly ground pepper to taste
Flour for dredging
4 tablespoons butter
3 tablespoons olive or peanut oil
1 garlic clove, finely chopped
½ cup chopped onions
½ teaspoon rosemary
½ teaspoon thyme
1 bay leaf
½ cup dry red wine
½ cup beef stock

1 Remove all membranes from the kidney and place it in a small mixing bowl. Add water barely to cover and the vinegar. Let stand 2 hours.

2 Drain the kidney and wipe it dry. Cut into thin slices and sprinkle with salt and pepper. Dredge lightly in flour and brown quickly on all sides in hot butter and oil.

3 Add the garlic, onions and herbs and cook 5 minutes. Add the wine and beef stock and simmer 15 minutes longer. Serve with boiled potatoes.

ROGNONS DE VEAU EN CASSEROLE

4 SERVINGS

7 tablespoons butter
3 veal kidneys, trimmed
1 tablespoon minced shallots
½ cup dry white wine
1 tablespoon lemon juice
1½ tablespoons prepared mustard,
    preferably Dijon
½ cup beef gravy
Salt and freshly ground pepper to taste
3 tablespoons minced parsley

1 Heat 4 tablespoons of the butter in a flameproof casserole. Sauté the kidneys in the butter for about 10 minutes, turning them occasionally. Remove them to a hot plate.

2 Add the shallots to the pan in which the kidneys were cooked. Cook the shallots for 1 minute. Add the wine and lemon juice. Bring to a boil, scraping the drippings, and cook until the liquids have been reduced to ¼ cup. Remove the pan from the heat.

3 Mix the mustard with remaining butter and add by teaspoons to the reduced liquid, stirring. Add the beef gravy and salt and pepper.

4 Cut the sautéed kidneys into very thin crosswise slices. Sprinkle them lightly with additional salt and pepper and add them, with their juices, to the pan. Cook over low heat for 1 or 2 minutes to warm them, without allowing the sauce to boil. Shake the pan occasionally. Sprinkle with the parsley and serve in the casserole.

SAUTÉED CALF'S LIVER

6 SERVINGS

6 slices calf's liver, trimmed
Flour
Salt and freshly ground pepper to taste
3 tablespoons butter

1 Dredge the liver in flour seasoned with salt and pepper and sauté in the butter over medium heat until golden brown on both sides. Reduce the heat and cook to the desired degree of doneness. (Two minutes on each side will produce rare meat; 6 will produce well done.)

2 Transfer the liver to a heated platter and serve immediately.

Variations

FLAMED CALF'S LIVER

Sauté liver as above. After cooking, sprinkle with ¼ cup cognac and ignite. Transfer the liver to a heated platter and pour the pan juices over it.

CALF'S LIVER WITH ONIONS

Sauté 1 cup chopped onions in the butter until soft, then add the liver and sauté.

CALF'S LIVER WITH BACON

Cook 12 slices bacon until crisp. Drain and serve on top of the sautéed liver.

FEGATO ALLA VENEZIANA
SAUTÉED LIVER STRIPS WITH ONIONS

4 SERVINGS

3 tablespoons olive oil
2 cups thinly sliced onions
1½ pounds calf's liver, thinly sliced
Salt and freshly ground pepper to taste

1 Heat the oil in a large heavy skillet and add the onions. Cover and cook over low heat for about 30 minutes, until very soft and golden, not brown.

2 Meanwhile, cut away any tough fibers from the liver. Cut the liver into very thin (julienne) strips.

3 Add the liver strips to the onions and sauté over high heat for just 1 or 2 minutes, until the liver loses its raw look. Season with salt and pepper and serve immediately.

Note: One tablespoon red wine vinegar or dry vermouth may be added to the liver just before serving.

BRAISED LIVER

6 SERVINGS

1½ pounds (½-inch-thick) beef or pork liver
¼ cup flour
1½ teaspoons salt
¼ teaspoon freshly ground pepper
5 tablespoons butter
2 cups thinly sliced carrots
1 cup finely chopped onions
1 medium green pepper, diced
¼ cup beef stock

1 Cut the liver into serving pieces and dredge the pieces in the flour mixed with the salt and pepper.

2 Brown the liver in the butter in a heavy skillet. Arrange the carrots, onions and green pepper on top of the liver. Add the stock, cover, and cook slowly for 35 minutes, or until tender.

BRAISED SWEETBREADS

6 SERVINGS

3 pairs sweetbreads
1 teaspoon lemon juice
3 tablespoons butter
1 onion, sliced
1 carrot, sliced
1 bay leaf
Pinch of thyme
3 parsley sprigs
1 tablespoon flour
½ cup dry white wine
1 cup chicken stock
Salt and freshly ground pepper to taste
2 tablespoons dry sherry

1 Soak the sweetbreads in ice water 1 hour. Drain and place in boiling water to cover. Add the lemon juice and simmer 10 minutes. Drain and cool immediately in ice water. Remove all the connective and covering tissues.

2 Preheat the oven to 350°F.

3 Melt the butter in a flameproof casserole. Add the onions, carrots, bay leaf, thyme and parsley and cook slowly until the onions are golden.

4 Sprinkle the mixture with the flour, add the sweetbreads, wine, stock, salt and pepper and heat to simmering. Cover and transfer to the oven. Bake 20 minutes. Uncover and bake 10 minutes longer.

5 Transfer the sweetbreads to a platter. Stir the sherry into the liquid in the casserole and strain over the sweetbreads.

SWEETBREADS WITH MADEIRA

6 SERVINGS

3 pairs of sweetbreads
Salt
1 tablespoon vinegar, or lemon juice
18 small white onions, peeled
3 carrots, cut into strips
4 tablespoons butter
3 shallots, chopped
1½ cups brown sauce (page 551)
½ cup Madeira wine
Freshly ground pepper to taste

1 Soak the sweetbreads in ice water for several hours; drain. Bring them to a boil in 1 quart of water with 1 teaspoon salt and the vinegar. Lower the heat and simmer for 4 minutes. Drain and place in cold water. When cool, remove connective tissues and tubes but not the top membrane. Press under a weight for several hours.

2 Preheat the oven to 350°F.

3 Brown the onions and carrots lightly in 2 tablespoons of the butter in a skillet. Turn them into a shallow baking dish. Arrange sweetbreads over the vegetables.

4 In the same skillet, heat the shallots in the remaining butter and add the brown sauce. Add the wine and pour the mixture over the sweetbreads. Season with salt and pepper.

5 Bake for about 1 hour, basting frequently with the liquid in the pan.

SWEETBREADS IN INDIVIDUAL CASSEROLES

4 SERVINGS

3 pairs of sweetbreads
2 tablespoons lemon juice
2 teaspoons salt
1 small onion, minced
1/3 pound mushrooms, sliced
2 tablespoons butter
3 tablespoons flour
1 1/4 cups chicken stock
1/2 cup dry white wine
1/4 cup cream
Salt and freshly ground pepper to taste
Soft fresh bread crumbs
Melted butter

1 Soak the sweetbreads in ice water for 45 minutes; drain. Cover with boiling water containing the lemon juice and salt. Simmer for 15 to 20 minutes.

2 Drain the sweetbreads and cool immediately in ice water. Drain again, and break into small pieces, removing all connective tissues, membranes and tubes.

3 Sauté the onion and mushrooms in the butter until tender. Add the flour and cook over very low heat for a few minutes.

4 Preheat the oven to 500°F.

5 Add stock and wine to the mushrooms. Let the sauce thicken over low heat for 10 minutes. Add the cream and sweetbreads, season with salt and pepper, and continue to cook for another 6 minutes.

6 Spoon the mixture into individual casseroles. Sprinkle with bread crumbs and moisten with melted butter. Bake in the oven until the crumbs are golden brown.

BOILED BEEF TONGUE

ABOUT 8 SERVINGS

1 (4-pound) fresh or smoked beef tongue
1 onion, studded with 3 cloves
1 leek, or an extra onion
1 celery stalk, with leaves
4 parsley sprigs
1 bay leaf
1 tablespoon salt
Few whole black peppercorns

1 Wash the tongue and place it in a large kettle with the remaining ingredients. Add cold water just to cover. Cover tightly, bring to a boil, lower the heat and simmer until tender, about 3 1/2 hours.

2 Let tongue cool in its broth. When cool, remove it and cut off bones and gristle at the thick end of the tongue. Slit the skin from the thick end to the tip on the underside. Use a paring knife to loosen the skin at the thick end, and pull and peel off the skin from the thick end to the tip.

3 Return the tongue to the broth to reheat, if desired; or serve cold.

BRAISED TONGUE

1 (4-pound) fresh beef tongue
½ cup diced carrots
½ cup diced onions
½ cup diced celery
¼ cup diced white turnip
3 tablespoons butter
3 tablespoons flour
Salt and freshly ground pepper to taste
¼ cup chopped sour pickles

1 Wash the tongue, cover with water and simmer for about 2 hours. Drain the tongue and cool it. Reserve the cooking liquid.

2 Preheat the oven to 350°F.

3 Remove the skin, bones, roots and gristle from the tongue and place the meat in a deep casserole. Add the vegetables.

4 Melt the butter and blend in the flour. Stir in 3 cups of the cooking liquid slowly and bring to a boil. Add salt, pepper and the pickles and pour the sauce over the tongue.

5 Bake for 2 hours. Serve on a hot platter with the strained sauce from the casserole.

BRAISED OXTAIL

3 pounds oxtail, disjointed
Flour for dredging
Salt and freshly ground pepper to taste
3 tablespoons vegetable oil
1 cup diced carrots
1 garlic clove, minced
12 small whole white onions, peeled
2 cups dry red wine
1 bay leaf
Pinch of thyme
Beef stock
1 cup chopped mushrooms (optional)
Chopped parsley

1 Preheat the oven to 350°F.

2 Have the oxtail disjointed and roll in flour seasoned with salt and pepper. Brown the meat in the oil in a hot skillet and transfer it to a casserole.

3 Add the carrots, garlic and onions to the pan and brown well. Transfer to the casserole and add the wine and seasonings. Add enough beef stock to barely cover and sprinkle with salt and pepper.

4 Cover and bake 2½ to 3 hours, or until the meat is tender. If desired, sauté the mushrooms in butter and add to the casserole for the last ½ hour of cooking. Serve sprinkled with chopped parsley.

OXTAIL RAGOÛT

8 SERVINGS

4 oxtails, skinned and cut into pieces
4 tablespoons butter
¼ cup vegetable oil
2 cups finely chopped celery
¼ cup finely chopped parsley
2 garlic cloves, minced
1 bay leaf
2 carrots, scraped and chopped
2 tablespoons flour
1 cup beef stock
1 cup dry red wine
3 tablespoons cognac
1 pound ripe tomatoes, peeled, seeded and
    chopped, or 2 cups canned plum tomatoes,
    drained and chopped
Juice of ½ lemon
¼ teaspoon grated nutmeg
1 cup Madeira wine
Freshly ground pepper to taste

1 Preheat the oven to 350°F.
2 Brown the oxtails well in the butter and oil in a large skillet.
3 Line a buttered casserole with the celery and parsley. Add the garlic and bay leaf. Transfer the oxtails to the casserole.
4 Add the carrots to the skillet in which the oxtails cooked. Cook them, stirring, until light brown. Sprinkle with the flour; when it starts to brown, add a little stock. Stir to dissolve brown particles and scrape this mixture into the casserole.
5 Add the remaining stock to the casserole with the red wine, cognac and tomatoes. Cover. Bake for 2½ to 3 hours. Transfer the oxtails to a hot deep serving dish.
6 Strain the gravy but press as much as possible of the cooked vegetables through the sieve. Bring the strained sauce to a boil and add the lemon juice, nutmeg, Madeira and pepper. Simmer for 5 minutes. Pour the sauce over the oxtails and sprinkle them with additional chopped parsley.

◆

TRIPE A LA CREOLE

4 TO 6 SERVINGS

2 pounds honeycomb tripe
1 teaspoon salt
½ teaspoon sugar
2 cups canned tomatoes
1 (10-ounce) can (1¼ cups) tomato purée
1 green pepper, diced
2 medium onions, diced
½ cup chopped celery
1 garlic clove, minced
¼ teaspoon freshly ground pepper
Dash of cayenne
½ cup minced boiled ham
1 pound mushrooms, sliced

1 Wash the tripe several times under running water. Cut it into julienne strips. Place the strips in a large pan and cover with cold water. Bring to a boil and add ½ teaspoon of the salt and the sugar. Cover and simmer for about 3 hours, until the tripe is tender. Drain.
2 Add the tomatoes, tomato purée, green pepper, onions, celery, garlic, remaining salt, the pepper and cayenne to the tripe. Cover and simmer for 20 minutes.
3 Add the ham and mushrooms. Cover and simmer for 15 minutes longer.

Philadelphia Pepper Pot, page 95.

TRIPE A LA MODE DE CAEN

8 TO 10 SERVINGS

4 pounds honeycomb tripe
4 calf's feet
2 large carrots, scraped
1 onion, peeled
1 celery stalk
2 large leeks, split and washed well
Bouquet garni (10 peppercorns, 1 garlic clove,
    1 teaspoon thyme, 1 bay leaf, 1 clove and 2
    parsley sprigs, tied in cheesecloth bag)
Salt and freshly ground pepper to taste
2 large thin slices beef fat (obtained from
    the butcher)
Thick paste made with flour and water
½ cup aged Calvados

1 Heat the oven to 300°F.
2 Wash the tripe carefully in several changes of cold water. Drain and slice the tripe into pieces 2 inches square.
3 In two separate kettles, cover the tripe with cold water and the calf's feet with cold water. Bring each to a boil. Immediately add 2 cups of cold water to each kettle to stop the cooking. Drain.
4 Line a large earthenware casserole or tripe pot with the blanched calf's feet and cover with the tripe. Add the carrots, onion, celery, leeks and bouquet garni. Sprinkle with salt and pepper. Cover with cold water and top with the beef fat. The lid of the casserole or pot should have a small hole to permit escape of steam.
5 Cover the pot with the lid and prepare a thick paste with flour and water. Seal the cover with the paste. Bring to boiling point on top of stove, then place in oven. Bake 12 hours.
6 Break and discard the pastry seal. Uncover and discard the vegetables and bouquet garni. Transfer the tripe to a serving casserole and add the meat from the calf's feet, discarding the bones. Skim the fat from the liquid and season with salt and pepper. Add the Calvados and strain the liquid through a double thickness of cheesecloth over the tripe. Serve piping hot with boiled potatoes on the side.

Game

HASSENPFEFFER

6 TO 8 SERVINGS

4 pounds rabbit, cut into serving pieces
1½ cups mild vinegar
1½ cups water
1 cup red Bordeaux wine
2 cups sliced onions
2 teaspoons salt
1 teaspoon dry mustard
1 teaspoon freshly ground pepper
1 tablespoon mixed pickling spices
8 whole cloves
3 bay leaves
Flour
5 tablespoons butter
1 tablespoon sugar
1 cup sour cream

1 Place the rabbit in a large bowl. Add the vinegar, water, wine, onions, salt, mustard, pepper, pickling spices, cloves and bay leaves. Refrigerate 24 hours or longer, turning the rabbit occasionally.

2 Remove the rabbit, dry the pieces well, dust them lightly with flour and brown in the butter in a heavy saucepan or Dutch oven.

3 Strain the marinade and add to the rabbit. Cover, bring to a boil, lower the heat and simmer until tender, about 40 minutes.

4 Arrange the rabbit on a heated platter. Add the sugar to the broth and correct the seasonings. Blend 6 tablespoons flour with a little water. Stir into the broth and cook, stirring, 1 minute. Just before serving, stir in the sour cream. Reheat but do not let boil. Pour over the rabbit and serve with buttered noodles.

Rabbit or Hare Pâté, page 31.

Venison is considered the most desirable of game and it may be prepared in many ways. The flesh of a very young deer is as tender as beef; young venison steak, for example, is delicious when sautéed briefly in butter and sprinkled with parsley. With older deer, it is better to marinate the meat for several hours or several days in a well-seasoned marinade. This has the effect not only of flavoring the meat but of making it tender as well.

♦

VENISON GOULASH

6 SERVINGS

2 pounds venison (any cut) cut into 1½-inch
   cubes
3 tablespoons flour
3 tablespoons vegetable oil
1 large onion, sliced or chopped fine
2 garlic cloves, chopped
1 quart boiling water or stock
½ cup red wine
1 (6-ounce) can tomato paste
1 tablespoon Hungarian paprika
Salt to taste
1 cup sour cream (optional)

1 Roll the meat in the flour, pressing the flour into the cubes.

2 Heat the oil in a skillet, add the onion and garlic and cook until browned. Add the meat and brown well. Add all the remaining ingredients except the sour cream. Stir well, cover and simmer gently until the meat is tender, 2 to 3 hours, adding more stock, water or wine if necessary.

3 Just before serving, stir in the sour cream. Serve with red cabbage cooked with apples, and buttered noodles, or boiled new potatoes covered with sour cream.

BIGOS
POLISH HUNTER'S STEW

8 SERVINGS

½ ounce dried mushrooms
1 cup boiling water
2½ pounds sauerkraut
3 slices of lean bacon, diced
1 large onion, finely chopped
½ cup chopped parsley
1 tablespoon flour
2 cups canned tomatoes, drained
½ pound kielbasa, cut into ⅛-inch slices
1½ pounds leftover cooked game, cut into
    1½-inch cubes
1 cup leftover meat gravy
Salt and freshly ground pepper to taste
2 teaspoons sugar (optional)
1 cup Madeira wine

1 Wash the mushrooms and pour the boiling water over them. Let stand for 20 minutes.

2 Wash and drain the sauerkraut and place it in a large heavy kettle with a tight-fitting lid. Pour the liquid in which the mushrooms soaked over the sauerkraut. Trim off any tough stems and cut the mushrooms into strips. Add the mushrooms to the sauerkraut and cover. Simmer slowly for 30 minutes.

3 Cook the bacon slightly and add the onion and parsley. Cook until the onion is golden but do not let the bacon become crisp. Add the flour and stir in a little juice from the kettle containing the sauerkraut. Pour the mixture into the sauerkraut and mix well. Add the tomatoes.

4 Fold the meats into the sauerkraut and add the gravy. Add seasonings, the sugar and Madeira. Bring to a boil. Remove from the heat and let stand in a cool place, or refrigerate. Traditionally, this dish is served on the second day, reheated, with boiled potatoes. It may be kept and served several days later.

SAUCE VENAISON

ABOUT 3 CUPS

4 cups chopped bones and trimmings from
    venison or other game
¾ cup chopped carrots
¾ cup chopped onions
½ cup chopped celery
⅓ cup vegetable oil
¼ cup flour
5 cups boiling beef stock
1 cup dry white or red wine
3 tablespoons tomato paste
4 parsley sprigs
1 bay leaf
¼ teaspoon thyme
1 teaspoon peppercorns, coarsely ground,
    or more
½ cup red currant jelly
½ cup cream

1 Brown the bones, trimmings, carrots, onions and celery in the oil in a large skillet. Using a slotted spoon, remove them to a platter and reserve.

2 Add the flour to the skillet and brown it slowly, stirring. If necessary, add more oil. Remove the skillet from the heat and stir in the stock, wine and tomato paste.

3 Pour the sauce into a kettle. Add the browned bones and trimmings. Bring to a boil. Tie the parsley, bay leaf and thyme in a cheesecloth bag and add it to the sauce. Simmer, skimming occasionally to remove fat and foam, for about 3 hours. Strain the sauce through a sieve lined with cheesecloth.

4 Let the sauce cool and skim off all remaining fat. When ready to use, bring the sauce to a boil and add the peppercorns. At this point the sauce is called *poivrade*. Also, at this point the sauce may be frozen. To freeze, simply pour the sauce into airproof plastic bags or other freezer

Continued

containers. Cover or seal, leaving a small amount of air space for expansion and freezing. Defrost the sauce before proceeding.

5 Stir the jelly into the sauce. When it is melted and thoroughly blended, stir in the cream. Heat the sauce to the boiling point and serve with roasted or broiled venison or other game.

♦

VENISON CHOPS WITH MUSHROOMS

4 TO 8 SERVINGS

8 tender venison chops
Salt and freshly ground pepper to taste
¼ pound butter
½ pound mushrooms, thinly sliced
⅓ cup dry white wine
¾ cup brown sauce (page 551)
8 thin slices of ham

1 Sprinkle the venison chops with salt and pepper. Heat half of the butter in a large heavy skillet and brown the chops in it on both sides. Preferably the chops should be served rare, particularly if the venison is tender. Transfer the chops to a warm serving platter.

2 Add 2 more tablespoons of the butter to the skillet and add the mushrooms. Cook, stirring, until mushrooms are wilted. Sprinkle with pepper and add the wine. Stir to dissolve the brown particles clinging to the bottom and sides of the skillet. Stir in the brown sauce and simmer briefly.

3 Meanwhile, heat the ham in the remaining butter. Top each chop with a slice of ham. Pour the sauce over the chops and serve immediately.

ROAST HAUNCH OF VENISON

10 TO 12 SERVINGS

1 (6-pound) haunch of venison
1 bottle claret or Burgundy wine
1 large onion, sliced
1 garlic clove, crushed
1 bay leaf
3 juniper berries
6 strips of fat bacon

1 If the lower part of the leg is used, remove the shank bone from the venison. Place the meat in a large bowl and marinate overnight in the wine with the onion, garlic, bay leaf and juniper berries.

2 Preheat the oven to 450°F.

3 Remove the meat from the marinade and skewer and tie it into a compact shape. Strain and reserve the marinade. Insert a thermometer in the thickest portion of muscle and place the meat on a rack in an open roasting pan. Place the bacon strips on top of the meat.

4 Roast the meat 20 minutes. Reduce the oven temperature to 325°F and cook 15 to 18 minutes per pound to an internal temperature of 140°F for very rare; 150°F for medium well done. While the meat is roasting, baste occasionally with the marinade.

7

Vegetables

STEAMED VEGETABLES

Vegetables steamed with very little water lose a minimum of vitamin and mineral content and consequently retain most of the flavor. This is the method of choice if the vegetable is to be chilled and served with a sauce such as vinaigrette.

Leafy greens such as spinach and kale should be washed thoroughly in several waters, drained and steamed in only the water that clings to the leaves. Asparagus, green and yellow snap beans, broccoli, cauliflower, fennel, leeks, yellow summer squash and zucchini are particularly delicious steamed. Wash and trim the vegetables; asparagus and leeks need careful cleaning to remove any sand. Separate broccoli and cauliflower into flowerets. Very small squash may be cooked whole, and larger squash may be halved, quartered, sliced or cut into uniform cubes. Asparagus, snap beans and leeks should be tied into bundles with soft string.

Put the prepared vegetable in a large skillet or saucepan with a tight-fitting cover; a double-boiler bottom with the top reversed is ideal for whole asparagus stalks. Add ½ to 2 inches (depending on the depth of the vessel) of boiling salted water, enough to fill the pan with steam. Add a little more boiling water during the cooking if the pan becomes dry, but there should be very little water remaining in the pan when the vegetable is done. Steam the vegetable until just tender, for 5 to 8 minutes if the vegetable is cut up, for 8 to 10 minutes if it is whole.

VEGETABLES VINAIGRETTE

Chilled cooked vegetables with vinaigrette sauce make an excellent vegetable dish for summer menus. They can also be served as a salad course or as one of the dishes in a selection of appetizers. Some of the vegetables that are well suited to this preparation are asparagus, celery knobs, leeks, onions, potatoes and spinach *en branche*. Raw mushrooms in vinaigrette sauce make an excellent appetizer as well as a flavorful accompaniment to cold meats.

Vegetables to be served this way should be cooked in boiling salted water, or steamed, until just tender, not mushy, then chilled. Spoon basic vinaigrette (page 576) over them and serve. Or, for a more pronounced flavor, marinate the vegetable in the sauce for 30 minutes or longer before serving.

For salads, arrange the prepared vegetable on a bed of endive or shredded lettuce or on several whole leaves of romaine, raddichio or Boston lettuce.

◆

STEAMED ARTICHOKES

8 SERVINGS

8 large artichokes
Juice of 2 lemons
8 coriander seeds (optional)

1 Trim the tough outer leaves and stalks from the artichokes. Trim the tips of the other leaves with scissors. Rub all cut portions with lemon juice. Drop the vegetables into boiling salted water to cover. Add the coriander seeds and remaining lemon juice.

2 Simmer, covered, until the outer leaves pull off easily, about 40 minutes. Serve hot with melted butter, hollandaise or mousseline sauce; or cold with basic vinaigrette (page 576).

STUFFING ARTICHOKES

1 Wash the artichoke and, using a sharp knife or scissors, cut off the top third of the vegetable.

2 Pull off the tough outside leaves around the base and discard. Using the fingers, open the center leaves carefully. Turn the artichoke over on a chopping board or other flat surface and press down firmly at the base to cause the leaves to spread open farther.

3 Turn the artichoke right side up and pull the yellow and yellow-white leaves from the center.

4 Sprinkle the center, fuzzy portion of the vegetable with lemon juice to keep it from darkening. Using a soup spoon or other substantial spoon, carefully scrape and pull the fuzzy and prickly portion from the heart of the artichoke. It is important that the last bit of this "choke" be removed, because if swallowed it creates an unpleasant sensation in the throat.

5 Sprinkle the smooth, scraped artichoke bottom with additional lemon juice.

6 Using a sharp, heavy knife, cut off the stem of the artichoke flush with the base. The stem may be peeled and cooked and, when it is tender, used in the filling.

7 Stand the artichokes in a deep kettle or saucepan so that they fit snugly together, or tie each with a string so that they will retain their shape.

8 Add salt, lemon juice and boiling water to cover. Cook, covered, 20 to 30 minutes, or until partly tender.

9 Using 2 spoons, remove the artichokes from the water and turn upside down to drain. When partly cool, fill the centers with stuffing and bake as directed.

Note: You may also stuff artichokes between the leaves, eliminating the need for steps 4 and 5.

BEEF-STUFFED ARTICHOKES

6 SERVINGS

6 medium artichokes
1 tablespoon vegetable oil
¾ pound ground beef
½ cup chopped onions
3 tablespoons chopped fresh parsley
1 cup soft bread crumbs
1 egg, beaten
1 teaspoon salt
⅛ teaspoon freshly ground pepper
¼ teaspoon ground ginger
¼ teaspoon oregano
6 slices fresh tomato
2 tablespoons olive oil
2 tablespoons buttered bread crumbs
2 tablespoons lemon juice

1 Prepare the artichokes for stuffing (opposite). Preheat the oven to 350°F.

2 In a skillet heat the oil, add the beef and onions and sauté until brown. Remove from the heat and stir in the parsley, soft crumbs, egg, ½ teaspoon of the salt, the pepper, ginger and oregano. Spoon the filling into the artichoke centers and top with a slice of tomato.

3 Combine the olive oil and remaining salt. Brush the artichokes and tomatoes with the mixture, place in a shallow baking pan and sprinkle with buttered crumbs. Fill the pan with boiling water to the depth of 1 inch and add the lemon juice. Cover closely with foil and bake 1 hour.

SHRIMP-STUFFED ARTICHOKES

4 SERVINGS

4 medium artichokes
1 cup shrimp, cooked, shelled and deveined
1½ cups soft bread crumbs
¼ cup finely chopped onions
½ teaspoon salt
Lemon juice
1 egg, beaten
Olive or vegetable oil

1 Prepare the artichokes for stuffing (page 369). Preheat the oven to 350°F.

2 Cut the shrimp into small pieces and combine with crumbs, onions, salt, 2 teaspoons of lemon juice and the egg. Spoon the mixture into the artichokes.

3 Place the artichokes in a small baking pan and pour boiling water around them to the depth of 1 inch. Add 1 tablespoon lemon juice and brush the artichokes generously with oil. Cover with foil and bake 30 minutes.

Artichokes à la Grecque, page 449.

MARINATED ARTICHOKES

6 SERVINGS

6 small artichokes
2 garlic cloves
1 teaspoon salt
2 cups water
1 celery stalk, with leaves
1 bay leaf
2 parsley sprigs
3 tablespoons olive oil
10 peppercorns
Juice of 1 lemon
Pinch of thyme

1 Trim the artichokes and cut off the sharp points with kitchen shears.

2 Mash the garlic with the salt and place in a kettle with the artichokes and water.

3 Cut the celery stalk into halves and tie it into a neat bundle with the bay leaf and parsley. Add to the kettle along with the remaining ingredients. Bring to a boil and simmer until artichokes are tender, 20 minutes or longer, depending on the size of the artichokes. Let the artichokes cool in the marinade. Discard the celery bundle. Serve artichokes well chilled, each with a little of the marinade.

ARTICHOKE HEARTS VS. ARTICHOKE BOTTOMS Artichoke hearts and artichoke bottoms are not the same. The heart (such as that purchased frozen) consists of a portion of the heart, the "choke" removed, and a few tender leaves. The bottom is precisely that. It is the bottom of the vegetable with all leaves and choke removed.

COOKING ARTICHOKE BOTTOMS

4 SERVINGS

4 large artichokes
1 lemon, halved
2 teaspoons flour
1 teaspoon salt

1 Trim off the tough outer leaves of the artichokes. Using a sharp kitchen knife, slice off the stems of the artichokes. Immediately rub cut surface with the lemon. Neatly slice through the vegetables parallel to the base to leave an artichoke bottom less than 1 inch thick. Immediately rub cut surface with lemon.

2 Squeeze the remaining lemon juice into a saucepan. Add the flour and blend well with a wire whisk to make a paste. Add water, a little at a time, stirring until flour is thinned and well blended. Drop the artichoke bottoms into the pan and add enough water to cover them. Add salt. Bring to a boil, cover, and simmer for 25 minutes or longer, until artichokes are tender. Drain.

3 When the artichokes are cool enough to handle, remove the fuzzy "choke" from the center by pulling and scraping with a spoon. If artichoke bottoms are to be served hot, they may be reheated in hot salted water before serving.

ARTICHOKE BOTTOMS WITH MUSHROOM SAUCE

8 SERVINGS

2 tablespoons butter
2 tablespoons olive oil
1/4 pound mushrooms, diced
Salt and freshly ground pepper to taste
Tarragon to taste
1/2 cup cream
1 egg yolk, lightly beaten
1 tablespoon lemon juice
16 artichoke bottoms, freshly cooked and hot

1 In a skillet heat the butter and oil, add the mushrooms and cook until almost tender. Season with the salt, pepper and tarragon. Stir in the cream, egg yolk and lemon juice. Do not boil, but blend thoroughly over low heat.

2 Arrange the artichoke bottoms on a serving platter and spoon the mushroom sauce over them.

Artichokes Mock Benedict, page 112.

ARTICHOKES CLAMART

8 SERVINGS

8 artichoke bottoms, freshly cooked and hot
1 cup puréed green peas
4 tablespoons butter, melted

1 Preheat the oven to 450°F.
2 Arrange the artichoke bottoms in a buttered shallow baking dish. Spoon a heaping tablespoon of puréed peas into the center of each. Pour the butter over the purée.
3 Bake until artichokes are thoroughly heated and peas are slightly brown on top.

◆

ARTICHOKE HEARTS AND MUSHROOMS ITURBI

6 SERVINGS

2 (9-ounce) packages frozen artichoke hearts
4 tablespoons butter
1 pound mushrooms, sliced
½ cup chicken stock, or half sherry
   and half stock
Salt and freshly ground pepper to taste
Pinch of oregano to taste

1 Defrost the artichoke hearts by heating them with the butter in a skillet over low heat.
2 Add the mushrooms when the artichoke hearts are tender. Add the stock and cook for 10 minutes or less, until the mushrooms are done. Season with salt, pepper and oregano.

*The Jerusalem artichoke is not an artichoke at all, but is actually related to the sunflower, called **girasole** in Italian. Through some slip of nomenclature, **girasole** turned into **Jerusalem**. Recently, as this neglected vegetable has become more popular in this country, it has been called **sunchoke**.*

◆

JERUSALEM ARTICHOKES

4 SERVINGS

1 pound Jerusalem artichokes
Salt to taste
4 tablespoons butter, melted
1 tablespoon finely chopped parsley or chives
Lemon juice to taste

1 Scrub the artichokes and pare them. Drop them in water to cover and add salt. Bring to a boil and simmer 25 to 35 minutes, or until tender.
2 Drain the artichokes and add the melted butter, chopped parsley or chives and lemon juice. Serve in place of boiled potatoes.

ASPARAGUS

Remove the tough ends of the asparagus. Peel the stalks a few inches up from the end toward the tips. Stand the stalks in the lower part of a double boiler or deep kettle. Add boiling salted water to a depth of 2 inches, cover with the upper portion of the boiler or a lid and cook until just tender, 8 to 10 minutes. (If it is more convenient, asparagus may be cooked in a heavy skillet with a tight-fitting cover.) Drain and serve with melted butter or with hollandaise sauce (page 554). Allow 2 pounds for 4 servings.

◆

ASPARAGUS VINAIGRETTE

Pour basic vinaigrette (page 576) over hot or cold cooked asparagus and let stand 1 hour, turning the asparagus once.

ASPARAGUS WITH FRESH TOMATO SAUCE

6 SERVINGS

⅓ cup mayonnaise
1¼ teaspoons lemon juice
¼ teaspoon salt
Pinch of white pepper
⅓ cup diced, peeled tomatoes
3 pounds freshly cooked asparagus

1 For the sauce, combine the mayonnaise, lemon juice, salt and pepper in the top part of a double boiler. Stir over hot, not boiling, water until heated through.

2 Stir in tomatoes and serve over hot, freshly cooked asparagus.

◆

ASPARAGUS WITH BROWN BUTTER SAUCE

4 SERVINGS

4 tablespoons butter
3 tablespoons lemon juice
2 pounds fresh asparagus, steamed
Chopped fresh parsley for garnish

Heat the butter in a small saucepan until it just starts to turn a hazelnut brown. Add the lemon juice and pour the sauce over the hot asparagus. Garnish with chopped parsley.

ASPARAGUS POLONAISE

Vegetables polonaise means that they are sprinkled with buttered bread crumbs and sieved egg.

4 SERVINGS

6 tablespoons butter
¼ cup fine bread crumbs
2 pounds asparagus, steamed
1 hard-cooked egg, sieved
Chopped parsley to garnish

1 In a saucepan melt the butter, add the crumbs and sauté until light brown.
2 Sprinkle the crumbs and butter over hot, freshly cooked asparagus and then sprinkle with the sieved hard-cooked egg and chopped parsley.

♦

ASPARAGUS AU GRATIN

6 SERVINGS

4 tablespoons butter
¼ cup flour
1¾ cups chicken stock
¼ cup half-and-half
¾ cup grated cheddar cheese
¼ cup grated Parmesan cheese
Salt and freshly ground pepper to taste
36 hot, freshly cooked asparagus spears

1 In a saucepan melt the butter, add the flour and stir with a wire whisk until blended. Meanwhile, bring the chicken stock and half-and-half to a boil and add all at once to the butter-flour mixture, stirring vigorously with the whisk until the sauce is thickened and smooth. Add the cheddar, Parmesan, salt and pepper and stir until the cheeses melt.
2 Place alternate layers of sauce and asparagus in a buttered casserole, ending with a layer of sauce. Sprinkle with additional Parmesan cheese and brown quickly under a preheated broiler or bake in a preheated 450°F oven for 5 minutes.

Asparagus Salad, page 451.

♦

ASPARAGUS, MILANESE STYLE

4 SERVINGS

2 pounds fresh asparagus
2 tablespoons butter
¼ teaspoon freshly ground pepper
¼ cup grated Parmesan cheese

1 Preheat the oven to 350°F.
2 Wash the asparagus; remove the hard ends of the stalks and the scales. Place in a saucepan with ½ inch of boiling water. Bring to the boiling point and cook, uncovered, for 5 minutes. Drain.
3 Place a layer of the cooked asparagus in a buttered 1-quart casserole. Dot with butter and sprinkle with pepper. Repeat, using remaining asparagus, butter and pepper. Sprinkle the top with Parmesan cheese. Bake for 5 minutes. Serve hot.

GREEN BEANS

Remove ends and strings from beans. They may be left whole, snapped into 1-inch lengths or French cut into thin, lengthwise strips. Cook, covered, in a small amount of boiling salted water until barely tender. Drain and serve with melted butter. Allow 1 pound (about 3 cups) for 4 servings.

♦

GREEN BEANS WITH WATER CHESTNUTS

4 SERVINGS

Sauté 1 cup water chestnuts, drained and coarsely chopped, in 3 tablespoons butter about 3 minutes. Pour over 1 pound hot, drained beans and season with salt and a pinch of oregano.

Green Bean Salad, page 453.
Pasta with Pesto and Green Beans, page 498.

GREEN BEANS A LA NIÇOISE

6 SERVINGS

½ cup olive oil
1 onion, sliced thin
1 cup canned Italian plum tomatoes
½ green pepper, chopped
½ cup chopped celery
¼ cup water
1 teaspoon salt
¼ teaspoon freshly ground pepper
2 cloves
1 bay leaf
6 parsley sprigs
½ teaspoon chervil
1 pound green beans, cooked until tender
    and drained

1 In a skillet heat the oil, add the onions and cook until golden brown. Add the tomatoes, green pepper, celery, water, salt and pepper.

2 Tie the cloves, bay leaf, parsley and chervil in a small cheesecloth bag and add to the vegetables. Simmer, uncovered, about 25 minutes. Add the beans and continue simmering until the beans are hot. Remove the spice bag.

SAVORY GREEN BEANS

6 SERVINGS

1½ pounds green beans
¼ cup oil
1 garlic clove, crushed
1 tablespoon chopped onions
¾ cup diced green pepper
¼ cup boiling water
1 teaspoon salt
1 tablespoon chopped basil
½ cup grated Parmesan cheese

1 Leave the beans whole, or cut into 1-inch pieces.

2 Heat the oil and garlic in a heavy pan. Add the onions and green pepper and cook slowly 3 minutes. Add the beans, water, salt and basil, cover and simmer until the beans are tender, about 15 minutes if whole.

3 Stir in half the cheese, turn the mixture into a serving dish and sprinkle with the remaining cheese.

◆

HERBED GREEN BEANS

4 SERVINGS

1 pound fresh green beans, cut into
    1-inch lengths
4 tablespoons butter
¼ cup minced onions
½ garlic clove, minced
¼ cup minced celery
¾ teaspoon salt
¼ teaspoon rosemary
¼ teaspoon basil

1 Soak the green beans in cold water for 15 minutes.

2 Melt the butter in a 1½-quart saucepan. Sauté the onions, garlic and celery in it until tender.

3 Add the drained beans, cover, and cook over low heat for 15 to 20 minutes. Add seasonings.

◆

GREEN BEANS WITH DILL

4 SERVINGS

1 pound fresh green beans
2 tablespoons peanut oil
1 tablespoon butter, melted
Salt to taste
1 teaspoon lemon juice
1 tablespoon finely chopped dill

1 Trim the beans, pinching off the tips at both ends. Break or cut the beans into 2-inch lengths. Rinse the beans and drain.

2 Put the oil into a saucepan with a tight-fitting lid and add the beans. Do not add other liquid. Cover and cook over low to medium heat, shaking the saucepan frequently. Cook for 15 to 20 minutes, until the beans are crisp tender. Pour the beans into a vegetable dish and pour the butter over them. Add salt and lemon juice and sprinkle with the chopped dill.

SNAP BEANS WITH TOMATOES AND PARMESAN

6 SERVINGS

3 slices of bacon, chopped
½ cup chopped onions
2 cups of 2-inch pieces of cooked snap beans,
    green or yellow
4 large tomatoes, cubed
¼ teaspoon salt
⅛ teaspoon freshly ground pepper
¼ cup grated Parmesan cheese

1 Preheat the oven to 350°F.
2 Fry the bacon and remove it from the skillet. Sauté the onions in the bacon fat until just tender.
3 Combine the onions, bacon, beans, tomatoes, salt and pepper. Place in a greased casserole, top with grated cheese, and bake until the cheese is brown, 10 to 15 minutes.

♦

FRESH LIMA BEANS

Cut off the rounded edges of the lima beans and shell like peas. Place the beans in a small amount of boiling salted water, cover and boil rapidly until tender, 20 to 30 minutes. Allow 2 pounds (2½ cups shelled) or more for 4 servings.

LIMA BEANS WITH FRESH HERBS

4 SERVINGS

Season 2 pounds hot, drained lima beans with 2 tablespoons butter and 2 tablespoons chopped parsley, dill or coriander.

♦

LIMA BEANS WITH CREAM

4 SERVINGS

2 tablespoons butter
2 cups shelled fresh lima beans, cooked
Salt and freshly ground pepper to taste
2 teaspoons chopped parsley
Pinch of hot red pepper flakes
½ cup half-and-half or cream

1 Melt the butter and add the beans, salt, pepper, parsley and hot red pepper flakes.
2 Purée the beans in a food processor and add the cream. Reheat, if necessary.

CREOLE LIMA BEANS

5 SERVINGS

2 slices of bacon
1 medium onion, chopped
¼ cup chopped green pepper
2 cups canned tomatoes
1 teaspoon sugar
2 cups cooked baby lima beans, drained
Salt and freshly ground pepper to taste

1 Sauté the bacon until crisp and remove from the pan. Add the onions and
pepper to the fat in the pan and cook until
tender but not brown.

2 Add the tomatoes and sugar and
cook about 15 minutes, stirring occasionally. Add the beans and season with salt
and pepper.

3 Simmer a few minutes longer. Serve
hot, sprinkled with the crumbled bacon.

◆

BEETS

Trim the tops from beets but leave about 1
inch of stem intact. This will keep them
from bleeding. Put the beets in a saucepan
and add water to cover and salt to taste.
Bring to the boil and cook for 25 to 45 minutes, or until tender. Cooking time will depend on the age and size of the beets.
Drain the beets and peel them. One pound
of beets will yield about 2 cups of sliced
beets, or 3 to 4 servings.

HARVARD BEETS

4 TO 6 SERVINGS

2½ cups sliced cooked beets
⅓ cup sugar
2 teaspoons cornstarch
¼ cup vinegar
1 tablespoon butter

1 Drain the beets, reserving ¼ cup of
the liquid.

2 Combine the sugar and cornstarch
and stir in the vinegar and beet liquid (or
water). Cook, stirring, over low heat until
the mixture is thickened and smooth.

3 Add the beets and the butter and
cook until heated through.

◆

GINGERED BEETS

ABOUT 4 SERVINGS

⅓ cup sugar
¾ teaspoon ground ginger
2 teaspoons cornstarch
¼ cup cider vinegar
2½ cups cooked or canned baby beets, drained
2 tablespoons butter
1 tablespoon chopped parsley

1 Blend the sugar, ginger and cornstarch and gradually add the vinegar, stirring until smooth. Cook over medium
heat, stirring, until thickened. Add the
beets and butter and simmer 10 minutes
longer, stirring occasionally.

2 Serve piping hot, sprinkled with
chopped parsley.

BEETS WITH ORANGE

½ cup sugar
1 tablespoon cornstarch
½ teaspoon salt
½ cup cider vinegar
2 tablespoons water
Grated rind and juice of 1 orange
3½ cups cooked or canned small beets, drained
2 tablespoons butter

   1 In a saucepan mix the sugar, cornstarch, salt, vinegar and water and bring to a boil. Stir until clear.
   2 Stir in the orange rind and juice and the beets. Heat gently and, before serving, stir in the butter.

PICKLED BEETS

1 cup vinegar
1 teaspoon salt
1 garlic clove, minced
½ cup brown sugar
2 teaspoons mixed whole pickling spices
8 to 12 medium beets, cooked, cooled, and
   sliced or quartered

Combine the vinegar, salt, garlic, sugar and spices in a saucepan. Bring to a boil, simmer for 2 or 3 minutes, and pour over the beets. Cool and chill.

Note: The pickled beets may be stored in the refrigerator for up to 2 weeks.

Ukrainian Borscht, page 62.
Russian Borscht, page 63.
Chlodnik, page 63.
Quick Cold Beet Soup, page 64.
Beet Salad, page 451.
Beet-Cabbage Relish, page 593.
Beet Preserves, page 608.

BROCCOLI

Wash broccoli well and drain. Remove and discard the large coarse leaves and cut off the tough lower parts of the stalk. If stalks are large, cut lengthwise into halves or quarters. Stand the stalks upright in a deep kettle, add 1 inch boiling salted water, cover and cook until stalks are just tender, about 10 minutes. Or slice the stalks and steam for a few minutes, then add the flowerets and steam a few minutes longer. One bunch (about 1½ pounds) yields 4 servings.

♦

BROCCOLI WITH CAPERS

Sprinkle hot drained broccoli with capers and melted butter mixed with a little of the juice from the caper bottle.

♦

BROCCOLI AMANDINE

4 SERVINGS

Cook 1 large bunch of broccoli (see page 380); drain and arrange on a heated serving platter. To 6 tablespoons melted butter add lemon juice to taste and ¼ cup coarsely chopped toasted almonds. Sprinkle over the broccoli.

BROCCOLI WITH BLACK OLIVES

4 SERVINGS

1 bunch (about 1½ pounds) fresh broccoli, trimmed
3 tablespoons olive oil
1 garlic clove, chopped fine
Salt and freshly ground pepper to taste
¼ cup small black olives, pitted and cut into small pieces
3 tablespoons grated Parmesan cheese

1 Parboil the broccoli about 2 minutes in a small amount of salted water. Drain.

2 Heat the oil, add the garlic and sauté until light brown. Add the broccoli and season with salt and pepper. Cook slowly over low heat 10 minutes, adding a little of the water in which the broccoli was cooked if the pan gets too dry.

3 Add the olives and heat 2 minutes longer. Serve immediately sprinkled with the grated cheese.

BROCCOLI WITH ANCHOVY-CHEESE SAUCE

6 SERVINGS

1 bunch (about 1½ pounds) broccoli
1 teaspoon salt
Anchovy-cheese sauce (page 571)
Anchovies for garnish

1 Wash and trim the broccoli, remove stem ends and cut into portions of similar size.

2 Place broccoli in a saucepan with 1 inch of boiling water containing the salt. Bring to a boil and cook, uncovered, for 5 minutes. Cover and boil for 10 to 15 minutes longer, or until broccoli is barely tender. Drain.

3 Top with anchovy–cheese sauce. Garnish with anchovies.

Cream of Broccoli Soup, page 64.
Broccoli Salad, page 452.
Fusilli with Broccoli, page 499.

BROCCOLI RING

6 SERVINGS

1 bunch (about 1½ pounds) broccoli
2 tablespoons butter
2 tablespoons flour
1 cup cream
4 eggs, separated
Pinch of grated nutmeg
Salt and freshly ground pepper to taste

1 Preheat the oven to 350°F.

2 Wash and trim the broccoli and cut it into small pieces. Steam the broccoli until tender. Chop the broccoli until fine and reserve.

3 Melt the butter and stir in the flour, using a wire whisk. When blended, add the cream, stirring vigorously with the whisk. When thickened and smooth, combine with the broccoli. Remove from the heat and stir in the slightly beaten egg yolks, the nutmeg, salt and pepper.

4 Beat the egg whites until thick and fold them into the broccoli mixture.

5 Generously butter a 1-quart ring mold and lightly flour it. Pour the mixture into the mold and set the mold in a larger pan. Pour about 1 inch of boiling water around the bottom of the mold. Bake the ring for 30 minutes, or until puffed and set.

BRUSSELS SPROUTS

Remove any wilted leaves from the sprouts and cut a gash in each stem from tip toward sprout. Rinse thoroughly. Bring the sprouts to a boil with enough salted water to cover. Cover and simmer 5 to 10 minutes until just tender. One quart of sprouts yields about 6 servings.

♦

BRUSSELS SPROUTS WITH CARAWAY SEEDS

6 SERVINGS

1½ pounds (1 quart) Brussels sprouts
Chicken stock
3 tablespoons butter
2 teaspoons caraway seeds
¼ teaspoon salt
⅛ teaspoon ground pepper

1 Wash the Brussels sprouts, trim off the tough outer leaves and cut a small cross in the bottom of each.
2 Pour chicken stock to a depth of 1 inch in a saucepan. Bring the stock to a boil and add the sprouts. Return to the boil, cover and simmer 5 to 10 minutes, or until just tender. Drain and add remaining ingredients. Toss lightly and serve at once.

BRUSSELS SPROUTS WITH BROWN BUTTER

6 SERVINGS

Heat 3 tablespoons of butter over low heat until it begins to brown. Add 1 tablespoon of lemon juice and pour the mixture over 1 quart of hot, cooked Brussels sprouts. If desired, sprinkle with ¼ cup shredded toasted almonds.

♦

BRUSSELS SPROUTS WITH CHESTNUTS

6 SERVINGS

1 quart Brussels sprouts
1½ teaspoons salt
1 tablespoon finely chopped onions
Boiling beef or chicken stock
4 tablespoons butter
⅔ cup cooked chestnuts

1 Wash and trim the sprouts. Soak them in 4 cups cold water containing 1 teaspoon of the salt for 20 minutes. Drain.
2 Place in a saucepan with the onions, stock and remaining salt. Bring to a boil and cook, covered, for 5 to 10 minutes, until tender. Drain.
3 Melt the butter, add the chestnuts, and cook until butter is golden. Pour over sprouts and toss lightly to mix sprouts and chestnuts.

BRUSSELS SPROUTS A LA CRÈME

4 TO 6 SERVINGS

1 quart Brussels sprouts
2½ teaspoons salt
2 tablespoons butter
2 teaspoons finely chopped onions
3 tablespoons flour
1 cup chicken stock
½ cup half-and-half
⅛ teaspoon freshly ground white pepper
Dash of grated nutmeg
1 teaspoon chopped parsley

1 Wash and trim the sprouts. Soak them in 4 cups cold water containing 1 teaspoon salt for 20 minutes. Drain.

2 Cook the sprouts, uncovered, in 1 inch of fresh boiling water containing 1 teaspoon salt for 5 to 10 minutes, until tender. Drain.

3 Melt the butter in a saucepan and cook the onions in it until soft but not brown. Add the flour and stir and cook until it turns golden.

4 Stir in the stock, half-and-half, remaining salt, the white pepper and nutmeg. Cook over low heat, stirring constantly, until thickened. Stir in chopped parsley. Serve the cream sauce over the Brussels sprouts.

CHINESE CABBAGE WITH MUSTARD

4 TO 6 SERVINGS

1 large head (2 pounds) Chinese cabbage
2 tablespoons dry mustard
2 tablespoons light soy sauce
2 teaspoons vinegar

1 Discard any tough outer leaves of the cabbage. Cut the remainder into 1-inch slices across the head and boil in water to cover 1 minute. Drain.

2 Mix the remaining ingredients in a serving bowl, add the cabbage and toss to coat it evenly. Cover and cool. Serve well chilled.

◆

BUTTERED CABBAGE

Remove and discard discolored outer leaves from green cabbage. Wash, core, and cut into shreds or wedges. Cook, covered, in a small amount of boiling salted water or stock until just tender, 5 to 10 minutes. Drain well. Season with salt and freshly ground pepper and serve with melted butter.

CABBAGE A LA BRETONNE

4 SERVINGS

1 medium-size cabbage
2 cups beef stock
2 eggs, well beaten
¾ cup half-and-half
½ teaspoon salt
Freshly ground pepper and grated nutmeg
   to taste
3 tablespoons olive oil
3 tablespoons tarragon vinegar
2 teaspoons sugar
Paprika

   1 Cut the cabbage into 8 wedges and cook in the stock until tender. Drain and keep warm.
   2 Mix the eggs, half-and-half, salt, pepper and nutmeg.
   3 Heat the oil, vinegar and sugar to boiling in the top of a double boiler over direct heat. Add, stirring, to the egg mixture. Return to the double boiler and cook over simmering water, stirring constantly, until thickened.
   4 Remove the core from the cabbage wedges and discard. Place the cabbage in a warm bowl and cover with the sauce. Sprinkle with paprika. Let stand a few minutes before serving.

CABBAGE IN SOUR CREAM

4 OR MORE SERVINGS

2 tablespoons butter
1 small cabbage, shredded
1 egg, beaten
1 cup sour cream
2 tablespoons sugar
3 tablespoons vinegar or lemon juice
Salt and freshly ground pepper to taste

   1 Melt the butter in a large skillet. Add the cabbage and cook, covered, until tender but not brown.
   2 Mix the egg, sour cream, sugar, vinegar, salt and pepper. Pour over the cabbage and heat, stirring, until almost simmering; do not boil. Serve at once.

Cabbage Green-Tomato Relish, page 592.
Spiced Cabbage, page 592.

◆

CABBAGE IN CARAWAY CREAM

4 SERVINGS

1 small firm green cabbage
2 tablespoons butter
1 teaspoon salt
1 garlic clove, minced
1 teaspoon caraway seeds
1 teaspoon sugar
1½ tablespoons vinegar
½ cup sour cream

   1 Trim the cabbage and shred it coarsely.
   2 Heat the butter in a skillet. Add the cabbage, salt and garlic and stir well.

Cover tightly and steam for 10 minutes. Water is not necessary if the cover is tight enough.

3 Remove cover and add the caraway seed, sugar and vinegar. Mix well. Stir in the sour cream and heat thoroughly but do not boil. Serve immediately.

◆

STUFFED CABBAGE

Cabbage is seldom thought of as company food, and perhaps its esteem in this regard is best illustrated by an incident in the life of a young Rumanian couple living in the United States.

Some time ago, when their funds were particularly low, they had invited to dinner a gentleman whose liking for steaks was well known. They were unable to provide his favorite dish and decided instead to serve one of their own—stuffed cabbage. But the husband struck on an idea.

"Maria," he said, "when we are seated at dinner, you come from the kitchen and say, 'Ion, what do you suppose happened? The steak fell on the floor.' I will say, 'No matter, Maria, we can have the stuffed cabbage.' "

When the night in question arrived and they were seated at the table the wife came from the kitchen and said, "Ion, what do you suppose happened? The stuffed cabbage fell on the floor."

"Maria," he said, "you mean the steak fell on the floor."

"No, Ion," she reiterated, "the stuffed cabbage fell on the floor."

Although it is not proposed that stuffed cabbage will ever replace steak as a national favorite, the dish can be a culinary delight. And it can be presented in a fashion to give it unusual eye appeal. Here is a European method of stuffing cabbage leaves to make them symmetrical with no strings attached.

1 Pull off the tough outer leaves from the cabbage and cut out the bottom core of the head with a paring knife. Cook the vegetable in boiling salted water to cover 5 minutes, or until the leaves separate easily. Invert and drain well.

2 Separate the individual leaves and dry them.

3 Place a square of cheesecloth on a flat surface. In the center of it place one of the large cabbage leaves, curly edge up. Insert a smaller cabbage leaf in the first and fill the smaller leaf with 1 or 2 tablespoons of the stuffing.

4 Bring the 4 corners of the cheesecloth together and twist the ends shut. This will shape the stuffed leaves into a compact round.

5 Remove the cheesecloth immediately and arrange the stuffed cabbage in a casserole with the sealed edge of the vegetable down.

6 Continue stuffing the leaves until all have been filled. The same square of cheesecloth may be used repeatedly.

ARMENIAN STUFFING
FOR CABBAGE LEAVES
6 SERVINGS

1 large cabbage
½ cup olive oil
2½ cups chopped onions
½ cup rice
½ cup water
½ cup finely chopped parsley
¼ cup raisins
¼ cup pistachios
¼ cup tomato paste
1 teaspoon salt
¼ tablespoon allspice
¼ teaspoon cinnamon
¼ teaspoon freshly ground pepper
2 cups chicken stock

1 Prepare the cabbage for stuffing as on page 385.

2 In a skillet heat the oil, add the onions and cook gently until golden brown. Add the rice and cook, covered, over low heat ½ hour. Stir occasionally.

Continued

3 Add the remaining ingredients except the cabbage and stock and cook 5 minutes longer.

4 Strain the liquid into a heavy round casserole. Stuff the cabbage leaves with the rice mixture.

5 Arrange the stuffed leaves in the casserole and weight down with an inverted plate that fits loosely inside the casserole. Add enough chicken stock to reach the rim of the plate and simmer until done, about 30 minutes.

BEEF STUFFING FOR CABBAGE LEAVES
ABOUT 8 SERVINGS

1 large cabbage
1½ tablespoons butter
1½ tablespoons olive oil
½ cup chopped onions
1 garlic clove, minced
1 pound ground chuck
2 cups cooked rice
3 tablespoons minced parsley
½ teaspoon thyme
1 teaspoon salt
¼ teaspoon freshly ground pepper
1 cup beef or chicken stock
1 cup tomato sauce
1 bay leaf
Lemon slices

1 Prepare the cabbage for stuffing as on page 385. Preheat the oven to 350°F.

2 In a skillet heat the butter and oil, add the onions and garlic and cook until the onions are transparent. Remove to a platter. Add the meat to the skillet and cook until light brown. Return onions and garlic to skillet.

3 Add the rice, parsley, thyme, salt and pepper. Mix well and fill the cabbage leaves with the mixture.

4 Arrange the stuffed leaves in a casserole and add the combined stock and tomato sauce and the bay leaf. Cover and bake 1 hour, adding more liquid if necessary.

5 Transfer the cabbage to a warm serving platter, garnish each serving with a lemon slice and sprinkle with additional parsley. Surround with the sauce remaining in the casserole, discarding the bay leaf.

JULIE SAHNI'S STUFFED CABBAGE WITH GINGER SAUCE

The ground meat dish called *keema* makes an excellent stuffing for cabbage. The cabbage is served with an uncommonly good fresh ginger sauce.

4 TO 6 SERVINGS

Indian keema with ginger (page 326)
1 small (1½ to 2 pounds) cabbage
Salt to taste
3 tablespoons vegetable oil
1½ cups thinly sliced onions
1¼ cups finely chopped ripe tomatoes, or
  1 cup canned crushed tomatoes with
  their liquid
1 tablespoon shredded ginger
1 lemon, ends trimmed, peeled, seeded
  and thinly sliced
Freshly ground pepper to taste
1½ cups water

1 Prepare the keema and set it aside.

2 Cut away and discard the tough bottom and center core of the cabbage. Drop the cabbage into boiling water to cover to a depth of 1 inch. Add salt and let cook 5 minutes. Drain thoroughly, cored side down. When cool enough to handle, separate the leaves. Set aside 15 or so leaves to be stuffed. Finely shred the remaining leaves and set the shreds aside.

3 Heat the oil in a saucepan and add the onions. Cook, stirring, until the onions start to take on color, about 5 minutes. Add the shredded cabbage, tomatoes, ginger, lemon, salt, pepper and water. Cook 2 minutes and set this sauce aside

4 Preheat the oven to 375°F.

5 Place 1 large cabbage leaf on a flat surface (if the leaf is torn, place another leaf atop it). Add about 2½ tablespoons of the ground meat filling and fold the leaf over to enclose the filling, jelly-roll fashion, tucking in the ends. There should be 12 to 14 finished cabbage rolls.

6 Spoon about one third of the pulpy tomato sauce over the bottom of a baking dish large enough to hold the rolls in 1 layer compactly. Pour the remaining sauce overall, equally distributing the cabbage shreds. Cover closely with foil and place in the oven. Bake 50 minutes. Remove the foil and bake 10 minutes longer.

♦

HOT CABBAGE SLAW

4 SERVINGS

3 cups shredded green or white cabbage
1 teaspoon salt
1 tablespoon butter
½ cup milk
1 teaspoon caraway seeds
½ teaspoon tarragon, or more
Freshly ground pepper to taste

1 Put the cabbage in a 1-quart pan. Rinse and drain. Sprinkle with the salt, cover, and place over medium heat. When the cover is hot to the touch, reduce the heat to low and cook for 5 minutes.

2 Add butter, milk and caraway seeds. Add the tarragon and pepper and stir to blend. Bring to a boil. Serve hot.

BRAISED RED CABBAGE

2 onions, sliced
2 tablespoons oil or bacon drippings
1 red cabbage, finely shredded
2 large tart apples, peeled and diced
½ cup red currant jelly
1 bay leaf
6 allspice berries
Salt and freshly ground pepper to taste
⅔ cup red wine, or more
24 fresh chestnuts, peeled (see page 189)

1 Preheat the oven to 325°F.

2 Sauté the onions in the oil in a heavy stainless-steel or porcelainized-iron casserole until tender.

3 Add the cabbage, apples, jelly, bay leaf, allspice, salt, pepper and ½ cup of the wine.

4 Cover tightly and bake for 2 hours, adding more of the wine if necessary to prevent sticking. Stir occasionally.

5 Add the chestnuts about 1 hour before the end of cooking time. Add a little more wine if cabbage seems dry. Remove the bay leaf and allspice before serving.

Pickled Red Cabbage, page 605.

GERMAN-STYLE RED CABBAGE

1 small head of red cabbage
2 tart red apples, cored but not peeled
2 tablespoons bacon fat or lard
Salt and freshly ground pepper to taste
3 tablespoons red wine vinegar
1 tablespoon brown sugar

1 Remove the outer leaves of the cabbage and discard. Quarter, core and grate the cabbage into a skillet.

2 Slice the unpeeled apples and add to the cabbage. Add the fat, salt and pepper and bring to a boil with just enough water to cover. Cover, reduce the heat and simmer until tender but still crisp, about 15 minutes. Drain, reserving the liquid.

3 Mix the vinegar and sugar and stir into the reserved liquid. Cook, stirring, until blended. Stir in the cabbage and serve hot.

BUTTERED CARROTS

Scrape and peel the carrots; leave whole or cup up, as desired. Cook, covered, in a small amount of boiling water until tender. (Cooking time will depend on the size and age of the vegetables.) Drain well and season with salt, freshly ground pepper and melted butter. Allow 1 pound of carrots for 4 servings.

◆

CAROTTES VICHY

6 SERVINGS

1½ pounds carrots, trimmed and scraped
Salt and freshly ground pepper to taste
1 teaspoon sugar
¼ cup water
4 tablespoons butter
Chopped parsley to garnish

1 Cut the carrots into very thin rounds. There should be about 4 cups. Put them in a skillet and add salt, pepper, sugar, water (Vichy water if you want to be authentic) and butter.

2 Cover with a round of buttered wax paper and cook over moderately high heat, shaking the skillet occasionally. Cook about 10 minutes, until carrots are tender, the liquid has disappeared and the vegetables are lightly glazed. Take care they do not burn. Serve sprinkled with chopped parsley.

Cream of Carrot Soup, page 65.
Pickled Carrots, page 603.

ORANGE-GLAZED CARROTS

4 SERVINGS

3 tablespoons orange juice
1½ tablespoons sugar
4 tablespoons butter
6 cloves
¼ teaspoon salt
4 cups hot cooked sliced carrots
Chopped fresh parsley

Combine the orange juice, sugar, butter, cloves and salt in a saucepan. Cook until the butter is melted and the sauce is hot. Remove and discard the cloves. Pour the mixture over the carrots and serve garnished with the parsley.

CARROT TZIMMES

6 TO 8 SERVINGS

2 pounds carrots
½ teaspoon salt
¾ cup honey
1 tablespoon lemon juice
2 tablespoons flour
2 tablespoons butter, melted

1 Scrape the carrots and slice them into very thin rounds. Cook the carrot rounds in salted water to cover for about 8 minutes, until they are almost tender.

2 Add the salt, honey and lemon juice. Simmer until the liquid in the pan is reduced to about half of its original volume.

3 Blend the flour into the butter. Add to the carrots, stirring. Bring the mixture to a boil and simmer for 1 minute.

Note: If this recipe is prepared for the menu for Rosh Hashanah, instead of butter use vegetable shortening or chicken fat.

CARROTS WITH ARTICHOKE HEARTS

6 SERVINGS

½ pound fresh mushrooms, quartered
1 tablespoon olive oil
1½ tablespoons butter
Salt and freshly ground pepper to taste
2 tablespoons minced shallots or scallions
1 (9-ounce) package frozen artichoke hearts, cooked
1½ pounds carrots, braised in butter
⅓ cup beef stock
2 tablespoons minced parsley, or combination of parsley and chives

1 Sauté the mushrooms in the oil and butter in a skillet for 4 or 5 minutes, until very light brown. Season with salt and pepper.

2 Stir the shallots and artichoke hearts into the mushrooms and toss for 2 or 3 minutes over moderately high heat. Fold in the carrots.

3 Add the stock to the mixture. Cover and cook slowly for 4 or 5 minutes, until the stock has almost completely evaporated. Correct seasoning if necessary.

4 Put the vegetables in a hot serving dish and sprinkle with the parsley.

CARROTS AND POTATOES MOUSSELINE

4 TO 6 SERVINGS

6 carrots, scraped and quartered
3 medium potatoes, peeled
3 tablespoons butter
½ cup cream
Grated nutmeg to taste

1 In separate saucepans cook the carrots and potatoes in boiling salted water until tender. Drain.

2 Force the vegetables through a food mill and return them to one of the saucepans. Add the butter and beat with a wooden spoon. Add the cream while beating and season with a little nutmeg. Serve hot.

Cauliflower, broccoli, Brussels sprouts, cabbage and kale are cousins under the leaf. The finest heads of cauliflower are firm to the touch and range in color from chalk to creamy white. The outer leaves should be firm, fresh and green. The leaves are thoroughly edible. Good taste in cauliflower has nothing to do with size and relative sizes have little to do with age.

Marie Jeanne Bécu, the Countess du Barry, the court favorite of Louis XV, gave her royal name to many dishes made with cauliflower. The name du Barry on a menu almost invariably denotes cauliflower in some form.

◆

CAULIFLOWER

Trim the cauliflower, removing outer leaves and part of the core and cutting off any blemishes. Score the core with a knife to facilitate cooking. Place in a kettle of boiling salted water to cover and add 1 teaspoon of lemon juice. Cover and simmer 20 minutes, or until just tender when tested with a fork. Do not overcook. (The cauliflower may be broken into flowerets and steamed for about 5 minutes.) Allow 1 large head for 4 servings.

◆

CAULIFLOWER WITH ANCHOVY BUTTER

Combine ¼ pound melted butter with ½ teaspoon anchovy paste. Blend well and pour over freshly cooked cauliflower.

CAULIFLOWER POLONAISE

Cook a large head of cauliflower until tender and drain. Place in a serving dish and cover lightly with ½ cup fresh bread crumbs that have been browned in 2 tablespoons butter. Sprinkle with 1 tablespoon chopped hard-cooked egg and 1 teaspoon chopped parsley.

♦

MEXICAN-STYLE CAULIFLOWER

4 TO 5 SERVINGS

1 medium cauliflower, separated into flowerets
1½ cups tomato sauce
2 tablespoons chopped parsley
¼ teaspoon cinnamon
⅛ teaspoon ground cloves
1 tablespoon capers
2 tablespoons chopped olives
3 tablespoons grated Monterey Jack cheese
2 tablespoons fine bread crumbs
1 tablespoon olive oil

1 Preheat the oven to 425°F.
2 Cook the cauliflower, covered, in a small amount of boiling salted water until barely tender. Drain.
3 Mix the tomato sauce, parsley, spices, capers and olives. Pour a little of the sauce into a heatproof dish, add cauliflower and cover with remaining sauce.
4 Sprinkle with the cheese, crumbs and oil and bake until brown.

CAULIFLOWER WITH CAPER SAUCE

6 SERVINGS

1 large cauliflower
1¼ teaspoons salt
Cornstarch
3 tablespoons butter
3 tablespoons lemon juice
1 tablespoon grated onion
⅛ teaspoon freshly ground pepper
1 teaspoon turmeric
2 tablespoons capers
Chopped parsley

1 Remove the stem and leaves from the cauliflower. Place the cauliflower in a saucepan with 1 inch of boiling water containing 1 teaspoon of the salt. Bring to a boil and cook, uncovered, for 5 minutes. Cover and cook for 20 minutes longer, or until cauliflower is tender, turning once.
2 Drain the liquid from the cauliflower and measure it. There should be about 1 cup. Blend in 1 teaspoon cornstarch for each ½ cup liquid.
3 Add the butter, lemon juice, onion, pepper, turmeric and remaining salt to the liquid. Cook, stirring, until sauce has thickened. Add the capers. Pour the sauce over cauliflower and garnish with parsley.

CAULIFLOWER WITH MUSTARD SAUCE

1 medium cauliflower
¾ cup heavy cream
¾ cup mayonnaise
Salt to taste
1½ tablespoons prepared mustard, preferably Dijon or Düsseldorf
Juice of ½ lemon, or more
Paprika

1 Remove the stem and leaves from the cauliflower. Steam the cauliflower whole until it is barely tender. Drain and keep warm.

2 Whip the cream and set aside briefly.

3 In a mixing bowl combine the mayonnaise, salt, mustard and lemon juice. Whip until blended; fold in the whipped cream. Pour sauce over cauliflower or serve it separately. Sprinkle with paprika.

Cauliflower Pickle, page 604.
Cauliflower Salad Napoletana, page 452.

CAULIFLOWER MORNAY

6 SERVINGS

1 large cauliflower, cut into flowerets
¼ cup butter
2 tablespoons flour
1 cup chicken stock
1 cup cream
Salt and freshly ground white pepper
2 egg yolks, lightly beaten
2 tablespoons grated Parmesan cheese

1 Cook the cauliflower in salted water until just tender. Drain well. Turn into a hot serving dish or casserole.

2 While the cauliflower is cooking, make a sauce of 2 tablespoons of the butter, the flour, stock and cream. Season with salt and pepper to taste.

3 Mix egg yolks with a bit of the sauce and add, stirring, to the sauce. Add the cheese and remaining butter. Mix until the cheese has melted.

4 Serve over the cauliflower; or use a heatproof casserole, sprinkle the top with extra grated cheese, and broil to a golden brown.

In the United States celery is rarely thought of as a vegetable to cook. The French, however, serve braised celery often as an accompaniment for roast meats.

♦

CELERY BRAISED IN WHITE WINE

4 TO 6 SERVINGS

6 celery hearts
2 tablespoons olive oil
2 tablespoons butter
½ teaspoon salt
⅛ teaspoon freshly ground pepper
½ cup dry white wine
¼ cup chicken stock

1 Cut off most of the leaves and remove the rough outer stalks of the celery. Cut each heart lengthwise into halves. Wash thoroughly and drain on paper toweling.

2 Heat the oil and butter in a skillet large enough to hold all the celery pieces in one layer. Arrange the pieces, flat side down, in the skillet and cook over low heat until lightly browned. Turn the pieces over and sprinkle with half of the salt and pepper. Brown the rounded side, turn over and sprinkle with the remaining salt and pepper.

3 Pour the wine and stock into the pan, cover, and simmer gently until the celery is tender. Remove the celery to a heated serving plate. Reduce the cooking liquid a little and spoon some of it over the celery. Sprinkle with chopped parsley or chives or paprika.

Celery Relish, page 595.

CREAMED CELERY

4 SERVINGS

2 cups sliced celery
Salt and freshly ground pepper to taste
2 tablespoons butter
1 tablespoon chopped onions
2 teaspoons flour
½ cup cream
¼ cup chicken stock

1 Place the celery, salt, pepper and butter in a saucepan with a tight-fitting cover. Cover and cook slowly, shaking the pan often, until the celery is almost tender, about 15 minutes. Add the onions and continue cooking until tender. If the cover does not fit tightly it will be necessary to add a little water, but the celery should be almost dry at the end of the cooking time.

2 Blend in the flour and gradually add the cream and chicken stock. Bring to a boil and cook, stirring, until thickened.

Variations

CREAMED CELERY AMANDINE

Add ¼ cup shredded, toasted almonds to the creamed celery.

SCALLOPED CELERY IN CHEESE SAUCE

Prepare the creamed celery and add ¾ cup grated cheddar cheese to the mixture. Stir until the cheese has melted. Turn into a casserole, sprinkle the top with additional grated cheese or with buttered coarse bread crumbs and brown under a preheated broiler or in a preheated 375°F oven.

PURÉE OF CELERY KNOB

Celery knob, a knobby tuber that has a celery-like flavor, is sometimes called celeriac and sometimes celery root.

4 TO 6 SERVINGS

4 large celery knobs
2 medium potatoes
Chicken stock
Salt and freshly ground pepper to taste
Half-and-half

1 Peel the celery knob and potatoes. Cut into quarters. Boil the celery and potatoes separately in salted water until tender, about 20 minutes. Do not overcook.

2 Purée the celery knob in a food processor, adding enough chicken stock to aid the blending. Or the celery knob may be put through a potato ricer.

3 Mash the potatoes and mix with the puréed celery. Season with salt and pepper and fold in enough half-and-half to ensure a smooth consistency.

Céleri Rémoulade, page 33.

CELERY KNOB PARMIGIANA

6 SERVINGS

4 celery knobs
1 tablespoon lemon juice
2 teaspoons salt
6 tablespoons butter, melted
½ cup grated Parmesan cheese
2 tablespoons chopped parsley

1 Preheat the oven to 425°F.

2 Peel the celery knobs and cut them into thin little sticks about 2 inches long. Drop the pieces into boiling water to cover with the lemon juice and salt added. Cook for about 10 minutes, or until just tender. Do not overcook. Drain.

3 Butter a baking dish large enough to hold the celery knobs. Arrange a layer of the drained pieces and sprinkle with some of the melted butter and some of the cheese. Continue to fill the dish with drained pieces, butter and cheese. If desired, each layer may be sprinkled with a little black pepper and paprika.

4 Bake for 15 minutes, or until the cheese is golden brown. Sprinkle a border of parsley around the edge and serve the celery knobs in the baking dish.

CORN ON THE COB

One of the commonest faults in cooking corn on the cob is overcooking it.

1 OR 2 EARS OF CORN PER PERSON

Ears of corn
Salt
Pepper butter (see below)

1 Bring enough water to the boil to more than cover the corn when it is added to the kettle. Add 1 tablespoon of salt for each quart of water.

2 Remove the husks from the corn and neatly break off or trim each end. Drop the corn into the boiling water and return to the boil. Turn off the heat immediately and let the corn stand in the water exactly 5 minutes. Serve with plenty of butter, or with chilled pepper butter.

PEPPER BUTTER

Crush 2 teaspoons peppercorns in a mortar or with the flat side of a skillet. Blend with ¼ pound softened butter and add salt to taste. Spoon into a serving bowl and chill.

Okra with Corn, page 412.

BAKED FRESH CORN

6 SERVINGS

3 tablespoons butter
3 tablespoons flour
1½ teaspoons salt
Dash of freshly ground pepper
1½ cups half-and-half
2¼ cups cooked (5 to 6 plump ears) corn
    cut from the cob
3 beaten eggs
¾ cup buttered bread crumbs
Paprika

1 Preheat the oven to 350°F.

2 Heat the butter in a saucepan, add the flour and blend with a wire whisk. Season with salt and pepper. Meanwhile, bring the half-and-half to a boil and add all at once to the butter-flour mixture, stirring vigorously with the whisk until the sauce is thickened and smooth. Remove the sauce from the heat and add the corn. Slowly add the beaten eggs, stirring constantly.

3 Pour the mixture into a greased 5- to 6-cup casserole and top with the bread crumbs. Sprinkle with paprika and place in a shallow pan of hot water. Bake 45 to 50 minutes.

Variation

CORN AND CHEESE PUDDING

Add 1 cup grated sharp cheddar cheese and 1 teaspoon dry mustard to the white sauce. Cook briefly until the cheese melts before adding the corn.

SHAKER CORN PUDDING

6 SERVINGS

2 cups grated (4 to 5 plump ears)
   uncooked corn
3 eggs
¼ cup sugar
Dash of grated nutmeg
½ teaspoon salt
⅛ teaspoon freshly ground pepper
2 cups milk
½ cup buttered soft fresh bread crumbs
2 tablespoons butter

1 Preheat the oven to 250°F.
2 Place the corn in a buttered baking dish. Beat the eggs well. Add the sugar, nutmeg, salt, pepper and milk; blend. Pour the mixture over the corn and sprinkle the top with the crumbs. Dot with the butter. Set the baking dish in a pan of boiling water and bake for 1 hour.

♦

CORN IN CREAM

6 SERVINGS

12 ears of corn, shucked
4 tablespoons butter
Salt and freshly ground pepper to taste
½ to ¾ cup cream

1 Cut or grate the kernels from corn cobs. Heat butter in a saucepan and add the corn kernels. Cook for 3 to 5 minutes.
2 Season corn with salt and pepper and stir in the cream. Heat thoroughly and serve.

CORN CREOLE

4 TO 6 SERVINGS

6 ears of corn
2 tablespoons butter
2 scallions, trimmed and sliced
2 tablespoons chopped green pepper
1 large tomato, peeled and finely chopped
Salt and freshly ground pepper to taste

1 Cut the corn kernels from the cobs. Heat 1 tablespoon of the butter and add the corn, scallions and green pepper. Cook for 3 minutes.
2 Add the tomato, salt and pepper. Cover and cook for 5 minutes, or until the corn is tender. Stir in the remaining butter and serve.

Corn and Crabmeat Chowder, page 66.
Corn and Watercress Soup, page 66.
Corn Salad, Mexican Style, page 453.
Old-fashioned Fresh Corn Relish, page 593.
Ohio Corn Relish, page 594.
Corn and Tomato Relish, page 594.

CORN, OKRA AND TOMATO CASSEROLE

6 TO 8 SERVINGS

4 cups (about 8 plump ears) fresh corn cut
   from the cobs
1 cup sliced fresh okra
1 cup soft fresh bread crumbs
¼ cup finely chopped onions
2 teaspoons sugar
1 teaspoon salt
½ teaspoon freshly ground pepper
¼ cup bacon drippings or butter
2 cups milk
4 large eggs, lighly beaten
6 medium or 3 large tomatoes
2 tablespoons butter, melted

1 Preheat the oven to 350°F.

2 Combine vegetables, crumbs, onions, sugar, seasonings, drippings and
milk in a saucepan. Stir and cook for 5
minutes, or until thickened. Remove from
heat and stir a little of the hot mixture into
the eggs, then add eggs to the remaining
hot mixture. Turn into a buttered 2-quart
casserole.

3 Bake for 1 hour and 10 minutes, or
until the mixture is firm.

4 Cut tomatoes into ½-inch slices. Arrange slices over the top of the casserole
15 minutes before end of baking time.
Brush top with melted butter and sprinkle
with additional salt and pepper.

FRESH CORN FRITTERS

24 (2-INCH) FRITTERS

6 ears of corn
¼ cup flour
2 tablespoons sugar
½ teaspoon salt
⅛ teaspoon freshly ground pepper
1 egg, lightly beaten
2 tablespoons shredded mild cheddar cheese
Oil for deep frying

1 Cut the corn off the cob by running
the point of a sharp knife lengthwise
down the middle of each row of kernels,
cutting the kernels into halves. Shave a
thin layer of kernels off the entire cob. Repeat, taking off another layer. Clean off
the remainder by scraping the cob with the
bowl of a tablespoon.

2 Mix the corn with the flour, sugar,
salt and pepper. Blend in the egg and
cheese.

3 Heat the oil to 365°F. Drop the corn
mixture into the oil by teaspoons. Cook
until golden brown. Drain on paper
toweling.

CORN TAMALES

6 SERVINGS

6 ears of corn
½ cup flour
1 egg, lightly beaten
½ cup shredded mild cheese
3 tablespoons sugar
½ teaspoon salt
⅛ teaspoon freshly ground pepper
¼ cup raisins

1 Remove the shucks and silk from the ears of corn. Reserve 12 large strips of shucks. Cut the corn from the cob according to directions in the recipe for corn fritters (see opposite page). Reserve 3 of the scraped cobs.

2 Combine the cut corn, flour, egg, cheese, 2 tablespoons of the sugar, the salt, pepper and raisins. Mix well.

3 For each tamale, use 2 large shucks, placing them side by side lengthwise, overlapping the edges about 1 inch. Place ¼ cup of the corn mixture in the center of each. Fold the lengthwise edges over the top. Fold the ends under.

4 Place the tamales in a saucepan with the 3 reserved scraped corn cobs, the remaining sugar and boiling water to cover. Cook slowly, covered, for 1¼ hours, until the filling is firm. Discard the cobs.

CUCUMBER OVALS

Trim the ends from the cucumbers and cut the cucumbers into 2-inch lengths. Cut each section lengthwise into quarters. Using a paring knife, carefully cut away the skin and seeds, leaving only the firm flesh. Place the pieces in a saucepan and add boiling water to cover. Cook for 1 minute and drain. Return the cucumber to the saucepan and add butter, salt and pepper to taste. Toss until butter melts. Sprinkle with parsley and serve hot. Allow 1 large cucumber for 2 servings.

STUFFED CUCUMBERS

3 SERVINGS

3 large cucumbers
4 tablespoons butter
2 tablespoons finely chopped onions
¼ cup soft fresh bread crumbs
½ cup minced cooked chicken
1 tablespoon slivered toasted almonds
¼ teaspoon salt
⅛ teaspoon freshly ground pepper
¼ teaspoon thyme
Chicken stock

1 Preheat the oven to 375°F.

2 Peel the cucumbers, cut them into 2-inch lengths and scoop out the seeds with an apple corer or small sharp knife. Place the cucumbers in boiling salted water, simmer for 3 minutes and drain.

3 Melt 2 tablespoons of the butter, add the onions, and sauté until tender but not brown. Add the crumbs, chicken, almonds, salt, pepper and thyme. Moisten the chicken mixture with a little stock.

4 Stuff the cucumber tubes with the chicken mixture and arrange them in a buttered casserole. Sprinkle the remaining butter, melted, over the cucumbers. Add stock to casserole to come halfway up the cucumber pieces.

5 Bake for about 20 minutes, until the cucumbers are just tender.

Cold Cucumber Soup, page 67.
Cucumber Yogurt Relish, page 599.
Sweet Cucumber and Green Tomato Pickle, page 604.
Cucumber Salad, page 453.
Swedish Cucumber Salad, page 454.

Some cooks, particularly Italians, salt eggplant before cooking and let it drain to get rid of excess moisture. I have never found that this improved either texture or flavor, so I do not recommend it.

♦

BROILED EGGPLANT

4 SERVINGS

2 garlic cloves, minced
1 teaspoon grated onions
½ teaspoon salt
¼ cup olive oil or melted butter
1 medium eggplant

1 Mix the garlic, onions, salt and oil.

2 Peel the eggplant and cut into ½-inch slices. Place on a greased baking sheet and brush with the seasoned oil. Broil in a preheated broiler about 5 inches from the source of heat for 5 minutes, basting once with the seasoned oil.

3 Turn the slices, using a pancake turner, and brush with remaining oil mixture. Broil until tender, about 2 minutes longer.

4 Serve plain or with tomato sauce.

Variation

EASY EGGPLANT PARMIGIANA

Boil the eggplant slices as directed. When tender transfer to a baking dish. Spread with tomato sauce and sprinkle generously with grated Parmesan cheese. Top each piece with a thin slice of mozzarella or mild American cheese and boil until light brown and bubbly. Serve as a luncheon or supper entrée.

STUFFED EGGPLANT

3 medium eggplants
2 tablespoons olive oil
1 medium onion, chopped
2 garlic cloves, minced
1 green pepper, chopped
1 pound ground round
½ cup grated Romano cheese
¼ cup dry bread crumbs
2 tablespoons tomato paste
1¼ teaspoons salt
½ teaspoon oregano
¼ teaspoon freshly ground pepper
Basic tomato sauce (page 561)

1 Boil the eggplants in a large kettle of water, covered, for 15 minutes. Drain and cut in half lengthwise. Carefully remove the pulp, leaving a shell ½ inch thick.

2 Preheat the oven to 350°F.

3 In a skillet heat the oil, add the onions, garlic and green pepper and sauté until just tender. Remove to a bowl. Sauté the beef until it loses its pink color. Drain and add to the bowl.

4 Chop the eggplant pulp and combine with the sautéed mixture. Add remaining ingredients except tomato sauce and mix well. Fill the shells with the mixture and place in a greased baking pan. Brush the tops with additional oil and bake about 45 minutes. Serve with tomato sauce.

FRENCH-FRIED EGGPLANT STICKS

1 large eggplant
¾ cup fine dry bread crumbs
6 tablespoons grated Parmesan cheese
2½ teaspoons salt
¼ teaspoon freshly ground pepper
2 eggs, beaten
2 tablespoons milk
Oil for deep frying

1 Peel the eggplant and cut it into ½-inch crosswise slices. Cut each slice into ½-inch strips. Set aside.

2 Combine the crumbs, cheese, salt and pepper. Beat the eggs with the milk. Dip eggplant sticks into crumb mixture, then into egg mixture, and again into crumb mixture.

3 Fry sticks in oil heated to 375°F. Drain on paper toweling. Serve hot.

Ground Beef with Eggplant, page 295.
Salata Melitzanas, page 454.
Eggplant and Sesame Salad, page 455.
Eggplant Chutney, page 600.
Eggplant Relish, page 599.

AUBERGINES A LA BOSTON

Aubergines à la Boston is eggplant in one of its most elegant forms, in a Gruyère cheese sauce. It is somewhat tedious to prepare but the game is worth the candle.

8 SERVINGS

2 medium eggplants
2½ teaspoons salt
¼ teaspoon freshly ground pepper
5 tablespoons flour
¼ cup vegetable or olive oil
3 tablespoons butter
1 cup finely chopped onions
Pinch of cayenne
¾ cup milk
2 tablespoons grated Gruyère or Swiss cheese
2 tablespoons grated Parmesan cheese
¼ cup cream
1 teaspoon dry mustard
1 cup sliced mushrooms

1 Cut the unpeeled eggplants in half lengthwise. Cut gashes in the pulp and sprinkle each half with ½ teaspoon of the salt. Let stand 30 minutes.

2 Squeeze out the water and wipe dry. Mix the pepper and flour and dredge each half in the mixture. Reserve the remaining flour.

3 In a large skillet, heat half the oil, add 2 eggplant halves, cut side down, and cook slowly, covered, 10 minutes. Turn and cook 10 minutes longer. Remove from the pan and repeat the process with the remaining oil and eggplant.

4 In a saucepan heat 2 tablespoons of the butter, add the onions and cook until transparent. With a wire whisk stir in the reserved flour, the remaining salt and the cayenne. Add the milk and cook, stirring, until thickened.

5 Mix the cheeses and add half to the sauce. Blend in 3 tablespoons of the cream and the mustard. Sauté the mushrooms in the remaining butter and add.

6 Scoop out the eggplant pulp, leaving a shell ½-inch thick. Chop the pulp coarsely and add to the sauce. Mix well and spoon into the shells. Sprinkle the tops with the remaining cheese and broil until brown. Before serving, pour the remaining cream over the top. Serve hot.

Eggplant-Lamb Casserole, page 335.
Moussaka à la Grecque, page 334.
Moussaka à la Turque, page 333.

♦

EGGPLANT FRITTERS

4 SERVINGS, OR 3½ DOZEN HORS D'OEUVRES

1 small eggplant
¼ cup water
1 egg, beaten
1 small onion, grated
½ teaspoon salt
⅛ teaspoon freshly ground pepper
⅓ cup flour
1 teaspoon baking powder
2 tablespoons milk or tomato sauce, approximately
Oil for deep or shallow frying

1 Peel and cube the eggplant. Place in a saucepan with the water and cook, covered, until tender. Drain well and mash.

2 Stir in egg, onion, salt and pepper.

3 Mix the flour and baking powder and stir into the eggplant mixture. Add enough milk to make a drop batter.

4 Drop the batter by tablespoonfuls into oil heated to 360°F and cook until brown on all sides. Drain on paper towels.

EGGPLANT PARMIGIANA

6 SERVINGS

2 cups olive oil
1 garlic clove, minced
1 cup chopped onions
5 cups drained and chopped Italian tomatoes,
    fresh or canned
½ teaspoon basil
Salt and freshly ground pepper to taste
2 tablespoons flour
1 whole egg, beaten
2 eggplants, peeled and cut into ½-inch slices
1 cup grated Parmesan cheese
½ cup diced mozzarella cheese
Butter

1 Heat ¼ cup of the olive oil in a heavy skillet, add the garlic and onions and sauté until the onions are transparent. Add the tomatoes, basil, salt and pepper and cook, stirring occasionally, 30 minutes.

2 Preheat the oven to 350°F.

3 Combine the flour, egg and ¼ teaspoon salt. Dip the eggplant slices in the batter and fry in the remaining oil until light brown on both sides.

4 Place alternate layers of eggplant, sauce and cheeses in a large casserole. Dot the top with butter and bake 30 minutes.

Pasta with Eggplant, page 486.

BAKED MARINATED EGGPLANT

4 TO 6 SERVINGS

¾ cup olive oil
3 tablespoons lemon juice or vinegar
Salt and coarsely ground pepper
½ teaspoon minced garlic
2 tablespoons anchovy paste
1 large eggplant
¾ cup grated sharp cheddar cheese

1 Preheat the oven to 400°F.

2 Combine the oil, lemon juice, salt, pepper, garlic and anchovy paste. Beat with a fork or rotary beater until well blended.

3 Pare the eggplant and slice it crosswise into ½-inch rounds. Pour the oil mixture over the slices and let stand for 15 minutes, turning occasionally. If necessary, baste occasionally with the mixture.

4 Place the slices on a baking sheet lined with foil and bake for 10 to 15 minutes, turning once. Sprinkle with the cheese and place under the broiler until cheese melts.

ITALIAN EGGPLANT

4 TO 6 SERVINGS

1 large eggplant
2 slices of bacon, cubed
1 onion, minced
1 large tomato, peeled, seeded and chopped
½ cup chopped celery
1 egg, beaten
Salt and freshly ground pepper to taste
8 black olives, pitted and sliced (imported
     black olives are best)
6 flat anchovy fillets, chopped
¾ cup soft fresh bread crumbs
½ cup grated Parmesan or Romano cheese

1 Preheat the oven to 325°F.
2 Peel and cube the eggplant. Steam the cubes over hot water for 5 to 10 minutes, or until nearly tender.
3 Cook the bacon until crisp. Mix the crisp pieces with the eggplant, onions, tomato, celery, egg, salt, pepper, olives, anchovies and half the crumbs.
4 Pour the mixture into a greased baking dish. Combine the remaining crumbs with the cheese and sprinkle over the top of the casserole. Bake for 30 minutes.

What a pity that most of us in this country know Belgian endive only as a salad ingredient. Once a taste for cooked endive is acquired, the skillet takes precedence over the salad bowl.

◆

BRAISED ENDIVE

4 SERVINGS

8 heads of endive
Juice of ½ lemon
4 tablespoons butter
1 teaspoon salt
⅓ cup water
1 teaspoon sugar

1 Trim off and discard any discolored leaves from the outside of the endive. Place the heads in 1 layer in a heavy skillet and add the lemon juice, 1 tablespoon of the butter, the salt, water and sugar. Cover and bring to a boil. Cook over moderate heat for 25 to 30 minutes, until endive are tender.
2 Drain the endive and press gently to remove any excess moisture.
3 Heat the remaining butter in the skillet and brown the endive in it on all sides. They should be a light caramel color when cooked. Serve with roasted meats.

Variation

BRAISED ENDIVE WITH WALNUTS

Brown ¼ cup chopped walnuts in 1 tablespoon butter and spoon over the cooked endive.

SAUTÉED ESCAROLE

4 SERVINGS

2 pounds escarole
¼ cup olive oil
1 clove garlic, minced
Salt and freshly ground pepper
Olive oil and vinegar (optional)

1 Trim the escarole and discard any tough or bruised leaves. Trim off the root end. Cut the head of escarole into quarters. Rinse well. Shake escarole to remove any excess moisture.

2 Heat the ¼ cup oil in a large saucepan and add the garlic. Let it cook briefly, then add the escarole. Do not add any water except that which clings to the leaves. Cover and cook for 10 to 15 minutes, stirring occasionally so that the cooking will be even.

3 Sprinkle with salt and pepper. Serve with olive oil and vinegar, if desired. Sautéed escarole may also be served cold with oil and vinegar.

The pungent and pleasing flavor of anise or licorice found widely in Italian and Scandinavian cuisine usually comes from the seeds, leaves and bulbous stems of the fennel plant, an aromatic herb of the parsley family. The seeds of the common fennel are used in sweet pickles, cookies, apple pies and candy. The chopped feathery green leaves add color and flavor to sauces for fish, particularly herring, mackerel and salmon, and the leaves make an excellent addition to salads.

Fennel may be eaten raw, like celery. To serve it raw, trim the coarse outer leaves and cut the bulb into quarters, slices or julienne strips.

Fennel is also delicious cooked, and it may be substituted in any recipe for celery.

◆

FENNEL WITH LEMON AND SPICES

4 TO 6 SERVINGS

2 cups water
6 tablespoons olive oil
⅓ cup lemon juice
Salt to taste
10 whole peppercorns
10 whole coriander seeds
2 tablespoons minced shallots or onions
5 parsley sprigs
1 small stalk of celery
¼ teaspoon thyme
¼ teaspoon fennel seed
4 small heads of fennel

Continued

1 Combine the water, oil, lemon juice, salt, peppercorns, coriander seeds and shallots in a large saucepan. Tie the parsley, celery, thyme and fennel seed in cheesecloth and add to the liquid. Cover, bring to a boil and simmer 10 minutes.

2 Trim off the top leaves and tough outer stalks of the fennel. Cut the vegetable into quarters and add to the saucepan. Cover and simmer until the fennel is tender, 30 to 40 minutes.

♦

FENNEL AU GRATIN

4 SERVINGS

1 large head of fennel, or 3 small
5 tablespoons butter
3 tablespoons flour
1½ cups milk
½ teaspoon salt
¼ teaspoon freshly ground pepper
¼ cup grated Parmesan cheese
½ cup soft fresh bread crumbs

1 Preheat the oven to 375°F.

2 Wash the fennel, trim it and cut it into 1-inch lengths. Steam the fennel over boiling water for about 10 minutes, or until barely tender.

3 Melt 3 tablespoons of the butter, blend in the flour, and gradually stir in the milk. Season with the salt and pepper and bring to a boil, stirring. Add the cheese and stir to melt.

4 Spread half of the crumbs over the bottom of a greased shallow 1-quart casserole. Place the steamed fennel pieces over the top and pour the sauce over all. Top with remaining crumbs and dot with remaining butter. Bake for 20 minutes, or until bubbly hot.

Variation

ENDIVE AU GRATIN

Pour boiling water over 8 heads of endive, add salt to taste, cover and cook until almost tender, about 20 minutes. Proceed with step 3 as for fennel, opposite.

♦

COLCANNON WITH KALE

6 SERVINGS

2 pounds white potatoes
1 teaspoon salt
3 cups finely cut kale
3 tablespoons minced onions
3 tablespoons butter
⅛ teaspoon freshly ground white pepper
1 to 2 tablespoons milk

1 Preheat the oven to 400°F.

2 Peel the potatoes and cut them into quarters. Place in a saucepan with 1 inch of boiling water containing ½ teaspoon of the salt. Cover and cook for 15 to 20 minutes, until the potatoes are tender. Drain and mash.

3 Meanwhile, cook the kale until tender in 1 inch of boiling water containing ½ teaspoon of the salt. Drain.

4 Sauté the onions in half the butter. Combine the onions with the mashed potatoes, drained kale, pepper, and milk. Beat until smooth.

5 Turn the mixture into a shallow baking dish, dot with the remaining butter, and place in the oven. Heat for 15 to 20 minutes.

COOKED GREENS

All greens should be washed well before cooking.

Most greens, if they are fresh and young, can be cooked in the liquid that clings to the leaves after they are drained. Place the greens in a kettle with a close-fitting lid and simmer until tender, 3 to 10 minutes. Drain well and season with salt to taste. Serve with melted butter and, if desired, a little lemon juice. Edible greens include spinach, beet tops, dandelions, mustard greens, turnip greens and most members of the lettuce family.

If the greens are not particularly young, it is best to cook them until tender in a kettle with an inch or so of lightly salted water. In the South, greens are frequently cooked with salt pork for an hour or more.

OVEN-BRAISED LETTUCE

6 SERVINGS

6 small heads of Boston lettuce
3 slices of bacon
2 tablespoons finely chopped onions
2 tablespoons finely chopped carrot
1 cup beef stock
Salt and freshly ground pepper to taste
Chopped parsley
Melted butter

1 Preheat the oven to 325°F.

2 Wash the lettuce and cook, covered, in a small amount of boiling salted water 2 minutes. Drain and press lightly with a dry cloth. Cut each head in half.

3 Line the bottom of a buttered casserole with the bacon and sprinkle with the chopped onions and carrot. Tuck the tops of the lettuce under and place flat on top of the vegetables. Add the stock and sprinkle with salt and pepper.

4 Cover with buttered wax paper or foil and bake 45 minutes.

5 Transfer the lettuce to a warm serving dish and keep hot. Reduce the liquid in the casserole and pour over the lettuce. Before serving, sprinkle with parsley and melted butter.

BRAISED LEEKS

4 SERVINGS

---

12 leeks
2 tablespoons butter
1 small white onion, minced
2 cups chicken stock
Salt and freshly ground pepper to taste

1 Cut the tops off the leeks, leaving 1 or 2 inches of leaves. Trim the roots. Use the leek tops in soup. Cut the stalks in half lengthwise and wash thoroughly under running water, holding the leaves apart. Tie the leeks with string.

2 In a skillet, heat the butter, add the onion and sauté until golden brown. Add the leeks, stock, salt and pepper. Cover and simmer until the leeks are tender, about 15 minutes. Serve hot, or chill and serve with a vinaigrette.

Leeks Vinaigrette, page 456.
Leek and Potato Purée, page 515.
Vichyssoise à la Ritz, page 70.
Cock-a-Leekie, page 92.
Leek and Sausage Pie, page 108.
Stir-Fry Beef with Leeks, page 275.

MUSHROOMS IN OIL WITH PARSLEY

4 SERVINGS

---

1 pound large mushrooms
¾ cup olive oil
1 teaspoon salt
¼ teaspoon freshly ground pepper
¼ cup chopped parsley
1 garlic clove, minced
1 shallot, minced
¼ cup soft fresh bread crumbs

1 Wash and slice the mushrooms, cutting through caps and stems. Marinate the mushrooms for 1 hour in ½ cup of the olive oil containing the salt and pepper.

2 Heat the remaining oil in a heavy skillet. Drain the mushrooms and sauté them in the hot oil for about 5 minutes, until just tender.

3 Add the remaining ingredients and toss lightly. Serve immediately.

SHERRIED MUSHROOMS

4 SERVINGS

12 large mushroom caps
Lemon juice
4 tablespoons butter
1 garlic clove, minced
2 tablespoons grated Gruyère or Parmesan
    cheese
6 tablespoons soft fresh bread crumbs
¼ teaspoon grated nutmeg
2 tablespoons finely chopped parsley
1 tablespoon finely chopped chives
Salt and freshly ground pepper to taste
¼ cup dry sherry, approximately

1 Preheat the oven to 350°F.

2 Remove the stems from the mushrooms. Chop the stems and sprinkle the caps with lemon juice.

3 Melt half of the butter in a small saucepan and cook the chopped stems until wilted. Add the garlic. Stir in the cheese, crumbs, nutmeg, parsley, chives, salt and pepper.

4 Stuff the caps with this mixture and arrange them in a buttered baking dish. Sprinkle lightly with sherry and dot with remaining butter. Bake for 15 minutes.

Stuffed Mushrooms, page 35.
Mushrooms Stuffed with Liver, page 36.
Mushrooms Stuffed with Snails, page 37.
Cream of Mushroom Soup, page 68.
Julie Wilson's Wild Rice and Mushroom Soup, page 67.
Mushrooms à la Grecque, page 36.
Salade Forestière, page 456.
Pauline Trigère's Mushroom Spaghetti, page 500.
Penne with Wild Mushroom Sauce, page 501.
Pickled Mushrooms, page 607.
Mushroom-Rice Ring, page 539.

MUSHROOM PIE

4 OR 5 SERVINGS

4 tablespoons butter
1 or 2 medium onions, chopped
1 pound whole button mushrooms or large
    mushrooms, sliced
1 tablespoon flour
½ cup half-and-half
1 tablespoon cognac or sherry
Salt and freshly ground pepper to taste
Pastry for a 2-crust (8-inch) pie

1 In a skillet heat the butter, add the onions and sauté until transparent.

2 Wipe the mushrooms with a damp cloth. Trim off the ends of the stems. Add to the onions and cook, stirring occasionally, 4 or 5 minutes. Stir in the flour, add the half-and-half and bring to a boil, stirring.

3 Stir in the cognac, salt and pepper. Cool while making the pastry.

4 Preheat the oven to 450°F.

5 Line a pie plate with pastry. Prick well with a fork and bake 10 to 12 minutes, until golden.

6 Place the trimmings on the remaining dough, pat and then roll to ⅛-inch thickness. Using a pastry wheel or knife, cut into strips about ½-inch wide.

7 Turn the cooled mushroom mixture into the cooked pie shell. Arrange the strips of pastry over the top in lattice fashion, pressing the ends to the rim of the pie. For a glazed top, brush the pastry with milk or egg diluted with a little water.

8 Bake until the crust is brown, about 20 minutes.

BROILED MUSHROOM CAPS

3 SERVINGS

2 tablespoons fine bread crumbs
1 tablespoon chopped parsley
1 teaspoon minced garlic
12 large mushroom caps
2 tablespoons vegetable oil
Salt and freshly ground pepper to taste

   1 Mix together the crumbs, parsley and garlic.
   2 Brush the mushroom caps with oil and roll in the crumbs. Sprinkle with the salt and pepper.
   3 Preheat the broiler. Broil the mushrooms under moderate heat, about 5 minutes on each side. Sprinkle with more oil, if necessary. Serve as a garnish for meats.

◆

PAPRIKA MUSHROOMS

6 SERVINGS

3 tablespoons butter
1 medium onion, chopped
¾ pound mushrooms, sliced
1 teaspoon Hungarian paprika
½ teaspoon salt
⅛ teaspoon freshly ground pepper
1½ tablespoons flour
¾ cup sour cream

   1 In a skillet heat the butter, add the onions and sauté until golden. Add mushrooms and cook, stirring, 3 to 4 minutes.

   2 Stir in the seasonings and flour. Cook 5 minutes, then remove from the heat. Stir in the sour cream and heat gently. Do not let boil.

◆

SAUTÉ OF WELL-SEASONED MUSHROOMS

3 SERVINGS

3 tablespoons butter
½ pound mushrooms, chopped or sliced
Salt and freshly ground pepper to taste
1 onion, finely chopped
1 garlic clove, crushed
1 teaspoon finely chopped parsley

   1 In a skillet heat 2 tablespoons of the butter, add the mushrooms and cook until golden brown. Season with salt and pepper. Remove the mushrooms from the pan.
   2 Add the remaining butter and heat. Add the onion, garlic and parsley and cook, stirring, about 2 minutes over high heat. Do not let brown.
   3 Return the mushrooms to the pan and reheat.

SWISS MUSHROOMS

4 TO 6 SERVINGS

1 tablespoon chopped shallots or scallions
7 tablespoons butter
1 pound mushrooms
Juice of ½ lemon
1 tablespoon chopped parsley
1 egg yolk
¼ cup flour
1 cup milk
1 cup half-and-half
¼ teaspoon grated nutmeg
Salt and freshly ground pepper to taste
¾ cup grated Gruyère or Swiss cheese

1 Preheat the oven to 350°F.

2 Cook the shallots in 3 tablespoons of the butter, stirring, for about 3 minutes. Do not brown.

3 Chop the mushrooms fine and add them to the skillet. Sprinkle them immediately with the lemon juice and stir in the parsley. Cook, stirring, for about 15 minutes, until almost a paste. Remove from the heat. When slightly cool, stir in the egg yolk.

4 Melt the remaining butter in a saucepan and stir in the flour, using a wire whisk. When mixture is blended, add the milk and half-and-half, stirring rapidly with the whisk. When mixture is thickened and smooth, season with the nutmeg, salt and pepper. Stir in the mushrooms.

5 Make a layer of the mushroom mixture in a buttered casserole. Cover with half the cheese. Add remaining mixture and sprinkle with remaining cheese. Bake for 15 to 20 minutes, until light brown and heated through. Final browning may be done under the broiler.

MUSHROOMS FLORENTINE

4 TO 6 SERVINGS

12 to 16 large mushrooms
¼ pound butter, melted
1½ tablespoons minced onions
1 garlic clove, minced
¾ cup puréed cooked spinach
½ cup minced cooked chicken or ground cooked pork
¼ teaspoon grated nutmeg
½ teaspoon salt
⅛ teaspoon freshly ground pepper
2 tablespoons grated Parmesan cheese

1 Preheat the oven to 375°F.

2 Wash the mushrooms and remove the stems. Dip the caps into 6 tablespoons of the melted butter and place them upside down in a buttered baking dish.

3 Chop the mushroom stems and sauté them, along with the onions and garlic, in the remaining butter for about 10 minutes, until soft but not brown.

4 Add the spinach, chicken, nutmeg, salt and pepper to the sautéed mixture.

5 Fill the mushroom caps with the spinach mixture. Sprinkle the grated cheese over the top of the filling. Bake for 15 minutes. Serve hot.

BOILED OKRA

Choose young, tender pods not more than 2½ inches long. Wash the okra and cut off the stems without cutting into the pods. Cook, covered, in a small amount of boiling salted water until the okra is tender but not excessively soft, about 8 minutes. Drain.

Some southern cooks insist that a little acid (vinegar or lemon juice) added to the water in which the okra is boiled cuts its mucilaginous quality.

Boiled okra may be dressed with lemon juice and melted butter. Or it may be cooled, marinated in a vinaigrette and served with mayonnaise. One pound will serve 3 to 4 people.

◆

CREOLE OKRA

4 SERVINGS

2 tablespoons butter or bacon drippings
¼ cup minced onions
3 tablespoons minced green pepper
1½ cups sliced okra
2 cups peeled and chopped tomatoes
Pinch of basil
Salt and freshly ground pepper to taste

1 Heat the butter, add the onions and green pepper and cook until soft but not brown.

2 Add the okra and sauté over moderate heat about 5 minutes, stirring constantly.

3 Reduce the heat, add the remaining ingredients and simmer, covered, about 20 minutes. Add a small amount of water if necessary to prevent scorching and to give a moist consistency.

OKRA WITH CORN

6 SERVINGS

4 tablespoons butter
2 medium green peppers, seeded and diced
½ cup minced scallions, tops included
1½ cups (about 4 plump ears) corn
    cut from the cob
1½ cups sliced okra
⅔ cup boiling water
½ teaspoon salt
⅛ teaspoon freshly ground pepper

1 Heat the butter in a skillet, add the peppers and scallions and sauté 2 to 3 minutes.

2 Add the remaining ingredients, cover and simmer until the vegetables are tender, about 5 minutes. Stir occasionally to prevent burning.

◆

FRIED OKRA

6 SERVINGS

3 dozen okra pods
2 eggs, lightly beaten
2 tablespoons milk
¾ teaspoon salt
½ cup fine dry bread crumbs
6 tablespoons vegetable oil

1 Boil the okra pods until almost tender, about 5 minutes. Drain.

2 Mix the eggs with the milk and salt. Dip the pods in the crumbs, then in the egg mixture, then again in the crumbs.

3 Heat the oil in a skillet, add the okra and sauté until brown, turning once.

Chicken-Okra Gumbo, page 154.

ONIONS BAKED IN THEIR SKINS

ALLOW 2 ONIONS PER SERVING

Wash medium onions, dry and bake in a preheated 375°F oven until tender, about 1½ hours.

Cut a slice from the root end of each onion and squeeze out the center. Discard the skins. Season with butter, salt and freshly ground black pepper to taste.

♦

ONIONS WITH CREAM AND SHERRY

6 SERVINGS

12 medium onions, sliced
⅔ cup cream
3 tablespoons sherry
½ teaspoon or more salt
Freshly ground pepper to taste
3 tablespoons butter

1 Boil the onions until tender yet firm, about 5 minutes. Drain and turn into a greased baking dish.

2 Preheat the oven to 350°F.

3 Mix the cream, sherry, salt and pepper and pour over the onions. Dot with butter.

4 Cover and bake 30 minutes.

CREAMED ONIONS

Creamed onions are a most appetizing dish and almost as traditional as turkey on many Thanksgiving tables. An interesting variation includes a sprinkling of thyme as noted below.

6 SERVINGS

18 small white onions
3 tablespoons butter
3 tablespoons flour
1½ cups milk
⅓ cup chopped parsley
¼ teaspoon paprika

1 To prevent weeping, cook the onions in their skins until tender, 20 minutes or longer. Drain and peel.

2 In a saucepan melt the butter, add the flour and stir with a wire whisk until blended. Meanwhile, bring the milk to a boil and add all at once to the butter-flour mixture, stirring vigorously with the whisk until the sauce is smooth and thickened. Add sauce to the onions and reheat. Sprinkle with parsley and paprika.

Variations

CHEESE

Add ½ cup grated sharp cheddar cheese to the sauce before adding the onions.

MUSHROOMS

Sauté ½ pound sliced mushrooms in butter and add to the sauce with the onions.

THYME

Stir 1 teaspoon or less of thyme into the sauce and omit the paprika.

FRENCH-FRIED ONIONS

Allow 1 large onion per serving. Cut the onions into ¼-inch slices, cover with a mixture of half water and half milk and let stand 30 minutes.

Drain the onions and dry on paper toweling. Dredge the onions in flour and brown in deep fat heated to 360°F.

Drain on paper toweling and sprinkle with salt to taste. Serve immediately.

♦

BAKED ONIONS

4 SERVINGS

8 (2-inch diameter) onions
¾ teaspoon salt
⅛ teaspoon freshly ground pepper
2 tablespoons butter
½ cup beef or chicken stock
1 tablespoon flour
2 tablespoons cold water
Fresh parsley for garnish

1 Preheat the oven to 375°F.
2 Peel the onions. Place them with the salt and boiling water to cover in a saucepan. Bring to the boiling point, cover, and cook for 5 minutes. Drain the onions and place them close together in a 1-quart casserole. Sprinkle with pepper, dot with butter, add the stock, and bake for about 45 minutes, until tender.
3 Mix the flour and water to a smooth paste and blend with the liquid around the onions. Bake for about 5 minutes longer, until the sauce is slightly thickened. Garnish with parsley.

BAKED ONIONS WITH PORK AND SCALLIONS

4 TO 8 SERVINGS

4 large onions
3 tablespoons butter
1 garlic clove, minced
¼ pound lean pork, ground
½ cup soft fresh bread crumbs
¼ cup chopped scallions, green part included
1 tablespoon chopped parsley
Salt and freshly ground pepper to taste

1 Preheat the oven to 350°F.
2 Peel the onions and cut them into halves crosswise. Scoop out part of the inside but leave a thick shell and cavity for stuffing. Chop the scooped-out onion.
3 Melt 1 tablespoon of the butter and cook the chopped onion and garlic in it briefly, stirring.
4 Combine the pork, crumbs, scallions, parsley, salt and pepper in a mixing bowl. Add the onion and garlic mixture and blend well. Sprinkle the 8 onion halves with salt and stuff them with equal amounts of the filling.
5 Rub the bottom of a baking dish with the remaining butter. Arrange the stuffed onions on it and cover closely with foil.
6 Bake for 1 hour, until onions are tender and meat is thoroughly cooked. Serve as is or, if desired, with a tomato sauce.

ONIONS AU GRATIN

4 SERVINGS

1 pound small whole white onions, or large
    onions sliced
2 tablespoons butter
2 tablespoons flour
½ cup cream or milk
Salt and freshly ground pepper to taste
¼ cup chopped parsley
1 cup coarse bread crumbs, buttered, or ¼ cup
    grated Parmesan cheese

1 Peel the onions and boil them in lightly salted water until just tender. Drain well, reserving ½ cup cooking liquid.

2 Melt the butter in a saucepan, add the flour and blend with a wire whisk. Meanwhile, bring the cream to a boil and add all at once to the butter-flour mixture, while stirring vigorously with the whisk. Add the reserved cooking water, salt, pepper and parsley.

3 Add the onions to the sauce and turn the mixture into a casserole. Sprinkle with buttered crumbs or grated cheese, or a mixture of both.

4 Brown under a preheated broiler or, if the dish has been prepared ahead, bake uncovered in a preheated 375°F oven until heated through and brown on top.

Variation

VEGETABLES AU GRATIN

Substitute any cooked vegetables such as peas, spinach or celery or a mixture of vegetables for part of the onions.

Onion Soup with Cheese, page 70.
Onion Relish, page 597.
Pickled Onions, page 606.

QUICK ONION KUCHEN

4 SERVINGS

2 tablespoons butter
4 large onions, sliced
2 eggs, beaten
1 cup sour cream
¼ teaspoon salt
Freshly ground pepper to taste
½ teaspoon caraway seeds (optional)
4 slices of rye bread
2 to 4 slices of bacon, halved

1 Preheat the oven to 375°F.

2 Heat the butter, add the onions and sauté until tender.

3 Mix the eggs, sour cream, salt, pepper and caraway seed.

4 Place the bread in a shallow greased baking dish and cover with the onions. Pour the sour cream mixture over the onions and place the bacon on top.

5 Bake until the bacon is crisp, about 25 minutes. Serve piping hot.

GLAZED ONIONS

4 SERVINGS

20 small white onions
3 tablespoons butter
1 to 2 teaspoons sugar
¼ teaspoon salt

1 Place the unskinned onions in a saucepan, add 1 inch boiling water, cover and cook until tender, about 20 minutes. Drain, cool and slip off the skins.

2 Heat the butter in a saucepan or skillet, add the onions, sprinkle with the sugar and salt and cook slowly, shaking the pan or turning the onions until they become a light golden brown.

ONIONS STUFFED WITH NUTS

6 SERVINGS

6 large Spanish or Bermuda onions
2 tablespoons butter
1¼ cups coarsely chopped Brazil nuts
    (or filberts, pecans or peanuts)
1 cup (packed) coarse dry bread crumbs
    or cooked rice
1 egg, lightly beaten
¼ teaspoon thyme
Salt and freshly ground pepper to taste
Buttered bread crumbs

1 Peel the onions without cutting off root ends, so onions will remain whole. Cut a thick slice from the top of each. Boil the onions and the top slices in a large quantity of salted water until just tender, about 30 minutes. Drain and cool. Scoop out the centers to form cups, leaving ⅓- to ½-inch-thick walls. Save the centers and invert the cups to drain.

2 Preheat the oven to 375°F.

3 Chop the top slices and onion centers. In a skillet heat the butter, add the chopped onion and cook until most of the liquid that forms in the skillet evaporates. Add the remaining ingredients except the buttered crumbs and mix well.

4 Stuff the onions with the mixture and top with the buttered crumbs. Place in a pan and add water barely to cover the bottom. Bake until the crumbs are brown, 20 to 30 minutes. Serve with tomato, mushroom or cheese sauce.

ONIONS STUFFED WITH MUSHROOMS

6 SERVINGS

6 large onions
4 tablespoons butter
½ green pepper, chopped
½ pound mushrooms, chopped
1 cup cooked rice
Salt and freshly ground pepper to taste
Soy sauce, curry powder or other desired
    seasoning
¼ cup sifted bread crumbs or grated
    Parmesan cheese

1 Prepare the onions for stuffing (see opposite page). Preheat the oven to 375°F.
2 Heat half of the butter in a skillet, add the pepper and mushrooms and cook briefly. Add the rice, seasonings and chopped onion. Stuff the onion shells with the mixture.
3 Sprinkle the tops with the crumbs and dot with bits of the remaining butter.
4 Place in a pan and add water barely to cover the bottom. Bake until the crumbs are brown, 20 to 30 minutes.

Note: One cup cooked meat, poultry, fish or shellfish may be substituted for the mushrooms.

BUTTERED PARSNIPS

Wash and peel parsnips. Leave whole, or slice if desired. Cook in a small amount of boiling salted water, covered, until tender, about 20 minutes for whole parsnips. Drain and serve with salt, freshly ground pepper and melted butter. Allow 1½ pounds for 4 servings.

♦

CANDIED PARSNIPS

6 SERVINGS

6 parsnips, peeled
½ cup brown sugar, firmly packed
1 teaspoon salt
½ cup orange juice
1 teaspoon grated orange rind
4 tablespoons butter

1 Boil the parsnips until almost tender, about 15 minutes. Drain and slice.
2 Preheat the oven to 375°F.
3 Arrange the parsnips in layers in a greased casserole, sprinkling the layers with some of the sugar, salt, juice and rind and bits of butter. Bake 25 to 30 minutes.

BUTTERED FRESH PEAS

Shell peas just before cooking and place in a small amount of boiling salted water. Add a pinch of sugar, if desired. Cover and simmer until just tender (cooking time will depend on the size and age of the peas). Drain and season with salt and melted butter. One pound of peas will yield about 1 cup shelled.

♦

PURÉED GREEN PEAS

6 TO 8 SERVINGS

2 packages frozen peas, cooked
¼ teaspoon sugar
3 tablespoons butter
¼ cup flour
½ cup cream
Salt and freshly ground pepper to taste
¼ cup sour cream

1　Rub well-drained peas through a sieve or purée in a food mill. Add the sugar.

2　In a saucepan melt the butter, blend in the flour and cook, stirring, until light brown. Add the pea purée and cream and bring to a boil, stirring constantly.

3　Season with salt and pepper, mix well and stir in the sour cream.

Cream of Curried Pea Soup, page 69.
Pasta with Fresh Peas, page 486.

FRESH PEAS, FRENCH STYLE

4 SERVINGS

2 cups shelled peas (about 2 pounds in the shell)
6 tiny white onions, peeled
5 to 6 lettuce leaves, shredded
3 parsley sprigs, tied together
½ teaspoon salt
Pinch of sugar
3 tablespoons butter
¼ cup water
1 teaspoon flour

1　In a saucepan combine the peas, onions, lettuce, parsley, salt, sugar and 2 tablespoons of the butter. Mix together and add the water.

2　Cover closely and cook over medium heat until all but a little of the moisture evaporates, about 20 minutes.

3　Cream together the remaining butter and the flour. Add to the liquid in the pan and shake the pan in a circular movement to mix it in (stirring with a utensil breaks the peas). When the liquid has thickened and returned to a boil, remove the pan from the heat. Remove the parsley and serve.

♦

FRIED SWEET PEPPERS

4 SERVINGS

6 sweet peppers, a mixture of green, red and yellow
1 tablespoon butter
1 tablespoon olive oil
Salt and freshly ground pepper to taste
Oregano to taste

1 Wash the peppers and cut them into quarters. Remove stems, seeds and membranes.

2 Heat the butter and olive oil in a large skillet and add the quartered peppers. Cook, covered, for 10 minutes. Uncover and cook, stirring occasionally, for 10 minutes longer, until the peppers are tender.

3 Season with salt, pepper and oregano. Serve immediately.

◆

RICE-STUFFED GREEN PEPPERS

6 SERVINGS

6 large green peppers
¼ cup finely chopped onions
2 tablespoons butter
4 cups cooked rice
¼ cup finely chopped parsley
1 cup grated cheddar cheese
Salt and freshly ground pepper to taste
⅓ cup chicken stock

1 Preheat the oven to 350°F.

2 Hollow out the peppers and remove the seeds. Place the peppers in a colander or sieve and lower into a large pan of boiling water. Leave them in the water for about 5 minutes. Drain.

3 Sauté the onions in the butter until tender. Combine the onions with the rice, parsley, cheese, salt and pepper. Stir in the stock and fill the pepper cases with the mixture.

4 Place the filled peppers in a buttered baking dish, add ¼ cup water and bake for about 15 minutes, or until peppers are barely tender and filling is piping hot. Serve with tomato sauce, if desired.

MEAT-STUFFED GREEN PEPPERS

6 SERVINGS

6 large green peppers
¼ cup olive oil
½ cup chopped onions
1 garlic clove, finely chopped
¾ pound ground veal, beef or pork, or a combination of the three
¾ cup grated Parmesan cheese
2 cups cooked rice
3 tablespoons chopped parsley
Salt and freshly ground pepper to taste
3 tablespoons red wine
¾ cup tomato juice or stock

1 Preheat the oven to 350°F.

2 Trim the stem ends from the peppers and carefully remove the seeds and pith.

3 In a large skillet heat the oil, add the onions and garlic and sauté until the onions are transparent. Add the meat and stir until it is no longer red.

4 Stir in the remaining ingredients except the tomato juice and let cool slightly. Stuff the peppers with the mixture.

5 Place the peppers in a greased baking dish and pour the tomato juice around them. Bake until the peppers are tender, 30 to 40 minutes. Baste occasionally with the pan liquid, adding more liquid to the pan as necessary.

Roasted Peppers, page 34.
Ed Giobbi's Sweet Red Pepper Sauce for Pasta, page 490.
Italian Pepper Salad, page 457.
Henry Creel's Pepper Hash, page 595.
Pickled Sweet Red Peppers, page 606.
Veal with Peppers, Italian Style, page 316.

PIMIENTOS STUFFED WITH CORN

4 SERVINGS

1¼ cups cooked corn
¾ cup soft bread crumbs
1 tablespoon chili sauce
1 to 2 tablespoons grated onions
3 tablespoons butter, melted
Salt and freshly ground pepper to taste
4 whole canned pimientos, rinsed and
    well drained

1 Preheat the oven to 450°F.
2 Mix the corn, crumbs, chili sauce, onions, 2 tablespoons of the butter, salt and pepper.
3 Stuff the pimientos with the mixture and place in a shallow buttered baking dish. Top each with ¼ tablespoon of the remaining butter and bake 15 minutes.

Note: Any ground meat, poultry or fish may be substituted for the corn.

GLAZED PUMPKIN

6 TO 8 SERVINGS

1 (3-pound) pumpkin
¼ cup orange juice
¾ cup firmly packed brown sugar
¾ teaspoon cinnamon
½ teaspoon salt
4 tablespoons butter, melted

1 Peel and seed the pumpkin. Cut it into chunks and steam it on a rack in a pot with a tight-fitting cover for 20 minutes, until the pumpkin is nearly tender. Drain the chunks well.
2 Preheat the oven to 400°F.
3 Arrange the pumpkin chunks in one layer in a greased shallow baking dish. Mix the orange juice, sugar, ½ teaspoon of the cinnamon and the salt and spoon the syrup over the pumpkin. Drizzle with the melted butter.
4 Bake for 25 minutes, until the pumpkin is tender and glazed. Sprinkle the remaining cinnamon over the pumpkin before serving.

PUMPKIN RING

8 SERVINGS

1 (3-pound) pumpkin
¼ cup milk
¼ cup fresh bread crumbs
4 tablespoons butter, melted
3 eggs, well beaten
1 tablespoon grated onion
½ teaspoon salt
⅛ teaspoon freshly ground pepper

1 Cut the pumpkin into halves. Remove the seeds, stringy portion and outside shell. Cut into small pieces. Cover with boiling water and cook until tender, about 20 minutes. Drain and mash thoroughly, or put through a coarse sieve or food mill.

2 Preheat the oven to 350°F.

3 Add the remaining ingredients to the pumpkin and mix well. Pack the mixture into a buttered 1-quart ring mold. Set the mold in a pan of hot water and bake until firm, about 45 minutes.

4 Turn out on a serving dish and fill the center with buttered peas, tiny whole onions or creamed mushrooms.

BAKED PUMPKIN WITH GINGER

8 SERVINGS

1 (3-pound) pumpkin
4 tablespoons butter
¼ cup light brown sugar, firmly packed
3 tablespoons finely chopped preserved ginger
¼ teaspoon salt
⅛ teaspoon freshly ground pepper

1 Preheat the oven to 350°F.

2 Halve the pumpkin. Remove the seeds and stringy portion. Cut into 2-inch diamonds. Pare each piece, then score deeply.

3 Melt the butter in a saucepan. Add the remaining ingredients and cook over low heat, stirring, until the sugar dissolves.

4 Arrange the pumpkin in a single layer in a shallow baking dish. Brush with the sugar mixture and bake, uncovered, until tender, about 45 minutes, basting frequently.

SCALLIONS WITH CHEESE SAUCE

4 SERVINGS

4 bunches scallions, trimmed
¾ cup chicken stock
2 tablespoons butter
2 tablespoons flour
¼ cup half-and-half
¼ teaspoon salt
Dash of cayenne or Tabasco sauce
½ cup grated cheddar cheese

1 Cook the scallions, covered, in the stock until just tender. Drain and keep warm. Reserve the liquid.

2 Melt the butter, add the flour and stir with a wire whisk until blended. Meanwhile, bring the reserved liquid and the half-and-half to a boil and add all at once to the butter-flour mixture, stirring vigorously with the whisk. Season with salt and cayenne. Add the cheese and stir until melted.

3 Place the scallions on a warm plate and cover with the cheese sauce.

La Fonda del Sol's Pumpkin Soup, page 69.

The French use the name **Florentine** *for almost all spinach dishes, supposedly because the fields around Florence once were green with the vegetable. When one sees eggs Florentine, fish Florentine, or mushrooms Florentine on a menu, it is safe to assume that the foods in question are served on a bed of spinach, either puréed or en branche.*

The water content of spinach is formidable, and because of this it should be cooked only in the water that clings to its leaves after it is washed. Use a saucepan with a tight-fitting cover. One pound of spinach will reduce to just over a cup after cooking.

◆

CREAMED SPINACH

4 TO 6 SERVINGS

3 pounds fresh spinach
4 tablespoons butter
¼ cup flour
1 tablespoon grated onion
2 cups chicken stock or milk
1 teaspoon salt
¼ teaspoon freshly ground pepper
Hard-cooked eggs

1 Wash the spinach several times in cold water to remove all sand; discard any tough stems. Place the spinach in a kettle with only the water that clings to the leaves; cover. Cook until spinach is wilted, then drain and chop very fine.

2 Heat the butter in a skillet. Add the flour and onion and cook, stirring, until brown. Gradually add the stock, stirring constantly until thickened and smooth.

3 Add the spinach, salt and pepper; simmer for several minutes. Garnish with chopped egg whites and riced egg yolks.

SPINACH WITH SESAME SEEDS

4 SERVINGS

3 pounds fresh spinach
¼ cup sesame seeds
2 tablespoons light soy sauce
Juice of ½ lemon
Freshly ground pepper to taste

1 Preheat the oven to 350°F.

2 Wash the spinach and discard any tough stems. Place the spinach in a saucepan with only the water that clings to the leaves. Do not season. Cover, bring to a boil, and cook just until leaves wilt, stirring once or twice. Drain well and keep warm.

3 Meanwhile, scatter the sesame seeds in a small skillet and bake for 5 to 10 minutes, until brown, stirring occasionally. Remove from the oven.

4 Place spinach in a serving dish and add toasted sesame seeds and remaining ingredients.

SPINACH WITH SAUTÉED MUSHROOMS

4 SERVINGS

2 small onions, chopped
2 tablespoons butter
2 pounds fresh spinach
1 cup sliced mushrooms
2 teaspoons lemon juice
1 teaspoon salt
¾ teaspoon sugar
⅛ teaspoon freshly ground pepper

1 Sauté the onions in 1 tablespoon of the butter.

2 Wash the spinach and cut off and discard the root ends and any tough stems. Chop the spinach coarsely and add to the onions. Cover and cook over medium heat for 10 minutes.

3 Sauté the mushrooms in the lemon juice and remaining butter. Add to the spinach along with the seasonings. Toss lightly. If desired, garnish with additional sautéed sliced mushrooms. Serve immediately.

ITALIAN SPINACH

3 pounds spinach, well washed and trimmed
1 tablespoon butter
1 tablespoon olive oil
1 garlic clove, finely chopped
Salt to taste
¼ teaspoon cayenne
Coarsely grated Parmesan cheese

1 Cut the spinach into coarse shreds. Plunge into boiling salted water to cover and parboil 30 seconds. Drain well and place in a baking dish.

2 In a skillet heat the butter and olive oil. Add the garlic, salt and cayenne and cook over low heat 5 minutes. Combine the oil mixture with the spinach and sprinkle with cheese and additional butter, melted. Brown quickly under a broiler.

Spinach Salad, page 444.
Spinach Soup with Yogurt, page 71.
Cream of Spinach Soup, page 71.
Spinach and Endive Salad, page 445.

SPINACH MOLD

3 cups chopped drained cooked spinach
⅔ cup fine dry bread crumbs
½ cup minced onions
2 tablespoons butter
⅛ teaspoon freshly ground pepper
½ teaspoon salt
⅛ teaspoon grated nutmeg
½ cup grated Swiss cheese
5 eggs
1 cup milk, scalded

1 Preheat the oven to 325°F. Generously oil a 1-quart ring mold.

2 Combine the spinach and crumbs in a mixing bowl.

3 Cook the onions in the butter in a covered skillet for 10 minutes. Add to the spinach mixture. Add the pepper, salt, nutmeg and cheese.

4 Lightly beat the eggs. Add the hot milk to the eggs, stirring constantly. Add to spinach mixture and mix well.

5 Pour the mixture into the prepared mold and set the mold in a pan of hot water. Bake for 35 minutes, or until a knife plunged into the center comes out clean.

6 Allow the mold to rest for 5 minutes before unmolding onto a warm serving platter.

For vegetable lovers, the squash family is a bountiful blessing, for this genus of edible gourd includes such diverse members as white pattypans or cymlings, yellow crooknecks and dark green zucchini. The small green acorn squash, the giant blue-gray Hubbards and even the familiar orange pumpkins are relatives. One may use any one of the orange-fleshed fall varieties in place of another and they can be glazed or candied in the same way that sweet potatoes are prepared. The smaller species, such as zucchini, cymlings and acorn squash, with their seed-filled hollow centers, are well designed for stuffing preparations and their bland flavors combine successfully with a wide variety of seasonings.

♦

BAKED ACORN SQUASH

6 SERVINGS

3 acorn squash
Grated nutmeg or ground ginger to taste
Salt and freshly ground pepper to taste
3 teaspoons brown sugar, or more
6 teaspoons butter
6 teaspoons sweet sherry (optional)

1 Preheat the oven to 325°F.
2 Split the squash into halves and scoop out the fibers and seeds.
3 Sprinkle the cavity of each half with nutmeg, salt, pepper, brown sugar and a teaspoon of butter. Bake for 30 to 45 minutes, or until flesh is tender. Five minutes before serving, add a teaspoon of sherry to each cavity.

PATTYPANS STUFFED WITH VEAL

8 SERVINGS

4 white pattypan squash
¼ cup olive oil
1 onion, finely chopped
2 garlic cloves, minced
1 pound veal, ground
2 tart green apples, peeled, cored and diced
1 cup soft fresh bread crumbs
¼ cup grated Parmesan cheese
2 tablespoons pine nuts, chopped
½ teaspoon thyme
Salt and freshly ground pepper
Chicken stock

1 Preheat the oven to 350°F.
2 Wash the squash. Cut a small slice from both stem and blossom ends and cut the squash into halves horizontally. Steam in a colander over a pan of boiling water for 10 minutes. Scoop out the seeds and discard them. Scoop out some of the squash to enlarge the hollow, but do not cut through the bottom. Chop the scooped-out vegetable. Turn the hollowed-out halves upside down to drain.
3 Heat the oil in a skillet and sauté the onion and garlic until tender but not brown. Add the veal and cook until the meat loses its color, stirring occasionally.
4 Add the apples, crumbs, cheese, nuts, thyme, salt, pepper and chopped squash. Mix well. Fill the squash halves with the mixture.
5 Place the filled squash in a shallow baking dish. Pour in the stock until it reaches a depth of 1 inch. Bake for 25 minutes, or until the squash is tender and the stuffing hot.

BAKED BUTTERNUT SQUASH

ALLOW ½ POUND PER SERVING

Preheat the oven to 400°F.

Cut butternut squash in half lengthwise, and then across into quarters. Remove the seeds and fibers and brush cut surfaces with melted butter.

Place on a baking sheet, cover with foil and bake until almost tender when tested with a knife, about 25 minutes. Uncover, brush again with butter, and continue baking until tender and light brown.

♦

GLAZED BUTTERNUT SQUASH

4 SERVINGS

1 (2-pound) butternut squash
½ cup brown sugar, firmly packed
½ teaspoon cinnamon
¼ teaspoon grated nutmeg or ground ginger
¼ teaspoon salt
3 tablespoons butter, melted

1 Peel, seed and slice the squash. Place on a rack in a pot with a tight-fitting cover, add water to cover bottom of pot, cover and steam until squash is nearly tender, 12 to 15 minutes. Drain the squash well.

2 Preheat the oven to 400°F.

3 Arrange the squash in 1 or 2 layers in a greased shallow baking dish. Mix sugar, spices and salt and sprinkle over the squash. Drizzle with the melted butter.

4 Bake until the squash is tender and somewhat glazed, 15 to 20 minutes. For a deeper glaze, broil a few minutes.

MASHED SQUASH

4 SERVINGS

1 butternut or acorn squash
2 tablespoons butter
1 to 2 teaspoons brown sugar
¼ teaspoon salt
Milk

1 Peel the squash and cut into slices of even thickness. Remove the seeds.

2 Place the squash slices on a rack in a pot with a tight-fitting cover, add water to cover the bottom of the pot and steam, covered, until tender, 15 to 20 minutes.

3 Lift the squash to a bowl or drain off the water. Mash or put through a food mill. Add butter, brown sugar, salt and enough milk, if needed, to make mixture soft and fluffy. Reheat before serving.

SCALLOPED SUMMER SQUASH WITH CHEESE

4 TO 5 SERVINGS

3 tablespoons butter
1 onion, minced
1 garlic clove, minced
1 green pepper, chopped
4 medium tomatoes, peeled and chopped
½ teaspoon salt
Freshly ground pepper to taste
1½ pounds summer squash
1 cup grated Parmesan cheese

1 Heat the butter, add the onion, garlic and green pepper and sauté until tender and light brown. Add the tomatoes, salt and pepper and cook, stirring occasionally, while preparing the squash.

2 Peel the squash if the skin is not tender and cut into slices or cubes. Put in a saucepan with ½ cup boiling water, cover tightly and cook until the squash is just tender. Drain well.

3 Preheat the oven to 350°F.

4 Turn half the squash into a deep pie plate or casserole. Cover with half the tomato sauce and half the cheese. Repeat the layers.

5 Bake until the cheese topping is bubbly and beginning to brown.

SUMMER SQUASH WITH OREGANO

4 SERVINGS

1½ pounds yellow summer squash
1 garlic clove, sliced
1 tablespoon olive oil
1 large tomato, peeled and quartered
1 teaspoon salt
½ teaspoon oregano
Freshly ground pepper to taste
2 tablespoons chopped parsley

1 Scrub the squash with a stiff brush and slice crosswise into thin slices.

2 Sauté the garlic in the oil in a 1½-quart pan for 1 minute. Add the sliced squash and continue to cook for 1 minute while turning the slices gently in the oil. Stir in the tomato, salt and oregano.

3 Cover and cook over low heat for 12 to 15 minutes. Sprinkle with pepper and garnish with parsley.

SQUASH WITH ONIONS AND SOUR CREAM

1 cup finely chopped onions
2 tablespoons butter
2 pounds yellow summer squash
1 teaspoon salt
½ cup sour cream
Freshly ground pepper to taste
½ cup soft fresh bread crumbs
2 tablespoons melted butter

1 Preheat the oven to 350°F.
2 Cook the onions in the butter until golden, stirring almost constantly.
3 Scrub and trim the squash and cut them into cubes. Cook squash in 1 inch of boiling water containing the salt for 5 to 10 minutes, or until tender. Put the squash through a food mill or ricer.
4 Combine the puréed squash, onions and sour cream and season the mixture with additional salt and pepper to taste. Spoon it into a casserole and top with crumbs. Dribble the butter over it.
5 Bake for 10 to 15 minutes, or until the casserole starts to bubble. Place it briefly under the broiler until crumbs are brown.

BROILED TOMATOES WITH OLIVES

6 SERVINGS

6 medium tomatoes
½ cup chopped cooked ham
½ cup chopped green olives
Chopped basil
3 tablespoons olive oil

1 Halve the tomatoes and leave inverted a few minutes to drain. Preheat the broiler. Arrange them, cut side up, in a shallow heatproof dish.
2 Mix the ham and olives and place a rounded tablespoon of the mixture on each tomato half. Sprinkle with basil and spoon the oil over the top.
3 Broil about 3 inches from high broiler heat until the tops are brown, about 10 minutes.

◆

SAUTÉED TOMATO SLICES

ALLOW ½ TO 1 TOMATO PER SERVING

Dip firm tomato slices into slightly beaten egg, then into fine cracker crumbs. Sprinkle with salt and pepper.
Brown on both sides in hot melted butter in a heavy skillet, about 10 minutes.

STEWED TOMATOES WITH SWEET BASIL

4 SERVINGS

5 large ripe tomatoes
6 tablespoons butter
Salt and freshly ground pepper to taste
10 basil leaves, cut in thin strips
2 cups toasted bread cubes

1 Drop the tomatoes into boiling water for 10 seconds, then skin the tomatoes and remove the seeds. Dice the flesh and place in a saucepan. Add the butter, salt and pepper. Cover and stew slowly about 5 minutes, stirring occasionally.

2 Add the basil and cook 10 minutes longer. Add the bread cubes and mix well. Cook until the tomatoes are soft. The crumbs will take up the excess liquid.

DEVILED TOMATOES

4 SERVINGS

4 tomatoes, halved
Salt and freshly ground pepper to taste
Cayenne to taste
2 tablespoons buttered bread crumbs
2 tablespoons butter
½ teaspoon prepared mustard
Dash of Tabasco sauce
2 teaspoons Worcestershire sauce
1 teaspoon sugar
1½ tablespoons red wine vinegar
1 egg yolk

1 Place the tomato halves on a baking sheet, cut side up. Sprinkle lightly with salt, pepper and cayenne, and then with the crumbs. Set aside.

2 Melt the butter in a very small saucepan. Add the mustard, Tabasco, Worcestershire, sugar, vinegar and a sprinkling of salt. Bring to a boil.

3 Beat the egg yolk and add a little of the vinegar mixture while stirring. Return to the saucepan and cook over low heat until thickened, stirring constantly.

4 Broil the tomatoes until the crumbs are brown and serve with a spoonful of sauce on each half.

Cold Tomato Soup, page 72.
Fresh Tomato Soup, page 72.
Cream of Tomato Soup, page 73.
Tomato Dill Soup, page 74.
Gazpacho, page 74
Tomatoes Antiboise, page 120.
Herbed Tomato Salad, page 458
Tomatoes Stuffed with Basil, page 461.
Tomato and Onion Salad, page 461.
Cherry Tomato and Sour Cream Salad, page 462.
Uncooked Tomato Relish, page 597.
Spicy Tomato Catsup, page 602.

TUNA-STUFFED BAKED TOMATOES

6 SERVINGS

6 large tomatoes
2 slices crumbled bread, crusts removed
1 (7-ounce) can tuna, flaked
6 anchovies, chopped
1 small garlic clove, minced
1 tablespoon chopped basil
Salt to taste
3 tablespoons dry bread crumbs or grated
    Parmesan cheese
3 tablespoons butter, melted

1 Preheat the oven to 375°F.
2 Cut the tops from the tomatoes and discard. Scoop out the pulp and mince it, or rub it through a coarse sieve. Invert the tomatoes to drain.
3 To the tomato pulp add the bread, tuna, anchovies, garlic and basil. Mix well.
4 Salt the tomato cups lightly and fill them with mixture.
5 Toss the crumbs in the butter until well mixed and sprinkle over the top.
6 Place the tomatoes in an oiled baking dish and bake about 20 minutes.

TOMATOES STUFFED WITH CHICKEN LIVERS

8 SERVINGS

8 firm tomatoes
Salt and freshly ground pepper
½ pound fresh mushrooms
4 tablespoons butter
1 medium onion, minced
½ cup soft fresh bread crumbs
1 tablespoon chopped parsley
1½ pounds chicken livers
2 tablespoons dry white wine

1 Preheat the oven to 350°F.
2 Wash and dry the tomatoes. Cut off a thin slice from the stem end of each tomato and scoop out the pulp. Season the tomato shells lightly with salt and pepper and reserve; reserve half of the pulp.
3 Wipe the mushrooms and reserve 8 of the caps. Chop the remaining mushrooms. Melt 2 tablespoons of the butter and in it sauté the mushroom caps briefly. Remove mushrooms from the pan and set aside. Add the onion and chopped mushrooms to the butter left in the pan and cook for 3 minutes. Add the bread crumbs, reserved tomato pulp, parsley, 1 teaspoon salt and ⅛ teaspoon pepper. Cook for 3 minutes longer.
4 Cut the chicken livers into bite-size pieces and sauté them in the remaining butter. Add them to the crumb mixture along with the wine; blend well. Fill the tomato shells generously with the mixture. Dot with additional butter and top with the mushroom caps.
5 Place in a well-buttered baking pan and bake for 20 minutes.

Note: If desired, the dish can be completely assembled and refrigerated overnight before baking.

CUCUMBER-STUFFED TOMATOES

6 SERVINGS

2 cucumbers
2 teaspoons grated onions
4 teaspoons lemon juice
4 tablespoons butter
¼ cup water
Salt and freshly ground pepper to taste
6 tomatoes
Buttered soft fresh bread crumbs

1 Preheat the oven to 400°F.

2 Peel and seed the cucumbers and cut them into ½-inch cubes. Put in a saucepan and add the onions, lemon juice, butter, water and seasonings. Simmer for 5 minutes.

3 Remove the seeds and pulp from the tomatoes and drain them. Fill the tomatoes with the cooked cucumber mixture. Sprinkle with bread crumbs. Bake for about 10 minutes, until the tomatoes are tender and the crumbs are brown.

COLD RICE-STUFFED TOMATOES

6 SERVINGS

½ cup rice
¼ cup vegetable oil
1 tablespoon vinegar
Salt and freshly ground pepper to taste
1 teaspoon minced onion
1 tablespoon minced parsley
6 medium tomatoes
Boston or romaine lettuce

1 Cook the rice according to package directions. When tender and while still hot, add the oil and toss lightly. Add the vinegar, salt, pepper, onion and parsley. Toss lightly and let stand, covered, at room temperature 3 hours.

2 At serving time, cut the stem ends off the tomatoes. Hollow them out and mix the flesh with the rice. Pile the mixture lightly in the tomatoes and set on a bed of lettuce. If desired, serve with mayonnaise.

PAULA'S COLD TOMATOES

6 SERVINGS

2 pounds spinach, cooked briefly, thoroughly
    drained and finely chopped
4 tablespoons olive oil
2 medium onions, finely chopped
½ cup pine nuts
2 garlic cloves, finely chopped
Salt and freshly ground pepper to taste
6 medium tomatoes
Sugar
Chopped basil to taste

1 Preheat the oven to 350°F.

2 Drain the spinach thoroughly, then squeeze out the remaining moisture.

3 In a skillet heat 2 tablespoons of the oil and sauté the onions briefly until pale golden in color. Add pine nuts and garlic and sauté 1 minute. Remove from the heat.

4 Add the spinach, the remaining oil, the salt and pepper.

5 Cut the stem ends from the tomatoes, hollow them out and sprinkle the insides with salt, pepper, a little sugar and basil. Stuff the tomatoes with the spinach mixture.

6 Arrange the tomatoes in a baking pan and bake until they wrinkle, about 15 minutes. Chill. At serving time, bring to room temperature.

FRIED GREEN TOMATOES

4 TO 6 SERVINGS

¼ cup flour
1 tablespoon cornmeal
½ teaspoon salt
4 large green tomatoes, unpeeled
¼ cup vegetable oil
4 tablespoons butter
Sugar
Freshly ground pepper to taste

1 Mix flour, cornmeal and salt. Wash and core the tomatoes and slice them. Coat the slices with the flour mixture.

2 Brown on one side in hot oil and butter; sprinkle with sugar. Using a spatula, carefully turn each slice over to brown the other side. Sprinkle the brown side with pepper. Do not overcook or the slices will fall apart. Serve immediately.

HOW TO HOME-DRY TOMATOES

Home-dried tomatoes are not quite on a par with imported Italian bottled-in-oil sun-dried tomatoes. But they are an excellent substitute and easy to prepare, although their oven-drying time may range from 6 to 8 hours longer. They may also be dried in a vegetable-and-fruit dehydrator, which takes from 6 to 24 hours.

Select red, ripe unblemished plum tomatoes. Cherry tomatoes may be dried in a similar fashion, but they are much more tedious to prepare. Cut each tomato lengthwise in half and scoop out the seeds of each half. If desired cut away and discard the small dark stem end. Use paper toweling to blot the cut surface of each tomato to remove any excess surface liquid.

Sprinkle the cut surface of each tomato half with a small amount of kosher salt. One teaspoon should be sufficient for 20 tomato halves.

If the tomatoes are to be dried in the oven, preheat the oven to 200°F. If they are to be dried in an electric food dehydrator, preheat it to about 140°F. To many professionals minds the oven drying yields a preferable end result. But the dehydrator will produce tomatoes with a much brighter hue.

For oven drying, line a baking sheet with foil. Arrange the tomato halves skin side down on the foil. If a dehydrator is used, arrange the tomato halves skin side down on one of the racks.

For oven drying, place the baking sheet on one or two of the upper racks. Let bake 6 hours or longer; the commonest drying time is about 7½ hours. Check the tomatoes often to prevent burning or overcooking. When ready, the tomato halves should be shriveled and the skin a bit leathery. They will have lost most of their natural liquid, which will be concentrated.

They will be almost dry but not crisp or brittle. Use your own judgment and continue cooking until properly dried. Let them stand uncovered until they have reached room temperature. (See instructions for How to Package Home-Dried Tomatoes in Oil, opposite).

If an electric food dehydrator is used, cook according to the manufacturer's instructions. Or cook about 2 hours and reduce the dehydrator temperature to 130°F. Continue cooking until the tomatoes are shriveled and the skin somewhat leathery. The total drying time may well be in excess of 12 hours. When ready, the tomatoes will be only slightly moist in the center. They will be almost dry but not crisp or brittle. Let the tomatoes stand uncovered until they have reached room temperature.

HOW TO PACKAGE HOME-DRIED TOMATOES IN OIL Place the dried tomatoes in a shallow dish and sprinkle them lightly with 1 tablespoon vinegar, preferably balsamic vinegar. Turn until the pieces are lightly coated. Let stand briefly and pour off the vinegar. Cut 1 peeled garlic clove into thin slices and set aside.

Arrange the tomato halves, standing them on end, in a sterilized 1-cup (½ pint) glass jar with a screw top. As you work, arrange the garlic slices between the tomato pieces. If you wish you may insert sprigs of fresh herbs such as thyme, rosemary or the leaves of fresh basil in the jar.

Pour approximately ⅓ cup olive oil, or enough to cover the top of the tomatoes, over all and tightly seal the top of the jar. The tomatoes will keep for an indefinite period of time. Once the jar is opened, it must be refrigerated.

Rigatoni with Proscuitto and Sun-dried Tomato Sauce, page 487.
Pesto Sauce with Sun-dried Tomatoes, page 498.

STEAMED WHITE TURNIPS

ALLOW 2 POUNDS FOR 4 SERVINGS

Peel young white turnips and dice in large cubes. Cook in boiling salted water to cover until soft, about 30 minutes. Drain and toss in a little butter, shaking the pan frequently. Serve sprinkled with chopped parsley.

Turnip Soup, page 75.

PURÉED RUTABAGAS
YELLOW TURNIPS

ALLOW 2 POUNDS FOR 4 SERVINGS

Peel rutabagas and cut into cubes. Cook in boiling salted water to cover until soft, about 30 minutes. Drain well.

Purée in a food processor.

Return to the pan and reheat to dry out the surplus water. Add butter and cream and stir until the purée has the consistency of mashed potatoes. Add salt and pepper to taste.

TURNIPS WITH POULETTE SAUCE

6 SERVINGS

2 pounds white or yellow turnips
½ teaspoon salt
Sauce poulette (page 566)
Chopped freshly parsley

1 Peel the turnips and cut them into ½-inch slices. Cut the slices into ½-inch strips.

2 Place strips in a saucepan with 1 inch of boiling water containing the salt. Bring to the boiling point, uncovered, and boil for 5 minutes. Cover and cook for about 15 minutes, until tender.

3 Drain the turnips and toss them lightly with sauce poulette. Garnish with parsley.

RUTABAGA PUDDING

6 SERVINGS

2 cups (about 1¼ pounds) mashed cooked
    rutabagas
2 tablespoons butter
1 cup soft fresh bread crumbs
¼ teaspoon mace
⅛ teaspoon freshly ground pepper
1 teaspoon salt
1 tablespoon sugar
⅛ teaspoon ground ginger
½ cup milk
1 egg, beaten
1 tablespoon butter, melted

1 Preheat the oven to 350°F.

2 Combine the rutabagas, butter, crumbs, mace, pepper, salt, sugar, ginger and milk. Beat in the egg. Turn the mixture into a buttered 1-quart casserole and brush the top with the melted butter. Bake for about 45 minutes, until brown.

BAKED ZUCCHINI AND TOMATOES

6 TO 8 SERVINGS

2 cups chopped onions
1 green pepper, cored, seeded and chopped
½ cup chopped celery
2 garlic cloves
4 tablespoons butter
4 cups chopped peeled tomatoes, fresh or canned
1 bay leaf
1 tablespoon chopped basil, or 1 teaspoon dried
¼ cup chopped parsley
Salt and freshly ground pepper to taste
4 zucchini
½ cup flour
¼ cup olive oil
¾ cup soft fresh bread crumbs
¼ cup grated Parmesan cheese

1 In a medium-size kettle cook the onions, pepper, celery and garlic in 3 tablespoons of the butter until onions are translucent. Add the tomatoes, bay leaf, basil, parsley, salt and pepper. Simmer for 30 minutes.

2 Preheat the oven to 450°F.

3 Scrub and trim the zucchini and cut them into 1-inch rounds. Dredge the rounds in flour, then shake to remove excess. Quickly brown the rounds in the oil and transfer to paper toweling to drain. Add the drained slices to the tomato mixture and continue to cook for about 10 minutes, until zucchini is tender but not mushy.

4 Pour the mixture into a 2-quart baking dish and sprinkle with a mixture of the crumbs and cheese. Dot with remaining butter. Bake until thoroughly hot and bubbling. The top should be golden brown.

ZUCCHINI, ARMENIAN STYLE

6 SERVINGS

2 pounds zucchini, washed and trimmed
1 cup ground lamb, preferably shoulder, or 1 pound lamb patties
½ cup rice
1 small onion, chopped fine
1 tablespoon chopped parsley
½ cup stewed tomatoes
Salt and freshly ground pepper to taste

1 Peel the zucchini and cut into 3-inch lengths. Scoop out the centers. Soak the vegetable in cold salted water about ½ hour.

2 Mix the lamb with the rice, onion, parsley, tomatoes, salt and pepper.

3 Drain the zucchini and fill the hollows with the lamb mixture. Arrange in a saucepan and add water to the depth of 1 inch. The water should not reach more than halfway up the sides of the zucchini.

4 Cover the pan tightly and simmer over low heat until the rice is tender, about 1 hour. Check from time to time to see that the water has not evaporated.

ZUCCHINI WITH HERBS

6 SERVINGS

3 large or 6 small zucchini
1 tablespoon butter
2 tablespoons vegetable oil
1 tablespoon minced shallots or onions
1 teaspoon minced tarragon,
    or ½ teaspoon dried

1 Wash and dry the zucchini. Trim off the ends and cut the zucchini into 1-inch lengths. Cut each length through the center into two.

2 Heat the butter and oil in a large skillet, add the shallots and zucchini and sauté 5 to 10 minutes. Add the tarragon. Toss together and serve immediately.

ZUCCHINI WITH ALMONDS ALLA ROMA

This is a recipe I discovered on a visit to Italy in midsummer. We ate it in a small, relatively new restaurant in Rome called Tre Scalini. The dish consists of small, square-shaped pieces of zucchini (including the skin) sautéed in olive oil and topped with golden brown slices of almonds and grated Pecorino cheese. A marvelous first course or side dish.

4 SERVINGS

3 (½-pound) zucchini
½ cup olive oil
¾ cup sliced blanched almonds
1½ teaspoons minced garlic
Salt to taste
6 tablespoons grated Pecorino Romano
    or Parmesan cheese

1 Trim off the ends of each zucchini. Hold each zucchini upright and slice down to make ¼-inch-thick slices all around. Each slice should be about 1 inch wide. Slice the firm white center portion into similar slices. Discard the seeded center portion.

2 Stack the slices and cut them into 1-inch or slightly smaller squares. There should be about 3½ cups.

3 Heat the oil in a skillet and add the almonds. Cook over moderate heat, stirring constantly, for a few seconds until the pieces are golden brown. Remove the pieces with a slotted spoon and drain on paper toweling.

4 Pour off all but ¼ cup of oil and add the zucchini pieces, garlic and salt. Stir and toss the pieces about 2 minutes, or until they are crisp tender.

5 Spoon equal portions of the zucchini onto 4 individual plates. Sprinkle with equal amounts of the almonds and cheese and serve immediately.

Zucchini à la Grecque, page 462.

ZUCCHINI
AU BON GOUT

6 SERVINGS

6 small whole zucchini, scrubbed and trimmed
1½ cups peeled, chopped tomatoes
¾ cup bread cubes, cooked in butter until crisp
Salt and freshly ground pepper to taste
Grated Parmesan cheese

1 Preheat the oven to 450°F.

2 Simmer the zucchini in a little water until barely tender, 8 to 10 minutes. Drain and, when cool, cut in half lengthwise. Scoop out the seeds from each half and invert the halves on paper toweling to drain.

3 Arrange the zucchini, cut side up, in a baking dish and fill the cavities with equal parts chopped tomatoes and croutons. Sprinkle with salt, pepper and cheese.

4 Bake until heated through. Just before serving, brown under the broiler.

LES COURGETTES
FLORENTINE

6 SERVINGS

3 medium zucchini, washed and trimmed
2 pounds fresh spinach, well washed
    and trimmed
2 tablespoons butter
2 tablespoons flour
½ cup milk
½ cup cream
¼ cup grated Gruyère or Parmesan cheese
¼ teaspoon grated nutmeg
Salt and freshly ground pepper to taste

1 Peel the squash and halve lengthwise. Scoop out the centers. Cook it in a little salted water until barely tender.

2 Meanwhile, cook the spinach until barely tender. Drain and chop coarsely.

3 Preheat the oven to 350°F.

4 In a saucepan melt the butter, add the flour and stir with a wire whisk until blended. Meanwhile, bring the milk and cream to a boil and add all at once to the butter-flour mixture, stirring vigorously with the whisk until the sauce is thickened and smooth.

5 Remove the sauce from the heat and stir in the remaining ingredients. Stir in the chopped spinach and spoon the mixture into the squash halves.

6 Arrange the squash in a baking dish and sprinkle with additional grated Parmesan cheese and melted butter. Bake until heated through. Just before serving, brown quickly under the broiler.

ZUCCHINI STUFFED WITH HAM

6 SERVINGS

1 cup ground ham
½ cup soft bread crumbs
½ teaspoon dry mustard
½ teaspoon salt
⅛ teaspoon freshly ground pepper
2 tablespoons minced onions
½ cup grated cheddar cheese
2 pounds zucchini
¼ cup oil
1 garlic clove, crushed
1½ teaspoons cornstarch
½ cup tomato sauce

1   Preheat the oven to 350°F.
2   Combine the ham, crumbs, mustard, salt, pepper, onions and cheese.
3   Wash the zucchini thoroughly and cut into 3-inch lengths. Scoop out the centers with an apple corer, leaving a shell ¼ inch thick. Stuff with the ham mixture.
4   Place the zucchini in a baking pan and add the oil and garlic. Cover and bake until the squash are tender, 45 to 55 minutes. Remove from the pan.
5   Mix the cornstarch with the tomato sauce and stir into the pan. Cook over low heat until thickened. Skim off the excess fat and spoon the sauce over the zucchini.

ZUCCHINI IN A SKILLET

4 SERVINGS

2 tablespoons vegetable oil
1 medium onion, sliced
1 cup chopped tomatoes, canned or fresh
¾ teaspoon salt
Freshly ground pepper to taste
½ bay leaf
3 medium zucchini, cut into 1-inch pieces

1   Heat the oil, add the onion and sauté until transparent. Add the tomatoes, salt, pepper and bay leaf. Simmer 5 minutes.
2   Add the zucchini to the sauce, cover and simmer until tender, 8 to 10 minutes.

RATATOUILLE NIÇOISE

This dish from the Riviera may be eaten hot or cold. Cold, it may serve as an appetizer. Add garlic according to conscience and social engagements.

5 TO 6 SERVINGS

⅓ cup olive oil
2 or more garlic cloves, peeled and chopped
2 cups (1 large) sliced onions
3 cups (2 medium) sliced zucchini
4 cups (1 small) cubed, peeled eggplant
3 tablespoons flour
2 green peppers, seeded and cut into strips
1½ cups canned plum tomatoes
1 tablespoon capers
Salt and freshly ground pepper to taste

1 Heat the oil in a large skillet, add the garlic and onions and sauté until the onions are transparent.

2 Meanwhile, slice the squash and peel and cube the eggplant. Flour the pieces lightly.

3 Add the squash, eggplant and green peppers to the skillet, cover and cook slowly about 30 minutes.

4 Add the tomatoes and capers and simmer, uncovered, until the mixture is thick, about 10 minutes. Season with salt and pepper. Serve hot or cold.

VEGETABLE MEDLEY

4 SERVINGS

2 tablespoons olive oil
½ garlic clove, crushed
½ cup chopped green pepper
½ cup chopped onion
2 cups sliced yellow squash
1 cup cut green beans
1 cup whole-kernel corn
1 teaspoon salt
1 teaspoon chili powder
1 tablespoon lemon juice
Freshly ground pepper to taste

1 Heat the oil in a 1½-quart saucepan. Add the garlic, green pepper and onion; sauté for 3 to 5 minutes.

2 Add the squash, green beans and corn. Cover the pan and cook over low heat for 20 minutes. Add salt, chili powder, lemon juice and pepper.

Minestrone, page 61.
Ed Giobbi's Vegetable Lasagne, page 482.

PETJEL
MIXED VEGETABLES WITH PEANUT SAUCE

6 SERVINGS

3 tablespoons peanut butter
1½ cups water
1 garlic clove, minced
1 tablespoon brown sugar
¼ teaspoon cayenne pepper
1 tablespoon lemon juice
Salt to taste
1 cup sliced cabbage
1 cup diced green beans
1 pound spinach, cleaned and trimmed
1 cup bean sprouts

1 Combine the peanut butter, water, garlic, brown sugar, cayenne and lemon juice in a saucepan. Bring to a boil, reduce heat and simmer for 2 minutes. Add salt and cool.

2 Boil the cabbage and beans in salted water to cover for 20 minutes. Add the spinach and simmer for 5 minutes. Add the bean sprouts and cook, stirring, for 1 minute. Drain. Place vegetables on a large serving dish. Top with the sauce and serve immediately.

◆

VEGETABLE RAGOÛT

4 SERVINGS

2 large sweet red bell peppers
1 small zucchini
1 (about 6-ounce) white onion
¼ pound mushrooms
1 carrot
1 tablespoon olive oil
1 tablespoon butter
1½ cups finely shredded (julienned) leeks
Freshly ground pepper to taste
¼ cup chicken stock

1 Cut each pepper in half and cut away the core and seeds. Cut the pepper into quarters and cut each quarter into thin strips. There should be about 2 cups.

2 Cut the zucchini into slices about ¼ inch thick. Stack the slices and cut them into ¼-inch strips. There should be about 1 cup.

3 Peel the onion and cut it in half lengthwise. Place each half, cut side down, on a flat surface and slice thin. There should be about 2 cups.

4 Break off the mushroom stems and set aside. Place the caps on a flat surface and, holding a knife parallel to the cutting surface, cut each cap in half. Cut the caps crosswise into thin strips. Cut the mushroom stems lengthwise into thin slices. Cut the slices into thin strips. There should be about 2 cups of mushroom strips.

5 Trim and scrape the carrot. Cut it lengthwise into ¼-inch-thick slices. Cut the slices crosswise in half. Cut the slices lengthwise into very thin julienne strips. There should be about 1 cup.

6 Heat the oil and butter in a small heavy casserole and add the onion and carrot. Cook, stirring, about 1 minute. Add the leeks and cook 1 minute, stirring.

7 Add the peppers, zucchini, and mushrooms and cook, stirring, about 1 minute. Add the black pepper and stock and cover closely. Continue cooking 8 minutes.

8

Salads

An old culinary chestnut states that it takes four persons to make a sauce for salads: a spendthrift for oil, a miser for vinegar, a counselor for salt and a madman to stir the ingredients.

Whatever the qualifications for delivering a creditable salad dressing, the salad itself is no better than the greens that go into it. The rules for their preparation are relatively simple. The greens should be garden fresh and totally free from blemish. When brought into the kitchen they should be washed carefully in cold running water, then shaken firmly but gently to remove excess moisture. A little moisture goes a long way in helping to crisp the leaves; a lot of moisture shortens storage life.

The lettuce then should be placed in a clear plastic bag layered with paper toweling and refrigerated until ready for use.

Because warmth can wilt the fragile leaves, salads should be tossed in chilled bowls and served on chilled plates. Salad dressings may be made in advance, although many responsible chefs and home cooks prefer to toss the greens with each dressing ingredient separately at the last moment. There seems to be an advantage in this. When the oil is added first and the greens are tossed, the leaves are individually coated with a film. The lemon juice or vinegar then is added, then the salt and freshly ground black pepper. The coating of oil is said to discourage wilting.

MIXED GREEN SALAD

4 SERVINGS

1 egg yolk
1 teaspoon prepared mustard, preferably Dijon
2 tablespoons wine vinegar
6 tablespoons olive oil
1 tablespoon finely chopped shallots or sweet onion
Salt and freshly ground pepper to taste
4 cups mixed salad greens (escarole, romaine, watercress), in bite-size pieces

Combine the egg yolk with the mustard and beat in the wine vinegar with a fork. Add the oil, shallots and seasoning to taste and stir rapidly until well blended. Pour the sauce over the salad greens and toss well. Serve on chilled plates.

◆

SALAD FOR ONE

1 SERVING

1½ to 2 cups salad greens, cut into bite-size pieces
Salt to taste
1 garlic clove, halved
½ teaspoon dry mustard
2 teaspoons wine vinegar, approximately
2 tablespoons olive oil, approximately
Freshly gound pepper to taste

1 Rinse the greens in cold water and drain well.

2 Sprinkle the bottom of a salad bowl with salt and rub with garlic halves. Discard the garlic.

3 Add the mustard and vinegar. Let stand for 10 minutes. Add the greens, toss lightly, and sprinkle with oil. Toss, sprinkle with pepper and serve.

CAESAR SALAD

ABOUT 6 SERVINGS

Salt to taste
1 garlic clove, peeled
1 teaspoon dry mustard
1 tablespoon lemon juice
Tabasco sauce to taste
3 tablespoons olive oil
3 bunches of romaine
1 tablespoon grated Parmesan cheese
1 can anchovies, drained
1 egg, boiled for 60 seconds
½ cup croutons

1 Sprinkle the bottom of a wooden salad bowl with salt and rub it with the garlic. Add the mustard, lemon juice and Tabasco and stir with a wooden spoon until the salt dissolves.

2 Add the olive oil and stir rapidly until the liquid blends.

3 Wash the romaine well and dry the leaves with a towel. Tear the leaves into bite-size pieces and add them to the salad bowl. Sprinkle with Parmesan cheese, add the anchovies and break the egg over the salad.

4 Sprinkle with the croutons (bread cubes toasted lightly in olive oil) and mix gently but thoroughly with a wooden fork and spoon.

WILTED DANDELION GREENS

3 TO 4 SERVINGS

4 cups coarsely shredded dandelion greens
4 strips of bacon, diced
3 tablespoons mild vinegar
2 teaspoon sugar
½ teaspoon salt
Dash of freshly ground pepper
¼ teaspoon dry mustard

1 Tough roots or stems should be removed from the greens before shredding them. Place the greens in a large bowl.

2 Cook the bacon until crisp. Add the remaining ingredients to the bacon and fat and heat, stirring, until the sugar has dissolved.

3 Pour the mixture over the dandelion greens and toss well.

Variation

WILTED LETTUCE

Prepare as above, substituting for dandelion greens an equal quantity of lettuce cut into bite-size pieces.

ITALIAN TOSSED SALAD

Salt to taste
1 garlic clove, peeled
¼ cup olive oil
1 tablespoon lemon juice or wine vinegar
1 tablespoon mayonnaise
1 teaspoon dry mustard
Freshly ground pepper to taste
1 head of romaine or other lettuce,
*   cut into bite-size pieces*
1 fennel bulb, cut into julienne strips
*   (optional)*
⅓ cup walnuts, coarsely chopped, or
*   3 anchovy fillets, chopped fine*
1 tablespoon capers
2 hard-cooked eggs, sliced
Grated Parmesan cheese (optional)

1 Sprinkle the bottom of a salad bowl with salt and rub with the garlic. Add the oil, lemon juice, mayonnaise, mustard and pepper and stir with a wooden spoon until well blended.

2 Add the romaine, fennel, walnuts, capers and sliced eggs and toss lightly with a fork and spoon. If desired, sprinkle with grated Parmesan cheese.

SPINACH SALAD

1 pound spinach
Salt to taste
1 garlic clove, peeled
2 tablespoons lemon juice
6 tablespoons olive oil
Freshly ground pepper to taste
2 hard-cooked eggs, cut into wedges
½ red onion, sliced thin

1 Wash the spinach well in several changes of clear water. Pull away the tough stems and discard. Drain the spinach leaves and chill in a damp, clean cloth. Tear into bite-size pieces.

2 Sprinkle the bottom of a salad bowl with salt and rub with the garlic. Add the lemon juice and olive oil and chill the bowl. When ready to serve, add the spinach and sprinkle with pepper. Garnish with egg and onion rings and toss lightly with a fork and spoon.

Variations

SPINACH AND AVOCADO SALAD

Prepare spinach salad as above and toss lightly with the onion rings, the eggs (coarsely chopped) and a large avocado, seeded and diced. Serve immediately.

SPINACH AND BACON SALAD

Cut 6 slices of bacon into small cubes and fry until crisp. Toss the spinach salad and sprinkle with the crumbled bacon.

SPINACH AND MUSHROOM SALAD

Slice ¼ pound mushrooms and toss with the spinach.

SPINACH AND ENDIVE SALAD

12 SERVINGS

2 pounds baby leaf spinach
¾ pound Belgian endive
1 cup Italian olive oil
½ cup tarragon vinegar
2 tablespoons mayonnaise
1 tablespoon lemon juice
1 tablespoon coarsely ground pepper
1 tablespoon salt
1 tablespoon oregano
1 tablespoon basil
½ tablespoon Worcestershire sauce
½ tablespoon Hungarian paprika
⅛ pound Roquefort cheese, crushed

1 Wash the spinach in several changes of water to make certain that no sand clings to the leaves. Cut the large leaves into bite-size pieces. Cut the endive into bite-size pieces.

2 Combine the remaining ingredients and blend well. Pour enough salad dressing over the salad greens to coat greens lightly. Toss well. There should be no dressing on the bottom of the bowl when the salad is served.

CURLY ENDIVE WITH BACON DRESSING

4 TO 6 SERVINGS

1 head curly endive (chicory)
1 scallion, finely chopped, green part included
3 slices of bacon
½ cup cream
2 egg yolks, well beaten
Salt and freshly ground pepper to taste
1 teaspoon sugar
3 tablespoons wine vinegar
Chopped parsley

1 Remove the core from the endive and cut the leaves into bite-size pieces. Drop them into cold water and rinse well. Drain in a salad basket or on paper toweling. Place the endive in a salad bowl, sprinkle with scallion, and set aside.

2 Cut the bacon into small cubes and cook in a skillet until bacon is crisp but not burned. With a slotted spoon remove the bacon and dry on paper toweling. Sprinkle the bacon over the salad greens.

3 Blend the cream and egg yolks and pour the mixture into the skillet. Add salt, pepper, sugar and vinegar and cook over very low heat, stirring constantly, until mixture thickens slightly. Do not boil or it may curdle. Cool slightly. Pour the sauce over the endive and toss. Sprinkle with parsley.

CHEF'S SALAD
A L'ADAM

ABOUT 4 SERVINGS

½ cup wafer-thin slices of sweet onion
    (Bermuda or Italian)
½ cup strips of Gruyère or Swiss cheese
    (matchlike strips about 1 inch long)
½ cup ham strips (matchlike strips about 1
    inch long)
½ cup strips of green pepper (matchlike strips
    about 1 inch long)
4 tablespoons peanut oil
3 tablespoons olive oil
3 tablespoons wine vinegar
Salt and freshly ground pepper to taste
2 cups mixed greens

Combine all ingredients except greens and
mix well. Add seasonings to taste. Let
stand in the refrigerator overnight. Serve
with mixed greens.

♦

CHICORY AND
FENNEL SALAD

6 SERVINGS

Salt to taste
1 garlic clove, peeled
½ cup olive oil
1 tablespoon wine vinegar
1 tablespoon mayonnaise
Freshly ground pepper to taste
1 head of chicory, cut into bite-size pieces
1 fennel bulb, cut in small thin strips
2 anchovy fillets, chopped
1 teaspoon capers
1 hard-cooked egg, sliced

1 Sprinkle the bottom of a salad bowl
with salt and rub it with the garlic. Add
the oil, vinegar, mayonnaise and pepper.
Stir with a wooden spoon until well
blended.
2 Add the remaining ingredients and
toss lightly with a fork and spoon.

♦

MIXED GREEN SALAD
WITH PRESERVED
DUCK

6 SERVINGS

10 cups loosely packed mixed salad greens, cut
    into large bite-size serving pieces
½ cooked, browned confit de canard
    (preserved duck) half a breast, 1 leg
    with thigh attached, gizzard, heart
    and so on (see page 178)
1 teaspoon minced garlic
1 teaspoon Dijon mustard
2½ tablespoons red wine vinegar
6 tablespoons salad oil, preferably walnut oil
Salt and freshly ground pepper to taste

1 Put the salad greens into a mixing
bowl.
2 Cut the fat from the duck pieces. Cut
off and reserve the lean duck meat and cut
it into bite-size pieces. Discard the bones.
3 Put the garlic, mustard and vinegar
in a mixing bowl and blend with a wire
whisk. Gradually add the oil while beating with the whisk. Season with salt and
pepper.
4 Pour the mixture over the salad
greens and toss to blend. Spoon the mixture onto 6 salad plates and arrange equal
portions of the duck meat over each.

SALAD WITH HOT GRILLED QUAIL

4 SERVINGS

16 cups, approximately, mixed salad greens
    such as spinach, chicory, watercress, curly
    endive, radicchio and romaine, cut or torn
    into bite-size pieces
4 grilled quail (page 185)
2 tablespoons Dijon mustard
1 tablespoon finely chopped shallots
1 teaspoon minced garlic
¾ cup corn or peanut oil
¼ cup balsamic vinegar
Salt and freshly ground pepper to taste

1 Rinse, pat dry and prepare the salad greens and put them into a large salad bowl.

2 Prepare and cook the quail.

3 Put the mustard, shallots and garlic in a small bowl and gradually add half of the oil, stirring vigorously with a wire whisk. Still beating add the remaining oil alternately with the vinegar. Add salt and pepper.

4 Pour the dressing over the salad and toss. Arrange the salad greens on each of 4 salad plates. Arrange 1 freshly cooked quail in the center of each serving.

GREEK SALAD

12 SERVINGS

Salt to taste
1 garlic clove
2 heads Boston lettuce, shredded
1 romaine lettuce, shredded
3 celery hearts, diced
6 radishes, sliced
1 bunch scallions, sliced
1 cucumber, thinly sliced
1 green pepper, cut into thin rings
12 oil-cured black olives
½ pound feta cheese, diced
½ cup olive oil
Juice of 2 lemons
Salt and freshly ground pepper to taste
½ teaspoon oregano
1 tablespoon minced parsley
8 anchovy fillets
3 tomatoes, cut into wedges
Parsley sprigs for garnish

1 Rub a large salad bowl with salt and garlic. Discard the garlic.

2 In the salad bowl, combine the lettuces, celery, radishes, scallions, cucumber, green pepper, olives and cheese.

3 Beat the olive oil with the lemon juice and pour over the salad. Toss and season with salt and pepper. Sprinkle the salad with the oregano and parsley.

4 Arrange the anchovy fillets radiating from the center with the tomato wedges. Garnish with parsley sprigs.

WATERCRESS AND RADISH SALAD

4 SERVINGS

2 bunches of watercress
1 bunch of radishes
1 teaspoon salt
1 garlic clove, halved
1 teaspoon dry mustard
1 tablespoon wine vinegar
¼ cup olive oil

1 Rinse the watercress under cold water and shake well to remove excess moisture. Trim the radishes well, wash and dry.

2 Place the salt in the bottom of a salad bowl and rub it with the garlic clove around bottom and sides of the bowl. Discard the garlic. Add the mustard and vinegar and stir to blend. Let stand for 10 minutes to develop mustard flavor. Add the oil and blend with a fork.

3 Chop the tops and part of the stems of the watercress and place in the bowl. Slice the radishes and add them. Toss well and serve immediately.

◆

WATERCRESS AND ORANGE SALAD

6 SERVINGS

2 bunches of watercress
3 heads of Belgian endive
2 oranges, peeled and sectioned
2 shallots, finely chopped
½ cup olive oil
2 tablespoons lemon juice
Salt and coarsely ground pepper

1 Wash the watercress and trim off the stems. Place the watercress tops in a large salad bowl. Trim off the ends of the endive and cut into 1-inch lengths. Add to the watercress. Top with the orange sections.

2 Combine the shallots, oil and lemon juice in a measuring cup and add salt and pepper to taste. Blend well with a fork. Pour the sauce over the greens and toss gently.

◆

WATERCRESS AND ENDIVE SALAD

6 TO 8 SERVINGS

1 large bunch watercress
6 heads Belgian endive
½ cup olive oil
3 tablespoons wine vinegar
¼ teaspoon salt
⅛ teaspoon paprika
Freshly ground pepper to taste
1 teaspoon minced onion

1 Before untying the bunch of watercress, cut off part of the stems to make short sprays. Discard the stems. Untie the bunch.

2 Crisp the watercress sprays and endive in ice water about 15 minutes before using. Dry gently with paper toweling.

3 Cut the endive heads in half lengthwise, beginning at the root ends. Cut into bite-size pieces.

4 Combine the olive oil, vinegar, seasonings and onion. Mix well.

5 Place the endive and watercress in a salad bowl and sprinkle with the salad dressing. Toss lightly.

COLESLAW WITH CARAWAY

It is startling how caraway enlivens the flavor of coleslaw.

8 SERVINGS

4 cups (1½ pounds) shredded cabbage
2 to 3 tablespoons finely chopped onion
Salt and freshly ground white pepper to taste
1 tablespoon lemon juice
1 cup mayonnaise
Dash of Tabasco sauce
1 tablespoon caraway seeds

1 Sprinkle the cabbage with the chopped onion, salt and pepper.

2 Combine the lemon juice, mayonnaise and Tabasco and toss with the cabbage and caraway.

Hot Cabbage Slaw, page 387.

♦

CREOLE SALAD

6 TO 8 SERVINGS

6 small zucchini
3 tomatoes, chopped
1 green pepper, finely chopped
1 avocado, peeled and cubed
2 scallions, chopped
1 teaspoon salt
½ teaspoon sugar
½ teaspoon freshly ground pepper
Olive oil and wine vinegar to taste

Wash the zucchini thoroughly. Do not peel, but cut it into wafer-thin slices. Toss with remaining ingredients except oil and vinegar and let sit for 1 hour. Serve with olive oil and wine vinegar.

SALADE RUSSE

Salade Russe is a combination of equal parts cooked vegetables—carrots, turnips, celery root, beets and potatoes—cut into small cubes, plus cooked green peas.

The vegetables are marinated lightly in French dressing, drained and then mixed with enough mayonnaise to bind them together.

Anchovy and Pimiento Salad, page 35.

♦

ARTICHOKES A LA GRECQUE

3 SERVINGS

3 medium artichokes
1 fennel branch, minced (optional)
1 celery stalk, minced
3 cups water
½ cup olive oil
Juice of ½ lemon, or 2 tablespoons vinegar
½ teaspoon salt
Few coriander seeds
4 peppercorns

1 Cut the artichokes into quarters. Remove the prickly choke and trim the pointed ends of the leaves until the leaves are about 1 inch long.

2 Mix the remaining ingredients in a pan and bring to a boil. Add the artichokes and cook, covered, until tender, 15 to 20 minutes.

3 Cool the artichokes in the cooking liquid and serve in it.

Asparagus Vinaigrette, page 373.

MEXICAN AVOCADO SALAD

6 SERVINGS

2 tablespoons olive oil
2 tablespoons vinegar
⅛ teaspoon salt
Dash of freshly ground pepper
3 medium avocados
2 tablespoons lemon juice
Crisp salad greens
1 medium orange, peeled and sliced
1 small onion, thinly sliced
¼ cup sliced pimiento-stuffed green olives

1 Combine the olive oil, vinegar, salt and pepper; blend well.

2 Cut the avocados into halves and peel them. Brush all over with the lemon juice.

3 Arrange avocados on the salad greens. Top with orange, onion and olive slices. Pour the dressing over the salad.

AVOCADO AND GRAPEFRUIT SALAD

4 SERVINGS

1 large ripe avocado
2 tablespoons lemon juice
1 large grapefruit
Boston, romaine or Bibb lettuce leaves
½ teaspoon dry mustard
¼ cup olive oil
1 shallot, finely chopped, or 1 tablespoon
    finely chopped chives
½ teaspoon minced garlic
Salt and freshly ground pepper to taste

1 Peel and pit the avocado and cut it into strips. Sprinkle with 1 tablespoon of the lemon juice. Peel the grapefruit and cut it into sections; remove any seeds.

2 Line 4 salad plates with a single layer of lettuce leaves. Arrange alternate strips of avocado and grapefruit sections symmetrically over the lettuce. Chill.

3 Combine the remaining lemon juice and the mustard and let stand for 10 minutes. Combine with the oil, shallot and garlic and blend well, beating with a small fork. Adjust the seasonings to taste.

4 When ready to serve, spoon the sauce over the avocado and grapefruit. This is an excellent salad to serve with highly spiced dishes such as chili con carne or curries.

ASPARAGUS SALAD

6 SERVINGS

2 pounds asparagus, cut into 4-inch lengths
½ cup olive oil
2 tablespoons wine vinegar
¼ teaspoon salt
⅛ teaspoon freshly ground pepper
2 teaspoons chopped parsley
Chicory
2 hard-cooked egg yolks, sieved
1 tablespoon capers
Ripe olives

1 Early in the day, cook the asparagus until barely tender. Cool. Place it in a shallow dish. Combine the oil, vinegar, salt, pepper and parsley and pour mixture over the asparagus. Chill in the refrigerator.

2 Just before serving, place the asparagus on a bed of chicory. Sprinkle the cut ends with the egg yolks and top with the capers. Garnish with the olives.

♦

BEET SALAD

6 SERVINGS

6 medium beets, cooked
2 cups shredded dandelion greens, or arugula
6 heads of Belgian endive, cut up
½ cup basic vinaigrette (page 576)
Salt and freshly ground pepper to taste

Drain and cool the beets, peel them, and cut them into thin slices. Put the slices in a bowl with the greens, pour the dressing over all and toss gently. Add salt and pepper.

BEET AND ONION SALAD

6 SERVINGS

6 medium beets, cooked
1 medium onion, sliced tissue-thin
3 whole cloves
¼ cup olive oil
3 tablespoons cider vinegar, or more
1 teaspoon sugar, or more
Salt and freshly ground pepper to taste

1 Drain and cool the beets, trim them and slip off the skins with a paring knife. Cut the beets into thin slices and chill them.

2 Add the onion slices to the beets and toss with the remaining ingredients.

BROCCOLI SALAD

5 OR 6 SERVINGS

1 bunch (1½ to 2 pounds) broccoli
½ cup basic vinaigrette (page 576)
Romaine lettuce leaves
⅓ cup mayonnaise
¾ teaspoon lemon juice
Anchovy fillets for garnish

1 Cook the broccoli until just tender, drain and chill. Marinate the broccoli in the basic vinaigrette for 1 hour or longer.

2 Arrange the romaine leaves on individual salad plates. Place the marinated broccoli on romaine just before serving.

3 Combine the mayonnaise with the lemon juice and spoon the mixture over the broccoli. Garnish with anchovy fillets.

CAULIFLOWER SALAD NAPOLETANA

6 SERVINGS

1 medium head of cauliflower
1 teaspoon salt
2 tablespoons olive oil
1 cup wine vinegar
½ teaspoon freshly ground pepper
¼ teaspoon basil
6 anchovy fillets, diced
2 tablespoons capers
¼ cup chopped black olives

1 Break the cauliflower into flowerets. Place in a saucepan with 1 inch of boiling water containing the salt. Simmer, uncovered, for 5 minutes. Cover and cook for 5 to 6 minutes longer, only until flowerets are crisp tender. Drain the flowerets and rinse in cold water. Place in a salad bowl.

2 Combine the oil, vinegar, pepper and basil. Mix well and pour over cauliflower. Add anchovies, capers and olives. Toss lightly. Sprinkle with addititional capers, if desired, before serving.

GREEN BEAN SALAD

ALLOW 1 POUND FOR 4 SERVINGS

Dress cooked green beans while still warm with oil, vinegar, salt and freshly ground black pepper. Season with chopped dill or parsley and chopped scallions. Chill.

◆

CORN SALAD, MEXICAN STYLE

6 SERVINGS

4 to 6 ears of fresh corn
½ cup diced green pepper
¼ cup diced pimiento
1 cup diced fresh tomatoes
1 teaspoon salt
¼ cup herb dressing II (page 576)
Lettuce
Red onion rings

1 Boil the ears of corn for 6 to 8 minutes before cutting the kernels off the cobs. Measure out 2 cups corn and combine it with the green pepper, pimiento and tomatoes.

2 Just before serving, add the salt and salad dressing. Toss lightly. Turn into a salad bowl lined with lettuce. Garnish with onion rings.

CUCUMBER SALAD

6 SERVINGS

¾ cup sour cream
1 tablespoon chopped onion or chives
½ teaspoon salt
Freshly ground pepper to taste
½ teaspoon ground cumin
2 tablespoons vinegar
2 medium cucumbers, pared, seeded and sliced
    thin (about 3 cups)
Lettuce or other greens
Paprika

1 Mix the sour cream, onion, salt, pepper, cumin and vinegar. Add the cucumbers and toss lightly.

2 Serve on lettuce or other greens with a garnish of paprika.

Note: This salad, without greens, may be served as an accompaniment to fish.

SWEDISH CUCUMBER SALAD

6 SERVINGS

4 (about 1¾ pounds) cucumbers
6 tablespoons white vinegar
6 tablespoons sugar
¾ cup water
Salt and freshly ground pepper, preferably
    white, to taste
¼ cup finely chopped parsley
1 tablespoon finely chopped dill

1 Peel the cucumbers and cut them in half lengthwise. Scrape out the seeds. Cut the halves crosswise into thin slices. There should be about 5 cups. Put the slices in a bowl.

2 Blend the vinegar, sugar, water, salt and pepper in a small saucepan and bring to the simmer. Stir until the sugar dissolves. Pour the liquid over the cucumbers. Let stand until cool. Chill.

3 Sprinkle with parsley and dill and toss to blend.

Variation

THAI CUCUMBER SALAD

Follow the recipe for Swedish cucumber salad, but in step 1 add 2 tablespoons finely shredded, trimmed, seeded hot pepper (preferably red) to the cucumber slices. Omit the parsley and dill. Sprinkle the cucumber slices with ⅓ cup finely chopped coriander leaves.

SALATA MELITZANAS
EGGPLANT SALAD

6 TO 8 SERVINGS

1 large eggplant
1 small onion, chopped
Salt and freshly ground pepper to taste
½ cup olive oil
1½ tablespoons wine vinegar
Chopped parsley, tomato wedges and black
    olives for garnish

1 Preheat the oven to 350°F.

2 Bake the eggplant for about 1 hour, or until soft.

3 Remove the skin from the eggplant and chop the flesh. Combine the eggplant, onion, salt, pepper, olive oil and vinegar. Mix well. Garnish with parsley, tomato wedges and olives.

EGGPLANT AND SESAME SALAD

4 SERVINGS

2 tablespoons sesame seeds
¼ cup olive oil
1 large eggplant
2 garlic cloves, minced
2 tablespoons lemon juice
Chopped dill
Salt and freshly ground pepper to taste
Parsley

1 Preheat the oven to 400°F.

2 Sauté the sesame seeds in 1 tablespoon of the oil until they are light brown. Set aside.

3 Bake the eggplant for about 45 minutes, or until tender. Wash under running water and remove the skin very carefully. Let the eggplant drain.

4 Chop or mash the eggplant with a wooden spoon or blend in a food processor. Add the garlic, lemon juice and remaining oil to the eggplant. Season with dill, salt and pepper. Top with the sesame seeds and a sprinkling of parsley.

BELGIAN ENDIVE SALAD

6 SERVINGS

6 heads of Belgian endive
½ cup fresh walnuts, whole or broken
2 firm sweet apples
Juice of 1 lemon
6 tablespoons olive oil, approximately
Salt to taste

1 Trim away a little of the end of each head of endive. Cut the endive into bite-size bits and place in a colander or salad basket. Rinse thoroughly in cold water, then shake colander to dry endive.

2 Put the endive in a salad bowl and sprinkle with the walnuts.

3 Core and peel the apples and cut them into bite-size bits or thin slices. Add the apples to the salad bowl and immediately sprinkle with lemon juice. Toss.

4 Add the oil and salt and toss again. If desired, add more oil. Serve immediately.

LEEKS VINAIGRETTE

6 medium or large (3½ to 4 pounds) leeks
Basic vinaigrette (page 576)

1 Peel off and discard any very tough outer leaves of the leeks. Carefully trim off the stem end of each leek at the base, cutting away the roots. Cut each leek crosswise, leaving a base of the white part 6 or 7 inches in length.
2 Split leeks lengthwise, starting about 1 inch from the root end. Drop the leeks into cold water and let stand several minutes. Rinse well to make certain there is no dirt or sand between the leaves. Drain well.
3 Tie the leeks, 3 to a bundle, with string.
4 Bring enough water to the boil to cover the leek bundles when added. Drop the bundles into the water and bring to the boil. Cover closely and let cook 7 minutes. Drain thoroughly. Serve lukewarm or at room temperature with the sauce vinaigrette spooned over.

SALADE FORESTIÈRE

1 pound fresh white mushrooms
¼ cup fresh lemon juice, or more
¼ cup chopped parsley
½ cup olive oil
Salt and freshly ground pepper to taste
4 cups mixed salad greens (chicory, endive
    and Boston lettuce)

1 Trim the stems and wipe the mushrooms with damp paper toweling. Slice the mushrooms through caps and stems into very thin slices.
2 Pour the lemon juice over the slices and add the parsley, oil, salt and pepper. Chill the mushrooms.
3 Toss mushrooms and marinade with the greens and serve.

♦

CHINESE RADISHES

20 radishes, sliced
1 green pepper, slivered
2 tablespoons white vinegar
1½ tablespoons soy sauce
1 tablespoons sugar

Combine the ingredients and chill thoroughly. Serve with barbecued dishes.

HEART OF PALM AND AVOCADO SALAD

12 SERVINGS

1 large head of romaine
1 large head of escarole
6 scallions, or 2 medium onions
4 ripe avocados
2 tablespoons lemon juice
2 (1-pound) cans (4 cups) hearts of palm
Pimiento strips
Tarragon French dressing (page 577)

1 Wash the salad greens, drain well and wrap in a clean towel to absorb all the water. Tear the salad greens into bite-size pieces and place in a large salad bowl.

2 Wash the scallions and slice them, green part included. Arrange them in the center of the salad; if onions are used, slice thin and arrange them in the center of the salad.

3 Peel the avocados and cut lengthwise into ¼-inch slices. Sprinkle with the lemon juice. Cut the drained hearts of palm into ¼-inch rounds.

4 Arrange the avocados and hearts of palm on the greens. Garnish with the pimiento strips. Just before serving, toss with the dressing.

ITALIAN PEPPER SALAD

4 SERVINGS

2 large green peppers
4 tablespoons olive oil
1 tablespoon wine vinegar
Salt and freshly ground pepper to taste
8 anchovy fillets (optional)

1 Char the peppers on the outside by holding them on the tines of a fork in a moderately high flame of a gas burner, or do this in the broiler. Turn them until they are black all over. Cool under running water and rub off the outer charred membrane.

2 Halve the peppers, remove and discard the seeds. Slice into thin lengths. Add the oil, vinegar, salt and pepper. Let stand 30 minutes at room temperature before serving. If desired, garnish each serving with crisscrossed anchovies.

Note: Italians like this salad best when made with White Caps, a slender, long yellowish-green pepper that becomes locally available in August. It is more tender than familiar types.

RADISH SALAD

4 SERVINGS

2 cups radishes
½ cup white vinegar
2 teaspoons salt
Olive oil
Freshly ground pepper to taste
2 tablespoons capers
1 canned chili pepper, cut into strips

1 Slice the radishes and marinate in the vinegar and salt 3 hours. Drain.

2 Mix the radishes with olive oil to taste, sprinkle with pepper and garnish with the capers and chili pepper.

♦

ENSALADA DE CEBOLLA BURRIANA
ONION SALAD WITH ANCHOVIES AND OLIVES

6 SERVINGS

Slice 3 or 4 sweet Spanish onions (or sweet red Italian onions) very thin. Soak them in salted water with ice cubes for 30 minutes. Drain the onions and wring out in a linen towel. Arrange in a large salad bowl, sprinkle with oil and wine vinegar, and garnish with anchovy fillets and pitted ripe black olives.

Not only is the tomato the most versatile of vegetables, there is also none other with more perceptible differences in flavor and texture. Off season they are tasteless, but when summer comes they are something to feast on. The small cherry tomatoes that are available even during the winter months have a surprising depth of flavor and make a colorful garnish for almost any salad.

The most elegant way to serve any tomato, large or small, is to peel it in advance. This is easily done if the tomatoes are dipped quickly into boiling water and allowed to stand for precisely 10 seconds. If they stand longer than that, they start to cook and their texture is spoiled. Remove them from the water and skin them with a paring knife. The operation is not as tedious as it may sound.

♦

HERBED TOMATO SALAD

4 SERVINGS

¼ cup olive oil
3 tablespoons fresh lemon juice
¾ teaspoon salt
Freshly ground pepper to taste
1 tablespoon chopped onion
½ garlic clove, minced
1 teaspoon paprika
1 teaspoon chopped mint
3 large ripe tomatoes, sliced

Combine oil, lemon juice, salt, pepper, onion, garlic, paprika and mint. Beat with a fork and refrigerate for 30 minutes. Pour the dressing over the tomatoes and serve.

PANZANELLA

One of the tastiest salads for summer is of Tuscan origin and it is called *panzanella*. It is made with red, ripe tomatoes, celery, cucumber and onion and a handful of fresh basil leaves. Oddly enough it also contains pieces of bread that have been soaked in water and squeezed to extract most of the liquid.

The name *panzanella* is said to refer to the Roman word *panza*, which means "belly." The theory goes that it was served in the homes of Italian peasants as a first course to fill their appetites before the more costly main courses were served.

4 SERVINGS

3 ounces bread with crusts left on (see note)
2 large red, ripe tomatoes, about 1¼ pounds
1 tablespoon minced garlic
4 to 6 hearts of celery stalks
¾ cup diced, seeded cucumber
1 small red onion, peeled
½ cup diced sweet red pepper
½ cup diced sweet yellow pepper
12 flat anchovy fillets
2 tablespoons drained capers
12 basil leaves
Salt and freshly ground pepper to taste
2 tablespoons white vinegar (apple cider
    vinegar works well)
¼ cup olive oil

1 Cut or break the bread into 2-inch cubes. There should be about 2 cups loosely packed. Put the cubes in a mixing bowl and add cold water to cover. Let stand 10 minutes.

2 Meanwhile, cut away and discard the core of each tomato. Cut the tomatoes into ¾-inch cubes. There should be about 3 cups. Put the tomatoes into a salad bowl. Add the garlic.

3 Cut the celery stalks crosswise into thin ½-inch cubes. There should be about 1 cup. Add this to the salad bowl.

4 Add the cucumber to the bowl.

5 Cut the onion lengthwise in half. Cut the halves crosswise into thin slices. You will need 1 cup. Add this to the bowl. Add the diced red and yellow peppers.

6 Cut the anchovy fillets crosswise into thirds. Add these to the bowl. Add the capers.

7 The basil leaves may be coarsely chopped or they may be left whole. Add the leaves to the bowl.

8 Drain the bread and squeeze it gently between the hands to get rid of much of the moisture. Do not make the bread mushy. Break the soaked bread into smaller pieces and add to the salad. Sprinkle with salt and pepper.

9 Sprinkle the salad with the vinegar and oil and toss well.

Note: The bread for this recipe should be of excellent quality, a bit firm and coarsely textured. Pita bread works very well.

♦

SLICED TOMATO SALAD

Dip large garden-ripe tomatoes in boiling water to loosen skins. Peel. Slice them thick and dress with oil, vinegar, salt and chopped basil.

SALADE PROVENÇALE

2 medium heads of Boston or romaine lettuce
2 large ripe tomatoes, cut into bite-size wedges
1 onion, thinly sliced
1 or 2 garlic cloves, minced
2 tablespoons finely chopped chives
1 tablespoon chopped basil
1 dozen pitted green olives
1 dozen pitted black olives
1 teaspoon prepared mustard, preferably
    Dijon or Düsseldorf
2 tablespoons wine vinegar
7 tablespoons olive oil
Salt and freshly ground pepper to taste
Radishes for garnish

1 Core the lettuce and cut or tear the leaves into bite-size pieces. Place them in a salad bowl and add the tomatoes, onion, garlic, chives, basil and the green and black olives.

2 Blend the mustard with the vinegar and sprinkle over the salad. Toss lightly, then add the oil, salt and pepper and toss again. If desired, add more vinegar, oil, or both, and toss again. Garnish with radishes.

TOMATO-CUCUMBER SALAD PLATTER

6 tomatoes
2 tablespoons finely chopped basil
3 tablespoons finely chopped parsley
6 tablespoons finely chopped onion
6 cucumbers
⅓ cup wine or tarragon vinegar
⅔ cup olive oil
1 teaspoon salt
1 teaspoon sugar
3 tablespoons capers
Snipped dill

1 Peel the tomatoes; cut in halves. Combine the basil, parsley and onion and sprinkle over the tomato halves.

2 Peel the cucumbers; slice. Combine the vinegar, oil, salt and sugar and pour over the cucumber slices.

3 To serve, drain the cucumber slices. Arrange in center of platter, sprinkle with the capers and dill. Arrange the tomato halves around edge.

TOMATOES STUFFED WITH BASIL

6 SERVINGS

6 ripe tomatoes
Salt
1 cup basil leaves, closely packed
1 garlic clove
¾ cup pine nuts
½ cup grated Parmesan cheese
⅓ cup olive oil

1 Peel the tomatoes, core them and cut a slight depression in the center for stuffing. Squeeze the tomatoes gently to remove most of the seeds. Turn them upside down on a small layer of salt to drain.

2 Meanwhile, combine the remaining ingredients in the container of a food processor and blend until well puréed.

3 Salt the tomatoes both inside and out and spoon equal portions of the basil mixture into the center of each. Serve at room temperature.

TOMATO AND ONION SALAD

4 SERVINGS

1 cup sliced red onions
4 ripe medium tomatoes, sliced
½ cup chopped parsley
¼ cup olive oil
2 teaspoons lemon juice
2 teaspoons wine vinegar
1 teaspoon chopped basil
½ teaspoon sugar
Salt and freshly ground pepper to taste

Arrange alternate slices of onions and tomatoes on a chilled serving dish and sprinkle with remaining ingredients, which have been mixed well.

CHERRY TOMATO AND SOUR CREAM SALAD

6 OR MORE SERVINGS

1 pint cherry tomatoes
1 teaspoon dry mustard
3/4 cup sour cream
Salt to taste
Cayenne to taste
2 tablespoons finely chopped basil
1/4 cup finely chopped scallions,
    green part included

1 Remove the stems from the tomatoes and peel them.

2 Place the mustard in a mixing bowl and stir in a little of the sour cream to form a paste. Blend in the remaining sour cream. Add salt and cayenne. Gently stir in the cherry tomatoes. Chill. When ready to serve, sprinkle with basil and scallions.

ZUCCHINI A LA GRECQUE

6 SERVINGS

4 zucchini, trimmed and scrubbed
1 cup water
1/4 cup olive oil
1 garlic clove
1 bay leaf
1 tablespoon finely chopped parsley
1 tablespoon finely chopped tarragon,
    or 1 teaspoon dried
1 tablespoon lemon juice
1/2 teaspoon salt
Dash of Tabasco sauce
Pinch of thyme
Freshly ground pepper to taste

Cut the zucchini into slices 1/4 inch thick. Place with the remaining ingredients in a saucepan. Cover and bring to a boil. Turn off the heat and let cool, then refrigerate. Serve as an hors d'oeuvre or as a salad on lettuce leaves.

Potatoes generally have either a mealy texture or a firm waxy texture when cooked. For salads select the thin-skinned waxy potatoes because they will not crumble when they are sliced or cubed, or use new potatoes. Cook the potatoes in the skins to retain the most flavor and cool them only until they can be handled before peeling and slicing them. If the dressing is added to the potatoes while they are still warm, the salad will be much more flavorful.

♦

POTATO SALAD

6 SERVINGS

3 tablespoons olive oil
1 tablespoon wine vinegar
Salt and freshly ground pepper to taste
2 cups cubes of warm cooked potatoes
1 cup finely chopped celery
⅓ cup mayonnaise
3 tablespoons minced parsley
2 hard-cooked eggs, coarsely chopped
1 tablespoon minced shallots
1 tablespoon dry mustard

1 Combine the oil, vinegar, salt and pepper. Pour the dressing over the warm potatoes. Toss lightly and chill.

2 Add the remaining ingredients and toss again.

WARM POTATO SALAD

4 TO 6 SERVINGS

8 medium potatoes
1 teaspoon salt
½ teaspoon freshly ground pepper
¼ cup wine vinegar
2 tablespoons beef stock
2 tablespoons dry white wine
½ cup vegetable oil
1 tablespoon chopped tarragon
1 tablespoon chopped parsley

1 Cook the potatoes in boiling salted water until tender but still firm, about 20 minutes.

2 Peel the potatoes while still warm and cut into slices ¼ inch thick. Place in a salad bowl.

3 In another bowl, combine the salt, pepper, vinegar, stock and wine. Mix until the salt dissolves. Add the remaining ingredients and mix well. Pour over the potatoes and toss gently but thoroughly, until all the liquid is absorbed.

SOUR CREAM POTATO SALAD

4 SERVINGS

¼ cup sour cream
¼ cup mayonnaise
3 cups peeled and diced cooked potatoes
2 tablespoons chopped scallions,
    green part included
1 tablespoon snipped dill
Dash of Tabasco sauce
Salt and freshly ground pepper to taste
Celery seed to taste
Lettuce or other greens

1 Mix the sour cream and mayonnaise. Add to the potatoes.

2 Mix in the other ingredients except the greens. When thoroughly and lightly mixed, heap on a bed of the greens.

SPRING POTATO SALAD

8 SERVINGS

1 pound new potatoes, cooked and peeled
2 tablespoons lemon juice
1 tablespoon vinegar
1 tablespoon vegetable oil
1 teaspoon salt
¼ teaspoon freshly ground pepper
½ head of Boston lettuce
½ head of romaine
3 scallions, chopped, green part included
1 cup diced celery
½ cucumber, sliced
2 tablespoons mayonnaise
2 medium tomatoes for garnish

1 Dice the potatoes while still warm and combine with 1 tablespoon of the lemon juice, the vinegar, oil, salt and pepper. Let the potatoes marinate in the refrigerator for at least 1 hour.

2 Tear the lettuce and romaine into bite-size pieces and place in a salad bowl along with the scallions, celery, cucumber and marinated potatoes. Mix the remaining lemon juice with the mayonnaise. Add to the salad and toss lightly. Garnish with tomato slices or wedges.

GERMAN POTATO SALAD WITH SOUR CREAM

4 SERVINGS

1 pound (about 4 medium) potatoes, boiled
1 teaspoon sugar
½ teaspoon salt
¼ teaspoon dry mustard
⅛ teaspoon freshly ground pepper
2 tablespoons vinegar
1 cup sour cream
½ cup thinly sliced cucumber (optional)
Paprika

1 Slice potatoes while still warm. If new potatoes are used, slice in their jackets. Old potatoes should be peeled.

2 Mix the sugar, salt, mustard, pepper and vinegar. Add the sour cream and cucumber and mix. Pour over the potatoes and toss lightly until all the potatoes have been coated with dressing. Turn into a serving dish and sprinkle with paprika. Serve warm or cool.

POTATO SALAD WITH ANCHOVIES

12 SERVINGS

5 pounds new potatoes
1 bunch of scallions, chopped
1 (5-ounce) can pimientos, drained
   and cut into strips
3 (2-ounce) cans flat anchovy fillets, diced
¼ cup olive oil
¼ cup wine vinegar
1 tablespoon lemon juice
Salt and freshly ground pepper to taste

1 Cover the potatoes with boiling salted water, bring to a boil and simmer for about 20 minutes, until barely tender. Drain, peel and cut into ¼-inch slices.

2 While the potatoes are still warm, place them in a large bowl. Add the scallions, pimientos and anchovies along with the oil from the can.

3 Combine the remaining ingredients and pour over the salad. Toss to mix and chill for at least 2 hours.

LENTIL SALAD

6 SERVINGS

1 cup lentils
1 onion, studded with 2 cloves
½ bay leaf
3 cups water
1 teaspoon salt
2½ tablespoons olive oil
1½ tablespoons wine vinegar
1 onion, minced
2 tablespoons minced parsley
Freshly ground pepper to taste
Quartered tomatoes

1 Place the lentils, the onion studded with cloves and the bay leaf in a saucepan. Add water and salt and simmer until tender, 30 to 40 minutes. Drain and discard the bay leaf and onion.

2 Add the oil, vinegar and minced onion. Let cool to room temperature.

3 At serving time add the parsley and pepper and mix lightly. Garnish with tomatoes.

NAVY BEAN SALAD

6 SERVINGS

2 cups cooked white navy beans
¼ cup olive oil
Juice of 1 lemon
Salt and freshly ground pepper to taste
Chopped parsley, dill and mint to taste
4 scallions, chopped
1 tomato
1 hard-cooked egg

1 Drain the beans.

2 Place the oil, lemon juice, salt and pepper in a salad bowl and blend thoroughly.

3 Add the beans and mix well. Scatter chopped parsley, dill, mint and scallions over the beans. Garnish with tomatoes and egg, cut into quarters.

CHICK-PEA SALAD

4 cups cooked chick-peas
¾ cup peanut oil
¾ cup olive oil
¼ cup lemon juice
¼ cup red wine vinegar
¼ cup finely chopped scallions
1 garlic clove, minced
2 tablespoons finely chopped parsley

1 Drain the chick-peas thoroughly. Combine the remaining ingredients and stir well. Add the chick-peas.

2 Let marinate in the refrigerator for 2 or 3 hours. Serve on a bed of Boston lettuce leaves, sprinkled with additional chopped parsley. Leftover chick-peas may continue to marinate in the refrigerator for several days.

CHICK-PEA SALAD WITH HORSERADISH

2 cups cooked chick-peas, drained
¼ cup chopped pimiento
½ cup chopped green pepper
1 cup chopped celery
Salt and freshly ground pepper to taste
½ to ¾ cup mayonnaise
2 to 3 tablespoons prepared horseradish
Lettuce

1 Combine the chick-peas, pimiento, green pepper, celery, salt and pepper and toss lightly. Combine the mayonnaise and horseradish and stir into the mixture.

2 Just before serving arrange on crisp lettuce.

WINTER SALAD

6 TO 8 SERVINGS

1 cup cooked lima beans
1 cup cooked green beans, cut into
    1-inch lengths
1 cup cooked field peas, speckled beans
    or black-eyed peas
½ cup thinly sliced water chestnuts
1 medium red onion, chopped or cut into
    thin rings
¼ cup wine vinegar
½ to 1 garlic clove, minced
¾ cup plus 2 tablespoons olive oil
Salt and freshly ground pepper to taste
24 cherry tomatoes
¼ cup chopped parsley

1 The vegetables for this dish should be freshly cooked and not overcooked. They should be tender but still somewhat crisp. Combine the lima beans, green beans, field peas, water chestnuts and onion in a bowl.

2 Combine the vinegar, garlic, oil, salt and pepper. Beat with a wire whisk until well blended. Pour the sauce over the vegetables and refrigerate for several hours or overnight.

3 When ready to serve, toss lightly but thoroughly. Garnish with cherry tomatoes and sprinkle with chopped parsley.

FAVA BEAN SALAD

6 TO 8 SERVINGS

1½ cups shelled fava beans
1 large onion, quartered
8 cups cold water, approximately
1 teaspoon sugar
Salt to taste
6 tablespoons lemon juice
6 tablespoons salad oil
1 tablespoon sour cream
1 bunch scallions, trimmed and chopped
2 tablespoons chopped dill
2 tablespoons chopped parsley
6 imported black olives
6 radish roses

1 Soak the beans overnight in a generous amount of water, or cover beans with water, bring to a boil for 2 minutes, cover and let stand for 1 hour.

2 Drain the beans and rinse well, then place in a saucepan with the onion and the 8 cups of cold water. Bring to a boil and simmer, stirring frequently, until tender. Add more water as necessary. When the beans are done, most of the water should be absorbed.

3 When the beans are thoroughly tender, remove them from the heat. Mash the beans with a potato masher or put them through a food mill. Add the sugar, salt, 2 tablespoons of the lemon juice, 2 tablespoons of the oil and the sour cream. Let cool. Garnish with the scallions, dill, parsley, olives and radishes. Chill.

4 Blend the remaining lemon juice with the remaining oil and salt to taste and serve separately.

PINTO BEAN SALAD

6 SERVINGS

1 cup dried pinto beans
1 carrot, scraped and sliced
1 small onion, studded with 4 cloves
2 garlic cloves, minced
Salt and freshly ground pepper to taste
½ cup finely chopped onion
1 tablespoon coarsely chopped parsley
9 tablespoons olive oil
3 tablespoons wine vinegar
1 (7-ounce) can tuna fish, packed in oil

1 Soak the beans overnight in cold water to cover, or cover beans with water, bring to a boil for 2 minutes, cover and let stand for 1 hour.

2 Drain the beans and place them in a large saucepan. Add water to cover to 1 inch over the top of the beans. Add the carrot, onion studded with cloves, one of the garlic cloves, the salt and pepper. Bring to a boil and simmer 1 to 1½ hours, or until the beans are tender but not mushy. Chill.

3 Drain the beans and place them in a mixing bowl. Add the chopped onion, parsley, salt, pepper, remaining garlic clove, oil and vinegar. Toss. Cut tuna fish into bite-size pieces and toss fish with the beans. Serve cold.

LIMA BEAN AND MUSHROOM SALAD

6 SERVINGS

1 (10-ounce) package frozen lima beans
½ pound mushrooms
6 scallions, finely chopped
1 tablespoon chopped parsley
½ teaspoon marjoram
3 tablespoons wine vinegar
⅓ cup olive oil
1 garlic clove, minced
½ teaspoon salt
¼ teaspoon freshly ground pepper
⅛ teaspoon dry mustard
Salad greens

1 Cook the lima beans according to package directions and drain. Trim the mushrooms, wash and dry thoroughly. Cut the mushrooms into thin slices.

2 Combine the beans, scallions, parsley, marjoram, vinegar, oil, garlic, salt, pepper and mustard. Allow to marinate for at least 30 minutes.

3 Add the mushrooms and toss lightly. Pile the mixture atop salad greens.

CHICK-PEAS RÉMOULADE

6 SERVINGS

2 cups dried chick-peas
Salt
2 anchovy fillets
1 garlic clove, minced
1 tablespoon capers, chopped
1 teaspoon finely chopped shallots or scallions
2 tablespoons finely chopped parsley
¼ to ½ cup mayonnaise
Salt and freshly ground pepper
Lemon juice
Parsley sprigs for garnish

1 Cover the chick-peas with water, bring to a boil, and drain. Add fresh water to cover and salt to taste. Bring to a boil again.

2 Simmer the peas for 2 to 2½ hours, until they are tender. Let cool in the cooking liquid; drain.

3 Chop the anchovies and garlic together and blend with the capers, shallots and parsley. Use just enough mayonnaise to bind the mixture. Add seasonings and lemon juice to taste. Fold in the drained chick-peas and chill. Garnish with parsley sprigs.

BEANS AND TUNA VINAIGRETTE

6 TO 8 SERVINGS

2 cups (1 pound) dried pea beans
    or navy beans
1 garlic clove
2 teaspoons salt
¼ teaspoon freshly ground pepper
2 cups finely chopped scallions
¾ cup olive oil
2 tomatoes, peeled, seeded and chopped
¼ cup chopped parsley
1 (7-ounce) can tuna fish, flaked
3 tablespoons wine vinegar
3 or 4 drops of Tabasco sauce
Salt and freshly ground pepper to taste

1 Wash the beans, cover with cold water and soak overnight. Or cover beans with water, bring to a boil for 2 minutes, cover and let stand for 1 hour.

2 Place the beans in a saucepan with enough of the water they were soaked in just to cover them. Add the garlic, the 2 teaspoons of salt and the ¼ teaspoon of pepper. Bring to a boil and simmer for 45 minutes, or until barely tender; drain.

3 Meanwhile, sauté the scallions in ⅓ cup of the oil until just wilted. Add the tomatoes and cook for 1 minute longer. Add to the drained beans. Add parsley and tuna, gently mix and chill.

4 Just before serving, combine the remaining oil with the vinegar and Tabasco and pour over the bean salad. Season with salt and pepper.

KIDNEY BEAN AND EGG SALAD

6 SERVINGS

2 cups canned kidney beans, drained
½ cup diced celery
¼ cup sweet pickle relish
2 hard-cooked eggs, sliced
1 tablespoon finely chopped onion
Basic vinaigrette (page 576) to taste
Lettuce

1 Combine the kidney beans, celery, pickle relish, eggs and onion.

2 Pour dressing over the bean mixture and toss lightly. Chill thoroughly and serve on crisp lettuce.

◆

RICE SALAD VINAIGRETTE

4 SERVINGS

1 cup cooked rice
1 cup cooked green peas
½ cup olive oil
¼ cup minced parsley
¼ cup minced onion
2 tomatoes, peeled, seeded and cubed
3 tablespoons wine vinegar, or less
1 tablespoon finely chopped basil,
    or 1 teaspoon finely chopped mint

Combine all the ingredients in a mixing bowl. Mix well and chill thoroughly before serving.

Note: One cup of leftover meat or poultry sliced into thin strips may be substituted for the peas.

COLD RICE WITH SHRIMP

5 SERVINGS

1 cup rice
3 scallions
1 bunch of chives
½ onion
1½ cups cooked small shrimp
1 cup mayonnaise
Pinch of ginger
Salt and lemon juice to taste
Lettuce
Toasted sesame seeds

1 Cook the rice according to package directions and cool.

2 Chop the scallions, chives and onion fine. Add to the cold cooked rice. Add the shrimp and mayonnaise. Season to taste with the ginger, salt and lemon juice and refrigerate until serving time.

3 Heap on lettuce and garnish with sesame seeds.

COLD RICE RAVIGOTE

2 cups rice
2 small green peppers
3 pimientos, chopped
1 cup mayonnaise
½ teaspoon curry powder
Salt to taste
1 teaspoon lemon juice
Lettuce
Sliced pimientos
Minced chives

1 Cook the rice according to package directions and cool.

2 Seed and chop the green peppers. Add to the rice. Add the pimientos.

3 Mix the mayonnaise with the curry powder, salt and lemon juice. Mix into the rice and pimiento mixture and chill. Serve on lettuce garnished with sliced pimientos and chives.

Note: One pound of flaked crabmeat may be substituted for 1 cup of the rice.

RICE AND HAM VINAIGRETTE

1½ cups long-grain rice
1 cup finely diced cooked ham
½ cup finely chopped parsley
¼ cup finely chopped chives
1 tablespoon chopped capers
½ cup peanut oil
2 tablespoons olive oil
1 egg yolk
3 tablespoons wine vinegar
Salt and freshly ground pepper to taste

1 Cook the rice in 2 quarts of boiling salted water until it is tender. Drain in a colander, place the colander over boiling water and steam the rice briefly until it is fluffy and the grains stand apart. Refrigerate the rice.

2 When the rice is thoroughly chilled, combine it with the ham, parsley, chives and capers in a large mixing bowl. Refrigerate while preparing the sauce.

3 Combine the peanut oil, olive oil, egg yolk and vinegar in a small bowl. Whip the mixture with a wire whisk until the sauce reaches the consistency of a thin mayonnaise. Season with salt and pepper.

4 Toss the vinaigrette sauce with the rice-ham mixture until all the grains of the rice are coated. If necessary, add more oil or vinegar. Adjust seasonings to taste.

RICE SALAD A LA FRANÇAISE

4 SERVINGS

1 cup cooked rice, chilled
2 tomatoes, cored, peeled and cut into
    small cubes
6 radishes, trimmed and thinly sliced
½ cup finely chopped onions
½ cup finely chopped celery heart
4 small beets, cooked, peeled and cut into
    thin strips
¼ cup sliced green olives
Salt and freshly ground pepper to taste
½ teaspoon curry powder
1 teaspoon mustard, preferably
    Dijon or Düsseldorf
2 tablespoons wine vinegar, approximately
7 tablespoons olive oil, approximately

1 In a salad bowl combine the rice with the tomatoes, radishes, onions, celery heart, beets and olives. Sprinkle with salt and pepper.

2 Combine the curry powder, mustard and vinegar and sprinkle the mixture over the salad. Toss salad briefly and sprinkle with the oil. Toss again. If desired, add more vinegar, oil or both.

TABBOULEH SALAD WITH TOMATOES

One of the most interesting salads is a specialty of Lebanon known as *tabbouleh* (sometimes spelled *tabboule*). It is made with cracked wheat, which is also called bulgur, and is now found on many grocery and supermarket shelves. Tabbouleh makes a marvelously healthy salad when combined with freshly squeezed lemon juice, a lot of chopped parsley and a judicious amount of olive oil. This version also has chopped lettuce among its ingredients.

6 TO 8 SERVINGS

¾ cup medium-fine cracked wheat (bulgur)
4 tablespoons olive oil
¾ cup chicken stock
3 cups salad greens such as romaine, Boston
    or Bibb lettuce, cut into bite-size pieces
½ cup peeled and seeded cubed tomatoes
1 cup coarsely chopped parsley, preferably
    Italian, or flat-leaf
¼ cup finely chopped mint
¾ cup chopped scallions
2 tablespoons lemon juice, or more
Freshly ground pepper to taste

1 Put the cracked wheat in a small 1-quart saucepan and add 2 tablespoons of olive oil. Stir to coat the grains evenly. Set aside and let stand several minutes.

2 Add the stock to the cracked wheat and cook over very low heat, stirring occasionally, about 1 minute. Remove the saucepan from the heat and set aside to cool.

3 Put the cracked wheat in a 2-quart mixing bowl and, using the fingers, break up any lumps. Add the chopped salad greens, tomatoes, parsley, mint, scallions, lemon juice, the remaining 2 tablespoons of olive oil and the pepper. Blend well. Add more lemon juice if desired.

FRUIT SALAD

18 SERVINGS

8 seedless oranges
2 lemons
4 cups sugar
2½ cups water
4 grapefruit
8 bananas
Juice of 1 lemon
2 Spanish melons
2 ripe pineapples
1 bunch of black grapes
1 bunch of white grapes
2 pints strawberries

1 With a swivel-bladed vegetable scraper, peel off the skins of the oranges and lemons. Discard the lemon pulp, or reserve for another use. Cut the peel into the thinnest possible strips. Add to the sugar and water in a saucepan. Simmer for about 30 minutes, until the rinds are transparent. Chill the sauce with rinds.

2 Peel the grapefruit. Section the grapefruit and oranges. Peel and score the bananas with fork tines and cut into thick slices. Marinate the grapefruit, oranges and bananas in the lemon juice for 10 minutes.

3 Cut the melons into balls and the pineapples into chunks. Skin and pit the black grapes; skin the white grapes. Combine with the strawberries and add to the marinated fruits. Chill.

4 Mix all the fruits with the sugar and citrus-rind sauce just before serving.

CANTALOUPE FLOWER SALAD

6 SERVINGS

1 large cantaloupe
2 cups mixed fresh fruits (pitted cherries,
    blueberries, strawberries, raspberries
    or pineapple wedges)
Belgian endive leaves
Fresh peach, pear or apricot slices
Orange French dressing (page 577)

1 Slash the cantaloupe part of the way down in 6 sections so that it slightly opens out like the petals of a flower. Remove the seeds and chill the fruit.

2 Place the melon on a serving plate and fill it with the mixed fresh fruits. Surround it with endive leaves and overlapping slices of peaches, pears or apricots.

3 Serve a slice of melon with mixed fruit and endive and pour some dressing over each serving.

9

Pasta

If Italy had contributed nothing but pasta dishes to the world of cuisine, that would have been sufficient for immortality.

Pasta is a food with a welcome versatility. There are, of course, hundreds of shapes that pasta may take, from acini di pepe *("peppercorn") to* ziti. *The roster includes* amorini *("little cupids"),* capelli di prete *("priests' hats"),* lancette *("little spears"),* lingue di passero *("sparrow's tongue"),* occhi di lupo *("wolf's eyes"),* fusilli, tufoli, *and the kind known as* vermicelli *("little worms"). The* vermicelli *come in strands even thinner than* spaghettini, *which are a slender version of* spaghetti, *which means "little strings."*

Commercial pasta is made with flour and water, and many imported brands are excellent. But for any of the flat noodles— fettuccine, lasagne, cannelloni, tagliatelle *—there's nothing better than homemade pasta, made with flour and eggs, rather than water. Many food stores also make good fresh pasta dough. The trick is to cook it only a few minutes for large pieces, like* lasagne, *and only seconds for noodles.*

◆

FRESH PASTA DOUGH

ABOUT 1 POUND OF DOUGH

3 cups sifted flour, preferably semolina
4 eggs

1 Place the flour in a bowl, add the unbeaten eggs and mix with the hands until the dough can be gathered into a rough ball.

2 Turn out on a smooth surface and knead until all the crumbly particles have been incorporated. The dough should be very stiff. The addition of more flour may be essential to achieve this.

3 Divide the dough into thirds and, using one portion at a time, roll with a floured rolling pin into a very thin sheet. Let stand, covered with a towel, ½ hour or more. Roll the sheet of dough as for a jelly roll and cut into strips of desired width. Lay out to dry well and store as needed.

4 To make the noodles in a pasta machine, divide the dough into thirds and press each into a flat rectangle. Use one piece at a time, keeping the remainder covered to prevent drying. Set the dial on the machine for the widest opening and run the dough through several times, gradually decreasing the size of the opening. As the strip of dough lengthens, fold it in half for each successive rolling.

5 Shape and fill the dough immediately for stuffed pasta. For noodles, let it dry briefly before running through the cutter.

Variations

FETTUCCINE

Cut the folded dough into ⅛-inch strips.

TAGLIATELLE

Cut the folded dough into ¼-inch strips.

LASAGNE

Cut the almost paper-thin sheet of dough into rectangular strips about 3 inches wide and 8 inches long.

CANNELLONI

Cut the almost paper-thin sheet of dough into pieces about 4 inches square.

MANICOTTI

Cut the sheets of dough into 3-inch squares.

FETTUCCINE ALFREDO

Fresh pasta dough makes this traditional dish even more sublime. Be sure to have the butter, half-and-half and cheese at room temperature.

4 SERVINGS

1 pound fresh pasta dough, cut for fettuccine
¼ pound butter, cut into 8 parts
Freshly ground pepper to taste
1 cup half-and-half
¼ pound grated Parmesan cheese
2 large white Italian truffles, sliced (optional)

1 Cook the noodles in 2 quarts of boiling salted water for 3 to 4 minutes. Drain and place in a dry pan.

2 Gently heat the noodles. Toss them gently while adding the butter and grinding the pepper over them.

3 Add the half-and-half and allow to heat thoroughly, tossing once or twice, until most of the half-and-half has been absorbed.

4 Add the cheese and the truffles. Heat, still tossing gently, for 2 to 3 minutes, until the noodles are evenly coated with the melted cheese. Serve immediately.

Variation

FETTUCCINE ALLA ROMANA

Add 1 cup freshly cooked peas and ½ cup finely shredded prosciutto to the fettuccine with the cheese. Eliminate the truffles.

FRESH PASTA WITH SPINACH AND PROSCIUTTO

6 SERVINGS

1½ pounds spinach
1 tablespoon lemon juice
3 tablespoons butter
1 tablespoon finely chopped onion
1 garlic clove, minced
3 tablespoons flour
1 cup half-and-half
Salt and freshly ground pepper to taste
⅛ teaspoon grated nutmeg
1 pound fresh pasta dough, cut ¼ inch wide
½ cup finely chopped prosciutto or cooked ham
½ cup buttered soft fresh bread crumbs

1 Preheat the oven to 350°F.

2 Wash the spinach carefully and cook in a covered pan in only the water clinging to the leaves until just tender. Drain and chop. Add the lemon juice.

3 Melt the butter and sauté the onion and garlic in it until tender. Blend in the flour. Gradually stir in the half-and-half and bring to a boil, stirring. Season with salt, pepper and nutmeg.

4 Cook the noodles until barely tender and drain.

5 Add the spinach to the sauce and mix well. Toss the noodles, spinach mixture and prosciutto together and place in a buttered shallow casserole. Top with the crumbs. Bake for 15 to 20 minutes, or until very hot and light brown.

FRESH PASTA
WITH MUSHROOMS

4 SERVINGS

1 pound mushrooms, thinly sliced
3 tablespoons butter
Salt to taste
1/4 teaspoon freshly ground pepper
1 cup soft fresh bread crumbs
1/2 pound fresh pasta dough, cut 1/4 inch wide
2 tablespoons finely minced parsley

1 Cook the mushrooms in 2 tablespoons of the butter until they are light brown. Sprinkle with salt and pepper.

2 In a small skillet cook the crumbs in the remaining tablespoon of butter, stirring until brown.

3 Cook the noodles until barely tender and drain. Turn them onto a hot platter and toss with the mushrooms. Sprinkle with bread crumbs and parsley and serve immediately.

♦

FRESH PASTA
WITH CHICKEN
AND MUSHROOMS

4 TO 6 SERVINGS

1/4 pound butter
1/3 cup flour
2 1/2 cups chicken stock
3/4 cup half-and-half
1/4 cup dry white wine
2 teaspoons salt
1/4 teaspoon freshly ground white pepper
1 cup sliced fresh mushrooms
6 mushroom caps

1 cup cooked ham cut in thinnest possible strips (julienne)
1/2 pound fresh pasta dough, cut 1/4 inch wide
2 cups diced cooked chicken
1/3 cup grated Parmesan cheese

1 Preheat the oven to 350°F.

2 Melt half the butter in a saucepan. Blend in the flour with a whisk. Gradually add the chicken stock, stirring constantly with the whisk. Add the half-and-half and cook, stirring, until the sauce is thickened and smooth. Add the wine, salt and pepper.

3 Sauté the sliced mushrooms, mushroom caps and ham in the remaining butter.

4 Cook the noodles until barely tender and drain. Add to the sauce along with the sliced mushrooms, chicken and ham. Turn the mixture into 4 or 6 greased individual casseroles. Top each with a mushroom cap and sprinkle with Parmesan cheese. Heat in the oven until the cheese is melted and golden brown, about 10 minutes.

♦

PARSLEYED NOODLES

6 SERVINGS

1 pound wide noodles
1/4 cup finely chopped parsley
4 tablespoons butter, melted
Salt and freshly ground pepper to taste

1 If using homemade noodles, cook for 2 or 3 minutes in boiling salted water. If using packaged noodles, cook according to directions on box.

2 Drain the noodles and combine with the remaining ingredients, tossing gently.

FETTUCCINE ALFREDO

Fresh pasta dough makes this traditional dish even more sublime. Be sure to have the butter, half-and-half and cheese at room temperature.

4 SERVINGS

1 pound fresh pasta dough, cut for fettuccine
¼ pound butter, cut into 8 parts
Freshly ground pepper to taste
1 cup half-and-half
¼ pound grated Parmesan cheese
2 large white Italian truffles, sliced (optional)

1 Cook the noodles in 2 quarts of boiling salted water for 3 to 4 minutes. Drain and place in a dry pan.

2 Gently heat the noodles. Toss them gently while adding the butter and grinding the pepper over them.

3 Add the half-and-half and allow to heat thoroughly, tossing once or twice, until most of the half-and-half has been absorbed.

4 Add the cheese and the truffles. Heat, still tossing gently, for 2 to 3 minutes, until the noodles are evenly coated with the melted cheese. Serve immediately.

Variation

FETTUCCINE ALLA ROMANA

Add 1 cup freshly cooked peas and ½ cup finely shredded prosciutto to the fettuccine with the cheese. Eliminate the truffles.

FRESH PASTA WITH SPINACH AND PROSCIUTTO

6 SERVINGS

1½ pounds spinach
1 tablespoon lemon juice
3 tablespoons butter
1 tablespoon finely chopped onion
1 garlic clove, minced
3 tablespoons flour
1 cup half-and-half
Salt and freshly ground pepper to taste
⅛ teaspoon grated nutmeg
1 pound fresh pasta dough, cut ¼ inch wide
½ cup finely chopped prosciutto or cooked ham
½ cup buttered soft fresh bread crumbs

1 Preheat the oven to 350°F.

2 Wash the spinach carefully and cook in a covered pan in only the water clinging to the leaves until just tender. Drain and chop. Add the lemon juice.

3 Melt the butter and sauté the onion and garlic in it until tender. Blend in the flour. Gradually stir in the half-and-half and bring to a boil, stirring. Season with salt, pepper and nutmeg.

4 Cook the noodles until barely tender and drain.

5 Add the spinach to the sauce and mix well. Toss the noodles, spinach mixture and prosciutto together and place in a buttered shallow casserole. Top with the crumbs. Bake for 15 to 20 minutes, or until very hot and light brown.

FRESH PASTA
WITH MUSHROOMS

4 SERVINGS

1 pound mushrooms, thinly sliced
3 tablespoons butter
Salt to taste
¼ teaspoon freshly ground pepper
1 cup soft fresh bread crumbs
½ pound fresh pasta dough, cut ¼ inch wide
2 tablespoons finely minced parsley

   1 Cook the mushrooms in 2 tablespoons of the butter until they are light brown. Sprinkle with salt and pepper.
   2 In a small skillet cook the crumbs in the remaining tablespoon of butter, stirring until brown.
   3 Cook the noodles until barely tender and drain. Turn them onto a hot platter and toss with the mushrooms. Sprinkle with bread crumbs and parsley and serve immediately.

♦

FRESH PASTA
WITH CHICKEN
AND MUSHROOMS

4 TO 6 SERVINGS

¼ pound butter
⅓ cup flour
2½ cups chicken stock
¾ cup half-and-half
¼ cup dry white wine
2 teaspoons salt
¼ teaspoon freshly ground white pepper
1 cup sliced fresh mushrooms
6 mushroom caps

1 cup cooked ham cut in thinnest possible strips (julienne)
½ pound fresh pasta dough, cut ¼ inch wide
2 cups diced cooked chicken
⅓ cup grated Parmesan cheese

   1 Preheat the oven to 350°F.
   2 Melt half the butter in a saucepan. Blend in the flour with a whisk. Gradually add the chicken stock, stirring constantly with the whisk. Add the half-and-half and cook, stirring, until the sauce is thickened and smooth. Add the wine, salt and pepper.
   3 Sauté the sliced mushrooms, mushroom caps and ham in the remaining butter.
   4 Cook the noodles until barely tender and drain. Add to the sauce along with the sliced mushrooms, chicken and ham. Turn the mixture into 4 or 6 greased individual casseroles. Top each with a mushroom cap and sprinkle with Parmesan cheese. Heat in the oven until the cheese is melted and golden brown, about 10 minutes.

♦

PARSLEYED NOODLES

6 SERVINGS

1 pound wide noodles
¼ cup finely chopped parsley
4 tablespoons butter, melted
Salt and freshly ground pepper to taste

   1 If using homemade noodles, cook for 2 or 3 minutes in boiling salted water. If using packaged noodles, cook according to directions on box.
   2 Drain the noodles and combine with the remaining ingredients, tossing gently.

ROMAN NOODLES

4 SERVINGS

1 small garlic clove
2 tablespoons olive oil
¾ pound mushrooms, sliced
1 or 2 anchovy fillets, minced
2 tablespoons butter, softened
Salt and freshly ground pepper to taste
½ pound freshly cooked noodles, drained
¼ cup grated Parmesan cheese

1 Brown the garlic lightly in the oil. Remove the garlic and sauté the mushrooms in the oil about 5 minutes.

2 Cream the anchovies with the butter, add to the mushrooms and season with salt and pepper. Reheat.

3 Mix the mushrooms with hot noodles and serve with Parmesan chese.

♦

DUTCH NOODLES

2 TO 3 SERVINGS

½ cup blanched almonds
3 tablespoons butter
3 tablespoons poppy seeds
1 tablespoon lemon juice
½ pound freshly cooked noodles, drained
Salt and cayenne to taste

1 Sliver the almonds and sauté until brown, or brown in a 350°F oven.

2 Melt the butter, add the almonds, poppy seeds and lemon juice and pour over the noodles. Add salt and cayenne and toss together.

CARAWAY NOODLE RING WITH TUNA

6 SERVINGS

½ pound freshly cooked noodles, drained
1 tablespoon caraway seeds
5 tablespoons butter, at room temperature
3 tablespoons flour
1 cup milk
¾ cup cream
2 (6-ounce) cans tuna fish
¾ teaspoon salt
Freshly ground pepper and cayenne to taste
¼ teaspoon thyme
Parsley sprigs to garnish

1 Put the noodles in a bowl. Add the caraway seeds and 2 tablespoons of the butter. Toss lightly and turn into a buttered 1½-quart ring mold. Set the mold in a pan of hot water to keep warm.

2 Melt the remaining butter in a saucepan and stir in the flour. Add the milk, stirring with a wire whisk. When the mixture is thickened and smooth, add the cream. Simmer for 5 minutes, stirring occasionally.

3 Drain the tuna and flake it. Add it to the sauce. Add the seasonings and mix well. Turn out the noodle ring on a hot platter and fill the center with tuna and sauce. Garnish with parsley.

BAKED NOODLES WITH TOMATOES AND MOZZARELLA

4 SERVINGS

¼ pound butter, melted
¼ cup olive oil
1 garlic clove, minced
½ cup finely chopped onions
2 tablespoons tomato paste
1 (20-ounce) can (2½ cups) Italian-style
    plum tomatoes
Salt and freshly ground pepper to taste
½ teaspoon oregano
1 pound fresh pasta dough, cut into
    ½-inch-wide noodles
½ pound mozzarella cheese, cubed
¼ cup grated Parmesan cheese

1 Preheat the oven to 350°F.
2 Place 4 tablespoons of the butter and oil in a heavy skillet and sauté the garlic and onions in it until tender but not brown.
3 Add the tomato paste, tomatoes, salt and pepper. Bring to a boil and simmer, uncovered, for 20 minutes. Force through a food mill or strainer. Add the oregano.
4 Cook the noodles until barely tender and drain.
5 Mix the noodles with the mozzarella cheese and the remaining 4 tablespoons butter. Place in the bottom of a buttered casserole. Pour the sauce over the top and sprinkle with the Parmesan cheese. Bake for 15 to 20 minutes, or until the dish is bubbly hot.

NOODLE PUDDING

8 SERVINGS

3 eggs, separated
¼ pound butter, melted
2 tablespoons sugar
1 pound creamed cottage cheese
1 cup sour cream
½ pound freshly cooked noodles, drained
½ cup soft fresh bread crumbs
Butter

1 Preheat the oven to 375°F.
2 Beat the egg yolks until light. Add the melted butter and sugar and beat until well mixed. Fold in the cottage cheese, sour cream and drained noodles.
3 Beat the egg whites until stiff and fold into the noodle mixture. Place in a buttered 2-quart casserole. Sprinkle the top with the crumbs and dot generously with butter. Bake for 45 minutes.

LASAGNE

10 TO 12 SERVINGS

½ pound sweet Italian sausages
½ cup water
1 pound ground beef
2 eggs, beaten
4 tablespoons chopped parsley
Salt and freshly ground pepper to taste
¼ cup dry bread crumbs
1 tablespoon plus ¼ cup grated
    Parmesan cheese
5 cups tomato sauce for lasagne
    (see following recipe)
1 pound ricotta cheese
1 pound fresh pasta dough, cut for lasagne
2 tablespoons olive oil
1 pound mozzarella cheese, cut into
    ½-inch cubes

1 Prick the sausages all over with a fork. Put in a frying pan with the water. Cover, bring to a boil and cook for 10 minutes. Uncover, prick the sausages again with a fork and cook until the water evaporates, turning the sausages to brown. Drain on paper toweling.

2 Combine the ground beef, 1 of the beaten eggs, 2 tablespoons of the parsley, the salt, pepper, crumbs and 1 tablespoon of the Parmesan cheese. Mix well and shape into 2-inch meatballs.

3 Brown the meatballs on all sides in the same skillet in which the sausage cooked.

4 Add the sausages and meatballs to the tomato sauce, cover and simmer for 1 hour.

5 In a bowl, combine the ricotta, remaining beaten egg and 2 tablespoons parsley.

6 Remove the sausages from the tomato sauce and slice into thin rounds. Remove the meatballs, cut into quarters and slice into thin pieces.

7 Preheat the oven to 350°F.

8 Cook the lasagne in boiling salted water until barely tender. Rinse in cold water to stop the cooking. Toss with the olive oil to keep from sticking.

9 Cover the bottom of a 9 × 12-inch glass baking dish with a thin layer of tomato sauce. Cover with a layer of lasagne noodles, then all the ricotta mixture, another layer of lasagne, then three quarters of the mozzarella. Combine the sausage and meatball slices and spread over the cheese. Sprinkle with about ½ cup tomato sauce. Top with the rest of the mozzarella and sprinkle with ¼ cup Parmesan.

10 Cover the baking dish with foil and bake for 45 minutes. Uncover and cook for 15 minutes longer. Let sit for 30 minutes before cutting into squares. Serve with the remaining tomato sauce on the side.

Note: When the lasagne is ready for the oven and covered closely with foil, it may at that point be frozen. Do not defrost before baking. It must be baked from the frozen state for 2½ hours at 350°F.

TOMATO SAUCE FOR LASAGNE
ABOUT 5 CUPS

1 tablespoon olive oil
1 cup finely chopped onions
2 garlic cloves, minced
5 cups canned crushed tomatoes
3 tablespoons tomato paste
1 tablespoon chopped basil
1 teaspoon salt
1 teaspoon sugar
1 teaspoon oregano
Freshly ground pepper to taste

Heat the oil and sauté the onions until light brown. Add the garlic and cook another minute. Add the remaining ingredients and stir well.

ED GIOBBI'S VEGETABLE LASAGNE

6 TO 8 SERVINGS

2½ pounds eggplant, cut into
   ¼- to ½-inch-thick slices
Salt to taste
1 (9-ounce) package frozen artichokes
6 tablespoons olive oil
2 cups coarsely chopped onions
2 cups thinly sliced carrots
1 tablespoon finely chopped garlic
4 cups chopped, peeled tomatoes, or canned,
   drained tomatoes
1 teaspoon oregano, crumbled
2 tablespoons finely chopped basil, or
   1 tablespoon dried
4 whole cloves
Freshly ground pepper to taste
1 pound mushrooms, thinly sliced
Flour for dredging
Vegetable oil for frying
1 cup stock or water
1 cup walnuts
1 pound dried lasagne, preferably of Italian
   origin

1 Sprinkle the eggplant slices with salt and let drain for 1 hour. Rinse the slices and pat dry.

2 Drop the artichokes into boiling water. When the water returns to a full boil, drain and set aside.

3 Heat 3 tablespoons of olive oil in a medium-size saucepan and add the onions and carrots. Cook, stirring, until the onions are wilted and add the garlic. Cook about 1 minute, stirring, and add the tomatoes, oregano, basil, cloves, salt and pepper.

4 Cover and simmer 30 minutes, stirring often from the bottom to prevent sticking. Pour the sauce into the container of a food processor and blend. Return the sauce to the pan and add the artichokes. Cover and simmer 15 minutes longer.

5 Heat the remaining 3 tablespoons of olive oil in a skillet and add the mushrooms, salt and pepper. Cook over high heat, stirring, until mushrooms start to brown. Using a slotted spoon, remove the mushrooms and drain on paper toweling.

6 Dredge the eggplant slices in flour, a few slices at a time, and shake off excess. Heat ¾ inch of vegetable oil in a large skillet and add the eggplant slices, a few at a time. Cook until light brown on both sides. As they cook transfer them to paper toweling to drain. Repeat until all the slices are cooked.

7 Preheat the oven to 400°F.

8 Carefully remove the artichokes from the sauce and set them aside. Pour 2 cups of the sauce into the container of a food processor (if there is more than 2 cups, reserve the remaining sauce for a future use). Add the stock and the walnuts. Blend to a creamy consistency.

9 Meanwhile, cook the lasagne 5 to 6 minutes in a large quantity of boiling, salted water until it is al dente. Drain and rinse under cold running water.

10 Use a 12 × 12 × 3-inch baking dish. Add 1 layer of lasagne and 1 layer of eggplant slices. Pour some of the sauce over the eggplant and arrange a few artichoke hearts over all. Add another layer of lasagne and spread the mushrooms on top. Add another layer of lasagne, a layer of eggplant and sauce. Continue making layers of eggplant, sauce and lasagne until all the ingredients are used. Add a final layer of pasta and more sauce. If the dish seems too dense, add a little more stock or water.

11 Cover the dish closely with foil and place in the oven. Bake 30 minutes.

CANNELLONI
ALLA NERONE

ABOUT 3 DOZEN CANNELLONI, OR
APPROXIMATELY 12 SERVINGS

3 chicken breasts, boned
¼ pound plus 4 tablespoons butter
7 chicken livers
10 slices prosciutto
2 cups grated Parmesan cheese
½ cup flour
1 quart milk, scalded
1 cup cream
¼ teaspoon white pepper
Salt to taste
1 pound fresh pasta dough, cut for cannelloni

1 In a skillet, sauté the chicken breasts in 4 tablespoons of the butter until the breasts are light brown.

2 Sauté the chicken livers briefly in the same skillet.

3 Grind the chicken breasts, livers and prosciutto, using the finest knife of a food grinder. Or chop in a food processor. Add 1 cup of the grated Parmesan cheese and mix.

4 In the top of a double boiler melt the remaining ¼ pound butter, add the flour and stir with a wire whisk until blended. Add the scalded milk to the butter-flour mixture, stirring vigorously with the whisk. Cook over boiling water, stirring, until thickened. Add the cream to the sauce and season with white pepper and salt.

5 Add about 1 cup of the sauce to the ground meat mixture and mix well.

6 Cook the cannelloni squares in a large quantity of boiling water until tender, 8 to 10 minutes. Drain and spread the squares on damp towels.

7 Spread about 2 tablespoons meat filling on each square and roll tightly. Arrange the rolls of filled dough in two layers in three 12 × 7½-inch buttered baking dishes. Sprinkle each layer with some of the remaining Parmesan cheese and cover with some of the reserved sauce. (This preparation may be done ahead.)

8 Dot the top of each dish with bits of additional butter and bake in a preheated 375°F oven until the tops are light brown, 20 minutes or longer.

◆

SPINACH-CHICKEN
FILLING FOR PASTA

ABOUT 3 CUPS

1 cup minced cooked chicken
1 cup chopped cooked spinach, well drained
½ cup fresh bread crumbs
⅓ cup grated Parmesan cheese
¼ cup cream
1 garlic clove, finely chopped
2 eggs, beaten
2 teaspoons finely chopped parsley
½ teaspoon nutmeg
Salt and freshly ground pepper to taste

Combine the ingredients and mix well. Use as a filling for cannelloni, lasagne, manicotti or ravioli.

STUFFED MANICOTTI

12 SERVINGS

1 pound fresh pasta dough, cut for manicotti
Melted butter
2 onions, chopped
3 garlic cloves, chopped
2 tablespoons olive oil
½ pound mushrooms, chopped
1½ pounds chopped lean beef (may be
    part veal)
1½ cups chopped mozzarella
1 cup soft bread crumbs
1 egg, lightly beaten
1½ teaspoons salt
½ teaspoon oregano
¼ teaspoon freshly ground pepper
3 to 4 cups basic tomato sauce (page 561)
1 cup grated Parmesan cheese

1 Cook the pasta in a large quantity of rapidly boiling salted water until half done. Drain and rinse in cold water. Return it to the pot and toss with a small amount of melted butter to prevent it from sticking together.

2 Preheat the oven to 350°F.

3 Brown the onions and garlic lightly in the oil. Add the mushrooms and cook until wilted. Using the hands, blend the onion mixture with the beef, cheese, crumbs, egg, salt, oregano and pepper. Using a teaspoon, stuff the manicotti with the mixture.

4 Cover the bottoms of two 8-cup, shallow rectangular casseroles with a thin layer of tomato sauce and arrange a layer of the stuffed pasta on top. Cover lightly with more sauce and sprinkle generously with Parmesan cheese. If necessary, repeat the layers.

5 Bake about 30 minutes.

PASTA WITH RICOTTA AND PARSLEY

6 SERVINGS

5 medium onions, chopped
4 garlic cloves, minced
½ green pepper, minced
¼ cup olive oil
1½ cups minced parsley, tightly packed
1 teaspoon salt
Freshly ground pepper to taste
½ teaspoon oregano or thyme
½ cup sweet or sour cream
2 cups ricotta cheese
1 pound pasta (shells, elbows or other
    small forms)

1 Sauté the onions, garlic and green pepper in the oil until light brown, stirring often. Add the parsley, salt, pepper and oregano and cook, stirring, until the parsley is wilted but not brown.

2 Add the sour cream and mix. Add the ricotta and heat to serving temperature. To prevent curdling, do not heat to simmering.

3 Meanwhile, cook pasta until al dente. Drain well, return to the pot and add the sauce. Toss until well mixed. Adjust the seasonings and serve on a hot platter.

ZITI WITH FRESH HERBS

4 SERVINGS

1 tablespoon finely chopped parsley
1 tablespoon finely chopped tarragon
1 tablespoon finely chopped chives
1 tablespoon finely chopped chervil, or use
    1 additional teaspoon each of chopped
    tarragon and parsley
Salt to taste
1 pound ziti
2 tablespoons butter
2 tablespoons olive oil
½ cup grated Parmesan cheese

1 Combine the parsley, tarragon, chives and chervil in a small bowl.

2 Bring 2 quarts of water to the boil in a kettle and add salt. Add the ziti and cook about 12 minutes. Drain.

3 Return the ziti to the kettle and add the butter and oil. Toss briefly and add the herb mixture. Toss and serve immediately with the grated cheese on the side.

SPAGHETTI CARBONARA

4 SERVINGS

¼ pound bacon, cut into 1-inch lengths
3 tablespoons olive oil
1½ cups chopped onions
½ cup finely chopped parsley,
    preferably Italian
1 cup finely diced fontina cheese
⅔ cup finely shredded prosciutto
    or Virginia ham
2 egg yolks, lightly beaten
Hot red pepper flakes to taste
1 pound spaghetti
Freshly ground pepper
1 cup grated Parmesan cheese

1 Heat the bacon pieces in a heavy skillet and cook, stirring frequently, until crisp. Using a slotted spoon, transfer the bacon to paper toweling to drain.

2 Pour off almost all the fat from the skillet, but do not wash the skillet. Add the olive oil and onions. Cook the onions until tender.

3 Prepare the parsley, fontina cheese, prosciutto and egg yolks and keep these ingredients, plus the bacon bits and red pepper flakes, close at hand. Have a hot dish ready for tossing the spaghetti and hot bowls ready to receive the portions.

4 Cook the spaghetti in boiling salted water to the desired degree of doneness. The moment it is done, empty it into a colander. Drain quickly, then pour the spaghetti into the hot dish.

5 Add the onions, bacon bits, parsley, fontina cheese, prosciutto, beaten yolks and red pepper flakes and toss quickly and thoroughly with a fork and spoon. Serve in hot bowls and pass the pepper and Parmesan cheese.

PASTA WITH EGGPLANT

4 TO 6 SERVINGS

1 medium eggplant
Salt to taste
Olive or vegetable oil
1 teaspoon finely chopped garlic
1 tablespoon finely chopped parsley,
    preferably Italian
1½ to 2 cups peeled, cored, chopped tomatoes
Hot red pepper flakes to taste
1 pound pasta (penne or ziti), cooked
    and drained

1 Cut off the ends of the eggplant and discard. Cut the eggplant into ¼-inch rounds. Place in a mixing bowl and sprinkle with salt. Let stand about ½ hour, then squeeze the eggplant slices to remove most of the moisture.

2 Add about ¼ inch of oil to a skillet and cook the slices on all sides until golden brown, adding more oil as necessary. Drain the slices on paper toweling.

3 Heat 4 tablespoons of oil in a skillet and add the garlic. Cook briefly and add the parsley, tomatoes and red pepper flakes. Simmer about 10 minutes, or until the oil separates from the tomatoes.

4 Meanwhile, cut the eggplant slices into thin strips. Add the strips to the sauce and cook about 3 minutes. Serve with the hot pasta.

PASTA WITH FRESH PEAS

4 SERVINGS

¼ pound prosciutto
1 medium onion
1 garlic clove, peeled
1 (3-inch) piece of celery
1 cup parsley, preferably Italian
¼ cup olive oil
3 tablespoons butter
1½ pounds fresh peas
⅓ cup chicken or beef stock
1 large tomato, peeled, seeded and chopped
2 tablespoons chopped basil
Salt and freshly ground pepper to taste
1 pound spaghetti or linguine, cooked
    and drained
Grated Parmesan cheese

1 On a chopping board, mince together the prosciutto, onion, garlic, celery and parsley.

2 Heat together the olive oil and butter. Cook the minced ingredients in it over medium heat about 5 minutes.

3 Add the peas and stock. Cover and simmer, stirring occasionally, until the peas are tender. Toward the end of the cooking time, add the tomato and basil. Season with salt and pepper. If there is too much liquid, cook uncovered to allow for evaporation. The peas should be dry, not soupy.

4 Toss the pasta with the pea mixture and serve with grated Parmesan cheese.

RIGATONI WITH PROSCIUTTO AND SUN-DRIED TOMATO SAUCE

The following dish may be made with canned tomatoes, but it is much better prepared mid-summer when red, ripe tomatoes are at the peak of their flavor. The addition of sun-dried tomatoes makes this a rich and delicious sauce.

4 SERVINGS

1 pound ripe tomatoes, peeled, seeded and
    cut into ½-inch cubes
½ pound zucchini, ends trimmed, cut into
    ¼-inch slices
¼ pound prosciutto, or sliced cooked ham,
    cut into very thin julienne strips
1 teaspoon finely chopped jalapeño, or other
    hot green chili
1 cup finely chopped onions
1 tablespoon minced garlic
¾ cup grated Parmesan cheese
4 packed-in-oil sun-dried tomatoes, cut into
    small cubes (there should be about ¼ cup)
2 tablespoons olive oil
4 tablespoons butter
Salt and freshly ground pepper to taste
½ cup cream
½ teaspoon hot red pepper flakes
1 pound rigatoni

1 Prepare the fresh tomatoes, zucchini, prosciutto, chili, onions, garlic, cheese and sun-dried tomatoes and set aside in separate batches.

2 Heat the oil and 2 tablespoons of the butter in a saucepan and add the onions, garlic and chili. Cook, stirring, until onions are wilted. Add the prosciutto and cook, stirring 1 minute. Add zucchini and cook, stirring occasionally, about a minute longer. Add the fresh tomatoes and cook about 10 minutes. Add salt, pepper, 3 tablespoons of the cheese, the cream, sun-dried tomatoes and red pepper flakes. Cook to heat thoroughly.

3 Meanwhile, bring about 3 quarts of water to the boil. Add the rigatoni and cook until the pasta is al dente. Drain the pasta and return it to the hot pot. Add the remaining 2 tablespoons of butter and toss to blend well. Spoon the pasta into 4 hot soup bowls and spoon equal amounts of the sauce over the top of each serving. Serve with the remaining Parmesan on the side.

◆

SPAGHETTI WITH SAUCE BOLOGNESE

8 SERVINGS

1 cup dried white mushrooms
1 pound ground chuck
2 large onions, chopped
¼ pound prosciutto, sliced very thin
2 tablespoons butter
2 tablespoons olive oil
4 cups Italian plum tomatoes
1 small can tomato paste
2 pounds spaghetti, cooked and drained
Grated Parmesan cheese

1 Wash the mushrooms well and soak in tepid water. When soft, chop fine and add to the meat.

2 Sauté the onions and prosciutto in the butter and oil over low heat until the onions are golden. Add the beef and mushroom mixture. Cook, stirring, until the meat is brown. Add the tomatoes and tomato paste and allow to simmer slowly, uncovered, about 1 hour, or until the sauce is thick.

3 Serve over hot pasta with grated Parmesan on the side.

SPAGHETTI ALL' AMATRICIANA

The following dish is frequently listed on menus as *spaghetti alla matriciana* but it actually takes its name from the little town of Amatrice in the Sabine Hills.

4 SERVINGS

1 tablespoon olive oil
1 tablespoon butter
¼ pound (about 8 slices) bacon, cut into
    1-inch lengths
1 onion
½ cup dry white wine
2 cups chopped peeled tomatoes
Salt and freshly ground pepper to taste
2 tablespoons finely chopped basil
¼ cup finely chopped parsley
1 pound spaghetti, cooked to the desired
    degree of doneness
Grated Parmesan cheese

1 Heat the oil and butter in a skillet and add the bacon. Cook, stirring, until bacon is rendered of its fat.

2 Meanwhile, cut the onion in half and cut each half into the thinnest possible slices. Cook the onion, stirring, until wilted, about 10 minutes.

3 Add the wine and cook, stirring occasionally, until wine evaporates. Add the tomatoes, salt and pepper and cook 30 minutes. Add the basil and parsley and cook 10 minutes longer. Serve with spaghetti and Parmesan cheese.

SPAGHETTI WITH COGNAC TOMATO SAUCE AND SOUR CREAM

4 SERVINGS

2 tablespoons olive oil
2 tablespoons butter
2 cups finely chopped onions
1 teaspoon finely chopped garlic
1 pound ground round or sirloin steak
Salt and freshly ground pepper to taste
1 (35-ounce) can of tomatoes with tomato
    paste, or 5 cups canned tomatoes and
    3 tablespoons tomato paste
¾ cup beef stock
1 hot dried red pepper (optional)
2 tablespoons finely chopped parsley
1 pound spaghettini, spaghetti or vermicelli
2 tablespoons cognac
4 to 8 tablespoons sour cream
¾ cup grated Parmesan cheese

1 Heat the oil and butter in a casserole and when it is hot, add the onions and garlic, stirring. Cook until the onions are wilted and start to brown and add the meat, salt and pepper. Cook, stirring and breaking up lumps in the meat with the side of a large spoon. When there are no more lumps and the meat has lost its raw color, add the tomatoes, stock, red pepper and parsley. Cook, stirring occasionally, 45 minutes to 1 hour, or until sauce is thickened.

2 Meanwhile, cook the pasta to the desired degree of doneness.

3 Add the cognac to the spaghetti sauce and bring to the boil. Serve the spaghetti piping hot with the sauce on the side or toss the spaghetti with the sauce and serve. Pass the sour cream and grated cheese separately.

SPAGHETTI WITH MEATBALLS IN TOMATO SAUCE

4 SERVINGS

5 cups basic tomato sauce (page 561)
¾ pound ground lean beef, preferably sirloin
½ cup bread crumbs, preferably made from
    whole wheat bread
1 egg, beaten
1 tablespoon half-and-half
2 tablespoons grated Parmesan cheese
2 teaspoons minced garlic
¼ cup finely chopped parsley
¼ cup finely chopped basil
½ teaspoon grated lemon rind
¼ teaspoon grated nutmeg
Salt and freshly ground pepper to taste
¼ cup olive oil
1 pound spaghetti, cooked to the desired
    degree of doneness

1 Prepare the tomato sauce and bring to the boil.

2 Put the meat in a mixing bowl and add the crumbs, egg, half-and-half, cheese, garlic, parsley, basil, lemon rind, nutmeg and salt and pepper. Blend well with the fingers. Shape the mixture into 12 balls of more or less the same size.

3 Heat the oil in a skillet large enough to hold the meatballs without crowding. Brown the meatballs on all sides. As they brown, transfer them to the tomato sauce. Let simmer 15 minutes or longer.

4 Serve the meatballs in the sauce with the drained spaghetti.

SPAGHETTI WITH VEAL-AND-DILL MEATBALLS

It is curious how certain herbs and spices seem particularly suited to or "marry well" with one meat or another. Chicken, for example, goes notably well with tarragon, beef with marjoram, pork with rosemary, and so on. Dill makes a fine liaison when combined with veal.

6 SERVINGS

¾ pound twice-ground lean veal
3 to 5 tablespoons olive oil
⅓ cup finely chopped onions
2 teaspoons minced garlic
¼ cup finely chopped dill
1 tablespoon finely chopped parsley
⅛ teaspoon grated nutmeg
Salt and freshly ground pepper to taste
¼ cup freshly grated Parmesan cheese
2 tablespoons beaten egg
½ cup fresh bread crumbs
½ cup flour
4½ cups basic tomato sauce (page 561)
1 pound spaghetti, cooked to the desired
    degree of doneness

1 Put the meat in a mixing bowl.

2 Heat 2 teaspoons of the oil in a small skillet and add the onions and garlic. Cook, stirring, until wilted. Let cool. Scrape the mixture into the bowl with the meat.

3 Add the dill, parsley, nutmeg, salt, pepper, cheese and egg. Add the crumbs and blend well, using the fingers.

4 Shape the mixture into 18 balls of equal size. Dredge the balls in the flour and shake off excess.

5 Heat 2 tablespoons of the oil in a skillet large enough to hold the balls in 1 layer without crowding. Add the meatballs and cook, adding a little more oil if necessary to prevent sticking, until the balls are brown on all sides.

Continued

6 Meanwhile, bring the tomato sauce to a boil and add the meatballs. Cook 20 minutes.

7 Serve the meatballs and sauce with hot, freshly cooked spaghetti.

◆

SPINACH LINGUINE WITH FRESH TOMATO SAUCE AND BASIL

4 SERVINGS

2 pounds ripe tomatoes
2 tablespoons olive oil
2 teaspoons minced garlic
¼ teaspoon hot red pepper flakes
Salt to taste
¾ pound fresh or dried green linguine
2 tablespoons butter
¼ cup finely chopped basil

1 Bring 4 quarts of water to the boil.

2 Meanwhile, remove and discard the core from the tomatoes. Cut the tomatoes into ½-inch or slightly smaller cubes. There should be about 2½ cups.

3 Heat the oil in a saucepan and add the garlic. Cook briefly without browning and add the tomatoes, red pepper flakes and salt.

4 Add salt to the kettle of water. Add the linguine and stir. If fresh pasta is used, cook it 1 to 1½ minutes. If dried pasta is used, cook until al dente, 8 to 10 minutes.

5 Drain the pasta and return it to the kettle. Stir in the butter and add the tomato mixture. Blend and sprinkle with the basil.

ED GIOBBI'S SWEET RED PEPPER SAUCE FOR PASTA

4 SERVINGS

2 very red, unblemished sweet red peppers, about ½ pound
2 tablespoons olive oil
2 cups coarsely chopped onions
2 teaspoons minced garlic
½ teaspoon hot red pepper flakes
1 cup chicken stock
Salt and freshly ground pepper to taste
¼ cup chopped basil
1 pound cooked pasta
Grated Parmesan cheese

1 Cut the peppers lengthwise in half. Scrape away and discard the stems, veins and seeds. Chop the peppers coarsely. There should be about 2 cups.

2 Heat the oil in a large saucepan and add the peppers. Cook, stirring, about 5 minutes. Add the onions, garlic and red pepper flakes and cook, stirring, 2 minutes longer. Add the stock, salt and pepper. Cover and cook 15 minutes.

3 Ladle the sauce into the container of a food processor and blend thoroughly. Return the mixture to the saucepan and bring to the boil. Cook about 2 minutes and stir in the basil. Serve with 1 pound pasta cooked to the desired degree of doneness. Serve the cheese on the side.

TOMATO, MUSHROOM AND ANCHOVY SAUCE FOR PASTA

4 SERVINGS

1 very red, unblemished sweet red pepper
¼ pound mushrooms
2 tablespoons butter
2 teaspoons minced garlic
1 cup canned crushed tomatoes
Salt and freshly ground pepper to taste
¼ teaspoon hot red pepper flakes
4 bottled-in-oil, sun-dried tomatoes, cut into small cubes, (there should be about ¼ cup)
2 tablespoons anchovy paste or finely chopped anchovy fillets
¼ cup cream
¼ cup chopped basil
1 pound cooked pasta
Grated Parmesan cheese

1 Cut the pepper in half lengthwise. Scoop away and discard the core, veins and seeds. Cut the pepper into thin strips. There should be about ¾ cup.

2 Cut the mushrooms into thin slices. There should be about 1½ cups.

3 Heat the butter in a saucepan and add the mushrooms. Cook, stirring, until the mushrooms soften. Add the garlic and cook briefly. Add the crushed tomatoes, salt, pepper and red pepper flakes. Simmer about 10 minutes.

4 Add the pepper strips and simmer about 5 minutes. Add the sun-dried tomatoes and anchovy paste. Stir to blend. Add the cream and basil and bring to the boil. Serve over 1 pound freshly cooked pasta and with the cheese on the side.

SPAGHETTI WITH FRESH TUNA SAUCE

Broiled or grilled fresh tuna has become the favorite fish for countless Americans over the past decade or so. Leftover cooked fresh tuna is excellent when used for cold sandwiches, certain soups and in pasta sauces. This is one version with tomatoes and black olives.

4 SERVINGS

½ pound cooked fresh tuna
2 tablespoons anchovy paste, or finely chopped anchovy fillets
1 tablespoon butter, at room temperature
10 small (about ⅓ cup) black olives, preferably imported from Italy or Greece
3 tablespoons olive oil
1 tablespoon minced garlic
2 cups canned crushed, or finely chopped fresh ripe tomatoes
¾ cup bottled clam juice
Salt and freshly ground pepper to taste
2 tablespoons finely chopped parsley
2 tablespoons finely chopped basil
½ teaspoon hot red pepper flakes
2 tablespoons drained capers
1 pound spaghetti, spaghettini or capellini
¾ cup grated Parmesan, or Pecorino Romano cheese

1 Cut the tuna into bite-size pieces. There should be about 3 cups.

2 Blend the anchovy paste with the butter and set aside.

3 If the olives are not pitted, pit them. Coarsely chop the olives.

4 Heat 2 tablespoons of the oil in a saucepan and add the garlic. Cook, stirring, until the garlic starts to brown, then add the tomatoes and clam juice. Add salt, pepper, parsley, basil and red pepper flakes. Let simmer, stirring often, about 20 minutes over low heat. Stir in the anchovy butter, olives and capers. Add tuna and fold gently to blend.

Continued

5 Meanwhile, bring about 3 quarts of water to the boil and add salt. Cook the pasta until it is al dente. Drain immediately and return the pasta to the kettle. Add 1 tablespoon of olive oil and stir to blend. Spoon into 4 heated pasta plates and spoon equal portions of the tomato sauce over all. Serve with the cheese on the side.

◆

FETTUCCINE WITH ORIENTAL LOBSTER SAUCE

4 TO 6 SERVINGS

1 pound fresh or dried fettuccine or linguine
  (see note)
2 (1-pound) lobsters, or 1 pound medium
  raw shrimp
Salt to taste
¼ cup plus 2 tablespoons olive oil
¼ cup Vietnamese (nuoc mam) or Thai
  (nam pla) fish sauce, available where
  Oriental ingredients are sold
1½ teaspoons minced garlic
1 tablespoon finely chopped shallots
2 tablespoons finely chopped coriander
1 tablespoon finely chopped mint, or 1
  teaspoon dried and crumbled
8 scallions, trimmed and cut crosswise into
  ½-inch pieces
1 tablespoon finely chopped hot green chilies,
  such as jalapeño or serrano
1 tablespoon honey
½ teaspoon freshly ground pepper
4 teaspoons finely shredded fresh ginger
½ cup finely chopped scallions
½ pound broccoli, top part only, cut into
  bite-size pieces

16 snow peas, stringed as necessary
1 cup skinned, seeded tomatoes cut into
  thin julienne strips

1 Bring about 4 quarts of water to the boil in a kettle for the pasta. In another kettle, cook the lobsters or shrimp. Add salt to each kettle.

2 Drain the lobsters and remove the meat from both tails and claws. Cut the lobster meat into large bite-size pieces. If using shrimp, shell and devein them and leave them whole.

3 In a saucepan, combine ¼ cup of the olive oil, the fish sauce, garlic, shallots, coriander, mint, the scallion pieces, chilies, honey and pepper. Blend well with the wire whisk. Add the ginger and chopped scallions. Add the broccoli and snow peas and cook, stirring, about 1 minute. Add the tomatoes and cook, stirring, about 1 minute. Add the lobster or shrimp and stir to blend. Cover and keep warm.

4 Meanwhile, drop the pasta into boiling water. If fresh pasta is used, cook about 1½ minutes. If dried pasta is used, cook 7 to 9 minutes, or to the desired degree of doneness.

5 Drain the pasta and return it to the kettle. Add 2 tablespoons of olive oil and toss. Serve equal portions of the pasta with equal portions of the lobster sauce. Serve immediately.

Note: This dish is especially good with black pasta, which is made with the "ink" coloring of squid. The ink imparts a subtle, covetable flavor to the pasta. Squid pasta, or black pasta, is widely available in fine food specialty shops in many metropolitan areas. It is best served with a fish or sea-food sauce.

LINGUINE WITH LOBSTER

6 SERVINGS

2 (1½-pound) live lobsters
⅓ cup olive oil
1 garlic clove, minced
1 small onion, chopped
1 teaspoon salt
¼ to ½ teaspoon cayenne
Freshly ground pepper to taste
1 cup peeled and chopped tomatoes
2 tablespoons tomato paste
2 tablespoons water
⅔ cup dry white wine
1½ tablespoons chopped parsley
1 teaspoon oregano
1 pound pasta, cooked and drained

1 Cut the spinal cord of each lobster by inserting a knife where the tail and body meet. Turn the lobsters on their backs and split lengthwise. Cut each tail crosswise into 3 pieces. Cut off the claws and crack them.

2 Heat the oil in a large skillet, add the lobsters and cook over high heat 3 or 4 minutes, or until they are red. Add the garlic, onion and seasonings and cook, stirring, 2 minutes.

3 Add the tomatoes and tomato paste blended with the water and cook, turning the lobster pieces constantly, about 1 minute.

4 Add the wine, parsley and oregano and cook about 10 minutes, turning the lobster frequently.

5 To serve, drain the sauce onto hot linguine and toss to coat the pasta. Place on a platter and garnish with lobster.

SPAGHETTI WITH CRABMEAT

4 SERVINGS

4 tablespoons butter
½ cup chopped onions
½ cup chopped celery
2 garlic cloves, minced
2 tablespoons finely chopped parsley
2 fresh tomatoes, peeled, seeded and chopped
1 cup tomato sauce
Salt and freshly ground pepper to taste
1 teaspoon paprika, or more
1 pound crabmeat, picked over well to remove
    any bits of shell or cartilage
1 pound spaghetti
Grated Parmesan cheese

1 Heat the butter in a saucepan. Add the onions, celery and garlic. Cook until onions are wilted. Add the parsley, tomatoes, tomato sauce, salt, pepper and paprika. Simmer for 20 minutes, stirring occasionally.

2 Add crabmeat and heat thoroughly.

3 Cook the spaghetti until it is al dente. Dress the spaghetti with the sauce and serve the cheese separately.

PASTA WITH SHRIMP

4 SERVINGS

2 tablespoons olive oil
1 large onion, sliced thin
2 garlic cloves, minced
4 cups canned Italian tomatoes
1½ pounds small shrimp, shelled and deveined
Pinch of oregano
Salt and freshly ground pepper to taste
1 pound tagliarini or spaghettini, cooked
   and drained

1 Heat the oil and sauté the onion until it is transparent. Add the garlic and continue cooking over low heat about 3 minutes. Add the tomatoes and cook over fairly high heat 12 minutes, leaving the pot uncovered.

2 Add the shrimp and season with the oregano. Reduce the heat and simmer about 5 minutes. Add salt and pepper to taste. Serve over the hot pasta.

Note: Two cups of any of the following may be used in place of the shrimp: shelled raw clams without juice; raw oysters, cut into pieces; crabmeat; lobster meat, cut into pieces; raw baby squid, sliced thin.

Singapore-Style Shrimp with Noodles, page 268.

LINGUINE WITH CLAMS AND BASIL

2 SERVINGS

16 cherrystone clams, the smaller the better
6 cups water
Salt to taste
½ pound linguine, spaghettini or capellini
½ cup half-and-half
4 tablespoons butter
2 teaspoons minced garlic
½ cup coarsely chopped basil
¼ cup grated Parmesan cheese
Freshly ground pepper to taste

1 Open the clams or have them opened, reserving both the clams and their juices. Coarsely chop the clams and refrigerate. There should be about ⅓ cup clams and about ⅔ cup juice.

2 Pour the juice into a kettle and add the water and salt. Bring the liquid to the boil and add the linguine, stirring constantly until it is softened and boils freely. Cook until it is al dente, or to the desired degree of doneness.

3 As the pasta cooks, pour the half-and-half into a small saucepan and bring to the simmer.

4 Heat 2 tablespoons of the butter in a skillet or a small saucepan and add the garlic. Cook briefly, stirring, and add the clams and hot half-and-half. Remove from the heat.

5 When the linguine is done, drain it, return it to the kettle. Add remaining butter, tossing lightly to coat the strands. Add the clam mixture, basil, cheese, salt and pepper. Toss and serve immediately with a pepper mill on the side.

GAEL GREENE'S LINGUINE WITH WALNUTS

When Gael Greene, the distinguished restaurant critic, gave this recipe to me some years ago, she added a note: "Save this recipe for summer and fall when there is plenty of fresh basil in the garden."

2 TO 4 SERVINGS

6 ounces goat cheese, preferably Montrachet
    or Bucheron
1 cup grated Parmesan, or Pecorino Romano
    cheese, or a blend of both
¾ cup cream
2 tablespoons olive oil
2 tablespoons butter, at room temperature
2 tablespoons minced garlic
⅔ cup broken walnuts
1 cup closely packed basil leaves,
    finely chopped
Salt to taste
½ pound linguine or spaghettini
Freshly ground pepper to taste

1 Put the goat cheese in the bowl of a food processor. Add ⅓ cup of the Parmesan cheese and the cream. Blend thoroughly. Set aside.

2 Heat the oil and butter in a small heavy skillet and add the garlic and walnuts. Cook, stirring, until the walnuts start to take on color. Take care not to burn the nuts and garlic. Remove the skillet from the heat, add the basil and stir to blend. Set aside.

3 Meanwhile, bring about 3 quarts of water to the boil and add salt. Add the linguine and cook, stirring often, until al dente.

4 Scoop out and reserve ¼ cup of the hot pasta liquid.

5 Drain the pasta immediately and return it to the pot. Add the reserved cooking liquid, the cheese mixture, the basil-walnut mixture, salt and pepper. Serve on very hot pasta plates with the remaining Parmesan cheese on the side.

♦

PASTA WITH RED CLAM SAUCE

8 SERVINGS

2 tablespoons olive oil
3 garlic cloves, finely chopped
1 onion, chopped
2 celery stalks, chopped
¼ teaspoon thyme
¼ teaspoon basil
½ teaspoon oregano
Salt and freshly ground pepper to taste
2 cups canned tomatoes
1 can tomato paste
1½ cups water
2 cups fresh or bottled clam juice
2 cups minced clams, fresh or canned
4 tablespoons butter
½ cup chopped parsley
2 pounds fusilli, or other pasta, cooked
    and drained

1 In a heavy kettle, heat the oil, add the garlic, onions and celery and cook until the onions are transparent. Add the thyme, basil, oregano, salt, pepper, tomatoes, tomato paste and water. Bring to a boil, reduce the heat and simmer gently, uncovered, 1 hour.

2 After 30 minutes, add the clam juice.

3 Five minutes before serving add the clams and cook gently. Stir in the butter and parsley. Reheat until the butter melts. Serve with hot pasta.

PASTA WITH ANCHOVY AND CLAM SAUCE

4 SERVINGS

3 salted whole anchovies, or 8 canned
    flat anchovy fillets
2 dozen cherrystone clams in the shell
¼ cup olive oil
3 tablespoons butter
3 garlic cloves, minced
2 shallots, finely chopped
¼ cup finely chopped parsley, preferably
    Italian
½ teaspoon chopped rosemary
½ cup dry white wine
Freshly ground pepper to taste
Salt (very little, because the clams and
    anchovies are salty)
1 pound linguine or other pasta, cooked
    and drained
Hot red pepper flakes (optional)

1 If salted whole anchovies are used, wash them in cold running water to remove most of the external salt and any tiny scales that may be present. Use the fingers to pull the fillets from the bone. Discard the bones. Set the fillets aside.

2 Open the clams or have them opened and reserve both the clams and 1 cup of clam juice. Finely chop the clams (there should be about ¾ cup) and set aside.

3 Heat the oil and butter in a skillet. Add the garlic and shallots and cook until light brown. Add the anchovies and stir until they dissolve. Add the parsley, rosemary, reserved clam juice and white wine and bring to a boil. Add pepper and a tiny bit of salt and simmer about 15 minutes.

4 Add the chopped clams and cook 5 minutes. Serve piping hot over the freshly cooked pasta. Serve red pepper flakes on the side, if desired, but no cheese.

CONCHIGLIETTE WITH GORGONZOLA

4 TO 6 SERVINGS

4 tablespoons butter
¼ pound Gorgonzola, or blue cheese, cut into
    cubes or crumbled
1½ cups half-and-half
2 tablespoons cognac or other brandy
3 tablespoons tomato purée
⅓ cup coarsely chopped basil
½ cup broken or coarsely chopped walnuts
Salt to taste
1 pound small pasta shells (No. 22) or
    orecchiette ("little ears")
1½ cups grated Parmesan cheese

1 Melt the butter in a saucepan and add the Gorgonzola, stirring with a whisk. When the cheese is melted add the half-and-half, cognac, tomato purée, basil and walnuts.

2 Bring about 4 quarts of water to a boil in a kettle and add salt. Add the pasta and cook until al dente. Drain the pasta immediately and return to the kettle. Add the Gorgonzola sauce and ¾ cup of the Parmesan cheese. Toss to blend and spoon into 4 heated pasta plates. Serve with the remaining Parmesan on the side.

MUSSELS WITH LINGUINE

4 SERVINGS

1½ pounds (about 40) mussels
2 (about 1½ pounds) ripe tomatoes
Salt to taste
1 pound linguine
3 tablespoons butter
1 tablespoon minced garlic
Freshly ground pepper to taste
¼ teaspoon hot red pepper flakes
½ cup cream
¼ cup finely chopped basil
1 tablespoon olive oil

1 Pull off and discard the stringy beard from each mussel. Rinse and scrub the mussels well. Drain.

2 Put the mussels in a 2-quart kettle with a heavy bottom and cover with a tight-fitting lid. It is not necessary to add liquid. Cook the mussels over high heat. Shake the kettle and toss the mussels up and down to redistribute them. Let cook 3 or 4 minutes until all the mussels have opened.

3 Line a bowl with a fine sieve and line the sieve with cheesecloth. Pour in the mussels and their liquid. There should be ½ cup or more liquid. When the mussels are cool enough to handle, remove the meat from the shells. Set aside.

4 Meanwhile, drop the tomatoes into a basin of boiling water and let stand about 10 seconds. Drain. Cut away and discard the core. Pull away and discard the skin. Remove the seeds. Cut the tomatoes into small cubes. There should be about 2 cups.

5 Bring about 3 quarts of water to the boil and add salt. Add the linguine, stirring until it is limp. Cook 11 to 12 minutes, or until tender.

6 As the pasta cooks, heat the butter in a saucepan and add the garlic. Cook briefly without browning and add the tomatoes, salt, pepper and red pepper flakes. Cook about 2 minutes and add the cream and reserved mussel liquid. Bring to the boil and remove from the heat. Stir in the basil.

7 Drain the pasta and return it to the kettle. Stir in the oil and toss. Pour in the sauce and toss to blend.

Pesto within the past two decades has become very much a part of American culture. It will keep a week or longer tightly sealed and refrigerated and it is simple to freeze for later use. The best-known version of pesto is made with mashed or blended fresh basil leaves with garlic and pine nuts. When you make the basic version it is easy to alter the flavor by the addition of such ingredients as sun-dried tomatoes or anchovies. Pesto is generally served as a sauce for pasta, but it is excellent in vegetable soups, tomato in particular, and in certain sauces.

♦

PESTO SAUCE

ABOUT ¾ CUP

2 cups (about 2 ounces) basil leaves,
    stems removed
2 large garlic cloves, peeled
3 tablespoons pine nuts, preferably
    lightly toasted
⅓ cup grated Parmesan cheese
⅓ cup olive oil
Salt to taste

1 Rinse the basil leaves in cold running water. Drain and pat dry with paper toweling. Pack them compactly inside a 2-cup measure. Press firmly without crushing the leaves.

2 Put the leaves into the container of a blender or food processor.

3 Put the garlic cloves between 2 sheets of wax paper and smash them with a flat mallet or the bottom of a clean metal skillet. Scrape the garlic into the blender or processor.

4 Add the pine nuts, cheese, oil and salt. Blend thoroughly until the sauce has

a liquid consistency. Use immediately or scrape the sauce into a 1-cup jar with a screw top lid. Seal and refrigerate until ready to use. It will keep for 1 or 2 weeks. Or freeze the sauce. It will keep indefinitely.

Variations

PESTO SAUCE WITH SUN-DRIED TOMATOES

Prepare the basic pesto sauce, but add 3 (about 1 ounce) packed-in-oil sun-dried tomatoes or home-dried tomatoes (page 433). Add the tomatoes while blending the basil and oil.

PESTO SAUCE WITH ANCHOVIES

Prepare the basic pesto sauce, but add 3 flat anchovy fillets, or 1 tablespoon anchovy paste, while blending the basil and oil.

♦

PASTA WITH PESTO AND GREEN BEANS

4 SERVINGS

1 pound fettuccine or other pasta
Salt to taste
1 medium potato, cut into small cubes
¼ pound green beans, cut French style
    (slivered)
1 tablespoon butter
½ cup pesto sauce (opposite)
Grated Parmesan cheese

1 Bring a kettle of water to a boil and add the pasta and salt. Add the vegetables immediately and cook until the pasta is done to taste. Drain into a colander and empty the pasta and vegetables onto a hot platter. Toss with the butter.

2 Add the pesto and mix quickly. Serve piping hot, with cheese on the side.

♦

PASTA WITH RICOTTA

6 TO 8 SERVINGS

2 pounds spinach
1 pound fresh ricotta cheese
3 eggs, lightly beaten
2/3 cup grated Parmesan cheese
1/3 cup chopped parsley, preferably Italian
2 teaspoons salt
1/2 teaspoon freshly ground pepper
3 cups marinara sauce (page 564)
1 pound tubelike pasta such as macaroncelli, ziti or penne

1 Preheat the oven to 375°F.

2 Pick over the spinach, trimming away and discarding tough stems. Rinse the leaves well and drain. Cook the spinach briefly, tightly covered, in the water that clings to the leaves. Stir the spinach as it cooks just until the leaves are wilted. Drain well in a colander. When the spinach is cool enough to handle, press it to remove most of the moisture and chop.

3 Combine the spinach, ricotta, eggs, Parmesan cheese, parsley, salt, pepper and marinara sauce. Blend.

4 Bring a large quantity of water to a boil and add the pasta, stirring rapidly. Cook, stirring, for 2 minutes, then drain the pasta in a colander and add to the ricotta mixture. Pour the mixture into a baking dish and bake 25 to 30 minutes, or until the pasta is tender but not mushy. Do not overcook. Serve with additional Parmesan cheese on the side.

FUSILLI WITH BROCCOLI

4 SERVINGS

6 cups broccoli flowerets and sliced stems
6 tablespoons olive oil
2 teaspoons finely chopped garlic
1/4 teaspoon hot red pepper flakes
1/3 cup chicken stock
Salt and freshly ground pepper to taste
1 pound fusilli, cooked and drained

1 Cook the broccoli in boiling water for about 3 minutes. It should remain slightly crisp. Drain the broccoli and run under cold water to stop the cooking.

2 Heat the oil in a skillet and add the garlic. Cook briefly and add the broccoli. Toss to heat through. Add the red pepper flakes, stock, salt and pepper and bring to the boil.

3 Toss the fusilli with the hot sauce.

RIGATONI WITH BLACK OLIVE PURÉE

4 TO 6 SERVINGS

2 cups black olives, preferably of Italian or
  Greek origin
1 cup chicken stock
1 pound rigatoni
2 tablespoons olive oil
½ to ¾ cup grated Parmesan cheese

1 If the olives are not pitted, pit them, using a paring knife or a cherry pitter. Discard the pits.

2 Put the olives into the container of a food processor or, preferably, a blender. Purée as fine as possible. If a blender is used, turn the speed to liquefy.

3 Put the olive liquid into a small saucepan and add the stock. Bring to the simmer and keep warm briefly until ready to use.

4 Cook the rigatoni to the desired degree of doneness. Drain thoroughly and add the olive oil. Pour in olive mixture and toss. Serve each portion sprinkled with Parmesan cheese.

PAULINE TRIGÈRE'S MUSHROOM SPAGHETTI

4 SERVINGS

4 medium onions
6 tablespoons butter
2 pounds mushrooms, sliced
1½ teaspoons salt
Freshly ground pepper to taste
¼ teaspoon grated nutmeg
1 cup cream
1 pound spaghetti
Grated Parmesan cheese

1 Cut the onions into very thin slices. Melt 3 tablespoons of the butter in a heavy skillet and add the onions. Cook, stirring, until the onions have a delicate brown color.

2 Cover the skillet and cook the onions for 1 hour over very low heat. Stir occasionally.

3 In a second skillet melt the remaining 3 tablespoons of butter and sauté the mushrooms in it until tender. Season with salt and pepper and add to the onions.

4 Add the nutmeg and keep the sauce hot until ready to serve. Five minutes before serving add the cream and heat, but do not boil or the sauce will curdle.

5 Cook the spaghetti to the desired degree of doneness and drain. Mix thoroughly with the sauce at the last minute. Serve hot, with grated Parmesan cheese if desired.

PASTA WITH CHICKEN LIVERS AND MUSHROOMS

4 SERVINGS

4 tablespoons butter
1 onion, finely chopped
½ cup finely chopped celery
2 garlic cloves, minced
½ bay leaf
¼ teaspoon thyme
Cayenne to taste
2 cups Italian plum tomatoes, chopped
½ teaspoon sugar
½ pound chicken livers, trimmed and
    quartered
1 cup thinly sliced mushrooms
2 tablespoons flour
1 cup beef or chicken stock
1 pound fettuccine or spaghetti

1 Melt 2 tablespoons of the butter in a saucepan and add the onions, celery and garlic. Cook, stirring, until onions are translucent. Add the bay leaf, thyme, cayenne, tomatoes and sugar. Simmer, stirring occasionally, for about 30 minutes.

2 Meanwhile, heat the remaining 2 tablespoons of butter and cook the chicken livers and mushrooms in it, stirring, until chicken livers are light brown.

3 Sprinkle with flour and stir in the stock. Bring to a boil. When thickened and smooth, add the mixture to the tomato sauce. Continue to cook for 15 minutes.

4 Cook the pasta to the desired degree of doneness and drain. Serve hot with the sauce.

PENNE WITH WILD MUSHROOM SAUCE

4 TO 6 SERVINGS

1 pound wild mushrooms such as shiitake, hen
    of the woods or oyster mushrooms
2 tablespoons olive oil
3 tablespoons butter
6 tablespoons coarsely chopped shallots
1¾ cups chicken stock
⅓ pound fontina or provolone cheese at room
    temperature, cut into ¼-inch cubes (there
    should be about 1 cup)
¾ cup grated Parmesan cheese
½ cup finely chopped basil
½ teaspoon finely chopped thyme
Salt to taste
1 pound penne or ditalini

1 Rinse the mushrooms and pat dry with paper toweling. Cut the mushrooms into thin slices or bite-size pieces.

2 Heat 1 tablespoon of the oil in skillet and add the mushrooms. Cook, stirring frequently, about 5 minutes. Add half of the butter and the shallots, stirring to blend. Cook about 5 minutes longer and add the stock. Bring to the boil and add the fontina cheese. Let cook over relatively high heat about 5 minutes. Stir in the remaining butter and the Parmesan cheese. Stir to blend well. Add ¼ cup of the basil and the thyme and stir.

3 Meanwhile, bring about 3 quarts of water to the boil and add salt. Add the penne and cook until al dente. Reserve about ¼ cup of the cooking liquid. Drain the pasta immediately and return it to the pot. Add the reserved pasta liquid and remaining 1 tablespoon of olive oil and stir to blend. Transfer equal portions of the pasta onto each of 4 to 6 hot pasta plates. Spoon equal portions of the mushroom sauce onto each serving and sprinkle each serving with the remaining basil.

ANGEL'S HAIR PASTA WITH PROSCIUTTO AND WILD MUSHROOMS

4 SERVINGS

½ pound wild mushrooms such as morels,
    chanterelles, shiitake or oyster mushrooms
    (or use an equal amount of cultivated
    mushrooms)
¾ pound ripe tomatoes
¼ pound thinly sliced prosciutto
½ pound snow peas
Salt to taste
2 tablespoons olive or vegetable oil
Freshly ground pepper to taste
1 tablespoon minced garlic
1 teaspoon finely chopped jalapeño pepper
1 rosemary sprig, or ½ teaspoon dried
½ pound angel's hair pasta (capelli d'angelo),
    or vermicelli
½ cup cream
2 tablespoons butter
¾ cup grated Parmesan cheese
½ cup shredded basil

1 Rinse the mushrooms and pat them dry. Cut off and reserve the stems. Cut the mushroom caps into thin strips. There should be about 4 cups altogether.

2 Cut away the cores of the tomatoes. Cut the tomatoes into ½-inch cubes.

3 Cut the prosciutto into very thin julienne strips.

4 Pull off any tough strings from the pea pods. Put the pea pods in a saucepan and add water to cover. Bring to the boil and simmer 1 minute. Drain.

5 In a kettle, bring 3 quarts of water to the boil for the pasta. Add salt to taste.

6 Meanwhile, heat the oil in a casserole and add the mushrooms, salt and pepper. Cook, stirring, about 3 minutes and add the garlic, jalapeño and prosciutto. Stir for 1 more minute. Add the rosemary.

7 Add the pasta to the boiling water and stir until the strands are submerged. Cook about 4 minutes, or to the desired degree of doneness. Scoop out and reserve ½ cup of the cooking liquid. Drain the pasta and return it to the kettle.

8 Add the tomatoes to the mushroom mixture and stir. Add the cream and bring to the boil. Add the pasta and pea pods. Add the reserved pasta liquid, butter, ¼ cup of the cheese and the basil and toss to blend. Serve in 4 heated pasta plates with the remaining cheese on the side.

◆

SPAGHETTI WITH BACON AND MUSHROOM SAUCE

4 SERVINGS

8 slices of bacon, cut into small cubes
4 tablespoons butter
1 cup thinly sliced mushrooms
2 cups canned tomatoes, preferably Italian
    plum tomatoes, drained and chopped
¼ cup finely chopped parsley
½ cup dry white wine
Salt and freshly ground pepper to taste
¼ teaspoon hot red pepper flakes
1 pound spaghetti, cooked and drained

1 Cook the bacon in a skillet until it is rendered of most of its fat. Drain off the fat and add the butter. Sauté the mushrooms in it briefly.

2 Add the tomatoes, parsley, wine, salt, pepper and red pepper flakes to the skillet. Simmer for 30 minutes.

3 Taste the sauce and, if desired, add more salt. Combine the sauce with the spaghetti and serve immediately.

◆

MEXICAN PASTA CASSEROLE

4 SERVINGS

1 pound pork sausage
¾ cup diced onions
¾ cup diced green peppers
3½ cups canned tomatoes
2 cups sour cream
2 tablespoons sugar
1 tablespoon chili powder
1 teaspoon salt
½ pound penne or other tubular pasta

1 In a large skillet brown the sausage, onions and green peppers. Drain off excess fat.

2 Stir in the tomatoes, sour cream, sugar, chili powder and salt. Add the pasta, cover the skillet, and simmer until the pasta is tender.

PASTA E FAGIOLI
MACARONI AND BEANS

8 SERVINGS

1 pound dried navy beans or other
  small white beans
1 beef bone
¼ cup olive oil
2 garlic cloves, peeled
1 tablespoon chopped basil
2 teaspoons salt
½ teaspoon freshly ground pepper
1 cup beef stock
3 tomatoes, peeled and chopped
1 pound medium macaroni
2 tablespoons minced parsley
Grated Parmesan cheese

1 Pick over the beans, wash thoroughly and cover with water. Allow to soak overnight, or bring to a boil, simmer for 2 minutes, and allow to stand for 1 to 2 hours before proceeding.

2 Add the beef bone to the beans, bring to a boil and simmer for 2 hours, or until the beans are tender.

3 Heat the oil in a small pan and sauté the garlic in it. Add the basil, salt, pepper, stock and tomatoes and bring the mixture to a boil. Pour into the cooked beans.

4 Cook the macaroni according to package directions. Drain and reserve the liquid. Add the macaroni to the beans and cook for 5 to 10 minutes longer. Adjust the consistency of the dish by crushing some of the beans if it is too moist or by adding some of the reserved liquid if it is too dry. Discard any remaining liquid. Serve sprinkled with the parsley and the cheese.

BEEF AND MACARONI CASSEROLE

8 SERVINGS

¼ cup olive oil
⅓ cup finely chopped onions
2 garlic cloves, minced
1½ cups diced celery
1½ pounds beef chuck, ground
½ cup beef stock
1 (6-ounce) can tomato paste
1 (19-ounce) can (2½ cups) Italian-style
  tomatoes
2 teaspoons salt
½ teaspoon freshly ground pepper
1 pound fresh mushrooms, sliced
½ teaspoon oregano
1 tablespoon chopped basil
8 ounces small elbow macaroni, cooked
  and drained
1 (10-ounce) package frozen spinach, cooked
  and drained
½ cup buttered soft fresh bread crumbs
⅓ cup grated Parmesan cheese

1 Heat 2 tablespoons of the oil in a large heavy skillet. Sauté the onions in it until tender and golden. Add the garlic, celery and beef and cook until the meat loses its red color.

2 Add the stock, tomato paste, tomatoes, salt and pepper. Bring mixture to a boil and simmer for 1 hour, stirring occasionally. Add more stock if the mixture becomes too thick.

3 Preheat the oven to 350°F.

4 Heat the remaining 2 tablespoons oil and sauté the mushrooms briefly. Add to the sauce with the oregano, basil, macaroni and spinach. Pour into a buttered 3-quart casserole. Top with the crumbs mixed with the cheese. Bake for 30 minutes, or until bubbly hot and light brown.

*Stuffed noodle dumplings appear in four cuisines that are otherwise unrelated. The four dishes are the **wonton** of China, the **pelmeny** of Russia, the **kreplach** of Jewish cookery and the **ravioli** of Italy. Each of the dishes is made with a wafer-thin dough that is used to envelop such foods as meat or cheese. The dumplings are then simmered in broth or water and are served either as soup garnish or with a sauce. All of these dishes are delicious and hearty and are particularly suited to winter menus.*

♦

PASTA DOUGH FOR DUMPLINGS

Although the ingredients for this dough are the same as those for homemade noodles, the method of preparing the dough is different.

ABOUT 1 POUND

3 cups sifted flour
4 eggs

1 Place the flour on a board and make a depression in the center. Break the eggs into the hole.

2 With the hands, work the eggs into the flour until dough forms a ball. Knead the dough until it is smooth and elastic. Let it stand, covered with a towel, for 1 hour.

3 Roll the dough out on a lightly floured board until it is very thin. Stretch it over the rolling pin until it is paper-thin and translucent.

WONTON

4 SERVINGS, 16 WONTON

½ pound pasta dough for dumplings
  (opposite page)
½ pound pork, ground
1 tablespoon dry sherry
2 tablespoons soy sauce
½ teaspoon sugar
½ cup cold water
3 cups chicken stock
1 scallion, chopped

1 Roll out the dough until it is paper-thin. Cut into 4-inch squares.

2 Mix together the pork, sherry, 1 tablespoon of the soy sauce and the sugar.

3 Place 1 teaspoon of the mixture in the middle of each square. Fold over at the center, pressing the edges together. Fold lengthwise again. Pull the corners one over the other and press them together with a little water. When properly folded, the wonton resembles a nurse's cap.

4 Drop the wrapped wonton into 3 quarts of boiling water and bring to a boil again. Wontons will rise to the surface. Add the cold water and bring to a boil again to make sure that the filling is cooked. Drain and reserve.

5 Heat the stock. Add the remaining soy sauce. Drop the reserved wontons and the scallion into the broth and serve as soup.

SIBERIAN PELMENY

3 DOZEN (3-INCH) PELMENY, OR 5 DOZEN (2-INCH) PELMENY

1 pound pasta dough for dumplings
  (opposite page)
¾ pound beef chuck, ground
½ onion, finely chopped
½ teaspoon salt
¼ teaspoon freshly ground pepper
4 cups beef stock
1 egg white

1 Roll out the dough until it is paper-thin. Cut into 2- or 3-inch circles.

2 Mix together the beef and onion. Season with salt and pepper and moisten with 1 or 2 tablespoons of the stock.

3 Place 1 teaspoon of the filling in the center of each circle, moisten the edges with the egg white and fold over to form a crescent shape.

4 Bring remaining stock to a rolling boil and drop in the pelmeny. Cook for about 15 minutes. The pelmeny may be eaten in the soup or served separately with melted butter or sour cream.

KREPLACH

ABOUT 7 DOZEN

½ pound pasta dough for dumplings
  (page 504)
1 cup cheese filling (see following recipe)
4 cups vegetable stock

1 Roll out the dough and cut it into 1½-inch squares. Place ½ teaspoon of the cheese filling in the center of each square and pinch together into triangular puffs.

2 Bring the stock to a rolling boil. Drop in the kreplach and cook for 10 to 15 minutes. When cooked, kreplach will rise to the surface. Serve in the soup.

CHEESE FILLING
ABOUT 1 CUP

1 cup ricotta, or pot cheese
1 egg
2 tablespoons fine dry bread crumbs
¼ teaspoon salt
Dash of freshly ground pepper

Mix all the ingredients together with a fork.

Ravioli has become one of the ultimate dishes in many American homes and restaurants, but is considered by many to be a bit too tedious to prepare if you have to roll out the pasta dough. Many restaurants in this country and abroad now resort to a shortcut. The "dough" is now obtainable in already-cut rounds. They are called **suey gow** *or* **goyza,** *and in Oriental kitchens they are used to make the dumplings known as* **jao-tze** *or pot stickers. Wonton skins also work well for ravioli. Instructions for their use is indicated in the ravioli recipes outlined here.*

◆

LOBSTER RAVIOLI

The ravioli should be prepared just before cooking time. Do not prepare them in advance.

4 SERVINGS

2 (1¼-pound) lobsters
Salt to taste
2 tablespoons butter
¼ cup finely chopped onions
2 tablespoons finely chopped shallots
2 tablespoons flour
½ cup dry white wine
1 cup crushed tomatoes
1 cup fish stock or bottled clam juice
½ teaspoon tarragon
1 small bay leaf
¼ teaspoon thyme
Freshly ground pepper to taste
¼ teaspoon hot red pepper flakes
Cornmeal
48 suey gow (goyza) or wonton skins,
  approximately, available where Chinese
  foods are sold
1 egg yolk
2 tablespoons water
½ cup cream
1 tablespoon cognac

1 Drop the lobsters into boiling water to cover and add salt. Cook the lobsters 7 minutes and drain. Arrange the lobsters head down, letting the curved tails rest on the side of the kettle.

2 When the lobsters have reached room temperature, remove the meat from the shell. Place the meat on a flat surface and chop it fine. Save the soft body part of the shells, discarding the hard claw portions. Crush the soft portions using a heavy mallet.

3 Heat the butter in a heavy saucepan and add the onions and shallots. Cook until wilted. Add the crushed lobster shells and sprinkle with flour. Stir to blend. Add the wine, tomatoes, stock, tarragon, bay leaf and thyme. Bring to the boil, stirring. Add salt, pepper and red pepper flakes. Let cook 10 minutes.

4 Pour the mixture into a food mill and press to extract as much liquid from the solids as possible. There should be about 2½ cups of sauce.

5 Add ½ cup of the sauce to the chopped lobster and stir to blend. Set the remaining sauce aside.

6 When you work with the suey gow wrappers or the wonton skins, keep them covered as you work, otherwise they dry out quickly. Sprinkle a flat surface with cornmeal. Lay out 24 of the wrappers on this surface. Spoon equal portions of the lobster mixture (about 1 tablespoon each) onto the center of each wrapper.

7 Beat the yolk with the water and brush this mixture around each spoonful of the filling. Top each with a second wrapper and press around the filling to seal as neatly as possible. The ravioli may be cooked at this point. It is preferable, however, to use the top, unsharp edge of a biscuit cutter to press around the filling to help seal the wrappers. Choose a cutter to fit around the filling neatly and compactly. Press down gently to seal without cutting. Choose a slightly wider biscuit cutter and, placing it sharp side down, cut around the filling to make a round ravioli. Pull away and discard the excess dough. Carefully lift up each ravioli and place it on the surface previously sprinkled with cornmeal. Cover with a squeezed-out damp cloth until ready to cook.

8 When ready to cook, bring the reserved sauce to the simmer. Add the cream and cognac. Ideally, you should put the sauce through a fine sieve or food mill and reheat.

9 Bring about 3 quarts of water to the boil and add salt to taste. Add the ravioli. Let cook about 3 minutes.

10 Drain the ravioli and serve immediately with the sauce.

◆

SALMON RAVIOLI

4 SERVINGS

¾ pound raw skinless, boneless salmon
Salt and freshly ground pepper to taste
4 tablespoons finely chopped scallions
1 tablespoon finely chopped dill
2 tablespoons lemon juice
1 tablespoon olive oil
Cornmeal
48 suey gow (goyza) or wonton skins
Beurre blanc (pages 555–556)

1 Cut the salmon into small cubes and place on a flat surface. Chop it fine. Put the salmon in a bowl and add the salt, pepper, scallions, dill, lemon juice and olive oil. Refrigerate.

2 Fill and cook the ravioli as for lobster ravioli (page 506). Drain and serve with beurre blanc.

PORK RAVIOLI

4 SERVINGS

1 tablespoon butter
¼ cup finely chopped onions
1 tablespoon finely chopped scallions
½ teaspoon ground cumin
¼ pound mushrooms, finely chopped
Juice of ½ lemon
Salt and freshly ground pepper to taste
¾ pound ground lean pork
1 teaspoon sesame oil
1 teaspoon dark soy sauce
1 egg yolk
2 tablespoons chopped coriander
Cornmeal
48 suey gow (goyza) or wonton skins

1 Heat the butter in a saucepan and add the onions, scallion and cumin. Cook, stirring, until wilted. Add the mushrooms and stir. Sprinkle with lemon juice, salt and pepper. Cook 1 minute and add the pork. Cook, stirring and chopping down with the side of a heavy metal spoon to break up any lumps. Cook until meat loses its raw look.

2 Remove from the heat and let cool slightly. Stir in the sesame oil, soy sauce, egg yolk and coriander. Let stand until cool. Chill in the refrigerator.

3 Fill and cook the ravioli as for lobster ravioli (page 506). Drain and serve with a tomato sauce.

RAVIOLI WITH FOIE GRAS

4 SERVINGS

¾ pound cooked, ready-to-eat fresh foie gras,
    available in luxury food shops
2 or 3 fresh or canned black truffles, available
    in luxury food shops
16 wonton skins, available in many
    supermarkets and Chinese groceries
3 cups chicken stock

1 Cut the foie gras into 16 cubes, all more or less the same size. Refrigerate.

2 Drain the truffles. Cut 1 of them into 16 or more thin slices, each of approximately the same thickness.

3 Finely chop enough of the remaining truffles to make 1 tablespoon.

4 Place the wonton skins on a flat surface, about 4 at a time, keeping the remaining skins covered with a damp cloth as you work. Place 1 piece of foie gras slightly off center on each wonton skin. Sprinkle with a small amount of chopped truffle on top of each piece of foie gras, keeping the chopped pieces near the center. Using a pastry brush, brush around the inside perimeter of each wonton skin. Fold 1 corner of each skin across the filling to match the opposite corner. Press all around the outside edges of the wonton to seal firmly. Use a biscuit cutter and press around the angled edges of each wonton to make it round in shape.

5 Heat 4 soup bowls.

6 Bring the stock to the simmer in a saucepan and add the filled wonton. When the broth returns to the simmer, let cook 1 minute without boiling. Using a slotted spoon, remove the wonton and put 4 in each soup bowl. Spoon equal amounts of the simmering broth into each plate. Garnish each serving with 4 or more truffle slices.

There are many forms of gnocchi, a dish that cannot be described in a word. The closest approximation is dumpling. Gnocchi may be made with potatoes, farina or, as in gnocchi Parisienne, with cream puff paste.

♦

GNOCCHI PARISIENNE

4 TO 5 SERVINGS

6 tablespoons butter
6 tablespoons flour
2 cups milk
½ cup cream
Salt and freshly ground pepper to taste
Cream puff paste (see following recipe)
Grated Parmesan cheese
Melted butter

1 Preheat the oven to 350°F.
2 Melt the butter in a saucepan, add the flour and stir with a wire whisk until blended. Meanwhile, bring the milk to a boil and add all at once to the butter-flour mixture, stirring vigorously with the wire whisk. Stir in the cream and season with salt and pepper.
3 Bring 6 quarts lightly salted water to a boil and fill a pastry bag fitted with a round tube (size 12) with the cream puff paste. Hold the bag over the boiling water and, as the paste comes through, cut it off in 1-inch lengths. Poach the paste 3 to 4 minutes; remove from water to drain.

4 Butter a shallow casserole or au gratin dish and add a thin layer of the cream sauce. Add 1 or 2 layers of the gnocchi, covering each with the cream sauce. Sprinkle each layer with grated Parmesan cheese and the top with melted butter.
5 Bake 15 to 20 minutes.

CREAM PUFF PASTE FOR GNOCCHI

4 tablespoons butter
½ cup water
¼ teaspoon salt
Pinch of grated nutmeg
½ cup flour
2 eggs

1 Bring the butter, water, salt and nutmeg to a rapid boil. Add the flour all at once and, stirring rapidly with a wooden spoon, lift the pan a few inches from the heat. Continue stirring 30 seconds, or until the paste comes away from the sides of the saucepan and forms a rough ball in the center. Remove from the heat.
2 Add the eggs, one at a time, beating vigorously after each addition until the paste is smooth.

GNOCCHI PARMIGIANA

ABOUT 6 SERVINGS

3 cups milk
¼ pound butter
1 teaspoon salt
¾ cup farina
2 cups grated Parmesan cheese
1 egg, lightly beaten

1 Combine 2 cups of the milk, 4 tablespoons of the butter and the salt in a saucepan and bring to a boil. Mix the farina with the remaining milk and add to the boiling mixture. Cook, stirring, until thickened. Remove from heat.

2 Add 1 cup of the cheese and the egg and mix well. Turn into a 9-inch-square pan, cool and then chill until firm.

3 Preheat the oven to 425°F.

4 Cut the mush into small rounds, squares or diamonds and arrange in a greased shallow baking dish, preferably having only 1 layer with each shape of cereal slightly overlapping. Melt the remaining butter, pour over the top and sprinkle with the remaining cheese.

5 Bake until the top is golden brown, about 25 minutes.

GNOCCHI WITH POTATOES

5 TO 6 SERVINGS

3 medium potatoes
2 egg yolks
½ teaspoon salt
1 cup flour, approximately
1½ cups basic tomato sauce (page 561)
1 cup or more grated Parmesan cheese

1 For gnocchi, use a dry, mealy type of potato. Boil the potatoes in their jackets, peel and mash. Add the egg yolks and salt; whip until fluffy. Add the flour and mix, then knead until smooth, adding more flour as necessary to prevent sticking.

2 Divide the dough into 6 parts and shape each into a long roll about ½ inch in diameter. Cut into pieces about 1 inch long and press with the thumb or a fork. Sprinkle lightly with flour.

3 Add about a third of the gnocchi at a time to 6 quarts boiling salted water and cook about 5 minutes. Remove to a heated bowl and keep warm. Repeat until all the gnocchi have been cooked.

4 Add 1 cup of the tomato sauce and ½ cup of the cheese and toss lightly. Turn onto a serving platter and pour the remaining sauce over the top. Sprinkle with the remaining cheese.

10

Potatoes, Legumes, Rice and Grains

Potatoes

BAKED POTATOES

Thoroughly wash and dry potatoes. Grease lightly. Place on a rack in a preheated 425°F oven and bake until tender when tested with a fork, 40 to 60 minutes. When potatoes are done, remove from oven, split open and top with butter or sour cream. Season to taste with salt and freshly ground pepper.

♦

STUFFED POTATO FOR ONE

1 SERVING

Bake a large potato. When baked, split it into halves, scoop out the flesh and reserve one of the scooped-out shells. Put the flesh through a ricer and season with butter, salt, pepper and a touch of grated nutmeg. Add a little cream, blend well, and use the mixture to stuff the reserved shell. Sprinkle with about ¼ cup grated sharp cheddar cheese and place in a small baking dish. Bake in a 350°F oven until the potato is heated through and the cheese is melted.

ROQUEFORT CHEESE–STUFFED BAKED POTATOES

6 SERVINGS

6 large baking potatoes
½ to ¾ cup sour cream
¼ cup crumbled Roquefort cheese
Salt and freshly ground pepper to taste
4 scallions, minced, green part included
Paprika

1 Preheat the oven to 425°F.
2 Thoroughly wash and dry the potatoes. Bake until soft, 40 to 60 minutes.
3 Cut a slice from the top of each potato and scoop out the potato, being careful not to break the skin. Mash the potato well and beat in the sour cream, Roquefort cheese, salt and pepper. Add more sour cream, if necessary, to make the potatoes light and fluffy. Stir in the scallions.
4 Spoon the potato mixture into the shells, mounding it slightly. Place potatoes on a baking sheet. Dust the tops with paprika and return to the oven until light brown.

POTATOES-IN-THE-SHELL SOUFFLÉ

6 large baking potatoes
1½ teaspoons salt
⅛ teaspoon freshly ground pepper
Dash of grated nutmeg
2 tablespoons butter
3 tablespoons hot milk
1 egg, separated
Finely grated sharp aged cheddar cheese
Parsley for garnish

1 Preheat the oven to 425°F.
2 Scrub the potatoes. Prick the potatoes with a knife or skewer and bake them until tender, 40 to 60 minutes.
3 Cut a slice off the top of each potato; discard slices. Scoop out the insides and mash until fluffy with the seasonings, butter and hot milk. Beat in the egg yolk. Beat the egg white until stiff and fold into the potato mixture. Refill potato shells with this mixture. Sprinkle with grated cheese.
4 Lower the oven temperature to 350°F and bake the potatoes for about 25 minutes, until brown. Garnish with parsley.

STRAW POTATOES

4 large (about 1½ pounds) Idaho potatoes
Oil for deep frying
Salt

1 Peel the potatoes and drop them into cold water to cover.
2 Cut the potatoes into ⅛-inch slices. Stack the slices, a few at a time, and cut the potatoes into shreds about ⅛ inch thick. Drop the shreds into cold water as they are prepared.
3 Drain potatoes well in a colander.
4 Heat the oil to about 360°F in a deep fryer. Add the potatoes, a few handfuls at a time, and cook them, stirring frequently, until they are crisp and golden brown. Drain on paper toweling and sprinkle with salt.

DUCHESSE POTATOES

6 SERVINGS

2 *pounds (about 6 medium) potatoes*
3 *tablespoons butter*
Salt and freshly ground pepper to taste
¼ *teaspoon grated nutmeg*
2 *whole eggs*
2 *egg yolks*

1 Peel the potatoes and cut in half. Cook in boiling salted water to cover until soft but still firm.

2 Drain well and put through a food mill or a potato ricer. Beat the potatoes with a wooden spoon until smooth.

3 Add the butter, salt, pepper, nutmeg and eggs, which have been lightly beaten with the egg yolks. Whip until fluffy.

Note: The potatoes may be made in advance and kept ready if they are brushed with melted butter to keep a crust from forming. The potatoes may be put through a pastry tube to use as a garnish for a meat or fish dish. They may be shaped decoratively with a pastry tube and browned under a broiler flame. They are also used in making potato croquettes.

MASHED POTATOES— WITH VARIATIONS

4 SERVINGS OR 2½ CUPS

4 *medium (1¼ pounds) potatoes*
½ *onion*
2 *tablespoons butter*
¼ *to* ½ *cup hot milk (may be partly half-and-half)*
Salt and freshly ground pepper to taste

1 Peel the potatoes and cut into cubes; there should be about 3½ cups. Cover with boiling salted water, add the onion, cover and cook until the potatoes are tender but not mushy. Drain the potatoes thoroughly and discard the onion. Return the potatoes to the pan and shake over low heat to dry.

2 Mash the potatoes thoroughly, until no lumps remain, using a potato masher, food mill or electric mixer. Return to the pan and place over low heat. Beat in the butter and add the milk, little by little, beating constantly with a wooden spoon or an electric beater. Season with salt and pepper.

Note: Mashed potatoes may be held a short time over hot water in the top of a double boiler. Excessive heat develops an off-taste.

Variations

WITH CHEESE

Spread the mashed potatoes about 2 inches thick on a buttered heatproof platter. Sprinkle the top generously with grated cheese (Parmesan or a good Swiss) and brush with melted butter. Or spread with whipped cream to which grated cheese has been added. Slide under the broiler to brown.

WITH SCALLIONS

Omit the onion in cooking the potatoes. Add ⅓ cup minced scallions to the mashed potatoes.

WITH MUSHROOMS

Sauté ½ pound sliced mushrooms in 2 tablespoons butter and add to the mashed potatoes.

LUNCHEON DISH POTATOES

Grease individual muffin cups, fill with hot mashed potatoes and make a depression in the top of each portion. Drop an egg in each depression. Bake in a preheated 375°F oven until the eggs are set.

♦

HASH BROWN POTATOES

6 SERVINGS

3 cups chopped cooked potatoes
1½ tablespoons flour
¾ teaspoon salt
½ cup half-and-half
4 tablespoons butter
Chopped parsley

1 Mix the potatoes with the flour and salt. Add the half-and-half and blend well.

2 Heat half of the butter in a heavy skillet and pour in the potato mixture, spreading evenly. Cook slowly until brown underneath. Invert on a plate, add the remaining butter to the pan and gently slide the potatoes back into the skillet, cooked side up. Brown the underside. Serve garnished with parsley.

LEEK AND POTATO PURÉE

6 SERVINGS

5 large (about 1½ pounds) pototoes
2 tablespoons butter
4 cups finely chopped leeks, rinsed
    and well drained
½ cup milk
Salt and freshly ground pepper to taste
⅛ teaspoon grated nutmeg

1 Peel the potatoes and cut them into quarters. There should be about 4 cups. Put them in a saucepan and add cold water to cover. Bring to a boil and let cook until tender, 15 to 20 minutes. Drain well.

2 Put potatoes through a food mill or ricer (a food processor is not recommended because the potatoes will become gummy or "ropey").

3 Meanwhile, heat 1 tablespoon of the butter in a skillet and add the chopped leeks. Cover closely and cook, stirring frequently, until softened, about 10 minutes. Add the leeks to the potatoes.

4 Heat the milk in a very small saucepan. Stir the leeks and potatoes with a wooden spoon while gradually adding the milk. Add the remaining tablespoon of butter and season with salt, pepper and nutmeg. Heat briefly and serve.

SCALLOPED POTATOES WITH SOUR CREAM

4 SERVINGS

4 medium potatoes
1 cup sour cream
2 eggs, well beaten
2 tablespoons milk
3 tablespoons chopped chives
½ teaspoon salt
Dash of freshly ground pepper
1 cup shredded sharp cheddar cheese

1 Preheat the oven to 350°F.

2 Cook the potatoes in lightly salted water until just tender. Allow to cool slightly, then peel and slice. There should be 3 cups of sliced potatoes. Arrange the potatoes in a buttered shallow 1½-quart baking dish.

3 Combine the sour cream with the beaten eggs, milk, chives, salt and pepper. Pour over the potatoes in the baking dish and sprinkle with the cheese.

4 Bake for about 30 minutes, until heated through and light brown.

Colcannon with Kale, page 406.
Potato Salad, page 463.
Warm Potato Salad, page 463.
German Potato Salad with Sour Cream, page 465.
Spring Potato Salad, page 464.
Potato Salad with Anchovies, page 465.

NEW POTATOES WITH SOUR CREAM DRESSING

Like fresh asparagus and shad, new potatoes are evidence of spring.

6 SERVINGS

2 pounds new potatoes
¾ cup sour cream
⅛ teaspoon ground white pepper
1 tablespoon chopped dill

1 Scrape the potatoes and place in a saucepan with ½ inch boiling salted water. Cover, return to a boil and cook over medium heat until done, about 25 minutes. Shake the pan occasionally. Drain, remove the cover and cook a few minutes to evaporate any excess water.

2 Combine the sour cream, pepper and dill and toss lightly with the potatoes.

BRAISED NEW POTATOES AND CARROTS WITH DILL

6 SERVINGS

12 medium-size new potatoes
1 teaspoon salt
3 tablespoons butter
⅓ cup water
2 cups of ¼-inch slices of carrot
1 tablespoon chopped dill

1 Wash and scrape the potatoes; leave them whole. Place them in a saucepan with the salt, butter and water. Cover and cook for 20 minutes over low heat.

2 Add the carrots. Cover and cook for 15 minutes longer, or until carrots and potatoes are tender. Add dill and mix lightly. Serve hot.

JANSSON'S TEMPTATION
FRESTELSE

8 SERVINGS

4 to 6 (about 2 pounds) Idaho potatoes
1 (3½-ounce) can anchovy fillets or sprats
    (available in specialty food shops and where
    fine imported foods are sold)
1½ cups thinly sliced onions
Freshly ground pepper to taste
1½ cups cream
2 tablespoons butter

1 Preheat the oven to 350°F.

2 Peel the potatoes and cut them into ¼-inch-thick slices. Stack the slices and cut them into ¼-inch-thick strips to resemble french fries. There should be about 8 cups.

3 Cover the bottom of a baking dish (an oval dish measuring 13 × 8 × 2 inches is ideal) with half the potatoes. Drain the anchovies, reserving the liquid, and arrange them symmetrically over the layer of potatoes. Pour the reserved anchovy liquid evenly over all.

4 Scatter the onion slices over the top and sprinkle with pepper. Scatter the remaining potatoes evenly over all. Pour half the cream over and sprinkle with more pepper. Dot the top with butter and place in the oven. Bake about 30 minutes, or until the potatoes are light brown on top. Pour the remaining cream on top and continue baking 15 to 30 minutes longer, or until the potatoes are tender.

POTATO-CHEESE CHARLOTTE

6 SERVINGS

½ cup chopped onions
2 tablespoons butter
3 cups grated raw potatoes
2 eggs, beaten
1½ teaspoons salt
1 teaspoon paprika
⅛ teaspoon pepper
1 cup grated sharp cheddar cheese
2 slices of white bread

1 Preheat the oven to 350°F. Butter a 1-quart casserole.

2 Sauté the onions in the butter until limp. Mix with the potatoes, eggs, salt, paprika, pepper and cheese.

3 Soak the bread in water until soft. Squeeze dry and add to the potato mixture. Mix well.

4 Turn into the prepared casserole and bake for 1 hour.

PIERRE FRANEY'S POTATO PANCAKES

The best potato pancakes I have tasted are those prepared by my colleague for many years, Pierre Franey. Potato pancakes occur, of course, in many international cuisines. These are easy to make and quite special. If they are made thin and cooked until golden brown and crusty, they are excellent served with a touch of sour cream and fresh caviar.

4 SERVINGS

3 (about 1¼ pounds) potatoes
Salt to taste
1 tablespoon butter
⅓ cup half-and-half
2 eggs, lightly beaten
⅓ cup flour
¼ cup finely chopped onion
½ teaspoon minced garlic
2 tablespoons finely chopped parsley
Freshly ground pepper to taste
2 tablespoons vegetable oil

1 Put the potatoes in a saucepan and add cold water to cover and salt. Bring to the boil and cook until tender, 20 to 30 minutes. Drain and peel the potatoes and put them through a food mill or potato ricer.

2 In a mixing bowl combine the mashed potatoes, butter, half-and-half, eggs, flour, onion, garlic, parsley, salt and pepper. Blend well.

3 Heat the oil in a skillet, preferably nonstick. Spoon about ¼ cup of the potato mixture into 3 to 4 mounds into the oil. Flatten the mounds to make patty shapes. Cook 3 to 4 minutes, or until golden brown on one side. Turn and cook 3 to 4 minutes on the second side, or until golden brown. Do not overcook or pancakes will be dry to the taste. Serve hot.

POTATOES RISSOLÉES

8 SERVINGS

8 large potatoes, peeled
2 tablespoons butter
4 tablespoons vegetable oil
Salt to taste
Chopped parsley

1 Using a melon ball cutter, scoop rounds from large, firm potatoes. Cook the potato balls in boiling salted water 8 to 10 minutes. Drain well on paper toweling.
2 In a saucepan heat the butter and oil, add the potatoes and sauté until golden brown. Shake the pan frequently so that the potatoes brown evenly.
3 Sprinkle with salt and chopped parsley and serve.

♦

SWEDISH POTATO CAKES

6 SERVINGS

2 cups hot seasoned mashed potatoes
1 egg
1 tablespoon minced onion
1 tablespoon minced dill or parsley
⅛ teaspoon grated nutmeg
4 tablespoons butter

1 Mix the potatoes and egg and beat thoroughly until mixture is fluffy. Blend in the onion, dill and nutmeg and shape into 6 flat cakes.
2 Heat the butter in a large skillet and brown the cakes in it until crisp and brown on both sides.

DEVONSHIRE POTATO-MUSHROOM PIE

6 SERVINGS

3 cups seasoned mashed potatoes
1½ cups sliced fresh mushrooms
¼ cup chopped onions
2 tablespoons butter
1 teaspoon lemon juice
¼ teaspoon salt
Dash of freshly ground white pepper
½ cup sour cream

1 Preheat the oven to 350°F.
2 Place half of the mashed potatoes in a buttered 9-inch pie plate.
3 Sauté the mushrooms and onion in the butter. Add the lemon juice, salt and pepper and spoon over the potato layer. Spread with sour cream. Top with remaining potatoes.
4 Bake for 45 minutes, until brown. To serve, cut into wedges.

♦

GERMAN FRIED POTATOES

6 SERVINGS

3 tablespoons vegetable oil
4 cups thinly sliced raw potatoes
1 large onion, sliced
1 teaspoon salt

Heat the oil in a large skillet. Add the sliced potatoes and onion. Cover the skillet and cook, turning occasionally, until the potatoes are tender and golden. Season with salt.

GRATIN SAVOYARD

6 large baking potatoes
1 large or 2 small celery knobs
Butter
1¼ cups grated Gruyère or Swiss cheese
1 teaspoon salt
Freshly ground pepper to taste
¾ cup beef or chicken stock

1 Preheat the oven to 375°F.

2 Peel potatoes and celery knobs and cut them into even slices about ⅛ inch thick.

3 Butter a baking dish well and arrange alternate layers of celery knob, potato and cheese, using about 1 cup of the cheese. Begin and end the layers with potatoes. Sprinkle with salt and pepper and pour the stock over all.

4 Bake for 1 to 1¼ hours, until potatoes are tender and most of the liquid is absorbed. Sprinkle with remaining cheese and return to the oven until cheese melts.

RAGOÛT OF POTATOES PROVENÇALE

6 TO 8 SERVINGS

¼ pound onions
¾ pound green peppers
¼ pound mushrooms
4 to 6 (about 1½ pounds) potatoes
2 tablespoons olive oil
1 teaspoon minced garlic
Salt and freshly ground pepper to taste
1 (1-pound) can of tomatoes with tomato paste, preferably imported
1 tablespoon finely chopped basil
2 tablespoons finely chopped parsley
12 black olives, preferably imported

1 Coarsely chop the onions; there should be about 3 cups. Core, seed and cut the green peppers into 1-inch cubes; there should be about 2 cups. Thinly slice the mushrooms; there should be about 3 cups.

2 Peel the potatoes and cut them in half or quarter them, depending on their size. The pieces should measure about 1 × 2 inches.

3 Heat the oil in a deep saucepan and add the onions. Cook, stirring, until wilted. Add the garlic and cook briefly, stirring. Add the green peppers and cook about 3 minutes. Add the mushrooms, salt and pepper. Cook, tossing and stirring, about 2 minutes over high heat.

4 Add the potatoes and cook about 2 minutes, stirring. Add the tomatoes with tomato paste, basil and parsley. Cover and cook about 15 minutes.

5 Pit the black olives and add to the ragoût. Continue cooking until the potatoes are tender, 15 to 20 minutes.

SWEET POTATOES MOUSSELINE

6 TO 8 SERVINGS

4 medium (about 2 pounds) sweet potatoes
½ teaspoon grated nutmeg
¾ teaspoon salt
Dash of ground cloves
¼ cup sugar
2 tablespoons butter
1 egg, well beaten
¼ cup cream
1 tablespoon grated orange rind
½ teaspoon grated lemon rind
2 tablespoons light brown sugar

1 Preheat the oven to 450°F.
2 Cook the unpeeled whole sweet potatoes in boiling water to cover for 20 to 30 minutes, until tender. Slip off the skins and mash the potatoes until smooth.
3 Add the nutmeg, salt, cloves, sugar, 1 tablespoon of the butter, the egg, cream and grated rinds to the mashed potatoes. Beat until fluffy.
4 Turn the mixture into a buttered 1-quart casserole. Melt the remaining butter and brush the top of the mixture. Sprinkle with brown sugar. Bake for about 35 minutes, until brown.

CANDIED SWEET POTATOES

6 SERVINGS

4 to 6 sweet potatoes
1 cup granulated brown sugar
1 teaspoon salt
2 tablespoons butter
¼ cup water
¼ teaspoon cinnamon
⅛ teaspoon grated nutmeg

1 Preheat the oven to 350°F.
2 Parboil the sweet potatoes for 15 minutes; peel and slice them. Place in a buttered 1½-quart round baking dish.
3 Make a syrup by combining sugar, salt, butter, water and spices and boiling for 3 minutes. Pour syrup over potatoes.
4 Bake for 1¼ hours, basting frequently.

Note: One-half cup of the brown sugar may be replaced with ¼ cup honey.

SWEET POTATO SOUFFLÉ

2 pounds sweet potatoes
½ teaspoon grated nutmeg
Pinch of ground cloves
¼ teaspoon salt
¼ cup light brown sugar
2 tablespoons butter
¼ cup cream
3 eggs, separated

1 Preheat the oven to 400°F.

2 Cook the sweet potatoes in boiling water until tender. Drain, peel and mash until smooth.

3 Add the spices, salt, sugar, butter and cream. Beat together. Add the egg yolks. Beat the egg whites until stiff and fold them into the mixture.

4 Bake in a buttered soufflé mold or casserole for about 35 minutes, or until soufflé is well risen and brown. If desired, brush the top of the soufflé with melted butter and sprinkle lightly with light brown sugar before baking.

BRANDIED SWEET POTATOES

4 medium sweet potatoes
⅔ cup brown sugar, firmly packed
¼ cup water
2 tablespoons butter
¼ cup seedless raisins, or ½ cup chopped apple (optional)
¼ cup cognac

1 Wash the sweet potatoes but do not peel. Boil in water to cover until barely soft, about 15 minutes. Drain, cool and peel. Slice into a greased casserole.

2 Preheat the oven to 350°F.

3 Bring to a boil the brown sugar, water, butter and raisins. Add the cognac and pour the mixture over the potatoes.

4 Bake, uncovered, 30 minutes, basting several times with the syrup in the casserole.

Legumes

NEW ENGLAND BAKED BEANS

ABOUT 12 SERVINGS

4 cups dried navy (pea) beans
1 piece (8 ounces) salt pork, streaked with lean
¼ cup molasses
2 tablespoons sugar
½ teaspoon salt
1 teaspoon dry mustard
¼ teaspoon ground ginger
2 cups boiling water, or more

1 Pick over the beans, discarding split or discolored ones and any foreign matter. Wash the beans well, cover them with water and let stand overnight, or use the quick-soaking method on page 78.

2 Drain the beans, cover them with fresh water and cook slowly until the skins wrinkle when a few in a spoon are blown on. Rinse the beans with cold water and place in a 4-quart bean pot.

3 Preheat the oven to 250°F.

4 Pour boiling water over the salt pork, scrape the rind until white and score in ½-inch strips without cutting through the skin. Press the pork gently into the top of the beans.

5 Mix molasses, sugar and seasonings well and add 1½ cups of the boiling water. Pour over beans and cover pot.

6 Bake for about 9 hours, adding a little boiling water about every hour, or when needed. The water should never cover the beans but should appear as tiny bubbles above the beans.

Note: If desired, an onion may be placed in the bean pot before the beans are added.

JAMAICAN BAKED BEANS

4 SERVINGS

2 cups dried white pea beans
¾ pound salt pork, cut into ½-inch cubes
1 teaspoon salt
1 small onion, studded with 4 cloves
½ cup brown sugar or molasses
¼ cup dark rum
2 teaspoons dry mustard
1 teaspoon freshly ground pepper
Pinch of thyme

1 If unprocessed beans are used, soak them in 1 quart of water overnight. Soak the salt pork in cold water to cover 2 hours.

2 Drain the beans and put them in a large kettle. Add enough water to reach 2 inches above the beans. Add the salt and bring to a boil. Lower the heat and simmer the beans until they are barely tender. This will require 30 to 40 minutes for unprocessed beans, 20 minutes for the quick-cooking variety. Drain well.

3 Preheat the oven to 250°F.

4 Place the onion in the center of an earthenware casserole. Cover with a layer of half of the drained beans and add a layer of half of the salt pork. Add the remainder of the beans and top with the remaining salt pork.

5 Combine the sugar, rum, mustard, pepper and thyme and add to the beans. Add boiling water barely to cover and top the casserole with a tight-fitting lid. Bake 4 to 5 hours, or until tender, adding a little boiling water as necessary to keep the beans sufficiently moist. Uncover the casserole and let the beans cook 30 minutes longer without additional water.

FLAGEOLETS WITH ONIONS AND TOMATOES

6 TO 8 SERVINGS

2 cups flageolets or dried white beans
1 onion, studded with 5 or 6 cloves
¼ pound salt pork
1 large carrot, scraped and cut in half
2 thyme sprigs, or ½ teaspoon dried
1 bay leaf
Salt to taste
2 tablespoons butter
1¼ cups chopped onions
1 shallot, finely chopped
1 teaspoon finely chopped garlic
1 teaspoon finely chopped thyme
3 cups peeled and coarsely chopped tomatoes
2 tablespoons chopped parsley

1 Place the flageolets in a kettle and add water to cover to the depth of about 1 inch. Soak overnight. You can also use the quick-soaking method on page 78.

2 Drain the beans and return them to the kettle. Add 2 quarts of water, the whole onion, salt pork, carrot, thyme sprigs, bay leaf and salt. Bring to a boil and simmer 45 minutes to 1 hour.

3 Remove the salt pork and cut it into small cubes; reserve. Continue to cook the beans 30 minutes longer, or until tender. Different varieties require different lengths of cooking time.

4 Heat the butter in a skillet and cook the salt pork cubes until golden brown, stirring occasionally. Add the chopped onions, shallot, garlic and chopped thyme. When the onions are wilted, add the tomatoes and cook, stirring frequently, until the mixture is thickened.

5 Remove the carrot and whole onion and drain the beans, but reserve the bean liquid. Add the beans to the tomato sauce and stir gently. Let simmer about 10 minutes. If the beans seem too dry, use a little of the reserved bean liquid to moisten. Serve beans hot, sprinkled with parsley.

Pasta e Fagioli, page 503.

◆

BLACK BEANS IN RUM

6 SERVINGS

1 pound dried black beans
1 large onion, chopped
2 garlic cloves, minced
3 celery stalks, diced
1 minced carrot
Small herb bouquet (bay leaf, thyme and
    parsley, tied in cheesecloth)
Salt and freshly ground pepper to taste
3 tablespoons butter
6 tablespoons dark rum
Sour cream

1 Soak the beans overnight in water to cover, or use the quick-soaking method on page 78.

2 Add vegetables and seasonings and simmer slowly until the beans are almost tender. Discard the herb bouquet.

3 Preheat the oven to 350°F.

4 Place the beans and their juice in a bean pot or casserole. Add the butter and 3 tablespoons of the rum. Cover and bake until the beans are tender, about 2 hours. Add the remaining rum and serve piping hot with cold sour cream.

CUBAN BLACK BEANS

8 TO 10 SERVINGS

1 pound black beans, soaked overnight
1 large green pepper, cored, seeded and
    quartered
1 medium onion, quartered
8 coriander sprigs
1 teaspoon oregano
1 bay leaf
¼ pound salt pork, quartered
1½ cups sofrito (see following recipe)
¼ cup vinegar
1 teaspoon sugar

    1 Drain the beans and add water to cover to a depth of 1½ inches.

    2 Add the green pepper, onion, coriander, oregano, bay leaf and salt pork. Simmer the beans 1½ hours, or until tender, adding more water as necessary. When the beans are cooked, they should be somewhat liquid without being soupy. Add the sofrito.

    3 Using a wooden spoon, break up a few of the beans, crushing them against the side of the cooking utensil. This will thicken the beans. Add the vinegar and sugar and bring to a boil. Serve with rice.

SOFRITO
ABOUT 1½ CUPS

1 cup coarsely chopped onions
1 cup coarsely chopped green pepper
½ cup olive oil
1 garlic clove, minced

Combine all the ingredients in a skillet and cook until the vegetables are tender.

Black Bean Soup, page 77.
Picadillo with Rice and Beans, page 291.

PURÉE OF BLACK BEANS WITH SOUR CREAM

8 SERVINGS

1 cup dried black beans
1 onion, chopped
1 green pepper, chopped
1 garlic clove, minced
2 tablespoons olive oil
1 bay leaf
½ teaspoon salt
¼ teaspoon freshly ground pepper
1½ tablespoons wine vinegar
Sliced Italian red onions
Sour cream

    1 Pick over and wash the beans. Prepare them according to the quick-soaking method on page 78, using 3½ cups water.

    2 Sauté the onion, pepper and garlic in the olive oil until wilted. Add to beans.

    3 Add bay leaf and salt and pepper and cook, covered, for about 2 hours, until the beans are tender. Add water as needed to prevent sticking. Beans should be fairly dry when done.

    4 Add vinegar to the beans and purée the mixture in a food processor. Reheat. Serve with red onions and sour cream.

RED BEANS AND RICE

6 SERVINGS

1 pound dried kidney or other red beans
½ pound salt pork, sliced
1 large onion, chopped
¼ cup minced celery, with a few leaves
¼ cup minced parsley
Salt and freshly ground pepper to taste
4 cups hot cooked rice

1 Soak the beans in water to cover overnight; or use the quick-soaking method on page 78. Drain.

2 Place the beans in a large pot with the salt pork and water to cover. Cover the pot and simmer for ½ hour.

3 Add the vegetables and seasonings and cook until the beans are done, 1 to 1½ hours. Serve with hot rice.

NAVY BEANS AND RICE, ITALIAN STYLE

4 SERVINGS

½ cup dried navy beans
1 onion, chopped
1 celery stalk with leaves, chopped
2 tablespoons olive oil
1 cup canned tomatoes, undrained
1 teaspoon salt
Pinch of cayenne
½ cup rice
2 tablespoons grated Parmesan or
    Romano cheese
2 tablespoons chopped basil or parsley

1 Soak the beans overnight in water to cover; or use the quick-soaking method on page 78. Simmer until tender, adding more water as needed.

2 Brown the onions and celery in the oil and add to the beans. Add the tomatoes, salt, cayenne and water to cover.

3 Add the rice, cover tightly and cook until the rice is tender, about 15 minutes. Add water as needed. When cooked, the mixture should have the consistency of a thick stew. Stir in the cheese and basil and serve hot.

LOUBIA
SAVORY WHITE BEANS

ABOUT 4 SERVINGS

1 cup dried Italian cannellini
   (white kidney beans)
7 garlic cloves, peeled
1 parsley sprig
½ teaspoon salt
3 tablespoons olive oil
1 large tomato, unpeeled and quartered
Freshly ground pepper to taste
1½ tablespoons flour
1 tablespoon ground cumin, or more
2 tablespoons paprika, or more

  1 Soak the beans overnight in 4 cups of water. You can also use the quick-soaking method on page 78.
  2 Drain the beans; add fresh water to a level 1 inch above the beans. Add 2 of the garlic cloves, the parsley and the salt. Cover and cook until the beans are tender. Remove the parsley and garlic.
  3 Heat the oil and add the tomato and 2 more garlic cloves and cook over high heat until slightly thickened. Sprinkle with salt and pepper. Remove the garlic and stir in the flour. Stir the sauce well and add a little of the cooking liquid from the beans. Add this sauce to the beans.
  4 Crush a few of the beans with the back of a spoon. Add the cumin and salt and pepper. Mince the remaining garlic and stir into the beans with the paprika.

DAL

8 OR MORE SERVINGS

1 pound dried split peas
5 cups water
1 teaspoon salt
½ to 1 teaspoon curry powder
1 cup canned Italian peeled tomatoes, or
   4 medium fresh tomatoes, peeled and
   chopped
2 medium onions, chopped
¼ cup vegetable oil
1 garlic clove, minced
2 tablespoons mustard seed

  1 Combine the peas, water, salt, curry powder, tomatoes and onions. Bring to a boil and simmer, covered, about 45 minutes, or until the peas are tender and the consistency is that of thick pea soup.
  2 Add the remaining ingredients and simmer 10 minutes longer. This dish can be kept several days in the refrigerator and reheated, adding a little water each time. Serve as a side dish with curried foods.

CHICK-PEA CASEROLE

12 OR MORE SERVINGS

4 cups dried chick-peas
Salt to taste
2 tablespoons vegetable oil
2 medium onions, sliced
2 large tomatoes, chopped
1 cup tomato paste
1 cup water
1 teaspoon ground coriander
1 teaspoon cumin seed
1 teaspoon cayenne
¼ teaspoon turmeric
Hot cooked rice
Onion rings for garnish
Chopped coriander for garnish

1 Soak the chick-peas overnight in water to cover. Drain and add water to cover to a depth of 1½ inches. Add salt and simmer 2 hours or longer, until the chick-peas are tender. Or use the quick-soaking method on page 78.

2 Meanwhile, heat the oil in a saucepan, add the onions and cook until wilted. Add the tomatoes, tomato paste, water and spices. Add the chick-peas and simmer 30 minutes longer. Serve hot over rice, garnished with onion rings and coriander.

Hummus, page 23.
Caldo Gallego, page 77.
Chick-Pea Salad with Horseradish, page 467.
Chick-Peas Rémoulade, page 470.
Chick-Pea Salad, page 467.
Navy Bean Salad, page 466.

LENTILS WITH TOMATOES

3 TO 4 SERVINGS

1 cup lentils
8 cups water
Salt to taste
1 onion, finely chopped
1 green pepper, finely chopped
¼ cup olive oil
3 pimientos, chopped
2 cups peeled, chopped tomatoes
Freshly ground pepper to taste

1 Rinse the lentils in cold water and drain. Bring the 8 cups water to a boil and add the lentils and salt. Simmer 20 minutes, or until tender. Drain.

2 Cook the onions and green pepper in the oil until wilted. Add the pimientos and stir. Add the tomatoes and salt and pepper. Stir in the lentils and cook, uncovered, ½ hour. Serve hot.

Lentil and Macaroni Soup, page 79.

CHEDDAR CHEESE AND LENTIL LOAF

5 SERVINGS

2 cups cooked lentils, drained
1 cup soft bread crumbs, packed
½ pound cheddar cheese, grated
½ small onion
1 egg, slightly beaten
1 tablespoon butter, softened
½ teaspoon salt
¼ teaspoon freshly ground pepper
¼ teaspoon thyme

1 Preheat the oven to 350°F.
2 Combine all the ingredients and mix thoroughly.
3 Bake in a greased 9 × 4 × 3-inch loaf pan 45 minutes. Serve with tomato sauce.

CURRIED LENTILS

4 SERVINGS

1 cup lentils
3 cups water or stock
2 large onions, chopped
Salt to taste
3 tablespoons butter or oil
1 garlic clove, minced
1 teaspoon curry powder

1 Combine the lentils and water. Add 1 of the onions and salt and bring to a boil. Reduce the heat and simmer, covered, until the lentils are tender, 30 to 40 minutes. Drain.
2 In a skillet heat the butter, add the remaining onion and the garlic and cook until they begin to brown. Add to the lentils. Add the curry powder and cook until the lentils are very tender, about 10 minutes longer.
3 Serve plain or in a border of rice that has been garnished with sliced lemon or sliced chicken.

Lentil Salad, page 466.

FRIJOLES REFRITOS
CRISP FRIED BEANS

8 SERVINGS

1 pound dried red kidney beans
6 cups water
1 teaspoon salt
½ cup bacon drippings or lard, approximately
2 chorizos (Spanish sausages)
4 ounces cheddar cheese, cubed or grated

1 Pick over the beans, wash thoroughly and cover with the water. Allow to soak overnight; or use the quick-soaking method on page 78.

2 Add the salt, bring to a boil, cover and simmer for about 2 hours, or until the beans are tender. Mash the beans with a potato masher, add the drippings and heat the mixture until all the fat is absorbed, stirring frequently.

3 Skin the sausages, break them into pieces and fry in a small amount of the drippings.

4 Add the cheese and sausages to the beans. Reheat until crisp around the edges.

Minestrone, page 61.
Canadian Pea Soup, page 78.
Dutch Split Pea Soup, page 78.
Chicken and Kidney Bean Casserole, page 161.
Duck with Beans, page 179.
Southwest Beef and Beans, page 292.
Fava Bean Salad, page 468.
Beans and Tuna Vinaigrette, page 470.
Kidney Bean and Egg Salad, page 471.

ROMAN BEANS WITH SAGE

6 TO 8 SERVINGS

1 pound dried Roman, or cranberry, beans
¼ cup olive oil
1 tablespoon minced garlic
6 cups cold water
2 to 4 sage leaves, depending on their potency
Salt and freshly ground pepper to taste

1 Put the beans in a bowl and add water to cover to a depth of about 2 inches above the top of the beans. Soak overnight. Or use the quick-soaking method on page 78.

2 Heat the oil and add the garlic. Cook briefly. Drain the beans and add them. Add the water, sage, salt and pepper. Cook, uncovered, for about 1 hour.

3 Serve the beans with their pot juice spooned over. Sprinkle each serving with olive oil, if desired.

PINTO BEANS

8 SERVINGS

1 pound dried pinto beans
1 large onion, chopped
½ pound of salt pork
Salt

1 Soak the beans in water to cover for about 1 hour, then drain them.

2 Cover again with water about 2 inches above the beans, add the onions and salt pork and simmer until the beans are tender, about 2 hours. Add salt to taste.

Pinto Bean Salad, page 469.

Rice

In the Far East rice is coveted as the staff of life. The Italians rave about risotto, and rice is the accepted ne plus ultra *accompaniment for fried chicken in the Deep South. Rice originated in India and China a few millennia ago and came to Europe via Egypt and Greece. Oddly enough the French were among the last to appreciate its virtue, the reason being, according to gastronomic theory, that the early Gallic chefs succumbed to the temptation to stir it too often and cook it too long.*

There are dozens of kinds of rice including the long grain, short grain, oval grain and round grain, each bearing a different name. Wild rice is not botanically rice at all, but another sort of cereal, and it is native to the United States. Genuine rice of Eastern origin was introduced to this country in 1694.

The peoples of the world who depend on rice as a major nourishment eat it cooked from rough unpolished grains; that way it is more nutritious. When polished rice is used and cooked in a great quantity of water, the vitamins and whatever else go down the drain. Rice should be cooked in a minimum of stock or water, just enough for the grains to absorb and become tender. As the rice cooks, it should not be uncovered or disturbed with fork or spoon. According to the Chinese the rice is done when "eyes" form on the surface of the rice.

BAKED RICE

4 SERVINGS

2 tablespoons butter
¼ cup finely chopped onions
1 cup rice
3 sprigs of parsley
1 bay leaf
½ teaspoon thyme
1½ cups chicken stock

1 Preheat the oven to 400°F.
2 Heat 1 tablespoon of the butter in a saucepan and add the onions. Cook, stirring, until the onions wilt. Add the rice and stir until the grains are coated.
3 Tie the parsley, bay leaf and thyme in a piece of cheesecloth and add it along with the stock. When the stock comes to a boil, cover the pan and put it in the oven. Bake the rice for exactly 17 minutes.
4 Remove and discard the herbs. Add the remaining tablespoon of butter and toss lightly to blend.

Note: The rice may also be cooked over low heat on top of the stove for the same amount of time.

Variation

SAFFRON RICE

Add ¼ teaspoon saffron in place of the bouquet garni.

BOILED RICE FOR ONE

ABOUT 1 CUP

1 cup water
½ cup rice
Salt

1 Place the water in a saucepan with a close-fitting cover and bring to a boil.
2 Pour in the rice, add a little salt and stir once with a fork. Cover closely and cook, without raising the lid, for exactly 17 minutes. Remove from the heat and serve immediately.

♦

RICE AND OLIVE CASSEROLE

4 SERVINGS

2 cups cooked rice
½ cup finely chopped parsley
1 small onion, finely chopped
1 garlic clove, minced
1 cup milk
2 eggs, lightly beaten
Salt and freshly ground pepper to taste
⅓ cup sliced pimiento-stuffed green olives
¼ cup grated Parmesan cheese

1 Preheat the oven to 375°F.
2 In a mixing bowl combine the rice, parsley, onion, garlic, milk, eggs, salt and pepper. Mix well and turn into a buttered 1-quart casserole.
3 Arrange the olives over the top of the casserole and sprinkle with the cheese. Bake for 40 minutes.

RICE WITH ZUCCHINI AND PEAS

8 SERVINGS

4 tablespoons butter
2 tablespoons finely chopped onions
2 young, tender zucchini, cut into small cubes
    (there should be about 1½ cups)
¾ cup peeled, cubed fresh tomatoes
2 cups rice
2 cups water
Salt and freshly ground pepper to taste
½ cup chicken stock
2 thyme sprigs, or 1 teaspoon dried
2 parsley sprigs
½ bay leaf
2 tablespoons chopped pimientos
2 cups cooked green peas

1 Preheat the oven to 400°F.

2 Melt 2 tablespoons of the butter in a flameproof casserole and add the onions. Cook, stirring, until the onions are wilted. Add the zucchini and tomatoes and stir. Cook until most of the liquid evaporates. Add the rice and stir.

3 Add the water, salt, pepper and stock and bring to a boil on top of the stove. In a piece of cheesecloth tie together the thyme, parsley and bay leaf and add it. Cover and bring to a boil once more.

4 Place the casserole in the oven and bake 18 minutes, or until the moisture is absorbed and the rice is tender. Off the heat remove the bouquet and add the pimiento, green peas and remaining 2 tablespoons butter and toss until all is incorporated.

RICE WITH CHICKEN LIVERS AND MUSHROOMS

6 SERVINGS

4 tablespoons butter
1 tablespoon finely chopped onion
½ teaspoon minced garlic
1 cup rice
½ bay leaf
1½ cups chicken stock
Salt to taste
¼ pound chicken livers, picked over and cubed
1½ cups diced mushrooms
4 pimientos, chopped
2 black truffles (optional)

1 Preheat the oven to 350°F.

2 Melt 2 tablespoons of the butter in an ovenproof saucepan or casserole with lid. Add the onion and garlic and cook briefly without browning.

3 Add the rice and bay leaf and cook, stirring, about 2 minutes. Add the stock and salt and bring to a boil. Cover closely and bake exactly 17 minutes.

4 Meanwhile, melt the remaining butter in a skillet and add the chicken livers. Cook, stirring, over moderate heat until the livers lose their red color. Add the mushrooms and cook until most of the liquid evaporates. Do not overcook or the livers will become too dry.

5 When the rice is cooked, stir in the liver and mushroom mixture, pimientos and truffles.

RICE WITH PEAS

4 TO 6 SERVINGS

¼ cup wild rice
¾ cup white rice
1 teaspoon salt
4 tablespoons butter
2 shallots, minced
1 garlic clove, minced
1½ pounds fresh green peas, shelled
Salt and freshly ground pepper to taste

1 Place the wild rice in a saucepan and add boiling water to cover. Cover and let stand for 20 minutes. Drain and repeat 3 times or more, until rice is almost tender. Use fresh boiling water each time.

2 Add the white rice, salt and 2½ cups water to the wild rice. Cover and cook over low heat for 25 to 30 minutes, or until the water is absorbed and rice is tender.

3 In a small saucepan melt the butter and cook the shallots and garlic in it for about 2 minutes. Simmer the peas in water without salt until tender.

4 Combine the rice, butter and peas and toss briefly. Season with salt and pepper and serve hot.

CURRIED RICE

6 SERVINGS

5 tablespoons butter
1 cup finely chopped onions
3 tablespoons curry powder
2 tablespoons flour
1½ cups chicken stock
1 cup cream
½ cup milk
3 cups cooked rice

1 Melt the butter in a large skillet. Sauté the onions in it until golden. Blend in the curry powder and flour and stir until a smooth paste forms.

2 Gradually add the stock, cream and milk. Mix well, stirring, until the sauce is thickened and smooth.

3 Add the rice, turning it over gently in the sauce until all the liquid is absorbed. Cook lightly for 5 minutes. Serve very hot, with a sprinkling of curry powder.

Arroz con Polla, page 160.
Cold Rice-stuffed Tomatoes, page 431.
Cold Rice with Shrimp, page 471.
Cold Rice Ravigote, page 472.
Rice Salad Vinaigrette, page 471.
Rice and Ham Vinaigrette, page 472.
Rice Salad à la Française, page 473.

FRIED RICE WITH SHRIMP

6 SERVINGS

4 to 6 tablespoons vegetable oil
½ cup Chinese cabbage or finely diced celery
½ cup sliced water chestnuts
½ cup thinly sliced scallions
2 tablespoons finely chopped parsley
3 cups cooked rice
½ cup smoked ham (preferably Smithfield)
*   cut into small cubes (optional)*
Salt and freshly ground pepper to taste
3 tablespoons soy sauce or to taste
2 cups cooked, shelled shrimp
2 tablespoons water
4 eggs

1 Heat 2 tablespoons of the oil in a wok or large skillet and add the vegetables. Cook quickly, stirring occasionally, 3 or 4 minutes.

2 Add the parsley, rice and ham and mix well, adding more oil if necessary. Season with salt, pepper and soy sauce.

3 Add the shrimp and cook, stirring, until heated through.

4 Heat 2 tablespoons of the oil in a separate skillet, add the water to the eggs and beat, then let them cook without stirring to make a pancake. Do not turn. Cut the pancake into thin strips and sprinkle over the fried rice.

PORK FRIED RICE WITH GINGER

4 SERVINGS

6 tablespoons peanut oil
2 eggs, lightly beaten
⅓ pound (about 1 cup) pork or beef, ground
1 teaspoon grated fresh ginger
2 cups cooked rice
Salt and freshly ground pepper to taste
¼ cup chopped scallions
12 lettuce leaves

1 Heat 2 tablespoons of the oil, add the eggs and scramble to the soft stage.

2 Heat 2 additional tablespoons of oil in a wok or large skillet and add the pork. Cook, stirring, until the meat is thoroughly cooked. Add the ginger and stir. Add the rice, salt and pepper and cook, stirring rapidly to blend all the ingredients. When the rice is piping hot, mix in the remaining oil, the scallions and the egg, broken up roughly. Spoon portions of the hot fried rice into the lettuce leaves, roll with the fingers and serve immediately.

RICE A LA GRECQUE

ABOUT 4 CUPS

3 tablespoons butter
1 onion, chopped
1 small garlic clove, crushed
3 or 4 leaves of green lettuce, shredded
2 fresh pork sausages, sliced
3 mushrooms, sliced
3 tomatoes, peeled, seeded and diced
1 cup rice
2 cups boiling water or chicken stock
1 teaspoon salt
Dash of freshly ground pepper
½ cup cooked peas
1 diced pimiento
2 tablespoons raisins, sautéed in butter

1 Melt 2 tablespoons of the butter in a large saucepan and brown the onion in it. Add the garlic, lettuce, sausages, mushrooms and tomatoes. Add the rice and mix well together.

2 Add the boiling water, salt and pepper, cover tightly and cook over low heat 20 minutes. Mix well with a fork and add the remaining ingredients. Serve with lamb or poultry, or use for stuffing poultry or veal.

RISOTTO

Risotto, an affectionate or diminutive term for *riso*, or "rice," meaning "little rice," is one of the dishes most closely identified with Milan, and there are many ways to cook it. Basically, however, it is rice cooked in a broth, frequently with saffron, and it is always served with grated cheese. In Italy, it is served like pasta as a first course. The short-grain rice called *arborio* is essential for a good risotto.

4 TO 6 SERVINGS

6 tablespoons butter
3 tablespoons finely chopped onions
1 garlic clove, finely chopped
2 cups arborio rice
Salt and freshly ground pepper to taste
1 teaspoon chopped stem saffron
5 cups chicken stock
½ cup dry white wine
¾ cup grated Parmesan cheese

1 Heat 2 tablespoons of the butter in a fairly large casserole. Add the onions and garlic and cook until onions are wilted. Add the rice, salt, pepper and saffron and stir to coat the grains.

2 Meanwhile, heat the stock and keep it at the simmer.

3 Add the wine to the rice and cook, stirring occasionally, until all the wine has evaporated.

4 Add 1 cup of the hot stock to the rice mixture and cook, stirring occasionally and gently, until all that liquid has been absorbed. Add ½ cup more of the stock and cook, stirring occasionally, until it is absorbed. Continue cooking the rice in this fashion, adding ½ cup of stock every 3 or 4 minutes, just until each ladleful is absorbed. Remember that the rice must cook gently.

5 When all the stock has been added and absorbed, after about 25 minutes, fold in the remaining butter and the cheese. The rice should be creamy, not dry.

Variations

RISOTTO RING

Turn the finished risotto into a well-buttered 6-cup ring mold and press the rice down gently. Invert at once on a serving plate or keep warm in a pan of hot water until ready to serve.

CHICKEN LIVER RISOTTO

Brown 5 or 6 chicken livers, cut into eighths, in the butter and remove. Cook the onions and garlic, then add ½ cup chopped mushrooms and cook 3 minutes. Add the rice and continue with recipe. When the risotto is done, stir in the chicken livers and 2 tablespoons chopped parsley with the butter and cheese.

◆

RISOTTO FOR ONE

ABOUT 1 CUP

1 tablespoon butter
2 tablespoons finely chopped onions
¼ garlic clove, minced
½ cup arborio rice
1 cup boiling chicken stock

1 Heat the butter in a small saucepan with a tight-fitting cover. Add the onions and garlic and cook, stirring, until the onions are translucent. Add the rice and cook, stirring, until rice is golden.

2 Add the stock and cover. Cook, without uncovering, for exactly 20 minutes. Remove from the heat and let stand until ready to serve.

RISOTTO WITH ESCAROLE AND CHEESE

4 TO 6 SERVINGS

2 cups finely shredded escarole
6 tablespoons butter
⅓ cup finely chopped onions
2 cups arborio rice
⅓ cup dry white wine
Salt and freshly ground pepper to taste
4 to 5 cups simmering chicken stock
1½ cups fontina cheese, cut into cubes
¼ cup cream
¼ cup grated Parmesan cheese

1 Prepare the escarole and set aside.

2 Heat 2 tablespoons of the butter in a saucepan and add the onions. Cook, stirring, until the onions are wilted. Add the rice and cook, stirring, about 1 minute. Add the escarole and wine and cook, stirring, about 2 minutes, or until the wine is absorbed. Season with salt and pepper.

3 Start adding the stock about ½ cup at a time, stirring from the bottom, and cook until the stock has been absorbed. Immediately add another ½ cup of stock and cook, stirring, until absorbed. Continue adding stock and stirring until the rice is tender and creamy, but the inner core of the grain must retain a certain resilience to the bite.

4 Add the fontina, cream and Parmesan. Stir quickly from the bottom to blend.

MARVIN DAVID'S RISOTTO WITH PROSCIUTTO AND WILD MUSHROOMS

4 TO 6 SERVINGS

½ cup dried Italian mushrooms, preferably
  porcini
2 cups hot water
4 cups chicken stock
4 tablespoons butter
1 tablespoon olive oil
1 cup finely chopped onions
2 cups arborio rice
¾ cup finely shredded prosciutto
¾ cup grated Parmesan cheese

1 Place the mushrooms in a mixing bowl and add the hot water. Let stand 20 minutes or longer until softened.

2 Drain, but reserve both the mushrooms and their soaking liquid, by lining a mixing bowl with a sieve and adding a double thickness of cheesecloth. Pour in the mushrooms and their liquid. Squeeze the mushrooms into the cheesecloth-lined sieve. Pour the strained liquid into a saucepan and bring to the boil. Cook until reduced to about 1 cup. Add the chicken stock and bring to a simmer. Keep the broth at a bare simmer until it is all used.

3 Cut the mushrooms in half and set aside.

4 Heat 2 tablespoons of the butter and the oil in a heavy saucepan and add the onions. Cook, stirring, until onions start to brown. Add the rice and cook, stirring, until rice is coated.

5 Add 1 cup of stock and cook, stirring, about 2 minutes, or until the stock is absorbed.

6 Add ½ cup of the stock and cook, stirring, about 1 minute. Add the prosciutto and another ½ cup of the stock.

Cook, stirring, until the stock is absorbed, 2 to 3 minutes.

7 Continue cooking, adding ½ cup of stock as needed, for 20 minutes or slightly less. When the rice is nearly finished add the mushroom pieces. Continue adding stock and stirring until the rice is tender and creamy, but the inner core must retain a certain resilience to the bite.

8 Stir in the remaining 2 tablespoons of butter and the cheese and serve.

◆

RICE WITH ASPARAGUS

5 TO 6 SERVINGS

2½ pounds asparagus
½ cup dry white wine
1 cup rice
Salt and freshly ground pepper to taste
½ cup each grated Parmesan and Gruyère
  cheese, mixed
6 tablespoons butter

1 Cook the asparagus until tender in boiling salted water. Drain but reserve 1 cup of liquid in which vegetable was cooked.

2 Cook the rice in the wine and reserved water seasoned with salt and pepper.

3 Layer the cooked rice with the asparagus in a shallow buttered dish, saving the best-looking spears to arrange on top. Sprinkle with cheeses, dot with butter and broil until the cheese has melted and the top is brown.

MUSHROOM-RICE RING

6 SERVINGS

1 cup rice
2 cups water
1 teaspoon salt
½ pound mushrooms
2 tablespoons butter
¼ cup hot stock or water
Freshly ground pepper to taste

1 Combine the rice with the water and salt and bring to a strong boil. Reduce the heat to very low, cover and cook 15 minutes, or until the water is absorbed and the rice is dry and flaky.

2 Preheat the oven to 350°F.

3 Chop the mushrooms and sauté them in the butter for 3 minutes. Add the stock.

4 Combine the rice and mushroom mixture and season with salt and pepper.

5 Spoon the mixture into a greased 7-inch ring mold and set in a pan containing 1 inch hot water. Bake 30 minutes.

6 Invert the rice on a platter and fill with seasoned vegetables.

RICE AND CHEESE CROQUETTES

6 SERVINGS

3 tablespoons butter
3 tablespoons flour
1 cup milk
1 cup shredded sharp cheddar cheese
2 teaspoons grated onion
½ teaspoon salt, approximately
½ teaspoon dry mustard
⅛ teaspoon freshly ground pepper
Dash of cayenne or Tabasco sauce
2 cups cooked rice
2 cups sifted bread crumbs
1 egg beaten with 2 tablespoons water
Oil for deep frying
Onion-pimiento sauce (page 567)

1 Melt the butter in a saucepan, add the flour and stir with a wire whisk until blended. Meanwhile, bring the milk to a boil and add all at once to the butter-flour mixture, stirring vigorously with the whisk. Add the cheese, onion and seasonings and mix well. Add the rice and fold into the sauce. Chill.

2 Shape the mixture into 12 croquettes, roll in crumbs, then in beaten egg and again in crumbs. Let the croquettes dry.

3 Heat enough oil to cover the croquettes to 385°F and fry until golden brown. Drain on paper toweling. Serve with onion-pimiento sauce.

RICE WITH CHILI PEPPERS AND CHEESE

6 SERVINGS

1 cup rice, cooked
2 cups sour cream
Salt to taste
½ pound Monterey Jack cheese, cut into
    small cubes
1 (6-ounce) can peeled green chili peppers,
    drained and cut into thin strips
Butter
½ cup grated Parmesan cheese

1 Preheat the oven to 350°F.

2 Combine the rice with the sour cream and season with salt. Spread half the mixture in the bottom of a buttered casserole.

3 Sprinkle the rice mixture with the Monterey Jack cheese and strips of chili pepper. Top with the remaining rice mixture and dot with butter. Sprinkle with the Parmesan cheese.

4 Bake, uncovered, 30 minutes and serve immediately.

EGG PILAF

6 TO 8 SERVINGS

2 cups rice
4 cups chicken stock
Salt to taste
6 eggs
¼ pound butter, melted
Freshly ground pepper to taste

1 In a saucepan combine the rice, chicken stock and salt. Bring to a boil and cover. Reduce the heat and cook slowly for about 20 minutes, until all the liquid is absorbed.

2 Beat the eggs with a whisk or rotary beater and add them all at once to the rice. Add the butter immediately. Stir well without returning the pan to the heat. The heat of the rice will set the eggs. Season with pepper and serve immediately.

ARMENIAN RICE PILAF

It is curious how one food as basic as rice can gain in taste and texture when allied with another food as basic as thin spaghetti. This is a centuries-old Armenian specialty—rice combined with spaghettini, vermicelli or capellini. Before blending and simmering, the strands of pasta are sautéed briefly in a little oil until they turn golden brown.

6 SERVINGS

1 tablespoon vegetable oil
Enough thin spaghetti such as capellini,
    vermicelli or spaghettini to make ½ cup
    when broken into 2-inch lengths
¾ cup rice
1½ cups chicken stock
Salt to taste
2 tablespoons butter

1 Heat the oil in a saucepan and add the pieces of pasta, stirring. Cook until the strands are golden brown. Do not burn.

2 Add the rice and stir. Add the stock and salt and bring to a boil. Cover and let simmer 17 minutes. Stir in the butter.

PILAF

8 SERVINGS

⅓ cup finely chopped onions
6 tablespoons butter
2¼ cups rice
4½ cups boiling chicken stock
Salt and freshly ground pepper to taste

1 Preheat the oven to 375°F.

2 Sauté the onions in the butter in a heavy casserole until tender and transparent but not brown.

3 Add the rice and continue to cook over low heat, stirring occasionally, until rice grains turn opaque. Do not allow rice to brown.

4 Add the stock and season with salt and pepper. Cover tightly and bake for 5 minutes. Reduce the heat to 350°F and bake for 15 to 20 minutes longer, or until rice has absorbed all the stock.

Variations

MUSHROOM PILAF

Sauté ½ pound mushrooms, sliced, in 4 tablespoons butter and add to pilaf before serving.

NUT PILAF

Add ¼ cup toasted cashews to pilaf before serving.

BROWN RICE

4 SERVINGS

1 cup brown rice
2 tablespoons butter
1 tablespoon chopped onions
¼ teaspoon minced garlic
1¾ cups water or chicken stock
Salt and freshly ground pepper to taste
1 bay leaf
1 parsley sprig
1 thyme sprig, or ¼ teaspoon dried

1 Rinse the rice and set aside.

2 Melt 1 tablespoon of the butter in a saucepan and add the onions and garlic. Cook, stirring, until the onions are wilted.

3 Add the rice, water, salt, pepper, bay leaf, parsley and thyme. Bring to the boil and cover closely. Let simmer 40 minutes.

4 Remove from the heat. Discard the bay leaf and parsley and thyme sprigs. Fluff the rice with a fork and stir in the remaining butter.

FLUFFY WILD RICE

3 TO 4 SERVINGS

Wash ½ cup wild rice in cold water. Cover with 2 cups boiling water. Cover and let stand 20 minutes. Drain and repeat 3 more times, until rice is tender. Use fresh boiling water each time and add 1½ teaspoons salt the last time. Season with pepper and stir in generous amounts of butter.

This rice may be kept warm in the oven or in a double boiler (cover if held longer than 5 minutes).

◆

WILD RICE, MINNESOTA STYLE

6 SERVINGS

4 to 5 cups chicken stock
1½ cups wild rice, washed
1½ cups shredded celery
¾ cup chopped onions
¼ pound mushrooms, chopped
1 pimiento, chopped
Salt and freshly ground pepper to taste

1 Preheat the oven to 375°F.

2 Place all the ingredients except 1 cup of the stock in a 6-cup greased casserole. Cover tightly and bake about 1½ hours, adding more stock as necessary.

WILD RICE WITH SNOW PEAS

4 SERVINGS

1 cup wild rice
2 scallions
1 tablespoon butter
1 teaspoon salt
2 cups or more chicken stock
¼ pound snow peas
4 large mushrooms
1 (4-ounce) can water chestnuts, drained
2 tablespoons vegetable oil
½ teaspoon salt
¼ teaspoon freshly ground pepper
¼ cup toasted almonds

1 Wash the rice thoroughly, changing the water several times. Cut the green part of the scallions diagonally into 2-inch lengths. Chop the white part of the scallions fine.

2 Melt the butter in a large saucepan. Add the minced white part of the scallions and sauté until tender. Add the rice, salt and 2 cups stock. Bring to a boil, stir once and reduce the heat. Cover tightly and cook over low heat until the rice is tender and the liquid is absorbed, about 35 minutes. If necessary add more stock as the rice cooks.

3 Meanwhile, remove the ends and strings from the peas. Cut the mushrooms and water chestnuts into thin slices.

4 Heat the oil in a large skillet. Add the green part of the scallions, peas, mushrooms and water chestnuts and sauté only until the mushrooms are tender.

5 Transfer the cooked rice and vegetable mixture to a casserole. Add salt and pepper and sprinkle with almonds. Mix lightly and keep hot for serving in a very low oven.

VIVIAN BUCHER'S WILD RICE, MUSHROOM AND ORZO SALAD

8 TO 10 SERVINGS

½ pound wild rice
Salt
¼ cup olive oil
8 to 10 ounces fresh mushrooms, thinly sliced
½ pound (about 1 cup) orzo or riso
Freshly ground pepper to taste
¼ cup finely chopped parsley

1 Rinse the wild rice and drain well. Bring about 6 cups of water to a boil and add salt. Add the rice and cook, partially covered, until the rice is tender and "blossoms," 40 to 50 minutes. Drain.

2 Meanwhile, add 1 tablespoon of the oil to a heavy casserole and add about half of the mushrooms. Cook over moderately high heat until the mushrooms give up their liquid. Cook until this liquid evaporates. Pour and scrape the mushrooms as they are cooked into a large mixing bowl. Repeat with another tablespoon of oil and the remaining mushrooms.

3 Add the drained wild rice to the mushrooms and stir to coat with oil.

4 Meanwhile, bring about 4 cups of water to a boil and add salt. Add the orzo and cook about 9 minutes, or until tender. Drain. Add the orzo to the mushrooms and wild rice. Add the remaining oil and the salt and pepper. Add the parsley. Toss and stir to blend thoroughly. Serve at room temperature.

Grains

BARLEY AND MUSHROOM CASSEROLE

4 SERVINGS

1 large onion, chopped
½ pound mushrooms, sliced
5 tablespoons butter
1 cup pearl barley
2 cups beef or chicken stock

1 Preheat the oven to 350°F.

2 Cook the onions and mushrooms in the butter until onions are wilted and mushroom juices have evaporated. Add the barley and brown lightly. Pour the mixture into a buttered casserole. Pour 1 cup of the stock over the barley and cover. Bring to a boil.

3 Bake the casserole, covered, for 25 to 30 minutes. Add remaining stock. Continue to cook, covered, for 15 minutes or longer, until liquid is absorbed and barley is tender.

KASHA, OR BUCKWHEAT GROATS

6 SERVINGS

2 tablespoons butter
½ cup finely chopped onions
2 cups chicken stock
1 cup kasha, or buckwheat groats
1 teaspoon paprika
1 egg, firmly beaten
Salt to taste

1 Heat the butter in a saucepan and add the onions. Cook, stirring, until onions start to take on color. Do not brown. Add the stock and bring to the simmer.

2 Put the kasha in a nonstick skillet and add the paprika and egg. Cook, stirring constantly, over low heat until the grains are coated with egg. The grains should remain separate. Cook until the grains are light brown.

3 Pour in the simmering stock and salt and cover closely. Cook over low heat about 15 minutes, or until the liquid has been absorbed and the kasha is tender.

BULGUR PILAF

4 TO 6 SERVINGS

1 cup bulgur, preferably large grain (No. 3)
3 tablespoons butter
1/3 cup finely chopped onions
1/2 cup finely chopped heart of celery
2 teaspoons minced garlic
1/2 teaspoon chopped marjoram,
    or 1/4 teaspoon dried
1 3/4 cups chicken stock
Salt and freshly ground pepper to taste
1 tablespoon finely chopped parsley

1 Put the bulgur in a sieve and run under cold running water. Drain.

2 Heat 2 tablespoons of butter in a saucepan and add the onions, celery and garlic. Cook briefly until the onions are wilted and stir in the marjoram.

3 Add the bulgur and stir to coat. Add the stock, salt and pepper. Cover and simmer 20 to 25 minutes, stirring occasionally from the bottom to prevent burning. Cook until all the liquid is absorbed. Stir in the remaining tablespoon of butter and the parsley.

Tabbouleh Salad with Tomatoes, page 473.

COUSCOUS

There is an outstanding North African ingredient that is becoming increasingly available in this country in supermarkets and grocery stores. It is called *couscous* and it is a pasta—perhaps the tiniest pasta shape of all—and it is the easiest of all to cook. You simply add it to a simmering broth (with or without herbs of your own choice), cover closely and remove it from the heat. At the end of 5 minutes it is ready to serve. The proportion of couscous to liquid is 1 cup of pasta to 1 1/2 cups of liquid. Serve as a side dish, like rice.

4 SERVINGS

1 1/2 cups chicken stock
1 tablespoon butter
1 tablespoon finely chopped parsley or other
    sweet herb
1 cup quick-cooking couscous

1 Bring the stock to a boil in a saucepan and immediately add the butter, parsley and couscous. Cover closely.

2 Remove saucepan from the heat and let stand 5 minutes. Serve immediately.

Note: Chopped onion, tomato or other vegetables can be cooked briefly in butter before adding the stock.

Cornmeal is more widely revered in the American South and Southwest than in other sections of the country, but one exception is the famed scrapple of the Pennsylvania Dutch. Italians, particularly those of southern Italy, have a keen appetite for polenta, which is made of cornmeal mush and served with cheese, tomato sauce or other savory adornments. The only trick to cooking polenta is to stir it constantly when adding it to the boiling water.

◆

BASIC POLENTA

ABOUT 4 CUPS, OR 4 SERVINGS

1 quart water
1 teaspoon salt
1 cup cornmeal

1 Bring about 2½ cups of water to a boil in the top part of a double boiler over direct heat. Add the salt.

2 Mix the cornmeal with the remaining water and add to the boiling water. Reduce the heat and cook, stirring constantly, until the mixture boils.

3 Place the pan over boiling water and cook, covered, about 45 minutes, stirring occasionally.

Variations

POLENTA WITH GORGONZOLA

Turn hot polenta into a serving dish. Make a depression in the center and fill it with butter and Gorgonzola cheese (3 tablespoons or more of butter and 3 to 4 ounces of cheese). Spoon butter and cheese over each serving of polenta.

POLENTA WITH BEL PAESE

Turn hot cooked polenta into a greased 9 × 9-inch pan and spread to make a layer about ½ inch thick. Chill. Cut into cubes, place in a greased shallow baking dish and sprinkle with bits of Bel Paese cheese and butter. Bake in a preheated 400°F oven until the polenta is hot and light brown, or about 25 minutes.

GRILLED POLENTA

Turn hot cooked polenta into a greased 9 × 9-inch pan. Spread to make a layer about ½ inch thick. Chill. Turn the polenta out of the pan and cut into squares, rectangles or as desired. Place the pieces on a cookie sheet that has been lined with foil and broil until brown and well crisped on both sides. If desired, brush with melted butter during broiling.

POLENTA LAYERS

1 cup cornmeal
4 cups water
Salt
1 medium onion, chopped
1 garlic clove, minced
½ green pepper, chopped
2 tablespoons vegetable oil
1 pound chopped beef
½ cup soft bread crumbs
1 egg
Freshly ground pepper

1 Mix the cornmeal with 1 cup of the water. Bring the remaining water to a boil with the salt. Stir in the cornmeal and cook, stirring, over moderate heat until thick.

2 Preheat the oven to 350°F.

3 Sauté the onion, garlic and green pepper in the oil until tender. Add the beef, crumbs, egg and additional salt and pepper to taste. Mix well.

4 Turn half the cornmeal mush into a greased 8×4×3-inch loaf pan and spread evenly. Arrange the meat mixture on top and cover with the remaining mush.

5 Cover the pan with a piece of oiled foil and bake about 1 hour. Serve with a tomato sauce.

POLENTA WITH MUSHROOMS

2 cups cornmeal
2 cups cold water
6 cups boiling water
3 teaspoons salt
4 cups sliced fresh mushrooms
½ cup diced onions
1 garlic clove, minced
2 teaspoons lemon juice
4 tablespoons butter
⅛ teaspoon freshly ground pepper
⅓ cup half-and-half
¾ cup grated Parmesan cheese
6 mushroom caps (optional)

1 Combine the cornmeal and cold water. Pour into a saucepan containing the boiling water and 2 teaspoons of salt, stirring constantly. Cook until thickened, stirring frequently. Cover and continue to cook over low heat for 10 minutes. Turn into a loaf pan (9 × 5 × 3 inches) and let stand until cold and firm.

2 Preheat the oven to 350°F.

3 Sauté the mushrooms, onions and garlic in the lemon juice and butter. Add the remaining teaspoon of salt and the pepper.

4 Remove the cold cornmeal mush from the pan. Split lengthwise into halves to form 2 layers. Return the lower half to the pan. Cover with the sautéed mushroom mixture and pour the half-and-half over all. Sprinkle with the cheese. Top with remaining cornmeal layer.

5 Bake for 30 minutes. If desired, 10 minutes before the baking time is up, dip mushroom caps into melted butter and arrange over the top of the polenta as a garnish. Serve as a main dish.

GARLIC CHEESE GRITS

6 TO 8 SERVINGS

1 cup regular or quick-cooking grits
¼ pound butter
¾ cup grated sharp cheddar cheese
½ cup milk
3 eggs, well beaten
2 tablespoons finely chopped jalapeño peppers
2 teaspoons Worcestershire sauce
½ teaspoon minced garlic
¼ teaspoon cayenne or Tabasco sauce
Salt and freshly ground pepper to taste

1 Preheat the oven to 350°F.

2 Cook the grits according to package directions. Regular grits require 25 to 30 minutes of slow cooking; quick-cooking grits will take 3 to 5 minutes.

3 While hot add the remaining ingredients and stir to blend well. Pour the mixture into a buttered 2-quart casserole and bake 30 to 40 minutes, or until set.

FRIED GRITS

6 TO 8 SERVINGS

2 cups freshly cooked grits
1 tablespoon butter, melted
2 eggs, lightly beaten
Salt and freshly ground pepper to taste
¾ cup flour
¼ cup peanut or corn oil, or bacon drippings

1 Butter the inside of an 8 × 8-inch baking dish.

2 Scrape the grits into the dish and smooth the top to make a layer about ¾ inch thick. Cover with the melted butter. Refrigerate several hours or overnight until the grits are firm. Cut the grits into squares.

3 Beat the eggs with salt and pepper. Blend the flour with salt and pepper. Dip the squares first in the egg and then in flour to coat well. Shake off excess.

4 Heat the oil in a heavy skillet and cook the squares on one side until golden brown. Turn and cook the other side until golden brown and heated through.

Sauces, Salad Dressings, Composed Butters, Marinades and Stocks

SAUCE BÉCHAMEL

Béchamel, or white sauce, is a foundation sauce of French cuisine. If the home cook could learn to make but one sauce, this would be the most valuable because it is the basis for countless dishes. It may be made with milk alone or enriched with additional cream, or part of the liquid may be stock.

ABOUT 2 CUPS

---

4 tablespoons butter
¼ cup flour
2 cups milk
2 thin slices of onion
2 parsley sprigs
3 tablespoons cream
Salt and freshly ground pepper to taste
Dash of grated nutmeg

1 Heat the butter in a saucepan and stir in the flour. Cook, stirring with a wire whisk, until thoroughly blended.

2 Scald the milk with the onion and parsley. Strain it into the butter-flour mixture, stirring constantly with the wire whisk. When the mixture is thickened and smooth, add the cream.

3 Season the sauce with salt and pepper and add nutmeg.

Variations

THIN WHITE SAUCE

Follow directions above, using 2 tablespoons butter and 2 tablespoons flour.

THICK WHITE SAUCE

Use 6 tablespoons each of flour and butter.

SAUCE MORNAY

Add 1 cup grated Gruyère cheese to the hot sauce and stir over low heat until melted. Season with mustard and Worcestershire sauce to taste.

CHEDDAR CHEESE SAUCE

Add 1½ cups grated sharp cheddar to the hot sauce and stir over low heat until melted. Stir in 2 teaspoons lemon juice.

SAUCE VELOUTÉ

Substitute chicken, beef or fish stock for the milk and proceed as for white sauce.

MUSTARD SAUCE

Combine 1 teaspoon dry mustard with the flour when making the white sauce.

FRESH HERB SAUCE

Add 2 teaspoons freshly chopped herbs, such as parsley or dill.

DRIED HERB SAUCE

Add ½ teaspoon dried herbs, such as thyme or oregano.

◆

SAUCE PÉRIGUEUX

The words *périgueux* and *périgord* relate to a region of France that is famous for its harvest of black truffles. Sauce périgueux is probably the most famous of all truffle sauces.

ABOUT 2 CUPS

---

2 cups brown sauce (opposite page)
1 small (1-ounce) can truffles
2 tablespoons cold butter

Heat the brown sauce and add the liquid from the can of truffles. Chop the truffles and add them to the sauce. Bring to a boil and remove from the heat. Stir in the cold butter and serve hot with grilled beef, veal or chicken dishes.

BROWN SAUCE OR SAUCE ESPAGNOLE

There is nothing more French than the sauce that is known as *espagnole*. It is one of the foundation sauces of French cuisine and is nearly as important as wine, shallots, butter and cream. In most recipes written in English, *espagnole* is translated as "brown sauce." Brown sauce is easy to prepare, but it is time-consuming. It frequently is combined with a reduction of butter, shallots and wine as an accompaniment to grilled meats, poultry and game. It is also used to enrich stews and ragoûts.

There is nothing that is a perfect substitute for brown sauce, but the closest approximation is canned beef gravy, which may be used in any recipe calling for brown sauce.

ABOUT 2 QUARTS

---

5 pounds veal bones
1 large onion, quartered
5 small carrots, peeled and quartered
2 celery stalks with leaves, coarsely chopped
½ teaspoon thyme
1 teaspoon crushed peppercorns
3 bay leaves
3 garlic cloves, unpeeled
1 tablespoon salt
½ cup flour
3 quarts water
1¼ cups tomato purée
½ cup chopped green part of leeks, well washed
3 sprigs of parsley

1 Preheat the oven to 475°F.

2 Combine the bones, onion, carrots, celery, thyme, peppercorns, bay leaves, garlic and salt in a large roasting pan. Place in the oven and bake 45 minutes. Reduce heat if necessary to prevent bones from burning. Sprinkle with flour and bake 15 minutes longer.

3 Transfer the ingredients to a large kettle and add 2 cups of water to the roasting pan. Cook over moderate heat, stirring, to dissolve brown particles that cling to the bottom and sides of the pan. Pour liquid from roasting pan into the kettle and add remaining water, tomato purée, leeks and parsley. Bring to a rapid boil, reduce heat and simmer for 2 hours. Add more liquid if necessary and skim often to remove fat and foam as it rises to the surface. Cool and strain. This sauce may be frozen and defrosted as necessary. Or it may be stored tightly sealed for several weeks in the refrigerator.

◆

SAUCE BERCY

This sauce is named for a well-known quarter of Paris, which was at one time famous as a center of commerce for wines. Wine is obviously an essential ingredient.

ABOUT 2 CUPS

⅓ cup finely chopped shallots
3 tablespoons butter
¾ cup plus 2 tablespoons dry white wine
1½ cups brown sauce (opposite)
1 teaspoon each of chopped tarragon and parsley

1 Cook the shallots in 1 tablespoon of the butter until they are golden brown.

2 Add ¾ cup of the dry white wine and cook until it is reduced by half. Add the brown sauce and cook for 10 minutes.

3 Strain through a sieve and bring to the boil. Turn off the heat and stir in the remaining 2 tablespoons cold butter. Add remaining wine and the herbs. Serve hot.

MADEIRA SAUCE

ABOUT 1¼ CUPS

2 tablespoons butter
2 tablespoons finely minced shallots
1½ cups brown sauce (page 551)
2 tablespoons lemon juice
¼ cup Madeira wine

1 Melt the butter in a saucepan and sauté the shallots for 5 minutes, taking care that the butter does not brown.
2 Add the brown sauce and lemon juice. When the liquid boils, add the wine and simmer gently 5 minutes.

Variation

SAUCE AU PORTO

Substitute port for the Madeira wine.

BORDELAISE SAUCE

Red wine is, obviously, the wine to be used in dishes named bordelaise. Preferably the wine should be a good Bordeaux, but any fine red wine will do.

ABOUT 2 CUPS

2 tablespoons butter
2 tablespoons minced shallots
¾ cup dry red wine
1½ cups brown sauce (page 551)
2 tablespoons lemon juice
2 tablespoons minced parsley
Salt and cayenne to taste

1 Melt the butter in a saucepan and cook shallots until they are transparent.
2 Add the wine and simmer until reduced one half. Add the remaining ingredients and heat thoroughly. Serve with roasted and sautéed meat dishes.

Note: For a variation, place ½ cup sliced beef marrow in a saucepan and barely cover with water. Add salt to taste and bring to a boil. Cook in barely simmering water for 2 minutes. Add the poached marrow to the bordelaise sauce and serve hot.

BÉARNAISE SAUCE

1½ CUPS

1 teaspoon chopped shallots
1 small tarragon sprig, chopped
2 peppercorns
Pinch of salt
¼ cup tarragon vinegar
5 egg yolks
¼ pound plus 4 tablespoons butter, melted
Pinch of cayenne
1 teaspoon minced tarragon

1 Simmer the shallots, tarragon sprig, peppercorns and salt in the vinegar over low heat until the vinegar has been reduced by two thirds. Cool to lukewarm.

2 Add the egg yolks and beat briskly with a wire whisk. Place over low heat and gradually add the butter. Whisk until the sauce thickens. Strain. Season with cayenne and stir in the minced tarragon.

Variation

SAUCE CHORON

Simmer 1 cup chopped tomatoes until reduced by half. Add to the béarnaise with the cayenne and tarragon.

QUICK BÉARNAISE

This sauce can be made in a blender or food processor, but the blender seems to work better.

¾ TO 1 CUP

2 tablespoons white wine
1 tablespoon tarragon vinegar
2 teaspoons chopped tarragon
2 teaspoons chopped shallots or onion
¼ teaspoon freshly ground pepper
¼ pound butter
3 egg yolks
2 tablespoons lemon juice
¼ teaspoon salt
Pinch of cayenne

1 Combine the wine, vinegar, tarragon, shallots and pepper in a skillet. Bring to a boil and cook rapidly until almost all the liquid disappears.

2 In a small saucepan heat the butter to bubbling, but do not brown.

3 Place the egg yolks, lemon juice, salt and cayenne in the container of a blender. Cover the container and flick the motor on and off at high speed. Remove the cover, turn the motor on high and gradually add the hot butter.

4 Add the herb mixture, cover and blend on high speed 4 seconds.

SAUCE MALTAISE

A sauce maltaise is nothing more than an orange-flavored version of béarnaise. It is named, of course, for the island of Malta.

___

ABOUT ¾ CUP

___

3 egg yolks
1 tablespoon lemon juice
¼ cup orange juice
¼ teaspoon salt
⅛ teaspoon freshly ground white pepper
¼ pound butter, melted and hot, but not
    brown
1 tablespoon grated orange rind

1 Place the egg yolks, lemon juice, 1 tablespoon of the orange juice, the salt and pepper in a blender.

2 Turn the motor on low speed and gradually add the butter in a steady stream. Blend for about 15 seconds, or until the sauce is smooth and well blended.

3 Remove to a warm sauceboat and fold in the remaining orange juice and the grated rind. Serve over cooked broccoli, asparagus or cauliflower.

HOLLANDAISE SAUCE

Holland is a land of butter; small wonder this sauce is called hollandaise.

___

ABOUT 1 CUP

___

3 egg yolks
1 tablespoon cold water
¼ pound soft butter
¼ teaspoon salt
½ teaspoon lemon juice, or to taste

1 Combine the egg yolks and water in the top of a double boiler and beat with a wire whisk over hot (not boiling) water until fluffy.

2 Add a few spoonfuls of butter to the mixture and beat continually until the butter has melted and the sauce starts to thicken. Care should be taken that the water in the bottom of the boiler never boils. Continue adding the butter, bit by bit, stirring constantly.

3 Add the salt and lemon juice. For a lighter texture, beat in a tablespoon of hot water if desired.

Variation

MUSTARD HOLLANDAISE

Combine 2 teaspoons dry mustard with 1 teaspoon water and let stand for 10 minutes. Add to the sauce along with the salt. Omit the lemon juice.

QUICK HOLLANDAISE

ABOUT ¾ CUP

Heat ¼ pound butter to bubbling, but do not brown. Into a blender put 3 egg yolks, 2 tablespoons lemon juice, ¼ teaspoon salt and a pinch of cayenne. Turn motor on low speed and add hot butter gradually. Blend about 15 seconds, or until sauce is thickened and smooth.

◆

SAUCE MOUSSELINE

This is hollandaise with whipped cream.

2 CUPS

½ pound butter, at room temperature
3 egg yolks
½ teaspoon salt
Juice of 1 lemon
½ cup heavy cream, whipped

1 Cut the butter into 3 parts. In the top of a double boiler combine 1 part of the butter with the beaten egg yolks. Place over hot, nearly boiling, water and beat constantly with a wire whisk until the butter has melted.

2 Add the second part of the butter and repeat the process; then add the third, beating constantly. When the sauce thickens, season with salt and lemon juice.

3 If the sauce begins to curdle while it is being made, add a little boiling water and continue beating until the sauce is smooth again. Fold the whipped cream into the sauce and serve at once.

With the advent of nouvelle cuisine in the middle of the twentieth century, beurre blanc, or "white butter sauce," made its debut in America. It can be made with or without cream, but the cream helps to stabilize the sauce. It is an incredibly simple sauce to make, and, unfortunately, very calorific. If desired, you may stir in any finely chopped sweet herb to this sauce, such as tarragon, parsley or dill, after the butter is added. You may also add a touch of lemon or lime juice.

◆

BEURRE BLANC WITHOUT CREAM

1 CUP

¼ cup finely chopped shallots
3 tablespoons white vinegar
2 tablespoons dry white wine
¼ pound cold, unsalted butter
Salt and freshly ground pepper, preferably
    white, to taste

1 Combine the shallots, vinegar and wine in a saucepan and bring to the boil. Simmer until the liquid is reduced by about one half. Remove the saucepan from the heat.

2 Cut the butter into 1-inch cubes.

3 Return the saucepan to the heat and add the cubes of butter, a few at a time, stirring vigorously with a wire whisk. Continue adding the butter, beating constantly until the sauce is hot. Add salt and pepper.

BEURRE BLANC WITH CREAM

ABOUT 1 CUP

9 tablespoons cold, unsalted butter
¼ cup finely chopped shallots
3 tablespoons white vinegar
2 tablespoons dry white wine
½ cup cream
Salt and freshly ground pepper, preferably
    white, to taste

1 Cut the butter into 9 equal slices of 1 tablespoon each.

2 Heat 1 tablespoon of butter in a saucepan and add the shallots. Cook briefly, stirring. Add the vinegar and wine and simmer until the liquid is reduced by one half. Pour in the cream and bring to the simmer.

3 Cook, stirring constantly, over low heat while adding the remaining butter slices, a few at a time. Add salt and pepper to taste.

MAYONNAISE

ABOUT 2 CUPS

2 egg yolks
2 teaspoons Dijon mustard
½ teaspoon salt
Pinch of cayenne
¼ cup wine vinegar or lemon juice
1 cup olive oil
1 cup vegetable oil

1 Beat the yolks until thick and lemon colored. Add the seasonings and half of the vinegar. Beat well.

2 Mix the oils and add, while beating, drop by drop at first and then in a gradually increasing amount as the mixture thickens. Do not overbeat.

3 Slowly add the remaining vinegar and beat well. Chill.

♦

GREEN MAYONNAISE

ABOUT 2 CUPS

Combine 1½ cups mayonnaise with ¾ cup minced greens—a mixture of spinach, watercress, parsley, chives or tarragon. Greens may be puréed in a food processor to make a smoother sauce.

♦

CURRIED MAYONNAISE

Add 1 tablespoon of curry powder (or more to taste) to each cup of mayonnaise.

FOOD PROCESSOR MAYONNAISE

The most expeditious way to prepare a mayonnaise is through the use of the food processor. The end result is equal to that made by hand.

ABOUT 1½ CUPS

2 egg yolks
Salt to taste
2 teaspoons Dijon mustard
1¼ cups vegetable or olive oil
2 teaspoons or more vinegar or lemon juice
Freshly ground pepper to taste

1 Place the yolks in the container of a food processor. Add the salt and mustard and pulse the food processor for just a second.

2 With the motor running, add the oil in a thin stream. Add the remaining ingredients, processing just enough to blend.

TARTAR SAUCE

ABOUT 1¼ CUPS

1 cup freshly made mayonnaise
1 teaspoon mustard, preferably
  Dijon or Düsseldorf
2 tablespoons finely chopped sour pickles
  (cornichons)
2 tablespoons finely chopped drained capers
1 tablespoon finely chopped chives
1 tablespoon finely chopped tarragon (optional)
Lemon juice

Combine mayonnaise and mustard and all the chopped ingredients. Stir in lemon juice to taste. If the sauce seems too thick, it may be thinned by beating a little cold water into it. Serve with fish and shellfish.

♦

AÏOLI
GARLIC MAYONNAISE

2 CUPS

2 to 4 garlic cloves, minced
2 egg yolks
½ teaspoon salt
Freshly ground pepper to taste
2 cups olive oil

1 Place the garlic in a mixing bowl and add egg yolks, salt and pepper. Beat rapidly with a wire whisk or rotary beater.

2 Gradually add the oil, while beating. Add it drop by drop at first and then in a gradually increasing amount as the mixture thickens. Chill. This is fine as a dip for raw vegetables. It can also be served with steamed fish, fresh cod in particular.

GREEN GODDESS SAUCE

2 CUPS

1 cup freshly made mayonnaise
1 garlic clove, minced
3 anchovies, chopped
¼ cup finely cut chives, or scallions, green
    part included
¼ cup chopped parsley
1 tablespoon lemon juice
1 tablespoon tarragon vinegar
½ teaspoon salt
Freshly ground pepper to taste
½ cup sour cream

Blend all the ingredients except the sour cream. Fold in the sour cream. Serve with chilled cooked fish.

◆

MAYONNAISE AND COGNAC SAUCE

This is a sauce of European origin. It is delectable with cold seafood appetizers such as shrimp, crabmeat or lobster. It may be spooned over but it is best served on the side. It would go well with cold sliced meats or potatoes or with cold pieces of chicken or fish.

¾ CUP

¾ cup freshly made mayonnaise
1 teaspoon tomato paste
1 teaspoon cognac

Combine the ingredients.

SAUCE GRIBICHE

The origin of the name of this sauce is obscure. It contains many flavors including herbs, onion and hard-cooked egg. It goes with many dishes including such bistro foods as calf's head and boiled beef and with cold cooked fish or seafood.

ABOUT 2 CUPS

1 egg yolk
Salt and freshly ground pepper to taste
1 teaspoon prepared mustard, preferably
    Dijon or Düsseldorf
3 tablespoons wine vinegar
½ cup olive oil
½ cup vegetable oil
¼ cup finely chopped parsley
3 tablespoons chopped chives
2 tablespoons finely chopped shallots
1 tablespoon finely chopped onions
1 teaspoon finely chopped tarragon,
    or ½ teaspoon dried
¼ teaspoon thyme
1 hard-cooked egg, sieved or finely chopped

1 This sauce is made like a mayonnaise. Place the egg yolk in a mixing bowl and add salt, pepper, the mustard and vinegar. Immediately begin whipping the mixture with a wire whisk or rotary beater. Add the oils, a few drops at a time, then continue to add in a steady stream, beating constantly. The sauce should become thicker all the time.

2 Stir in the remaining ingredients. If a thinner sauce is desired, add a small amount of cold water.

SAUCE VERTE, OR SALSA VERDE

A green sauce is known as *sauce verte* in France and *salsa verde* in Italian. With minor variations they are identical. Green sauce goes well with boiled beef, cold sliced boiled potatoes and freshly steamed fish and seafood.

ABOUT 2 CUPS

1 cup finely chopped onions
½ cup chopped watercress leaves
½ cup coarsely chopped spinach
2 tablespoons chopped parsley
1 tablespoon chopped chives
6 tablespoons balsamic or red wine vinegar
1 cup olive oil
Salt and freshly ground pepper to taste

1 Put the onions, watercress, spinach, parsley and chives into the container of a food processor. Blend well. Add the vinegar and, with the motor running, add the oil in a steady stream.

2 Season the sauce with salt and pepper and blend.

HOT HERB SAUCE FOR BOILED BEEF

ABOUT 2 CUPS

4 tablespoons butter
¼ cup flour
2 cups beef stock, heated
2 egg yolks, beaten lightly
2 tablespoons chopped capers
1 tablespoon finely chopped parsley

1 Melt the butter and stir in the flour. Add the hot stock, beating vigorously with a wire whisk. When the mixture is thickened and smooth, simmer for 5 minutes, stirring occasionally.

2 Remove from the heat and add gradually to the egg yolks. Return to the heat and add the capers and parsley. Heat briefly and serve hot with boiled beef.

RÉMOULADE SAUCE I
MAYONNAISE BASE

ABOUT 2½ CUPS

2 cups tart mayonnaise
1 garlic clove, minced
2 hard-cooked eggs, finely chopped
1 tablespoon finely chopped tarragon,
    or 1 teaspoon dried
1 tablespoon finely chopped parsley
1 teaspoon strong prepared mustard,
    preferably Dijon or Düsseldorf
1 teaspoon anchovy paste

Blend all the ingredients well and let stand
1 to 2 hours before serving.

♦

RÉMOULADE SAUCE II
VINAIGRETTE BASE

ABOUT 1 CUP

3 tablespoons wine vinegar
1 to 2 tablespoons prepared mustard,
    preferably Dijon or Düsseldorf
2 tablespoons minced scallions
2 tablespoons minced celery
1 teaspoon grated horseradish
1 tablespoon minced parsley
½ cup plus 1 tablespoon olive oil
Dash of cayenne
Salt and freshly ground pepper to taste

Combine the vinegar with the mustard,
scallions, celery, horseradish and parsley.
Beat in the olive oil, a little at a time, and
season with cayenne, salt and pepper.
Serve as a sauce for cold boiled shrimp.

SOUR CREAM–DILL SAUCE

ABOUT 2 CUPS

1 egg
2 tablespoons finely chopped dill
4 teaspoons lemon juice
1 teaspoon grated onion
½ teaspoon salt
Pinch of freshly ground pepper
Pinch of sugar
1½ cups sour cream

Beat the egg until fluffy and lemon colored. Add the remaining ingredients,
blending in the sour cream last. Stir until
blended and chill.

SPANISH SAUCE

2 CUPS

1 large onion, minced
2 tablespoons chopped green pepper
1 small garlic clove, minced
2 tablespoons butter
2 cups canned Italian plum tomatoes
¼ cup stuffed olives, chopped
1 teaspoon salt
½ bay leaf
¼ teaspoon freshly ground pepper
Pinch of ground cloves

1 Sauté the onion, green pepper and garlic in the butter until light brown, stirring often.

2 Chop the tomatoes in the can, using a knife. Add the tomatoes and their juices and remaining ingredients to the sautéed mixture and simmer, partly covered, until thick, or about 30 minutes. Stir occasionally. Adjust the seasonings and remove the bay leaf.

3 Place 2 tablespoons of the sauce on an omelet before rolling it. Garnish with more sauce.

The most versatile of vegetables is the tomato. Who could do without it? Here is a repertory of tomato sauces that would do credit to Italy, the Mediterranean or Mexico.

◆

BASIC TOMATO SAUCE

ABOUT 5 CUPS

3½ cups canned tomatoes, preferably imported
3 tablespoons olive oil
1 cup finely chopped onions
1½ tablespoons minced garlic
5 tablespoons tomato paste
1½ teaspoons crushed oregano
¼ teaspoon hot red pepper flakes
Salt and freshly ground pepper to taste
6 tablespoons finely chopped basil
¼ cup finely chopped parsley
1 cup beef stock

1 If the tomatoes are not of the crushed variety, put them into the container of a food processor and blend.

2 Heat the oil in a saucepan and add the onions and garlic. Cook briefly while stirring. Do not brown. Add the tomatoes, tomato paste, oregano, red pepper flakes, salt, pepper, basil, and parsley. Stir and bring to the boil. Add the stock and cook 30 minutes.

Continued

Variations

MEAT TOMATO SAUCE

Brown ½ pound chopped beef in the oil after cooking the onions and garlic.

TOMATO AND WINE SAUCE

Substitute 1 cup dry red wine for the tomato paste.

◆

TOMATO SAUCE WITH CHILI POWDER

ABOUT 2 CUPS

5 tablespoons butter
¼ cup finely chopped onions
1 teaspoon minced garlic
1 teaspoon chili powder
½ teaspoon thyme
2 tablespoons flour
¼ cup dry white wine
1 cup crushed tomatoes
¾ cup chicken stock
Salt and freshly ground pepper to taste

1　Heat 1 tablespoon of the butter in a saucepan and add the onions and garlic. Cook, stirring, until onions are wilted. Add the chili powder and thyme and sprinkle with the flour, stirring. Add the wine, tomatoes, stock, salt and pepper. Cook, stirring, 10 minutes.

2　Put the sauce through a sieve or food mill. Reheat and swirl in the remaining butter.

TOMATO SAUCE WITH HERBS

This is an excellent and easily made tomato sauce good any season of the year, but particularly so when fresh herbs are on the market. The sauce may be served over pasta and is the ideal filling for a roulade of crabmeat (page 115).

3 CUPS

2 tablespoons olive oil
1 cup finely chopped onions
1 tablespoon minced garlic
1 (28-ounce) can (3 cups) imported
　Italian tomatoes
¼ teaspoon finely chopped thyme,
　or ⅛ teaspoon dried
¼ teaspoon finely chopped savory,
　or ⅛ teaspoon dried
¼ cup finely chopped basil
¼ teaspoon finely chopped oregano,
　or ⅛ teaspoon dried and crushed
1 bay leaf
Salt and freshly ground pepper to taste
¼ teaspoon hot red pepper flakes
¼ cup cream

1　Heat the oil in a saucepan and add the onions and garlic. Cook, stirring, about 5 minutes without browning. Add the tomatoes, thyme, savory, basil, oregano and bay leaf. Add salt, pepper and red pepper flakes. Simmer about 20 minutes, or until slightly thickened.

2　Pour the sauce into the container of a food processor and blend thoroughly. Return the sauce to the saucepan and add the cream. If desired, add a touch more red pepper flakes.

FRESH TOMATO–GINGER SALSA

ABOUT 2 CUPS

3 (about 1½ pounds) red ripe tomatoes
1 tablespoon safflower oil
1½ teaspoons finely grated fresh ginger
1½ teaspoons rice wine vinegar
Salt and freshly ground pepper to taste

1 Cut away and discard the cores of the tomatoes. Cut each tomato crosswise in half and press or scoop out the seeds. Cut the tomato into ¼-inch cubes and put the pieces in a bowl.

2 Add the remaining ingredients and stir to blend. Serve at room temperature.

SALSA CRUDA
A MEXICAN TABLE SAUCE

ABOUT 3 CUPS

2 cups drained, canned tomatoes
½ cup finely chopped onions
¼ cup finely chopped coriander
1 tablespoon chopped canned jalapeño peppers with seeds
1 tablespoon finely chopped fresh jalapeño peppers with seeds
2 tablespoons liquid from bottled or canned jalapeño peppers
Salt and freshly ground black pepper

1 Blend the tomatoes to a coarse pulp in a food processor or electric blender. Pour them into a mixing bowl. Add the onions and coriander and blend well.

2 Add the hot peppers, a small amount at a time, to the tomatoes. Add them according to the desired strength. Add the jalapeño liquid and salt and pepper. Serve with any suitable Mexican or Tex-Mex food. Or serve as a dip with tostadas.

PICO DE GALLO
A FIERY HOT CHILI SAUCE

This is a cold, exceedingly hot sauce that bites the palate and tongue. It goes well with many Mexican dishes, including chili con carne and huevos rancheros, but should be added a little at a time to suit the individual palate. *Pico de gallo* translates roughly as "rooster's beak."

ABOUT 2½ CUPS

½ cup finely chopped jalapeño peppers
* with seeds*
½ cup finely chopped onions
½ cup seeded, unpeeled, diced tomatoes
⅓ cup finely diced avocado
3 tablespoons finely chopped coriander
2 tablespoons lime juice
1 teaspoon olive oil
Salt and freshly ground pepper to taste

Combine all the ingredients in a mixing bowl and serve at room temperature. Serve with any suitable Mexican or Tex-Mex food.

SALSA MEXICANA

ABOUT 4 CUPS

4 cups peeled fresh tomatoes or canned Italian
* plum tomatoes*
¼ cup canned green chilies, finely chopped
¼ cup wine vinegar
2 garlic cloves, minced
2 tablespoons vegetable oil
2 tablespoons finely chopped parsley
2 teaspoons chopped basil
1 teaspoon thyme
1 teaspoon oregano
Salt and freshly ground pepper to taste

Chop the tomatoes and combine with the remaining ingredients. Chill. Serve with any suitable Mexican or Tex-Mex dish.

◆

MARINARA SAUCE

ABOUT 3 CUPS

1 garlic clove, minced
½ cup chopped onions
2 tablespoons olive oil
4 cups canned Italian tomatoes
½ cup chopped parsley
4 whole basil leaves, or 1 teaspoon dried
½ teaspoon oregano
Salt and freshly ground pepper to taste

1 Cook the garlic and onions in the oil until golden brown.

2 Put the tomatoes into the container of a food processor and blend thoroughly. Combine all the ingredients and simmer, uncovered, until thickened, about 1¼ hours.

MUSHROOM SAUCE
BROWN

ABOUT 2½ CUPS

½ pound mushrooms
1 tablespoon finely chopped shallots
    or scallions
4 tablespoons butter
¾ cup brown sauce (page 551)
½ cup Madeira wine
1 cup cream
1 teaspoon strong prepared mustard
Salt and freshly ground pepper to taste

1 Cook the mushrooms and shallots in 3 tablespoons of the butter until dry.

2 Combine the brown sauce and wine. Cook for 10 minutes. Add the cream and cook for 5 minutes longer. Remove from heat and stir in the mustard, remaining butter, salt, pepper and the mushrooms and shallots.

◆

MUSHROOM SAUCE
WHITE

ABOUT 2 CUPS

4 tablespoons butter
¼ pound mushrooms, sliced
½ small onion, minced
3 tablespoons flour
1¼ cups milk
1 teaspoon salt
⅛ teaspoon freshly ground white pepper

Melt the butter in a saucepan. Add the mushrooms and onion and sauté until the mushrooms are tender. Blend the flour with the milk and add to the saucepan. Cook over low heat, stirring constantly, until thickened. Add salt and pepper.

◆

MUSHROOM-WINE SAUCE

3 CUPS

2 tablespoons butter
1 tablespoon chopped parsley
½ garlic clove, chopped fine
1 small onion, chopped
1 tablespoon flour
1 cup chicken stock
⅛ teaspoon grated nutmeg
¾ pound mushrooms, thinly sliced
¼ cup dry sherry

1 In a saucepan, heat 1 tablespoon of the butter, add the parsley, garlic and onion and cook over medium heat 3 minutes. Stir in the flour. Gradually add the stock, stirring constantly. Add the nutmeg.

2 In a skillet heat the remaining butter, add the mushrooms and sauté briefly. Combine with the sauce and simmer 15 minutes. Add the wine and bring to a boil. Serve with roast meats or poultry.

SAUCE POIVRADE

Grilled venison and other meats are well complemented by a sauce pungently flavored with peppercorns. The heat is slightly assuaged by currant jelly.

ABOUT 1½ CUPS

8 peppercorns, crushed
½ cup vinegar
1 cup brown sauce (page 551), or leftover
    thickened gravy
2 tablespoons red currant jelly

1 Mix together peppercorns and vinegar and simmer, uncovered, until reduced to ¼ cup.
2 Add brown sauce and simmer ½ hour. Add jelly. Strain.

SAUCE POULETTE

The word *poulette* is related to *poule*, which means "chicken" in French. It is a chicken sauce enriched with cream and egg yolk and frequently flavored with dry sherry. The sauce is excellent with poached foods, especially chicken and veal.

ABOUT 1½ CUPS

½ cup sliced fresh mushrooms
1 tablespoon finely chopped onions
3 tablespoons butter
1 teaspoon lemon juice
2 tablespoons flour
1 cup chicken stock
¼ cup cream
½ teaspoon salt
Dash of freshly ground white pepper
¼ cup dry sherry
1 egg yolk

1 Sauté the mushrooms and onions in the butter and lemon juice. Blend in the flour. Add the stock and cream and cook, stirring vigorously with a wire whisk, until the mixture is thickened and smooth. Add the seasonings and wine.
2 Beat the egg yolk with a little of the sauce and add to the remaining sauce in the pan. Cook for 1 minute.

BUTTER SAUCE FOR SHELLFISH

8 SERVINGS

1 pound butter
3 to 4 tablespoons lemon juice
1 tablespoon Worcestershire sauce
½ teaspoon Tabasco sauce

Melt the butter over low heat. Add the remaining ingredients and beat well with a fork. Distribute among 8 individual serving cups and serve with steamed hard-shell crabs, boiled lobster, etc.

◆

CAPER SAUCE

Capers are remarkably tasty tidbits; they are the buds of the caper plant and are normally found pickled in vinegar. A caper sauce goes well with many boiled foods including tongue and boiled beef.

ABOUT 2½ CUPS

3 tablespoons vegetable oil
3 tablespoons flour
1½ cups beef stock
½ cup cream
2 tablespoons or more capers
Salt and freshly ground pepper to taste

1 Heat the oil in a saucepan, add the flour and stir with a wire whisk until blended. Meanwhile, bring the stock to a boil and add all at once to the butter-flour mixture, stirring vigorously with the whisk. Cook, stirring, until thickened.
2 Add the cream, capers, salt and pepper. Reheat before serving; do not boil.

CHUTNEY SAUCE FOR HAM

ABOUT 1 CUP

½ cup bottled chutney, chopped
½ cup sugar
¼ cup water
2 tablespoons lemon juice

Mix all the ingredients and simmer until syrupy. Serve hot with hot baked ham.

◆

ONION-PIMIENTO SAUCE

This is a tasty sauce that complements cooked ham and croquettes made with pork, chicken or veal.

ABOUT 2½ CUPS

1 medium onion, minced
3 tablespoons butter
3 tablespoons flour
1 cup chicken stock
½ cup cream
2 tablespoons chopped pimiento
2 teaspoons chopped parsley
Salt and freshly ground white pepper to taste

1 Sauté the onion in the butter until tender but not brown. Add the flour and blend with a wire whisk. Add the stock and cream and cook, stirring, until the sauce boils.
2 Add the pimiento, parsley, salt and pepper. Purée in a food processor.

FLEMISH SAUCE FOR POACHED FISH

¾ TO 1 CUP

4 tablespoons butter
2 teaspoons prepared mustard,
    preferably Dijon
Juice of 1 lemon
Salt and freshly ground pepper to taste
2 teaspoons chopped parsley
1 teaspoon chopped chives
¼ teaspoon grated nutmeg
4 egg yolks

1 In a saucepan, combine the butter, mustard, lemon juice, seasonings and herbs. Place the saucepan in a skillet containing simmering water (or use a double boiler) and stir with a wire whisk until the butter has melted.

2 Beat the egg yolks until thick and lemon colored and stir them into the butter-mustard mixture. Continue beating vigorously over barely simmering water until the sauce thickens. Serve immediately over poached fish.

FRENCH QUARTER SAUCE

ABOUT ¾ CUP

6 tablespoons olive oil
3 tablespoons strong prepared mustard,
    preferably Dijon or Düsseldorf
2 tablespoons cider vinegar
1 garlic clove, minced
6 anchovy fillets
1 tablespoon finely chopped parsley
1 tablespoon finely chopped chives
½ teaspoon salt

Put all the ingredients in a food processor and blend until well mixed. Chill thoroughly. If desired, combine with 1 finely sieved hard-cooked egg. Serve over chilled shrimp.

◆

HORSERADISH SAUCE

ABOUT 1½ CUPS

3 tablespoons butter
3 tablespoons flour
1½ cups boiling beef stock
Horseradish to taste

1 Melt the butter in a saucepan, add the flour and stir with a wire whisk until blended.

2 Add the boiling liquid all at once, stirring vigorously with the whisk until the mixture is smooth and thickened. Season with horseradish. Serve with boiled beef or tongue.

COLD HORSERADISH DRESSING

1¼ CUPS

2 to 4 tablespoons finely grated horseradish
1 cup sour cream
1 teaspoon sugar
Pinch of salt
Pinch of freshly ground pepper
1 tablespoon finely chopped dill

Mix together all the ingredients except the dill. Chill and, before serving, garnish with the dill. Serve with smoked trout or whitefish or cold meats. This is also good as a dip for vegetables.

◆

COLD HORSERADISH SAUCE A LA DRESDEN

ABOUT 2½ CUPS

1 cup heavy cream, whipped
½ cup freshly shredded horseradish
2 teaspoons sugar
Salt and freshly ground pepper to taste

Mix all the ingredients and chill well before serving. Serve with smoked trout or whitefish.

DIABLO SAUCE

¾ CUP

2 tablespoons butter
¼ cup chopped scallions
1 hard-cooked egg yolk, crushed
2 tablespoons olive oil
2 tablespoons dry sherry
1 tablespoon tarragon vinegar
1 teaspoon dry mustard
1 teaspoon anchovy paste
Salt and Tabasco sauce to taste

Heat the butter and cook the scallions in it for 3 minutes. Add the remaining ingredients and bring to a boil. Let stand until ready to use.

◆

CUMBERLAND SAUCE

ABOUT 1½ CUPS

½ cup currant jelly
Grated rind and juice of 2 lemons
Grated rind and juice of 1 orange
¼ cup port wine
¼ teaspoon ground ginger
⅛ teaspoon grated nutmeg

Combine all the ingredients in a saucepan and bring to the boil, stirring. Let cool. Chill and serve with cold tongue or game dishes.

LEMON SAUCE

ABOUT 1¾ CUPS

4 tablespoons butter
2 tablespoons flour
¼ cup lemon juice
1 cup boiling water
¼ teaspoon salt
Dash of Tabasco sauce
½ cup whipped sweet or sour cream,
    approximately

Melt 3 tablespoons of the butter in a sauce-pan. Stir in the flour and let cook for 2 minutes. Add the lemon juice and boiling water; stir and cook until smooth and thickened. Simmer for 5 minutes and add the salt and Tabasco. Just before serving, add the cream and remaining 1 tablespoon butter, melted. Serve over vegetables.

◆

PARSLEY SAUCE

ABOUT 1¼ CUPS

¾ cup olive or vegetable oil
3 tablespoons plus 1 teaspoon lemon juice
Salt and freshly ground pepper to taste
¼ cup chopped parsley
2 tablespoons finely chopped onions
¼ teaspoon minced garlic
¼ teaspoon oregano

1 Combine the oil, lemon juice, salt and pepper in a small saucepan. Stir briskly to blend and heat thoroughly. Do not boil.

2 Remove the sauce from the heat, let cool almost to lukewarm and add the remaining ingredients. Serve with fish.

ANCHOVY SAUCE

ABOUT ¾ CUP

½ cup olive oil (may be half butter)
8 garlic cloves, chopped
2 (2-ounce) cans flat anchovies, undrained
3 tablespoons chopped parsley

1 Heat the oil in a skillet and add the garlic. Reserving 5 anchovies for garnish, add the remainder to the oil and cook, stirring, until the garlic is light brown and the anchovies have disintegrated.

2 Pour the sauce over hot drained pasta and toss well until mixed. Add the parsley and toss. Or use for garnish with the reserved anchovies.

Variations

BAGNA CAUDA

Add to the oil in the anchovy sauce above ¼ pound butter and sliced truffle. Serve over boiled meats or vegetables.

GREEN ANCHOVY SAUCE

Sauté contents of 1 can anchovies, drained, in ½ cup olive oil along with 1 minced onion and 1 small minced green pepper. When onion is golden, add ¼ cup minced parsley. Spoon over hot cooked pasta and sprinkle with grated Parmesan cheese.

ANCHOVY-CHEESE SAUCE

ABOUT 1 CUP

1½ tablespoons butter
1½ tablespoons flour
1½ cups milk
Dash of freshly ground white pepper
¾ cup shredded cheddar cheese
6 anchovies, chopped

Melt the butter and stir in the flour. Remove from the heat and add the milk, stirring. Cook until thick. Add the pepper, cheese and anchovies. Heat only until cheese is melted. Serve with broccoli or other vegetable.

♦

TUNA FISH SAUCE

This is a simplified version of the sauce used for vitello tonnato. It may be served with poached veal, chicken or turkey.

1 CUP

1 medium garlic clove, peeled and sliced
3 to 4 ounces (about half a 7-ounce can) tuna
  and the oil in which it was packed
2 well-drained anchovies
¼ cup olive oil
2 tablespoons vinegar
1 tablespoon chopped onion
1 tablespoon half-and-half
Chopped rind of ½ lemon

Combine the ingredients in a food processor and blend until puréed.

CURRY SAUCE

ABOUT 1½ CUPS

4½ tablespoons butter
1 garlic clove, minced
⅓ cup finely chopped onions
⅓ cup finely chopped celery
3 tablespoons chopped carrot
2 tablespoons flour
2 tablespoons curry powder
½ bay leaf
2 parsley sprigs
2 thyme sprigs, or ½ teaspoon dried
1¾ cups chicken stock
Salt and freshly ground pepper to taste

1 Heat 3 tablespoons of the butter in a saucepan and add the garlic, onions, celery and carrot. Cook, stirring, until the onions are wilted. Add the flour and cook, stirring, about 3 minutes. Stir in the curry powder, bay leaf, parsley and thyme.

2 Using a wire whisk, continue to stir briskly while adding the stock. Simmer, covered, stirring occasionally, about 30 minutes. Put the mixture, including the soft vegetables, through a fine sieve, using a wooden spoon. Swirl in the remaining butter by rotating the pan gently and add salt and pepper. Serve with seafood crêpes (page 122) or with any cooked seafood.

ASPARAGUS SAUCE

ABOUT 2 CUPS

1 tablespoon butter
1 tablespoon olive oil
1 tablespoon finely chopped shallots
1 cup coarsely chopped cooked asparagus
⅓ cup dry white wine
1 cup chicken stock
2 tablespoons cream

1 Heat the butter and oil in a saucepan
and add the shallots. Cook, stirring, for 30
seconds. Add the chopped asparagus,
wine and stock. Bring to the simmer. Add
the cream and let cook 5 minutes, stirring
occasionally.

2 Pour the sauce into the container of a
food processor and blend thoroughly. Return the sauce to the saucepan and reheat.
Serve with poached or grilled fish or
chicken.

Variation

CARROT SAUCE

Substitute 1 cup of cubed cooked carrots
for the asparagus.

WATERCRESS SAUCE

ABOUT 1¼ CUPS

1 bunch watercress
½ cup finely chopped green part of scallions
⅓ cup vegetable oil
1 egg yolk
1 tablespoon Dijon mustard
2 teaspoons white vinegar
Tabasco sauce to taste
Salt and freshly ground pepper to taste

1 Pull or cut off enough watercress
leaves and upper tender stems to make 1¼
cups, loosely packed. Reserve the remaining watercress for another use. Put the 1¼
cups into a food processor container.

2 Add the chopped scallions and the
oil and blend as fine as possible.

3 Put the yolk, mustard and vinegar
into a mixing bowl and start beating with
a wire whisk. Add the watercress mixture,
a tablespoon or so at a time, beating rapidly with the whisk. Beat until thickened.
Add Tabasco, salt and pepper.

CUCUMBER SAUCE

1½ CUPS

1 cup finely chopped peeled and seeded
    cucumbers
½ teaspoon salt
2 teaspoons sugar
1 tablespoon cider vinegar
⅛ teaspoon freshly ground pepper
½ cup heavy cream, whipped

1 Combine the cucumbers and salt. Let
stand at least 1 hour.

2 Drain cucumbers and mix with
sugar, vinegar and pepper. Just before
serving fold in the whipped cream. Serve
over fish.

◆

DILL SAUCE

¾ CUP

½ cup finely chopped dill
½ cup finely chopped green part of scallions
½ cup vegetable oil
1 egg yolk
1 tablespoon Dijon mustard
2 teaspoons white vinegar
Tabasco sauce to taste
Salt and freshly ground pepper to taste

1 Put the dill and scallions into the
container of a food processor and add the
oil. Blend thoroughly.

2 Put the yolk, mustard and vinegar
into a mixing bowl and start beating with
a wire whisk. Add the dill-scallion mixture, a tablespoon or so at a time, beating
rapidly with the whisk. Beat until thickened. Add Tabasco, salt and pepper.

SAUCE ROUILLE

The word *rouille* in French means "rust." This
garlic-flavored sauce, which is excellent with
broiled fish or in fish soups, is called rouille
because of its darkish-red color, which derives
from saffron and paprika.

ABOUT 6 CUPS

2 medium potatoes, baked, mashed
    while warm
3 garlic cloves, minced
3 egg yolks
½ teaspoon paprika
½ teaspoon saffron
2 cups peanut oil
1 cup cream
Salt and freshly ground pepper to taste

1 Spoon the mashed potatoes into the
mixing bowl of an electric mixer. Add the
garlic, yolks, paprika and saffron and beat
well.

2 Meanwhile, warm the oil and cream
and start adding the oil to the potato mixture while beating on low speed. Add the
oil and cream alternately until the sauce
has the consistency of mayonnaise. Season with salt and pepper and beat at high
speed for 30 seconds. Serve with poached
fish or spoon a dab or so into fish soups.

SAUCE AURORE

The word *aurore* in French means "dawn." This cream sauce is so called because it has a pink or pale red dawn-colored tinge. It is excellent with fish.

2 CUPS

5 tablespoons butter
¼ cup flour
1 cup hot milk
½ cup fish stock
½ cup cream
1 tablespoon tomato paste
Salt and freshly ground pepper to taste
Lemon juice to taste

1 Heat 3 tablespoons of the butter in a heavy enamelware or stainless-steel saucepan. Blend in the flour and cook slowly for 2 minutes. Remove from the heat.

2 Beat in the hot milk with a wire whisk, blending thoroughly. Beat in the fish stock, ¼ cup of the cream and the tomato paste. Boil, stirring, for 1 minute. Thin out with remaining cream, adding 1 tablespoon at a time. Season with salt, pepper and lemon juice. Remove from heat.

3 Just before serving, beat in the remaining butter, 1 tablespoon at a time. Serve with poached or baked fish.

SEAFOOD COCKTAIL SAUCE

This cocktail sauce is traditional American and is widely used, particularly in the South. It is fine with any seafood, including shrimp, crab and lobster, and is particularly good with oysters on the half shell.

ABOUT 1 CUP

1 cup tomato catsup
1 tablespoon Worcestershire sauce, or more
2 tablespoons prepared horseradish
¼ teaspoon Tabasco sauce
½ cup finely diced heart of celery
Salt and freshly ground pepper to taste
Lemon juice to taste

Combine catsup, Worcestershire, horseradish, Tabasco and celery. Add salt, pepper and lemon juice and chill.

♦

ORIENTAL SAUCE

ABOUT ¾ CUP

½ cup soy sauce
4 teaspoons vinegar or lemon juice
3 teaspoons sugar
1 teaspoon chopped fresh ginger

Combine all the ingredients and stir until the sugar is dissolved. Serve with 2 pounds of shrimp, cooked and deveined. As a serving idea, arrange the shrimp on a bed of fresh watercress surrounding the sauce.

SEAFOOD SAUCE

ABOUT 3 CUPS

1 tablespoon butter
2 shallots, finely chopped
1 tablespoon flour
¾ cup tomato juice
½ cup milk
2 tablespoons sherry
½ cup cream
1 to 1½ pounds cooked lobster, shrimp or
    crab, cut into small pieces

1 Melt the butter and sauté the shallots in it until they are tender but not brown.

2 Add the flour, stirring. Add tomato juice and milk, stirring rapidly with a wire whisk. Bring to the boil, stirring with the whisk, and simmer 1 minute. Stir in the sherry and cream.

3 Add the seafood and stir to blend. Reheat but do not boil. Serve immediately.

MUSTARD-CHEESE SAUCE

ABOUT 2 CUPS

1¼ teaspoons dry mustard
1 teaspoon water
4 tablespoons butter
¼ cup flour
2 cups milk
½ teaspoon salt
¼ teaspoon freshly ground black pepper
1 cup shredded cheddar cheese
1 teaspoon lemon juice

1 Combine the mustard with the cold water and let stand for 10 minutes to develop flavor.

2 Melt the butter in a saucepan and blend in the flour. Gradually add milk. Stir and cook until the sauce is of medium thickness.

3 Add the salt, mustard mixture, pepper, cheese and lemon juice. Heat only to melt cheese.

Salad Dressings

BASIC VINAIGRETTE

The most important oil and vinegar sauce in the Western world goes by the name of vinaigrette, or French dressing. On its home territory it is called *sauce salade*. Almost any good quality vinegar may be used, but the best is balsamic vinegar.

½ CUP

2 tablespoons vinegar, preferably
   balsamic vinegar
2 teaspoons Dijon mustard
6 tablespoons olive oil
Salt and freshly ground pepper to taste
1 teaspoon minced garlic

1 Put the vinegar and mustard in a bowl and stir with a wire whisk. Gradually add the oil, stirring rapidly with the whisk.

2 Stir in the salt, pepper and garlic.

HERB DRESSING I

ABOUT 3 CUPS

2 cups vegetable oil
½ cup tarragon vinegar
½ cup chopped parsley
¼ cup dry red wine
2 garlic cloves, peeled and split
2 teaspoons salt
2 teaspoons chopped basil
1 teaspoon paprika
½ teaspoon dry mustard
½ teaspoon freshly ground pepper

Combine all ingredients and shake well. Discard garlic before using. Use over salad greens, sliced tomatoes, cucumbers, etc.

♦

HERB DRESSING II

ABOUT ⅔ CUP

½ cup vegetable or olive oil
4 fresh basil leaves, chopped
3 tablespoons wine vinegar
1 tablespoon finely chopped onion
1 tablespoon water
1 tablespoon finely chopped parsley
½ teaspoon salt
⅛ teaspoon thyme
⅛ teaspoon marjoram

Combine all the ingredients in a jar with a tight-fitting lid. Shake vigorously. Let stand 10 minutes. Serve over crisp salad greens.

TARRAGON FRENCH DRESSING

½ CUP

5 tablespoons olive oil
3 tablespoons red wine vinegar
2 teaspoons salt
2 teaspoons chopped tarragon, or ½ teaspoon
  crumbled dried
¼ teaspoon freshly ground pepper
1 garlic clove

1 Combine oil, vinegar, salt, tarragon and pepper.
2 Peel garlic, cut into halves and add to dressing. Let the dressing stand for several hours before using.
3 Remove and discard garlic. Mix the dressing well and pour over salad just before serving.

♦

ORANGE FRENCH DRESSING

1 CUP

½ cup vegetable oil
¼ cup orange juice
2 tablespoons lemon juice
2 tablespoons shredded apples or pears
1 teaspoon sugar
¼ teaspoon dry mustard
⅛ teaspoon salt
Chopped rind of 1 orange
Dash of freshly ground white pepper

Combine all ingredients and beat with a rotary beater or blend in a food processor. This is an excellent dressing for fruit salads.

GRAPEFRUIT FRENCH DRESSING

2 CUPS

1½ teaspoons salt
1 teaspoon paprika
⅛ teaspoon freshly ground white pepper
1 teaspoon minced tarragon
1 teaspoon sugar
1 cup vegetable oil
¾ cup grapefruit juice
3 tablespoons lemon juice

Combine the salt, paprika, pepper, tarragon, sugar and oil. Let stand for 1 hour. Add the grapefruit juice and lemon juice and store in the refrigerator until serving time.

♦

SHALLOT VINAIGRETTE

ABOUT ½ CUP

4 tablespoons olive oil
2 tablespoons finely chopped shallots
2 tablespoons balsamic vinegar
½ teaspoon minced garlic
Salt and freshly ground pepper to taste

Combine all the ingredients in a small bowl and beat briskly to blend. Cover and let stand 1 hour or longer. Leftover sauce may be bottled tightly and refrigerated for 1 or 2 days.

HORSERADISH CREAM DRESSING

ABOUT 1¾ CUPS

¾ cup cream
¼ cup wine vinegar
Salt and white pepper to taste
3 tablespoons grated horseradish
1½ teaspoons finely chopped shallots or onions

   1 Beat the cream until very stiff, then gradually beat in the wine vinegar.
   2 When the mixture is the consistency of mayonnaise, add the salt and pepper. Fold in the horseradish and shallots.

NORTH AFRICAN LEMON DRESSING

ABOUT 1 CUP

⅔ to ¾ cup olive oil
¼ cup lemon juice
2 garlic cloves, minced
Grated peel of 2 lemons
½ teaspoon salt
1 teaspoon sugar
½ teaspoon ground coriander
½ teaspoon ground cumin
½ teaspoon dry mustard
½ teaspoon paprika
⅛ teaspoon cayenne or Tabasco sauce

Combine all the ingredients in a jar with a tight-fitting lid. Refrigerate and shake well before using. Serve with fruit salads and cottage cheese, or with a salad made by alternating slices of tomatoes, sweet onions, cucumbers and sweet pepper rings.

LIME-MINT DRESSING

ABOUT 1 CUP

¾ cup olive oil or vegetable oil
¼ cup lime juice
1 teaspoon salt
1 teaspoon finely chopped parsley
1 teaspoon finely chopped mint
1 teaspoon finely chopped chives
1 teaspoon prepared mustard
¼ teaspoon white pepper

Mix all the ingredients, place a cube of ice in the dressing and beat until the mixture thickens to the consistency of medium cream sauce. Use for tossed greens or coleslaw.

ROQUEFORT CREAM MAYONNAISE

ABOUT 2 CUPS

½ cup cream
2 tablespoons Roquefort cheese
1 cup freshly made mayonnaise

Whip the cream until stiff. Crumble the cheese. Fold the whipped cream and cheese into the mayonnaise. Serve over greens or lettuce hearts.

NIÇOISE SAUCE

ABOUT 2¾ CUPS

¼ cup tomato paste
1 green pepper, seeded and finely chopped
1 teaspoon chopped tarragon and chives,
    mixed
2 cups freshly made mayonnaise

Combine the tomato paste with the green pepper, tarragon and chives. Fold into the mayonnaise and mix well.

◆

RUSSIAN DRESSING

This is a wholly American invention and it is curiously named. Some recipes call for caviar, which would give the name credibility. It is, however, optional.

ABOUT 1 CUP

1 cup mayonnaise, preferably freshly made
2 tablespoons chili sauce or tomato catsup
2 tablespoon diced pimiento
2 tablespoons black or red caviar (optional)
1 tablespoon finely chopped green olives
1 tablespoon finely chopped parsley
1 teaspoon Worcestershire sauce
Salt and freshly ground pepper to taste

Combine all the ingredients in a mixing bowl. Blend well.

RUSSIAN DRESSING A L'AUDELAN

ABOUT 2 CUPS

1½ cups freshly made mayonnaise
½ cup finely chopped cooked beets
1 tablespoon prepared horseradish
    or black caviar
Salt to taste

1 Mix the mayonnaise and the beets until the dressing is an even pink hue. If horseradish is used, mix it in thoroughly. Cavair should be folded in carefully but thoroughly. Add the salt.

2 Refrigerate the dressing at least 2 hours before serving.

◆

SOUR CREAM AND CUCUMBER SAUCE

ABOUT 1½ CUPS

1 cup sour cream
½ cup peeled, seeded and finely chopped
    cucumber
1 teaspoon finely chopped dill
1 teaspoon finely grated onion
½ teaspoon salt

Thoroughly mix all the ingredients. Refrigerate 1 to 2 hours before serving.

SEA GODDESS DRESSING

ABOUT 2 CUPS

1 garlic clove, minced
3 tablespoons minced anchovies
¼ cup finely minced chives
1 tablespoon lemon juice
1 tablespoon tarragon wine vinegar
½ cup sour cream
1 cup freshly made mayonnaise
⅓ cup finely chopped parsley
Salt and freshly ground pepper to taste

Combine the ingredients in the order given. Chill thoroughly. Serve with fish or seafood salads.

♦

MONA LISA DRESSING

ABOUT ½ CUP

½ teaspoon paprika
½ teaspoon horseradish
½ teaspoon dry mustard
½ cup mayonnaise
1 tablespoon cream

Add the paprika, horseradish and mustard to the mayonnaise and fold in the cream. If a lighter dressing is desired, the cream may be whipped. Use for hearts of lettuce or romaine.

Composed Butters

HERB BUTTER

ABOUT ¾ CUP

¼ pound butter, at room temperature
1 tablespoon lemon juice
3 tablespoons finely chopped fresh herb
 (parsley, tarragon, rosemary or other). Or
 use 1 to 3 teaspoons dried herb, depending
 on its strength.
Salt and freshly ground pepper to taste

1 Cream the butter and beat in the lemon juice, a little at a time.
2 Beat in the herb and season with salt and pepper. Chill, if desired.

Variations

BASIL BUTTER

Use 2 teaspoons lemon juice and 2 tablespoons fresh basil, or 1 teaspoon dried. The basil butter may be served on top of poached eggs, as a spread for hot biscuits, on freshly cooked vegetables and on top of fish. Eggs also may be fried in basil butter.

MAÎTRE D'HÔTEL BUTTER

Use parsley as the herb and beat in 1 teaspoon Worcestershire sauce with the lemon juice. Serve with grilled meats.

SNAIL BUTTER

Add 1 teaspoon each finely chopped garlic and shallots to the recipe for maître d'hôtel butter. Add, if desired, a little thyme and rosemary. Use for stuffing snails in the shell.

PARSLEY BUTTER

Use on broiled fish or meat.

TARRAGON BUTTER

Use on broiled fish or meat.

ROSEMARY BUTTER

Use on broiled lamb, chicken or pork.

GARLIC BUTTER

Use minced garlic to taste and serve on steak or lamb.

◆

CURRY BUTTER

ABOUT ½ CUP

¼ pound butter
½ teaspoon curry powder
Dash of freshly ground pepper
Dash of paprika

Cream the butter, add remaining ingredients and beat until fluffy. Store in the refrigerator in a covered glass jar until ready to use. Recream before using. Use as a substitute for regular butter in making sandwiches or serve on broiled meats or fish.

FISH BUTTERS

MUSTARD BUTTER
½ CUP

Melt 6 tablespoons butter and add 2 tablespoons prepared mustard. Serve on broiled salmon.

ANCHOVY-TOMATO BUTTER
½ CUP

To 4 tablespoons creamed butter add 4 anchovies, chopped fine; 1 teaspoon tomato paste; ½ garlic clove, mashed, and a pinch of black pepper. Use on smelts, mackerel, salmon, etc.

PIQUANT BUTTER
½ CUP

Cream 6 tablespoons butter and add 1 teaspoon Worcestershire sauce, 2 teaspoons finely chopped chutney and 2 teaspoons chili sauce. Serve on broiled fish steaks.

ANCHOVY BUTTER
½ CUP

Melt ¼ pound butter and carefully pour it into another pan, leaving the residue behind. To the clarified butter add 10 anchovy fillets, drained of oil and minced, 1 teaspoon minced parsley and the juice of 1 lemon.

TABASCO ROQUEFORT STEAK SPREAD

ENOUGH FOR 2 (4-OUNCE) STEAKS

3 ounces Roquefort cheese
2 tablespoons butter
½ teaspoon Tabasco sauce

Cream all ingredients together until well blended. Spread over charcoal-grilled steak.

◆

MUSHROOM BUTTER

ABOUT 2 CUPS

½ pound fresh mushrooms, sliced
4 tablespoons plus ¼ pound butter
3 tablespoons sherry or cognac
¼ teaspoon freshly ground pepper
¼ teaspoon salt

1 Sauté the mushrooms in 4 tablespoons of the butter 5 minutes. Turn them occasionally to brown all sides.

2 Put the mushrooms and pan juices into the container of a food processor. Add the remaining ingredients and blend until smooth. Serve on grilled meats.

RED WINE BUTTER FOR STEAK

ABOUT ½ CUP

2 teaspoons minced shallots
9 ounces (1⅛ cups) dry red wine
4 tablespoons butter, at room temperature
1 teaspoon chopped parsley
Salt and freshly ground pepper to taste

1 Cook the shallots and wine together in a shallow open pan until the liquid has reduced to one quarter the original amount. Remove from the heat and cool.

2 Cream together the butter and parsley. Combine it with the wine-shallot mixture and season with salt and pepper.

3 Keep the creamed butter covered and under refrigeration. Add as desired to hot broiled meat.

◆

SESAME SEED AND LEMON BUTTER

ABOUT ½ CUP

5 tablespoons butter, melted
2 tablespoons toasted sesame seeds
1 tablespoon lemon juice
Salt and freshly ground pepper to taste

Combine all ingredients and heat. Serve with hot vegetables.

HERBED CAPER BUTTER

¼ CUP

4 tablespoons butter
2 teaspoons capers, chopped if large
½ teaspoon oregano
⅛ teaspoon freshly ground pepper

Combine all ingredients in a small sauce-pan. Heat until butter is melted. Serve over cooked vegetables such as broccoli, Brussels sprouts, cabbage, cauliflower and snap beans

◆

SAVORY PECAN BUTTER

1 CUP

¼ pound butter, melted
½ cup chopped toasted pecans
3 tablespoons lemon juice
2 tablespoons chopped chives
½ teaspoon salt
¼ teaspoon freshly ground pepper
¼ teaspoon marjoram

Combine all the ingredients and heat just enough to blend the flavors. Serve over cooked vegetables.

Marinades and Basting Sauces

MARINADE

ABOUT ½ CUP

¼ cup soy sauce
3 tablespoons sherry
1 tablespoon brown sugar
2 small slices of fresh ginger, diced
1 garlic clove, crushed

Combine all the ingredients. Use the mixture to marinate spareribs, shrimp or beef kebabs.

◆

DANIEL BOULUD'S MARINADE FOR BEEF

ABOUT ¾ CUP

¼ cup finely chopped shallots
¼ cup dry red wine
2 tablespoons red wine vinegar
1½ tablespoons olive oil
1 tablespoon minced garlic
1 tablespoon cracked or coarsely ground pepper
1 teaspoon finely chopped rosemary
½ teaspoon sugar

Combine all the ingredients in a flat dish and add red meat, such as flank steak. Let stand 30 minutes, turning the meat occasionally. Cook the meat on a preheated grill, basting occasionally with the sauce.

MARINADE FOR SMOKED OR BARBECUED FOODS

2½ CUPS

1 (12-ounce) bottle or can of beer or ale
1 cup soy sauce
¼ cup vegetable oil
2 tablespoons finely minced chopped onion
2 tablespoons sugar
2 tablespoons vinegar
1 teaspoon dry mustard
½ teaspoon ground ginger
½ teaspoon cinnamon

Mix all ingredients in a food processor. Pour over butterfish, bluefish, salmon or swordfish steaks in a shallow pan. Marinate for 2 to 3 hours, stirring occasionally. Drain and smoke. Makes enough marinade for 2 to 3 pounds of fish.

♦

BASTING SAUCE FOR DUCK

ABOUT 1¼ CUPS

½ cup soy sauce
½ cup sherry
¼ cup honey, Chinese bead molasses or syrup from a jar of preserved ginger
1 garlic clove, minced
1 teaspoon grated fresh ginger

Combine all ingredients in a saucepan, bring to a boil and remove from the heat. Use to baste a duck, every 15 minutes, as it roasts or turns on the spit.

BARBECUE SAUCE

ABOUT 4 CUPS

4 large onions, sliced
⅓ cup olive oil
1 (6-ounce) can tomato paste, or 1 (14-ounce) bottle tomato catsup
1 parsley sprig
1 thyme sprig
1 bay leaf
1 garlic clove, minced
2 cups vinegar
½ bottle Worcestershire sauce
2 tablespoons sugar
1 dried hot pepper pod
Salt and cayenne to taste

Sauté the onions in the olive oil until soft. Add the tomato paste, parsley, thyme, bay leaf and garlic and let simmer for 30 minutes. Add remaining ingredients and let simmer until the desired flavor and thickness are attained. If a smooth sauce is preferred, the sauce may be puréed in a food processor.

GREEN PEPPER BARBECUE SAUCE

1¼ CUPS

½ cup diced green pepper
½ cup cider vinegar
2 slices lemon
2 tablespoons brown sugar
2 tablespoons finely chopped onion
2 tablespoons chili sauce
2 tablespoons vegetable oil
1½ teaspoons chili powder
1 teaspoon dry mustard
1 teaspoon salt
⅛ teaspoon cayenne

Combine all ingredients in a pan. Cook for 3 minutes. Use for basting spareribs, chops and chicken.

♦

BARBECUE SAUCE FOR SPARERIBS

ABOUT 2 CUPS

1 medium onion, chopped
1 garlic clove, minced
1 cup canned tomatoes
¼ cup vinegar
¼ cup Worcestershire sauce
¼ cup brown sugar
2 teaspoons prepared mustard
1 teaspoon salt
1 teaspoon chili powder
1 teaspoon celery seed
1 teaspoon lemon juice

Combine all the ingredients in a saucepan and simmer for 30 minutes. Use as a basting sauce for spareribs.

AVERY ISLAND BARBECUE SAUCE

2½ CUPS

2 tablespoons butter
1 medium onion, chopped
1 garlic clove, minced
1 (28-ounce) can (3½ cups) tomatoes
1 (6-ounce) can tomato paste
2 slices of lemon
1 bay leaf
½ cup chopped celery with leaves
⅓ cup vinegar
¼ cup chopped green pepper
3 tablespoons molasses
2 teaspoons dry mustard
2 teaspoons Tabasco sauce
½ teaspoon salt
½ teaspoon ground cloves
½ teaspoon allspice

Melt the butter in a saucepan. Add the onions and garlic and cook until the onions are tender but not brown. Add the remaining ingredients and simmer for 30 minutes. Let stand until cool. Strain if desired. Use to brush hamburgers, chicken, spareribs or sausages during baking, broiling or grilling.

Lime Barbecue Sauce, page 134.

SOUTHERN BARBECUE SAUCE

ABOUT 2¼ CUPS

1 (14-ounce) bottle tomato catsup
¼ pound butter
Juice and rind of 1 lemon
1 garlic clove, minced
1 tablespoon Worcestershire sauce

Combine all ingredients in a saucepan and bring to a boil. After the butter melts, simmer for 5 minutes and remove from the heat. Remove the lemon rind and use the sauce for basting poultry, fish or meats.

◆

BASTING SAUCE FOR SPIT-ROASTED LEG OF LAMB

ABOUT 1¼ CUPS

½ cup olive oil
½ cup red wine
8 juniper berries, crushed (optional)
1 bay leaf, crushed
1 teaspoon sugar
1 teaspoon chopped rosemary,
    or ½ teaspoon dried
¼ teaspoon ground ginger
¼ teaspoon cayenne
¼ teaspoon grated nutmeg
1 thyme sprig, or ¼ teaspoon dried
Salt and freshly ground pepper to taste

Combine all the ingredients in a saucepan, bring to a boil and remove from the heat. Use to baste leg of lamb.

Stocks (or Broths)

BEEF STOCK

A good stock is the basis for literally thousands of the world's finest dishes. Although the preparation of beef stock is time-consuming it is not a complicated procedure. It can be made in large quantities and, given sufficient storage space, frozen for future use.

3 QUARTS BEFORE CONCENTRATION

3 pounds shin of beef
2 marrow bones
3 pounds beef chuck, cut into thirds
3 quarts water
1 teaspoon salt
6 peppercorns
1 large onion, peeled or unpeeled, studded
    with 4 cloves
1 large or 2 small leeks
1 bay leaf
½ teaspoon thyme
2 carrots, washed and trimmed
2 parsley sprigs
2 celery stalks
1 white turnip, quartered (optional)

1 Remove the meat from the shinbone and reserve. Place the shinbone and marrow bones in boiling water to cover, cook 5 minutes and drain well.

2 Place the bones and all the meat including the trimmings in a large kettle. Add 3 quarts of water. Bring to a rolling boil and reduce the heat. Skim the surface to remove the foam and fat. Continue skimming until the foam ceases to rise.

3 Add the salt, peppercorns and onion. Trim the leek and split down the center toward the root without cutting through. Wash well under cold running water. Place the bay leaf in the center of the leek and sprinkle with thyme. Tie the cut portion with string and add to the simmering liquid. Add the carrots, parsley, celery and turnip.

4 Cover loosely and simmer gently 4 or 5 hours.

5 Strain the liquid through a double thickness of cheesecloth. (The meat may be used for hash.) Taste the stock and, if a richer, more concentrated flavor is desired, simmer uncovered until it reaches the desired flavor.

6 Cool quickly by placing the kettle in cold water. Chill the stock until the fat solidifies. Skim off the fat.

◆

LAMB STOCK

ABOUT 3 QUARTS

2 to 3 pounds neck of lamb, cut into pieces
Lamb bones
4 quarts water
2 onions, sliced
1 teaspoon salt
½ teaspoon freshly ground pepper

1 Place all the ingredients in a large kettle. Bring to a boil, cover and simmer for 3 to 4 hours.

2 Strain, cool and chill the stock. Before using it, discard the layer of fat that has risen to the top.

CHICKEN STOCK

8 CUPS

4 pounds bony chicken parts, such as necks, backs and wings
4 quarts water
2 onions, peeled, each studded with 2 cloves
4 allspice berries
1 teaspoon peppercorns, crushed lightly
4 cups coarsely chopped leeks
¼ pound mushrooms, coarsely chopped
1 tomato, cut into quarters
2 cups coarsely chopped celery, leaves included
2 cups coarsely chopped scraped carrots
2 thyme sprigs
1 bay leaf
2 garlic cloves, crushed

1 Put the chicken parts in a kettle and run cold water over them until the water runs clear. Drain. Add the 4 quarts of water.

2 Add onions to the kettle. Add the allspice, peppercorns, leeks, mushrooms, tomato, celery, carrots, thyme, bay leaf and garlic. Bring to the boil and let simmer 3 hours, skimming the surface often to remove all traces of fat, scum and foam.

3 Strain the liquid. There should be about 13 cups. Discard the solids. Pour the liquid into a clean kettle and bring to the boil. Let simmer about 2 hours, or until reduced to 8 cups. Cool the stock and chill it, or freeze for future use.

◆

PORK BROTH

ABOUT 1 CUP

Put 1 pound cracked pork bones in 2 cups lightly salted water. Cover and simmer for 1 hour. Strain.

VEAL STOCK

3 QUARTS

1 large (3- to 4-pound) veal knuckle
1½ pounds veal, cut into pieces
5 quarts water
1 teaspoon salt
6 peppercorns
1 large onion, studded with 4 cloves
1 carrot, washed and trimmed
1 celery stalk with leaves
3 parsley sprigs
1 large bay leaf

1 Put the veal knuckle in boiling water, cook for 5 minutes and drain well.

2 Place the bone and meat in a large kettle. Add the cold water and bring to a boil. Reduce the heat. Skim to remove foam and fat and continue to simmer and skim until foam ceases to rise.

3 Add remaining ingredients, cover loosely and simmer gently for about 3 hours.

4 Lift the bones and meat from the liquid. (The meat may be used for hash.) Strain the liquid through a double thickness of cheesecloth.

5 Cool the stock and chill it. Remove the layer of fat from the surface before using the stock in recipes.

Note: If veal stock is to be used for aspic dishes, a calf's foot or two may be added to the kettle to give a greater amount of gelatin. Parboil the calf's feet with the veal knuckle before adding them to the kettle.

COURT BOUILLON

A court bouillon is any liquid used for poaching fish or shellfish. It may be merely salted water. The best court bouillon, however, is made with fish trimmings and herbs.

ABOUT 2 QUARTS

1 celery stalk
3 parsley sprigs
½ bay leaf
Bones and head of 1 white-fleshed fish
8 cups water
1 cup white wine, or ½ cup cider vinegar
1 small onion
10 bruised peppercorns
1 teaspoon salt
Pinch of thyme

Tie the celery, parsley and bay leaf together with string. Combine all ingredients in a deep saucepan or kettle and simmer, uncovered, 20 minutes. Strain the liquid through a double thickness of cheesecloth. Cool before using it for poached fish. Plunge shellfish into boiling court bouillon.

FISH STOCK

8 CUPS

2 pounds bones from a white-fleshed nonoily
    fish, including heads, if possible
1½ cups coarsely chopped celery
2 cups coarsely chopped onions
1 garlic clove, crushed unpeeled
2 cups chopped leeks
3 thyme sprigs
1 bay leaf
8 cups water
1 cup dry white wine
1 teaspoon peppercorns

   1 If fish heads are used, the gills must
be removed. Rinse the bones in cold
water.
   2 Combine the ingredients in a small
kettle and bring to the boil. Let simmer
about 20 minutes.
   3 Strain the broth and discard the solids.

Note: Leftover stock may be frozen for
later use.

FISH VELOUTÉ

ABOUT 5 CUPS

¼ pound plus 4 tablespoons butter
½ cup flour
5 cups hot fish stock

   1 Melt the butter in a large saucepan
and stir in the flour.
   2 When blended and smooth add the
fish stock and stir vigorously with a wire
whisk. When sauce is thickened and
smooth, cook about 1 hour, stirring occasionally.

Note: This sauce may be frozen and defrosted as needed. Or it will keep a week
or longer in the refrigerator.

♦

QUICK ASPIC FOR CHICKEN

ABOUT 4 CUPS

3 cups chicken stock
1 cup tomato juice
4 envelopes (4 tablespoons) unflavored gelatin
1 teaspoon sugar
2 eggshells, crushed
2 egg whites, lightly beaten
2 tablespoons cognac
Salt and freshly ground pepper to taste

   1 Combine stock, juice, gelatin, sugar,
eggshells and egg whites in a saucepan.
Heat slowly, stirring, until mixture boils
up. Remove from heat and stir in cognac,
salt and pepper.
   2 Strain the mixture through a sieve
lined with cheesecloth that has been
rinsed in cold water and wrung out.

QUICK ASPIC FOR FISH

ABOUT 2 CUPS

1½ cups fish stock or clam broth
½ cup tomato juice
2 envelopes (2 tablespoons) unflavored gelatin
¼ teaspoon salt
⅛ teaspoon freshly ground pepper
1 teaspoon sugar
1 egg white, lightly beaten
1 eggshell, crushed
2 tablespoons chopped parsley

1 Combine the stock, tomato juice, gelatin, salt, pepper, sugar, egg white and eggshell in a saucepan. Heat the mixture slowly, stirring constantly, until it boils up in the pan.

2 Strain the mixture through a sieve lined with cheesecloth that has been rinsed in cold water and wrung out. Pour into a shallow dish (8 × 8 inches) and chill.

3 When aspic is set, turn out onto a chopping board, add the parsley and chop the aspic fine.

QUICK ASPIC FOR BEEF

ABOUT 2 CUPS

2 cups beef stock
2 envelopes (2 tablespoons) unflavored gelatin
2 eggshells
2 egg whites
2 tablespoons cognac

1 Combine the stock, gelatin, eggshells and egg whites in a saucepan and bring to a boil, stirring constantly. When the boiling point is reached, remove from the heat.

2 Line a colander or sieve with cheesecloth that has been rinsed in cold water and wrung out.

3 Strain the liquid through the cloth and add the cognac. Let stand at room temperature until ready to use. If the mixture gels before it is used, it may be reheated over low heat.

12

Relishes, Pickles and Preserves

Relishes

Relish *is one of the most apt food words in the* *language. Relishes offer a fine contrast in fla-* *vors when served with savory dishes.*

♦

CABBAGE–GREEN TOMATO RELISH

ABOUT 4 PINTS

8 cups chopped green tomatoes
8 cups (1 large head) chopped cabbage
2 cups chopped onions
½ cup chopped sweet red pepper
2 tablespoons salt
½ teaspoon allspice
1 teaspoon celery seed
1 tablespoon mustard seed
⅓ cup firmly packed brown sugar
2 cups cider vinegar

1 Arrange the tomatoes, cabbage, onions and red pepper in layers in a large
saucepan, sprinkling each layer with salt.
Let stand overnight. Drain.

2 Add the allspice, celery seed, mustard seed, sugar and vinegar. Boil uncovered, stirring occasionally, until there is
just enough liquid left to moisten the ingredients well, or 25 minutes. Pack into
hot sterile jars, filling the jars to the top.
Seal.

SPICED CABBAGE

ABOUT 4 PINTS

16 cups (2 large heads) shredded cabbage
½ cup coarse salt
Cider vinegar
½ to 2 cups sugar, depending on
    sweetness desired
1 tablespoon white mustard seed
1 tablespoon prepared horseradish
1 teaspoon whole cloves
4 (3-inch-long) cinnamon sticks, broken

1 Place the cabbage in a stone crock or
enamel pan in layers with the salt. Let
stand overnight.

2 Press out all the juice and, if desired,
rinse the cabbage in cold water to reduce
the salt. Drain and measure.

3 In a saucepan, heat to simmering half
as much vinegar as there is cabbage. Add
the sugar, mustard seed and horseradish.
Tie the cloves and cinnamon in cheesecloth and add. Cook, stirring, until the
sugar is dissolved. Continue simmering 15
minutes. Discard spice bag.

4 Pack the cabbage loosely in hot clean
jars and fill to within ½ inch of the top of
the jar with the hot spiced vinegar. Seal
and process in boiling water (see below)
20 minutes.

Note: If desired, ¼ cup mixed pickling
spice may be substituted for the spices in
the recipe.

Boiling Water Bath: Adjust covers as manufacturer directs and place filled jars on a
rack in a kettle containing boiling water.
Add boiling water if needed to bring water
1 to 2 inches over the tops of the containers; do not pour boiling water directly on
top of glass jars. Cover the kettle. When
water returns to a rolling boil, begin to
count processing time. Boil gently and

steadily for the processing time recommended for the food you are canning. Add boiling water if necessary to keep containers covered during processing. Remove the jars from the kettle immediately when processing time is up and seal at once as manufacturer directs.

◆

BEET-CABBAGE RELISH

5 PINTS

1 cup chopped onions
4 cups shredded cooked beets
4 cups (1 small head) shredded cabbage
1 cup grated horseradish
4 teaspoons salt
1¾ cups vinegar
¾ cup sugar

1 Combine in a saucepan the onions, beets, cabbage, horseradish and salt.

2 Heat the vinegar, dissolve the sugar in it and add to the vegetables. Boil 10 minutes. Pack in hot sterile jars and seal.

To Sterilize Jars: Place washed jars in a large kettle and cover with warm water. Cover the kettle and boil 15 to 20 minutes. When ready to use, remove with tongs and drain. The jars should be hot when hot mixture is poured in to prevent breakage.

OLD-FASHIONED FRESH CORN RELISH

ABOUT 3 PINTS

16 large ears fresh corn
4 cups (1 small head) finely chopped cabbage
1 cup diced celery
2 cups diced green peppers
1½ cups chopped onions
1 garlic clove, minced
¾ cup sugar
¼ cup lemon juice
¾ cup water
1¼ cups cider vinegar
5 teaspoons salt
1 teaspoon celery seed
1½ tablespoons dry mustard
1 teaspoon turmeric
¼ teaspoon cayenne
¾ cup chopped pimiento

1 Cook the corn on the cob in boiling salted water to cover 2 to 3 minutes, using 1 teaspoon salt to 1 quart water. Cool the corn and cut from the cob.

2 Mix the corn with the cabbage, celery, green peppers, onions and garlic. Set aside while preparing the vinegar and spice mixture.

3 Combine the sugar, lemon juice, water, vinegar, salt and spices in a 5-quart kettle. Bring to a boil. Add the vegetables and cook 25 minutes, stirring frequently. Stir in the pimiento and heat.

4 Pack into hot sterile jars and seal at once. Keep 4 to 5 weeks before using.

CORN AND TOMATO RELISH

ABOUT 4 PINTS

12 large ears fresh corn, cut from the cob
4 cups chopped, peeled onions
4 cups chopped, peeled and seeded
   ripe tomatoes
4 cups chopped, peeled and seeded cucumbers
3 green peppers, seeded and chopped
3 sweet red peppers, seeded and chopped
6 small hot red peppers, seeded and chopped
1 bunch celery, trimmed of leaves and tough
   outer stalks and minced
2 tablespoons turmeric
4 cups vinegar
2 tablespoons mustard seed
1 cup sugar
1/3 cup salt

1 Combine all the vegetables in a large heavy saucepan.

2 Blend the turmeric with a little of the vinegar and add the mustard seed.

3 Dissolve the sugar and salt in the remaining vinegar. Add the vinegar and seasonings to the vegetables, bring to a boil and simmer, uncovered, 1 hour.

4 Pour into hot sterile jars and seal at once. Keep 4 or 5 weeks before using.

OHIO CORN RELISH

ABOUT 1½ PINTS

1 large cucumber, peeled, seeded and quartered
3 medium onions, peeled and quartered
1 green pepper, seeded and quartered
3 cups (about 12 ears) sweet corn,
   cut from the cob
2 medium tomatoes, peeled and seeded
1 cup sugar
1 cup cider vinegar
½ cup water
2 tablespoons salt
1½ teaspoons mustard seed
½ teaspoon freshly ground pepper
½ teaspoon turmeric

1 Put the cucumber, onions and green pepper through a food grinder, using a medium blade, or chop in a food processor. Combine with the corn and tomatoes in a large kettle.

2 Add the remaining ingredients, mix and bring to a boil. Stir almost constantly with a wooden spoon until the sugar dissolves. Cover and cook slowly over medium heat 45 minutes.

3 Pour into hot sterile jars and seal at once. Keep 4 to 5 weeks before using.

CELERY RELISH

5 PINTS

2 green peppers
2 sweet red peppers
1 pound (6 medium) onions
3 tablespoons salt
1¼ cups sugar
3 tablespoons mustard seed
½ teaspoon turmeric
⅔ cup light corn syrup
1⅔ cups distilled white vinegar
⅔ cup water
8 cups (5 medium bunches) sliced celery

1 Chop peppers and onions.
2 Combine salt, sugar, mustard seed and turmeric. Blend in the corn syrup, vinegar and water, cover and heat to boiling. Add vegetables, including celery. Simmer, covered, 3 minutes.
3 Pack into hot sterile jars, filling to within ⅛ inch of the top of the jar and making sure that the liquid covers the vegetables. Seal at once.

HENRY CREEL'S PEPPER HASH

4 PINTS

1 dozen medium sweet red peppers
1 dozen medium sweet green peppers
2 medium onions
4 cups boiling water
2 cups cider vinegar
2 cups sugar
½ teaspoon salt

1 Wash the red and green peppers, cut out the stems and remove the seeds. Put through a food chopper, using the coarse blade. Or coarsely chop in a food processor. There should be 7 cups of each.
2 Peel the onions and coarsely chop them.
3 Add the onions to the peppers. Add boiling water to cover and let stand 10 minutes. Drain in a bag overnight or 8 hours. Discard the liquid.
4 Add the vinegar, sugar and salt. Bring to the boiling point and boil 20 minutes. Pour into hot sterile jars and seal at once.

COOKED CRANBERRY-ORANGE RELISH

ABOUT 12 SERVINGS

1 pound cranberries, picked over and washed
2 cups sugar
½ cup water
½ cup orange juice
2 teaspoons grated orange rind
½ cup blanched almonds, slivered

1 Combine all the ingredients except the almonds in a saucepan and cook until the cranberries pop open, about 10 minutes.

2 Skim the foam from the surface and cool. Stir in the almonds just before serving.

♦

GINGERED CRANBERRY SAUCE

2 PINTS

4 cups cranberries, picked over and washed
1 cup water
2 cups sugar
Dash of salt
⅓ cup candied or preserved ginger, diced

1 Place the cranberries in a saucepan containing the water. Cover and bring to a boil. Cook for 6 to 8 minutes, until skins burst.

2 Remove the cranberry mixture from the heat and stir in the sugar, salt and ginger. Mix thoroughly. Cool and chill. Serve with poultry, pork, ham or veal.

CRANBERRY-ORANGE RELISH WITH RAISINS AND APPLES

This is an exceptionally tasty cranberry chutney or relish made with orange and ginger and given greater texture and flavor with the addition of raisins, apples and almonds.

6 CUPS

1 cup dark or golden raisins
2 cups sugar
2 tablespoons white vinegar
2 tablespoons shredded fresh ginger
2 tablespoons slivered orange zest
1 cup orange juice
6 cups (about 1½ pounds) cranberries, picked over and washed
1½ cups diced, peeled tart green apples
1 cup (about 5 ounces) slivered almonds, toasted

1 Put the raisins in a small bowl and pour boiling water over them to cover. Let stand 15 minutes or longer. Drain.

2 Meanwhile, put the sugar and vinegar in a heavy saucepan and cook over low heat, stirring constantly, until the syrup takes on a light, golden-brown color. Do not burn. Remove from the heat.

3 Add the ginger, orange zest and orange juice and bring to a boil, stirring constantly.

4 Add the cranberries and cook, stirring often, until the berries just begin to pop, about 5 minutes. Add the raisins, diced apples and almond slivers. Let cool.

CRANBERRY-APPLE SAUCE

2 PINTS

1 pound cranberries, picked over and washed
2 cups sugar
2 apples, peeled, cored and diced
½ teaspoon cinnamon
⅛ teaspoon allspice
⅛ teaspoon ground cloves

1 Place cranberries in a 2-quart saucepan. Add the sugar and apples.
2 Cover and place over medium heat. When the cover is hot to the touch, reduce the heat to low and cook for 12 minutes. Stir in the spices. Serve with pork, chicken or turkey.

♦

UNCOOKED TOMATO RELISH

4 PINTS

8 cups chopped, peeled and seeded tomatoes
1 cup chopped celery
1 cup mild cider vinegar
¾ cup chopped onions
½ cup chopped green pepper
3 tablespoons sugar
1 tablespoon mustard seed
2 teaspoons salt
¼ teaspoon grated nutmeg
¼ teaspoon cinnamon
¼ teaspoon ground cloves

Mix all the ingredients together thoroughly. Pour into sterile jars, cover and refrigerate. Use within 2 or 3 weeks.

ONION RELISH

ABOUT 6 SERVINGS

24 small white onions
⅓ cup olive oil
⅓ cup wine vinegar
1⅓ cups water
1 garlic clove, chopped
½ teaspoon salt
½ teaspoon dry mustard
½ teaspoon mustard seed
½ teaspoon freshly ground pepper
1 clove
1 teaspoon sugar
⅓ cup light raisins
Minced parsley or dill

1 Boil the unpeeled onions 5 minutes, drain and rub off the skins. Add the oil, vinegar, water, seasonings and sugar and simmer until the onions are just tender. Add the raisins and simmer 3 minutes longer. Chill.
2 Sprinkle generously with parsley or dill.

MANGO CHUTNEY

ABOUT 3 CUPS

1 or 2 not-too-ripe mangoes, or 3 or 4 tart,
  firm apples
½ cup coarsely chopped onions
1 teaspoon minced garlic
1 cup brown sugar
¼ cup lime juice
½ cup malt vinegar
Peel from ½ grapefruit, cut into ½-inch cubes
Peel from ½ orange, cut into ½-inch cubes
½ lemon, seeded and cut into ¼-inch cubes
1 cup dark raisins
¾ cup chopped pineapple
¼ cup pitted dates, prunes or chopped
  black figs
¾ teaspoon grated nutmeg
¾ teaspoon allspice
¾ teaspoon ground cloves
¾ teaspoon ground ginger
¼ teaspoon freshly ground pepper
¼ teaspoon hot red pepper flakes

1 Peel the mangoes or apples. Cut the flesh into ½-inch cubes. There should be 2 cups.

2 In a saucepan, combine the mangoes, onions, garlic, brown sugar, lime juice and vinegar. Bring to the boil and simmer for 10 minutes.

3 Add the grapefruit and orange peel, cubed lemon, raisins, pineapple, dates and all the spices. Bring to the boil and cook for 20 minutes.

4 Spoon the chutney into jars and seal. It will keep for an indefinite period in the refrigerator.

SWEET MIXED RELISH

ABOUT 6 PINTS

1 medium cabbage
7 green tomatoes
3 celery stalks
2 sweet red peppers
3 green peppers
1 tablespoon mustard seed
1 tablespoon celery seed
1 tablespoon salt
2 cups sugar, or more
1 quart mild cider vinegar

1 Put the cabbage, tomatoes, celery and red and green peppers through a food grinder, using the medium knife. Combine the vegetables in a large saucepan with the mustard seed, celery seed and salt. Add the 2 cups sugar, or more if a sweeter relish is desired, and the vinegar.

2 Cook slowly for about 2 hours, stirring occasionally. Pack into hot sterile jars and seal.

EGGPLANT RELISH

7 PINTS

2 (1-pound) eggplants
Olive or cooking oil
12 tomatoes, diced (there should be 12 cups)
1 (7-ounce) jar pitted green olives
1 cup sliced blanched almonds or pine nuts
1½ cups seedless raisins
½ cup drained capers
4 cups of 1-inch pieces of celery
1 tablespoon salt
1 teaspoon freshly ground pepper
½ cup sugar
1 cup wine vinegar

1 If eggplant is young and tender, do not peel. If not, peel. Cut into ½-inch cubes. Fry in hot oil 1 inch deep. Drain on paper toweling. Set aside.

2 Cook the tomatoes for 10 minutes, or until soft. Force through a sieve. Cut the olives into quarters. Combine tomatoes, olives, nuts, raisins, capers, celery, salt and pepper. Cook, uncovered, for 20 minutes, until celery is tender, stirring frequently.

3 Add sugar and vinegar. Cook for 5 minutes. Add the eggplant. Heat only until eggplant is hot.

4 Ladle into hot sterilized jars. Seal at once. Serve cold as a relish and sandwich filling or serve hot as a vegetable.

CUCUMBER YOGURT RELISH

ABOUT 3 CUPS

2 small cucumbers
½ teaspoon salt
2 tablespoons vinegar
¼ cup chopped scallions
2 cups yogurt

1 Score the skin of the cucumbers lengthwise with a fork. Cut the cucumbers into halves, discard the seeds and finely chop the cucumbers.

2 Sprinkle the chopped cucumbers with the salt and vinegar and let the mixture stand for 20 minutes. Drain, if necessary. Add the cucumbers and scallions to the yogurt. Serve with curries or spicy dishes.

EGGPLANT CHUTNEY

ABOUT 1½ CUPS

1 (1-pound) eggplant
2 teaspoons lemon juice
1 teaspoon olive or peanut oil
½ teaspoon salt

1 Place the unpeeled, untrimmed eggplant on the center of a gas burner. Using a very low flame, turn the eggplant every 2 or 3 minutes until the eggplant skin is slightly charred all over. Continue to cook on the flame about 10 minutes longer, or until the eggplant is thoroughly soft throughout.

2 Cover the flame with foil and place the eggplant on top. Continue cooking about 5 minutes.

3 Let the eggplant cool. Pull off and discard the skin. Place the pulp in a mixing bowl and add the remaining ingredients. Stir to blend and chill several hours.

OLIVE-VEGETABLE RELISH

ABOUT 2 PINTS

¼ cup wine vinegar
¾ cup vegetable or olive oil
1 tablespoon sugar
1 garlic clove, slivered
¼ teaspoon freshly ground pepper
½ teaspoon paprika
¾ cup pimiento-stuffed olives
¾ cup diced cauliflower
½ cup chopped celery
½ cup diced carrots
½ cup diced white turnips
½ cup small white onions
½ cup diced green pepper
½ cup diced summer squash
¼ cup chopped canned pimientos
1 tablespoon capers

1 Combine the vinegar, oil, sugar, garlic, pepper and paprika in a jar or bottle. Shake well to blend thoroughly.

2 Place the remaining ingredients in a mixing bowl. Pour the liquid mixture over them and mix well. Chill for at least 48 hours.

ATJAR KETIMUN
SWEET-AND-SOUR RELISH

8 SERVINGS

2 cucumbers, peeled, seeded and cut into
    1-inch slices
Salt
½ cup vinegar
3 tablespoons sugar
¼ cup water

1 Sprinkle the cucumbers lightly with salt and let stand for 20 minutes. Drain.

2 Heat the vinegar, sugar and water and boil for 2 minutes. Remove from heat and cool.

3 Add the cucumbers and let the mixture stand for several hours before serving.

Note: Halved red and white radishes and sliced bamboo shoots may be substituted for the cucumbers.

◆

HOT MUSTARD SAUCE

¼ CUP

Combine ¼ cup dry mustard with enough water to make a paste. Let the mixture stand for 10 minutes to develop flavor. Serve with Chinese dishes.

GRAPE AND GREEN TOMATO CHUTNEY

2 PINTS

2 pounds green tomatoes, sliced
4 tart apppples
⅔ cup chopped onions
2¾ cups dark brown sugar
2 cups cider vinegar
1 cup seedless raisins
½ teaspoon salt
½ teaspoon hot red pepper flakes
1 tablespoon mustard seed
1 teaspoon dry mustard
1 teaspoon finely choped fresh ginger
3 cups Thompson seedless grapes

1 Put the tomato slices in a 5-quart saucepan. Peel and dice the apples and add them to the tomatoes. Add the onions, sugar, vinegar, raisins and salt. Mix well. Cook over medium heat for about 30 minutes.

2 Add the red pepper flakes, mustard seed, dry mustard, ginger and grapes to the hot mixture. Cook for about 30 minutes longer, or until mixture is thickened.

3 Pack chutney into hot sterilized jars, preferably 1-cup size. Seal at once.

SAUCE PIQUANTE

ABOUT ½ CUP

3 tablespoons hot red pepper flakes
½ teaspoon cayenne
¼ cup olive oil
1 teaspoon paprika
3 or 4 saffron shreds

Crush the red pepper flakes with a mortar and pestle. Add the cayenne and enough boiling water to make a paste. Stir in the remaining ingredients and let stand until ready to use.

♦

SPICY TOMATO CATSUP

ABOUT 8 PINTS

12 pounds ripe tomatoes
1 cup chopped onions
1½ cups vinegar
1 cup sugar
½ teaspoon salt
1 tablespoon whole cloves
1 teaspoon black pepper
1 teaspoon mustard seed
½ teaspoon celery seed
¼ teaspoon cayenne
1 (3-inch-long) cinnamon stick, broken

1 Core and chop the tomatoes. Cook together tomatoes and onions until soft and press mixture through a fine sieve.

2 Return purée to heat and cook until reduced by half, stirring occasionally. Add remaining ingredients including spices tied in a bag. Continue cooking, uncovered, to desired consistency, about 4 hours. Discard spice bag. Seal in hot sterilized jars.

Pickled Vegetables and Fruits

PICKLED BEETS

ABOUT 3 PINTS

2 pounds beets
1½ cups cider vinegar
1½ tablespoons dry mustard
½ teaspoon salt
1¼ cups sugar
2 medium onions, sliced (optional)
2 teaspoon celery seed

1 Cook the beets in water to cover until tender. Drain, reserving 1 cup of the cooking water. Slip off the skins and slice.

2 Heat the vinegar and reserved cooking water to a boil. Mix the mustard, salt and sugar. Add to the vinegar and let boil again.

3 Arrange the beets and onions in layers in clean canning jars. Add the celery seed and cover with the hot vinegar mixture. Seal, cool and store in refrigerator. Let stand a few days before using. They will keep for weeks in the refrigerator.

SPICED PICKLED CANTALOUPE

2½ PINTS

¼ cup salt
8 cups cantaloupe meat, cut into
    1-inch squares
4 cups sugar
1 cup vinegar
2 or 3 (3-inch-long) cinnamon sticks
1½ tablespoons allspice berries
1½ tablespoons whole cloves
3 cups boiling water

1 Combine 1 quart cold water and the salt and stir to dissolve. Pour over the cantaloupe, cover and let stand 3 hours. Drain.

2 Add the sugar, vinegar and spices to the boiling water in a large enamel or stainless-steel pot. Bring to a boil, stirring until the sugar has dissolved. Add the drained cantaloupe meat and bring to a boil. Boil 10 minutes, cool, cover and let stand overnight.

3 Drain the syrup from the cantaloupe. Bring the syrup to a boil and boil 10 minutes. Add the cantaloupe and bring to a boil again. Reduce the heat and simmer gently for 45 minutes, or until the cantaloupe is clear and transparent. Pour immediately into hot sterile jars and seal at once.

PICKLED CARROTS

ABOUT 2 PINTS

4 cups small carrots of uniform size
3 cups white vinegar
½ cup water
1 cup sugar
3 tablespoons mixed pickling spice, tied in
    cheesecloth

1 Cook the carrots in water to cover until the skins slip off easily and the carrots are half done. Peel.

2 Boil together 10 minutes the vinegar, water, sugar and spices. Remove the spice bag.

3 Add the carrots and boil 2 to 4 minutes, or until almost tender. Pack in hot sterile jars and pour the syrup over them. Seal.

Variation

PICKLED SHOESTRING CARROTS
FOR COCKTAILS

Cut carrots after parboiling into uniform strips. Follow the above directions but do not boil the sticks in syrup; merely bring them to the boiling point, pack and seal.

SWEET CUCUMBER AND GREEN TOMATO PICKLE

7 HALF-PINT JARS

4 cups thinly sliced unpeeled cucumbers
4 cups thinly sliced green tomatoes
2 cups thinly sliced white onions
¼ cup salt
1 cup sugar
2 cups cider vinegar
1 tablespoon mustard seed
½ teaspoon celery seed
5 or 6 peppercorns
½ teaspoon turmeric

1 Arrange alternate layers of cucumbers, green tomatoes, onions and salt in a bowl. Let stand 6 to 8 hours, or overnight. Drain.

2 Combine the remaining ingredients in a 4-quart kettle and bring to a boil. Add the cucumbers, tomatoes and onions and boil until the vegetables are clear, 5 to 10 minutes.

3 Pack in hot sterile jars and seal at once.

CAULIFLOWER PICKLE

APPROXIMATELY 7 PINTS

2 large heads (approximately 4 pounds trimmed) cauliflower
1 pound (about 12) medium onions
¼ cup salt
¾ cup sugar
1 teaspoon turmeric
2 teaspoons mustard seed
1 teaspoon celery seed
1 small dried hot red pepper
½ teaspoon whole cloves
1½ cups white vinegar
1½ cups water

1 Wash the cauliflower and break into flowerets. Scald the onions, peel and slice. Mix with the cauliflower and salt and let stand overnight. Drain and rinse in cold water. If too salty; soak 1 hour in cold water and drain.

2 Combine the sugar, turmeric, mustard seed, celery seed and red pepper in an 8-quart kettle. Tie the cloves in a cheesecloth and add. Stir in the vinegar and water and boil 5 minutes.

3 Add the cauliflower and onions and boil until tender but still crisp, or 5 to 10 minutes. Remove and discard cheesecloth bag and red pepper. Pack at once into hot sterile jars with the boiling liquid. Seal at once.

PICKLED RED CABBAGE

This is an excellent quickly aged red cabbage. It is the creation of Len Allison, chef-owner of Manhattan's well-known Hubert's restaurant. It is spiced with juniper berries, allspice and bay leaf. Honey or sugar may be added to give it balance.

4 OR MORE SERVINGS

1¼ cups finely shredded, cored red cabbage
½ cup dry white wine
½ cup white vinegar
¼ cup sugar
⅛ teaspoon allspice
3 juniper berries
1 small bay leaf
Honey or sugar to taste (optional)
Lemon juice to taste (optional)

1 Bring enough water to the boil to cover the cabbage when it is added. Add the cabbage and let stand 30 seconds. Drain and put the cabbage in a glass bowl or jar.

2 Bring the wine, vinegar, sugar, allspice, juniper berries and bay leaf to the boil. If desired, add honey or sugar and lemon juice. Pour this over the cabbage. Let stand uncovered until cool. Chill overnight or longer. This pickle, properly refrigerated, will keep a week or longer.

QUICK DILL PICKLES

2 QUARTS

14 to 16 (3½-inch-long) cucumbers
2 tablespoons vinegar
4 garlic cloves, peeled
1 teaspoon whole mixed pickling spice
½ teaspoon mustard seed or celery seed
4 bay leaves
2 small bunches dill
2 grape leaves (optional)
1 quart water
½ cup coarse salt

1 Wash the cucumbers and drain. Pack in upright position in 2 sterile 1-quart jars. Add half the vinegar, garlic, pickling spice, mustard seed, bay leaves, dill and grape leaves to each jar.

2 Bring the water and salt to a boil and pour over the cucumbers, filling the jars to within ½ inch of the top. Seal at once. Let stand in refrigerator at least 1 week before using and use within 2 to 3 weeks.

PICKLED ONIONS

ABOUT 4 PINTS

3 pounds small white onions
½ cup salt
1 or more red chili peppers, seeded
    and quartered
½ teaspoon peppercorns
4 slices of fresh ginger
¼ to 1½ cups sugar (amount depends on
    whether cocktail onions or sweet onions
    are desired)
3 pints white vinegar

1 Place the unpeeled onions in boiling water to cover and let stand 2 minutes. Drain, cover with cold water and peel.

2 Dissolve the salt in 1 quart water in an enamel, steel or earthenware container. Add the onions and enough additional water to cover. Let stand overnight. Rinse in cold water and drain.

3 Heat to boiling enough water to cover the onions. Add the onions and cook 1 minute. Drain and arrange in hot clean jars in layers with peppers, peppercorns and ginger.

4 Bring the sugar and vinegar to a boil and pour over the onions to within ½ inch of the top of the jar. Seal.

PICKLED SWEET RED PEPPERS

3 PINTS

12 sweet red peppers
1 quart distilled white vinegar
2 cups sugar

1 Wash and seed the peppers and cut them into ½-inch strips

2 Boil the vinegar and sugar together 5 minutes.

3 While the vinegar-sugar mixture is boiling, pack the peppers into hot clean jars. Cover with the vinegar solution, filling to within ½ inch of the top of the jar. Adjust lids and process in boiling water bath (page 592) 10 minutes.

◆

MUSHROOM AND CELERY PICKLES

3 CUPS

1 pound small fresh mushrooms
2 teaspoons salt
1 cup sliced celery
⅔ cup olive or other salad oil
1 garlic clove, split
2 tablespoons lemon juice
2 tablespoons sliced pimiento-stuffed olives
2 tablespoons sliced ripe olives
1 tablespoon chopped fresh parsley
1 tablespoon capers
1 tablespoon wine vinegar

1 Wash the mushrooms and leave them whole. Cook them in 1 inch of boiling water containing 1 teaspoon of the salt for 10 minutes.

2 Drain the mushrooms. Add remaining ingredients and toss lightly. Refrigerate for several hours, overnight or for several days before serving. Use as a relish or as one of the dishes for antipasto or hors d'oeuvre.

♦

WATERMELON PICKLES

ABOUT 6 PINTS

Watermelon rind
Limewater, made with 2 quarts cold water and
  1 tablespoon lime (calcium oxide purchased
  in a drugstore)
2 tablespoons allspice
2 tablespoon whole cloves
10 (2-inch-long) cinnamon sticks
1 quart vinegar
4 pounds (9 cups) sugar

1 Select thick rind from a firm, not overripe, melon. Trim off the green skin and pink flesh. Cut into 2-inch cubes enough trimmed rind to measure 12 cups.

2 Soak for 1 hour in the limewater. Drain, cover with fresh water and boil until fork tender, 10 minutes or longer. Drain.

3 Tie the spices in cheesecloth, add the vinegar, 1 quart fresh water and sugar and bring to a boil. Add the watermelon rind and boil gently, uncovered, until clear. Add more water if the syrup becomes too thick. Remove the spice bag.

4 Pack the rind in hot sterile jars and fill almost to the top with syrup. Tightly seal the jars.

PICKLED MUSHROOMS

2 TO 3 CUPS

1 pound small fresh mushrooms
¾ cup olive oil
¼ cup tarragon vinegar
¼ cup finely chopped parsley
1 teaspoon chervil
1 garlic clove, minced
Salt and coarsely cracked pepper

1 Trim away the mushroom stems and use them for another purpose. Drop the mushroom caps into boiling salted water and simmer, covered, for exactly 45 seconds. Drain immediately. Put the mushrooms in a glass jar.

2 Combine the remaining ingredients and blend well with a fork. Pour the marinade over the hot mushrooms, cover and let stand in the refrigerator for 2 days. Use as a relish or as one of the dishes for antipasto or hors d'oeuvre.

Preserves and Conserves

KUMQUAT PRESERVES

3 PINTS

2 pounds kumquats
2 tablespoons baking soda
2 cups corn syrup
2 cups sugar
3½ cups water

1 Remove the stems and leaves from the kumquats. Wash well and drain. Place in a deep kettle, sprinkle with baking soda, cover with boiling water and let stand until cool.

2 Wash 3 times in fresh water, using a vegetable brush to remove the oil. Drain. Cut crosses ¼ inch deep in the stem and blossom ends. Drop 1 at a time into rapidly boiling water to cover. Cook until tender, about 10 minutes.

3 Prepare a syrup by boiling together the corn syrup, sugar and water for 10 minutes. Add the drained kumquats. Boil slowly, stirring occasionally, until the fruit is partly transparent and the syrup thickens (226°F on a candy thermometer), 20 to 30 minutes. Remove from the heat and cover. Let stand overnight.

4 Reheat to boiling and pack the kumquats into hot sterile jars. Bring the syrup again to a boil and pour it over the fruit to within ½ inch of the top. Seal immediately.

BEET PRESERVES

ABOUT 3 PINTS

2 pounds beets
4 cups sugar
1 tablespoon ground ginger
1 cup coarsely chopped or slivered almonds
3 lemons, quartered and sliced

1 Cook the beets until tender in just enough water to cover. Drain, peel and dice.

2 Combine the beets with the sugar, ginger and almonds in a deep kettle. Cook over very low heat about 30 minutes.

3 Add lemons and continue cooking 30 minutes longer. Turn into a sterile crock or jelly glasses.

♦

LEMON PRESERVES

ABOUT 5 HALF-PINTS

4 lemons
1 orange
Sugar

1 Remove the peel from the lemons and orange. Cut the peel into paper-thin julienne strips and combine with the sliced or chopped fruit. Discard seeds.

2 Add 1 cup water for each cup of pulp and peel. Let stand overnight.

3 Boil the mixture until the peel is tender. Cool.

4 Add 1 cup sugar for each cup of fruit and juice. Cook until the syrup gives a jelly test—2 drops form on the edge of a metal spoon and drop off simultaneously. Stir occasionally. Pour into hot sterile half-pint jars. Seal at once.

PRESERVED ORANGE SLICES

6 large thin-skinned oranges
2 cups sugar
2 cups water
⅓ cup lemon juice
¼ cup cognac (optional)

1 Wash the oranges and cut into ½-inch slices. Cover with boiling water and cook until tender, or about 1 hour. Drain, discarding the water.

2 Boil together the sugar and 2 cups water 5 minutes, stirring until the sugar is dissolved. Add the lemon juice and orange slices and simmer until the orange rind is tender and translucent, or about 1 hour. Add water as necessary.

3 Place the orange slices in hot sterile jars. Cover with the boiling syrup, add the cognac and seal.

SPICED ORANGE WEDGES

4 oranges, unpeeled
½ teaspoon baking soda
2 cups sugar
1¼ cups water
½ cup vinegar
12 cloves
3 (2-inch-long) cinnamon sticks

1 Cover the oranges with water. Add the baking soda and bring to a boil. Boil 20 minutes, or until easily pierced with a fork. Drain and cut into 8 wedges.

2 Combine the sugar with the water, the vinegar, cloves and cinnamon. Stir over low heat until the sugar has dissolved. Boil 5 minutes.

3 Add the orange wedges and simmer about 20 minutes. Cool, cover and refrigerate. Serve with fresh or smoked pork or duck.

PICKLED SECKEL PEARS

ABOUT 4 QUARTS

8 pounds Seckel pears
10 (2-inch-long) cinnamon sticks
2 tablespoons whole cloves
2 tablespoons allspice berries
4 pounds (9 cups) sugar
1 quart cider vinegar
2 cups water

1 Wash the pears, remove the blossom ends only and prick the skins; or peel if desired.

2 Boil the pears 10 minutes in water to cover; drain.

3 Tie the spices in cheesecloth. Combine the sugar and vinegar with the water, add the spices and boil 5 minutes. Add the pears, cover and cook 10 minutes longer, or until the pears are tender. Let stand overnight.

4 Remove the spice bag and reheat to boiling. Pack the pears in hot sterile jars. Return syrup to a boil and pour it over the pears, filling the jars to the top. Seal.

SPICED QUINCES

ABOUT 2 PINTS

2 pounds quinces
2 cups white or cider vinegar
1 cup water
3 cups sugar
2 (3-inch-long) cinnamon sticks
1 tablespoon whole cloves
Few pieces of fresh ginger

1 Peel and core the quinces. Cut them into slices, cover with boiling water and cook until almost tender when pierced with a knife. Drain.

2 Boil for 5 minutes the vinegar, water, sugar, cinnamon, cloves and ginger, stirring until the sugar is dissolved.

3 Add the quinces and cook until clear and tender.

4 Fill hot sterile jars with the quinces and cover almost to the top of the jars with boiling syrup. Seal immediately.

Variation

SPICED PEARS

Substitute hard pears for quinces. If a softer variety of pear—such as underripe Bartletts—is used, omit cooking in water and add the fruit directly to the syrup.

CRANBERRY FRUIT CONSERVE

ABOUT 4 (8-OUNCE) GLASSES

1 pound (4 cups) cranberries, picked over
   and washed
1½ cups water
1½ cups sugar
1 cup seeded raisins, chopped
1 apple, peeled, cored and chopped
Grated rind and juice of 1 orange
Grated rind and juice of 1 lemon
1 cup chopped walnuts

1 Cook the cranberries in the water until all the skins pop open. Add the sugar, raisins, apple, orange and lemon rind and juice. Boil together 15 minutes.

2 Remove from the heat and add the walnuts. Pack in hot sterile jars and seal with melted paraffin.

GRAPE CONSERVE

ABOUT 4 PINTS

4 pounds Concord grapes, washed
   and stemmed
1 orange
4 cups sugar
1 cup seedless raisins
½ teaspoon salt
1 cup chopped walnuts

1 Skin the grapes, reserving the skins. Boil the pulp 10 minutes, stirring often. Press through a sieve to remove the seeds.

2 Seed the orange and grind it coarsely. Add with the juice to the grape pulp. Add the sugar, raisins and salt.

3 Boil the mixture rapidly, stirring constantly, until thickened, or 10 minutes. Add the grape skins.

4 Boil 10 minutes longer. Add the nuts and reheat to boiling. Pack in sterile hot jars and seal.

Brandied tutti-frutti is an orchard in a crock. The time to start it is when the first perfect, firm-ripe fruit of summer comes on the market. As other fruits appear they are added to the crock and the end result is a fantastic dessert as is or a sauce for ice cream, puddings or cake.

Uses for Brandied Fruits: Use as a dessert or as a sauce for ice cream, cake or pudding. Or serve with crackers and cream cheese. In the South, brandied peaches are popular as an accompaniment to poultry and fresh and smoked hams. Use additional syrup to flavor puddings and sauces.

◆

◆

BRANDIED TUTTI-FRUTTI I

ABOUT 6 QUARTS

1 pound peaches
1 pound plums
1 pound pears
1 pound nectarines
3 pounds grapes (1 pound each green, red and blue)
7 pounds sugar

1 Wash perfect, firm-ripe fruit. Rub the fuzz off the peaches with a clean cloth. With a fork, prick all over the peaches, plums, pears and nectarines. Do not prick or seed the grapes.

2 In a stone crock of at least 8 quarts capacity, pack the fruits in layers with the sugar. Cover with the lid of the crock or wax paper and let stand in a cool place until syrup forms. Stir up the sugar in the bottom of the container every 3 days.

3 After a week, when the fruit floats in the syrup, press down with a plate and a nonmetal weight and cover with wax paper. Stir occasionally from the bottom until the sugar is dissolved.

4 Let the fruit stand until fermentation is complete, a month or so. Pack in sterile jars, seal and store in a cool place.

BRANDIED TUTTI-FRUTTI II

APPROXIMATELY 9 QUARTS

1 pint cognac
1 pint peeled, sliced pineapple
1 pint strawberries
1 pint cherries
1 pint raspberries
1 pound apricots
1 pound nectarines
1 pound peaches
1 pound grapes
Sugar

1 Pour the cognac into a stone crock of at least 2½-gallon capacity. Add the pineapple and an equal amount of sugar. Cover the crock tightly.

2 As each fruit comes into season, add it with an equal weight of sugar. Stir up the sugar from the bottom every 3 or 4 days to dissolve the sugar. If at any time fruits float in the syrup, weight down with a plate and nonmetal weight.

3 When the juice ceases to bubble after the last addition of fruit and sugar, transfer fruit and syrup to sterile jars and seal.

Note: The cognac is used at the beginning as a starter to help the fermentation. The crock must be kept in a cool dry place. All fruits should be added whole and unpeeled, unless otherwise stated. Apricots, nectarines and peaches should be pricked all over with a fork.

♦

BRANDIED PEACHES I

ABOUT 1 QUART

1 quart cling peaches
1 cup sugar
1 cup cognac

1 Rub fuzz from peaches, or peel if desired. Pack into a clean quart jar in layers with the sugar until the jar is about three-quarters full.

2 Add the cognac and seal. Turn the jar upside down every day for 4 or 5 days to distribute and dissolve the sugar. Let stand about 3 months before using.

♦

BRANDIED PEACHES II

Wash perfect peaches, ripe but not soft. Rub off the fuzz with a clean cloth. Do not peel. Prick each peach twice with a fork.

For each pound of peaches use 1 cup each water and sugar. Combine the water and sugar and heat slowly until the sugar is dissolved. Bring to a boil and boil 1 minute.

Add the peaches to the syrup and boil until the peaches are tender, 5 to 7 minutes.

Pack the peaches in hot sterile jars and fill three quarters full with the syrup. Finish filling with brandy. Seal and store in a cool place 1 month before using.

One pound of medium peaches fills a pint jar.

♦

SPICED APPLES

6 PINTS

5 pounds (15 medium) firm apples
6 cups sugar
2 cups white vinegar
4 cinnamon sticks, broken into 1-inch pieces
2 teaspoons whole cloves

1 Peel, quarter and core the apples.

2 Combine the sugar, vinegar, cinnamon and cloves and heat to boiling. Add the apples and boil gently, uncovered, until tender but not broken.

3 Pack into hot sterile jars, filling to within ¼ inch of the top and making sure the syrup covers the fruit. Seal immediately.

SWEET PICKLED CRAB APPLES

6 PINTS

7 pounds crab apples
1 quart distilled white vinegar
8 cups sugar
¼ cup whole cloves
1 (3-inch-long) cinnamon stick
1½ teaspoons ground ginger

1 Wash crab apples and remove blossom ends. Prick each apple several times with a fork.

2 Heat the vinegar and sugar to boiling, add spices tied in cheesecloth and crab apples. Boil gently until the crab apples are tender but not broken. Remove the spice bag.

3 Pack the boiling mixture into hot sterile jars, filling to within ¼ inch of the top of the jar and making sure that the syrup covers the fruit. Seal immediately, cool and store.

APPLE BUTTER

4 PINTS

3 quarts fresh sweet cider
8 pounds juicy ripe apples
2½ cups brown sugar, packed
2 teaspoons cinnamon
½ teaspoon allspice
½ teaspoon ground cloves
½ teaspoon salt

1 Boil the cider in a big stainless steel or enamel kettle until the amount is reduced one half, or about 30 minutes.

2 Meanwhile, quarter and core the apples but do not peel them. Add to the reduced cider and cook over low heat until the apples are tender. Stir almost constantly. When the apples are cooked, force the mixture through a sieve and return to the kettle.

3 Add the sugar, spices and salt and cook over low heat until the mixture thickens, or about ½ hour. If necessary use a Flame Tamer to ensure low heat. Stir almost constantly.

4 Pour at once into hot sterile jars and seal.

Note: To test apple butter for doneness, pour a little on a cold plate. When no rim of liquid separates around the edge of the butter, it is sufficiently thick.

CONCORD GRAPE BUTTER

6 OR 7 (6-OUNCE) GLASSES

2 pounds Concord grapes
1½ tablespoons grated orange rind
1 cup water
2¼ cups sugar
½ teaspoon cinnamon
¼ teaspoon ground cloves
⅛ teaspoon grated nutmeg

1 Wash the grapes, drain and pull from the stems. Squeeze the pulp from the skins into a kettle, reserving the skins.

2 Cook the pulp slowly until soft, or about 10 minutes. Put through a sieve to remove the seeds.

3 Return the pulp to the kettle, add the orange rind and water and cook 10 minutes, stirring frequently with a wooden spoon. Add the skins and heat to boiling. Add the sugar and spices and cook over low heat, stirring frequently, until thick (see test for apple butter, opposite page).

4 Pour into hot sterile jars and seal at once.

Note: If desired, the mixture may be puréed in a food processor and reheated to boiling before canning.

Marmalades and Jellies

ENGLISH MARMALADE

7 TO 8 CUPS

2 pounds Seville or bitter oranges
1 large lemon
9 cups cold water
8 cups sugar

1 Slice and seed the unpeeled oranges and lemon as thin as possible. Cover with the cold water and let stand 24 hours.

2 Bring to a boil, add the sugar and remove from the heat. Stir until the sugar has dissolved. Let stand 24 hours.

3 Bring the mixture to a boil again and simmer gently 2 hours. When the peel is transparent and soft, bring to a rapid boil and cook about 30 minutes, or until 2 drops form on the edge of a metal spoon and drop off simultaneously. For a stiffer marmalade, continue cooking until the drops run together as they fall off.

4 Skim the foam from the surface and pour the marmalade into hot sterile jars. Seal tight with jar tops or cover with a thin layer of melted paraffin. If paraffin is used, add a second layer after the first layer has cooled. Store in a cool dry place.

RIPE TOMATO MARMALADE

ABOUT 5 PINTS

3 quarts peeled, seeded and sliced tomatoes
6 cups sugar
1 teaspoon salt
2 oranges
2 lemons
2 cups water
4 (3-inch-long) cinnamon sticks
2 teaspoons whole cloves

1 Mix the tomatoes, sugar and salt in a large kettle and set aside.

2 Peel the oranges and lemons and slice the peel very thin. Boil the peel in the water for 5 minutes and drain. Add peel to the tomatoes

3 Slice the orange and lemon pulp, remove the seeds and add to the tomatoes.

4 Tie the cinnamon and cloves in cheesecloth and add to the tomatoes.

5 Heat the tomato mixture to a boil. Cook rapidly, stirring almost constantly, until thickened, 45 minutes or longer.

6 Remove the spice bag. Pour the marmalade into hot sterile jars and seal. Store in a cool, dry, dark place.

Variation

GREEN TOMATO MARMALADE

Follow the cooking and canning directions for ripe tomato marmalade, omitting the oranges and spices and adding 4 additional lemons.

APPLE-TOMATO MARMALADE

ABOUT 5 CUPS

1 quart peeled, seeded and quartered tomatoes
1 quart peeled and chopped apples
2 lemons, seeded and ground
3 pounds (6 cups) sugar
1 ounce fresh ginger
4 whole cloves

1 Chop the tomatoes and drain in a sieve.

2 Add the apples and lemons to the drained tomatoes and cook 15 minutes.

3 Add the sugar and add the ginger and cloves tied in cheesecloth. Cook, stirring, until the sugar is dissolved; continue to cook until the mixture has the consistency of thin marmalade, stirring frequently. Remove the spice bag.

4 Pour into hot sterile jars and seal.

LIME MARMALADE

11 OR 12 CUPS

3 cups thinly sliced limes
1 cup thinly sliced lemons
2 quarts water
5 pounds (11¼ cups) sugar

1 Place the prepared fruits and water in an 8- to 10-quart kettle. Cover and cook until tender, 15 minutes or longer.

2 Add the sugar, stir until dissolved and boil rapidly about 45 minutes, until 2 drops form on the edge of a metal spoon and drop off simultaneously. For a stiffer marmalade, continue cooking until the drops run together as they fall off.

3 Skim the foam from the surface of the marmalade and fill hot sterile jars. Seal tight with jar tops or cover with a thin layer of melted paraffin and, when cool, add another layer. Store in a cool dry place.

PINEAPPLE MARMALADE

6 OR 7 CUPS

3½ cups shredded or ground (about
*   2 medium) fresh pineapples*
3 thinly sliced lemons
1 quart water
4½ cups sugar

1 Place the prepared fruits and water in a 6-quart kettle and let stand overnight. Boil until the lemon is tender, about 20 minutes.

2 Add the sugar, stir until dissolved and boil rapidly about 25 minutes, until 2 drops form on the edge of a metal spoon and drop off simultaneously. For a stiffer marmalade, continue cooking until the drops run together as they fall off.

3 Skim the foam from the surface and pour the marmalade into hot sterile jars. Seal tight with jar tops or cover with a thin layer of melted paraffin and, when cool, add another layer. Store in a cool dry place.

APPLE JELLY

6 CUPS

Use sour red-skinned apples. Cut out stem and blossom ends but do not peel or core. Cut crosswise in ¼-inch slices and measure or weigh. (One pound measures about 3 cups.) Place apples in pot and add enough water barely to cover apples, not over 2 cups per pound of fruit. Cook gently until apples are tender.

Turn apples into a cotton flannel jelly bag or several thicknesses of cheesecloth in a sieve and let juice drip several hours or overnight into a bowl.

To make a batch of jelly, measure 6 cups of apple juice and 4 cups of sugar. In a 3- or 4-quart kettle bring the juice to a boil. Add sugar and cook, stirring, until sugar is dissolved. Boil rapidly until the jellying point has been reached, 220° to 222°F, or until 2 drops form on the edge of a metal spoon and then run together to form a sheet. Skim off foam. Pour immediately into hot sterile glasses, filling them to within ¼ inch of the top. Pour a thin layer of melted paraffin over the top and cool. Add a second thin layer of paraffin, cool, cover with lid or foil and store in a cool place.

Variations

APPLE–ROSE GERANIUM JELLY

Place 2 rose geranium leaves in each glass before filling with boiling jelly.

APPLE-MINT JELLY

Before pouring jelly into glasses add green food coloring and about ½ teaspoon mint extract.

APPLE-PEELING JELLY

Substitute apple peelings and cores for sliced apples and proceed as directed for sliced apples. Six cups of peelings and cores yield about 1½ cups jelly.

◆

CRANBERRY JELLY

1 CUP

2 cups cranberries, picked over and washed
½ cup water
¾ cup sugar

Cook the cranberries in the water in a covered saucepan until the skins pop. Press the berries through a sieve, add the sugar, and cook for 3 to 5 minutes. Chill until firm.

13

Breads

Yeast Breads and Rolls

KNEADING BREAD

The cook who bakes good bread—firm, flavorful, fragrant—knows how to knead. The motion is simple but tricky to describe. When the dough, forming a sort of ball in shape, has been turned out of the bowl onto a lightly floured board, it should be folded over toward the cook, then pressed down and away from the cook with the heel of the hand. The ball is turned a quarter circle, the motion repeated, and so on until the texture is smooth and elastic. The board may be sprinkled lightly with additional flour from time to time; but no more flour should be kneaded in than is necessary. The kneading process takes 8 to 10 minutes.

An electric mixer with a dough hook is a great convenience in bread making. The bread dough should be kneaded for about 5 minutes with the hook.

Almost any bread can be made in a food processor fitted with the metal blade. Once the ingredients are mixed, process the dough until it pulls away from the sides of the container. The dough is then completely kneaded.

DISSOLVING YEAST

Yeast must be dissolved in liquid to make it active. The liquid should be warm (110 to 115°F) to be most effective.

ALLOWING DOUGH TO RISE

When making bread, the temperature of the dough should be kept as close as possible to 85°F. One good way to maintain this gentle warmth is to put the bowl of dough in an oven with just the pilot light on. Or stand the bowl of dough in a large pan or a sink filled with lukewarm water. As the water cools, reheat it by adding hot water, but do not keep the dough warm over a hot burner. Dough may be shaped when doubled in bulk and an impression remains when pressed with a finger.

SHAPING LOAVES

After the dough has risen, punch down and divide into portions for the desired number of loaves. Form into balls and allow to rest about 10 minutes on a lightly floured board. Shape into loaves by pressing the ball of dough into an oblong about $9 \times 7 \times 1$ inches. Fold each end of the oblong to the center, overlapping the ends slightly. Press each side down firmly and pinch along the center to keep the ends sealed and the dough in shape. Place the loaves, sealed edges down, in greased bread pans. Brush the tops with melted shortening, cover with a towel and let rise until doubled in bulk.

◆

FRENCH BREAD

1 LOAF

1 cup lukewarm water
1½ teaspoons salt
1 package (1 tablespoon) yeast
1 tablespoon soft shortening
3½ to 3¾ cups flour
Sesame or poppy seeds

1 Combine the water and salt; add the yeast and stir until yeast is well dissolved. Add the shortening.

2 Stir in the flour, ½ cup at a time. Continue adding enough flour to make a stiff dough.

3 When the dough begins to leave the sides of the bowl, turn it out onto a lightly floured board. Knead until the dough is smooth and elastic and does not stick to the board.

4 Place the dough in a greased bowl, turning once to bring the greased side up. Cover with a damp cloth and let rise in a warm place (80 to 85°F) until doubled in bulk, or 1½ to 2 hours. (Dough has doubled when 2 fingers, pressed into it, leave an indentation.)

5 Punch the dough down, fold over edges of dough and turn it upside down. Cover and let rise again until almost doubled in bulk, or 30 to 45 minutes.

6 Roll the dough into an oblong, 15 × 10 inches. Starting from a wide side, roll the dough up tightly as for a jelly roll. Pinch the edges together to seal. With a hand on each end of the roll, roll gently back and forth to lengthen the loaf and taper the ends.

7 Place the loaf diagonally on a baking sheet that has been lightly greased and sprinkled with cornmeal. With a sharp knife, make ¼-inch slashes in the dough at 2-inch intervals, or 1 lengthwise slash. Brush the top with cold water and let stand, uncovered, about 1½ hours. Brush again with cold water.

8 Bake in a preheated 425°F oven 10 minutes. Brush again with water, reduce oven temperature to 375°F and bake 10 minutes longer. Brush with water again, sprinkle with sesame or poppy seeds and continue baking until golden brown, 15 to 20 minutes longer.

Note: For more glaze and less crustiness, in place of the plain water brush with 1 egg white slightly beaten with 1 tablespoon water.

FRENCH BREAD CROÛTES

Preheat oven to 400°F. Place slices of French bread, ½ inch thick, on a baking sheet and butter generously on one side. Bake for 10 to 15 minutes, turning once. The croûtes are done when they are crisp and brown. Use for fish soup or as a base for slices or pieces of other foods.

Variations

GARLIC-FLAVORED CHEESE CROÛTES

Rub the outside of a crusty loaf of French bread with garlic. Cut the bread into slices ¼ inch thick. Brush the slices with oil and place on a baking sheet. Bake until golden. Turn once. Sprinkle with grated Parmesan or Swiss cheese and bake just until the cheese melts.

TABASCO CROÛTES

Preheat oven to 375°F. Cut French bread on the diagonal into ½-inch slices. Melt ¼ cup butter and stir in 1 garlic clove, minced, and ¼ teaspoon Tabasco sauce. Brush the mixture on the cut surfaces of the bread. Bake for 15 to 20 minutes, until hot and toasted.

CUBAN BREAD

This was one of the most popular breads among students at the late James Beard's cooking school in New York.

2 LOAVES

1 package (1 tablespoon) yeast
2 cups lukewarm water
1¼ tablespoons salt
1 tablespoon sugar
6 to 7 cups flour

1 Dissolve the yeast in the water and add the salt and sugar, stirring thoroughly.

2 Add the flour, 1 cup at a time, beating it in with a wooden spoon. Or use the dough hook on an electric mixer at low speed. Add enough flour to make a fairly stiff dough.

3 When the dough is thoroughly mixed, shape it into a ball, place in a greased bowl and grease the top. Cover with a towel and let stand in a warm place (80 to 85°F) until doubled in bulk.

4 Turn the dough out onto a lightly floured board and shape into 2 long, French-style loaves or round, Italian-style loaves. Arrange on a baking sheet heavily sprinkled with cornmeal and allow to rise 5 minutes.

5 Slash the tops of the loaves in 2 or 3 places with a knife or scissors. Brush the loaves with water and place them in a cold oven. Set the oven control at 400°F and place a pan of boiling water on the bottom of the oven. Bake the loaves until they are crusty and done, 40 to 45 minutes.

Garlic Bread, page 26.
Hot Herb Bread, page 26.

HIGH-PROTEIN BREAD

1 LOAF

1 package (1 tablespoon) yeast
1 cup lukewarm water
2½ cups flour
3½ tablespoons nonfat dry milk
3 tablespoons full-fat soy flour
2 teaspoons sugar
1½ teaspoons salt
2 teaspoons vegetable shortening

1 Dissolve yeast in water.

2 Combine all dry ingredients in a mixing bowl. Add the liquid and mix well. Add shortening and continue mixing until the dough is smooth.

3 Place the dough in a well-greased bowl, grease the top, cover and let rise in a warm place (80 to 85°F) for 1½ hours.

4 Punch dough down, fold over edges of dough and turn it upside down. Cover and let rise 15 to 20 minutes.

5 Shape dough into a loaf and place in a greased 9 × 4 × 3-inch loaf pan. Cover and let stand about an hour in a warm place until dough fills the pan.

6 Bake in a preheated 400°F oven about 50 minutes.

CROUTONS

Cut slices of bread into ½-inch cubes, or into smaller or larger cubes as desired. Dry them in a 325°F oven, or brush them with butter, oil or cheese, and toast them in the oven as for croûtes; or sauté them over moderate heat until golden brown.

Bread garnishes can be cut in other shapes, tiny rounds, triangles, crescents, etc. These little crusts can be prepared in the same way as the cubes.

◆

BREAD CRUMBS

Bread crumbs are used as a finishing garnish on the top of many dishes, and crumbs are an essential of the garnish or sauce called polonaise, which is especially good with vegetables such as asparagus, broccoli and Brussels sprouts. For directions for making soft fresh bread crumbs and fine dry bread crumbs, see page 187.

Whole wheat bread, which has been looked on with increasing favor in America, is easy to prepare and is improved if toasted walnuts and raisins are kneaded into the dough before baking. It is best made with an electric mixer equipped with a dough hook or in a food processor, because it is a bit too laborious to knead it by hand.

◆

100% WHOLE WHEAT BREAD

2 LOAVES

1 cup milk
¼ cup molasses
2 tablespoons vegetable shortening
2 teaspoons salt
1 package (1 tablespoon) yeast
1 cup lukewarm water
6 cups whole wheat flour, approximately

1 Scald the milk and place in a deep bowl with the molasses, shortening and salt. Cool to lukewarm.

2 Meanwhile, soften the yeast in ½ cup of the water. Add the remaining water to the milk mixture, and when it is lukewarm, stir in the yeast.

3 Sift the flour and return to the flour any bran remaining in the sieve. Set aside 1 cup. Add the remainder to the yeast mixture and stir until the flour is dampened. Add enough additional flour from the reserved cup to form a soft dough, stiff enough to leave the sides of the bowl and cling to the spoon in 1 ball.

Continued

4 Turn the dough out on a lightly floured board and knead until smooth and not sticky, about 5 minutes. Place in a greased bowl about 3 times the size of the dough. Turn the dough in the bowl and invert it so that the greased side is up. Cover with a towel and let rise in a warm place (80 to 85°F) until doubled in bulk, or about 2 hours.

5 Punch the dough down, fold in the edges, cover and let rise again in a warm place about 30 minutes.

6 Turn the dough out on a board and cut in half. Shape into balls and let stand, covered, 15 minutes. (This makes the dough easy to shape and gives the loaves a smooth crust.) Shape into loaves.

7 Place the loaves, smooth side up, in greased 9 × 4 × 3-inch loaf pans. Grease the tops, cover with a towel and let rise in a warm place until the dough comes slightly above the tops of the pans, or about 1½ hours.

8 Bake the loaves in a preheated 425°F oven 12 minutes. Reduce the heat to 350°F and bake about 50 minutes longer. The bread is done when it shrinks slightly from the sides of the pan. For a heavier crust, bake about 15 minutes longer. Turn out of the pans immediately and cool on a rack before storing.

Note: To shorten the time of rising by about an hour, 2 packages of yeast may be used instead of 1 package.

WHOLE WHEAT BREAD WITH WALNUTS AND RAISINS

1 LOAF

2 cups bread or all-purpose flour,
    approximately
1¼ cups whole wheat flour
¾ cup coarsely chopped toasted walnuts
¾ cup raisins, preferably black although
    golden may be used
1 teaspoon sugar
1¼ cups lukewarm water, approximately
1½ packages (1½ tablespoons) yeast
Corn, peanut or vegetable oil for
    greasing the bowl
1 tablespoon cornmeal
1 small egg white
2 tablespoons water

1 If the bread is to be blended and kneaded in an electric mixer equipped with a dough hook, put the bread flour and whole wheat flour, walnuts, raisins and sugar into the mixer's bowl and start beating, using the wire whip. Blend the water with the yeast and stir to dissolve. Start beating on low speed and when all the water is added, increase the speed to high. If the dough is too sticky, add a little more flour; if it is too dry, add a little more water. Beat 3 minutes. Remove the wire whip and install the dough hook. Beat on medium speed for an additional 6 minutes. Turn the dough out onto a lightly floured board and knead briefly.

2 If a food processor is used, put the bread flour, whole wheat flour, sugar and yeast into the bowl. With the motor on, pour the water gradually into the funnel. Blend until the dough pulls away from the sides. This may take 2 or 3 minutes. If the dough is too sticky add a little more flour; if it is too dry, add a little more water. Turn the dough out onto a lightly floured board and knead in the walnuts and raisins.

3 Lightly oil a mixing bowl and add the dough, turning it around and around until the entire surface is coated lightly with oil. Cover closely with a damp towel or clear plastic wrap and let stand in a warm place until doubled in bulk, about 1 hour.

4 Sprinkle the bottom of a baking sheet with cornmeal. Preheat the oven to 425°F.

5 Turn the dough out onto a lightly floured board and knead briefly. Shape the dough into a long sausage shape 16 or 17 inches long. Transfer the dough to the baking sheet. It may be necessary to place it on the diagonal. Use a razor blade or a very sharp knife to make 3 or 4 parallel, diagonal gashes—each about ½ inch deep —on top of the loaf. Beat the egg white with the water and brush all over the top of the dough to coat it lightly.

6 Half fill a cake pan or other heatproof receptacle with water. Bring it to the simmer.

7 Place the baking sheet in the oven and place the pan of water on the lower rack or bottom of the oven. Bake the loaf about 35 minutes, or until is is quite brown and crusty. When you rap on the ends of the loaf with your knuckles, it should have a slightly hollow sound.

8 Transfer the bread to a rack and let cool.

WHEATEN BREAD

2 LOAVES

2 packages (2 tablespoons) yeast
2 teaspoons granulated sugar
1⅓ cups lukewarm water
2 tablespoons butter, softened
2 teaspoons salt
¼ cup light brown sugar
1½ cups stone-ground whole wheat flour
3 cups all-purpose flour

1 Sprinkle the yeast and granulated sugar on the water. Let stand for 15 minutes.

2 Add the butter, salt, brown sugar, wheat flour and 2 cups of all-purpose flour to the yeast mixture. Mix with a wooden spoon until well blended.

3 Put the remaining flour on a board and turn the dough onto it. Knead the dough in the flour until the dough is smooth. Place it in a greased bowl and set in a warm place to rise. Let stand for about 3 hours, or until dough is doubled in bulk.

4 Grease 2 loaf pans (4 × 8 inches). Punch down the dough, shape it into 2 loaves and place in the pans. With a sharp knife score the top of the loaves as you would a ham. Set in a warm place to rise. Let stand for 1½ hours, or until doubled in bulk.

5 Preheat the oven to 375°F.

6 Brush the top of the dough with cold water. Bake the loaves for 35 minutes, or until they sound hollow when tapped on the bottom. Cool on a rack.

OLD-FASHIONED OATMEAL BREAD

3 LOAVES

2 cups milk
2 tablespoons vegetable shortening
¼ cup brown sugar, packed
1¼ teaspoons salt
1 package (1 tablespoon) yeast
¼ cup lukewarm water
2 cups regular rolled oats (not quick cooking)
5 to 6 cups flour

1 Scald the milk and stir in the shortening, brown sugar and salt. Stir until dissolved and cool to lukewarm.

2 In a large mixing bowl, soften the yeast in the water. Stir in the lukewarm milk mixture, add the oats and sufficient flour to make a soft dough.

3 Turn the dough out on a lightly floured board. Knead until smooth and elastic, or about 10 minutes; the dough will spring back when pressed with a finger.

4 Place the dough in a warm greased bowl, grease the surface, cover and let rise in a warm place (80°F) until doubled in bulk, or about 2 hours; the dough will retain a finger imprint when pressed.

5 Turn the dough out on a lightly floured board, divide into thirds and shape into loaves. Place the loaves, sealed edges down, in greased 9 × 5½-inch loaf pans. Brush the tops with melted shortening, cover and let rise until almost doubled in bulk, about 1 hour.

6 Bake in a preheated 400°F oven about 45 minutes.

7 Remove from pans and cool the baked loaves on racks.

PUMPERNICKEL BREAD

3 OR 4 LOAVES

1½ cups cold water
¾ cup cornmeal
1½ cups boiling water
1½ tablespoons salt
1 tablespoon sugar
2 tablespoons shortening
1 tablespoon caraway seeds (optional)
1 package (1 tablespoon) yeast
¼ cup lukewarm water
2 cups mashed potato, cooled
6 cups rye meal or flour
2 cups whole wheat flour, approximately

1 Stir the cold water into the cornmeal. Add to the boiling water and cook, stirring constantly, until thick.

2 Add the salt, sugar, shortening and caraway seeds. Let stand until lukewarm. Meanwhile, soften the yeast in the lukewarm water.

3 Add the potatoes and yeast to the cornmeal mixture. Add the rye meal and enough whole wheat flour to make a stiff dough, stirring first with a spoon, then with the hands.

4 Turn the dough out on a lightly floured board and knead until the dough is smooth and elastic and does not stick to the board.

5 Place the dough in a greased bowl, grease the surface, cover with a towel and let stand in a warm place (80° to 85°F) until doubled in bulk.

6 Divide the dough into 3 or 4 portions and form into loaves. Place, seam side down, in greased 9×4×3-inch loaf pans. Grease the tops of the loaves, cover and let rise until doubled in bulk.

7 Bake in a preheated 375°F oven about 1 hour.

Variation

SOUR DOUGH PUMPERNICKEL

After the dough has been kneaded the first time, put about 1 cup in a bowl. Cover and set aside at room temperature to ferment and sour for a week or so. When making a fresh batch of dough, add the sour dough to the liquids in place of the 1 package of yeast.

RYE BREAD

3 LOAVES

1 package (1 tablespoon) yeast
½ cup lukewarm water
3 cups rye flour
2 tablespoons honey
⅓ cup vegetable shortening
1 tablespoon salt
2 cups boiling water
5 to 5½ cups all-purpose flour
1 tablespoon caraway seeds, if desired
2 eggs, lightly beaten

1 Soften the yeast in the warm water. Combine the rye flour, honey, shortening and salt. Add the boiling water and blend well. Cool to lukewarm.

2 Add the softened yeast. Gradually stir in the all-purpose flour to make a soft dough. Add the caraway seeds. Turn the dough out on a floured board and let it rest for 10 minutes.

3 Knead the dough for about 10 minutes, until it is smooth and satiny. Place in a lightly greased bowl and turn once to grease the surface. Cover and let rise until doubled in bulk.

4 Punch the dough down, cover and let it rise again until almost doubled in bulk.

5 Divide the dough into 3 parts, form round loaves and place them on greased baking sheets.

6 Preheat the oven to 350°F.

7 Let the loaves rise until almost doubled. Brush them with lightly beaten egg. Bake for 35 to 40 minutes.

Note: The same recipe made with whole wheat flour instead of all-purpose flour will make a darker bread.

ONION RYE BREAD

3 LOAVES

2 cups milk
¼ cup sugar
4 teaspoons salt
¼ cup vegetable oil
1 package (1 tablespoon) yeast
1 cup lukewarm water
6 cups all-purpose flour
3 tablespoons caraway seeds
1 cup chopped onions
2½ cups rye flour, approximately
Cornmeal
Cream

1 Scald the milk and add the sugar, salt and oil. Stir until the sugar has dissolved and cool the mixture to lukewarm.

2 Soften the yeast in the water and add to the milk mixture. Add the white flour and mix well. Stir in the caraway seeds, onions and 2 cups of the rye flour and mix.

3 Turn the dough out on a surface sprinkled with rye flour and knead until smooth and elastic, adding enough additional rye flour to give a fairly stiff dough. Place in a greased bowl, grease the top, cover with a towel and let stand in a warm place (80° to 85°F) until doubled in bulk, about 1 hour.

4 Punch the dough down by folding the edges into the center. Cover and let rise again until doubled in bulk.

5 Grease three 9 × 4 × 3-inch loaf pans and sprinkle with cornmeal. Divide the dough into thirds, shape into loaves and place in the prepared pans. Brush the tops of the loaves with cream and then sprinkle with salt. Cover with a towel and let rise in a warm place until doubled in bulk, about 1 hour.

6 Bake in a preheated 350°F oven 1 hour, or until the loaves have a hollow sound when tapped. Turn out on a rack to cool.

SPIRAL BREAD

2 LOAVES

1 cup scalded milk
2 tablespoons sugar
2½ teaspoons salt
¼ cup vegetable shortening
1 cup lukewarm water
2 packages (2 tablespoons) yeast
7 cups flour
Melted butter or vegetable oil
Filling (see following recipes)

1 To the scalded milk add the sugar, salt and shortening. Stir and cool to lukewarm.

2 Pour water into a large bowl, add yeast and stir until dissolved. Add milk mixture.

3 Add 4 cups of flour, stir; then beat well. Add remaining flour and stir until dampened. Let stand 10 minutes.

4 Turn dough out onto a floured surface and knead until smooth, about 10 minutes. Place in a greased bowl, grease surface, cover and let rise in a warm place (80° to 85°F) until doubled in bulk, about 45 minutes.

5 Punch dough down, turn out on a smooth surface and let rest 10 minutes.

6 Grease two 9 × 5 × 3-inch loaf pans.

7 Cut dough in half and shape each half into a ball. Roll each into a rectangle about ¼ inch thick and almost 9 inches wide.

8 Brush with lightly beaten egg reserved from the selected filling recipe and then spread the filling over it to about 1 inch from the edges. Roll jelly-roll fashion and pinch edges to seal. Place in greased pans with seam side down.

9 Brush tops with melted butter or oil, cover with wax paper and let rise in a warm place until slightly higher in the middle than the edge, 50 to 60 minutes.

10 Meanwhile, preheat the oven to 400°F.

11 Cut gashes in top of loaves if desired. Place in oven and bake 1 hour. Turn out and cool on a rack.

HERB FILLING

2 cups finely chopped parsley
2 cups finely chopped scallions
1 large garlic clove, minced
2 tablespoons butter
2 eggs, lightly beaten
¾ teaspoon salt
Freshly ground pepper to taste
Tabasco sauce to taste

1 Cook parsley, scallions and garlic in butter over moderate heat, stirring often, until thoroughly wilted but not brown. Mixture should be reduced to about half the original volume. Cool.

2 Reserve about 2 tablespoons of the beaten eggs for later use in brushing over the dough. Add balance to vegetables and season with salt, pepper and Tabasco.

ANCHOVY FILLING

4 (2-ounce) cans anchovy fillets, drained
2 small garlic cloves, minced
2 tablespoons tomato paste
1 whole egg
1 egg yolk
Cayenne to taste
1 teaspoon paprika (for color)

1 Mash anchovies to a paste with the garlic. Add the tomato paste and mix.

2 Beat the egg with the egg yolk until well mixed. Reserve 2 tablespoons for later use. Add balance to anchovy mixture. Add cayenne and paprika.

ANADAMA BREAD

2 LOAVES

½ cup cornmeal
1 cup cold water
1 package (1 tablespoon) yeast
1½ cups boiling water
3 tablespoons butter
½ cup molasses
2 teaspoons salt
3 cups whole wheat flour
2½ to 3 cups all-purpose flour

1 Mix the cornmeal with ¾ cup cold water. Heat the remaining water to lukewarm and soften the yeast in it.

2 Add the cornmeal to the boiling water and stir over low heat until the mixture boils. Add the butter, molasses and salt and cool to lukewarm.

3 Combine the yeast with the cornmeal and mix. Add the whole wheat flour and enough white flour to give a fairly firm, nonsticky dough. Turn out on a floured board and knead until smooth and elastic.

4 Turn the dough into a greased bowl, grease the surface, cover with a towel and let rise in a warm place (80° to 85°F) until doubled in bulk.

5 Knead lightly again and shape into 2 loaves. Place in greased loaf pans or on greased cookie sheets. Brush with oil. Cover and let rise until doubled in bulk.

6 Bake in a preheated 400°F oven 15 minutes. Reduce the oven temperature to 375°F and bake about 35 minutes longer.

CRANBERRY ANADAMA BREAD

2 LOAVES

1½ cups cranberries, picked over and washed
1 tablespoon grated orange rind
¼ cup sugar
2 packages (2 tablespoons) yeast
½ cup lukewarm water
⅔ cup cornmeal
2½ cups boiling water
3 teaspoons salt
3 tablespoons vegetable shortening
½ cup molasses
7½ cups flour
1 tablespoon milk

1 Wash cranberries; put them through a food chopper, using the coarse blade. Add the orange rind and sugar. Let stand.

2 Soften the yeast in the warm water. Set aside.

3 Add the cornmeal to the boiling water. Cook for 3 minutes, or until thickened. Remove from heat and add the salt, shortening and molasses. Mix well. Cool to lukewarm.

4 Stir in the softened yeast and the cranberries. Add 5 cups of the flour and mix well. Knead in the remaining flour on a pastry board.

5 Continue kneading until dough is smooth and satiny. Place the dough in a greased bowl, turning to grease dough on all sides. Cover and let rise in a warm place for 1 hour, or until doubled in bulk.

6 Punch down dough, cover and let rest for 10 minutes. Shape the dough into 2 loaves. Place in 2 greased 9×5×3-inch loaf pans. Cover and let rise again in a warm place for about 45 minutes, until dough has doubled in bulk.

7 Preheat the oven to 375°F.

8 Brush the tops of the loaves with the milk. Bake for 45 minutes, or until done.

SWISS CHEESE LOAF

3 LOAVES

1½ cups milk, scalded
3 tablespoons sugar
1½ tablespoons salt
3 tablespoons butter
1 cup cold water
½ cup lukewarm water
2 packages (2 tablespoons) yeast
8 cups flour, approximately
1½ cups grated Gruyère cheese
3 teaspoons paprika
1 egg, beaten

1 Pour the milk into a large bowl. Add the sugar, salt and butter. Stir until butter melts. Stir in the cold water.

2 Place the warm water in a small warm bowl. Sprinkle with yeast and stir to dissolve. Add yeast to milk mixture. Add 5 cups of the flour and beat until smooth. Add enough remaining flour to make a stiff dough.

3 Turn dough out on a lightly floured board and knead for 8 to 10 minutes. Place in a greased large bowl and grease the top of the dough. Cover and let rise in a warm place, free from draft, for about 1 hour, until doubled in bulk.

4 Roll one third of the dough into a rectangle 10 × 12 inches. Sprinkle with one third of the cheese and paprika. Roll up on the long side and seal seam and edges. Place in a 9×5×3-inch loaf pan and brush with beaten egg. Cover and let rise again for about 1 hour, until doubled in bulk. Repeat with remaining dough, cheese and paprika.

5 Preheat the oven to 375°F.

6 Bake the loaves for 30 to 40 minutes, or until golden brown.

RAISIN-OAT CINNAMON BREAD

2 LOAVES

1¼ cups milk, scalded
1 cup uncooked rolled oats, either quick
   cooking or regular
¼ cup vegetable shortening
¾ cup sugar
1¼ teaspoons salt
1 package (1 tablespoon) yeast
1 egg, lightly beaten
2¾ cups flour, approximately
½ cup seedless raisins
1 teaspoon cinnamon
4 tablespoons butter, melted

  1 Pour 1 cup of the milk over the oats. Stir in the shortening, ¼ cup of the sugar and the salt, and cool to lukewarm.

  2 Cool the remaining milk to lukewarm, add the yeast and stir until dissolved. Add to the oats mixture.

  3 Stir in the egg, flour and raisins and mix to a soft dough. Turn dough out on a lightly floured board and knead until smooth and elastic. Shape into a ball and place in a clean greased bowl, turning once to grease the top.

  4 Cover and let rise in a warm place for about 1 hour, until doubled in bulk. Punch down, cover and let rest for 10 minutes. Divide dough into halves and shape into loaves. Place each in a greased 9×5×3-inch loaf pan. Cover and let rise again in a warm place for about 1 hour, until doubled in bulk.

  5 Preheat the oven to 350°F.

  6 Bake 45 to 60 minutes, or until loaves sound hollow when tapped on the bottom.

  7 Combine the remaining sugar with the cinnamon. While the loaves are still hot, brush with the melted butter and sprinkle tops, sides and ends with the sugar mixture.

SWEDISH COFFEE LOAVES

2 LOAVES

2 packages (2 tablespoons) yeast
¼ cup lukewarm water
5 tablespoons butter
⅓ cup sugar
2 teaspoons crushed cardamom seeds,
   or 1 teaspoon ground cardamom
½ teaspoon salt
¾ cup milk, scalded
1 egg
3½ to 4 cups flour
¾ cup raisins
Beaten egg for glaze

  1 Soften the yeast in the lukewarm water.

  2 Mix together the butter, sugar, cardamom, salt and hot milk. Cool until lukewarm. Add the egg, softened yeast and 2½ cups of the flour. Beat thoroughly.

  3 Add enough of the remaining flour, a little at a time, to make a soft dough. Set a little aside for kneading. Turn the dough out on a lightly floured surface and knead for about 10 minutes, until smooth and elastic.

  4 Place dough in a lightly buttered bowl, turning once to grease the surface. Cover and let rise in a warm place for about 1½ hours, until doubled in bulk. When light, punch down, turn out on a lightly floured surface and knead lightly.

  5 Mix the raisins with the dough and divide the mixture into 2 parts. Cut each half into 3 pieces of equal size. Roll the pieces into long ropes and braid 3 ropes together for each loaf. Place the loaves on a buttered cookie sheet. Cover with a towel and let rise again in a warm place for about 45 minutes, until doubled in bulk.

Continued

6 Preheat the oven to 375°F.

7 Brush the loaves with beaten egg; sprinkle with sugar and chopped nuts if desired. Bake for 20 to 25 minutes.

◆

BABKA

2 MEDIUM-SIZE LOAVES

2½ cups milk
6 cups flour, approximately
2 packages (2 tablespoons) yeast
½ cup sugar
1 teaspoon salt
16 egg yolks
¼ pound plus 4 tablespoons butter, softened
1 cup white sultana raisins
¼ cup rum
Confectioners' sugar

1 Bring 2 cups of the milk to a rolling boil. Add it to 1¼ cups of the flour, beating it in hard until the mixture is as fluffy as mashed potatoes. Cool to lukewarm.

2 Add the yeast to the remaining ½ cup of lukewarm milk. Stir in the sugar and salt and add to the cooled paste. Let the mixture rise for 20 minutes, or until it forms a light sponge. Stir it down.

3 Beat in the egg yolks and enough flour to make a soft sticky dough. Add the butter.

4 Knead the dough in the bowl until it is very smooth, shiny and elastic. The hand should be clean when it is pulled abruptly from the dough. Kneading by hand will take about 40 minutes, possibly longer. Or beat the dough in an electric mixer equipped with a kneading hook. When the dough has been beaten enough, clean the sides of the bowl, cover with a towel, and let the dough rise in a draft-free place until doubled in bulk.

5 Preheat the oven to 375°F. Grease 2 small kugelhopf molds or tube pans.

6 Stir the risen dough down. Work in the raisins. Fill the pans halfway, cover with a cloth and let the dough rise again until almost doubled in bulk. Bake in the preheated oven for 30 to 45 minutes, until the loaves are a deep golden brown.

7 Remove the loaves from the pans. Sprinkle them with rum and cool. Dust with confectioners' sugar when they are cool.

◆

SWEDISH JULBRØD
A Christmas bread from Sweden.

2 LOAVES, OR ABOUT 20 SERVINGS

2 packages (2 tablespoons) yeast
¼ cup lukewarm water
¾ cup milk, scalded and cooled to lukewarm
½ teaspoon salt
⅓ cup sugar
¼ pound butter, softened
3 eggs, lightly beaten
4¼ cups flour
1 cup raisins
1 cup sliced citron
1 cup blanched almonds
1 to 3 teaspoons cardamom seeds
¼ cup confectioners' sugar

1 Soften the yeast in the water. Add the milk, salt, sugar, butter and eggs, reserving 1 egg white.

2 Mix a little flour with the raisins and citron. Add ½ cup of the almonds, shredded.

3 Remove the papery covering from the cardamom seeds and crush the seeds. Add with one half of the flour to the yeast mixture and stir until smooth. Cover and let rise in a warm place (85°F) until doubled in bulk, or about 40 minutes.

4 Stir in the remaining flour and knead until smooth and elastic. Knead in the fruits and nuts. Turn the dough into a greased bowl, grease the top, cover and let rise about 30 minutes.

5 Cut the dough into sixths and roll each piece with the palms of the hands into a long strip. Braid 3 strips and shape into a ring on a greased baking sheet. Repeat for a second loaf.

6 Brush the loaves with the reserved egg white beaten with 1 tablespoon water. Cover with the confectioners' sugar and remaining almonds and let rise until doubled in bulk, or about 30 minutes.

7 Bake in a preheated 450°F oven for 10 minutes. Reduce the oven temperature to 350°F and bake about 20 minutes longer.

PANETTONE
The traditional Italian Christmas bread.

1 LARGE LOAF

2 packages (2 tablespoons) yeast
1 cup lukewarm water
¼ pound butter, melted
2 teaspoons salt
½ cup sugar
2 eggs, beaten
3 egg yolks, beaten
5½ cups flour, approximately
1 cup thinly sliced citron
1 cup seedless raisins

1 Soften the yeast in the water.

2 Mix the butter, salt, sugar, eggs and egg yolks. Add the yeast and butter mixture to 5 cups flour and stir until blended. Knead on a floured board until smooth and free from stickiness, adding more flour as needed. The dough should be soft. Knead in the citron and raisins.

3 Place the dough in a greased bowl, grease the surface, cover with a towel and let rise in a warm place (80° to 85°F) until doubled in bulk, or about 2 hours.

4 Knead the dough again until smooth. Place in a greased 3-quart pudding pan or other round pan, brush the top with melted butter, cover and let rise again until doubled in bulk, or about 40 minutes. Using a sharp knife, cut a deep cross in the top of the loaf.

5 Bake in a preheated 425°F oven until the surface begins to brown, or about 8 minutes. Reduce the oven temperature to 325°F and bake about 1 hour longer.

HOLIDAY FRUIT BREAD

2 LOAVES

2 packages (2 tablespoons) yeast
¼ cup lukewarm water
1 cup milk, scalded
½ cup sugar
2 teaspoons salt
5 tablespoons butter
3 eggs
5 cups flour, approximately
1 cup raisins
¾ cup chopped candied cherries
¼ cup chopped candied citron
1 tablespoon water

1 Soften the yeast in the lukewarm water.

2 Place the milk, sugar, salt and butter in a mixing bowl and stir to dissolve the sugar and melt the butter. Cool to lukewarm. Stir in the yeast and 2 of the eggs, lightly beaten.

3 Add enough flour to make a soft dough. Turn the dough out on a lightly floured board and knead for about 10 minutes, until smooth and satiny. Place in a clean greased bowl, turning to grease the top of the dough. Cover with a towel and set in a warm place for about 1 hour, until doubled in bulk.

4 Punch dough down and let rest for 10 minutes. Knead in the raisins, cherries and citron until well mixed. Divide the dough into halves and shape into 2 loaves. Place in 2 greased 4½ × 8½ × 2½-inch loaf pans. Cover and let rise until doubled in bulk.

5 Preheat the oven to 375°F.

6 Beat the remaining egg with the tablespoon water and brush over the tops of the loaves. Bake for about 40 minutes, or until the loaves are golden brown and sound hollow when tapped on the bottom. Cool on wire racks.

Note: The halves of dough may be shaped into braids or into ring shapes to lend variety.

♦

BRIOCHE

18 TO 24 BRIOCHES

1 package (1 tablespoon) yeast
⅓ cup lukewarm water
2 to 3 tablespoons sugar
4 cups flour, approximately
½ pound butter, softened
1 teaspoon salt
7 eggs
½ cup milk, scalded and cooled

1 Soften yeast in ⅓ cup lukewarm water. Add 1 teaspoon sugar and 1 cup flour. Mix and then knead until smooth. Place ball of dough in a bowl and cover with additional lukewarm water. Let rise until ball floats in water, 1 hour or less.

2 Put remaining flour in a large bowl. Add the ball of dough, half the butter, the remaining sugar, salt and 2 of the eggs, lightly beaten. Mix well with the fingers, adding enough milk to give a soft, non-sticky dough. Turn out on a lightly floured board and knead until smooth.

3 Work in the remaining butter and 2 more eggs. Repeat the kneading. Lift the dough and slap or bang it on the table until it is very smooth.

4 Add 2 more eggs, work them into the dough and repeat the kneading and banging on the table.

5 Shape the dough into a ball and place it in a greased bowl. Cover and let rise in a warm place (80° to 85°F) until doubled in bulk.

6 Punch and stir the dough down. Shape into a ball, place in a clean greased bowl, cover tightly with foil and chill overnight or slightly longer.

7 To shape the brioche, turn the dough out onto a floured board. Cut off about one sixth and reserve for the topknots of the buns. Divide remainder of the dough into 18 to 24 portions and shape each into a ball. Place in greased brioche pans or muffin tins (2¾ × 1¼ inches deep). Cut reserved dough into the same number of small balls. Dampen a finger slightly and make a depression in the center of each large ball. Place a small ball in each of the depressions. Cover and let rise in a warm place until doubled in bulk, or about 1 hour.

8 Preheat the oven to 450°F and place rack near bottom.

9 Lightly beat remaining egg and brush over the tops of the brioche. Place in oven and bake until brown, about 15 minutes.

◆

CHEESE BRIOCHE

1 BRIOCHE RING OR 12 SMALL BRIOCHES

¼ cup lukewarm water
1 package (1 tablespoon) yeast
2 cups flour
4 teaspoons sugar
½ teaspoon salt
3 eggs
¼ pound butter, melted
¼ pound Swiss cheese, shredded

1 Place the lukewarm water in a large warm bowl. Sprinkle with yeast. Stir to dissolve. Add ½ cup of the flour and mix well. Cover and let rise in a warm place, free from draft, for about 20 minutes, until doubled in bulk.

2 Combine remaining flour, the sugar and salt. Stir in eggs and beat until smooth. Stir in butter and the yeast mixture. Beat until smooth. Stir in the cheese. Cover and let rise again for about 1 hour, until doubled in bulk.

3 Punch dough down; cover with wax paper and a damp towel. Chill overnight.

BRIOCHE RING

4 Shape chilled dough into a roll. Fit into a greased 9-inch ring mold. Cover and let rise again for about 1 hour, until doubled in bulk.

5 Preheat the oven to 375°F.

6 Bake for about 45 minutes, or until golden brown. Remove from pan; cool slightly on rack. Serve warm.

INDIVIDUAL BRIOCHES

4 Shape 12 tiny balls out of one sixth of the chilled dough. Shape remainder into 12 large balls. Place large balls in greased brioche pans or muffin tins. With a dampened finger, make a depression in each large ball and insert a tiny ball. Cover and let rise in a warm place, free from draft, for about 1 hour until doubled in bulk.

5 Preheat the oven to 450°F.

6 Bake for about 15 minutes, or until golden brown. Serve warm.

CROISSANTS

Croissants, the traditional French breakfast bread, can be made from several doughs. Here is one made with a yeast dough.

ABOUT 18 ROLLS

1 package (1 tablespoon) yeast
¾ cup lukewarm milk
2 cups flour
½ teaspoon salt
¼ pound butter
1 egg yolk

1 Dissolve the yeast in the milk.

2 Sift together the flour and salt and stir in the yeast mixture. Knead until smooth and elastic.

2 Place the dough in a greased bowl, grease the top of the dough and let rise in a warm place (85°F) until doubled in bulk.

4 Roll the dough out in a long strip, dot with bits of the butter and fold into thirds. Turn so that an open edge is nearest. Pat and roll into another long strip, fold into thirds, wrap in wax paper and chill well.

5 Roll the chilled dough out and fold the ends to the center. Fold again as above, wrap and refrigerate. Remove and repeat the process a fourth time.

6 The last time, roll the dough out a little thinner (about ⅛ inch) but do not fold. Cut into triangles and brush 1 tip of each with beaten egg yolk mixed with a little water. Roll from the wide end to the tip, pressing to seal. Shape into half-moons.

7 Place on well-buttered cookie sheets, cover with wax paper and let rise until doubled in bulk.

8 Brush the tops with beaten egg yolk and bake in a preheated 425°F oven 20 to 25 minutes. Serve hot or cold.

CRUMPETS

ABOUT 16 CRUMPETS

2 cups lukewarm water
1 package (1 tablespoon) yeast
¼ cup mashed potatoes (optional)
¾ teaspoon salt
1¾ cups sifted flour, approximately

1 Pour the water into a 2-quart bowl. Add yeast and let stand until softened. Add potatoes, salt and flour. Mix well, using a wooden spoon, and then beat 3 minutes. The batter should be thin. Cover and let stand in a warm place 30 minutes.

2 Beat again 3 minutes and let stand 30 minutes longer. Repeat process once more.

3 Place a griddle over medium heat, grease it lightly and arrange 6 greased crumpet rings on it. When the griddle is hot, beat the batter briefly and spoon it into the rings, filling each about one third full.

4 Bake until the surface is dry and the bottom is brown. Remove rings, turn crumpets and brown the second side very lightly. Cool on a rack.

5 Toast to heat. Serve with plenty of butter and, if desired, jam.

NUT TWISTS

2 DOZEN TWISTS

½ cup milk
½ cup vegetable shortening
3 tablespoons sugar
1½ teaspoons salt
1 teaspoon vanilla extract
2 packages (2 tablespoons) yeast
¼ cup lukewarm water
3 cups flour
3 eggs
¾ cup finely chopped nuts
½ cup sugar
1 teaspoon cinnamon

1 Scald the milk and combine with the shortening, sugar and salt. Cool to lukewarm. Add the vanilla and the yeast dissolved in the lukewarm water and mix well.

2 Blend in 1½ cups of the flour and beat until smooth. Cover and let rest for 15 minutes.

3 Add the eggs, one at a time, beating well after each addition. Blend in the remaining flour and mix thoroughly. The dough should be quite soft. Cover dough and let rise in a warm place (80° to 85°F) about ½ hour.

4 Combine the nuts, sugar and cinnamon.

5 Divide the dough into small pieces with a tablespoon. Roll each piece in the sugar-nut mixture and stretch it to about 8 inches in length. Twist into desired shapes.

6 Place on a greased baking sheet and let rise until almost doubled in bulk.

7 Bake in a preheated 375°F oven 12 to 15 minutes.

BASIC ROLLS

ABOUT 36 ROLLS

2 cups milk
¼ cup vegetable shortening or butter
¼ cup sugar
2 teaspoons salt
2 packages (2 tablespoons) yeast
¼ cup lukewarm water
5 to 6 cups sifted flour
Melted shortening or butter

1 Bring the milk to a boil. Add shortening or butter, sugar and salt and cool to lukewarm.

2 Soften yeast in the lukewarm water and add to milk mixture.

3 Add about half of the flour, mix and beat well. Add enough remaining flour to make a soft dough.

4 Turn out on a floured board, let rest 10 minutes and then knead until smooth, about 10 minutes.

5 Place dough in a greased bowl, grease surface, cover and let rise in a warm place (80° to 85°F) until doubled in bulk.

6 Turn dough out on a floured board and knead lightly until surface is smooth. Shape as desired (see following variations) and place 1 inch apart on a greased baking sheet. Brush with melted butter, cover with a towel and let rise until doubled in bulk, 30 to 40 minutes.

7 About 10 minutes before rolls have risen preheat oven to 375°F.

8 Brush rolls with additional melted butter, milk or egg diluted with a tablespoon of water and bake 15 to 20 minutes, or until brown.

Continued

Variations

PARKER HOUSE ROLLS

Roll dough to ¼- to ½-inch thickness and cut into 2-inch rounds. Using the dull edge of a knife, make a crease slightly off center across each roll. Invert rolls, brush with melted butter and fold larger "half" over smaller half.

BISCUIT ROLLS

Roll dough ½ inch thick and cut into 2-inch rounds.

HAMBURGER ROLLS

Roll dough ½ inch thick and cut with a 3-inch cutter.

CRESCENT ROLLS

Using one quarter of the dough at a time, roll dough into a round ¼ inch thick. Use a 9-inch pan as a guide and cut the dough into a perfect circle. Cut into 10 or 12 pie-shaped wedges, brush very lightly with melted butter and roll jelly-roll fashion, beginning with the outer edge. Curve each roll into a crescent on the baking sheet.

FINGER ROLLS

Shape dough into balls 1 to 1½ inches in diameter. Roll and stretch under the hands until 3 to 4 inches long.

CLOVERLEAF ROLLS

Cut risen dough in half and shape each half into a roll about 12 inches long. Cut into 1-inch pieces and divide each piece into thirds. Shape into balls. Grease 2-inch muffin cups, place 3 balls in each, brush the tops with melted butter and let rise until doubled in bulk.

CINNAMON BUNS

Follow directions for shaping and filling whole wheat cinnamon buns (opposite page).

QUICK WHOLE WHEAT ROLLS

ABOUT 2 DOZEN ROLLS

1¼ cups milk
¼ cup sugar
2½ teaspoons salt
3 tablespoons honey or molasses
4 tablespoons butter or vegetable shortening
2 packages (2 tablespoons) yeast
¼ cup lukewarm water
3½ cups whole wheat flour

1 Scald the milk and combine with the sugar, salt, honey and butter. Cool to lukewarm.

2 In a large bowl soften the yeast in the water. Add the lukewarm milk mixture and stir in enough flour to make a stiff dough.

3 Turn the dough out on a lightly floured surface and knead until smooth. Place in a greased bowl, grease the surface of the dough, cover with a towel and let rise in a warm place (80° to 85°F) until doubled in bulk, about 45 minutes.

4 Turn the dough out on an unfloured surface and shape into rolls (see basic roll variations, opposite). Brush the tops with melted butter, cover and let rise in a warm place until doubled in bulk, about 1 hour. Bake in a preheated 400°F oven about 20 minutes.

ST. LUCIA'S CARDAMOM BUNS

18 BUNS

2 packages (2 tablespoons) yeast
½ cup lukewarm water
⅓ cup sugar
2 teaspoons salt
1 teaspoon ground cardamom
¼ pound butter
¾ cup milk, scalded
1 large egg
4⅓ cups sifted flour
Raisins
1 egg white, beaten only until foamy

1 Soften the yeast in the lukewarm water.

2 Place the sugar, salt, cardamom and butter in a large bowl. Add hot milk, mix well and cool to lukewarm. Stir in the yeast, egg and 2 cups of the flour. Beat until batter falls in sheets from a spoon.

3 Add remaining flour and knead dough on a lightly floured board for about 5 minutes, until creamy and satiny.

4 Place in greased bowl, turning dough to bring greased surface to top. Cover and let rise in a warm place (80° to 85°F) for 45 to 50 minutes, until dough is doubled in bulk.

5 Punch down dough and shape into a ball. Cover and let rest for 10 minutes.

6 Pinch off pieces of dough and roll into 12-inch lengths ½ inch thick. Curl each end and put 2 rolls together back to back. Stick a raisin in the center of each curl. If desired, form the rolls of dough in the shape of an S, coiling or curling the ends. Stick a raisin in each coil.

7 Place the buns on a greased baking sheet. Brush with the egg white. Cover and let rise in a warm place (80° to 85°F) for about 40 minutes, until doubled in bulk.

8 Preheat the oven to 400°F.

9 Bake the buns for 10 to 12 minutes.

◆

WHOLE WHEAT CINNAMON BUNS

18 BUNS

Quick whole wheat roll dough (opposite page)
Melted butter
1½ cups brown sugar, packed
1 tablespoon cinnamon
¼ teaspoon grated nutmeg
⅔ cup raisins
Confectioners' sugar icing (page 705)

1 Follow the directions for the roll dough through the first rising. Turn out the dough onto a floured board, divide in half and roll each half into a thin rectangle about ¼ inch thick and 10 inches long. Brush with butter.

2 Mix the sugar, cinnamon and nutmeg. Sprinkle half the mixture and half the raisins on each sheet of dough. Roll tightly as for a jelly roll and cut each roll into 9 equal portions. Place the buns, cut sides up, in two 8- or 9-inch greased round or square pans and brush with melted butter. Cover with wax paper and let rise until doubled in bulk, about 1 hour.

3 Bake in a preheated 350°F oven about 30 minutes. Serve warm, plain or sprinkled with confectioners' sugar, or cool and glaze with confectioners' icing.

Quick Breads

BAKING POWDER BISCUITS

12 TO 15 BISCUITS

2 cups flour
2½ teaspoons baking powder
1 teaspoon salt
⅓ cup vegetable shortening
⅔ cup milk, approximately

1 Preheat the oven to 425°F.

2 Sift the flour, baking powder and salt into a mixing bowl.

3 With a pastry blender or 2 knives cut in shortening until mixture has the texture of coarse cornmeal.

4 Stir mixture gently with a fork while adding the milk. Use enough milk to form a dough that is soft but not sticky.

5 Knead on a lightly floured board until smooth, or about 20 strokes. Roll dough on the board until it is ½ inch thick. Cut with a floured biscuit cutter and place on a baking sheet at 1-inch intervals.

6 Bake 12 to 15 minutes, or until golden brown.

Variations

CHEESE BISCUITS

Cut ½ cup grated sharp American cheese into the flour mixture with the shortening.

HAM OR BACON BISCUITS

Add ⅔ cup ground cooked ham or 6 slices cooked bacon, crumbled, to the flour-shortening mixture before adding the milk.

HERBED BISCUITS

Add 2 tablespoons each chopped chives and pimiento and 1 tablespoon chopped parsley to the flour-shortening mixture before adding the milk.

ORANGE BISCUITS

Cut 2 tablespoons grated orange rind into the flour mixture with the shortening. Top each biscuit with a cube of sugar that has been dipped in orange juice.

DROP BISCUITS

Increase milk to 1 cup. Stir the dough lightly until just blended and drop by spoonfuls onto a greased baking sheet.

WATERCRESS BISCUITS

Add coarsely chopped leaves (washed and thoroughly dried) from one bunch of watercress to the dry ingredients.

BUTTERMILK BISCUITS

ABOUT 15 BISCUITS

2 cups flour
1 teaspoon salt
1 teaspoon baking powder
½ teaspoon baking soda
¼ cup vegetable shortening
¾ cup buttermilk, approximately

1 Preheat the oven to 425°F.

2 Sift together the dry ingredients. Cut in the shortening until the mixture resembles coarse cornmeal.

3 Add enough buttermilk, while stirring lightly with a fork, to make a soft dough that separates from the sides of the bowl and forms a mound when stirred.

4 Turn onto a lightly floured board and knead lightly about 30 seconds. Roll to ½-inch thickness and cut into rounds, using a floured biscuit cutter. Transfer to baking sheets and bake 12 to 15 minutes.

WHOLE WHEAT BACON BISCUITS

ABOUT 14 BISCUITS

1 cup whole wheat flour
1 cup all-purpose flour
1 tablespoon baking powder
¾ teaspoon salt
⅓ cup vegetable shortening
½ cup crumbled crisp cooked bacon
¾ cup milk, approximately

1 Preheat the oven to 450°F.

2 Mix together the whole wheat flour, all-purpose flour, baking powder and salt in a bowl. Cut in the shortening.

3 Add the bacon and mix to a soft dough with the milk. Turn out on a lightly floured board and knead for ½ minute so that dough is no longer sticky.

4 Roll out to ½-inch thickness, cut into 2-inch rounds and place on an ungreased cookie sheet. Bake for about 15 minutes.

BASIC MUFFINS

12 (3-INCH) MUFFINS

2 cups flour
4 tablespoons sugar
1 tablespoon baking powder
½ teaspoon salt
2 eggs, well beaten
1 cup milk
¼ pound butter, melted and cooled slightly

1 Preheat the oven to 400°F.
2 Sift together the flour, sugar, baking powder and salt.
3 Mix the eggs, milk and butter. Add the liquid mixture to the dry ingredients and stir only until the flour is moistened. Do not beat the batter until smooth.
4 Spoon into well-greased muffin tins, filling the cups about two thirds full. Bake about 20 minutes and serve immediately.

Variations

BACON MUFFINS

Add ½ cup crisp chopped cooked bacon to sifted dry ingredients.

CHEESE MUFFINS

Eliminate sugar and add ⅔ cup grated sharp American cheese to the sifted dry ingredients. Sprinkle with paprika before baking.

CRANBERRY MUFFINS

Mix ¾ cup chopped cranberries and ¼ cup sugar. Add to the dry ingredients.

NUT MUFFINS

Add ¾ cup finely chopped nuts to sifted dry ingredients.

DATE MUFFINS

Add ½ cup sliced, pitted dates to sifted dry ingredients.

UPSIDE-DOWN MUFFINS

In the bottom of each muffin cup place ½ teaspoon butter and 1 teaspoon brown sugar. Add a few nuts or raisins or 1 stewed dried fig or apricot. Cover with batter and bake as directed.

◆

BUCKWHEAT MUFFINS

12 MUFFINS

¼ cup vegetable shortening
3 tablespoons sugar
2 tablespoons molasses
1 egg, unbeaten
1½ cups flour
2 teaspoons baking powder
½ teaspoon baking soda
½ teaspoon salt
¾ cup fine buckwheat groats
1 cup buttermilk
¼ cup cut, seeded raisins

1 Preheat the oven to 425°F.
2 Cream the shortening until fluffy. Add the sugar and molasses and beat until light. Beat in the egg.
3 Sift together the flour, baking powder, baking soda and salt. Add to the creamed mixture. Add the groats and buttermilk and stir only until the dry ingredients are moistened. Add the raisins.
4 Fill greased 2½-inch-deep muffin pans one-half to two-thirds full and bake until the muffins are brown and done, or about 20 minutes. Serve hot.

FRESH CORN MUFFINS

15 MUFFINS

2 eggs, well beaten
1 cup milk
¼ cup vegetable shortening, melted
1 cup (2 or 3 ears) fresh corn cut from the cobs
1½ cups flour
1 teaspoon salt
3 teaspoons baking powder
2 tablespoons sugar
¾ cup cornmeal

1 Preheat the oven to 400°F. Grease muffin pans well with shortening.
2 Combine the eggs, milk, shortening and corn in a mixing bowl.
3 In another bowl sift together the flour, salt, baking powder and sugar. Blend with the cornmeal and stir into the corn mixture.
4 Fill the muffin pans two-thirds to three-quarters full with the mixture. Bake for 25 minutes, or until done. Serve hot.

ONION SQUARES

9 SQUARES

2 cups sliced onions
3 tablespoons butter
2 cups flour
2 teaspoons baking powder
1 teaspoon salt
¼ cup vegetable shortening
2 tablespoons chopped parsley, or ½ teaspoon caraway seeds
1 cup milk
⅓ cup sour cream

1 Preheat the oven to 425°F.
2 Cook the onions, covered, in butter until tender. Cool.
3 Sift together the flour, baking powder and salt. Chop in the shortening until the mixture resembles coarse cornmeal.
4 Add the parsley and milk and stir until all the flour is moistened.
5 Turn into a well-greased 8-inch-square pan. Spread onions over the top and cover with sour cream.
6 Bake about 20 minutes. Cut into squares and serve hot.

TEA SCONES

16 SCONES

2 cups sifted flour
2 tablespoons sugar
3 teaspoons baking powder
½ teaspoon salt
5 tablespoons butter
1 egg, beaten
¾ cup milk, approximately

1 Preheat the oven to 425°F.

2 Sift together the flour, sugar, baking powder and salt.

3 Chop in the butter with a pastry blender until the flour-coated particles of butter are the size of coarse cornmeal.

4 Add the egg and about three quarters of the milk. Stir quickly and lightly, only until no flour shows. Add more milk if needed to make a soft dough.

5 Turn the dough out on a floured surface and knead gently about 15 times. Cut the dough in half. Shape each half into a ball, press each down into a round about ½ inch thick and cut into 8 wedges like a pie.

6 Place the wedges on a greased cookie sheet without allowing the sides to touch. Glaze, if desired, with lightly beaten egg. Bake until deep golden brown, about 12 minutes.

Note: Scones may be cut also into 2-inch rounds or into squares.

POPOVERS

An old recipe for popovers, typical of those in many early cookbooks, reads: "Get an iron pop-over pan blazing hot, grease it well and pour in the batter."

These cast-iron pans are found in few homes today, with the result that many home cooks are fearful of using substitutes. Fortunately, successful popovers can be baked in modern heavy aluminum tins, or oven glass and earthenware cups like custard cups. The chief requirement is that the cups be deeper than they are wide. If the cups are of aluminum or metal that heats quickly, they do not have to be preheated; if glass or earthenware cups are used, it is best to preheat them while mixing the batter. Heated cups are greased just before filling.

No skill is required in mixing popovers. Success depends on proper baking. The batter is thin—about as thick as heavy cream. In the hot oven the large amount of liquid forms steam, quickly causing the flour-egg mixture to expand and form a nearly hollow shell. This shell must be baked until it is rigid, to prevent collapse as the steam condenses on cooling. It is always a temptation to peek, but to prevent collapse the oven door should not be opened for at least 30 minutes of baking.

6 TO 8 POPOVERS

1 cup flour
½ teaspoon salt
2 eggs
1 cup milk
1 tablespoon vegetable oil

1 Heat the oven to 425°F. Grease aluminum popover pans and set aside. If glass or earthenware cups are used, place these on a baking sheet in the oven to heat; remove and grease just before filling.

2 Measure all ingredients into a bowl and beat with a rotary beater until mixture is very smooth.

3 Fill cups a little less than half full and bake in the preheated oven, without peeking, about 35 minutes, or until the sides are rigid to the touch. If drier popovers are desired, pierce each one with a knife and bake 5 minutes longer.

SPOONBREAD

3 cups milk
1½ cups sifted yellow cornmeal
8 tablespoons butter, melted
Salt to taste, if desired
4 eggs, separated
2 teaspoons baking powder

1 Preheat the oven to 350°F.

2 Bring 2 cups of the milk to the boil and gradually add the cornmeal in a steady stream, stirring rapidly with a wire whisk. Stir in the butter and salt. Cook over low heat, stirring almost constantly, about 10 minutes.

3 Scrape the mixture into a mixing bowl and let cool to lukewarm.

4 Beat the yolks until light and stir them into the mixture. Blend the baking powder with the remaining 1 cup of milk and stir it into the mixture.

5 Beat the egg whites until stiff and fold them into the mixture.

6 Butter a 1½-quart casserole and pour the mixture into it. Bake 40 minutes, or until a knife inserted in the center comes out clean. Serve immediately, with butter on the side.

SOUTHERN CORN BREAD

There are more recipes for corn bread than there are magnolia trees in the South. This is a family standard.

8 SERVINGS

⅓ cup flour
1½ cups sifted cornmeal
1 teaspoon baking soda
½ teaspoon salt
2 eggs
1 cup buttermilk
2 cups milk
1½ tablespoons butter

1 Preheat the oven to 350°F.

2 Sift the flour, cornmeal, baking soda and salt into a mixing bowl. Beat the eggs until foamy and stir them into the dry mixture. Stir in the buttermilk and 1 cup of the milk.

3 Heat the butter in a 9×2-inch black skillet and when it is very hot, but not brown, pour in the batter. Carefully pour the remaining 1 cup of milk on top of the batter without stirring. Place the skillet in the oven and bake 50 minutes, or until set and baked through. Slice into wedges.

QUICK CORN BREAD

1½ cups cornmeal
2 cups flour
2 tablespoons sugar
1 teaspoon salt
4 teaspoons baking powder
2 eggs
2 cups milk
¼ cup bacon drippings

1 Preheat the oven to 450°F.
2 Grease two 9-inch-square pans.
3 Sift the cornmeal, flour, sugar, salt and baking powder together into a mixing bowl. Stir in the lightly beaten eggs, the milk and bacon drippings until well mixed.
4 Spread in baking pans and bake for 30 minutes. Cool.

Note: If this is to be used as a stuffing, it is best if it is made a day ahead. This recipe will yield about 12 cups for stuffing.

CORN AND CHEESE BREAD

8 SERVINGS

1 cup canned cream-style corn
1 cup yellow cornmeal
3 eggs
Salt to taste
½ teaspoon baking soda
¾ cup buttermilk
⅓ cup melted vegetable shortening or oil
¾ cup grated sharp cheddar cheese
2 tablespoons butter

1 Preheat the oven to 400°F.
2 In a mixing bowl, combine the corn, cornmeal, eggs, salt, baking soda and buttermilk. Stir well and add the shortening and ½ cup of the cheese. Stir to blend.
3 Meanwhile, put the butter in a 9-inch skillet, preferably of black iron. Place it in the oven and heat until the butter melts without browning.
4 Pour the batter into the skillet. Sprinkle with the remaining cheese and bake 30 minutes, or until the bread is firm and golden brown on top.

CORN STICKS

½ cup yellow cornmeal
½ cup flour
2 tablespoons sugar
1½ teaspoons baking powder
Salt to taste
¾ cup plus 3 tablespoons cream
2 tablespoons butter, melted
1 egg, separated
1 tablespoon butter
½ cup corn kernels freshly cut from the cob

1 Preheat the oven to 425°F.

2 Select a standard mold for making corn sticks. Place it in the oven until thoroughly heated.

3 Meanwhile, combine the cornmeal, flour, sugar, baking powder and salt in a mixing bowl. Blend well.

4 Blend the cream, 2 tablespoons butter and egg yolk. Add this to the cornmeal mixture, stirring to blend.

5 Melt 1 tablespoon butter in a small skillet and add the corn. Cook, stirring, just until heated through. Stir this into the batter.

6 Beat the egg white and fold it into the mixture.

7 Brush the corn stick mold lightly with oil. Spoon an equal portion of the filling inside each corn stick mold.

8 Bake 15 to 20 minutes. Serve hot.

BOSTON BROWN BREAD

1 cup cornmeal
1 cup rye flour
1 cup whole wheat flour
2 teaspoons baking soda
1 teaspoon salt
2 cups buttermilk
¾ cup molasses
1 cup seedless raisins

1 Combine the cornmeal, flours, baking soda and salt in a mixing bowl.

2 Mix together buttermilk, molasses and raisins. Add to the dry ingredients; mix well.

3 Fill well-greased pudding molds or cans two-thirds full. (Dough will fill 3 No. 2 cans or 2 No. 2½ cans.) Cover with greased mold covers or can lids and then with foil.

4 Set on a rack in a large kettle with water halfway up the sides. Cover and cook for 3 hours, replenishing water as necessary.

SALT-RISING BREAD

2 LOAVES

2 medium potatoes, peeled and thinly sliced
2 tablespoons cornmeal
½ tablespoon sugar
1 teaspoon salt
2 cups boiling water
2 cups milk, scalded and cooled to lukewarm
⅛ teaspoon baking soda
8 cups flour, approximately
½ cup soft shortening or butter

1 Place the potatoes, cornmeal, sugar and salt in a 3-quart bowl. Add the boiling water and stir until the sugar and salt are dissolved. Cover with plastic wrap or foil. Set the bowl in a pan of warm water over the pilot light of a stove, or where it will stay at about 120°F, until small bubbles show in the surface, for 24 hours or longer.

2 Remove the potatoes to a sieve and press out excess moisture into the potato water still in the bowl.

3 Add the milk, baking soda and 4 cups of the flour to the bowl. Stir until smooth. Set the bowl again in the pan of warm water and let it stand for about 2 hours, until the sponge is almost doubled in bulk.

4 Chop the shortening or butter into 1 cup of the remaining flour. Add this to the sponge. Add enough additional flour, about 3 cups, to make a moderately stiff dough. Knead on a floured surface quickly and lightly. Do not let dough get cold.

5 Return the dough to the bowl, grease the surface of the dough and let it rise for about 2 hours, until doubled in bulk.

6 Turn the risen dough out on a lightly floured surface and shape into 2 loaves. Place in greased 9 × 5 × 3-inch loaf pans and grease the tops of the loaves. Let rise again for about 2 hours, until almost dou-bled in bulk, or slightly above the tops of the pans. Sprinkle the tops with cornmeal if desired.

7 About 15 minutes before the loaves have finished rising, preheat the oven to 400°F.

8 Bake the loaves for 15 minutes, then lower the oven temperature to 350°F and bake for about 35 minutes longer, or until the bread shrinks from the sides of the pans and is brown. Cool on a rack.

◆

APPLE BREAD

1 LOAF

2 cups flour
1 teaspoon baking powder
½ teaspoon baking soda
1 teaspoon salt
½ cup vegetable shortening
⅔ cup sugar
2 eggs
1 cup unpeeled, ground apples and juice
½ cup grated sharp cheese
¼ cup chopped nuts

1 Preheat the oven to 350°F.

2 Sift together the flour, baking powder, baking soda and salt.

3 Cream the shortening, add the sugar gradually and continue working until light and fluffy. Add the eggs, 1 at a time, beating about 1 minute after each addition. Add the apples, cheese and nuts and mix well.

4 Add the dry ingredients in 2 portions, mixing only until all the flour is dampened.

5 Turn into a greased 9 × 5 × 3-inch loaf pan. Push the batter well up into the corners of the pan, leaving the center slightly hollow. Bake 1 hour.

BANANA BRAN BREAD

2 LOAVES AND 2 CUSTARD CUPS

1 cup ready-to-eat bran cereal
1 cup mashed (2 to 3) ripe bananas
3 tablespoons vegetable shortening
½ cup sugar
¼ cup boiling water
1 egg
1½ cups flour
2 teaspoons baking powder
½ teaspoon baking soda
½ teaspoon salt

1 Preheat the oven to 350°F.
2 Measure the bran, mashed bananas, shortening and sugar into a bowl. Add the water and stir until well mixed. Add the egg and beat well.
3 Sift together the flour, baking powder, baking soda and salt. Add to the banana mixture, stirring only until combined.
4 Fill 2 greased cans (1-pound baked-bean cans) not more than two-thirds full. Bake any extra batter in greased custard cups.
5 Bake until a toothpick inserted in the center comes out clean, or 25 minutes for custard cups, 45 minutes to 1 hour for cans. Let cool 5 minutes, then remove from cans.

Gingerbread, page 691.

JOHN HARPER'S BANANA NUT BREAD

John Harper's banana nut bread has won awards at the Michigan State Fair, and he kindly shared the recipe with me. It is an excellent bread served warm from the oven or cut into slices and toasted for breakfast.

1 LOAF

½ cup vegetable shortening
¾ cup sugar
1 large egg
4 teaspoons lemon juice
2 cups flour
1 teaspoon baking soda
½ teaspoon salt
1 cup mashed (2 to 3) ripe bananas
½ cup walnuts, preferably black, broken or chopped coarsely

1 Preheat the oven to 350°F.
2 Put the shortening and sugar into the bowl of an electric mixer. Cream together until smooth and well blended. Beat in the egg and lemon juice.
3 Sift together the flour, baking soda and salt. Fold the mixture into the batter and blend well. Stir in the mashed bananas and walnuts. Pour the mixture into a 9×4×3-inch loaf pan and bake 60 to 70 minutes, or until a straw inserted in the center of the loaf comes out clean. Turn out on a rack to cool.

BANANA TEA BREAD

1 LOAF

1¾ cups sifted flour
2 teaspoons baking powder
¼ teaspoon baking soda
½ teaspoon salt
⅓ cup vegetable shortening
⅔ cup sugar
2 eggs, well beaten
1 cup mashed (2 to 3) ripe bananas
½ teaspoon cinnamon
Pinch of grated nutmeg

   1 Preheat the oven to 350°F.
   2 Sift together the flour, baking powder, baking soda and salt.
   3 Cream the shortening, add the sugar gradually and continue working until light and fluffy. Add the eggs and beat well. Add the flour mixture alternately with the bananas, a small amount at a time, beating after each addition until smooth. Stir in the cinnamon and nutmeg.
   4 Turn into a well-greased 8½ × 4½ × 3-inch loaf pan and bake about 70 minutes.

ORANGE HONEY BREAD

1 LOAF

2 tablespoons vegetable shortening
1 cup honey
1 egg, well beaten
1½ tablespoons grated orange rind
2½ cups flour
2½ teaspoons baking powder
½ teaspoon baking soda
½ teaspoon salt
¾ cup orange juice
¾ cup chopped nuts

   1 Preheat the oven to 325°F.
   2 Cream the shortening, add the honey and mix together thoroughly. Add the egg and orange rind.
   3 Sift the flour with the baking powder, baking soda and salt and add to the creamed mixture alternately with the orange juice, stirring only until flour is dampened. Add the nuts.
   4 Turn into a greased 9-inch loaf pan and bake 70 minutes.

ORANGE OATMEAL BREAD

1 LOAF

¾ cup plus 2 tablespoons sugar
1 orange, peeled and thinly sliced, with each
    slice cut into eighths
1½ cups flour
1 teaspoon salt
4½ teaspoons baking powder
¼ teaspoon baking soda
1 cup old-fashioned rolled oats
2 tablespoons butter, melted
2 eggs, lightly beaten
⅔ cup water
2 tablespoons grated orange rind

1 Preheat the oven to 350°F.

2 Sprinkle 2 tablespoons of the sugar over the orange pieces. Set aside.

3 Combine the flour, salt, baking powder, baking soda and remaining sugar in a bowl. Add the oats.

4 Combine the melted butter, eggs, water, orange rind and sweetened oranges and add to the dry ingredients, stirring just until blended. Pour into a greased 9 × 5 × 3-inch loaf pan and bake for 55 to 60 minutes. Cool on a rack.

CRANBERRY-NUT BREAD

1 LOAF

2 cups flour
2 teaspoons baking powder
½ teaspoon salt
½ teaspoon baking soda
4 tablespoons butter, softened
1 cup sugar
1 egg
1 tablespoon grated orange rind
½ cup chopped nuts
¼ cup chopped citron
½ cup fresh orange juice
1½ cups cranberries, picked over and washed

1 Preheat the oven to 350°F.

2 Sift together the flour, baking powder and salt.

3 Add the baking soda to the butter and mix well. Gradually blend in the sugar. Beat in the egg. Stir in the orange rind, nuts and citron. Add the flour mixture alternately with the orange juice.

4 Put the cranberries through a food chopper, using the coarse blade. Or coarsely chop in a food processor. Stir into the dough.

5 Turn into a well-greased, lightly floured 9 × 5 × 3-inch loaf pan and bake for 1 hour and 20 minutes. Cool.

STEAMED DATE AND HONEY BREAD

2 LARGE OR 3 SMALL LOAVES

1 cup cornmeal
1 cup rye flour
1 cup all-purpose flour
½ teaspoon salt
½ teaspoon cinnamon
1 teaspoon baking soda
½ cup light molasses
½ cup honey
1½ cups buttermilk, or 1½ cups milk mixed
    with 1½ tablespoons vinegar or lemon juice
1 cup pitted dates, quartered

1 Combine the cornmeal, flours, salt, cinnamon and baking soda in a mixing bowl. Stir in the molasses, honey and buttermilk. Fold in the dates.

2 Generously grease 2 coffee cans or 3 No. 303 cans fitted with covers (shelled nuts come in these cans). Spoon the batter into the cans and cover tightly with foil or the can covers.

3 Set the cans on a rack in a large pot or roaster equipped with a tight-fitting cover. Pour enough water into the large pot to come halfway up the height of the cans. Bring to a boil, reduce heat to low, cover the pot and steam the bread for 2½ hours in the coffee cans, or for 2 hours in the smaller cans. Remove from cans immediately and cool on racks.

SESAME TEA BREAD

1 LOAF

3 cups flour
1 teaspoon salt
2½ teaspoons baking powder
½ cup toasted sesame seeds
⅔ cup sugar
¼ cup vegetable shortening
2 eggs
1 teaspoon grated lemon rind
1½ cups milk
1 tablespoon untoasted sesame seeds

1 Preheat the oven to 350°F.

2 Sift the flour, salt and baking powder together and mix in the toasted sesame seeds.

3 Cream the sugar and shortening together until fluffy and beat in the eggs. Blend in the lemon rind and milk. Add all at once to the flour mixture and mix only until the ingredients are blended, about 30 strokes. Use the cut-and-fold method of mixing and stop halfway through to scrape down the bowl and spoon with a rubber spatula.

4 Turn the mixture into a well-greased, lightly floured 9×5×3-inch loaf pan. Sprinkle the untoasted sesame seeds over the top.

5 Bake 70 minutes. Cool. Serve with sweet butter or cream cheese.

SPICE BREAD

1 LOAF

1½ teaspoons aniseed
¾ cup water
½ cup honey
½ cup sugar
½ cup finely chopped citron
2¼ cups flour
1½ teaspoons baking soda
½ teaspoon salt
1 teaspoon cinnamon
Dash of ground cloves
1 teaspoon grated nutmeg

1 Preheat the oven to 350°F.

2 Combine the aniseed and water in a saucepan. Bring mixture to a boil. Add the honey, sugar and citron and stir until sugar is dissolved. Remove from the heat.

3 Sift together the remaining ingredients and fold in the liquid mixture. Turn the batter into a 9 × 5 × 3-inch loaf pan and bake for 1 hour. Serve buttered or with cream cheese.

Note: This bread improves if allowed to stand for 1 day.

NEW ENGLAND BUTTERMILK DOUGHNUTS

For tender doughnuts the dough must be soft, not nearly so stiff as for bread. Plenty of flour on the pastry cloth or board eliminates the handling that is undesirable. A deep-fat thermometer registers the right heat—375°F. Higher than that means the doughnuts cook on the outside and not within, and lower than that means they become fat soaked.

ABOUT 3 DOZEN (3-INCH) DOUGHNUTS

4½ cups flour
¼ teaspoon grated nutmeg
¼ teaspoon allspice
1½ teaspoons baking soda
1½ teaspoons cream of tartar
1½ teaspoons salt
3 eggs
1 cup sugar
3 tablespoons vegetable shortening, melted
1 cup buttermilk
Oil for deep frying

1 Sift together the flour, nutmeg, allspice, baking soda, cream of tartar and salt.

2 Beat the eggs until thick and lemon colored and gradually beat in the sugar. Add the melted shortening and buttermilk, then add the flour mixture. Mix well, chill and turn out on a well-floured board or pastry cloth.

3 Roll to ¼-inch thick; cut with a floured cutter.

4 Fry a few at a time in 375°F deep hot oil for 3 minutes, or until brown, first on one side and then on the other.

BASIC PANCAKES

ABOUT 1 DOZEN (5-INCH) PANCAKES

1 cup flour
2 teaspoons baking powder
2 tablespoons sugar
½ teaspoon salt
1 egg
½ to ¾ cup milk
2 tablespoons butter, melted and slightly
  cooled

1 Sift together the flour, baking powder, sugar and salt.

2 Beat the egg, milk and butter until blended.

3 Pour milk mixture into dry ingredients and stir only enough to moisten the dry ingredients. Do not beat or the pancakes will be tough.

4 Heat a griddle and lightly grease it. Drop the batter from the tip of a large spoon or a ¼ cup measure and bake until the entire surface of the pancake is dotted with holes. Turn and bake the other side just until light brown. Keep warm in a 200°F oven until all the pancakes are cooked.

WHOLE WHEAT PANCAKES

ABOUT 20 PANCAKES

¾ cup cake flour
1 cup whole wheat flour
1 teaspoon salt
2 tablespoons sugar
1¾ teaspoons baking powder
3 tablespoons molasses
2 eggs, lightly beaten
4 tablespoons butter, melted
1 cup milk

1 Combine the flours, salt, sugar and baking powder in a bowl. Mix together the molasses, eggs, butter and milk. Pour the liquid into the flour mixture and stir to make a fairly smooth batter.

2 Heat a griddle so that a drop of water sputters when it is dropped onto it. Lightly grease the griddle.

3 Spoon the batter onto the griddle to make cakes about 2½ inches in diameter. When the surface bubbles and the underside is brown, turn the cakes and brown the other side.

FRESH CORN PANCAKES

16 PANCAKES

4 to 6 ears of fresh corn
1 cup milk
2 tablespoons butter, melted
2 eggs, separated
⅔ cup flour
1 teaspoon sugar
1 teaspoon baking powder
½ teaspoon salt

1 Boil the ears of corn for 1 minute before cutting the kernels off the cobs. Measure out 2 cups of kernels and combine them with the milk, butter and egg yolks in a saucepan.

2 Sift together the flour, sugar, baking powder and salt. Add to the liquid ingredients and mix well.

3 Beat the egg whites until they stand in soft peaks. Fold into the mixture.

4 Fry the mixture on a hot well-greased griddle, using ½ cup batter for each pancake. Turn to brown on both sides. Serve with maple syrup or butter.

MINUTE SCALLION PANCAKES

2 LARGE PANCAKES

½ cup chicken stock
½ teaspoon salt
1 egg
⅔ cup flour
⅓ cup minced scallions
1 slice of bacon, cooked and minced, or
    1 tablespoon dried shrimp, minced
4 teaspoons vegetable oil

1 Combine the stock with ¼ teaspoon of the salt. Combine the stock mixture with the remaining ingredients except the oil. Mix in a bowl into a thin paste.

2 Place 2 teaspoons of the oil in a hot skillet over medium heat. Cover the bottom evenly by tipping around, or using a spatula. Pour half of the mixture from the bowl into the skillet, spread out flat and cover the bottom. Cook until edge is light brown, then turn to brown the other side.

3 Use the remaining oil and cook the remaining mixture in the same way. Serve hot as a snack or breakfast dish.

CORNMEAL PANCAKES

ABOUT 20 PANCAKES

1⅓ cups cornmeal
¼ cup flour
1 teaspoon salt
½ teaspoon baking soda
2 cups buttermilk
2 eggs
4 tablespoons butter, melted

1 Place the cornmeal, flour, salt and baking soda in a bowl. Mix the buttermilk and eggs together and stir into the dry ingredients. Stir in the melted butter.

2 Heat the griddle until a drop of water sputters on the surface. Lightly grease the griddle with shortening.

3 Pour or spoon the batter onto the griddle to make 2-inch pancakes. When the surface bubbles and the cakes are set and light brown on the underside, turn and brown the second side. These are very light pancakes and can be turned easily only if made small.

RAISED BUCKWHEAT PANCAKES

ABOUT 20 PANCAKES

2 teaspoons yeast
2 cups milk, scalded and cooled to lukewarm
2 cups buckwheat flour
½ teaspoon salt
2 tablespoons molasses
½ teaspoon baking soda, dissolved in
    ¼ cup lukewarm water
1 egg
¼ cup vegetable oil, or melted butter

1 Place the yeast in a bowl and gradually add the milk, stirring to dissolve. Stir in the flour and salt until the mixture is smooth. Cover with a towel and let stand at room temperature overnight or for about 12 hours.

2 Stir in the molasses, baking soda, egg and oil.

3 Heat a griddle until a drop of water sputters on the surface. Grease lightly with shortening.

4 Pour or spoon the mixture onto the griddle to make cakes about 2½ inches in diameter. Cook until surface bubbles and the cakes are set and light brown on underside. Turn and brown the other side.

RICE AND SESAME PANCAKES

24 (3-INCH) PANCAKES

¾ cup flour
1½ teaspoons baking powder
½ teaspoon sugar
¼ teaspoon salt
1 egg, separated
1 cup milk
2 tablespoons butter, melted
½ teaspoon vanilla extract
½ cup cooked rice
1 tablespoon toasted sesame seeds

1 Sift the flour, baking powder, sugar and salt together.

2 Combine the egg yolk, milk, butter and vanilla. Stir in the dry ingredients and beat until smooth. Fold in the rice and sesame seeds.

3 Beat the egg white until stiff but not dry and gently fold into the mixture.

4 Preheat a griddle or heavy skillet. Grease lightly with shortening or oil. Spoon the batter in tablespoons onto the hot griddle and cook until light brown on the underside. Turn and lightly brown the other side. Serve with preserves and sour cream.

SOUR CREAM PANCAKES

ABOUT 14 (5-INCH) PANCAKES

1 cup flour
½ teaspoon salt
½ teaspoon baking soda
1¼ cups sour cream, approximately
1 egg, slightly beaten

1 Sift together the flour, salt and baking soda.

2 Combine the sour cream and egg. Pour into the flour mixture and stir just enough to moisten the dry ingredients. Do not beat.

3 Heat a griddle or skillet, grease if necessary and drop the batter by spoonfuls onto it. When bubbles break on top of the cakes, turn and bake on the other side.

Variations

BUTTERMILK PANCAKES

Substitute 1 cup buttermilk for the sour cream and add 2 tablespoons melted butter when combining the milk and egg.

FRUIT AND NUT PANCAKES

Add to either sour cream or buttermilk batter ½ cup finely chopped apples or well-drained canned pineapple; or ½ cup chopped pecans or other nuts.

BUCKWHEAT BLINI

36 BLINI

1 cup milk
½ package (½ tablespoon) yeast
4 eggs, separated
½ teaspoon salt
1 teaspoon sugar
3 tablespoons butter, melted
1½ cups buckwheat flour

1 Scald milk and allow it to cool to lukewarm. Add yeast and stir until softened.

2 Beat the egg yolks until thick. Add the yeast mixture and remaining ingredients except egg whites. Mix thoroughly.

3 Set in a pan of warm water, cover and let rise until doubled in bulk, about 1¼ hours.

4 Beat egg whites stiff and fold gently but thoroughly into batter.

5 Preheat a lightly buttered griddle until it is hot. Using 1 tablespoon of batter for each pancake, cook until golden brown, turning once. If the blini begin to stick to the griddle, butter them lightly again. Serve with caviar and sour cream.

WHITE FLOUR BLINI

42 BLINI

2 cups milk
½ package (½ tablespoon) yeast
2 teaspoons sugar
3 cups flour
3 eggs, separated
5 tablespoons butter, melted
½ teaspoon salt

1 Scald the milk and allow it to cool to lukewarm. Add the yeast and stir until the yeast has softened.

2 Add the sugar and 1½ cups of the flour and mix well. Cover and set in a pan of warm water until doubled in bulk, about 1¼ hours.

3 Beat the egg yolks with the butter and salt. Add to the batter. Add the remaining flour and beat until smooth. Cover and let rise as before until doubled in bulk, approximately 30 minutes.

4 Beat the egg whites until stiff and fold into the batter. Let the mixture stand for 10 minutes.

5 Preheat a lightly buttered griddle until it is hot. Using 1 tablespoon of batter for each pancake, bake until golden brown on both sides, turning once. Serve with caviar and sour cream.

BASIC WAFFLE RECIPE

5 OR 6 WAFFLES

2 cups flour
3 teaspoons baking powder
1 teaspoon salt
2 tablespoons sugar
2 eggs, separated
1½ cups milk
6 tablespoons shortening, melted

1 Sift together the flour, baking powder, salt and sugar.

2 Beat egg yolks; add milk and melted shortening. Pour into flour mixture and stir just enough to moisten dry ingredients. Fold in egg whites, which have been beaten until stiff but not dry.

3 Grease a hot waffle iron and pour batter to 1 inch from edge. Bake 4 to 5 minutes. Serve hot with melted butter and syrup or honey.

♦

WHOLE WHEAT–NUT WAFFLES

ABOUT 6 WAFFLES

2 cups whole wheat flour
2 teaspoons baking powder
½ teaspoon salt
3 eggs, separated
1½ cups milk
¼ cup shortening, melted
½ cup chopped walnuts or filberts

1 Mix the flour with the baking powder and salt.

2 Beat the egg yolks and add the milk and shortening. Add to the flour mixture and mix until all the flour is moistened. Add the nuts.

4 Bake in a hot waffle iron and serve with melted butter and heated syrup.

♦

RYE FRITTERS

2 SERVINGS

1 cup all-purpose flour
1 cup rye meal (not regular rye flour)
1 teaspoon salt
1 teaspoon cinnamon
1 teaspoon baking powder
1 egg
2 teaspoons molasses
1 cup milk, approximately
Oil for deep frying

1 Sift together into a mixing bowl the flour, rye meal, salt, cinnamon and baking powder.

2 Beat the egg, add the molasses and pour into the flour mixture. Add ⅔ cup of the milk and mix thoroughly, adding more milk if necessary to make a medium stiff batter.

3 Drop the batter from a spoon slightly larger than a tablespoon into oil heated to 360°F. Fry about 2½ minutes on each side. Serve hot with maple syrup and sausages.

BREAD CRUMB DUMPLINGS

1 loaf of good-quality sliced white bread
¼ cup water
6 to 8 eggs, beaten
½ cup finely chopped parsley
½ cup finely chopped onion
½ teaspoon grated nutmeg
Salt to taste

1 Trim the crusts from the bread. Use the white part to make bread crumbs in a food processor.

2 Sprinkle enough of the water over the crumbs, tossing with a 2-pronged fork, barely to moisten. Add the eggs, tossing lightly with the fork. When well blended, add the remaining ingredients.

3 Drop by tablespoons atop bubbling stew or boiling stock. Cover the pan and steam for about 30 minutes. The dumplings should puff up and be very light.

TOMATO DUMPLINGS

1 cup flour
½ teaspoon salt
1½ teaspoons baking powder
½ teaspoon dry mustard
½ cup tomato juice

Sift the flour with the salt, baking powder and mustard. Gradually stir in the tomato juice. Drop by tablespoons atop bubbling stew or boiling stock; cover. Cook without lifting the lid for 15 minutes.

◆

HERB DUMPLINGS

1½ cups flour
2 teaspoons baking powder
1 teaspoon salt
½ teaspoon thyme
¼ teaspoon marjoram
2 tablespoons chopped parsley
1 egg, lightly beaten
⅔ cup milk

1 Mix together the flour, baking powder, salt, thyme, marjoram and parsley. Combine the egg and milk and stir into the flour mixture until flour is moistened.

2 Drop by tablespoons atop bubbling stew or boiling stock; cover. Steam for 10 minutes. Uncover and cook for 10 minutes longer.

14

Desserts

Pies and Pastries

MAKING SUCCESSFUL PIE PASTRY

An experienced cook tosses together a batch of pastry quickly and easily and invariably turns out well-shaped pies with tender, crisp and somewhat flaky crusts. Some of the tricks that may help the novice in successful pastry making follow:

CHOICE OF INGREDIENTS Use all-purpose flour, not cake flour. Lard and hydrogenated vegetable shortenings are better than butter or margarine because they yield a tenderer product. Cold or ice water aids in producing flakiness.

CHOICE OF UTENSILS A food processor makes pie pastry in seconds, although purists say the crust is not as flaky as when made by hand. If doing it by hand, a pastry blender is an efficient tool for chopping in fat, but 2 knives will produce the same results. If the fingers are used, the heat from the hand softens the fat excessively and it is apt to be rubbed into the flour so thoroughly that the pastry is lacking in flakiness. Perhaps a fork is the best utensil for mixing as the water is added. Glass pie plates give a darker-colored crust than aluminum.

AMOUNT OF WATER TO USE Fat particles coated with flour must be bound together with water, and for lightness there must be enough water present to form steam. The amount of water needed varies with the dryness of the flour. Use only enough water to dampen all the dough. Excess water toughens the crust and too little water makes it crumbly.

ROLLING THE DOUGH Pat the dough all over with a rolling pin so the particles will stick together and roll without cracking. To prevent kneading and toughening the pastry, roll it from center out toward the edge. A cloth-covered and well-floured board and rolling pin prevent sticking.

FITTING THE DOUGH IN THE PLATE For a well-shaped pie, fit the dough into the plate without stretching. When pressing it to the plate do so by working from the rim toward the center, lifting the pastry at the edge if necessary to give extra fullness inside the plate. To prevent bulging of pastry, press out all air spaces between dough and the plate.

TO PREVENT SOAKING OF THE BOTTOM CRUST Brush the dough with lightly beaten egg white or with shortening before adding the filling. Bake on the lower rack of a hot oven at least 10 minutes; for the whole time if the filling permits.

BASIC PIE PASTRY

PASTRY FOR 9-INCH DOUBLE-CRUST PIE,
OR 6 TARTS

2 cups flour
½ teaspoon salt
⅔ cup shortening
⅓ cup cold water, approximately

1 If using a food processor, put the flour, salt and shortening into the container. Start processing while pouring the water through the funnel. Add only enough water so that the dough holds together and can be shaped into a ball.

2 If using a pastry blender or 2 knives, chop in the shortening until the mixture resembles coarse cornmeal. Sprinkle water slowly over the top of the flour, while tossing the mixture up from the bottom of the bowl with a fork. After about three quarters of the water has been added, press the dampened part of the dough into a ball and set aside. Add only enough water to dampen the remaining flour mixture. Press all the dough together.

3 Divide the dough into 2 portions, one slightly larger than the other. If the kitchen is hot, chill the dough for ½ hour before rolling.

4 Place the larger ball of dough on a lightly floured pastry cloth or board, pat in all directions with a floured rolling pin and then roll from the center out in all directions, loosening the pastry and reflouring the cloth and rolling pin as necessary. Roll into a round ⅛ inch thick and 2 inches larger in diameter than the top of the pie plate.

5 Fold gently into quarters, place in the plate and unfold. Fit the dough into the plate loosely and press against the plate without stretching it. Trim the edge slightly larger than the outside rim of the plate. Add desired filling.

6 Stack the pastry trimmings on the remaining ball of dough and roll until about 1 inch larger than the top of the plate. Fold gently into quarters and cut several small gashes to allow steam to escape.

7 Moisten the rim of the lower crust, place top crust on the filled plate and unfold. Do not stretch the pastry. Tuck the rim of the top beneath the edge of the undercrust and flute with the fingers, making a tight seal.

8 Bake as directed for the filling used.

Variations

BAKED PIE SHELL

Line pie plate with pastry for bottom crust and prick well with a fork around bottom and sides. Bake in preheated 450°F oven 12 to 15 minutes, or until golden. Cool before adding desired filling.

LATTICE-TOP PIE CRUST

Roll dough for top crust into a circle and cut into ½-inch strips. Moisten the rim of the bottom crust with water and place half of the strips parallel on the filled pie shell, spacing evenly. Repeat with remaining strips in opposite direction. Attach strips firmly to rim.

TART SHELLS

Cut pastry into 5-inch rounds and fit over inverted muffin tins or custard cups; or line tart shells, fitting pastry loosely into pans and pressing it firmly around the sides. Prick well with a fork and bake in a preheated 450°F oven 10 to 15 minutes, or until golden brown.

SWEET PIE PASTRY

6 TART SHELLS, OR 2 (9-INCH) PIE SHELLS

2 cups flour
½ pound butter, at room temperature
2 egg yolks
2 tablespoons sugar
Grated rind of 1 lemon
Pinch of salt

1 Put the flour in a mixing bowl, make a well in the center and add the remaining ingredients.

2 Mix the center ingredients with the fingers of one hand or a pastry blender until blended. Quickly work in the flour. Add a small amount of ice water if necessary to moisten the dough so it can be gathered into a ball.

3 Wrap the dough in wax paper and chill 1 hour. Roll out the pastry, fit it into the plates and bake on the bottom shelf of a preheated 450°F oven until brown, about 15 minutes.

ALMOND CRUST

1 (9-INCH) CRUST

1½ cups blanched almonds
1 egg white
¼ cup sugar

1 Preheat the oven to 375°F.

2 Using a knife, chop the almonds fine. Or chop them briefly in a food processor.

3 Beat the egg white until stiff and gradually fold in the sugar. Fold in the chopped almonds and press the mixture firmly over the bottom and sides of an oiled 9-inch pie plate. Bake the shell until light brown. Remove to a rack and cool.

♦

BRAZIL NUT CRUST

1 (9-INCH) PIE CRUST

Brazil nuts
2 tablespoons sugar

1 Using a food processor, chop enough Brazil nuts to make 1 cup.

2 Blend the ground nuts with the sugar. Using the back of a tablespoon or the fingers, press the mixture against the bottom and sides of a 9-inch pie plate.

3 Bake the shell in a preheated 400°F oven until light brown, about 8 minutes. Cool.

VANILLA CRUMB CRUST

1 (9-INCH) PIE CRUST

1⅓ cups vanilla wafer crumbs
¼ cup sugar
5 tablespoons butter, melted

1 Preheat the oven to 400°F.
2 Combine the crumbs with the sugar and melted butter and mix thoroughly.
3 Press the mixture firmly against the sides and bottom of a 9-inch pie plate, using the back of a spoon.
4 Bake 5 minutes and cool.

Meringue Pie Crust, page 752.
Meringue Pie Topping, page 753.

◆

GRAHAM CRACKER CRUST

1 (8-INCH) SPRINGFORM PAN CRUST

15 graham crackers
1 tablespoon sugar
½ teaspoon cinnamon
4 tablespoons butter, melted

1 Break the crackers into quarters and place in the container of a food processor. Blend to crumbs and empty the crumbs into a bowl.
2 Stir in the sugar and cinnamon. Add the melted butter and mix until all the crumbs are moistened.
3 Press the crumbs against the sides and bottom of a buttered springform pan or 9-inch pie plate. Chill before adding the filling.

NUT-CRUMB CRUST

1 (8-INCH) SPRINGFORM PAN CRUST

⅔ cup graham cracker crumbs
¼ cup finely chopped nuts
2 tablespoons butter, melted
1 tablespoon sugar
¼ teaspoon cinnamon
¼ teaspoon grated nutmeg

1 Mix together all the ingredients.
2 Sprinkle half the crumb mixture on the bottom of an 8-inch springform pan. Turn a pie filling or cheesecake mixture into the pan and sprinkle with the remaining crumbs.

◆

CARDAMOM APPLE PIE

6 TO 8 SERVINGS

Pastry for a 2-crust pie
5 cups tart juicy apple slices
½ cup honey
2 tablespoons butter
¾ teaspoon ground cardamom
1 teaspoon vanilla extract

1 Preheat the oven to 350°F.
2 Line a 9-inch pie plate with a layer of pastry and arrange the apple slices over it.
3 Dribble honey over apples. Dot with the butter and sprinkle with cardamom and vanilla.
4 Arrange top pastry over apples and flute edges. Bake for 35 to 40 minutes.

APPLE–SOUR CREAM PIE

Pastry for a 1-crust pie
2 eggs
½ cup plus ⅓ cup sugar
½ cup plus 2 tablespoons flour
1 cup sour cream
1 teaspoon grated lemon rind
1 tablespoon lemon juice
⅓ cup seedless raisins
2½ cups sliced apples
¼ teaspoon grated nutmeg
3 tablespoons butter

1 Preheat the oven to 400°F.

2 Line a 9-inch pie plate with the pastry.

3 Beat the eggs and add the ½ cup of sugar, 2 tablespoons flour, the sour cream, lemon rind and juice. Add the raisins and apples; mix well. Pour into the pastry-lined pie plate. Bake for 10 minutes.

4 Combine the remaining flour and sugar and the nutmeg. Cut in the butter with 2 knives until the mixture is crumbly. Sprinkle on the apple filling and continue baking for 30 to 35 minutes, until the crumbs are brown and the filling is set. Chill.

NORMANDY APPLESAUCE PIE

1½ cups flour
2 eggs, separated
2 tablespoons granulated sugar
¼ pound butter, softened
Grated rind of 1 lemon
2 (15-ounce) jars (4 cups) thick applesauce
½ cup confectioners' sugar
2 or 3 drops of lemon juice
1 cup slivered almonds

1 Combine flour, well-beaten egg yolks, granulated sugar, butter and lemon rind. Blend well; chill for 2 hours.

2 Preheat the oven to 400°F.

3 Divide mixture into 2 portions, one twice as large as the other. Roll out the large portion to a thickness of ⅛ inch. Use to line a shallow oblong pan. Cover with the applesauce.

4 Roll out smaller portion of dough to fit top of pan. Cover pan with the dough and seal the edges.

5 Mix together the beaten egg whites, confectioners' sugar and lemon juice. Blend until smooth and spread over top of pasty. Sprinkle with slivered almonds.

6 Bake for about 30 minutes, until the top is crusty and brown. Serve hot or cold.

APPLE TART

This tart is really an upside-down pie because it is baked with the crust on top, then inverted. It can be served hot or cold.

6 TO 8 SERVINGS

½ pound butter
1 cup light brown sugar
3 cups apple slices
¼ cup blanched almonds
2 teaspoons lemon juice
¼ teaspoon cinnamon
4 teaspoons grated lemon rind
1¼ cups flour
1 teaspoon granulated sugar
1 egg, lightly beaten
Whipped cream, sweetened and flavored

1 Preheat the oven to 450°F.
2 Melt half the butter in a round or square heatproof skillet or baking dish (8 or 9 inches). Add the brown sugar and heat for 3 minutes, stirring, until the mixture has heavy bubbles. Cool until the sugar begins to set.
3 Cover the cooled sugar mixture with the apple slices in any desired pattern. Stud with the almonds. Blend the lemon juice, cinnamon and half of the grated rind and sprinkle the mixture over the apple slices.
4 Blend the flour and granulated sugar in a bowl. Add remaining lemon rind. Cut in remaining butter with fingers or a pastry blender until the mixture resembles coarse meal. Add the egg. Work the dough quickly, then gather into a ball.
5 With a floured rolling pin roll out the dough on a lightly floured board into a sheet that will fit the inside of the baking dish. Fit pastry over the apples but do not attach to the dish. Trim neatly.

6 Bake for 15 to 20 minutes, until pastry is golden brown. Cool for 2 minutes, then invert onto a serving platter. Serve with sweetened whipped cream flavored with vanilla, brandy or orange liqueur.

◆

BLACKBERRY AND APPLE PIE

6 TO 8 SERVINGS

Pastry for a 2-crust pie
3 cups fresh blackberries, picked over, washed and drained
1 cup thin slices of peeled green apples
2⅔ tablespoons quick-cooking tapioca
1 cup sugar
½ teaspoon cinnamon
2 tablespoons butter

1 Preheat the oven to 450°F.
2 Line a 9-inch pie plate with half of the pastry.
3 Combine the blackberries, apples, tapioca, sugar and cinnamon. Mix well and transfer to the prepared pie plate.
4 Dot the filling with the butter and cover with the remaining pastry. Seal and flute the edges. Pierce the pastry with the point of a knife to allow the steam to escape during baking.
5 Bake for 10 minutes. Reduce the heat to 350°F and bake for about 30 minutes longer, or until pastry is brown. The pie may be served either warm or cold, with whipped cream or ice cream.

BANANA–SOUR CREAM PIE

6 TO 8 SERVINGS

1½ cups sour cream
3 egg yolks
¾ cup sugar
2 tablespoons cornstarch
1 teaspoon vanilla extract
2 medium bananas
2 tablespoons lemon juice
1 baked 9-inch pie shell

1 Put the sour cream into the top part of a double boiler and heat over boiling water until moderately hot. The cream will get thinner as its heats.

2 Beat the egg yolks lightly in a mixing bowl and stir in the sugar and cornstarch. Gradually add the hot sour cream, stirring vigorously. Cook over boiling water for 15 to 20 minutes, until thick. Remove mixture from the heat, add the vanilla and cool.

3 Peel and slice the bananas and sprinkle with the lemon juice. Put half of the bananas on the bottom of the baked pie shell and spoon half of the cool filling over them. Cover with the remaining bananas and then the remaining filling. Chill for several hours before serving.

BLUEBERRY PIE

6 TO 8 SERVINGS

Pastry for a 2-crust pie
¾ cup sugar
3 tablespoons quick-cooking tapioca
Dash of cinnamon
4 cups blueberries
1 tablespoon lemon juice
1 teaspoon grated lemon rind
1 tablespoon butter

1 Preheat the oven to 425°F.

2 Line a 9-inch pie plate with half of the pastry.

3 Mix the sugar, tapioca and cinnamon. Sprinkle the mixture over the berries. Add lemon juice and rind. Spoon the berries into the prepared pie plate and dot with the butter.

4 Cut the remaining pastry into strips and make a lattice top for the pie. Trim edges, moisten, and border with a strip of pastry.

5 Bake on lower rack of the oven for about 50 minutes.

CHERRY TART

6 SERVINGS

2 (1-pound) cans (4 cups) pitted red
  sour cherries packed in water
1 cup sugar
2 tablespoons brandy (optional)
1½ cups flour
1½ teaspoons cinnamon
¼ pound butter
1 egg, beaten
4 teaspoons cornstarch
¼ teaspoon almond extract
Sweetened whipped cream

1 Drain the cherries. Sprinkle them with 10 tablespoons of the sugar and the brandy. Allow to stand for 1 hour, tossing occasionally.

2 Sift the flour together with the cinnamon and remaining sugar into a bowl. Cut in the butter with 2 knives or a pastry blender. Mix in the egg and work the mixture with the hands until it just holds together. Chill for 30 minutes.

3 Preheat the oven to 350°F.

4 Pat the crust mixture into an 8-inch pie plate or flan ring, making an even layer. Crimp the dough around a standing edge.

5 Drain the cherries. Measure the drained syrup and, if necessary, add water to make ¾ cup of liquid. Place ½ cup of the syrup in a pan and bring to a boil. Stir the cornstarch into the remaining ¼ cup of the syrup.

6 Pour the hot syrup over the blended cornstarch, return to the pan and cook over low heat, stirring, for 2 or 3 minutes. Add the almond extract.

7 Place the cherries in the tart shell or flan ring and pour the hot sauce over them. Bake for 50 minutes. Serve warm or cold, garnished with whipped cream.

CRANBERRY-PEAR PIE

6 TO 8 SERVINGS

Pastry for a 2-crust pie
2 cups cranberries, picked over and washed
⅓ cup water
3 tablespoons quick-cooking tapioca
1 cup sugar
Pinch of salt
3 cups diced fresh pears
2 tablespoons butter

1 Preheat the oven to 450°F.

2 Line a 9-inch pie plate with half of the pastry.

3 Place the cranberries and water in a saucepan. Cover and cook for 6 to 8 minutes, until the skins pop. Add the tapioca, sugar, salt and pears. Mix well and cool. Turn into the prepared pie plate and dot with the butter.

4 Cut the remaining pastry into strips and make a lattice top for the pie; or cover with solid pastry. Trim, turn under and flute the edge. Prick the crust to allow for escape of steam if a solid crust is used.

5 Bake the pie for 10 minutes. Reduce the heat to 350°F and cook for 30 minutes longer, until brown. Cool.

SOUTHERN PECAN PIE

8 SERVINGS

Pastry for a 1-crust pie
2 tablespoons flour
2 tablespoons sugar
3 eggs, lightly beaten
2 cups dark corn syrup
1 teaspoon vanilla extract
1 cup pecan halves

1 Preheat the oven to 425°F.

2 Line a 9-inch pie plate with the pastry.

3 Combine the flour and sugar and add to the beaten eggs, beating well. Add the corn syrup, vanilla and pecans, stirring well to blend.

4 Pour the pecan mixture into the pie shell and bake 10 minutes. Reduce the heat to 325°F and continue baking about 45 minutes.

HONEY PECAN PIE

8 SERVINGS

Pastry for a 1-crust pie
½ cup honey
½ cup white corn syrup
⅓ cup granulated sugar
⅓ cup light brown sugar
3 eggs, lightly beaten
4 tablespoons butter, melted
1 teaspoon vanilla extract
1 cup pecan halves

1 Preheat the oven to 375°F.

2 Line a 9-inch pie plate with the pastry.

3 Combine all the ingredients except the pecan halves. Pour into the prepared pie plate. Arrange the nut halves on top in any desired pattern.

4 Bake for 40 to 50 minutes, until the filling is set and the pastry golden brown. Cool and serve cold or slightly warm.

CHOCOLATE PECAN PIE

Pastry for a 1-crust pie
2 ounces (2 squares) unsweetened chocolate
3 tablespoons butter
1 cup light corn syrup
¾ cup sugar
3 eggs, lightly beaten
1 teaspoon vanilla extract
1 cup coarsely chopped pecans
½ cup heavy cream, whipped

1 Preheat the oven to 375°F.

2 Line a 9-inch pie plate with the pastry.

3 Melt the chocolate and butter in the top part of a double boiler over boiling water. Boil the syrup and sugar together for 2 minutes.

4 Blend the melted chocolate mixture and the syrup mixture and pour slowly over the beaten eggs, stirring constantly. Add the vanilla and pecans. Turn the mixture into the prepared pie plate.

5 Bake for 45 to 50 minutes, until the pie is completely puffed across the top. Cool. Serve topped with whipped cream.

PUMPKIN PIE

Pastry for a 1-crust pie
2 large or 3 small eggs
½ cup sugar
2 tablespoons molasses
Pinch of salt
1 teaspoon ground ginger
1 to 2 teaspoons cinnamon
¼ teaspoon ground cloves or allspice
2 cups puréed cooked pumpkin
1½ cups milk, half-and-half or evaporated milk

1 Prepare the pie shell with a fluted standing rim. Brush lightly with egg white or shortening.

2 Preheat the oven to 450°F.

3 Beat the eggs with the sugar, molasses, salt and spices until well blended. Add the pumpkin and milk and mix well. Adjust the seasonings.

4 Turn the mixture into the prepared crust and bake on the lower shelf of the oven 10 minutes. Lower the heat to 400°F and bake until a knife inserted in the center comes out clean, or about 30 minutes longer.

SOUR CREAM PUMPKIN PIE

6 SERVINGS

Pastry for a 1-crust pie
1 cup sugar
1 teaspoon cinnamon
½ teaspoon ground ginger
¼ teaspoon grated nutmeg
⅛ teaspoon ground cloves
1½ cups puréed cooked pumpkin
3 eggs, separated
1 cup sour cream
Whipped cream for garnish

1 Preheat the oven to 450°F. Prepare pie shell, prick the crust and bake until three fourths done. Reduce heat to 350°F.

2 Combine ½ cup of the sugar with the spices in the top of a double boiler. Blend in the pumpkin. Beat the egg yolks and stir into the mixture. Add the sour cream and mix well. Cook over hot, not boiling, water until thick, stirring constantly.

3 Beat the egg whites until they form soft peaks. Gradually beat in the remaining sugar. Fold into the pumpkin mixture.

4 Turn into the pie shell and bake 45 minutes, or until the top is brown. Serve with whipped cream, if desired.

SPICED RHUBARB PIE

6 TO 8 SERVINGS

Pastry for a 2-crust pie
5 cups of 1-inch pieces of rhubarb
1¼ cups sugar
3 tablespoons quick-cooking tapioca
2 tablespoons butter
½ teaspoon cinnamon
¼ teaspoon grated nutmeg
⅛ teaspoon ground cloves
Pinch of salt

1 Preheat the oven to 450°F.

2 Line a 9-inch pie plate with half of the pastry.

3 Mix the remaining ingredients and turn into the prepared pie plate.

4 Cut the remaining pastry into strips and make a lattice top for the pie. Trim, turn under and flute the edge.

5 Bake for 15 minutes. Reduce heat to 350°F and bake for about 30 minutes longer, until the rhubarb is tender and the crust is brown.

RASPBERRY PIE

8 SERVINGS

2 cups milk
1 vanilla bean
⅓ cup flour
½ cup sugar
Pinch of salt
4 egg yolks
1 whole egg
¼ cup heavy cream, whipped
Baked deep 9-inch pie shell
1 pint raspberries
½ cup red currant jelly

1 In a double boiler, scald the milk with the vanilla bean. Remove the bean.
2 Mix the flour, sugar and salt. Add a little of the scalded milk, stirring until smooth. Add to the remaining milk in the double boiler and cook, stirring, until thickened.
3 Beat together the egg yolks and the whole egg. Add a little of the hot mixture and stir until smooth. Add to the remaining sauce and cook over simmering water, stirring constantly, until the mixture has thickened.
4 Strain the mixture, cool and fold in the whipped cream. Turn into the baked pie shell and cover with raspberries.
5 Melt the jelly over very low heat, stirring, and pour evenly over the raspberries. Chill.

CHOCOLATE CHIFFON PIE

6 SERVINGS

1 envelope (1 tablespoon) unflavored gelatin
½ cup sugar
Pinch of salt
1 cup milk
2 eggs, separated
1 (6-ounce) package (1 cup) semisweet
    chocolate pieces
1 teaspoon vanilla extract
½ cup heavy cream, whipped
Brazil nut crust (page 664)

1 Combine the gelatin, half of the sugar and the salt in the top of a double boiler. Stir in the milk, egg yolks and chocolate pieces. Place over boiling water and cook, stirring constantly, until the gelatin has dissolved and the chocolate has melted, about 6 minutes.
2 Remove from the heat and beat with a rotary beater until the chocolate is blended. Stir in the vanilla and chill until the mixture mounds slightly when dropped from a spoon.
3 Beat the egg whites until stiff but not dry. Gradually add the remaining sugar and beat until stiff. Fold into the gelatin mixture. Fold in the whipped cream.
4 Turn the mixture into the prepared crust and chill until firm. Garnish with additional whipped cream and sprinkle with chopped Brazil nuts.

GERMAN SWEET CHOCOLATE PIE

ABOUT 6 SERVINGS

4 ounces sweet cooking chocolate
3 tablespoons hot coffee
1 teaspoon vanilla extract
1 cup heavy cream
Baked meringue pie crust (page 752)

1 Place the chocolate and coffee in a saucepan over low heat. Stir until the chocolate has melted. Cool.

2 Add the vanilla to the chocolate. Whip the cream to a soft consistency. Fold the chocolate mixture into the whipped cream and pile into the cooled meringue shell. Chill about 2 hours before serving.

Variation

BRANDIED GERMAN SWEET CHOCOLATE DESSERT

Make German sweet chocolate pie as directed but add 1 tablespoon cognac with the vanilla. If desired, omit the meringue shell and serve as a pudding in sherbet glasses. Chill as directed.

COCONUT CREAM PIE

6 TO 8 SERVINGS

½ cup sugar
3 tablespoons cornstarch
Pinch of salt
2 cups scalded milk
1 tablespoon butter
2 eggs, separated
1 teaspoon vanilla extract
1 cup grated coconut
Baked 9-inch or deep 8-inch pie shell

1 Preheat the oven to 325°F.

2 Mix ¼ cup of the sugar with the cornstarch and salt. Gradually stir in the scalded milk. Add the butter.

3 Cook the mixture in a double boiler, stirring constantly, until thickened.

4 Beat the egg yolks, add a little of the thickened mixture, blend and stir into the remaining hot mixture. Cook, stirring, until thickened. Cool slightly.

5 Add the vanilla and ¾ cup of the coconut. Turn into the baked pie shell.

6 Beat the egg whites until foamy. Gradually add the remaining sugar and beat until stiff but not dry. Spread over the filling, making sure that the meringue touches the crust at all points. Sprinkle with the remaining coconut and bake until light brown, or about 15 minutes. Cool before serving.

LEMON OR LIME MERINGUE PIE

1 cup sugar
Pinch of salt
¼ cup flour
3 tablespoons cornstarch
2 cups water
3 eggs, separated
1 tablespoon butter
¼ cup lemon or lime juice
Grated rind of 1 lemon or lime
Baked 9-inch pastry shell
Meringue pie topping (page 753)

1 Combine the sugar, salt, flour and cornstarch and gradually stir in the water. Cook, stirring constantly, until thickened and smooth.

2 Gradually stir hot mixture into beaten egg yolks, return to low heat and cook, stirring, 2 minutes. (Reserve egg whites for meringue topping.) Stir in butter, lemon juice and rind and cool slightly. Pour into baked pastry shell and cool. Top with meringue and brown in oven, as directed.

NANA'S BEST LEMON PIE

I have traveled often around America judging "Gourmet Galas" for the March of Dimes. The competition attracts many of the best cooks in each community. This lemon meringue pie is one of the best I have ever tasted. It is the recipe of Lord and Lady Barclay Ferguson, who were members of the diplomatic corps.

6 TO 8 SERVINGS

1½ cups plus 2 tablespoons sugar
¼ teaspoon cream of tartar
4 eggs, separated
1 tablespoon grated lemon rind
3 tablespoons lemon juice
2 cups heavy cream

1 Preheat the oven to 275°F.

2 Sift together 1 cup of the sugar and the cream of tartar. Beat the egg whites until stiff. Slowly fold in the sugar mixture and beat until well blended. Butter the bottom and sides of a 9-inch pie plate. Scrape the meringue mixture into the pie plate, building it up around the edges to fashion a shell. Place in the oven and bake 1 hour. Remove and place on a rack to cool.

3 Beat the egg yolks until light and lemon colored. Add ½ cup of the sugar. Add the lemon rind and lemon juice and beat to blend. Cook in the top of a double boiler until thickened, stirring constantly. Remove from the heat and let cool.

4 Whip half of the cream until stiff and fold this into the lemon filling. Pour this into the meringue shell. Chill until the filling is set.

5 Whip the remaining cream with the remaining 2 tablespoons of sugar and spoon on top of the filling. Chill, uncovered, 24 hours.

ORANGE CUSTARD PIE

Pastry for a 1-crust pie
4 eggs, lightly beaten
¾ cup sugar
1½ cups half-and-half, scalded
2 teaspoons grated orange rind
1⅔ cups orange juice
2 or 3 oranges, sectioned
1½ teaspoons cornstarch
3 tablespoons Grand Marnier

1 Preheat the oven to 425°F. Place the rack in the lower half of the oven.

2 Line a 9-inch pie plate with the pastry. Brush the pastry with a little of the beaten eggs and chill.

3 Mix remaining eggs with the sugar and half-and-half. Add orange rind and 1⅓ cups of the orange juice. Pour into the pastry-lined pie plate.

4 Bake for about 35 minutes, until a knife inserted into the center comes out clean. Arrange orange sections over the baked custard.

5 Mix remaining orange juice and the cornstarch. Cook, stirring, until thick. Add the liqueur and pour over oranges. Chill.

BUTTERSCOTCH PIE

6 tablespoons butter
1 cup dark brown sugar, packed
1¼ cups water
1 egg yolk
1 envelope (1 tablespoon) unflavored gelatin
¼ cup cold water
1 pint vanilla ice cream
Almond crust (page 664)
½ cup heavy cream, whipped
Slivered almonds, toasted

1 Melt the butter in a saucepan. Add the sugar and water and heat to a boil. Combine a little of the mixture with the lightly beaten egg yolk, then add to the mixture in the saucepan.

2 Soften the gelatin in cold water. Stir it into the sugar mixture until the gelatin dissolves. Add the ice cream, cut into pieces, and stir until melted.

3 Chill the mixture in the refrigerator until slightly thickened but not set. Turn into the prepared pie crust and chill until firmly set. When ready to serve, garnish with whipped cream and sprinkle with nuts.

VINEGAR PIE

6 TO 8 SERVINGS

4 egg yolks
2 egg whites
1 cup sugar
¼ cup flour
½ teaspoon each grated nutmeg, cinnamon,
    allspice and ground cloves
1 cup sour cream
3 tablespoons butter, melted
3 tablespoons cider vinegar
1 cup nuts (walnuts or pecans)
1 cup seedless raisins
Pastry for a 1-crust pie
Whipped cream

1 Preheat the oven to 450°F.
2 Beat the egg yolks.
3 Beat the egg whites until stiff. Fold in the sugar and mix with the yolks.
4 Sift the flour with the spices and add, alternately with the sour cream, to the egg mixture.
5 Combine the butter and vinegar and mix with the nuts and raisins. Add to the flour mixture.
6 Pour the mixture into a pastry-lined 9-inch pie plate and bake 10 minutes. Reduce heat to 400°F and bake 5 minutes. Reduce heat to 350°F and bake until the filling begins to set, or about 15 minutes.
7 Cool the pie and top with whipped cream.

APPLE STRUDEL

8 SERVINGS

1 package strudel leaves
6 tart apples, peeled and cored
Grated rind and juice of 1 lemon
1 cup raisins
1 cup chopped walnuts or almonds
1 cup sugar
1 teaspoon cinnamon
4 tablespoons butter, melted
¼ cup fine dry bread crumbs, toasted

1 Remove the strudel leaves from the refrigerator at least 3 hours before using.
2 Cut the apples into thin slices and mix with the lemon rind and juice. Add the raisins, walnuts, sugar and cinnamon and mix to combine.
3 Preheat the oven to 375°F.
4 Spread a large damp kitchen towel on a table. Open a sheet of strudel leaves and place on the cloth. Keep the remaining leaves covered to prevent drying. Brush the strudel sheet with melted butter and sprinkle with crumbs. Repeat this procedure with 3 more sheets of strudel leaves, placing each on top of the last.
5 Spread the nearest short edge of the leaves with the apple mixture, making a strip about 3 inches wide.
6 Loosely roll up the strudel, using the towel as an aid and folding in the sides of the strudel. Roll onto a greased baking sheet and brush the top with butter.
7 Bake until golden brown, 25 to 30 minutes. Slide onto a bread board and cut into 2-inch pieces.

RICOTTA PIE

8 SERVINGS

Pastry (see following recipe)
1¼ pounds ricotta cheese
⅓ cup sugar
Pinch of salt
4 eggs, separated
1 teaspoon almond extract
⅓ cup finely chopped citron
2 tablespoons kirsch
2 tablespoons orange juice
1 teaspoon grated orange rind
Confectioners' sugar

1 Preheat the oven to 400°F.

2 Prepare the pastry.

3 Force the cheese through a sieve. Stir in the sugar, salt, egg yolks, almond extract, citron, kirsch, orange juice and rind. Beat the egg whites until stiff but not dry and fold into the cheese mixture.

4 Pour the mixture into the pastry-lined pie plate. Use the pastry strips to make a lattice over the top. Finish with a stand-up edge and decorate.

5 Place in the oven and immediately reduce the heat to 375°F. Bake for about 45 minutes, or until the filling is set and a knife inserted into center comes out clean.

8 Turn off the heat and allow pie to cool to room temperature in the oven. Pie will fall somewhat as it cools. Sprinkle with confectioners' sugar. Chill.

PASTRY
2 (10-INCH) PIE CRUSTS

2½ cups flour
Pinch of salt
¼ cup sugar
¼ pound plus 4 tablespoons butter
1 egg yolk
3 tablespoons dry white wine or sherry

1 Place the flour, salt and sugar in a bowl. Blend in the butter with the fingertips or with a pastry blender until the mixture resembles coarse oatmeal.

2 Add the egg yolk, wine and enough cold water to gather the mixture into a ball. Chill the dough for 30 minutes to make it easier to handle.

3 Roll out two thirds of the dough on a lightly floured pastry cloth or board. Line a 10-inch pie plate. Roll out remaining dough to ⅛-inch thickness and cut with a pastry wheel into long strips ½ inch wide.

CREAM PUFF SHELLS

When cream puff paste (*pâte à choux*) is baked it is one of the apparent miracles of cuisine. The paste expands to many times its original size and a mass of air occurs in the center. Still, it is one of the easiest of foods to prepare. The only "secret" is to add the flour all at once and fearlessly to the water-butter mixture. Cream puff paste is not only baked; it may be deep fried to produce air-filled beignets soufflés.

10 LARGE PUFFS

1 cup water
¼ pound butter
Pinch of salt
1 cup flour
4 eggs
Pastry cream (page 706)

1 Preheat the oven to 450°F.

2 Combine the water, butter and salt and bring to a boil. Remove from the heat and add the flour all at once. Stir vigorously until the mixture leaves the sides of the pan and forms a ball around the spoon. If a ball does not form almost immediately, hold the saucepan over low heat and beat briskly a few seconds. Cool slightly.

2 Add the eggs, 1 at a time, and beat until the mixture is smooth and glossy after each addition.

4 Drop the mixture by rounded tablespoonfuls onto a greased baking sheet, leaving 2 inches between the puffs to permit spreading.

5 Bake 15 minutes. Reduce the heat to 350°F and bake until no bubbles of fat remain on the surface and the sides of the puffs feel rigid, about 30 minutes longer. Cool. Cut a cap off each puff and fill with pastry cream. Replace the cap.

Variations

ÉCLAIRS

Using a spoon or large round pastry tube, shape the cream puff mixture on a baking sheet to finger lengths. Bake, cool and slit each puff at the side. Fill with pastry cream and frost with melted chocolate or chocolate glaze.

BEIGNETS SOUFFLÉS

Flavor cream puff mixture with ¼ teaspoon orange extract or 1 tablespoon rum and drop by tablespoons into deep hot fat (370°F). Fry until brown on all sides. Serve hot, sprinkled with confectioners' sugar.

GREEK NUT ROLL A LA APHRODITE LIANIDES

35 TO 40 SLICES

1 cup finely chopped pecans
1 cup finely chopped walnuts
1 cup finely chopped almonds
¼ cup sugar
½ teaspoon ground cloves
½ teaspoon cinnamon
½ pound phyllo pastry
1 pound butter, melted
1 cup water
1 cup honey, preferably Greek
1 teaspoon lemon juice

1 Preheat the oven to 350°F.

2 Combine the nuts, sugar, cloves and cinnamon.

3 Brush 2 sheets of phyllo pastry with melted butter and arrange 1 sheet atop the other. Sprinkle with 2 tablespoons of the nut mixture. Repeat this procedure until there are 3 layers of pastry and nuts. Roll like a jelly roll. Continue to prepare the rolls until there are three.

4 Cut each roll into 1-inch slices. Place the slices on buttered baking sheets with sides.

5 Bake the nut rolls for 20 minutes, turn them over, and continue to bake for 15 minutes longer, until golden brown on both sides. Cool.

6 While the pastry is baking, make the syrup. Bring the water to a boil and stir in the honey. Blend well and add the lemon juice. Cool the syrup slightly. It should still be warm.

7 When the rolls are cool, dip each piece into the warm syrup. Serve at room temperature.

Cakes

ANGEL CAKE

12 TO 16 SERVINGS

1 cup sifted cake flour
1½ cups superfine sugar
1¼ cups (10 to 12) egg whites,
    at room temperature
1¼ teaspoons cream of tartar
Pinch of salt
1 teaspoon vanilla extract
¼ teaspoon almond extract

1 Preheat the oven to 325°F.

2 Sift the flour 4 times with ½ cup of the sugar.

3 Beat the egg whites until foamy. Add the cream of tartar and salt and beat until soft moist peaks form when the beater is withdrawn.

4 Add the remaining sugar, about 2 tablespoons at a time, beating it in after each addition. Add vanilla and almond extract.

5 Sift about ¼ cup of the flour-sugar mixture at a time over the meringue and cut and fold it in just until no flour shows.

6 Turn into an ungreased 10-inch tube pan and bake about 1 hour. Invert pan and let cake cool in pan.

SPONGE CAKE

1 (10-INCH) CAKE

6 eggs
1 tablespoon lemon juice
1 packed teaspoon grated lemon rind
1 cup sifted cake flour
Pinch of salt
1 cup sugar

1 Preheat the oven to 325°F. Lightly grease and flour the bottom, not the sides, of a 10-inch tube pan.

2 Break the eggs into the large bowl of an electric mixer, add the lemon juice and grated rind and beat the mixture at highest speed until soft peaks form, 12 to 16 minutes.

3 While the eggs are being beaten, sift together the flour and salt onto a piece of wax paper.

4 Continue beating the eggs at highest speed (after soft peaks form) and pour the sugar in a fine stream over them, taking 2½ to 3 minutes to add all the sugar.

5 Change to lowest speed and sift the flour and salt over the surface of the mixture as the bowl turns, taking 2½ to 3 minutes to add all the flour. Scrape the sides of the bowl and beat at lowest speed ½ minute.

6 Pour the batter into the prepared pan and bake 50 minutes, or until a toothpick inserted in the center comes out clean.

7 Invert the cake pan and set it on a rack to cool. Prop it up if necessary so that the air can circulate between the cake and the tabletop. Let the cake cool at room temperature before removing it from the pan.

POUND CAKE

According to tradition, the original pound cake was made with four pounds of ingredients. It contained a pound each of butter, sugar, flour and eggs. In whatever manner the pound cake came about, it is a delectable legacy from the standpoint of both flavor and texture. The cake has a firm texture and a tender crumb.

1 (9-INCH) TUBE CAKE

½ pound butter
1 teaspoon grated nutmeg
Pinch of salt
1⅔ cups sugar
5 eggs
2 cups sifted cake flour

1 Have all the ingredients at room temperature. Soften the butter and add the nutmeg and salt. Beat 4 minutes by electric beater or 8 minutes by hand.

2 Gradually blend in the sugar until fluffy, beating 2 minutes by electric beater or 8 minutes by hand.

3 Beat in 4 of the eggs, 1 at a time. Total beating time should be 1 minute by electric beater or 2 minutes by hand.

4 Stir in all the flour at one time and beat 2 minutes by electric beater or 5 minutes by hand.

5 Blend in the remaining egg, 15 seconds by electric beater or 33 strokes by hand. Turn the mixture into a well-greased, lightly floured 9×3½-inch tube cake pan.

6 Place in a cold oven and set the control to 300°F. If the cake is mixed by electric beater, bake 2 hours; if mixed by hand, bake 1½ hours. (Because the electric beater entraps a little more air into the batter, it produces a cake that is a little thicker and lighter.)

7 Cool the cake in the pan 10 minutes. Turn out on a wire rack to finish cooling.

GÉNOISE

The génoise is a superb French pastry. It does not contain a leavening agent other than the air that is beaten into the eggs. Originally it was necessary to beat the eggs by hand over low heat in order to give the eggs volume. With today's electric mixers the method is greatly simplified. It is important, however, that the eggs be at room temperature or warmer and that the mixing bowl of the electric mixer be warmed before the beating begins.

The power of electric mixers varies. Care should be taken that the mixer does not become overheated.

Finally, the utmost care must be taken when folding the flour and butter into the génoise batter.

2 (9-INCH) OR 3 (8-INCH) LAYERS

6 eggs, at room temperature
1 cup superfine sugar
1 teaspoon vanilla extract
4 tablespoons butter
1 cup sifted cake flour
Buttercream (page 701)
Praline powder (see following recipe)

1 Warm the bowl of an electric mixer. Beat the eggs with the sugar and vanilla at the highest speed until the mixture stands in stiff peaks when the beater is withdrawn. Depending on the power of the mixer, this should take from 5 to 30 minutes. It is important not to underbeat the mixture. Scrape the sides of the bowl with a rubber spatula from time to time so the ingredients will be well blended.

2 Meanwhile, grease two 9-inch or three 8-inch cake pans that are 1½ inches deep. Line the pans with wax paper and grease the paper. Melt the butter and cool to lukewarm. Preheat the oven to 350°F and place rack in the lower third of the oven.

3 Divide the flour into 6 to 8 portions and sift over the egg mixture a portion at a time. Use a rubber spatula to fold the flour in gently after each addition.

4 Add the butter, about a teaspoon at a time, and fold it in gently but completely.

5 Turn the batter into the prepared pans and bake 35 to 40 minutes. When done, the cake will rebound to the touch when pressed gently in the center.

6 Turn the cakes out onto a cooling rack, remove the paper and let cool. Frost with buttercream and praline powder.

PRALINE POWDER

1 cup sugar
⅛ teaspoon cream of tartar
⅓ cup water
1 cup blanched almonds

1 Boil the sugar, cream of tartar and water, stirring until the sugar dissolves. Add the almonds and cook without stirring until the almonds are brown and the syrup is a golden brown color. Turn into a buttered pan and cool until brittle.

2 Turn the brittle out of the pan, break into pieces and, using about a quarter at a time, cover with a towel and crush to a powder with a mallet or rolling pin. (Yields enough for use with buttercream over a 3-layer, 8-inch génoise).

To frost the génoise: Reserve half of the praline powder and add the remainder to the buttercream. Spread frosting between the layers and over the top and sides of the cake. Stand the cake on wax paper and toss the remaining powder over the sides, pressing it in gently. Any powder on the paper may be used for a border around the top of the cake. Chill the cake after frosting until ready to serve.

Variation

PETITS FOURS

Frost a sheet of génoise cake smoothly with buttercream. Cut the sheet with cookie cutters or a knife into desired shapes. Garnish with candied cherries cut in half or into sixths for petals of flowers, angelica cut into diamonds for leaves, whole or chopped nuts, candy sprinkles, melted chocolate, coconut, etc.

♦

ALL-PURPOSE CHIFFON CAKE

ABOUT 16 SERVINGS

2¼ cups sifted cake flour
1½ cups sugar
1 tablespoon baking powder
Pinch of salt
½ cup vegetable oil
5 egg yolks
2 teaspoons grated lemon rind
¾ cup water
2 teaspoons vanilla extract
1 cup egg whites
½ teaspoon cream of tartar
Lemon glaze (page 707) (optional)

1 Preheat the oven to 325°F. Put the rack in the lower half of the oven.
2 Sift together into a bowl the flour, sugar, baking powder and salt.
3 Make a well in the center of the flour mixture and add the oil, egg yolks, lemon rind, water and vanilla. Stir and beat until smooth.
4 In another bowl beat the egg whites with the cream of tartar until very stiff, much stiffer than for meringue.

5 Pour the egg yolk mixture gradually over egg whites, folding gently with a rubber spatula until just blended. Do not stir.
6 Pour the batter at once into an ungreased 10-inch tube pan. Bake for 65 to 70 minutes.
7 Immediately turn the tube pan upside down and place the tube over a funnel or other support so that the cake can hang in the pan free of the table until cool.
8 To remove cake from pan, loosen it from the tube and sides with a spatula and hit the edge of the pan on the table. Serve plain or top with lemon glaze.

Variation

CHIFFON LAYERS

For 2 square layers (9 × 9 × 1¾ inches), use the recipe for all-purpose chiffon cake and reduce the egg yolks to 4. Bake in a 350°F oven for about 35 minutes. Use one or both layers for party variety cakes (below) or as basis for other desserts.

PARTY VARIETY CAKES
24 SMALL CAKES

1 9-inch layer of all-purpose chiffon cake
Lemon filling (page 706)
Cream cheese icing (page 688)
Confectioners' sugar
Chopped nuts, colored coconut, candied fruits
    and candy sprinkles for garnish

1 Bake and cool the chiffon layer. Split it and fill it with lemon filling.
2 Cut the cake into halves and frost each half with the cream cheese frosting, or frost one half and sprinkle the other with confectioners' sugar.
3 Cut each frosted half-layer into thirds and then cut each of the thirds into 4 finger-shaped strips. Garnish as desired. Cut the sugar-sprinkled cake into finger-shaped strips, but serve it undecorated.

SPONGE ROLL

8 SERVINGS

4 eggs, at room temperature
¾ teaspoon baking powder
Pinch of salt
¾ cup granulated sugar
1 teaspoon vanilla extract
¾ cup sifted cake flour
Confectioners' sugar
1½ cups heavy cream, whipped
2 tablespoons orange liqueur
¼ cup pistachios, unsalted

1 Preheat the oven to 400°F. Line a greased jelly roll pan (15½ × 10½ inches) with parchment paper and grease again.

2 Beat the eggs together with the baking powder and the salt until very thick and light colored. Gradually beat in the granulated sugar. The mixture should form a ribbon as it drops from the beaters.

3 Stir in the vanilla and then fold in the flour gently. Pour the batter into the prepared pan, spread evenly, and bake for 13 minutes, or until done. Turn immediately onto a clean towel that has been generously sprinkled with confectioners' sugar.

4 Quickly remove the paper and roll, jelly-roll style, starting with the long side and enclosing the towel inside. Cool on a rack.

5 Combine the cream, ¼ cup of confectioners' sugar, the liqueur and the nuts. Unroll the cooled cake and spread with the cream mixture. Reroll, using the towel only as an aid. Sprinkle with additional confectioners' sugar and chill before serving.

Note: Instead of whipped cream, orange liqueur and pistachios, the cake can be spread with mocha buttercream (page 702). Reroll and sprinkle with confectioners' sugar and shaved unsweetened chocolate.

ONE-BOWL CHOCOLATE CAKE

12 SERVINGS

2 cups sifted cake flour
2 teaspoons baking powder
½ teaspoon baking soda
Pinch of salt
½ cup plus 2 tablespoons cocoa
1½ cups sugar
½ cup plus 2 tablespoons vegetable shortening
½ cup warm water
⅔ cup milk
2 eggs
1 teaspoon vanilla extract

1 Preheat the oven to 350°F.

2 Sift together in the bowl of an electric mixer the flour, baking powder, baking soda, salt, cocoa and sugar. Add the shortening, water, milk, eggs and vanilla and blend on very low speed until the ingredients are moistened. Mix 3 minutes on medium speed, scraping the bowl frequently to ensure complete blending. Do not include scraping time in the 3 minutes.

3 Pour the mixture into two 9-inch layer-cake pans that have been greased and lined with wax paper circles cut ⅛ inch smaller than the bottoms of the pans.

4 Bake until the cake rebounds when pressed gently in the center, 25 to 30 minutes. Cool in the pans on a cake rack 10 minutes before removing from the pans. Cool and frost as desired.

ANNELIESE RICHTER'S CHARLOTTE MALAKOFF AU CHOCOLAT
CHOCOLATE MOUSSE CAKE

One of the grandest chocolate desserts I have ever sampled was given me by a reader and fine cook named Anneliese Richter. It is a fabulous mousse cake adapted from a French classic called Charlotte Malakoff and is served with a sauce flavored with Grand Marnier.

10 TO 12 SERVINGS

¼ pound butter, at room temperature
1 cup sifted confectioners' sugar
3 large eggs, separated
4 tablespoons Grand Marnier, cognac or dark rum
½ teaspoon almond extract
½ pound semisweet chocolate morsels
½ cup grated blanched almonds
Pinch of salt
1 cup heavy cream, beaten until stiff
24 whole ladyfingers, split
Chocolate fondant icing (see following recipe)
Grand Marnier sauce (page 760) (optional)

1 Put the butter, sugar and egg yolks into the bowl of an electric mixture. Beat until light and lemon colored. Add 2 tablespoons of the Grand Marnier and the almond extract and beat to blend.

2 Put the chocolate into a small saucepan and set the saucepan in a bowl of simmering water. Heat the chocolate, stirring, until it is melted. Pour and scrape this into the butter and sugar mixture. Add the grated almonds and blend well.

3 Beat the egg whites until stiff, adding a pinch of salt. Fold them into the batter until no white streaks show. Fold in the whipped cream. Brush the flat portions of the ladyfingers with the remaining Grand Marnier.

4 This recipe will make 2 loaf cakes measuring about 8½ × 4¼ × 2½ inches or one 12 × 4½-inch pound cake pan. Line the bottom and sides of the pan or pans smoothly and neatly with foil to facilitate the unmolding. Line the bottom and sides of the prepared pan with ladyfingers, placing them close together, sides touching but not overlapping. Arrange them with the flat sides of the ladyfingers touching the pan. Pour and scrape the mousse into the pan. Slice off the ladyfingers sticking above the mold and arrange them neatly around the edges on top of the filling. Fill the center with more ladyfingers placed close together. Cover closely with clear plastic wrap and refrigerate several hours or overnight. When ready, unmold the cake onto a cake plate, frost with chocolate fondant icing or whipped cream sweetened and flavored with Grand Marnier, cognac or dark rum. Serve, if desired, with Grand Marnier sauce.

CHOCOLATE FONDANT ICING
1½ CUPS

½ pound (about 1⅓ cups) semisweet chocolate morsels
8 tablespoons unsalted butter
4 teaspoons honey

1 Combine the chocolate, butter and honey in a small mixing bowl.

2 Select a saucepan in which the bowl will fit snugly. Add an inch or so of water to the saucepan and bring to the boil. Place the bowl inside the saucepan, over but not in the boiling water. Let sit, stirring occasionally, until the chocolate is melted and blended with the other ingredients. Let cool to lukewarm.

3 Pour the icing evenly over the top of the mousse cake, letting the mixture run down the sides. Do not touch the top, but smooth out the sides with a metal spatula. Chill until the icing has hardened.

NORWEGIAN MOCHA CAKE

8 TO 10 SERVINGS

2 cups strong hot coffee
2 cups granulated sugar
2 tablespoons cocoa
1 cup seedless raisins, cut up
½ cup vegetable shortening
½ teaspoon vanilla extract
2 eggs
2 cups flour
Pinch of salt
2 teaspoons baking powder
1 teaspoon cinnamon
1 teaspoon grated nutmeg
½ teaspoon ground cloves
½ teaspoon baking soda
Confectioners' sugar

1 Preheat the oven to 350°F.
2 Combine the coffee, 1 cup of the granulated sugar, the cocoa and raisins in a saucepan. Bring to a boil and simmer for 10 to 15 minutes. Cool.
3 Cream the shortening and add remaining granulated sugar gradually, creaming until light and fluffy. Add vanilla. Add eggs separately, beating well after each addition.
4 Mix and sift the remaining ingredients, except the confectioners' sugar, and stir in. Spoon into a greased and floured pan (10 × 10 × 2 inches) or 10-inch tube pan. Bake for about 1 hour.
5 When cool, place paper lace doily on top. Sift confectioners' sugar onto doily; lift off carefully. Cut into squares to serve.

MARBLE CAKE

2 LOAVES

3 cups all-purpose flour
3 teaspoons baking powder
Pinch of salt
¼ pound plus 4 tablespoons butter
1½ cups sugar
3 large eggs
1 cup milk
½ cup molasses
1½ teaspoons cinnamon
½ teaspoon ground cloves
¼ teaspoon ground ginger

1 Preheat the oven to 350°F.
2 Sift together the flour, baking powder and salt. Set aside.
3 Cream the butter and sugar. Beat in the eggs, 1 at a time. Add the flour mixture alternately with the milk. Beat batter for 30 seconds.
4 Pour half of the batter into a bowl. Stir in the molasses and spices. Pour the light and dark batters alternately into 2 lightly floured well-greased loaf pans. Bake for 45 minutes, or until done. Cool. Frost, if desired.

SOUR CREAM FUDGE CAKE

12 SERVINGS

2 cups sifted cake flour
1½ cups sugar
1 teaspoon baking soda
Pinch of salt
⅓ cup vegetable shortening
1 cup sour cream
3 ounces (3 squares) unsweetened chocolate,
  melted
2 eggs
1 teaspoon vanilla extract
¼ cup hot water or hot coffee

1 Preheat the oven to 350°F. Grease the bottom of a 13 × 9 × 1½-inch pan, line with wax paper and grease the paper.

2 Sift together the flour, sugar, baking soda and salt. Add the shortening and sour cream and beat 2 minutes. Add the chocolate, eggs, vanilla and hot water and beat 2 minutes longer.

3 Turn the batter into the prepared pan and bake until the cake rebounds to the touch when pressed gently in the center, about 35 minutes.

4 Cool the cake in the pan 5 minutes. Turn out on a rack, remove the paper and cool. Frost as desired. To serve, cut into squares.

FRESH COCONUT CAKE

1 (9-INCH) CAKE

2¼ cups sifted cake flour
1½ cups sugar
4 teaspoons baking powder
Pinch of salt
½ cup vegetable shortening
1 cup coconut milk (page 147)
1 teaspoon vanilla extract
4 medium egg whites, unbeaten
Lemon curd (page 740)
Vanilla boiled frosting (page 700), or
  whipped cream
Freshly grated coconut

1 Preheat the oven to 350°F. Grease two 9-inch layer-cake pans, line with wax paper and grease the paper.

2 Into the bowl of an electric mixer sift the flour, sugar, baking powder and salt. Add the shortening, ¾ cup of the coconut milk and the vanilla. Beat 2 minutes at low to medium speed, scraping the bowl and beaters as necessary.

3 Add the egg whites and the remaining coconut milk and beat 2 minutes longer.

4 Turn the batter into the prepared pans and bake until a cake tester inserted in the center of the cake comes out clean, 20 to 30 minutes.

5 Cool the cake on a rack 10 minutes before removing from the pans.

6 When the cake is completely cool, spread lemon curd between the layers. Frost with vanilla boiled frosting, or with sweetened whipped cream. Sprinkle with freshly grated coconut.

CARROT AND RAISIN CAKE

12 SERVINGS

1½ pounds carrots, trimmed
2 cups sugar
4 eggs
1½ cups corn oil
2 cups flour
2 teaspoons baking powder
2 teaspoons baking soda
2 teaspoons cinnamon
Pinch of salt
2 teaspoons vanilla extract
½ cup raisins
½ cup walnuts broken into small pieces
Cream cheese icing (see following recipe)

1 Preheat the oven to 350°F.
2 Scrape and grate the carrots into fine shreds. There should be about 4 cups firmly packed.
3 Butter the inside of 3 round 9-inch layer-cake pans. Line each with a round of wax paper cut to fit neatly. Butter the paper. Sprinkle with flour and shake out excess. Set aside.
4 Beat the sugar and eggs until thickened. Beat in the oil gradually.
5 Sift together the flour, baking powder, baking soda, cinnamon and salt. Stir this into the egg mixture. Add the vanilla. Fold in the carrots, raisins and walnuts. Spoon equal amounts of batter into each of the prepared pans. Bake 35 to 40 minutes, or until the tops spring back when gently pressed with the fingers. Turn the cakes out onto a wire rack and let cool.
6 Meanwhile, prepare the icing. Use to frost the cake between the layers, around the sides and on the top.

CREAM CHEESE ICING
1½ CUPS

8 ounces cream cheese, at room temperature
¼ pound butter, at room temperature
1 teaspoon vanilla extract
2 cups sifted confectioners' sugar

Blend the cream cheese, butter, vanilla and sugar and beat well.

♦

LEMON CAKE

2 CAKES

½ pound butter
3 cups granulated sugar
5 egg yolks, beaten
4 cups all-purpose flour
1 cup milk
Grated rind and juice of 1 lemon
½ teaspoon baking soda
5 egg whites, stiffly beaten
Confectioners' sugar

1 Preheat the oven to 325°F.
2 Cream the butter, adding the granulated sugar gradually, until light and fluffy.
3 Add the remaining ingredients except the egg whites and confectioners' sugar and mix until well blended. Fold in the beaten egg whites. Divide the batter between 2 loaf pans (9 × 5 × 3 inches). Bake for 1 hour. Sprinkle with sifted confectioners' sugar and serve with ice cream.

APPLE-ORANGE NUT LOAF

2 LOAVES

2 large oranges
1 cup seedless raisins
2 cups applesauce
4 cups flour
4 teaspoons baking powder
4 teaspoons baking soda
2 cups sugar
Pinch of salt
1½ cups chopped walnuts or pecans
2 eggs, slightly beaten
6 tablespoons butter, melted

1 Preheat the oven to 350°F.

2 Squeeze the oranges. Chop the rind of the oranges and the raisins in a food processor. Add the orange juice and ground orange rind and raisins to the applesauce.

3 Sift together the flour, baking powder, baking soda, sugar and salt. Add the applesauce mixture and the nuts. Mix thoroughly and add the eggs and melted butter.

4 Grease 2 loaf pans (9 × 5 × 3 inches) and pour in the batter. Bake for 1¼ hours. Remove the cakes from the pans and cool on a wire rack. Let stand overnight before cutting.

PINEAPPLE UPSIDE-DOWN CAKE

6 SERVINGS

¼ pound plus 4 tablespoons butter
¾ cup brown sugar
3 (½-inch thick) slices of fresh pineapple, halved
¼ cup pecans
½ cup granulated sugar
1 egg
½ teaspoon vanilla extract
1½ cups all-purpose flour
1½ teaspoons baking powder
Pinch of salt
½ cup milk
Whipped cream

1 Preheat the oven to 375°F.

2 Melt the 4 tablespoons of butter in a 9-inch-square baking dish and sprinkle with the brown sugar. Arrange the pineapple slices and pecans in a design on top of the sugared butter.

3 Cream the remaining butter with the granulated sugar and beat in the egg and the vanilla. Sift together the flour, baking powder and salt and add alternately with the milk.

4 Spoon the batter carefully over pineapple slices. Bake for about 35 minutes, or until done. Let cake stand for 5 minutes before inverting onto a serving platter. Serve warm with whipped cream.

Note: Three fresh pears or peaches can be substituted for the pineapple slices. Peel the pears or peaches and cut in half.

CRUMB AND NUT CAKE

3 (8-INCH) LAYERS

1 cup vegetable shortening
1 cup sugar
4 eggs
2 teaspoons vanilla extract
3 cups fine graham cracker crumbs
1 cup finely chopped nuts
3 teaspoons baking powder
1 cup milk
Chocolate buttercream (page 701)

1 Preheat the oven to 350°F.

2 Blend the shortening, sugar, eggs and vanilla. Combine the crumbs, nuts and baking powder and add to the shortening mixture alternately with the milk. Pour into 3 greased 8-inch layer-cake pans 1¼ inches deep.

3 Bake 30 to 35 minutes. Turn out on a rack to cool. Put the layers together with the chocolate buttercream.

LEKACH
HONEY CAKE

35 TO 40 HONEY CAKES

4 eggs
1 cup sugar
1 cup honey
½ cup strong black coffee
2 tablespoons vegetable oil
3½ cups flour
1½ teaspoons baking powder
1 teaspoon baking soda
½ teaspoon allspice
½ teaspoon cinnamon
¼ teaspoon ground cloves
½ cup chopped nuts
½ cup raisins
½ cup citron, finely cut
2 tablespoons cognac
Buttercream (page 701)

1 Preheat the oven to 300°F. Line a 10 × 15 × 2¼-inch pan with wax paper.

2 Beat the eggs lightly. Add the sugar gradually and continue beating until the mixture is light and fluffy.

3 Combine the honey and coffee and stir it into the oil. Blend the mixture into the eggs and sugar.

4 Sift the flour, baking powder, baking soda and spices together. Stir in the nuts, raisins and citron and blend the mixture into the egg mixture. Stir in the cognac and pour the batter into the prepared pan.

5 Bake 1 hour. Cool and frost with buttercream, if desired. Cut into squares.

PAIN D'ÉPICE

1½ cups water
1 teaspoon aniseed
1 cup honey
1¼ cups sugar
3 teaspoons baking soda
4½ cups flour
Pinch of salt
1 teaspoon cinnamon
½ teaspoon grated nutmeg
3 tablespoons chopped citron
3 tablespoons chopped candied orange peel

1 Bring the water with the aniseed to a boil and set aside.
2 Preheat the oven to 350°F.
3 Add the honey and sugar to the water and stir until the sugar has dissolved. Add the baking soda.
4 Sift together the flour, salt, cinnamon and nutmeg. Add the citron and orange peel and mix. Add the honey mixture to the dry ingredients and stir until smooth.
5 Turn the mixture into two 8½ × 4½ × 2¾-inch greased loaf pans and bake about 1 hour.

GINGERBREAD

1 tablespoon cider vinegar
¾ cup milk
2 cups flour
2 teaspoons baking powder
¼ teaspoon baking soda
Pinch of salt
1½ to 2 teaspoons ground ginger
1 teaspoon cinnamon
¼ teaspoon ground cloves
⅓ cup vegetable shortening
½ cup sugar
1 egg
¾ cup dark molasses

1 Preheat the oven to 350°F. Grease an 8 × 8 × 2-inch pan.
2 Add the vinegar to the milk and set aside. Sift together twice the flour, baking powder, baking soda, salt and spices.
3 Cream the shortening, add the sugar gradually and cream well. Add the egg and whip until fluffy. Add the molasses and mix.
4 Add dry ingredients, about one quarter at a time, alternately with the (by this time) curdled milk. Stir only until mixed after each addition. Turn into prepared pan and bake 45 to 50 minutes, or until bread rebounds to the touch when pressed gently in the center.

GINGER ROLL

1¼ cups flour
⅓ cup granulated sugar
1¼ teaspoons baking soda
1 teaspoon each ground ginger, cinnamon,
     grated nutmeg and allspice
5 tablespoons butter, melted
⅓ cup molasses
1 egg, well beaten
½ cup warm water
Confectioners' sugar
1 cup heavy cream, whipped

1 Preheat the oven to 350°F. Grease a 10½ × 15½-inch jelly roll pan and line with paper; grease the paper.

2 Sift together twice the flour, sugar, baking soda and spices. Add the melted butter, molasses, egg and water and stir until smooth. Spread the mixture in the prepared pan. Bake until the cake rebounds when pressed with a finger, or 15 minutes.

3 Let the cake cook briefly in the pan. Cover with a thin cloth wrung out in cold water and finish cooling in the refrigerator.

4 Remove the cloth, sprinkle the cake with sugar, turn out on wax paper and remove the paper adhering to the under side of the cake.

5 Spread with whipped cream and roll. Wrap in wax paper and chill until ready to serve.

BANANA SHORTCAKE

3 cups flour
Pinch of salt
4 teaspoons baking powder
2 tablespoons sugar
¼ pound butter
1 cup milk, approximately
2 tablespoons butter, melted
1½ cups any marmalade
3 bananas, sliced
1 cup heavy cream, whipped

1 Preheat the oven to 425°F.

2 Sift together the flour, salt, baking powder and sugar. Using a pastry blender, chop in the ¼ pound butter until well mixed. Add the milk all at once and then more if necessary to give a soft dough. Turn the dough out on a floured surface and knead about 30 times.

3 Press half the dough into a greased 8 × 8-inch pan. Brush with the 2 tablespoons melted butter. Press the second half of the dough into an 8-inch square and place on top. Bake until brown, about 20 minutes.

4 Turn cake out on a rack and slide a cookie sheet between the layers. Place the bottom layer on a serving plate, spread generously with half the marmalade and cover with half the banana slices. Cover with the remaining shortcake and spread with marmalade and banana. Top with whipped cream.

Note: Almost any fresh fruit can be used in place of the bananas.

FRESH STRAWBERRY SOUR CREAM SHORTCAKE

6 SERVINGS

2 cups flour
3 teaspoons baking powder
Pinch of salt
¼ cup plus ⅓ cup sugar
1 (3-ounce) package cream cheese
2 tablespoons butter
1 egg, beaten
½ cup milk, approximately
1 quart fresh strawberries
1 cup sour cream

1 Preheat the oven to 450°F.
2 Sift together the flour, baking powder, salt and ¼ cup of the sugar. Add the cream cheese and butter, cutting them in with a pastry blender or 2 knives until the mixture resembles coarse cornmeal.
3 Pour the beaten egg into a measuring cup. Add enough milk to make ¾ cup and gradually stir into the flour mixture. Knead the dough about 20 seconds.
4 Pat half the dough into a greased round 8-inch layer-cake pan. Brush the surface with melted butter. Pat the remaining half of the dough over the top.
5 Bake until done, about 20 minutes. Remove to a cooling rack.
6 When the cake is cold, split the layers apart and place 1 on a large serving plate.
7 Wash, hull and slice the strawberries. Add ⅓ cup of the sugar and let stand 10 minutes. Spoon the strawberry mixture between and over the top of the shortcake layers.
8 Top with sour cream sweetened to taste.

Torten are a Viennese version of cake. Their texture is somewhat heavier than the typical American cake, but they are delicious nonetheless.

◆

APFELTORTE

6 TO 8 SERVINGS

½ pound butter
½ cup plus ⅓ cup sugar
1 egg, beaten
6 almonds, ground
1¾ cups flour
Pinch of salt
4 or 5 apples
¾ cup water
Whipped cream

1 Preheat the oven to 400°F.
2 Cream the butter and ⅓ cup of the sugar well. Add the egg and almonds. Sift in the flour and salt and mix smoothly. Spread two thirds of this dough in a deep 9-inch springform pan and bake 20 minutes. Let cool in pan.
3 Wash, pare, core and slice the apples into small sections.
4 Boil ½ cup of the sugar and the water together until the syrup spins a thread from the edge of the spoon. Place a few apple sections at a time in the syrup and cook until soft but not broken. Let apples cool.
5 Let the syrup cook a little longer to thicken it.
6 Arrange apple sections in neat rows on the torte and pour the syrup over them. Force the remaining dough through a pastry tube and decorate the top with a border and crisscross strips over the apples.

Continued

7 Return the torte to the hot oven and bake until the garnishing dough is done and beginning to turn golden brown.

8 Remove outer rim of pan and let the torte chill on the base. Serve with whipped cream.

◆

LINZERTORTE

12 SERVINGS

½ pound butter
1 cup flour
1½ cups unpeeled almonds, grated
½ cup granulated sugar
⅛ teaspoon ground cloves
⅛ teaspoon cinnamon
2 egg yolks
⅓ cup raspberry jam
½ egg white, lightly beaten
1½ tablespoons confectioners' sugar
Slivered almonds (optional)

1 Preheat the oven to 325°F.

2 Crumble or chop the butter into the flour. Add the almonds.

3 Mix the sugar with the cloves, cinnamon and egg yolks. Add to the flour mixture and knead the dough until smooth and well blended.

4 Turn two thirds of the dough into a 9-inch ungreased cake pan with a removable bottom. Press dough over the bottom and halfway up the sides. Spread with jam.

5 Roll egg-size balls of the remaining dough between the palms to make long rolls about ⅓ to ½ inch in diameter and about 8 inches long. Place the rolls on a baking sheet and chill until firm.

6 Using a spatula, lift the rolls and arrange lattice-style over the jam. Fasten to the dough around the rim of the pan by pressing lightly.

7 Brush with the egg white and bake on the lower rack of the oven about 1¼ hours.

8 Set the pan on a rack and partly cool the cake before removing the rim of the pan. Before serving, sprinkle the cake with confectioners' sugar and, if desired, slivered almonds.

◆

SACHER TORTE

This cake originated in the famed Sacher Hotel in Vienna.

6 TO 8 SERVINGS

5 tablespoons butter, at room temperature
6 tablespoons sugar
½ cup (3 ounces) semisweet chocolate pieces, melted
4 egg yolks
½ cup plus 1 tablespoon flour
5 egg whites
2½ tablespoons apricot jam

1 Preheat the oven to 325°F. Grease and lightly flour a deep 8-inch springform pan.

2 Cream the butter, add the sugar gradually and cream until fluffy. Add the chocolate and mix thoroughly, scraping the bottom of the bowl several times.

3 Add the egg yolks one at a time and mix well after each addition. Stir in the flour until no particles show.

4 Beat the egg whites until stiff but not dry and gently fold them into the batter until no white shows.

5 Turn the batter into the prepared pan and bake on the lower rack of the oven until the cake shrinks from the sides of the pan and rebounds to the touch when pressed gently in the center, or about 1¼ hours.

6 Let the cake stand 10 minutes on a cooling rack before turning out of the pan. (The cake will shrink slightly on cooling.) Turn the cake out on the rack, turn right side up and let it finish cooling.

7 Stand the rack and cake on wax paper and spread the top of the cake with jam. Pour any desired chocolate icing over the cake and spread it quickly to coat the top and sides.

◆

CHEESECAKE DE LUXE

8 SERVINGS

2½ pounds cream cheese
¼ teaspoon vanilla extract
1 teaspoon grated lemon rind
1¾ cups plus ⅓ cup sugar
3 tablespoons all-purpose flour
Pinch of salt
5 eggs
2 egg yolks
¼ cup cream
Crust (see following recipe)
1 quart strawberries
¼ cup water
1 tablespoon cornstarch
1 teaspoon butter

1 Preheat the oven to 475°F.

2 Beat cream cheese until fluffy. Add vanilla and lemon rind.

3 Combine 1¾ cups of the sugar, the flour and salt. Gradually blend into cheese mixture. Beat in eggs and egg yolks, one at a time, and the cream. Beat well.

4 Pour mixture into the prepared crust. Bake for 8 to 10 minutes.

5 Reduce the heat to 200°F. Bake for 1½ hours longer, or until set. Turn off heat. Allow cake to remain in the oven with door ajar for 30 minutes.

6 Cool on a rack. Chill.

7 To prepare the glaze, wash and hull the strawberries. Crush enough berries to make ½ cup. Boil the crushed berries, ⅓ cup of the sugar, the water and cornstarch 2 minutes, stirring. Add the butter. Strain and cool.

8 Arrange the whole berries over the top of the cheesecake and pour the glaze over the berries. Chill.

CRUST
FOR 1 (9-INCH) SPRINGFORM PAN

1 cup flour
¼ teaspoon sugar
1 teaspoon grated lemon rind
¼ pound butter
1 egg yolk, lightly beaten
¼ teaspoon vanilla extract

1 Preheat the oven to 400°F.

2 Combine flour, sugar and lemon rind. Cut in butter until mixture is crumbly. Add egg yolk and vanilla. Mix. Pat one third of the dough over the bottom of a 9-inch springform pan with sides removed. Bake for about 6 minutes, or until golden. Cool.

3 Butter the sides of the pan and attach to the bottom. Pat remaining dough around sides to a height of 2 inches.

REFRIGERATOR RUM CHEESECAKE

10 TO 12 SERVINGS

2 envelopes (2 tablespoons) unflavored gelatin
1 cup sugar
Pinch of salt
2 eggs, separated
1 cup milk
1 teaspoon grated lemon rind
1 tablespoon lemon juice
2 tablespoons light rum, or 2 teaspoons
   rum flavoring
3 cups (1½ pounds) creamed cottage cheese
Nut-crumb crust (page 665)
1 cup heavy cream, whipped

1 Mix the gelatin, ¾ cup of the sugar and the salt in the top of a double boiler.

2 Beat the egg yolks, add the milk and add to the gelatin mixture. Cook over boiling water, stirring, until the gelatin dissolves and the mixture thickens slightly, or about 10 minutes.

3 Remove the mixture from the heat and add the lemon rind, lemon juice and rum. Cool.

4 Whip the cottage cheese with an electric beater until smooth, or rub through a sieve into a large bowl. Stir in the cooled gelatin mixture. Chill, stirring occasionally, until the mixture mounds slightly when dropped from a spoon.

5 While the gelatin mixture is chilling, prepare the nut-crumb crust and set aside.

6 Beat the egg whites until stiff but not dry. Gradually add the remaining ¼ cup of sugar and beat until very stiff. Fold into the gelatin-cheese mixture. Fold in the whipped cream and turn into pan lined with the nut-crumb crust. Chill before serving.

CHOCOLATE CHEESECAKE

12 TO 14 SERVINGS

1½ cups graham cracker crumbs
5 tablespoons butter, melted
¾ cup sugar
8 ounces sweet cooking chocolate
1¼ pounds cream cheese, softened
Pinch of salt
1½ teaspoons vanilla extract
4 eggs, separated
2 cups heavy cream
½ cup flour
Shaved chocolate

1 Preheat the oven to 325°F. Lightly grease bottom and sides of a 9-inch springform pan.

2 Mix the crumbs with the butter and 2 tablespoons of the sugar. Sprinkle ¼ cup of the crumb mixture around the sides of the pan. Press remaining mixture onto the bottom.

3 Melt the chocolate in the top part of a double boiler over hot water. Remove from heat and cool slightly.

4 Mix cream cheese with salt, vanilla and half of the remaining sugar. Beat in egg yolks. Fold in the melted chocolate.

5 Beat the egg whites until they hold stiff peaks. Beat in remaining sugar, 1 tablespoon at a time, until well blended and very stiff.

6 Beat 1 cup of the cream until stiff and pour over the egg white mixture. Add cream cheese mixture. Sprinkle the flour on top and fold all the ingredients together gently.

7 Pour the mixture into the prepared pan. Bake for 1¼ hour. Do not open the oven door for 1 hour. Turn off heat at end of baking time and allow cake to remain in the oven with door closed for 3 to 4 hours. The cake may crack, but this is not detrimental to it.

8 Chill the cake. Remove the springform. Whip the remaining cream until stiff and spread over top of cake. Decorate with chocolate shavings.

◆

CHRISTMAS CHEESECAKE
A CHEESECAKE WITH CANDIED FRUIT FILLING

12 SERVINGS

½ pound candied fruit such as citrus, cherries, watermelon rind and so on
⅓ cup graham cracker crumbs, approximately
2 pounds cream cheese, at room temperature
½ cup cream
4 eggs
1¾ cups sugar
1 teaspoon vanilla extract

1 Preheat the oven to 300°F.

2 Cut the pieces of fruit into cubes, ¼ inch or smaller.

3 Butter the inside of a metal cake pan 8 inches wide and 3 inches deep. Do not use a springform pan. Sprinkle the inside with graham cracker crumbs. Shake out excess crumbs and set aside.

4 You may make the batter using a food processor or electric mixer. The processor is faster. Put the cream cheese, cream, eggs, sugar and vanilla into the container of a food processor or the bowl of an electric mixer. If the mixer is used, start beating the ingredients on low and, as the ingredients blend, increase the speed to high. If the processor is used, blend the ingredients thoroughly. Add the pieces of candied fruit and mix or blend.

5 Pour and scrape the batter into the prepared pan and shake gently to level the mixture.

6 Set the pan inside a wider pan and pour boiling water into the larger pan to a depth of about ½ inch. Do not let the edge of the cheesecake pan touch the sides of the larger pan. Set the pans thus arranged into the oven and bake 2 hours. At the end of that time, turn off the oven heat and let the cake remain in the oven for 1 hour longer.

7 Lift the cake out of its water bath and place it on a rack. Let stand at least 2 hours.

8 Place a round cake plate over the cake and carefully turn both upside down to unmold the cake. Serve lukewarm or at room temperature.

FOOD PROCESSOR CHEESECAKE

This is perhaps the quickest made cheesecake ever developed.

6 SERVINGS

1 envelope (1 tablespoon) unflavored gelatin
1 tablespoon lemon juice
Peel of 1 lemon
½ cup hot water or milk
⅓ cup sugar
2 egg yolks
8 ounces cream cheese
1 heaping cup crushed ice
1 cup sour cream
Graham cracker crust (page 665)

1 Place the gelatin, lemon juice, peel and water in the bowl of a food processor and blend briefly.

2 Add the sugar, egg yolks and cheese and blend. Add the ice and sour cream and blend until well mixed.

3 Pour the mixture into a 4-cup spring-form pan lined with one half of a recipe for graham cracker crust. Sprinkle the remaining graham cracker mixture over the top of the cake. Chill until set.

◆

HELEN McCULLY'S WHITE FRUITCAKE

1 (10-INCH) TUBE CAKE, OR 2 LOAVES

1½ pounds almonds, blanched and coarsely shredded
½ pound candied citron, chopped
¼ pound candied pineapple, chopped
¼ pound candied cherries, halved
½ pound golden raisins
4 cups flour
¾ pound butter
2 cups sugar
6 eggs, separated
¾ cup milk
¼ cup cognac
1 teaspoon almond extract
1 teaspoon cream of tartar

1 Preheat the oven to 275°F. Grease one 10-inch tube pan or two 9×5×3-inch loaf pans. Line with brown paper and grease the paper.

2 Mix together the almonds, fruits and ½ cup of the flour. Set aside.

3 Cream the butter until smooth, adding the sugar gradually. Beat the egg yolks lightly, add them to the creamed mixture and beat well.

4 Combine the milk, cognac and almond extract. Add to the creamed mixture alternately with remaining flour.

5 Beat the egg whites until foamy, then add cream of tartar. Continue beating until stiff. Pour the batter over the fruits and nuts. Mix well. Fold in egg whites.

6 Lift the batter into the prepared pans and press down firmly with the palm. Bake in tube pan 3¼ hours, or in loaf pans 2¼ hours.

7 Let stand 30 minutes. Turn the cakes upside down onto a wire rack. Peel off paper and store in an airtight container several days.

Note: This cake may be frosted with layers of almond paste (opposite page), milk frosting (opposite page) and confectioners' sugar icing (page 705).

NOVA SCOTIA BLACK FRUITCAKE

1 (10-INCH) TUBE CAKE, OR 2 LOAF CAKES

1 pound candied pineapple, shredded
1 pound golden raisins
½ pound seeded raisins
½ pound candied cherries, halved
4 ounces candied citron, coarsely chopped
4 ounces currants
2 ounces candied lemon peel, coarsely chopped
2 ounces candied orange peel, coarsely chopped
½ cup dark rum, cognac or sherry
4 ounces almonds, blanched and shredded
4 ounces walnuts or pecans, coarsely chopped
2 cups flour
½ teaspoon mace
½ teaspoon cinnamon
½ teaspoon baking powder
1 tablespoon milk
1 teaspoon almond extract
¼ pound butter
1 cup granulated sugar
1 cup brown sugar, packed
5 eggs

1 Mix the fruits. Add rum, cover and let stand overnight.

2 Preheat the oven to 275°F. Grease one 10-inch tube pan or two 9×5×3-inch loaf pans. Line with wax paper and grease the paper.

3 Combine the fruits, the nuts and ½ cup of the flour.

4 Sift together the remaining flour, mace, cinnamon and baking powder. Mix the milk with the almond extract.

5 Cream the butter until smooth, adding sugars gradually. Add the eggs, mix well and add the milk mixture. Add flour mixture; mix well.

6 Pour the batter over the fruits and nuts and mix thoroughly. Fill the pans and press batter down firmly.

7 Bake tube cake about 4 hours, loaves about 3 hours. Let cakes stand 30 minutes. Turn out onto a rack and peel off the paper.

8 Wrap cooled cakes in cheesecloth soaked in the rum. Place in a crock or deep kettle and cover tightly. As the cloth dries, dribble a little of the same liquor over it. Let ripen 1 month before frosting with a layer of each of the following two frostings. When dry, spread the milk frosting evenly with confectioners' sugar icing (page 705).

ALMOND PASTE
FROSTS 1 (10-INCH) CAKE OR 2 LOAF PANS

1 pound almonds, blanched
1 pound sifted confectioners' sugar
3 egg whites, lightly beaten
1 teaspoon almond extract

1 Grind the almonds fine.

2 Add remaining ingredients; mix thoroughly. Spread over the cake. Let dry.

MILK FROSTING
FROSTS 1 (10-INCH) CAKE OR 2 LOAF PANS

1 teaspoon butter
1½ cups sugar
1 tablespoon light corn syrup
½ cup milk
½ teaspoon almond extract

1 Cook the butter, sugar, corn syrup and milk to 234°F, stirring. Cool.

2 Add the almond extract and beat until of a soft fudge consistency. Spread over almond paste. Let dry.

ORANGE FRUITCAKE

1 (10-INCH) TUBE CAKE

2½ cups sifted cake flour
1 teaspoon baking powder
Pinch of salt
6½ ounces pitted dates, chopped
4½ ounces walnuts, chopped
½ pound butter
2 cups sugar
2 eggs
1 teaspoon baking soda
1 cup buttermilk
1 teaspoon vanilla extract
Grated rind and juice of 2 oranges

1 Preheat the oven to 300°F. Grease a 10-inch tube pan.

2 Sift together the flour, baking powder and salt. Stir several tablespoons of this mixture into the chopped dates and nuts.

3 Cream the butter until smooth, gradually adding 1 cup of the sugar. Add the eggs, 1 at a time, beating well after each addition.

4 Stir the baking soda into the buttermilk and add to the creamed mixture alternately with the flour mixture.

5 Add vanilla, dates, nuts and orange rind and mix well. Pour into pan and bake 1 hour and 20 minutes.

6 Meanwhile, boil together the orange juice and remaining 1 cup of sugar. When cake is done, pour over the top.

Note: This cake will keep 2 to 3 weeks if wrapped in foil or plastic wrap and stored in the refrigerator.

Frostings, Fillings and Glazes

VANILLA BOILED FROSTING

FROSTS TOPS AND SIDES OF 2 (8- OR 9-INCH) CAKE LAYERS

2½ cups sugar
⅓ cup light corn syrup
½ cup water
2 egg whites
1½ teaspoons vanilla extract

1 Bring to a boil the sugar, corn syrup and water, stirring until the sugar dissolves. Continue cooking to 242°F (syrup forms a firm ball in cold water).

2 In an electric mixer or a large bowl, beat the egg whites until stiff but not dry. Add the syrup in a fine stream while beating constantly.

3 Add the vanilla and continue beating until the frosting will hold its shape when dropped from the beater back into the bowl.

4 Spread the frosting quickly on the cake.

BUTTERCREAM

FROSTS TOPS AND SIDES OF 2 (9-INCH)
OR 3 (8-INCH) CAKE LAYERS

1 cup sugar
⅛ teaspoon cream of tartar
⅓ cup water
3 eggs
½ pound butter, at room temperature
1 teaspoon vanilla extract

1 Mix the sugar and cream of tartar.
Add the water and bring to a boil, stirring
until the sugar dissolves. Continue boiling
to 246°F (a drop of the mixture forms a firm
ball in cold water). Set aside to cool to
lukewarm.

2 Beat the eggs in an electric mixer or
with a rotary hand beater until fluffy. Add
the syrup slowly while beating. Beat until
cool.

3 Add the butter, a tablespoon at a
time, beating well after each addition. Beat
until very smooth and creamy. Chill until
firm enough to spread. After frosting, chill
the cake until ready to serve.

CHOCOLATE BUTTERCREAM I

FROSTS TOPS OF 2 (8-INCH) CAKE LAYERS

1 (6-ounce) package (1 cup) semisweet
    chocolate pieces
¼ cup boiling water or hot coffee
2 tablespoons confectioners' sugar
2 eggs, at room temperature
¼ pound butter, at room temperature
2 tablespoons rum

1 Place the chocolate in the container
of a food processor. Add the liquid and
process until chocolate has melted.

2 Add the sugar, eggs, butter and rum
and blend until smooth.

3 In warm weather, chill to spreading
consistency. Frost cake and refrigerate.

♦

CHOCOLATE BUTTERCREAM II

FROSTS TOPS OF 2 (8-INCH) CAKE LAYERS

1 (6-ounce) package (1 cup) semisweet
    chocolate pieces
¼ cup water
1 teaspoon instant coffee
¼ cup sugar
4 egg yolks
¼ pound butter, at room temperature

1 In the top of a double boiler heat the
chocolate, water, coffee and sugar. Stir occasionally until the mixture is smooth.

2 Beat in the egg yolks one at a time
and cook over boiling water 3 minutes,
stirring constantly. Remove from heat and
beat in the butter bit by bit.

MOCHA BUTTERCREAM

3 CUPS

1 cup sugar
⅓ cup water
¼ teaspoon cream of tartar
4 egg yolks
5 ounces semisweet chocolate
¼ cup strong coffee
¾ pound butter
2 tablespoons dark rum

1 Combine the sugar, water and cream of tartar in a heavy saucepan. Bring to a boil and boil rapidly until the syrup reaches 240°F on a candy thermometer.

2 Beat the egg yolks until fluffy. Gradually beat in the syrup and continue to beat until the mixture is stiff.

3 Melt the chocolate in the coffee over hot water. Beat into the egg yolk mixture.

4 Beat in the butter bit by bit. Stir in the rum. Chill until the buttercream has the right consistency for spreading.

VANILLA FROSTING

ABOUT 1½ CUPS

¼ pound butter
1 cup granulated sugar
¼ cup half-and-half
2 cups sifted confectioners' sugar,
    approximately
1½ teaspoons vanilla extract
Food coloring (optional)

1 Melt the butter, add the granulated sugar and half-and-half and stir thoroughly. Bring the mixture to a boil, stirring. Cool to room temperature.

2 Add the confectioners' sugar a little at a time, until frosting is of spreading consistency. Stir in the vanilla. Add a drop or two of food coloring to tint the frosting any desired color. Use immediately.

CHOCOLATE FROSTING I

ABOUT 1 CUP

½ cup semisweet chocolate bits
1 tablespoon butter
1½ tablespoons undiluted evaporated milk
2 tablespoons light corn syrup
½ teaspoon vanilla extract
1¾ cups sifted confectioners' sugar

1 Melt the chocolate bits in the top part of a double boiler over hot, not boiling, water.

2 Stir the butter, evaporated milk, corn syrup, vanilla and sugar into the melted chocolate. Blend until smooth.

◆

CHOCOLATE FROSTING II

ABOUT 1½ CUPS

4 ounces (4 squares) unsweetened chocolate
2¼ cups confectioners' sugar
¼ cup water
2 egg yolks
6 tablespoon butter, at room temperature

1 Melt the chocolate in a double boiler over hot water. Remove from the heat and add the sugar and water all at once. Blend well.

2 Add the egg yolks, one at a time, beating well after each addition. Beat in the butter, 1 tablespoon at a time.

FUDGE FROSTING

FROSTS TOPS AND SIDES OF
2 (9-INCH) CAKE LAYERS

3 cups sugar
3 tablespoons light corn syrup
1 cup milk
4 ounces (4 squares) unsweetened chocolate
5 tablespoons butter, at room temperature
1 teaspoon vanilla extract

1 Cook the sugar, syrup, milk and chocolate, stirring, until the sugar dissolves. Continue cooking to 232°F (the syrup forms a very soft ball in cold water). Stir occasionally to prevent scorching.

2 Remove from the heat, add the butter and cool without stirring until the bottom of the saucepan feels lukewarm.

3 Add the vanilla and beat until the frosting is creamy and barely holds its shape. Spread quickly on the cake before the frosting hardens.

LEMON OR ORANGE FROSTING

ABOUT 2 CUPS

1½ cups sugar
½ cup water
1½ tablespoons light corn syrup
2 egg whites
Pinch of salt
1½ tablespoons fresh lemon or orange juice
1 teaspoon vanilla extract
1 teaspoon grated lemon or orange rind

1 Boil sugar, water and corn syrup, stirring until sugar dissolves, and heat to 242°F on a candy thermometer.

2 Beat egg whites with salt until stiff. Add syrup gradually and beat until stiff. Add remaining ingredients and beat again until stiff.

CARAMEL FROSTING

FROSTS TOPS AND SIDES OF
2 (9-INCH) CAKE LAYERS

3 cups light brown sugar, packed
1 cup half-and-half
5 tablespoons butter, at room temperature
1 teaspoon vanilla extract

1 Cook the sugar and half-and-half, stirring, until the sugar dissolves. Continue cooking to 234°F (the syrup forms a very soft ball in cold water).

2 Remove from the heat, add the butter and cook without stirring until the bottom of the saucepan feels lukewarm.

3 Add the vanilla and beat until the frosting is creamy and barely holds its shape. Spread quickly on the cake before the frosting hardens.

◆

DECORATIVE FROSTING

ABOUT ½ CUP

Mix 1 lightly beaten egg white with 1 cup sifted confectioners' sugar and ¼ teaspoon vanilla extract. Add more sugar, bit by bit, until the frosting will hold its shape when piped or spread. If the frosting becomes too thick, add extra egg white.

COCONUT-PECAN FROSTING

FROSTS TOP AND BETWEEN LAYERS OF
3 (9-INCH) CAKE LAYERS

1 cup evaporated milk, or half evaporated milk
    and half fresh milk
1 cup sugar
3 egg yolks
¼ pound butter, at room temperature
1 teaspoon vanilla extract
1 cup flaked coconut
1 cup chopped pecans

1 Combine the milk, sugar, egg yolks, butter and vanilla in a saucepan. Cook over medium heat, stirring constantly, until the mixture thickens.

2 Add the flaked coconut and pecans. Beat until cool and of a spreading consistency.

◆

ROYAL ICING

ABOUT 1½ CUPS

Combine 2 lightly beaten egg whites and 1 tablespoon lemon juice in a mixing bowl. Gradually add about 3½ cups sifted confectioners' sugar, until the mixture is of spreading consistency. Cover the bowl with a damp cloth until icing is ready to use.

EASY PENUCHE ICING

FROSTS TOPS AND SIDES OF
2 (8-INCH) CAKE LAYERS

¼ pound butter
1 cup brown sugar, packed
¼ cup milk
1¾ to 2 cups sifted confectioners' sugar

1 Melt the butter in a saucepan, add the brown sugar and boil, stirring, over low heat 2 minutes. Add the milk and return to a boil, stirring constantly. Cool to lukewarm.

2 Gradually add the confectioners' sugar. Place the pan in ice water and stir until the icing is thick enough to spread. This is especially good for spice cakes.

◆

CONFECTIONERS' SUGAR ICING

ABOUT ½ CUP

Mix 4 teaspoons water with 1 cup sifted confectioners' sugar. Add ¼ teaspoon of any desired flavoring.

APRICOT FILLING

ABOUT 2 CUPS

½ cup sugar
3 tablespoons cornstarch
¼ cup undiluted frozen orange juice
  concentrate, thawed
1⅓ cups cooked or canned apricots, well
  drained

1 Combine the sugar and cornstarch in a saucepan; blend. Stir in the orange juice concentrate.

2 Purée the apricots in a food processor and add the purée to the sugar mixture.

3 Place over medium heat and bring to a boil, stirring constantly. Boil for about 30 seconds.

◆

CHOCOLATE FILLING

ABOUT 1½ CUPS

4 eggs, lightly beaten
¼ cup sugar
½ teaspoon cornstarch
4 ounces semisweet chocolate, melted
¼ pound butter, softened
½ cup finely ground walnuts (optional)
1 teaspoon vanilla extract

1 Mix together the eggs, sugar and cornstarch in the top part of a double boiler. Heat over boiling water, stirring, until mixture thickens. Do not boil. Cool.

2 Stir in the chocolate. Gradually beat in the butter, 1 tablespoon at a time.

3 Fold in the nuts and vanilla and stir until mixture is thick enough to spread.

LEMON FILLING

ABOUT ½ CUP

2 egg yolks, lightly beaten
½ cup sugar
2 tablespoons lemon juice
2 tablespoons butter
1 teaspoon grated lemon rind
1½ tablespoons cornstarch
3 tablespoons water

Cook all ingredients except cornstarch and water in the top part of a double boiler over boiling water, stirring until thick. Mix cornstarch with water, add to the pan, and cook, stirring, until thick.

◆

PASTRY CREAM

ABOUT 3 CUPS

⅓ cup sugar
3½ tablespoons cornstarch, or 6 tablespoons
  flour
6 lightly beaten egg yolks
2 cups milk
1 teaspoon vanilla extract

1 Mix sugar, cornstarch and egg yolks in a saucepan. Scald the milk and pour it gradually over the egg yolk mixture, stirring rapidly with a wire whisk.

2 Cook over low heat or in the top of a double boiler, stirring rapidly with the whisk, until the mixture is thickened and smooth. Do not allow the pastry cream to boil. Cool and stir in the vanilla.

APRICOT GLAZE

ABOUT 1 CUP

Heat 1 cup sieved apricot jam until it boils. Stir in 2 to 4 tablespoons cognac or other liqueur. Use the glaze while it is hot, on fruit tarts or on fruit-topped cheesecakes.

◆

CHOCOLATE GLAZE

ABOUT ½ CUP

Combine ½ cup semisweet chocolate morsels, 2 tablespoons light corn syrup and 1 teaspoon water in the top part of a double boiler. Place over hot, not boiling, water until chocolate is melted. Remove from heat and blend until smooth.

◆

LEMON OR ORANGE GLAZE

ABOUT 1¼ CUPS

3 tablespoons milk
2 tablespoons butter
2 cups sifted confectioners' sugar
3 tablespoons lemon or orange juice
1 teaspoon grated lemon or orange rind

1 Heat the milk and butter until the butter melts. Pour over the sugar and stir until smooth.
2 Add juice and rind. When the glaze is poured over a cake, it will run over the sides.

Cookies

ALMOND SQUARES

16 SQUARES

½ cup all-purpose flour
Pinch of salt
⅛ teaspoon baking soda
1 egg
1 cup brown sugar
½ teaspoon vanilla extract
1 cup blanched almonds

1 Preheat the oven to 325°F.
2 Sift the flour, salt and baking soda.
3 Beat the egg until it is light and foamy. Add the sugar and vanilla and beat well. Stir in the flour mixture and then the almonds.
4 Grease a shallow pan (8 × 8 × 2 inches) and spread the mixture into it with a spatula. Bake for 25 to 30 minutes, or until top is firm with a crust. While warm cut into squares, about 2 inches each. Cool before taking from the pan.

ALMOND MACAROONS

ABOUT 3 DOZEN

½ pound (1 cup) almond paste
1 cup confectioners' sugar
3 egg whites, approximately
½ teaspoon vanilla
Granulated sugar

1 Preheat the oven to 300°F.

2 Chop the almond paste, add the confectioners' sugar and work with the fingers until blended.

3 Add the egg whites, one at a time, blending well after each addition. Use only enough egg white to make a soft "dough" that will hold its shape when dropped from a spoon. Add the vanilla.

4 Force the mixture through a plain round pastry tube, well apart, in rounds on unglazed paper that has been fitted onto a cookie sheet. Sprinkle with granulated sugar.

5 Bake about 20 minutes. Remove the sheet of macaroons to a damp cloth, paper side down, to loosen the cookies for easy removal from the paper. Cool on a rack.

Variation

ROLLED MARZIPAN COOKIES

Prepare almond macaroon mixture using a minimum of egg white. The mixture must be stiff. Pat and roll to ¼-inch thickness on a board dusted with a mixture of equal measures of flour and confectioners' sugar. Cut into shapes, using a small floured cookie cutter. Bake as for almond macaroons, cool and ice with confectioners' sugar icing (page 705). If desired, before the frosting hardens, decorate with candied fruits, small candies or colored sugar.

BUTTER COOKIES

2 TO 2½ DOZEN COOKIES

¼ pound butter, at room temperature
⅓ cup sugar
1 egg
Pinch of salt
½ to 1 teaspoon vanilla extract
¼ teaspoon grated orange rind,
    or ⅛ teaspoon grated nutmeg
1 cup flour
Nuts (optional)

1 Preheat the oven to 375°F.

2 Cream the butter and sugar thoroughly. Add the egg, salt, vanilla and fruit rind and mix. Add the flour and mix well.

3 Shape the dough into small balls and flatten with the hand; or chill the dough and put it through a cookie press. Garnish with nuts if desired.

4 Place on a lightly greased cookie sheet and bake until the edges are light brown, or about 12 minutes.

KOURAMBIEDES
GREEK BUTTER COOKIES

These crumbly cookies, coated with confectioners' sugar, are traditionally served in Greek homes at all festive occasions. At weddings they are served as a good luck token.

ABOUT 4 DOZEN

½ pound butter, at room temperature
¾ cup confectioners' sugar
1 egg yolk
1½ tablespoons cognac or brandy
4½ cups cake flour, sifted twice

1 Cream the butter in an electric mixer until thick and lemon colored. Sift confectioners' sugar and add it gradually to the butter. Add egg yolk, creaming well. Add cognac.

2 Gradually work in the flour to make a soft dough that will roll easily in the palm of the hand without sticking. If sticky, refrigerate the dough for 1 hour.

3 Preheat the oven to 350°F.

4 Pat and shape the dough into balls 1½ inches in diameter. Place on ungreased baking sheet and bake until sandy colored (not brown), about 15 minutes. Cool and sift over generously with additional confectioners' sugar.

LADYFINGERS

ABOUT 18 WHOLE LADYFINGERS

½ cup sifted cake flour
⅔ cup sifted confectioners' sugar
Pinch of salt
3 eggs, separated
½ teaspoon vanilla extract

1 Preheat the oven to 350°F.

2 Sift together 3 times the flour, half of the sugar and the salt.

3 Beat the egg whites until stiff and gradually beat in the remaining sugar. Beat the egg yolks until thick and lemon colored and fold with the vanilla into the egg white mixture. Sift the flour mixture, one third at a time, over the eggs and fold in carefully.

4 Line ungreased baking sheets with unglazed paper. Press the batter through a pastry bag onto the paper, or shape with a spoon into strips about 4 × ¾ inches.

5 Bake 12 to 15 minutes, or until golden brown. Remove from paper with a spatula and cool on a rack.

GERMAN LEBKUCHEN

3 TO 4 DOZEN

4 eggs
2 cups sugar
2 cups honey
2½ cups blanched almonds, cut in small pieces
3 cups flour
½ teaspoon baking soda
1 tablespoon ground cloves
1 teaspoon cinnamon
½ cup candied orange peel
½ cup candied lemon peel
¼ cup citron

1 Beat the eggs well, add the sugar a little at a time and beat until light and fluffy. Add the honey and almonds and stir just enough to mix.

2 Sift the flour, baking soda and spices together, add the fruit cut in paper-thin strips and mix well so that the fruit is completely covered with flour. Combine the 2 mixtures and refrigerate to chill.

3 Preheat the oven to 350°F.

4 Spread the mixture ¼ inch thick on a buttered baking sheet and bake 30 minutes. Cool slightly and cut into desired shapes with cookie cutters.

MADELEINES

Marcel Proust immortalized these plain French sweets in *Swann's Way* when he wrote of them evocatively in a poetic passage that begins: "My mother, seeing that I was cold, offered me some tea. . . . She sent out for one of those short, plump little cakes called 'petites madeleines,' which look as though they had been molded in the fluted scallop of a pilgrim's shell. And soon . . . I raised to my lips a spoonful of the tea in which I had soaked a morsel of the cake."

3½ TO 4 DOZEN

4 eggs, at room temperature
Pinch of salt
⅔ cup granulated sugar
1 teaspoon vanilla
1 cup flour
¼ pound butter, melted and cooled

1 Grease well and flour pans for 4 dozen madeleines. If only half this many pans are available, cut the recipe in half and make it again. This is because the butter, on standing, settles to the bottom and causes a heavy rough layer. Place racks near the bottom of the oven and preheat the oven to 400°F.

2 Beat the eggs with the salt, adding sugar gradually, until the mixture stands in very stiff peaks. Add vanilla.

3 Sift about one quarter of the flour at a time over the egg mixture and fold it in until no flour shows.

4 Add the butter about a tablespoon at a time and fold it in as quickly as possible. Fill the prepared pans about three quarters full, place in oven immediately and bake until brown, about 10 minutes.

PRESSED COOKIES

6 DOZEN

½ pound soft butter
1 cup brown sugar, packed
½ cup granulated sugar
2 eggs, beaten
2 teaspoons vanilla
4 cups flour
Pinch of salt
1 teaspoon baking powder
½ teaspoon baking soda
2 tablespoons milk

1 Preheat the oven to 400°F.

2 Cream the butter with the sugars, add the eggs and vanilla and cream well.

3 Sift together the dry ingredients and add alternately with the milk to the creamed mixture. Mix well.

4 Force the dough through a cookie press onto an ungreased cookie sheet. Use different stencils in the press to give different shapes. Or the dough may be shaped into small balls, flattened with a fork and baked. Garnish with nuts, raisins and coconut, if desired.

5 Bake about 10 minutes.

SCOTCH SHORTBREAD

16 TO 20 WEDGES

¼ pound plus 3 tablespoons butter,
  at room temperature
½ cup confectioners' sugar
1½ cups plus 2 tablespoons flour
Pinch of salt

1 Preheat the oven to 325°F.

2 Cream the butter, add the sugar gradually and beat until fluffy. If desired, use an electric mixer at medium speed.

3 Sift the flour and salt into the creamed mixture and blend thoroughly with the hands.

4 Press the mixture into a 9-inch pie plate and pinch the edge to form a fluted rim. Prick the surface with a fork. Mark into 16 to 20 wedges, cutting about halfway through the dough.

5 Bake until firm when pressed gently in the center, or about 50 minutes; the shortbread should not be brown. In an aluminum pan bake on the lower rack; in a glass pan bake on the center rack.

6 Cool the shortbread in the pan. To serve, place right side up on a cutting board and cut in wedges where marked.

FLORENTINES

4 DOZEN

⅓ cup flour
Pinch of salt
¼ teaspoon baking soda
4 tablespoons butter
⅓ cup firmly packed brown sugar
2 tablespoons light corn syrup
1 egg, well beaten
½ teaspoon vanilla extract
½ cup flaked coconut
2 ounces semisweet chocolate

1 Preheat the oven to 350°F.

2 Sift together the flour, salt and baking soda.

3 Cream the butter and add the sugar gradually, creaming until light and fluffy. Add the corn syrup and egg and beat well.

4 Stir in the flour mixture, vanilla and coconut. Drop teaspoons of the dough about 2 inches apart onto a greased baking sheet. Spread into thin rounds.

5 Bake for 10 minutes. Remove at once from baking sheet. Cool.

6 Heat the chocolate in a double boiler over hot water until partly melted. Remove from hot water and stir rapidly until entirely melted. Dribble the melted chocolate in a lacy pattern over the cookies. Let stand for several hours, or until chocolate is firm.

MAIDA HEATTER'S CHOCOLATE-GINGER SANDWICH COOKIES

It is astonishing to think that less than twenty years ago, Americans were, by and large, unaccustomed to the use of fresh ginger. The only common ginger-based drinks or foods that came readily to mind were ginger ale, gingerbread, gingersnaps and, perhaps, ginger beer. Today, of course, fresh ginger is a staple commodity in many kitchens. One of the best cookies I have ever tasted are those of Maida Heatter, probably the greatest author of dessert books in America. These cookies are a treasure. The dough must be frozen before it is sliced and baked.

2 DOZEN

2 ounces peeled fresh ginger
½ pound butter, at room temperature
1 teaspoon vanilla extract
¼ teaspoon salt
⅛ teaspoon ground pepper, preferably white
1 cup firmly packed dark brown sugar
2 large egg yolks
1½ cups sifted unbleached flour
1 cup yellow cornmeal, preferably stone
    ground, available in health food stores
Grated rind of 2 lemons
½ pound semisweet chocolate

1 Cut the ginger into thin slices. Outfit a food processor with a metal chopping blade or use a very sharp, heavy knife to chop the ginger by hand. Chop it as fine as possible. There should be about ⅓ cup loosely packed.

2 In the large bowl of an electric mixer, combine the butter, vanilla, salt, pepper and sugar. Beat until thoroughly blended. Beat in the egg yolks and ginger. On low speed gradually beat in the flour and cornmeal.

3 Remove the bowl from the mixer and, using a wooden spoon, stir in the lemon rind.

4 Spread out a piece of plastic wrap about 15 inches long. Using a spoon, scoop out the dough into a strip measuring 10 or 11 inches long down the middle of the plastic. Fold the sides of the plastic wrap over the dough and with both hands, smooth over the plastic wrap to shape the dough into a neat, smooth log about 3½ inches wide and 1 to 1¼ inches high. When it is as smooth as possible, wrap it tightly at the ends and slide a flat-sided cookie sheet under the dough. Place the dough, on the cookie sheet, in the freezer. Let stand several hours, or until frozen solid.

5 Before baking, arrange the oven racks into 3 evenly spaced layers in the oven. Preheat the oven to 350°F. Line 2 cookie sheets with neatly cut sheets of parchment paper. Or use foil, placing it shiny side up.

6 With a sharp knife, cut the frozen dough into 48 slices, each about 3/16 inch thick. Arrange the slices at least 1 inch apart on the cookie sheets. Place in the oven and bake 15 to 17 minutes. As the cookies bake, reverse the sheets top to bottom and front to back once or twice to ensure even browning. The cookies are done when they are lightly colored along the very edges.

7 Remove the cookies from the oven and let stand about 1 minute. With a metal spatula, transfer the cookies to racks to cool.

8 Chop or grate the chocolate until it is fairly fine. Place it in the top of a small double boiler over warm water over low heat. Cover until the chocolate is partially melted, uncover and stir until completely melted.

9 Remove the top of the double boiler and let the chocolate stand briefly to cool slightly. Stir just to mix. Using a small spoon, place equal portions of the chocolate, ⅛ to ¼ inch thick, down the middle of each cookie on the flat (bottom) side. Keep the chocolate about ¼ inch away from the edges of each cookie. Place another cookie on top, pressing down slightly. Put on a small flat tray. Continue making the sandwiches. Refrigerate for a brief while, only until the chocolate becomes firm. Store.

◆

CHOCOLATE MERINGUES

ABOUT 8 DOZEN

6 ounces (1 cup) semisweet chocolate morsels
3 egg whites
1 cup sugar
⅓ cup graham cracker crumbs
½ teaspoon vanilla extract

1 Preheat the oven to 350°F.

2 Melt chocolate morsels over hot, not boiling, water. Remove from hot water and let cool for 5 minutes.

3 Beat the egg whites until stiff but not dry. Gradually add the sugar and beat until smooth and glossy. Fold in melted chocolate, the crumbs and vanilla.

4 Drop level teaspoons of the batter onto greased cookie sheets. Bake for 15 minutes. Serve with custards and ice creams.

SOFT CHOCOLATE COOKIES

3 DOZEN

1 cup shortening
2 cups firmly packed light brown sugar
Pinch of salt
1 teaspoon baking soda
¾ teaspoon cinnamon
½ teaspoon grated nutmeg
3 squares (3 ounces) unsweetened chocolate,
    melted
2 eggs
2½ cups flour
1 cup sour milk or buttermilk
1 cup chopped nuts
Nut halves for garnish

1 Cream the shortening with the brown sugar. Blend in the salt, baking soda, spices and melted chocolate. Beat in the eggs. Add the flour alternately with the milk; stir in the nuts. Chill the dough for at least 1 hour.

2 Preheat the oven to 375°F.

3 Drop teaspoons of the dough onto lightly greased cookie sheets. Bake for 15 to 18 minutes.

4 Press a nut half into the center of each cookie immediately after removing from the oven. Cool on wire racks.

BRANDY SNAPS

80 COOKIES

¼ cup light corn syrup
¼ cup molasses
¼ pound butter, at room temperature
1 cup flour
⅔ cup sugar
1 teaspoon ground ginger
2 teaspoons brandy

1 Preheat the oven to 300°F.

2 Heat the syrup and molasses to boiling. Remove from heat and add butter.

3 Sift together the flour, sugar and ginger. Add gradually, while stirring, to molasses mixture. Mix well. Add brandy.

4 Drop by half-teaspoonfuls 3 inches apart on a greased cookie sheet. Bake 10 minutes.

5 Remove from oven, loosen 1 cookie at a time and roll over handle of a wooden spoon. Slip off carefully. Serve filled with whipped cream, if desired.

BROWNIES

12 TO 18 BROWNIES

4 ounces (4 squares) unsweetened chocolate
5 tablespoons butter
2 eggs
1 cup sugar
½ cup flour
½ cup chopped walnuts or pecans
1 teaspoon vanilla extract
Pinch of salt

1 Preheat the oven to 350°F. Grease a 9 × 9-inch pan, line with paper and grease the paper.

2 Melt the chocolate and butter together. Beat the eggs with the sugar until fluffy and add to the chocolate mixture.

3 Add the flour, blend and add the nuts, vanilla and salt. Stir until well mixed.

4 Spread batter in prepared pan. If desired, garnish top with additional walnut or pecan halves. Bake for about 25 minutes. Cool in pan, turn out, remove paper and cut into squares or bars.

Variation

BLACK AND WHITE BROWNIES

Halve the amount of chocolate in the recipe above and add it, melted, to half the batter. Spread the white batter in a layer in the prepared pan, then pour chocolate layer over the top and spread evenly. Bake as above.

VIENNESE CRESCENTS

When this recipe was first published in the *New York Times*, one food authority wrote that it was, in her opinion, the greatest cookie recipe ever devised.

6 DOZEN CRESCENTS

½ vanilla bean
1 cup sifted confectioners' sugar
1 cup walnut meats
½ pound butter, at room temperature
¾ cup granulated sugar
2½ cups flour

1 Chop the vanilla bean. Pound it in a mortar or pulverize it in a blender with about 1 tablespoon of the confectioners' sugar. Mix with the remaining confectioners' sugar. Cover and let stand, preferably overnight. Reserve while cookies are baked.

2 Preheat the oven to 350°F.

3 Put the walnuts into the container of a food processor and chop until a paste forms. Add the butter, granulated sugar and flour and process until a smooth dough forms. Shape the dough, about a teaspoon at a time, into small crescents, about 1½ inches in diameter.

4 Bake on an ungreased cookie sheet until light brown, or 15 to 18 minutes. Cool 1 minute. While still warm, roll the cookies in the prepared vanilla sugar.

SOFT MOLASSES DROP COOKIES

ABOUT 3 DOZEN

½ cup vegetable shortening
½ cup brown sugar
½ cup molasses
1 egg
1¾ cups flour
1½ teaspoons baking powder
1 teaspoon cinnamon
1 teaspoon ground ginger
¼ teaspoon ground cloves
¼ teaspoon baking soda
1 teaspoon cider vinegar
2 tablespoons water
¼ cup buttermilk
1 cup raisins (optional)
Chocolate frosting I or II (page 703)

1 Preheat the oven to 350°F.
2 Beat the shortening and sugar until light and fluffy. Beat in the molasses, egg and 3 tablespoons of the flour.
3 Sift together the remaining flour and the other dry ingredients. Mix together the vinegar, water and buttermilk. Add alternately to the molasses mixture and beat batter until it is very smooth. Stir in raisins, if desired.
4 Drop teaspoons of the mixture onto greased cookie sheets. Flatten dough if desired. Bake for 12 to 15 minutes. Cool. Top each cookie with a dime-sized round of chocolate frosting.

OATMEAL THINS

ABOUT 2 DOZEN

½ cup flour
1½ cups rolled oats, either quick-cooking or old-fashioned
¼ cup superfine sugar
½ teaspoon baking soda
¼ pound butter
1 tablespoon maple syrup

1 Preheat the oven to 375°F.
2 Mix together the flour, oats, sugar and baking soda. Melt the butter with the syrup and add to the dry ingredients.
3 Place teaspoons of the batter 2 inches apart on greased cookie sheets. Bake for 8 to 10 minutes. Let stand for 1 or 2 minutes before removing to racks to finish cooling.

GINGERBREAD MEN

ABOUT 30 COOKIES

⅔ cup shortening
½ cup packed brown sugar
2 teaspoons ground ginger
1 teaspoon cinnamon
¼ teaspoon ground cloves or allspice
Pinch of salt
1 egg
¾ cup molasses
3 cups flour
1 teaspoon baking soda
½ teaspoon baking powder

1 Cream together the shortening, sugar, spices and salt. Add the egg and mix thoroughly. Add the molasses and blend.

2 Sift together twice the flour, baking soda and baking powder. Add to the molasses mixture and stir until blended. Chill.

3 Preheat the oven to 375°F.

4 Using a third to a quarter of the dough at a time, roll it to ⅛ inch or slightly thicker on a lightly floured pastry cloth with a floured rolling pin.

5 Cut with gingerbread man cutter or any other cutters desired. Transfer carefully to a greased baking sheet and repeat with remaining dough. Before baking, press raisins into the dough for eyes, nose and buttons on suit. Use half a slice of candied cherry for mouth.

6 Place in oven and bake 8 to 10 minutes. Cool on a rack. If desired, decorate with decorative frosting (page 704).

Variation

GINGERBREAD COOKIES

Roll the dough to ⅝ inch thickness on a floured pastry cloth or board. Using floured springerle boards or a rolling pin, press out the desired shapes and cut apart with a floured knife. Place on greased baking sheets and bake 10 to 12 minutes.

◆

NUTMEG HERMITS

5 DOZEN

4 cups flour
1 teaspoon baking soda
1½ teaspoons grated nutmeg
Pinch of salt
½ pound butter
2 cups soft brown sugar
4 eggs
¼ cup milk
2 cups seedless raisins
1 cup chopped pecans or walnuts

1 Preheat the oven to 375°F.

2 Sift together the flour, baking soda, nutmeg and salt. Cream the butter and brown sugar. Beat the eggs into the butter mixture. Add the flour mixture alternately with the milk. Stir in the raisins and nuts.

3 Drop teaspoons of the batter onto lightly greased cookie sheets. Bake for 12 to 15 minutes.

LAYERED NUT BARS

18 BARS OR 38 TEA-SIZE SQUARES

1 cup flour
1 cup finely packed brown sugar
½ cup shortening (may be half butter)
Topping (see following recipe)

1 Preheat the oven to 350°F.

2 Grease, line with paper and grease again a 9-inch-square pan.

3 Mix flour and sugar. Cut in shortening and mix till crumbly. Press into prepared pan and bake for 15 minutes. While this is baking, prepare the topping below.

4 When base has finished baking, pour topping over. Return to the oven and bake about 30 minutes.

5 Cool in the pan, turn out and cut into bars or squares. If desired, serve sprinkled with confectioners' sugar.

TOPPING

2 tablespoons flour
½ teaspoon baking powder
Pinch of salt
2 eggs
1 cup packed brown sugar
1 teaspoon vanilla extract
¾ cup chopped pecans or walnuts
1 cup flaked coconut

1 Combine the flour, baking powder and salt.

2 Beat eggs until very light. Add sugar gradually and beat until fluffy. Add vanilla.

3 Add flour mixture, mix and add nuts and coconut.

DATE AND NUT BARS

40 BARS

1 cup pecans or walnuts
½ cup dates
¾ cup flour
3 eggs
1½ cups brown sugar, firmly packed
¾ teaspoon baking powder
Pinch of salt

1 Preheat the oven to 350°F. Grease, line with paper and grease again a 10 × 10-inch pan.

2 Chop the nuts coarsely. Pit dates and chop. Add 1 tablespoon of the flour and mix with the fingers until dates are coated and mixed with nuts. Set aside.

3 Beat the eggs, add the sugar gradually and beat until fluffy.

4 Sift together the remaining flour, the baking powder and salt. Add to egg mixture and stir until well mixed. Stir the nuts and dates into the batter.

5 Spread in the prepared pan and bake for about 20 minutes, or until cake rebounds to the touch when pressed gently in the center. Cool slightly, turn out of pan and cut into bars 1 × 2½ inches.

Fruit Desserts

APPLE COMPOTE

6 SERVINGS

6 medium apples
3 tablespoons lemon juice, approximately
2 cups water
½ cup sugar
½ cup dry white wine
Rind of ½ lemon
1 (3-inch-long) cinnamon stick
⅓ cup currant jelly

1 Peel apples, halve them and core them. Rub them immediately with lemon juice to prevent discoloration. Drop them into 1 cup of the water.

2 Combine the remaining water with the sugar, wine and 1 tablespoon of the lemon juice. Add the apple halves, cover and simmer until fruit is tender but still firm. Remove fruit, place it in a glass bowl, cover and let stand until cool.

3 Add the lemon rind and cinnamon stick to the cooking liquid. Simmer until the sauce begins to thicken. Strain it over the apples and chill. Just before serving, dot with currant jelly.

APPLESAUCE

4 SERVINGS

2½ pounds slightly tart green apples
½ cup water
¼ cup sugar

1 Peel and core the apples. Cut them into thin slices (there should be about 6 cups) and put in a heavy saucepan. Add the water and sugar, cover and bring to a boil. Cook over low heat until the apples disintegrate, stirring occasionally.

2 Pour and scrape the mixture into the container of a food processor and purée until fine.

♦

GLAZED APPLES

6 SERVINGS

6 medium apples, peeled and cored
2 tablespoons lemon juice
1 tablespoon sugar
⅔ cup apple cider
1 cup currant jelly, melted
Crème fraîche (page 762), or whipped cream

1 Preheat the oven to 300° F.

2 Brush the apples with lemon juice. Dust them with sugar and set in a baking dish. Add the cider and bake 35 minutes, basting several times with the juice. Test the apples with a fork: they are cooked when they are soft inside but still hold their shape.

3 Mix the jelly with the juices in the bottom of the baking dish and pour over the apples to glaze them. Refrigerate and serve cold with crème fraîche.

CARAMEL APPLE SLICES

6 SERVINGS

6 medium apples
3 tablespoons lemon juice
3 tablespoons butter
3 tablespoons brown sugar
½ teaspoon cinnamon
Whipped cream

1 Pare and core the apples and cut them into eighths. Drop them into water mixed with the lemon juice.

2 Melt the butter in a heavy skillet with a tight-fitting cover and add the drained apples. Cover and cook over low heat 10 minutes, or until the apples soften.

3 Sprinkle with sugar and cinnamon and cook, uncovered, 15 to 20 minutes longer. Serve while warm with the whipped cream.

APPLE CRISP

6 SERVINGS

6 tart apples
1 cup sugar
½ teaspoon cinnamon
¼ teaspoon ground cloves
2 teaspoons lemon juice
¾ cup flour
Pinch of salt
6 tablespoons butter
¼ cup chopped nuts
Whipped cream, or ice cream

1 Preheat the oven to 350°F.

2 Peel, core and slice the apples into a bowl. Add ½ cup of the sugar, the spices and lemon juice. Mix lightly and pour into a buttered 1½-quart casserole.

3 Blend the remaining sugar, flour, salt and butter to a crumbly consistency. Add the nuts and sprinkle over the apple mixture. Bake 45 minutes, or until the apples are tender and the crust is a nice brown. Serve with whipped cream or ice cream.

APPLE OATMEAL CRISP

4 cups sliced tart cooking apples
1 tablespoon lemon juice
2 to 4 tablespoons sugar, depending on the
    tartness of the apples
1 cup rolled oats, either old-fashioned
    or quick-cooking
½ cup brown sugar
⅓ cup flour
5 tablespoons butter, melted
1 teaspoon cinnamon
Pinch of salt
Whipped cream

   1 Preheat the oven to 375°F.
   2 Place the apples in a greased shallow baking dish. Sprinkle with the lemon juice and sugar.
   3 Combine the remaining ingredients, except the whipped cream, and sprinkle over the apples. Bake for about 30 minutes, or until apples are tender. Serve hot or warm, with whipped cream.

APRICOTS WITH COGNAC

6 SERVINGS

1 pound dried apricots
⅔ cup sugar
Cognac to cover

Combine all the ingredients and let stand at least 24 hours. The flavor is improved if the fruit is allowed to steep in cognac for upward of a week. Serve chilled.

BANANAS CARIBBEAN

8 SERVINGS

4 medium bananas
¼ cup brown sugar, packed
½ cup fresh orange juice
¼ teaspoon grated nutmeg
¼ teaspoon cinnamon
½ cup sherry
1 tablespoon butter
2 tablespoons light rum

   1 Preheat the oven to 450°F.
   2 Peel the bananas and split them in half lengthwise. Place in a buttered 10×6×2-inch baking dish.
   3 Combine the sugar with the orange juice, spices and sherry. Heat and pour over the bananas. Dot with butter.
   4 Bake 10 to 15 minutes, or until the bananas are tender, basting once or twice.
   5 Remove from the oven and sprinkle with rum.

BAKED BANANAS A L'ORANGE

6 SERVINGS

3 firm ripe bananas
2 teaspoons cornstarch
2 tablespoons granulated sugar
⅓ cup fresh orange juice
1 tablespoon butter
1 tablespoon brown sugar
⅓ cup shredded coconut
Whipped cream, or vanilla ice cream (optional)

1 Preheat the oven to 375°F.
2 Peel the bananas and cut crosswise and lengthwise into halves. Arrange in a buttered shallow baking dish.
3 Combine the cornstarch, granulated sugar and orange juice. Pour the mixture over the bananas, coating well. Dot with butter and sprinkle with brown sugar and coconut.
4 Bake for 30 minutes, or until bananas are tender and sauce is slightly thick. Serve topped with whipped cream, or ice cream, if desired.

BLUEBERRY BETTY

6 SERVINGS

1 quart fresh blueberries
1 tablespoon lemon juice
¼ teaspoon cinnamon
1 cup flour
1 cup sugar
¼ pound butter
1 quart vanilla ice cream

1 Preheat the oven to 375°F.
2 Wash the berries and drain them in a colander. Place the berries in a 1½-quart casserole. Sprinkle with the lemon juice and cinnamon.
3 Sift flour and sugar together. With a pastry blender chop in the butter until it is crumbly. Sprinkle the mixture over the berries. Bake for 45 minutes. Serve with ice cream.

◆

PERLES DE CANTALOUPE AU RHUM

6 SERVINGS

1 large cantaloupe
¼ cup sugar
½ cup orange juice
2 tablespoons lemon juice
½ cup light rum

1 Cut the cantaloupe into halves and scoop out the seeds and stringy portion. Cut into melon balls.
2 Combine the sugar, orange juice, lemon juice and rum. Pour over the melon balls. Chill and serve.

CANTALOUPE ROYAL

6 SERVINGS

6 very small cantaloupes, of uniform size
1 pint vanilla ice cream, softened
½ cup heavy cream, whipped
1 tablespoon kirsch, or more
Fresh mint leaves
Fresh berries in season

1 Cut the cantaloupes into halves, remove the seeds and drain. Scoop out the inside of each cantaloupe, leaving a ¼-inch shell. Freeeze the shells overnight.

2 Chop 1 cup of the scooped-out cantaloupe meat very fine and blend it with the softened ice cream. (Any leftover cantaloupe meat can be reserved for use in fruit salads.)

3 Fold the whipped cream and kirsch into the ice cream mixture. Spoon into the frozen cantaloupe shells. If the ice cream mixture melts too much, freeze it until it is firm enough to spoon into the shells.

4 Freeze the filled shells until firm. The desert should have the consistency of ice cream. If it is too hard, let it stand at room temperature for about 30 minutes. Serve garnished with mint leaves and seasonal berries.

FIGS IN CRÈME DE CACAO

6 SERVINGS

1 dozen fresh figs
1 cup sour cream
2 tablespoons crème de cacao
½ teaspoon cocoa

1 Wash and drain the figs and, using a sharp knife, peel them.

2 Combine the sour cream and crème de cacao in a mixing bowl. Mix well. Dip the figs in the mixture, coating them entirely. Set the figs on end in a serving bowl. Dust with the cocoa and refrigerate to chill thoroughly.

♦

FRESH FIGS CURAÇAO

6 SERVINGS

12 fresh figs, peeled and quartered
1 tablespoon cognac
1 cup heavy cream, whipped
⅓ cup Curaçao

1 Marinate the figs in the cognac 30 minutes or longer.

2 Mix the cream and Curaçao. Fold in the figs and any cognac that they have not absorbed.

GINGERED FIGS

6 TO 8 SERVINGS

1 pound dried figs
2 lemons
1 large piece fresh ginger
Sugar
Cream

1 Wash the figs and clip off the stems. Add cold water to cover, 2 tablespoons lemon juice and 1 tablespoon very thinly sliced lemon rind.

2 Add the ginger and bring mixture to a boil. Boil until the figs are puffed and soft, or 20 to 30 minutes. Drain, reserving the liquid. Place the figs in a serving dish.

3 Measure the liquid and return it to the saucepan. Add half as much sugar as liquid and simmer until syrupy. Add 1 tablespoon lemon juice and 4 slices of lemon.

4 Pour the syrup over the figs, chill and serve with cream.

◆

AMBROSIA

Some people add cubed bananas or pineapple to ambrosia, but to a Southerner that is heresy.

6 SERVINGS

4 large oranges, preferably seedless
1 cup freshly grated coconut
1/3 cup confectioners' sugar

1 Peel the oranges and slice them or cut into sections. Remove any seeds, if necesssary.

2 Combine the oranges and the coconut and mix gently. Sprinkle with confectioners' sugar and refrigerate until ready to serve.

CHILLED SLICED ORANGES IN RED WINE

6 SERVINGS

3/4 cup sugar
1 cup water
1 cup dry red wine
2 cloves
1 (3-inch-long) cinnamon stick
2 slices of tangerine
2 slices of lemon
6 large navel oranges

1 Dissolve the sugar in the water and add the wine. Tie the cloves, cinnamon, tangerine and lemon in cheesecloth. Bring the wine mixture to a boil, add the cheesecloth bag and boil until the liquid becomes syrupy. Remove the bag and discard.

2 Meanwhile, skin the oranges and, with a sharp knife, cut off all the white membrane. Remove the segments. Add the fruit to the syrup and refrigerate until extremely cold.

3 Serve the dessert cold with a garnish, if desired, of slivered orange peel.

BAKED PAPAYA

6 SERVINGS

3 firm but ripe papayas
6 small pieces of vanilla bean
6 teaspoons butter
12 teaspoons brown sugar

1 Preheat the oven to 350°F.
2 Peel the papayas and split each in half. Remove the seeds.
3 Arrange the papaya halves, cut side up, in a baking dish with about ½ inch of water over the bottom. Dot the center of each papaya half with a small piece of vanilla bean, 1 teaspoon of butter and 2 teaspoons of sugar. Bake until tender, about 45 minutes.

♦

PEACH MELBA

6 SERVINGS

1 pint fresh or frozen raspberries
½ cup currant jelly
1½ teaspoons cornstarch
1 tablespoon cold water
3 peaches, peeled, poached and halved
  (page 726)
Vanilla ice cream

1 If using frozen raspberries, place them in a saucepan and allow to thaw. Mash the berries with a spoon, add the jelly and bring to a boil over low heat. Add the cornstarch mixed with the water and cook, stirring, until clear. Strain, if desired, and cool.
2 Place peach half, cut side up, in each of 6 individual dessert dishes. Top each with a scoop of ice cream and pour the cooled sauce over the top.

PEACHES IN WHITE WINE

4 TO 8 SERVINGS

8 unblemished firm ripe peaches
2 cups cold water
2 cups dry white wine
1 tablespoon lemon juice
1 cup sugar

1 Wash the peaches well and dry them, leaving the skin intact. The skin will give the peaches color as they cook.
2 Bring the water, wine, lemon juice and sugar to a boil in an enamelware or stainless-steel saucepan. Simmer until sugar is dissolved.
3 Drop the peaches into the boiling syrup. When the mixture returns to a boil, simmer until peaches are tender. The cooking time will depend on the texture of the peaches. Chill in the syrup.
4 To serve, peel the peaches and serve them in the syrup.

VANILLA-POACHED PEACHES OR PEARS

6 SERVINGS

6 firm ripe small peaches or pears
1 cup sugar
1 cup water
2 teaspoons lemon juice
Pinch of salt
1½ teaspoons vanilla extract, or 1 (2-inch)
    piece of vanilla bean

1 Peel the fruit, leaving them whole with stems intact.

2 Combine the sugar, water, lemon juice, salt and vanilla in a saucepan. Bring to a boil, add 3 peaches or pears, and cook, covered, 10 to 15 minutes for peaches, 20 minutes for pears, or until tender. Remove and reserve. Cook remaining fruit.

3 Return the first poached peaches or pears to the syrup and let all stand until cool. Chill. Remove vanilla bean if used.

PEARS BAKED IN GRENADINE

3 TO 6 SERVINGS

3 firm fresh pears
1 cup grenadine syrup
Juice of ½ lemon
Crème fraîche (page 762)

1 Preheat the oven to 325°F.

2 Peel the pears, leaving them whole with stem intact, or cut into halves lengthwise and remove cores. Place in a baking pan, cut side down.

3 Combine the grenadine with lemon juice. Pour over the pears. Bake the pears for 45 to 50 minutes, or until tender when tested with a toothpick. Baste frequently with the syrup.

4 Chill in refrigerator. Serve with the baking syrup and with crème fraîche.

PEARS BAKED WITH MINCEMEAT

6 SERVINGS

3 large ripe pears, peeled
6 heaping teaspoons mincemeat
⅓ cup sugar
½ cup water
Pinch of salt
1 tablespoon lemon juice
Cognac (optional)

1 Preheat the oven to 375°F.

2 Halve the pears and core them with a melon-ball cutter. Place the pear halves in a baking dish (10 × 5 × 2 inches). Fill each half with 1 heaping teaspoon of mincemeat.

3 Combine the sugar, water, salt and lemon juice in a saucepan. Bring to the boiling point, then pour over the pears. Cover the baking dish with foil. Bake for 1 hour, or until pears are tender, basting 3 times with the syrup. Remove the foil and bake 15 to 20 minutes longer, basting frequently.

4 Serve 1 pear half for each serving, with some of the syrup spooned over it. If desired, spoon 1 teaspoon cognac over each pear before serving.

Note: These pears would also make an admirable complement to baked ham.

PEARS A LA BORDELAISE

6 SERVINGS

6 fresh pears
Lemon juice
½ cup red Bordeaux wine
1 cup sugar
1 (3-inch-long) cinnamon stick
1 small piece of lemon peel
2 tablespoons rum or cognac (optional)

1 Peel and core the pears, cutting each into lengthwise halves. To prevent the pears from darkening, brush them with lemon juice or drop into water containing a little lemon juice.

2 In a saucepan combine the wine, sugar, cinnamon and lemon peel. Bring to a boil, stirring. Add 2 or 3 pear halves at a time and cook gently until tender. Repeat the process until all the pears have been cooked.

3 Cook the syrup until reduced to about half the original quantity. Pour over the pears and chill.

4 If desired, add rum before serving.

PRUNE WHIP WITH PORT WINE

6 SERVINGS

½ pound dried prunes
⅔ cup granulated sugar
Lemon rind
1 cup port wine
1 cup heavy cream
3 tablespoons confectioners' sugar
Slivered blanched almonds

1 Soak the prunes overnight in water to cover. Drain. Place them in a small kettle and add the granulated sugar, lemon rind and water to cover. Bring to a boil and cook until the prunes are tender.

2 Drain, leaving the prunes in the kettle. Add the port and cook 10 minutes longer. Remove the stones and purée the prunes in a food processor. Add a little more port if necessary to make the prunes moist and add more granulated sugar to taste.

3 Whip the cream and mix half of it with the prunes. Sweeten the remaining cream with confectioners' sugar and use as a garnish. Top with almonds.

CARDINAL STRAWBERRIES

4 SERVINGS

1 quart fresh strawberries
¼ cup raspberry jam
2 tablespoons sugar
¼ cup water
1 tablespoon kirsch
¼ cup slivered, blanched almonds

1 Wash and hull the strawberries.

2 Combine the jam, sugar and water in a saucepan and simmer about 2 minutes. Add the kirsch and chill.

3 Arrange the strawberries in 4 individual serving dishes. Pour the chilled raspberry sauce over the fruit and sprinkle with the slivered almonds.

◆

STRAWBERRIES WITH RUM CREAM

6 SERVINGS

1 quart whole fresh strawberries, hulled,
    rinsed and drained
½ cup granulated sugar
1 cup heavy cream
½ cup grated sweet chocolate
1 tablespoon confectioners' sugar
1 tablespoon light rum

1 Arrange the strawberries in a serving bowl and sprinkle with the granulated sugar. Chill until ready to serve.

2 Whip the cream and fold the chocolate and confectioners' sugar into it. Fold in the rum. Serve the cream with berries.

TANGERINES IN KIRSCH

ALLOW 1 PER SERVING

Peel tangerines and separate the segments. Arrange in a glass serving dish and sprinkle with confectioners' sugar. Sprinkle with kirsch and refrigerate 2 hours before serving.

♦

FRUIT MÉLANGE

4 TO 6 SERVINGS

Peel 2 peaches and 2 pears and cut into small dice. Combine with approximately 2 cups of berries such as blueberries, strawberries or raspberries. Sprinkle with 1 tablespoon lemon juice and ¼ cup sugar. Let stand until sugar dissolves. Add a spirit such as applejack, kirsch or cognac and serve chilled.

COMPOTE OF DRIED FRUITS WITH SAUCE A LA RITZ

6 SERVINGS

1 pound dried figs
1 pound dried apricots
1 cup red wine
½ cup water
1 cup sugar
1 tablespoon grated lemon rind
1 jar (about 8 ounces) brandied cherries
Sauce à la Ritz (see following recipe)

1 Soak the figs and apricots in cold water until they have plumped; drain.
2 Add the red wine, water, sugar and lemon rind to the fruits and cook slowly until tender. Add the cherries and chill.
3 Serve the compote with the sauce on the side.

SAUCE A LA RITZ
1½ CUPS

¼ cup milk
¾ cup cream
1 egg yolk
2 tablespoons sugar
¼ teaspoon vanilla extract
Kirsch to taste

1 Scald the milk and ¼ cup of the cream. Beat the egg yolk with the sugar until light. Gradually beat in the scalded milk and cream.
2 Place the mixture in the top part of a small double boiler and cook over hot water, stirring, until the mixture just coats the back of the spoon. Cool and chill.
3 Whip the remaining cream and fold into the mixture along with the vanilla. Fold in the kirsch.

MACEDOINE OF FRUIT IN VERMOUTH

6 SERVINGS

½ cup sweet or dry vermouth
¼ cup sugar
¼ teaspoon cinnamon
1 small to medium pineapple, cut into wedges
3 navel oranges, peeled and cut into sections
18 large grapes, halved and seeded

1 Combine the vermouth, sugar and cinnamon and let stand in the refrigerator 1 hour.

2 Pour off the liquid and discard the sugar sediment. Pour the liquid over prepared fresh fruit and marinate at least 1 hour in the refrigerator before serving.

Ice Cream and Sherbets

VANILLA ICE CREAM

1 QUART

6 egg yolks
1 cup sugar
4 cups milk
1 cup cream
1 vanilla bean, or 2 teaspoons vanilla extract

1 Put the egg yolks and sugar in a heavy saucepan. Beat with a whisk until pale yellow.

2 Combine the milk and cream in another saucepan. If the vanilla bean is used, split it and add it. Bring just to the boil.

3 Add about ½ cup of the milk mixture to the egg yolk mixture, beating rapidly. Add the remaining milk mixture, stirring rapidly. Scrape the black seeds from the center of the vanilla bean into the custard. Heat slowly, stirring and scraping all around the bottom with a wooden spoon. Bring the mixture almost, but not quite, to the boil. It should be smooth and custard-like; the correct temperature is 180°F.

4 Pour the custard into a cold mixing bowl, which will prevent further cooking. Let stand until room temperature. If the vanilla bean was not used, add the vanilla extract at this point.

5 Pour the mixture into the container of an ice cream freezer and freeze according to the manufacturer's instructions.

CHOCOLATE ICE CREAM

Prepare the vanilla ice cream, using only ¾ cup sugar. Melt 8 ounces (8 squares) semisweet or bitter chocolate in the top of a double boiler and add to the vanilla custard. Proceed as for vanilla ice cream.

◆

FRESH PEACH ICE CREAM

1 QUART

1 cup cream
2 cups milk
4 egg yolks
1 cup sugar
1 teaspoon vanilla extract
1 cup peeled and crushed ripe peaches

1 In a heavy saucepan, combine the cream, milk, egg yolks, ½ cup of the sugar and the vanilla. Cook over low heat, stirring constantly with a wooden spoon all around the bottom. Bring the mixture almost, but not quite, to the boil. It should be smooth and custardlike; the correct temperature is 180°F.

2 Pour the custard into a cold mixing bowl, which will prevent further cooking. Let stand until room temperature.

3 Add the remaining ½ cup sugar to the peaches and stir to dissolve.

4 Stir the peaches into the custard and pour the mixture into the container of an ice cream freezer. Freeze according to manufacturer's instructions.

FIG AND CASHEW ICE CREAM

One of the most glorious ice creams conceivable is made with fig preserves and cashews. It is irresistible both in flavor and texture. The most important thing is to make or buy the best fig preserves you can to put into your batter.

1 QUART

1 cup roasted cashews (see note)
3 egg yolks
½ cup sugar
2 cups milk
½ cup cream
½ teaspoon vanilla extract
1 (17-ounce) jar whole figs in heavy syrup
2 tablespoons cognac

1 Coarsely chop the cashews using a heavy knife.

2 Put the egg yolks and sugar in a heavy saucepan and beat with a whisk until pale yellow.

3 In another saucepan, combine the milk and cream. Bring just to the boil.

4 Add about ¼ cup of the hot mixture to the egg yolk mixture, mixing and beating rapidly. Add the remaining hot milk mixture, stirrring rapidly. Heat slowly, stirring and scraping all around the bottom with a wooden spoon. Bring the mixture almost, but not quite, to the boil. It should be smooth and custardlike. The correct temperature is 180°F.

5 Pour the mixture into a cold mixing bowl, which will prevent the custard from cooking further. Let stand until it reaches room temperature. Stir in the vanilla extract.

6 Drain the figs and put them into the container of a food processor. Blend. There should be about 1 cup. Add the figs to the custard. Add the chopped nuts and cognac.

Continued

7 Pour the mixture into the container of an ice cream freezer. Freeze according to the manufacturer's instructions.

Note: To roast cashews, preheat the oven to 375°F. Place unsalted cashews in a heat-proof pan or dish. Bake 5 minutes or slightly longer, stirring occasionally, until the nuts are golden brown.

♦

FRUIT OR BERRY ICE

1 QUART

3 pounds berries or soft-fleshed fruits,
  such as nectarines
1½ cups sugar, approximately

1 If berries are used, rinse, drain well and remove stems. If fruits are used, peel and remove the pits. Cut the flesh into chunks.

2 Put the berries or fruit into the container of a food processor and blend to a fine purée. There should be about 6 cups.

3 Scrape the purée into a mixing bowl and add the 1 cup of sugar. Blend well. Add more sugar to taste, depending on the tartness of the fruit.

4 Pour the purée into the container of an ice cream freezer and freeze according to manufacturer's instructions.

GRAPEFRUIT SHERBET

This sherbet is especially good with a touch of cold vodka poured over it.

1 QUART

2 cups sugar
4 cups water
2 cups grapefruit juice

1 Combine the sugar and water in a heavy saucepan and bring to the boil. Add the grapefruit juice and cool. Refrigerate until thoroughly chilled.

2 Pour the mixture into the container of an ice cream freezer and freeze according to the manufacturer's instructions.

PINEAPPLE SHERBET

1 PINT

1 (2-pound) very ripe fresh pineapple
2 tablespoons sugar
1 teaspoon lemon juice

1 Peel the pineapple and cut away any dark skin spots. For this recipe you will need only half of a prepared pineapple (wrap the remaining half in plastic wrap and set aside for a future use). Cut the half-pineapple into two pieces. Cut away and discard the center core. Cut the remaining flesh into 1-inch cubes. There should be about 2 cups.

2 Put the pineapple cubes, sugar and lemon juice into the container of a blender (a food processor may be used, but the mixture will not be as fine). Blend the mixture as fine as possible.

3 Pour and scrape the mixture into the container of an ice cream freezer and freeze according to manufacturer's instructions.

TANGERINES EN SURPRISE

This is a colorful and delicious dessert. Tangerine shells are hollowed out, filled with a tangerine sherbet mixture, then frozen. A sprig of mint serves as a "stem."

6 SERVINGS

10 to 12 tangerines
2 cups water
1 cup plus 2 tablespoons sugar
2 tablespoons corn syrup
2 tablespoons grated tangerine peel
2 tablespoons lemon juice
2 egg whites
Fresh mint sprigs

1 Cut the tops off 6 of the tangerines. With a spoon, gently scoop out the fruit sections. Reserve the shells and tops.

2 Remove the seeds from the sections and extract the juice by pressing the sections in a potato ricer. Use enough additional tangerine sections to make 2 cups of juice.

3 Combine the water, 1 cup of the sugar and the corn syrup and boil briskly 5 minutes. Add the grated tangerine peel and cool.

4 Add the tangerine and lemon juices to the syrup mixture. Strain the mixture through a fine sieve and pour into a shallow pan. Freeze until mushy.

5 When the ice is partly set, beat the egg whites with 2 tablespoons sugar until stiff. Fold into the ice and continue to freeze until the ice is solid.

6 Using an ice cream scoop, fill each tangerine shell with 2 scoops of the ice. Cover each with a tangerine top. Assemble in a pan, wrap with foil and return to the freezer until ready to serve. Garnish each with a sprig of mint before serving.

NO-COOK ICE CREAM

2½ cups sugar
4 eggs, well beaten
6 cups milk
4 cups cream
2 tablespoons vanilla extract
Pinch of salt

Gradually add the sugar to the eggs, beating constantly. Continue beating until mixture is thick. Add milk, cream, vanilla and salt. Mix thoroughly. Pour the mixture into the container of an ice cream freezer and freeze according to the manufacturer's directions.

Variations

STRAWBERRY, RASPBERRY, PEACH OR BANANA ICE CREAM

Substitute 4 cups puréed fresh fruit for 4 cups of the milk. Omit the vanilla. If desired, substitute almond extract.

NUT ICE CREAM

Add 2 cups chopped nuts to mixture.

Puddings, Custards and Other Desserts

BREAD-AND-BUTTER PUDDING

ABOUT 8 SERVINGS

3½ cups scalded milk
1 (1-inch) piece vanilla bean, or 1 teaspoon
    vanilla extract
4½-inch length of French bread (center
    portion, not the crusty end)
4 tablespoons butter, softened
½ cup seedless raisins
3 eggs
⅓ cup sugar
Pinch of salt
Grated nutmeg

1 In the top of a double boiler heat the milk and, if used, the vanilla bean. Place over simmering water and cook 15 minutes. Cool. Discard the vanilla bean, if used, or add the vanilla extract.

2 Cut the French bread into slices ¼ inch thick and spread butter on one side of each slice. Arrange the slices in a 6-cup casserole with the buttered side down, sprinkling the raisins between the layers.

3 Beat the eggs with the sugar and salt and add the scalded milk, stirring. Pour over the bread. Let stand 30 minutes. Sprinkle with nutmeg.

4 Set the casserole in a pan of hot water and bake in a preheated 350°F oven until a knife inserted in the center comes out clean, about 1 hour. Serve warm.

COFFEE BREAD-AND-BUTTER PUDDING

8 SERVINGS

1 cup strong coffee
1 cup half-and-half
2 cups milk
6 thin slices of raisin bread
Soft butter
2 eggs
½ cup sugar
Pinch of salt
1 teaspoon vanilla extract
¼ teaspoon grated nutmeg
Cream or whipped cream

1 Preheat the oven to 325°F.
2 Combine the coffee, half-and-half and milk; bring to scalding point.
3 Spread bread slices lightly with butter or margarine; do not trim off crusts. Cut into ½-inch cubes and add to coffee mixture.
4 Beat eggs lightly; add sugar and salt; mix well. Add bread mixture and vanilla.
5 Pour into a 1½-quart casserole. Sprinkle with the nutmeg.
6 Set the casserole in a pan of warm water. Bake for 1¼ hours, or until a knife inserted near rim of casserole comes out clean. Chill. Serve with plain or whipped cream.

NEW ENGLAND BREAD PUDDING

6 SERVINGS

3½ cups milk
4 tablespoons butter
2 cups dry bread cubes
½ cup sugar
2 eggs, lightly beaten
½ cup sherry
½ teaspoon cinnamon
½ teaspoon mace
½ teaspoon grated nutmeg
1 cup seedless raisins
½ cup thinly sliced citron (optional)

1 Preheat the oven to 375°F.
2 Scald the milk, add the butter and pour the hot liquid over the bread cubes. Soak about 5 minutes, then add the sugar, eggs, sherry and spices. Add the raisins and citron.
3 Pour the mixture into a buttered baking dish. Set the dish in a pan of hot water and bake until a knife inserted in the center comes out clean, or 1 hour.

HASTY PUDDING

1 quart milk
½ cup cornmeal
3 tablespoons butter
1 cooking apple, pared and diced
½ cup molasses
Pinch of salt
½ teaspoon grated nutmeg

1 Preheat the oven to 250°F. Butter a covered 2-quart baking dish.

2 Bring 1⅓ cups of the milk to a boil and gradually add the cornmeal, stirring constantly. Remove from the heat and add the butter, apple, molasses, salt and nutmeg. Mix well and add the remaining milk.

3 Pour the mixture into the baking dish and cover. Bake 3 to 3¼ hours.

4 Serve hot either plain or with cream, unsweetened whipped cream or vanilla ice cream.

Note: The classic pudding omits the apple.

CHOCOLATE PUDDING

2 cups half-and-half
1 cup milk
3 ounces (3 squares) unsweetened chocolate
2 tablespoons butter
⅔ cup sugar
3 tablespoons cornstarch
½ teaspoon vanilla extract

1 Combine the half-and-half and milk in a saucepan and bring almost to the boil.

2 Melt the chocolate and the butter in the top of a double boiler over hot water.

3 Combine the sugar and cornstarch and stir in ½ cup of the milk mixture. Blend well and add to the chocolate, mixing thoroughly.

4 Slowly add the chocolate mixture to the remaining milk mixture, stirring with a wire whisk. Bring to a boil, stirring constantly. Lower the heat and simmer about 5 minutes, stirring, until thickened and smooth.

5 Remove from the heat and stir in the vanilla. Pour the pudding into individual custard cups and cool.

VANILLA PUDDING

5 OR 6 SERVINGS

¼ cup cornstarch
½ cup sugar
Pinch of salt
3 cups milk
2 egg yolks
1½ teaspoons vanilla extract

1 In a bowl mix the cornstarch, sugar and salt. Add about ½ cup milk and mix. Heat remaining milk almost to simmering in a heavy saucepan over moderate heat.

2 Stir cornstarch mixture to blend it and add about half of the scalded milk to it while stirring. Return to milk in saucepan and cook, stirring, until the mixture boils.

3 Beat the egg yolks lightly. Add a small amount of the pudding mixture to the yolks, stirring constantly. Return all to the saucepan and cook, stirring, until thickened.

4 Add vanilla and turn the mixture immediately into a serving dish or into 5 or 6 custard cups. Cool and chill. Serve with a fruit sauce.

COCONUT PUDDING

8 SERVINGS

¼ pound plus 4 tablespoons butter
¾ cup sugar
1 whole egg plus 3 egg yolks, beaten
3 cups finely grated fresh coconut
1¼ cups half-and-half or undiluted
    evaporated milk
1½ teaspoons vanilla extract
1½ tablespoons lime juice
Meringue pie topping (page 753)

1 Preheat the oven to 350°F.

2 Cream together the butter and sugar until fluffy. Add the eggs, coconut, half-and-half and vanilla and mix well.

3 Butter 8 individual 6-ounce baking dishes and fill three-quarters full with pudding mixture. Set in a pan of hot water. Bake for about 45 minutes, until firm.

4 Remove and cool. Fold the lime juice into the meringue pie topping and spoon the meringue over the pudding. Return to the oven for 12 to 15 minutes to brown the meringue.

PUMPKIN PUDDING

6 SERVINGS

4 eggs, separated
1½ cups pumpkin purée
¾ cup half-and-half
2 to 4 tablespoons rum
¾ cup light brown sugar, packed
½ teaspoon each ground ginger, ground cloves
    and grated nutmeg
¾ teaspoon cinnamon
Pinch of salt
Whipped cream

1 Preheat the oven to 350°F.

2 Beat the egg whites until stiff.

3 Beat the egg yolks until thick and lemon colored. Combine the yolks with the pumpkin purée, half-and-half, rum, sugar and seasonings. Mix thoroughly until blended. Fold in the beaten egg whites.

4 Place the mixture in a buttered 1-quart soufflé dish. Set the dish in a pan of hot water and bake 40 to 45 minutes. Serve at once with sweetened, flavored whipped cream.

OLD-FASHIONED RICE PUDDING

6 SERVINGS

1 quart milk
¼ cup long-grain rice
½ cup sugar
Pinch of salt
½ cup seeded raisins (optional)
1 teaspoon vanilla extract
¼ teaspoon grated nutmeg

1 Preheat the oven to 300°F.

2 Mix the milk, rice, sugar and salt in a 6-cup buttered casserole and bake, uncovered, 2 hours, stirring the mixture every half hour.

3 If the raisins are not soft and fresh, let them stand in water to cover while the pudding bakes. Drain and add to the pudding. Add the vanilla and nutmeg and mix carefully.

4 Bake the pudding without stirring about ½ hour longer, or until the rice is very tender. Serve warm or cold.

LEMON RICE

3 cups milk
½ cup rice
½ cup granulated sugar
Grated rind of ½ lemon
2 tablespoons lemon juice
Pinch of salt
3 egg yolks, lightly beaten
4 egg whites
2 tablespoons confectioners' sugar

1 Place the milk and rice in the top part of a double boiler. Cook over hot water for about 30 minutes, until the rice is soft.

2 Preheat the oven to 425°F.

3 Add the granulated sugar, lemon rind, 1½ tablespoons of the lemon juice, the salt and egg yolks to the rice mixture. Cook, stirring gently, until thickened. Spoon into a well-buttered baking dish. Cool.

4 Beat the egg whites until soft peaks form. Beat in the confectioners' sugar and remaining lemon juice. Spoon over the pudding and bake for about 5 minutes, just long enough to brown the meringue.

COFFEE CREAM CHANTILLY

¼ cup sugar
½ cup very strong, hot black coffee
2 egg yolks, lighly beaten
1 cup heavy cream, whipped

1 Dissolve the sugar in the hot coffee. Pour the mixture over the egg yolks and stir to blend. Cook in the top part of a small double boiler over hot water, stirring constantly, until the mixture thickens like a custard.

2 Cool mixture and chill in the refrigerator until ready to use. Just before serving, fold in the whipped cream.

FRESH LIME CREAM

1 cup sugar
2 tablespoons cornstarch
Pinch of salt
1 cup water
¼ cup lime juice
1 egg, lightly beaten
1 teaspoon grated lime rind
1 teaspoon vanilla extract
1 cup heavy cream, whipped
Additional whipped cream and grated lime
    rind for garnish

1 Combine the sugar, cornstarch and salt in a saucepan or in the top part of a double boiler. Gradually stir in the water. Cook over hot, not boiling, water or over low direct heat until thickened, stirring constantly. Add the lime juice and cook until thickened.

2 Add a little of the hot mixture to the beaten egg and then stir it into the remaining hot mixture. Cook for 1 to 2 minutes over low heat, stirring constantly. Remove from the heat and add the grated lime rind and vanilla. Cool.

3 Fold in the whipped cream. Serve in sherbet glasses, garnished with additional whipped cream and a sprinkling of lime rind.

LEMON CURD

4 tablespoons butter
¾ cup sugar
2 eggs, lightly beaten
Juice of 2 lemons
Grated rind of 2 lemons

1 Cream the butter and gradually beat in the sugar.

2 Beat the eggs into the creamed mixture, then add the lemon juice and grated rind. Cook, stirring, over low heat until mixture thickens. This must be cooked over low heat and stirred constantly to keep it from curdling. If desired, use a double boiler.

3 Serve hot or cold, or use as a dessert filling.

LEMON FROMAGE WITH BLUEBERRIES

6 SERVINGS

3 whole eggs
2 egg yolks
½ cup sugar
Grated rind of 1 lemon
¾ tablespoon unflavored gelatin
¼ cup lemon juice
2 cups heavy cream
1 pint blueberries, washed well and
    sweetened to taste

1 Beat the eggs and egg yolks until lemon colored and frothy. While beating, add the sugar in a slow stream and continue to beat until mixture is thickened. Add the grated rind.

2 Combine the gelatin and lemon juice in a heatproof measuring cup. Place the cup over hot water and stir until gelatin dissolves. Add it to the egg mixture and beat well.

3 Whip the cream until it is stiff and fold it gently into the egg and lemon mixture. Pour the mixture into a 1-quart mold and chill for 4 hours. Unmold and serve with the sweetened blueberries.

CRÈME CELESTE

This is an egregiously rich cream dessert. It is like dipping your spoon into glorious, gossamer, heavenly manna. It is best served when fresh berries are in season—such fruits as raspberries or strawberries.

6 TO 8 SERVINGS

2 cups cream
¾ cup plus 2 tablespoons sugar
½ cup cold water
1 level tablespoon unflavored gelatin
2 cups sour cream
⅓ cup plus 2 tablespoons kirsch,
    framboise or brandy
1 pint (2 cups) fresh raspberries, strawberries,
    blueberries or other berries in season

1 Combine the cream and ¾ cup of the sugar in a small saucepan and heat gently, stirring often, until the mixture barely simmers. Remove from the heat.

2 Put the water in another small saucepan and sprinkle with the gelatin. Place this over low heat and stir until gelatin dissolves. Scrape this into the cream and sugar mixture, stirring to blend well.

3 Add the sour cream, beating with a wire whisk. Beat in ⅓ cup of the kirsch. Lightly oil the inside of a 5½- or 6-cup decorative mold. Pour in the cream mixture and chill several hours, preferably overnight in the refrigerator.

4 Meanwhile, trim off the stem ends or remove the stems of the berries. Put about ½ cup of the berries in the container of a food processor. Add the remaining 2 tablespoons of sugar and 2 tablespoons of kirsch and blend thoroughly. Pour the sauce over the remaining berries and stir. Chill. Unmold the dessert on a round plate (if necessary, cover the mold on all sides with a hot, rinsed out cloth).

5 When ready to serve, serve with the berries.

COFFEE BAVARIAN CREAM

4 TO 6 SERVINGS

1 envelope (1 tablespoon) unflavored gelatin
¼ cup cold water
2 eggs, separated
½ cup sugar
Pinch of salt
½ cup milk
½ teaspoon vanilla extract
½ cup strong black coffee
1 cup heavy cream

1 Soften the gelatin in the water.

2 Beat the egg yolks in the top part of a double boiler and add ¼ cup of the sugar and the salt. Gradually add the milk. Cook over hot water, stirring constantly, until slightly thickened.

3 Add the softened gelatin and stir until dissolved. Add the vanilla and coffee and chill until slightly thickened.

4 Beat the egg whites until stiff. Gradually add the remaining sugar, beating constantly. Whip the cream until slightly stiff. Fold into the gelatin mixture with the egg whites.

5 Pour the mixture into a 1-quart mold that has been rinsed out in cold water and chill until firm. Serve with fresh blueberries.

VANILLA BAVARIAN CREAM

8 TO 10 SERVINGS

1 envelope (1 tablespoon) plus 1½ teaspoons
    unflavored gelatin
⅓ cup cold water
6 egg yolks
¾ cup sugar
Pinch of salt
1½ cups milk
1½ teaspoons vanilla extract
1½ cups heavy cream, whipped
Fruit for garnish

1 Soften the gelatin in cold water and set aside.

2 Beat the egg yolks in the top of a double boiler until light and lemon colored. Gradually beat in the sugar. Add the salt.

3 Scald the milk and gradually stir it into the egg mixture. Cook over hot, not boiling, water until thickened, stirring constantly.

4 Blend in the softened gelatin and vanilla. Chill until the mixture begins to thicken, stirring occasionally to prevent a crust from forming on the surface.

5 Fold in the whipped cream and turn the mixture into a 1½-quart mold rinsed in cold water. Chill until firm.

6 When ready to serve, turn out on a serving plate. Garnish with strawberries, or other fruit.

CHARLOTTE RUSSE WITH KIRSCH

8 TO 10 SERVINGS

8 egg yolks
1 cup sugar
2 cups milk
1 (1-inch) piece vanilla bean
2 envelopes (2 tablespoons) unflavored gelatin
¼ cup cold water
¼ cup kirsch
2 cups heavy cream
12 ladyfingers, split

1 Combine the egg yolks and sugar and work the mixture with a wooden spoon until smooth. Bring the milk to a boil with the vanilla bean. Add it gradually to the yolk mixture, stirring rapidly with a wire whisk. Cook over boiling water until the mixture thickens.

2 Soften the gelatin in the cold water and add it to the custard, stirring until the gelatin dissolves. Remove the vanilla bean. Cool the custard but do not let it set. Add the kirsch.

3 Whip the cream until it stands in moist peaks and fold it into the custard.

4 Line a 2-quart mold with ladyfingers. Outline the bottom first by placing a small round of ladyfinger in the center. Cover the bottom with a daisy-petal pattern with the small round as a center. Stand ladyfingers side-by-side upright and close together around the sides. Pour the custard mixture into the mold and chill until set, about 2 hours. Unmold and serve. The charlotte may be served with fruit sweetened to taste and flavored with kirsch.

CARAMEL CUSTARD

5 SERVINGS

¾ cup sugar
3 eggs
Pinch of salt
2 cups milk, scalded
½ teaspoon vanilla extract

1 Preheat the oven to 350°F.

2 Heat ½ cup of the sugar slowly in a small heavy skillet, stirring constantly with a wooden spoon until the sugar melts, is free from lumps and turns a light caramel in color. Pour a spoonful of the syrup in each of 5 custard cups and let stand until slightly cooled.

3 Beat the eggs lightly with the remaining sugar and the salt. Add the milk slowly, while stirring. Add the vanilla. Strain and pour the strained mixture carefully into the prepared cups so as not to disturb the caramel.

4 Place the cups in a pan of hot water (the water should be almost level with the tops of the cups) and bake until a knife inserted in the center comes out clean, or about 40 minutes. Remove immediately from the water and cool quickly. Chill if desired.

5 To serve, run a knife around the edge of the custards, turn out and serve with whipped cream if desired.

CRÈME BRULÉE

3 cups cream
6 tablespoons granulated sugar
6 egg yolks
2 teaspoons vanilla extract
½ cup light brown sugar

1 Preheat the oven to 300°F.
2 Heat the cream over boiling water and stir in the granulated sugar.
3 Beat the egg yolks until light and pour the hot cream over them gradually, stirring vigorously. Stir in the vanilla and strain the mixture into a baking dish.
4 Place the dish in a pan containing 1 inch of hot water and bake until a silver knife inserted in the center comes out clean, or 35 minutes. Do not overbake; the custard will continue to cook from retained heat when it is removed from the oven. Chill thoroughly.
5 Before serving, cover the surface with the brown sugar. Set the dish on a bed of cracked ice and put the crème under the broiler until the sugar is brown and melted. Serve immediately or chill again and serve cold.

BAKED ORANGE CUSTARD

1 cup cream
1 cup orange juice
¼ cup sugar
3 eggs, lightly beaten
1½ teaspoons finely grated orange rind
Pinch of salt

1 Preheat the oven to 325°F.
2 Combine all the ingredients and blend well. Pour the mixture into custard cups and place in a pan of hot water.
3 Bake until a silver knife inserted in the center comes out clean, 40 to 50 minutes.

FLAN
SPANISH CARAMEL CUSTARD

12 SERVINGS

1¼ cups sugar
Pinch of salt
2 teaspoons vanilla extract
7 large eggs
½ cup cold milk
4 cups hot milk

1 Preheat the oven to 325°F.

2 Stir and cook ¾ cup of the sugar in a small saucepan over medium heat until it is melted and a light amber color. Pour it into a 1½-quart casserole, turning to coat all the bottom and as much of the sides as possible. If casserole is very cold, place in a pan of hot water to warm. This prevents the caramel from hardening before bottom and sides are coated.

3 Combine salt, vanilla and remaining ½ cup sugar. Mix well. Add the eggs and beat lightly with a rotary beater. Stir in the cold milk, then add the hot milk. Mix well.

4 Pour the custard into the caramel-coated casserole. Set in a pan of hot water. Bake in the oven for 1 hour and 20 minutes.

5 Remove from the oven and cool. Then chill. Just before serving, turn out into a shallow bowl or a slightly cupped serving plate that is about 2 inches larger than the flan. Slice and serve.

CINNAMON PUMPKIN FLAN

9 SERVINGS

1¼ cups plus 1 tablespoon sugar
Pinch of salt
1 teaspoon cinnamon
1 cup puréed cooked pumpkin
5 large eggs, lightly beaten
1½ cups undiluted evaporated milk
⅓ cup water
1½ teaspoons vanilla extract
½ cup heavy cream, whipped
¼ teaspoon ground ginger

1 Melt ½ cup of the sugar over low heat until the sugar forms a golden syrup. Stir constantly to prevent burning. Pour immediately into a shallow cake pan (8 × 8 × 2 inches) or a 9-inch pie plate, turning and rolling pan from side to side to coat with caramel. Set aside.

2 Preheat the oven to 350°F.

3 Combine ¾ cup of the remaining sugar with the salt and cinnamon. Add pumpkin and eggs. Mix well. Stir in the evaporated milk, the water and vanilla. Mix well and turn into the caramel-coated pan. Set in a pan of hot water. Bake for 1¼ hours, or until a knife inserted into the center of the filling comes out clean. Cool and chill.

4 To serve, run a spatula around the sides of the pan. Turn flan out onto a serving plate. Cut into squares or wedges. Combine the whipped cream with the remaining sugar and the ginger and spread over the squares.

CHOCOLATE MOUSSE

Mousse, of course, means "foam" in French. This mousse is the foamiest.

12 OR MORE SERVINGS

½ pound sweet chocolate
6 large eggs, separated
3 tablespoons water
¼ cup sweet liqueur, such as amaretto
    or Grand Marnier
2 cups heavy cream
6 tablespoons sugar

1 Cut the chocolate into small pieces and place in a saucepan over hot water. Cover and let melt over low heat.

2 Put the egg yolks in a heavy saucepan and add the water. Place the saucepan over very low heat while beating vigorously and constantly with a wire whisk. It is best to use a Flame Tamer to diffuse the heat and control it. When the yolks start to thicken, add the liqueur, beating constantly. Cook until the sauce achieves the consistency of a hollandaise or a sabayon, which it is. Remove from the heat.

3 Add the melted chocolate to the sauce and fold it in. Scrape the sauce into a mixing bowl.

4 Beat the cream until stiff, adding 2 tablespoons of the sugar toward the end of beating. Fold this into the chocolate mixture.

5 Beat the egg whites until soft peaks start to form. Beat in the remaining sugar and continue beating until stiff. Fold this into the mousse.

6 Spoon the mousse into a serving bowl and chill until ready to serve. If desired, garnish with whipped cream and grated chocolate.

FROZEN MOCHA MOUSSE

8 SERVINGS

3 ounces (3 squares) unsweetened chocolate
⅓ cup water
¾ cup sugar
Pinch of salt
3 egg yolks
1 tablespoon instant coffee powder
½ teaspoon vanilla extract
2 cups heavy cream, whipped

1 Place the chocolate and water in a saucepan and gradually bring to a boil, stirring. When chocolate is melted, add the sugar and salt and cook over low heat for 2 minutes. stirring constantly.

2 Place the egg yolks in a mixing bowl and beat with a whisk. Pour in the chocolate mixture, beating constantly. Add the coffee. Let the mixture cool.

3 Fold in the vanilla and whipped cream. Pour into refrigerator trays. Place in the freezer until firm.

FRESH TROPICAL MOUSSE

4 SERVINGS

Juice of ½ lemon
1 cup mashed papaya or mango
3 egg yolks
½ cup sugar
Pinch of salt
1½ envelopes (1½ tablespoons) unflavored gelatin
½ cup cold milk
1 cup heavy cream, whipped
2 tablespoons Cointreau or kirsch
1 pint fresh strawberries, washed and hulled

1 Add the lemon juice to the mashed fruit.

2 Beat the egg yolks, sugar and salt until thick and lemon colored. Add the fruit and mix well. Place in the top part of a double boiler and cook over boiling water, stirring, until the mixture thickens. Do not overcook.

3 Sprinkle the gelatin over the cold milk and add to the hot fruit mixture. Stir to dissolve the gelatin. Chill the mixture until it reaches the consistency of raw egg white.

4 Fold in the whipped cream and liqueur. Chill until set. Garnish with the fresh strawberries before serving.

OEUFS A LA NEIGE
FLOATING ISLAND

This is one of the most delectable of desserts. Mounds of egg white are poached in milk, then the milk is made into an English cream. The two are served together.

8 TO 10 MERINGUES

2 cups milk
1 vanilla bean
5 egg whites
⅔ cup sugar
Caramel (see next page)
English cream (see next page)

1 Pour the milk into an 8- or 9-inch skillet and add the vanilla bean. Over low heat let the milk warm to a point where bubbles appear around the edge.

2 Meanwhile, beat the egg whites until foamy. At this point, gradually start to add the sugar, continuing to beat until the egg whites are stiff.

3 Remove the skillet from the heat and drop the beaten egg whites on the milk in very large, rounded spoonfuls.

4 Return the skillet to very low heat; the surface of the milk should barely quiver. Cook the mounds of egg white 2 minutes. Using a skimmer or 2 forks, turn and cook 2 minutes on the other side, or until the meringues are firm to the touch.

5 Remove the meringues to a towel and drain. Reserve the milk and vanilla bean for the English cream.

6 Pile the meringues in a shallow bowl and chill. To serve the dessert, fill a crystal bowl with the chilled English cream, float the poached meringues on top and trickle the caramel over the meringues.

Continued

CARAMEL
ABOUT ½ CUP

½ cup sugar
¼ cup water

Melt the sugar in a small heavy skillet over very low heat, stirring constantly with a wooden spoon. Remove from the heat and add the water. Return the skillet to very low heat and simmer until the syrup is slightly thick and smooth. Trickle over the meringues.

Note: If desired, the caramel may be prepared in advance, kept at room temperature and reheated just before use.

ENGLISH CREAM
2½ CUPS

Milk reserved from cooking the meringues
½ vanilla bean, reserved from cooking the meringues
5 egg yolks
½ cup sugar

1 Strain the milk from the meringues into a 2-cup measure. Add enough fresh milk to fill it. Pour the milk into the top of a double boiler, add the half of vanilla bean and, over boiling water, heat the milk to a point where bubbles appear around the edge.

2 Blend the egg yolks with the sugar, using a fork. Add the hot milk gradually, stirring constantly.

3 Return the mixture, with the bean in it, to the top of the double boiler and cook over simmering water, stirring constantly, until the mixture thickens and coats a metal spoon.

4 Chill the mixture quickly by holding the top of the boiler in ice water; stir occasionally while the mixture cools. Strain and chill.

BOULES SUR CHOCOLAT

This is a variation of floating island but the poached meringues are on a chocolate custard.

12 SERVINGS

4½ cups milk
1 (4-inch) piece of vanilla bean, or 2 teaspoons vanilla extract
2¼ cups superfine sugar
8 egg whites, at room temperature
Chocolate custard (see following recipe)

1 Combine the milk with the vanilla bean and ¼ cup of the sugar. Slowly heat to simmering.

2 Meanwhile, beat the egg whites until stiff. Continue beating, adding the remaining 2 cups of sugar gradually, until the meringue holds its shape.

3 Using 2 spoons, drop egg-shaped balls of meringue on the simmering milk and simmer until they are firm, turning once. Carefully remove and set on a clean towel. Remove the vanilla bean and reserve the milk. If a bean is not used, add the extract.

CHOCOLATE CUSTARD
5 CUPS

⅔ cup sugar
⅔ cup cocoa
8 egg yolks
4 cups hot milk, reserved from the meringue

1 Mix the sugar, cocoa and yolks in a 6-cup saucepan. Slowly add the hot milk, while stirring, and cook over very low heat, stirring constantly, until the mixture coats a metal spoon.

2 Remove the mixture from the heat and cool. Pour into a glass serving bowl and set the meringues on top. Chill.

POTS DE CRÈME
A LA VANILLE

6 SERVINGS

6 egg yolks
½ cup sugar
2 cups half-and-half
1¼ teaspoons vanilla extract

1 Preheat the oven to 325°F.

2 Beat the egg yolks until light and lemon colored. Gradually beat in the sugar. Stir in ¼ cup of the half-and-half. Scald the remaining half-and-half and gradually stir into the mixture. Add the vanilla. Strain through a fine sieve into 6 individual ½-cup crème pots or custard cups. Cover with crème pot covers or foil.

3 Place in a baking pan on the lower rack of the oven. Pour enough boiling water into the pan to cover two-thirds of the pots or cups. Bake 15 minutes, or until a silver knife inserted into the center comes out clean. Cool and chill before serving.

POTS DE CRÈME
AU CHOCOLAT

4 SERVINGS

2 cups cream
4 ounces sweet chocolate, melted
3 egg yolks

1 Preheat the oven to 325°F.

2 Heat the cream in a double boiler over boiling water.

3 Add the chocolate and stir until the mixture is blended.

4 Beat the egg yolks and pour the hot cream over them, a little at a time, stirring vigorously.

5 Pour the mixture into crème pots or individual heatproof dishes. Place the pots in a pan of hot water about 1 inch deep. Bake until a knife inserted in the center comes out clean, or about 15 minutes. Chill.

◆

ZABAGLIONE

Zabaglione is one of the finest and most popular desserts in the Italian repertory. In French, it is called *saboyan*.

4 SERVINGS AS A DESSERT, OR 6 AS A SAUCE

6 egg yolks
6 tablespoons sugar
½ cup Marsala wine

1 Beat the egg yolks and gradually add the sugar, while beating, and the wine.

2 Place the mixture over boiling water and whip vigorously with a wire whisk until the custard foams up in the pan and begins to thicken. Do not overcook. Serve warm in sherbet glasses or as a sauce.

CHOCOLATE SOUFFLÉ

6 SERVINGS

2 tablespoons butter
2 tablespoons flour
¾ cup milk
Pinch of salt
2 ounces (2 squares) unsweetened chocolate
⅓ cup sugar
2 tablespoons cold coffee
½ teaspoon vanilla extract
3 egg yolks, lightly beaten
4 egg whites, stiffly beaten
Whipped cream

1 Preheat the oven to 375°F.
2 In a saucepan melt the butter, add the flour and stir with a wire whisk until blended. Meanwhile, bring the milk to a boil and add all at once to the butter-flour mixture, stirring vigorously with the whisk. Add the salt.
3 Melt the chocolate with the sugar and coffee over hot water. Stir the melted chocolate mixture into the sauce and add the vanilla. Beat in the egg yolks, one at a time, and cool.
4 Fold in the stiffly beaten egg whites and turn the mixture into a buttered 2-quart casserole sprinkled with sugar. Bake 30 to 45 minutes, or until puffed and brown. Serve immediately with whipped cream.

STRAWBERRY SOUFFLÉ

6 SERVINGS

2 cups sliced fresh strawberries, or frozen strawberries defrosted
½ cup orange juice
½ cup Curaçao
Sugar to taste
3 tablespoons butter
3 tablespoons flour
1 cup milk
4 eggs, separated
Whipped cream

1 Preheat the oven to 375°F.
2 Combine the strawberries, orange juice, Curaçao and sugar to taste.
3 In a saucepan melt the butter, add the flour and stir with a wire whisk until blended. Meanwhile, bring the milk to a boil and add all at once to the butter-flour mixture, stirring vigorously with the whisk. Stir in the lightly beaten egg yolks and cool.
4 Fold in stiffly beaten egg whites.
5 Drain the excess juice from the strawberries and reserve. Place the strawberry mixture in the bottom of a buttered soufflé dish sprinkled lightly with sugar. Pour the soufflé mixture on top and bake until puffed and golden brown, 30 to 45 minutes.
6 Serve immediately with whipped cream flavored with the reserved strawberry juice.

LEMON SOUFFLÉ

3 tablespoons flour
3 tablespoons butter, melted
¾ cup milk
¼ cup lemon juice
1½ teaspoons grated lemon rind
¼ cup granulated sugar
Pinch of salt
5 egg yolks, well beaten
5 egg whites, at room temperature
Confectioners' sugar

1 Preheat the oven to 350°F.

2 Blend the flour and butter in a saucepan. Gradually stir in the milk. Cook, stirring constantly, until the mixture is thickened and smooth. Remove from heat.

3 Stir the lemon juice and rind, granulated sugar and salt into the beaten egg yolks. Blend this mixture into the hot milk mixture.

4 Tie a 6-inch-wide strip of buttered wax paper around a well-greased 7-inch soufflé dish to form a collar. Dust dish and collar with granulated sugar.

5 Place the egg whites in a large mixing bowl and beat at highest speed until stiff but not dry. Gradually fold egg yolk mixture into beaten egg whites. Pour the mixture into the prepared dish.

6 Bake for about 40 minutes, or until golden brown. Remove collar at once and sprinkle soufflé with confectioners' sugar. Serve at once, with a custard sauce.

APPLE SOUFFLÉ WITH LEMON-NUTMEG SAUCE

6 SERVINGS

3 eggs, separated
½ cup sugar
1 teaspoon vanilla extract
⅛ teaspoon almond extract
4 tablespoons butter
¼ cup flour
1 cup milk
1 cup shredded apples
1 tablespoon lemon juice
½ cup cookie or cake crumbs
Lemon-nutmeg sauce (page 762)

1 Preheat the oven to 325°F.

2 Beat the egg yolks until thick and lemon colored. Stir in ¼ cup of the sugar and the vanilla and almond extract. Set aside.

3 Melt the butter in a saucepan. Stir in the flour and mix until smooth. Add the milk and cook over low heat, stirring constantly, until thick. Gradually stir in the egg yolk mixture.

4 Combine the shredded apples with the lemon juice and cookie crumbs and fold into the egg yolk mixture.

5 Beat the egg whites until soft peaks are formed. Gradually add the remaining sugar and continue beating until stiff. Gently fold the meringue into the apple mixture. Turn into an ungreased 1½-quart casserole or baking dish. Set in a pan of hot water and bake for about 1 hour, until done. Serve at once with lemon-nutmeg sauce.

Add to the list of foods that team together to multiply in goodness ice cream and old-fashioned meringue. They are a wonderful combination for summer desserts. Common to all meringues is a base of egg whites beaten until stiff and sweetened. The best-known meringue is that which is annually swirled atop some million pies. The delicate meringues to serve with ice cream are lightweight confections that are baked until crisp and dry, but are still as white and unblemished as suburban snow. The oven must be regulated to maintain a constant very low heat (225°F). At a higher temperature the meringues will brown. In an earlier era, meringues were often left to bake and dry overnight in the retained heat of an oven that had been turned off.

Meringues may be kept for days and even weeks in a dry place. Meringues that are imperfect and broken may be crumbled and combined with whipped cream as a topping for cakes and ice cream.

◆

MERINGUES, INDIVIDUAL AND PIE CRUST

1 MERINGUE PIE CRUST
AND 9 TO 12 INDIVIDUAL MERINGUES

7 egg whites, at room temperature
Pinch of salt
2¼ cups superfine sugar
1 teaspoon vanilla extract

1 Preheat the oven to 200° to 250°F. Grease and lightly flour an 8-inch pie plate, and cover a baking sheet with parchment paper.

2 Beat the egg whites with the salt until stiff. Continue to beat while adding 1½ cups of the sugar, 1 tablespoon at a time. Beat until the mixture no longer feels grainy when pressed between the fingers.

3 Fold the vanilla and the remaining sugar into the mixture.

4 Using about half of the mixture, spread a thin layer of meringue over the bottom of the prepared pie pan. Build up the sides with meringue to form a deep pie shell. Do not overlap onto the rim of the pan.

5 Form the remaining meringue into 9 to 12 ovals, using 2 serving spoons to shape them or putting the meringue through a pastry bag fitted with a plain tube. Place the ovals on the prepared baking sheet.

6 Bake the pie shell and the oval meringues for 45 to 60 minutes, or until dry but not brown. To complete the drying process, turn off the oven and allow the shell and meringues to cool slowly with the oven door ajar. In an oven with a pilot light, the shell and meringues may be left in overnight with the door closed.

◆

STRAWBERRY ANGEL PIE

8 TO 10 SERVINGS

Pile scoops of strawberry ice cream (2 quarts) into a baked 8-inch meringue pie crust (page 752). Garnish with whole fresh strawberries or strawberry sauce (page 757) or a combination of both.

MERINGUES GLACÉES

1 PER SERVING

Place 1 scoop of strawberry ice cream between 2 individual meringues (page 752). Top with strawberry sauce (page 757).

♦

MERINGUE PIE TOPPING

TOPPING FOR A 9-INCH PIE

3 egg whites
Pinch of salt
¼ teaspoon cream of tartar
1 teaspoon flavoring, such as vanilla extract
6 tablespoons sugar

1 Preheat the oven to 425°F.

2 Beat the egg whites with the salt until light and frothy. Add the cream of tartar and continue to beat until the whites are stiff enough to hold in peaks.

3 Add the vanilla extract and beat in the sugar, 1 tablespoon at a time, until meringue is stiff and glossy. No grains of sugar should be felt when a small amount of the mixture is rubbed between the fingers.

4 Pile the meringue lightly on cooled pie filling, spreading the meringue until it touches the edges of the pastry to prevent the meringue from shrinking. Bake for 5 to 6 minutes, until the top is brown.

Note: This amount of meringue is enough to cover the top and sides of an 8-inch, 2-layer cake.

COEUR A LA CRÈME

This is an enchanting dessert that must be made in a special heart mold. The molds are generally available wherever imported housewares are sold. This is a fine dish for Valentine's Day.

6 SERVINGS

1 pound cottage cheese
1 pound cream cheese, softened
Pinch of salt
2 cups cream
Crushed strawberries, fresh or frozen
  and defrosted

1 Combine thoroughly the cottage cheese, cream cheese and salt. Gradually add the cream, beating constantly until the mixture is smooth.

2 Turn the mixture into individual heart-shaped baskets or molds (which have been lined with one layer of cheesecloth) with perforated bottoms. Place on a deep plate and refrigerate to drain overnight. One large basket may be used.

3 When ready to serve, unmold the hearts onto chilled plates and serve with crushed sweetened strawberrries. Garnish, if desired, with whole fresh strawberries.

DACQUOISE

A fabulous dessert for spring menus is this elegant French creation made with baked meringue layers filled with buttercream.

6 TO 8 SERVINGS

5 eggs, separated
1/8 teaspoon cream of tartar
1 1/4 cups granulated sugar
1 1/2 cups ground blanched almonds
2 tablespoons flour
2 tablespoons sifted cornstarch
1/2 teaspoon vanilla extract
Buttercream (see following recipe)
Confectioners' sugar
Unsweetened chocolate

1 Preheat the oven to 250°F.

2 Place the egg whites in a mixing bowl. (Reserve the egg yolks for the buttercream.) Add the cream of tartar and beat until frothy. Gradually add 3/4 cup granulated sugar while beating. Continue to beat the meringue until it stands in stiff peaks when the beater is withdrawn from the mixing bowl.

3 Blend the remaining sugar, the almonds, flour, cornstarch and vanilla. Fold the mixture into the meringue.

4 Cut out two 8-inch circles of parchment paper and place them on a baking sheet. Or grease and flour a baking sheet and mark two 8-inch rings on it with the help of a layer-cake pan.

5 Spoon the meringue mixture into a pastry bag fitted with a plain tube with a 1/2-inch opening. Pipe the mixture out spirally from the center to cover the prepared circles. Bake the layers for 45 minutes. Cool.

6 Spread the buttercream between the cooled layers. Sprinkle sifted confectioners' sugar and shaved chocolate over the top.

BUTTERCREAM FOR DACQUOISE
1 1/2 CUPS

1 cup sugar
1/3 cup water
5 egg yolks
1/2 pound plus 4 tablespoons butter
2 tablespoons Grand Marnier
2 tablespoons instant coffee powder

1 Combine the sugar and water in a saucepan. Heat, stirring, to 236°F on a candy thermometer, or until the syrup spins a thread.

2 Beat the egg yolks until they are thick and pale. Gradually pour the syrup over them, beating all the time.

3 Beat in the butter. Add the liqueur and coffee powder. Chill the mixture until it is just thick enough to spread.

◆

BUDINO DI RICOTTA

This is an Italian ricotta cheese "pudding."

4 SERVINGS

1/2 pound ricotta
1/4 cup grated milk chocolate
1/4 cup finely chopped walnuts
2 tablespoons cream, approximately

1 Put the ricotta, chocolate and nuts into the container of a food processor and blend thoroughly. Add enough cream to make a smooth consistency.

2 Serve in sherbet glasses with cookies.

Crêpes are nothing more than French pancakes. They should be made in special crêpe pans, available wherever fine imported cooking utensils are sold. A crêpe pan is a small "spider" large enough for making one crêpe at a time.

♦

DESSERT CRÊPES

24 CRÊPES

3 cups flour
4 eggs
4 egg yolks
1 quart milk
2 teaspoons sugar
½ teaspoon salt
4 tablespoons butter

1 Mix the flour, eggs and egg yolks with a wire whisk. Add the milk, sugar and salt and beat until all the ingredients are thoroughly blended.

2 Melt the butter in a small container and skim off the foam. Pour off and reserve the fat, or clarified butter. Discard the sediment in the bottom of the container.

3 Heat a 4-inch skillet and brush it with the clarified butter. Pour in 1 tablespoon of the batter and tilt the pan immediately so that the batter will spread over the entire bottom of the pan. Cook the crêpe quickly on both sides.

4 Repeat the process until the crêpes are cooked, stacking them on a plate as they are finished. If the crêpes are to be served later, cover with wax paper to prevent drying.

CRÊPES SUZETTE

This is the best known of the dessert crêpe recipes.

4 TO 6 SERVINGS

4 lumps of sugar
1 orange
¼ pound butter
¼ cup Curaçao
¼ cup kirsch
12 dessert crêpes (opposite)

1 Rub the lumps of sugar on the orange skin until they are covered with the aromatic oil. Squeeze the orange and reserve the juice.

2 Crush the sugar with half of the butter and cream well.

3 Place the rest of the butter in a flat skillet or a chafing dish and, when it melts, add the orange butter. Add the orange juice and Curaçao and stir with a wooden spoon until well blended. Add the kirsch and ignite. Keep the sauce barely simmering over a spirit lamp or other low flame.

4 Add the crêpes one at a time and, using a fork and large spoon, turn each crêpe in the sauce, then fold into quarters. Serve hot.

CRÊPES ALASKA

Many desserts made with ice cream are called "Alaska." Here, ice cream is sandwiched between two crêpes, hot sauce is added and the effect is most unusual.

6 SERVINGS

4 lumps of sugar
1 orange
5 tablespoons butter
1 teaspoon lemon juice
¼ cup cointreau
¼ cup Grand Marnier
½ cup warmed cognac
12 warm dessert crêpes (page 755)
6 scoops of vanilla ice cream
½ cup slivered almonds, toasted

1 Rub the lumps of sugar on the orange skin until they are covered with the aromatic oil. Squeeze the orange and reserve the juice.

2 Crush the sugar with 3 tablespoons of the butter and mix until creamy.

3 Place the remaining butter in a flat skillet or in a chafing dish and add the lemon juice and liqueurs. Add the warmed cognac and ignite.

4 Place 1 crêpe on each of 6 dessert plates and top each crêpe with a scoop of vanilla ice cream. Cover with another crêpe and spoon the hot sauce over them. Sprinkle with toasted almonds.

CRÊPES WITH PINEAPPLE

This is an unusually delicious crêpe recipe. The crêpes are filled with a pastry cream and pineapple mixture.

6 SERVINGS

⅔ cup sugar
3½ tablespoons cornstarch
Pinch of salt
2½ cups milk
3 egg yolks, lightly beaten
1 teaspoon vanilla extract
2 tablespoons pineapple juice
1 tablespoon kirsch
6 dessert crêpes (page 755), at room temperature
Pineapple cubes

1 Mix the sugar, cornstarch and salt in a bowl. Scald the milk and pour over the dry ingredients, stirring constantly.

2 Place the mixture in a saucepan and cook over very low heat, stirring, until the mixture thickens. Cover and cook 10 minutes longer.

3 Add a little of the hot mixture to the egg yolks, stirring. Add the yolks to the remaining mixture and cook over hot water, stirring, until thickened, 2 minutes.

4 Cool the pastry cream and add the vanilla, pineapple juice and kirsch. Spoon the mixture down the center of the crêpes and roll. Garnish with pineapple cubes.

Dessert Sauces

STRAWBERRY SAUCE

ABOUT 2 CUPS

Put 1 quart fresh strawberries through a sieve, or purée in a food processor. Stir in 1 tablespoon lemon juice and sweeten with confectioners' sugar to taste. Raspberry sauce may be made in the same way.

◆

STRAWBERRY COMPOTE SAUCE

ABOUT 3½ CUPS

1 cup sugar
2 tablespoons cornstarch
1 pint fresh strawberries, sliced
¾ cup orange juice
1 medium banana, diced
1 medium orange, pared and cut into sections
¼ cup light rum (optional)

1 Combine the sugar and cornstarch and mix well.

2 Crush 1 cup of the strawberries and add to the sugar mixture along with the orange juice; mix well. Cook over medium heat, stirring constantly, until thickened and clear. Chill.

3 Add remaining strawberries and remaining ingredients and mix lightly but thoroughly. Serve over ice cream.

FRESH LINGONBERRY SAUCE

ABOUT 2 CUPS

2 cups fresh lingonberries
1 cup water
½ cup sugar

1 Wash and pick over the lingonberries, removing the stems, leaves and spoiled fruit.

2 Place the water and sugar in a saucepan over high heat and bring quickly to a boil. Boil the sugar syrup about 30 seconds, then add the berries. Reduce the heat and simmer gently 15 to 20 minutes. Cool and serve.

◆

FRESH RASPBERRY SAUCE

ABOUT 2 CUPS

2 cups raspberries
½ cup sugar, approximately
1 tablespoon cornstarch
1 tablespoon lemon juice
1 tablespoon cognac

1 Mix the raspberries with the sugar and heat, stirring frequently, to a boil. Press raspberries through a sieve to remove seeds. Add more sugar if desired.

2 Mix the cornstarch with the lemon juice and cognac. Heat the raspberry purée to a boil, stir in the cornstarch mixture and cook, stirring, until thickened.

3 Cool and serve over ice cream.

BLUEBERRY SAUCE

ABOUT 2 CUPS

¾ cup plus 1 tablespoon water
¼ cup sugar
1 tablespoon lemon juice
1 teaspoon cornstarch
1 cup blueberries

1 Bring ¾ cup of the water and the sugar to a boil and stir until the sugar has dissolved. Add the lemon juice.

2 Mix the cornstarch with 1 tablespoon water and add, stirring, to the syrup. Cook, stirring, 1 minute.

3 Add the blueberries and cook 2 or 3 minutes. Serve warm.

◆

BUTTERSCOTCH SAUCE

ABOUT 2 CUPS

1 cup dark corn syrup
1 cup sugar, or ½ granulated and
    ½ light brown sugar
½ cup half-and-half
2 tablespoons butter
Pinch of salt
1 teaspoon vanilla extract

1 Combine all the ingredients except the vanilla in a saucepan and cook over medium heat, stirring constantly, until the mixture comes to a full rolling boil. Boil briskly 5 minutes, stirring occasionally. Remove from the heat.

2 Add the vanilla and serve warm.

Note: The sauce may be stored in the refrigerator. To reheat, place in a pan of hot, not boiling, water, until the sauce has thinned to pouring consistency.

◆

CHERRY SAUCE

ABOUT 2½ CUPS

1 pound sweet cherries, pitted
½ cup water
⅓ to ½ cup light corn syrup or sugar
1 tablespoon cornstarch
Lemon juice
Kirsch, cognac, sherry or cherry liqueur
    (optional)

1 Place the cherries, ¼ cup of the water and the syrup in a saucepan and bring to a boil.

2 Blend the cornstarch with the remaining water and add, stirring, to the cherries. Cook, stirring, until clear, or about 1 minute.

3 Add lemon juice and kirsch to taste. Serve warm or cold over puddings or ice cream.

Note: The sauce may be stored in the refrigerator.

CARAMEL SAUCE

1½ CUPS

1¼ cups brown sugar
⅔ cup light corn syrup
4 tablespoons butter
½ cup cream
½ teaspoon vanilla extract

1 Combine the sugar, corn syrup and butter in a saucepan and stir over low heat until the sugar has dissolved. Continue cooking until the mixture forms a firm ball in cold water (242°F on a candy thermometer).

2 Remove the syrup from the heat and add the cream and vanilla. Cool. This sauce is recommended for vanilla and coffee ice cream.

♦

HOT FUDGE SAUCE

ABOUT 2½ CUPS

1 cup sugar
1 cup light corn syrup
½ cup cocoa
½ cup half-and-half or evaporated milk
3 tablespoons butter
Pinch of salt
1 teaspoon vanilla extract

1 Combine all the ingredients except the vanilla in a saucepan. Cook over medium heat, stirring constantly, until the mixture comes to a full rolling boil. Boil briskly 3 minutes, stirring occasionally.

2 Remove the mixture from the heat and add the vanilla. Serve warm.

Note: The sauce may be stored in the refrigerator. To reheat, place in a pan of hot, not boiling, water until the sauce has thinned to pouring consistency.

♦

BITTERSWEET FUDGE SAUCE

ABOUT 2½ CUPS

2 ounces (2 squares) unsweetened chocolate
1 (14-ounce) can sweetened condensed milk
Pinch of salt
½ cup hot water, approximately

1 Melt the chocolate in the top part of a double boiler. Add the condensed milk and stir over rapidly boiling water for about 5 minutes, until thickened.

2 Remove from the heat. Add the salt and enough hot water to soften the mixture to desired consistency. The sauce may be served warm or cold. It thickens on cooling but may be thinned again with water.

Variation

MOCHA SAUCE

Thin the fudge sauce with strong coffee in place of the water.

BITTER CHOCOLATE SAUCE

ABOUT 1½ CUPS

4 ounces (4 squares) unsweetened chocolate
2 tablespoons butter
2 tablespoons light corn syrup
6 to 8 tablespoons sugar
¾ cup milk
Pinch of salt

1 Melt the chocolate with the butter over hot water. Add the corn syrup and sugar and blend.

2 Add the milk and salt and cook, stirring, 10 minutes.

♦

BRANDIED FOAMY SAUCE

ABOUT 2 CUPS

¼ pound butter
1⅓ cups sifted confectioners' sugar
Dash of salt
1 egg, separated
2 tablespoons cognac
½ cup heavy cream, whipped
Pinch of grated nutmeg

1 Soften the butter and gradually blend in the sugar. Add the salt and egg yolk and beat well.

2 Cook over hot, not boiling, water, stirring constantly, until the mixture is light and fluffy, or 6 to 7 minutes. Remove from the heat and stir in the cognac. Chill.

3 Fold in the egg white, beaten until it stands in soft peaks. Fold in the whipped cream just before serving.

4 Serve over fruitcake and sprinkle with the nutmeg.

♦

GRAND MARNIER SAUCE

10 TO 12 SERVINGS

5 egg yolks
½ cup sugar
¼ cup Grand Marnier
1 cup heavy cream, stiffly beaten

1 Combine the egg yolks and sugar in a 2-quart mixing bowl that will fit snugly inside a slightly larger saucepan. Add about 2 inches of water to the saucepan. Bring the water to the boil and place the mixing bowl inside the saucepan. Place it over but not in the boiling water.

2 Beat the yolks and sugar vigorously with a wire whisk or electric mixer until the mixture becomes quite thick and pale yellow. Do not allow the yolk mixture to overheat or it will curdle. When ready, the sauce will coat a wooden spoon.

3 Remove the bowl from the saucepan and stir in 2 tablespoons of the Grand Marnier. Let the sauce stand until cool. Refrigerate until thoroughly chilled.

4 Fold the whipped cream into the sauce and stir in the remaining Grand Marnier.

HARD SAUCE

ABOUT 2 CUPS

½ pound sweet butter, softened
1 cup confectioners' sugar
¼ cup brandy, rum or sherry
½ teaspoon vanilla extract

Cream the butter and the sugar well. Add the brandy a few drops at a time and beat until fluffy. Beat in the vanilla and chill.

♦

ENGLISH CUSTARD

This is one of the best dessert sauces ever devised. Called *crème anglaise* in French, it is smooth, rich and elegant. It may be served hot or cold over cake, ice cream or fruits.

ABOUT 3 CUPS

6 egg yolks
¼ cup sugar
Pinch of salt
2 cups milk, scalded
Vanilla extract or sherry to taste

1 Beat the egg yolks until pale but not dry. Add the sugar, salt and milk. Cook and stir in the top part of a double boiler over simmering water. The water must never bubble into a boil.

2 When the custard reaches 175°F on a candy thermometer, it is done and must be removed from the heat, flavored with vanilla extract or sherry and put aside to use. If you do not own a candy thermometer, watch the stirring spoon. When it coats all over with the egg mixture and nothing drips from it, 175°F has been reached.

HONEY SAUCE

ABOUT 1 CUP

3 tablespoons butter
2 teaspoons cornstarch
⅔ cup honey
Whole toasted almonds (optional)

1 Melt the butter in a saucepan. Add the cornstarch and stir until smooth.

2 Add the honey and cook over low heat, stirring constantly, for about 5 minutes. Add almonds if desired.

3 Serve the sauce warm or cold over ice cream or unfrosted cake.

♦

MAPLE CREAM SAUCE

2½ CUPS

Boil 1 cup maple syrup down to ¾ cup. Cool. Fold into 1 cup heavy cream, whipped.

MOCHA CREAM SAUCE

ABOUT 2 CUPS

2 egg yolks
¼ cup sugar
Pinch of salt
½ cup strong coffee
1 cup heavy cream, whipped

1 Beat the egg yolks until somewhat thickened. Beat in the sugar and salt and stir in the coffee.
2 Cook over simmering water, stirring, until thickened. Chill; fold in the whipped cream.

♦

LEMON-NUTMEG SAUCE

1½ CUPS

½ cup sugar
1 tablespoon cornstarch
Pinch of salt
¾ cup water
¼ cup lemon juice
2 teaspoons lemon rind
½ teaspoon vanilla extract
¼ teaspoon grated nutmeg

1 Combine the sugar, cornstarch and salt in a saucepan. Stir in the water and cook, stirring constantly, until the mixture is thick and transparent. Remove from the heat and cool.
2 Stir in the lemon juice, lemon rind, vanilla and nutmeg. Serve over puddings and soufflés.

CRÈME FRAÎCHE
A THICKENED FRESH CREAM

ABOUT 1 CUP

1 cup cream
1 teaspoon buttermilk

Pour the cream into a jar or mixing bowl. Add the buttermilk and stir. Cover tightly with plastic wrap and let stand in a slightly warm place for 12 hours or longer, or until the cream is about twice as thick as ordinary heavy cream. Refrigerate and use as desired on fresh fruits, fruit pies and so on. Keep closely covered.

15
Table of Equivalents

Table of Equivalents

Anchovy fillets	2-ounce can	10–12 anchovies
Anchovy paste	2-ounce tube	2 tablespoons
Apples	1 pound (3 medium)	2½ cups pared and sliced
Apricots, dried	1 pound	3 cups
Asparagus	½ pound	6–8 stalks
	1 pound	3½ cups cut into 1-inch pieces
Bacon	1 pound	30 thin slices, 15 thick
	2 ounces	⅓ cup diced
Bananas	1 pound (3–4)	1½ cups mashed
		2 cups sliced
Barley	1 cup	3½ cups cooked
Beans, dried	½ pound (1 cup)	2–2½ cups cooked
Beans, fresh shell (fava, cranberry, lima)	1 pound	1 cup shelled
Bean sprouts, fresh	1 pound	3–4 cups
Beets	1 pound, trimmed	2 cups cooked and sliced
	15-ounce can or jar	2 cups
Blackberries	1 pint	2 cups
Blueberries	1 pint	3 cups
Bread crumbs	1 slice fresh bread	½ cup crumbs
	1 slice oven-dried	¼ cup fine crumbs
	8-ounce package	2¼ cups
Bulgur	1 cup	3½ cups cooked
Butter	¼ pound (1 stick)	8 tablespoons (½ cup)
	¼ pound	⅓ cup clarified butter
Cabbage, regular	2 pounds	9 cups shredded or sliced
		5 cups cooked
Chinese	1½ pounds	6–8 cups sliced
red	2 pounds	4 cups cooked
Carrots	1 pound (6–7)	3 cups sliced or shredded
		1⅓ cups cooked and puréed
		2½ cups diced
Celery	1 large rib (¼ pound)	½ cup sliced or chopped

Celery root (celeriac)	1 pound	3 cups grated or julienned
		1 cup cooked and puréed
Cheddar cheese	¼ pound	1 cup grated
Cherries	1 pound	2½ cups pitted
Chestnuts	1½ pounds	2½ cups peeled
	10-ounce can	about 25 whole chestnuts
Chicken	3½ pounds	3 cups cooked meat
	1 large boned breast	2 cups cooked meat
Chicken broth	13¾-ounce can	1¾ cups
Chick-peas, dried	1 cup	2½ cups cooked
Chocolate	1 ounce (1 square)	2 tablespoons grated
Clams	3 dozen	4 cups shucked
Cocoa	½ pound can	2 cups
Coconut	1 medium, fresh	4 cups shredded
	1 medium, fresh	2½ cups coconut milk
	3½-ounce can	1⅓ cups flaked
Corn	2 plump ears	1 cup kernels
Cornstarch	1 pound	3 cups
Couscous, quick-cooking	1 cup	2½ cups cooked
Crabmeat, fresh	1 pound	3 cups
Cranberries	12-ounce bag	3 cups
Cream	1 cup	2–2½ cups whipped
Cream cheese	3-ounce package	6 tablespoons
Cucumber	2 medium	3 cups sliced
Currants, dried	10-ounce package	2 cups
Dates, pitted	8-ounce package	1¼ cups chopped
Eggplant	1½ pounds	2½ cups diced and cooked
Eggs, large	5 whole	1 cup
	1 egg white	2 tablespoons
	8 egg whites	1 cup
	1 egg yolk	1 tablespoon
	14 egg yolks	1 cup
Figs, dried	1 pound	3 cups chopped
Flour, all-purpose	¼ ounce	1 tablespoon
	1 pound	3½ cups unsifted
cake	1 pound	4½ cups sifted
whole wheat	1 pound	3½ cups

Table of Equivalents

Garlic	2 medium cloves	1 teaspoon minced	Orange	1 medium	⅓ cup juice
Gelatin	1 envelope (¼ ounce)	1 tablespoon			2–3 tablespoons grated rind
Ginger, fresh	2-inch piece	2 tablespoons shredded	Oysters	1 quart, shucked	3 dozen
			Parmesan cheese	¼ pound	1 cup grated
Graham crackers	about 7	1 cup fine crumbs	Peaches	1 pound (4 medium)	2 cups peeled and sliced
Grapefruit	1 medium	⅔ cup juice	Pears	1 pound (3 medium)	2 cups sliced
Grits	1 cup	4 cups cooked			
Herbs	1 tablespoon fresh	1 teaspoon dried	Peas	1 pound	1 cup shelled
			Peppers, bell	1 large	1 cup chopped
Hominy	1 cup	4½ cups cooked	Pineapple	1 medium	3 cups cubed flesh
Jerusalem artichokes (sunchokes)	1 pound	2½ cups peeled and sliced	Plums	1 pound	2¼ cups halved and pitted
Kasha (buckwheat groats)	1 cup	2½ cups cooked	Potatoes, white	1 pound	3 cups sliced
					1½–2 cups mashed
Leeks	2 pounds	4 cups chopped	sweet	1 pound	3 cups sliced
		2 cups cooked			2 cups mashed
Lemon	1 medium	3 tablespoons juice	Prunes, dried	1 pound	2½ cups pitted
		2 teaspoons grated rind	Pumpkin, fresh	3 to 4 pounds	3½ cups cooked and puréed
Lentils, dried	1 cup	2½ cups cooked	Quince	1 pound (3 medium)	1½ cups chopped
Lime	1 medium	2 tablespoons juice			
		1 teaspoon grated rind	Raisins, seedless	4 ounces	¾ cup
	1 pound (8)	1 cup juice	Raspberries	1 pint	1¾–2 cups
Lobsters	2 pounds	½ pound cooked meat	Rhubarb	1 pound	2 cups cooked
			Rice, long-grain white	1 cup	3 cups cooked
Macaroni	8 ounces	4 cups cooked	brown	1 cup	4 cups cooked
Mangoes	4 medium	4 cups pulp	wild	1 cup	2 cups cooked
Milk, condensed	14-ounce can	1¼ cups	Romano cheese	¼ pound	1 cup grated
evaporated	5⅓-ounce can	⅔ cup	Saffron	1/20-ounce plastic bottle	1 tablespoon
Mushrooms	¼ pound fresh	1 cup sliced			
		1½ cups chopped	Scallions	1 bunch (6–7)	⅓ cup chopped (white part only)
	3 ounces dried	1 pound fresh			
Mussels	1 pound	16–20 mussels	Scallops, sea	½ pound	1 cup
Mustard	1 teaspoon dry	1 tablespoon prepared	Shallots	1 large (½ ounce)	1 tablespoon minced
Nectarines	1 pound (3–4)	2 cups sliced	Shrimp	1 pound	10–15 jumbo
Noodles	1 pound	7 cups cooked			16–20 large
Nuts	4 ounces	¾ cup chopped			25–30 medium
		1 cup ground			30–35 small
Oats	1 cup	2 cups cooked	Sour cream	8 ounces	1 cup
Okra	1 pound	5 cups	Spinach	2 pounds	1½ cups cooked and chopped
Onions	1 medium	½–¾ cup chopped	Split peas	1 cup	2½ cups cooked

Table of Equivalents

Squash, winter (acorn buttercup, butternut, Hubbard, turban)	3 pounds	3 cups cooked and puréed
Strawberries	1 pint	2 cups sliced
Sugar, brown	1 pound	2¼ cups packed
confectioners'	1 pound	3¾ cups unsifted
		4½ cups sifted
granulated	1 pound	2¼ cups
Swiss cheese	¼ pound	1 cup shredded
Tomatoes	1 pound (3–4 medium)	2½ cups peeled and seeded
	35-ounce can	2 cups drained pulp
Tomato paste	6-ounce can	¾ cup
	4½-ounce tube	5 tablespoons
Tomato sauce	8 ounces	1 cup
Turnips	1 pound (4)	2½ cups cooked
Water chestnuts	5-ounce can	15–17 water chestnuts
Wheat germ	12 ounces	3 cups
Yeast	1 cake compressed	1 package active dry
	1 envelope active dry	1 tablespoon
Zucchini	1 pound	3½ cups sliced
		2 cups grated and drained

Volume and Weight Equivalents

WEIGHT (common units)

1 ounce	28.35 grams
1 pound	453.59 grams
1 gram	0.035 ounces
1 kilogram	2.21 pounds

VOLUME (common units)

1 cup	16 tablespoons
	8 fluid ounces
	236.6 milliliters
1 tablespoon	3 teaspoons
	0.5 fluid ounce
	14.8 milliliters
1 teaspoon	4.9 milliliters
1 liter	1,000 milliliters
	1.06 quarts
1 bushel	4 pecks
1 peck	8 quarts
1 gallon	4 quarts
1 quart	2 pints
1 pint	2 cups
	473.2 milliliters

Formulas for metric conversions

Ounces to grams	multiply ounces by 28.35
Grams to ounces	multiply grams by .035
Pounds to grams	multiply pounds by 453.5
Pounds to kilograms	multiply pounds by .45
Cups to liters	multiply cups by .24
Fahrenheit to Centigrade	subtract 32 from Fahrenheit, multiply by 5, then divide by 9
Centigrade to Fahrenheit	multiply centigrade by 9, divide by 5, then add 32

Index

Aspics
  for beef, 590
  for chicken, 589
  for fish, 590
Atjar ketimun (sweet-and-sour
    relish), 601
Aubergines à la Boston, 402
Avery Island barbecue sauce, 585
Avgolemono soup (Greek egg-
    and-lemon soup), 91
Avocado(s)
  canapés, 18
  crab-stuffed, 114
  guacamole, 22
  salad
    Creole, 449
    grapefruit and, 450
    heart of palm and, 457
    lobster and, 113
    Mexican, 450
    spinach and, 444
  soup
    cold curried, 62
    Gerald, 61
  watercress ring, 119

Babka, 632
Bacon
  biscuits, 640
    whole wheat, 641
  calf's liver with, 357
  dressing, curly endive with,
    445
  fried shad roe with, 220
  and liver appetizers, 52
  muffins, 642
  and mushroom sauce,
    spaghetti with, 502
  mussels in, 39
  spaghetti carbonara, 485
  and spinach salad, 444
Bagel with cream cheese and
    salmon, 127
Bagna cauda, 570
Baked beans
  Jamaican, 523
  New England, 523
Baking powder biscuits, 640
Banana(s)
  baked, à l'orange, 722
  bread
    bran, 649
    nut, John Harper's, 649
    tea, 650
  Caribbean, 721
  ice cream, 734
  shortcake, 692
  sour cream pie, 668
Barbecued
  chicken, 135
  foods, marinade for, 584

Barbecued (cont.)
  lamb ribs, 325
  spareribs
    with beer and honey, 345
    Chinese, 344
  veal chops, 307
Barbecue sauces, 584
  Avery Island, 585
  green pepper, 585
  lime, 134
  Southern, 586
  for spareribs, 585
Barley and mushroom casserole,
    544
Basil
  butter, 580
  tomatoes stuffed with, 461
Bass, see Sea bass; Striped bass
Basting sauces
  for duck, 584
  for spit-roasted leg of lamb,
    586
  see also Barbecue sauces
Bavarian cream
  coffee, 742
  vanilla, 742
Bean(s)
  baked
    Jamaican, 523
    New England, 523
  beef and, Southwest, 292
  cassoulet, 179
  dried, 77
  duck with, 179–180
  fava, salad, 468
  flageolets with onions and
    tomatoes, 524
  kidney
    and chicken casserole, 161
    crisp fried (frijoles refritos),
      530
    and egg salad, 471
  macaroni and (pasta e fagioli),
    503
  minestrone, 61
  navy
    and rice, Italian style, 526
    salad, 466
  pinto, 531
    salad, 469
  red, and rice, 526
  Roman, with sage, 530
  snap, with tomatoes and
    Parmesan, 377
  and tuna vinaigrette, 470
  white, savory (loubia), 527
  see also Black bean(s);
      Chickpea(s); Green
      bean(s); Lima bean(s)
Bean curd, spicy pork and, 344
Bean sprouts, 268

Béarnaise sauce, 553
Béchamel sauce, 550
Beef, 274–303
  artichokes stuffed with, 369
  aspic for, 590
  and beans, Southwest, 292
  birds, stuffed, 280
  boiled, 285
    bollito misto, 286
    hot herb sauce for, 559
    pot au feu, 287
    Viennese, 286
  en casserole, 288
  chili con carne, 299
  chipped, creamed, with
    nutmeg, 303
  consommé à la Madrilène, 60
  cooked in beer (carbonnades
      flamande), 290–291
  corned
    and cabbage, 283
    glazed, 283
    hash, 284–285
    hash, red flannel, 285
    home-cured, 284
    Reuben sandwich, 128
  drippings, in Yorkshire
      pudding, 274
  émincé of, bourgeois, 280
  empanadas, 57
  feijoada, 341–342
  fillets with shrimp, 277
  filling
    for cream cheese pastry, 28
    for pirog, 56
  fried rice with ginger, 535
  goulash
    Budapest, 293
    Prague three-meat, 293
  green peppers stuffed with,
    419
  ground, with eggplant, 295
  hallacas, 300
  hamburgers
    with dill, 296
    grilled, for one, 296
    au poivre, 296
    potato roll, 297
    Roquefort, 296
  kebabs, 297
  keema with ginger, Indian,
      Julie Sahni's, 326–327
  kidney
    and steak pie, 356
    stew, 356
  liver
    braised, 358
    dumplings in soup, 94
  loaf
    Armenian, 298
    herbed meat, 298

Carrot(s) *(cont.)*
  and potatoes mousseline, 391
  and raisin cake, 688
  sauce, 572
  tzimmes, 390
  Vichy, 389
Cashew(s)
  and fig ice cream, 731–732
  Kung Pao shrimp with, 267
Casseroles
  barley and mushroom, 544
  beef, 288
    and beans, Southwest, 292
    and macaroni, 504
    and rice, Western, 295
  chicken and kidney bean, 161
  chick-pea, 528
  corn, okra and tomato, 398
  crabmeat, 248
  eggplant-lamb, 335
  moussaka
    à la Grecque, 334
    à la Turque, 333
  pasta, Mexican, 503
  pastel de choclo, 294–295
  rice and olive, 532
  rognons de veau, 357
  shepherd's pie, 332–333
  sweetbread (individual), 360
  turkey-filbert, 171
Cassoulet, 179
Catfish, deep-fried, 201
Catsup, spicy tomato, 602
Cauliflower, 391
  with anchovy butter, 391
  with caper sauce, 392
  fritto misto, 238
  Mexican-style, 392
  Mornay, 393
  with mustard sauce, 393
  pickle, 604
  polonaise, 392
  salad Napoletana, 452
Caviar
  lumpfish, sandwich, 129
  red
    celery with stuffing of, 33
    Madrilène, 60
    and sour cream dip, 22
  serving as appetizer, 14
Celery, 394
  braised in white wine, 394
  creamed, 394
    amandine, 394
  and mushroom pickles,
    606–607
  panzanella, 459
  with red caviar stuffing, 33
  relish, 595
  scalloped, in cheese sauce,
    394

Celery knob(s) (celeriac; celery
    root)
  céleri rémoulade, 33–34
  Parmigiana, 395
  purée of, 395
  salade Russe, 449
Chantilly, coffee cream, 739
Charlotte
  Malakoff au chocolat,
    Anneliese Richter's
    (chocolate mousse cake),
    685
  potato-cheese, 518
  Russe with kirsch, 743
Cheddar cheese
  artichokes mock Benedict,
    112
  asparagus au gratin, 374
  and clam canapés, 17
  and corn
    bread, 646
    pudding, 396
  creamed onions with, 413
  garlic grits, 548
  and lentil loaf, 529
  potato charlotte, 518
  and rice croquettes, 539
  sauce, 550
    anchovy, 571
    anchovy, broccoli with,
      381
    mustard, 575
    scallions with, 422
    scalloped celery in, 394
  and sherry spread, 20
  soufflé, 105
  straws, 25
  Welsh rabbit, 109
Cheese
  Bel Paese, polenta with,
    546
  biscuits, 640
  canapés
    baked, 17
    clam and, 17
    curried, 17
  croûtes, garlic-flavored, 621
  Danish, sandwich, 129
  feta
    Greek salad, 447
    shrimp baked with, 265
    spinach strudel, 53–54
  filling for kreplach, 506
  fritto misto, 239
  Gorgonzola
    conchigliette with, 496
    dip, 21
    polenta with, 546
  Hungarian, 24–25
  log, 19–20
  mashed potatoes with, 514

Cheese *(cont.)*
  Mozzarella
    baked noodles with
      tomatoes and, 480
    in carrozza, 109
  muffins, 642
  and mushroom omelet, 104
  rice with chili peppers and, 540
  ricotta
    budino di, 754
    pasta with, 499
    pasta with parsley and, 484
    pie, 678
  risotto with escarole and, 537
  roulade with crabmeat, 115
  straws, 25
  see also Cheddar cheese;
    Cream cheese; Gruyère;
    Parmesan; Roquefort;
    Swiss cheese
Cheesecakes
  chocolate, 696–697
  Christmas (with candied fruit
    filling), 697
  de luxe, 695
  food processor, 698
  refrigerator rum, 696
Chef's salad à l'Adam, 446
Cherry(ies)
  compote of dried fruits with
    sauce à la Ritz, 729
  sauce, 758
  soup, 76
  tart, 669
Chestnut(s)
  Brussels sprouts with, 382
  stuffing, 189
Chicken, 132–169
  with almonds, 157
  arroz con pollo, 160
  aspic for, 589
  baked
    herbed, 137
    summer-style, 138
  barbecued, 135
  bollito misto, 286
  breasts
    all'Alba, 138
    boning, 138
    breaded, 139
    Florentine, 139–140
    Kashmir, 142
    en papillote, 140
    Parmesan, 139
    with tarragon, 141
    Véronique, 141
    Viennese, 139
  broiled
    lime, 134
    for one, 134
    rosemary, 135

Chocolate *(cont.)*
  frosting, 703
  glaze, 707
  ice cream, 731
  mousse, 746
  pie
    chiffon, 673
    German sweet, 674
    pecan, 671
  pots de crème, 749
  pudding, 736
  sauce, bitter, 760
  soufflé, 750
  see also Fudge
Chorizo (Spanish hot sausage),
    352
  caldo gallego, 77
Choron sauce, 553
Choucroute garnie, Pierre
    Franey's, 346
Chowder
  clam
    Manhattan, 80
    New England, south-of-
      Boston style, 79
  corn and crabmeat, 66
  fish, 81
    Spanish, 84
  oyster, 88
Christmas
  cheesecake (with candied fruit
    filling), 697
  panettone, 633
  Swedish Julbrood, 632–633
Chupe, 236
Chutney(s)
  eggplant, 600
  grape and green tomato, 601
  mango, 598
  sauce for ham, 567
  see also Relishes
Cinnamon
  buns, 638
    whole wheat, 639
  pumpkin flan, 745
  raisin-oat bread, 631
Clam(s)
  aux blinis, 42
  Brazil nut spread, 21
  Burgundian, 243
  and cheese canapés, 17
  chowder
    Manhattan, 80
    New England, south-of-
      Boston style, 79
  fritters, 241
  linguine with basil and, 494
  Mexicaine, 242
  sauce
    anchovy and, pasta with,
      496

Clam(s) *(cont.)*
  red, pasta with, 495
  soup, Italian, 80
  steamed, 242
  stuffed
    baked, with garlic butter,
      38–39
    quahogs, 241
  washboiler clambake, 240
Cloverleaf rolls, 638
Club sandwich, 124
Cock-a-leekie, 92
Cocktail pizza, 58
Cocktail sauce, for seafood, 574
Coconut
  cream pie, 674
  fresh, cake, 687
  milk and cream, 147
  pecan frosting, 705
  pudding, 737
Cod(fish)
  baked, with potatoes, 202
  bouillabaisse, 234–235
  cacciucco (Italian seafood
    stew), 235
  cakes, 204
  cream of fish soup with
    vegetables, 82–83
  curried, 203
  loaf, 202
  mariner's stew, 211
  Provençale, 201
  salt, 203
    brandade de morue, 50
    poached, 201
    Portuguese-style, 203
Coeur à la crème, 753
Coffee
  Bavarian cream, 742
  bread-and-butter pudding, 735
  cream Chantilly, 739
  see also Mocha
Cognac
  apricots with, 721
  and mayonnaise sauce, 558
  Roquefort and, 20
  tomato sauce, spaghetti with
    sour cream and, 488
Colcannon with kale, 406
Coleslaw with caraway, 449
Collards, for feijoada, 341
Compote(s)
  apple, 719
  of dried fruits with sauce à la
    Ritz, 729
  strawberry, sauce, 757
Conchigliette with Gorgonzola,
    496
Confectioners' sugar icing, 705
Confit de canard (preserved
    duck), 178

Conserves
  cranberry, 611
  grape, 611
Consommé à la Madrilène, 60
Cookies, 707–718
  almond
    macaroons, 708
    squares, 707
  bars
    date and nut, 718
    layered nut, 718
  brandy snaps, 714
  brownies, 715
    black and white, 715
  butter, 708
    Greek (kourambiedes), 709
  chocolate
    ginger sandwich, Maida
      Heatter's, 712–713
    meringues, 713
    soft, 714
  florentines, 712
  German lebkuchen, 710
  gingerbread, 717
    men, 717
  ladyfingers, 709
  madeleines, 710
  molasses drop, soft, 716
  nutmeg hermits, 717
  oatmeal thins, 716
  pressed, 711
  rolled marzipan, 708
  Scotch shortbread, 711
  Viennese crescents, 715
Coq au vin, 158–159
Coquilles Saint-Jacques, 256–
    257
Corn
  baked fresh, 396
  on cob, 396
    washboiler clambake, 240
  in cream, 397
  Creole, 397
  fritters, 398
  muffins, 643
  okra and, 412
    and tomato casserole, 398
  pancakes, 655
  pastel de choclo, 294–295
  pimientos stuffed with, 420
  pudding
    cheese and, 396
    Shaker, 397
  relish
    fresh, old-fashioned, 593
    Ohio, 594
    tomato and, 594
  salad, Mexican style, 453
  soup
    chicken and, 90
    and crabmeat chowder, 66

Oatmeal
  apple crisp, 721
  bread
    old-fashioned, 626
    orange, 651
    raisin cinnamon, 631
  thins, 716
Oeufs à la neige (floating island),
    747–748
Oeufs au beurre noir, 98
Ohio corn relish, 594
Okra
  boiled, 412
  with corn, 412
  corn and tomato casserole, 398
  Creole, 412
  fresh tomato soup with, 73
  fried, 412
  gumbo
    chicken, 154
    seafood, 240
  lamb stew with, 330
Old House chiles rellenos, 34
Olive(s)
  beef with, 292
  black
    broccoli with, 380
    Grecian style, 15
    purée, rigatoni with, 500
  broiled tomatoes with, 428
  with dill, 16
  eggs stuffed with, 100
  mackerel with, 210
  mixed Italian, 15
  onion salad with anchovies
      and (ensalada de cebolla
      burriana), 458
  and rice casserole, 532
  spiced Spanish, 15
  vegetable relish, 600
Omelets, 101
  chasseur, 102
  cheese and mushroom, 104
  fillings for
    chicken liver and sage, 102
    spinach and sour cream,
        102–103
  Italian (frittata), 103–104
  for one, basic technique for,
      101
  Spanish, 103
Onion(s)
  baked, 414
    with pork and scallions, 414
    in their skins, 413
  with cream and sherry, 413
  creamed, 413
  French-fried, 414
  frittata, 103–104
  fritto misto, 238
  glazed, 416

Onion(s) *(cont.)*
  au gratin, 415
  kuchen, quick, 415
  panzanella, 459
  pickled, 606
  pimiento sauce, 567
  relish, 597
  rings, anchovies with, 33
  rye bread, 628
  salad
    with anchovies and olives
        (ensalada de cebolla
        burriana), 458
    beet and, 451
    tomato and, 461
  sandwiches, Irma's, 19
  in sauce for feijoada, 342
  soup with cheese, 70
  squares, 643
  stuffed
    with mushrooms, 417
    with nuts, 416
Orange(s)
  ambrosia, 724
  -apple nut loaf, 689
  baked bananas à l', 722
  beets with, 379
  biscuits, 640
  bread
    honey, 650
    oatmeal, 651
  carrots, glazed with, 389
  cranberry relish, cooked,
      596
    with raisins and apples,
        596
  custard
    baked, 744
    pie, 676
  duck à l', 175–176
  French dressing, 577
  frosting, 704
  fruitcake, 700
  glaze, 707
  marmalade, English, 615
  slices
    chilled, in red wine, 724
    preserved, 609
  and watercress salad, 448
  wedges, spiced, 609
Oriental
  lobster sauce, fettuccine with,
      492
  sardines, 217
  sauce, 574
  shrimp, 262
Orzo, wild rice and mushroom
    salad, Vivian Bucher's,
    543
Ossobuco, 317
Oven-braised lettuce, 407

Oxtail
  braised, 361
  ragoût, 362
Oyster(s)
  en brochette, 253
  broiled breaded, 253
  casino, 41
  cornmeal-fried, with mustard
      sauce, 254–255
  French-fried, 252
  fritto misto, 239
  on half shell, serving as
      appetizer, 14
  mignonette sauce for, 15
  pan roast Grand Central, 255
  Rockefeller, 41–42
  scalloped, old-fashioned, 254
  seafood gumbo, 240
  soup
    chowder, 88
    Hank Ketcham's, 89
    Mexican shellfish, with
        salsa, 84
    Spanish fish chowder, 84
  stew, 89
  stuffing, 190

Pain d'épice, 691
Pakistani pigeons and pilau, 182
Pancakes
  basic, 654
  blini
    buckwheat, 658
    white flour, 658
  buckwheat, raised, 656
  buttermilk, 657
  cornmeal, 656
  fresh corn, 655
  fruit and nut, 657
  potato, Pierre Franey's, 518
  rice and sesame, 657
  scallion, minute, 655
  sour cream, 657
  whole wheat, 654
Panettone, 633
Pan roast Grand Central, 255
Panzanella, 459
Papaya
  baked, 725
  fresh tropical mousse, 747
Paprika
  chicken paprikash, 152–153
  mushrooms, 410
Parker House rolls, 638
Parmesan
  celery knob Parmigiana, 395
  chicken, 139
  cream sauce, chicken in, 158
  eggplant Parmigiana, 403
    easy, 400
  endive au gratin, 406

Rice *(cont.)*
  with chili peppers and cheese,
    540
  curried, 534
  fried
    pork, with ginger, 535
    with shrimp, 535
  à la Grecque, 536
  green peppers stuffed with,
    419
  kedgeree, 111
  mushroom ring, 539
  navy beans and, Italian style,
    526
  and olive casserole, 532
  with peas, 534
  picadillo with beans and, 291
  pudding
    lemon, 739
    old-fashioned, 738
  red beans and, 526
  saffron, 532
  salad
    cold shrimp with, 471
    à la Française, 473
    and ham vinaigrette, 472
    ravigote, cold, 472
    vinaigrette, 471
  and sesame pancakes, 657
  shrimp with, 267
  tomatoes stuffed with, cold, 431
  with zucchini and peas, 533
  see also Pilaf (pilau); Risotto;
    Wild rice
Anneliese Richter's charlotte
    Malakoff au chocolat, 685
Ricotta
  budino di, 754
  pasta with, 499
    and parsley, 484
  pie, 678
Rigatoni
  with black olive purée, 500
  with prosciutto and sun-dried
    tomato sauce, 487
Risotto, 536–537
  chicken liver, 537
  with escarole and cheese, 537
  for one, 537
  with prosciutto and wild
    mushrooms, Marvin
    David's, 538
  ring, 537
Rock salt, 41
Rognons de veau en casserole,
    357
Rolled marzipan cookies, 708
Rolled picnic sandwiches, 18
Rolls (breads)
  basic, 637–638
  biscuit, 638

Rolls (breads) *(cont.)*
  cloverleaf, 638
  crescent, 638
  finger, 638
  hamburger, 638
  Parker House, 638
  whole wheat, quick, 638
Rolls, dessert
  ginger, 692
  Greek nut, à la Aphrodite
    Lianides, 680
  sponge, 684
Rolls, savory
  cheese roulade with crabmeat,
    115
  curried mushroom, 18
  hamburger potato, 297
  lobster, 124
  stuffed veal (braciolette
    ripiene), 313
Roman beans with sage, 530
Roman noodles, 479
Roquefort
  baked potatoes stuffed with,
    512
  cheese log, 19–20
  and cognac, 20
  cream mayonnaise, 578
  hamburger, 296
  shrimp stuffed with, 45
  strudel, 53
  Tabasco steak spread, 582
Rose geranium-apple jelly, 618
Rosemary butter, 581
Rotisserie Chinese duck, 177
Rouille sauce, 573
Royal icing, 705
Rum
  black beans in, 524
  cheesecake, refrigerator, 696
  cream, strawberries with, 728
  perles de cantaloupe au rhum,
    722
Rump roast with caraway seeds,
    281
Russian
  borscht, 63
  dressing, 579
    à l'Audelan, 579
  pirog, 54–56
  piroshki, 56
  shashlik, 325
Rutabaga(s)
  pudding, 434
  puréed (yellow turnips), 434
Rye
  bread, 627
    onion, 628
    stuffing, pork chops with,
      338
  fritters, 659

Sacher torte, 694–695
Saffron
  cream sauce, chicken in, 156
  rice, 532
  shrimp with, 265
Sage
  chicken liver with (omelet
    filling), 102
  cornmeal pastry, 172
Julie Sahni's Indian keema with
    ginger, 326–327
Julie Sahni's stuffed cabbage
    with ginger sauce, 387
St. Lucia's cardamom buns, 639
Salad(s), 441–74
  anchovy with pimiento, 35
  artichokes à la Grecque, 449
  asparagus, 451
  avocado
    grapefruit and, 450
    heart of palm and, 457
    Mexican, 450
    spinach and, 444
  beans and tuna vinaigrette,
    470
  beet, 451
    onion and, 451
  Belgian endive, 455
  broccoli, 452
  Caesar, 443
  cantaloupe flower, 474
  cauliflower, Napoletana, 452
  chef's à l'Adam, 446
  chick-pea(s), 467
    with horseradish, 467
    rémoulade, 470
  chicory and fennel, 446
  coleslaw with caraway, 449
  corn, Mexican style, 453
  Creole, 449
  cucumber, 453
    Swedish, 454
    Thai, 454
    tomato and, platter, 460
  curly endive with bacon
    dressing, 445
  eggplant
    salata melitzanas, 454
    sesame and, 455
  fava bean, 468
  forestière, 456
  fruit, 474
  Greek, 447
  green bean, 453
  heart of palm and avocado,
    457
  herring, 47
  with hot grilled quail, 447
  Italian
    pepper, 457
    tossed, 444